Medical Work, Medical Knowledge and Health Care

Medical Work, Medical Knowledge and Health Care

Edited by
Ellen Annandale, Mary Ann Elston and Lindsay Prior

Blackwell Publishing Ltd
9600 Garsington Road, Oxford, OX4 2DQ, UK
350 Main Street, Malden, MA 02148-5018, UK
550 Swanston Street, Carlton, Victoria 3053, Australia

Articles in this book were first published in the journal
Sociology of Health and Illness

British Library Cataloguing in Publication Data
A catalogue record for this title is available from the British Library

Library of Congress Cataloging in Publication Data
Applied for

ISBN: 0631223274

Typeset by Graphicraft Limited, Hong Kong
Printed and bound in the UK
Cover design: Design Deluxe
Cover photos: Imagestate

For further information on Blackwell Publishing, visit our website:
http://www.blackwellpublishing.com

Blackwell Publishing's policy is to use permanent paper from mills that
operate a sustainable forestry policy, and which has been manufactured
from pulp that is processed using acid-free and elementary chlorine-free
practices. Furthermore, Blackwell Publishing ensures that the text
paper and cover board used in all our journals has met acceptable
environmental accreditation standards.

Contents

Medical Work, Medical Knowledge and Health Care. Themes and Perspectives

Ellen Annandale, Mary Ann Elston and Lindsay Prior

Our approach stems from a profound belief that the needs of patients must be paramount. . . . The closer decisions are taken to the local community and those who work directly with patients, the more likely it is that patients' needs will be their prime objective. (DHSS 1979: 1)

Our vision is to move away from an outdated system of patients being on the outside, toward a model where the voices of patients, their carers and the public are heard through every level of the service, acting as a powerful lever for change and improvement. To give effect to this, the patient must be at the centre of everything the NHS does. (DoH 2001: 2)

Although they were written some twenty years apart, these two statements – both taken from policy documents announcing changes in the British National Health Service – have an almost identical vision: to put the patient at the heart of health care delivery. Medical work and the knowledge upon which it is based have undergone tremendous change over the twenty or so years that divide these two statements. Indeed, reform has become a way of life for health services, not only in the UK, but throughout the western world and beyond, as new policy initiatives challenge health practitioners to make changes in the way they organise their work. Amidst all of this change, working with patients remains a constant at the heart of medical work. From its early days sociology has also made patient care its subject matter. This is very apparent in the journal *Sociology of Health and Illness* which was first published in 1979, the same year in which 'putting patients first' became a watchword of British health policy. Throughout the years, papers in the Journal have made a major contribution to our understanding of the nature of medical knowledge and medical work in all its richness and variety. Although the specific topics that have been addressed have changed, as have the theoretical perspectives that have informed research, an overarching concern endures throughout; namely to show that far from being objective and politically neutral, medical work and medical knowledge are profoundly *social* in nature. From this perspective, sociologists have made links between the way in which medical work is organised and patients' experiences of care. Sociological research itself has often been politically engaged and concerned with improving the delivery of care to patients, even when it has consciously stopped short of making direct policy recommendations.

This Reader brings together a selection of readings on medical work, medical knowledge and health care which will be of interest to both sociologists and to health care practitioners. The articles span twenty years of scholarship published between 1980 and 2000. These twenty years and beyond have witnessed major changes in the delivery of health care and in the ways in which social scientists and health policy analysts have thought about medical work and medical knowledge. Indeed these changes have gone hand in hand with developments in health care – such as the emergence of new health technologies and reconfigurations in the health care division of labour – prompting new ways of thinking which in their turn feed into future research. Practical issues about the delivery of health care and theoretical perspectives are therefore intertwined. The best way to appreciate this is to look at how the topics that sociologists of health have been interested in have changed alongside changes in sociological approaches and in the social organisation of health care. Before we do this, we should note that when we use the terms 'medical knowledge' and 'medical work' we do so inclusively. That is, they are not intended to limit discussion to doctors' knowledge or to doctors' work, although sometimes this is the focus, but to refer to the knowledge and practice of all those engaged in patient care, including patients themselves, both in the formal health care system and informally in the home and elsewhere in the community. Since all of the articles in the Reader concern health care in the west, this introductory review will focus on only western societies.

Laying the foundations: early research

The sociology of knowledge helps us to understand how the way we think about health and health care is linked to time and place, that is to particular social contexts. Sociological thinking about medical knowledge and medical work during the 1960s and 1970s, for example, was influenced by the predominant sociological theories of the time and also by the way health care was organised. The sociology of health and illness was then in its infancy and very much concerned to establish its own distinct credentials. It did this by separating sociology's concern with *social factors* from medicine's concern with the *biological body*. For example, in his landmark publication *Profession of Medicine* (1970), Eliot Freidson proposed that illness could be thought of as a *biological* or *physical* state which exists independently of human knowledge and evaluation and also as a *social* state which is very much shaped by these same factors. Illness as a physical state, he argued, is the province of medicine, while health as a social state should be the province of the new discipline of the sociology of health and illness. By taking on this distinction, sociologists were carving out an intellectual domain all of their own (Strong 1979). A firm agenda was set for research on medical knowledge and medical work and this was to focus on how social factors shape the experience of health and health care. Although this remit was very broad and, as we will see, approached from a variety of different theoretical perspectives, it was crystallised in the concept of the 'biomedical model'.

Biomedicine

The 'biomedical model' brought social scientists' criticisms of modern medical knowledge and medical work together quite neatly in one overarching concept. Biomedicine was said to be *reductivist*, that is to assume that states of health and disease are natural phenomena which exist in the individual body; to operate inappropriately with a *simple cause-effect model* of illness (failing to appreciate that the causes of illness are complex and multifactorial); and to claim that medical work is *rational, objective and value free* (see Engel 1977, Mishler *et al.* 1981). This perspective is part and parcel of a wider 'industrial-capitalistic view of the world in which the idea that science represents an objective and value free body of knowledge is dominant' (Lock and Gordon 1988: 3). Although the biomedical model was precisely that – a model rather than a 'true to life' representation of everyday reality – it became the foundation upon which sociologists built their challenge to the nature and content of medical knowledge and its application in work with patients. As Mishler *et al.* (1981) put it, this new sociological perspective brought the medical approach into question and made it an object of enquiry in its own right. Even though the 'golden age' of medicine where doctors dominated other health occupations and had virtually complete control over the terms, conditions and content of their work was already waning by this time, it was the power of doctors and its consequences for patient care that captured sociologists' critical imagination in this early period. This meant more often than not that it was doctors, rather than other health care providers, such as nurses and midwives, who were the focus of research.

The development of this new and distinctly sociological approach to medical knowledge and medical work which was critical of the biomedical approach, led many early sociologists of health and illness into a strong alliance with the 'patients' perspective'. Certain topics came naturally to the fore. For example, many researchers were very uneasy about the power imbalance between the medical profession and patients. This meant that a lot of research of the 1970s was concerned with identifying the social organisational sources of the power of the medical profession and spelling out their negative consequences for patient care. The dominant sociological theories of the time – Parsonsian structural functionalism, Marxist political economy, and symbolic interactionism – provided quite different insights. In Parsons' (1951) analysis, the 'sick role' (patient's role) and the 'doctor's role' were seen as mutual, since each partner had a defined role to play in the recovery from illness. This reciprocity was essentially unequal given that the acquisition of medical knowledge and competence strongly favoured the doctor (Parsons 1975). Knowledge was the basis of power. Parsons' critics agreed with this, but stressed that doctors' knowledge is only one part of a much wider body of knowledge about health and health care. Everyday, or lay, health knowledge is also important. Since people actively interpret and give meaning to pain and other symptoms, often in consultation with friends and family, lay knowledge has an influence even *before* people reach the doctor's surgery or hospital emergency department. Lay knowledge also influences the way patients present their health problem to the doctor, as well as how they respond to any suggested treatments. Critics of Parsons stressed the contrasting perspectives of doctor and patient and argued that the doctor-patient relationship should be characterised as conflictual, rather than as reciprocal (see, for example, Bloor and Horobin 1975, Freidson 1961).

Empirical research
During the 1970s, sociologists opened the medical encounter up to direct sociological investigation. A rich and insightful body of predominantly qualitative research within the symbolic interactionist tradition revealed the conflicts and tensions that arise as patients and their doctors negotiate and bargain over aspects of care. As already noted, more often than not the sociologist's allegiance was to the patient. So much so that on occasion researchers even found it necessary to explain why they were *not* attending to the medical profession. This underscores the novelty of this new sociological approach and the implicit or explicit challenge to medicine that it posed. For example in *Going to See the Doctor*, Stimson and Webb explained that no research project can avoid the problem of bias in selection of research problems and methods, but that 'our choice of problem area and methods . . . was warranted in view of the paucity of research which deals with the patient as a person' (1975: vii). The patient, they argued, needs to be seen as a 'participant in medicine, rather than simply as a recipient of medical care' (*ibid*: 143). However, their study of interaction in general practice consultations led them to conclude that, although patients could exert control – for example, in how they presented themselves or in choosing not to follow prescribed treatments – their strategies were 'small scale and individualistic' (*ibid*: 143). In his book *Timetables* (1963), Roth analysed the conflicts and tensions over treatment timetables between patients who were hospitalised for tuberculosis and their doctors. From the doctor's point of view, the nature of the disease made it impossible to predict when a particular stage of treatment would be reached and therefore when a patient could be discharged home. Patients dealt with this unacceptable uncertainty by pressing for tentative predictions based on timetable norms of their own. These norms were a group product which developed out of 'the constant discussion among patients about the timing of events in their treatment and hospital life' (*ibid*: 60). Roth suggested that the actual timetable of treatment

resulted from the 'continual process of bargaining between patients and physicians over the question of when given points on the timetable will be reached' (*ibid*: 61).

The main reason why this kind of bargaining is possible, and also why tensions arise, is the inherent uncertainty, and hence malleability, of medical knowledge. Fox (1957, 2001) has stressed that certain elements of uncertainty are generic to medicine, irrespective of the historical period within which it is practised. Uncertainty stems from 'the impossibility of mastering the entire corpus of medicine's knowledge and skills; from the many gaps and limitations in medical knowledge and effectiveness that exist despite medicine's continuous advances; from difficulties associated with distinguishing between personal ignorance and ineptitude; and the lacunae and incapacitates of medicine itself' (Fox 2001: 237). The implications of these kinds of uncertainty for medical work have been appreciated for some time. For example, back in the early 1960s, Scheff argued that paralysing hesitation will arise unless doctors develop informal norms for handling uncertainty. One of the norms, or medical decision rules, that he identified was 'judging a sick person well is more to be avoided than judging a well person sick' (known as the 'type 2 error') (1963: 97). This norm, he argued, is based on the erroneous assumption that turning a well person into a sick person has little or no negative consequences. In actuality, he claimed, patients may organise their feelings and bodily reactions in accordance to a diagnostic label, particularly when they are in a confused or vulnerable state. The impact of uncertainty upon patient care was also studied by Davis (1960) in his research on children with poliomyelitis. He found that the real clinical uncertainty that existed in the early stages of diagnosis and treatment about the likely outcome for the patient (such as degree of paralysis), came to serve the purely managerial end of managing difficult interactions with parents. Specifically, the pretence of uncertainty on the part of doctors and nurses functioned to reduce the amount of time, effort and stressful personal involvement that a frank discussion of prognosis might entail. This meant that parents were left to look for cues and gradually figure the likely outcome out for themselves.

Studies of the medical encounter by symbolic interactionists like Roth and Davis focused on immediate work with patients. Other sociologists took a wider structural approach, locating medical work within the wider political economy of health care within society. McKinlay (1977: 461), for example, wrote of the profit making activities of industrial capitalism 'invading, exploiting, and ultimately despoiling any field of endeavour – with no necessary humane commitment to it – in order to seize and carry away an acceptable level of profit.' It was argued that through its practises medicine reinforced the (middle) class, (male) gender and (white) racial biases of society. Analysing the micro-politics of health care in doctor-patient interaction, Waitzkin and Stoeckle (1976) conceptualised the doctor as an agent of industrial capitalism, who reinforces capitalist ideologies such as individual personal responsibility for health, and mystifies the social origins of illness (*e.g.* in poverty, pollution and dangerous work conditions). The feminist work of this early period stressed the patriarchal nature of medicine and the sexist character of medical work. For example, studies of maternity care showed that obstetricians legitimate their control over childbirth by treating women as children who do not understand and cannot help themselves (*e.g.* Shaw 1974). More widely, research revealed how male doctors' preconceptions about women and their social roles negatively influence the advice and treatment that they receive. For example, Barrett and Roberts (1978) found that the primary definition of middle aged women held by British general practitioners was as housewives and mothers. This meant that when they presented with symptoms such as tiredness or anxiety, they were typically advised to cut down or give up paid work rather than to request that their husbands played a larger role in unpaid work in the home (for a wider review of this literature, see Clarke 1983). The partisan character of much sociological research is as apparent in feminist research as it was in early symbolic interactionist studies; the sociologist's explicit task is to disclose the negative consequences of medical control of women – such as undue clinical intervention in childbirth – and to encourage and support patient's efforts to take control of their own experience.

Even though their work was theoretically diverse, the sociologists who mapped out the field during these 'early years' had a shared conviction: that medical work should be viewed 'as socially organised practice rather than as an application of scientific knowledge' (Mishler *et al.* 1981: 99). Or, as Wright and Treacher (1981: 2) put it, that 'medical knowledge is a social construct'. Two common premises ran through this. First, that the medical knowledge which underpins practice is inherently uncertain and therefore open to manipulation in various ways. And second, that quality of patient care is directly related to how medical knowledge is conceptualised and applied. These premises were the platform upon which sociologists of various theoretical persuasions built their explicit or implicit recommendation that quality of patient care would improve if the power of the health care provider – notably the doctor – was diminished and the power of the patient increased. But this seemingly unshakeable sociological certainty was to be questioned in light of major changes that took place in the social organisation of health care and the place of patients, doctors, and other health care providers within it during the 1980s and 1990s.

Changes in the organisation of health care and new research agendas

If we were to propose a motif for recent sociological thinking about medical knowledge and medical work it would have to be: 'things are not as simple as they once seemed'. In retrospect, although insightful and groundbreaking, much of the early research of the 1960s and 1970s appears limited in scope and based on an overly simple sociological model of medical knowledge and medical work. At the heart of this model is an image of doctors as a rather uniform and all powerful profession dominating patients and the work of other practitioners, such as nurses. Current research is often quite different. Recent comments from Berg and Mol exemplify this. Medicine, they write,

> is not a coherent whole. It is not a unity. It is, rather, an amalgam of thought, a mixture of habits, an assemblage of techniques. Medicine is a heterogeneous coalition of ways of handling bodies, studying pictures . . . conducting conversations. Wherever you look, in hospitals, in clinics, in laboratories, in general practitioners' offices – there is multiplicity. (1998: 3)

Richness, complexity, multiplicity and the variety of medical knowledge and medical work are now the watchwords of sociological research. While the themes of the balance of power and control between various parties – and its implications for quality of patient care – are often still centre stage, the key characters are conceptualised in new ways. To understand why, we need to refer back to the guiding theme of this introductory review; that the topics sociologists are interested in have changed alongside changes in the organisation of health care and developments in sociological theory.

The major changes that have taken place in the organisation of western health care over the last twenty-five or so years are part of a wider restructuring of the welfare state and a re-conceptualisation of citizenship rights. There is now a strong expectation that collective rights and entitlements are balanced by individual duties, obligations and responsibilities (White 1999). The motto 'no rights without responsibilities' (Giddens 1998: 18) accords well with the wider social changes that have taken place since the 1970s. It has been argued that wide scale economic and social change – for example in the spheres of work and the family – have released individuals from the constraints of traditional social structures such as class, 'race', and gender. While once lives would have been more or less mapped out from birth, individuals are now expected to make their *own* lives amidst an array of choices. Beck and Beck-Gernsheim (2002: 31) refer to 'a social impetus toward individualisation of unprecedented scale and dynamism' since the mid twentieth century which 'forces people – for the sake of their survival – to make themselves the centre of their own life plans and conduct'. Individualism they argue is now *institutionalised* i.e. embedded within contemporary western societies. This is not to say that life choices are easily or freely made. On the contrary, in a society characterised by ever evolving and changing risks and uncertainties, life choices can seem very precarious and life itself quite chaotic (Giddens 1991). Nor does it mean that inequalities do not exist, rather that they are no longer so easily mapped along the dimensions of social class, 'race', age and gender.

In various ways, western government policies stress the need for health care to be more responsive to the *individual*. We can see this is in the new consumerist ethos, where patients are expected to hold health care providers to account for the quality of care that they provide at the same time that they have an obligation to be responsible for their own individual health and well-being. On their part, practitioners are expected to replace the tribal ethos which ties certain skills to certain professions such as medicine and nursing with more flexible or individualised working practices. Growing individualism therefore has a strong central steer, evident in the array of policy and practice guidelines surrounding medical work.

Since it represents a wider cultural shift, individualisation has in a sense been imported into health care from 'without'. But it also accords with the changes that have taken place within the organisation of health care itself. Developments in medical science such as in molecular biology, genetics and immunology, new diagnostic technologies and therapeutic techniques are all geared towards the prevention of illness, the treatment of illness, and even the avoidance of death by treating *the individual*. Similarly health promotion focuses on individual lifestyles much more than it does the collective social factors – such as pollution and unemployment – that undermine health. Moreover, the sheer complexity of medical science is leading to an increasingly stratified and arguably 'individualised' workforce divided by specialism, rank, training, skill and expertise. When differences by gender, age, and ethnicity are added to the picture then individual diversity seems an even more appropriate descriptor of medical work.

In this context the traditional depiction of the 'biomedical model' seems increasingly out of step with the complex realities of everyday practice. The health care division of labour is increasingly fluid and contested and no longer self evidently dominated by an all powerful medical profession. Stalwart guiding themes of the early sociology of medical knowledge and medical work have therefore been subject to revision in recent years. New conceptualisations of the health care division of labour have been central to this.

The health care division of labour
Although financial limitations and the need to work within a complex division of labour inevitably placed constraints on their work, during the 1950s, 1960s and into the 1970s doctors had a virtual mandate to control their own work and to direct patient care as they saw fit. In Britain, for example, this was enshrined in the new post-War National Health Service (NHS). The government promised that however the NHS was organised, 'the doctors taking part must remain free to direct their clinical knowledge and personal skill for the benefit of their patients in the way they feel to be best' (Ministry of Health 1944). In the USA, during the 'golden age' of medicine, at its height in the 1950s, doctors had virtually complete control over the terms, conditions and content of their work (Freidson 2001). In Britain the implicit compact or 'corporatist bargain' between government, the public and the

medical profession meant that, on their side, doctors accepted the government's right to set the budget and the broad national policy framework and, on its side, government accepted doctor's rights to autonomy and control over their work (Harrison and Ahmad 2000). Patients who were given healthcare rights, were usually willing to accept that 'doctor knows best' (Ham and Alberti 2002). As was discussed earlier, sociologists of medical work argued that under these circumstances the medical profession is liable to develop a 'self-deceiving view of the objectivity and reliability of its knowledge and of the virtues of its members' (Freidson 1970: 370). Errors of practice are likely to go undetected and alternative ways of thinking about health, illness and health care, such as those held by patients and practitioners not working within the biomedical model, are ruled out of court.

But these halcyon days of professional power were not to last. As Freidson (2001: 181) writes, by the last quarter of the twentieth century the status of medicine was 'so weakened that some asserted its proletarianization'. The implicit compact between the medical profession, the state and the public was fractured and, by the 1980s, sociologists were concerned less with the consequences of professional power and more with the reasons for its decline. Fuelled by well publicised errors of practice and mismanagement, the public in general were no longer willing to unquestionably trust doctors or to passively accept the biomedical model. This is reflected in the increasing popularity of 'alternative medicine' and the willingness to complain and challenge medical authority. In Britain, for example, complaints about clinical treatment, delayed or cancelled care, poor communication and staff attitudes have markedly increased. This mirrors a trend that began earlier in the USA and is now replicated in many other countries. This consumerist ethos is of course part and parcel of the wider individual reflexivity of late modern society. But it also accords well with a contractual 'rights and responsibilities' model of health care. Patients as consumers are part of a new mode of governance, a kind of 'consumerism by command from the centre' whereby governments mobilise popular opinion to put pressure on health care providers and hold them to account (Ham 2001: 233). So even though they are not natural allies – since the public is typically critical of the level of government funding and organisation of health care – the state and the public are drawn together in a challenge to medical power and autonomy.

Attempts to curb medical autonomy which began in the 1970s, developed in the 1980s and gained new momentum during the 1990s have been motivated by escalating costs and concerns about quality of care. Although the mechanisms for financing health care vary nationally, involving the state, insurers and patients in various ways, it is generally recognised that demographic changes, such as ageing populations, advances in medical science and rising public expectations are rapidly pushing up costs. Countries which have traditionally relied upon a free market model, such as the USA, are moving towards greater regulation and countries where health care has been centrally financed under a tax-system, such as Britain, are building in greater market competition to control costs. Although ultimately costs arise from wide societal changes, they are detected most easily at the level of individual care particularly in the work that doctors do in authorising patient requests, ordering diagnostic tests and undertaking treatments. This explains why doctors' work has been the major target of reform. An association has also been made between costs, medical autonomy and quality of care. Social scientists have recognised this for some time of course, pointing to the various ways in which social and political factors can impact upon care in negative ways. In the USA in particular a link has been made between doctors' own financial interests and treatment, such as unnecessary hysterectomies. The principle mechanism of cutting costs and improving quality has been greater managerial control over practice. This has taken several forms including *control over diagnosis and treatment*, such as decisions over what examinations, tests, drugs and procedures can be ordered through mechanisms like clinical guidelines, and *control over evaluation of care* such as peer review and audit and the use of 'performance indicators' (*e.g.* surgical mortality rates) (Harrison and Ahmad 2000: 130). In Britain these changes are part of a wider policy of 'clinical governance' through which NHS organisations are accountable for quality of services and safeguarding standards of care. But assaults on medical autonomy have arguably been most marked in the USA where the 'managed care revolution' has led to remarkable changes in the way that health care is organised and the way that doctors and other practitioners work. Health care has been consolidated into vast networks of doctors and hospitals and clinical decisions are now closely scrutinised and regulated by insurers and health care organisations (Bird *et al.* 2000).

There have also been significant changes in the work of other health care practitioners such as nurses, midwives and professions allied to medicine such as physiotherapists, occupational therapists and dieticians which are themselves partly bound up with attempts to curb medical autonomy and cut costs. The devolution of tasks that have traditionally been the prerogative of doctors to other practitioners has been a preferred strategy of those holding the health care purse strings such as insurers and government in recent years. So much so that it is currently presented as a panacea for all ills simultaneously helping to reduce costs (where, for example, nurses cost less than doctors), solve staffing problems, improve quality of care, and boost job satisfaction. In Britain for example, breaking the boundaries between professional groups and developing flexible working have become the new orthodoxies in health policy circles (Allen 2001).

The response from nursing and other professions allied to medicine to these changes has been mixed. On the one hand, expanding traditional jurisdictions can provide the opportunity for new roles such as nurse consultants, clinical nurse specialists and nurse practitioners to incorporate new skills and responsibilities into their practice. In the process it may help to excise nursing's traditional 'handmaiden role' and enhance professional standing. On the other hand, by becoming increasingly stratified by rank and specialism nursing may suffer a fate similar to medicine where, it has been argued, professional cohesion and the ability to fend off inroads into professional autonomy have been reduced through a process of divide and rule (Freidson 1989). In terms of everyday work, nurses and other practitioners could find themselves engaged in an increasingly technical and, for some, more routinised and therefore less skilled work which abandons the traditional 'core' caring role in favour of the 'biomedical approach' (Davies 2000). The growing sociological literature on these issues develops longstanding research on nursing's relationship to medicine. Back in the 1960s, for example, Stein (1967) referred to the 'doctor-nurse game'. He found that even though in some contexts nurses may have greater knowledge and expertise than doctors, they were discouraged from openly admitting this because to do so would have undermined prevailing norms of medical omniscience and nurses' obedience to doctors. Subsequent research has explored the changes that have taken place since the 1960s focusing on nurses' increasingly widespread dissatisfaction with subordination to medicine and their strategies for attaining greater autonomy (see, for example, Allen (2001) Porter (1995), Svensson (1996), Wicks (1998)). The question of whether new working patterns actually matter in terms of quality of patient care and how they impact on the quality of working life for staff, remains largely unanswered at the present time. But it is true to say that, in common with medicine, nursing has become an increasingly diverse and stratified profession.

The patient in the health care division of labour
During the 'early years', as we have seen, researchers generally maintained that a shift in the balance of power away from practitioners – particularly doctors – towards patients would improve quality of care. The changes that have taken place since the 1970s, such as the growth in consumerism and expectations of individual responsibility in health care have brought the patient's perspective to the fore. Challenges to medical autonomy in their turn, have done much to reduce the power of medicine. Over the years, within sociology too there has been a 'shift from a view in which the passive patient was locked into the doctor's all-knowing interventions to one in which the patient actively negotiates with a physician or other provider, inside or outside scientific medicine' (Olesen 2001: 255). New ways of thinking which appreciate that the division of labour concerns not only doctors and nurses but also individuals as workers in the service of their own care, have their roots in a number of developments within sociology during the 1980s. Feminist research in particular has been important in revealing the unpaid caring work that takes place between kin and others in the community (Graham 1993). In conceptualising patients as 'unpaid health workers', Stacey (1984) and others drew attention to the artificial divide between formal and informal care, and the cognate distinction between professional

and lay care. From within the symbolic interactionist tradition, Strauss *et al.* (1984: 977) stressed that patients are not only 'worked on' by doctors, nurses and others in hospitals, they also 'enter into the very process of being serviced themselves'. Although it may not be recognised as such, the work they undertake includes controlling symptoms and carrying out treatment regimens, personal housekeeping, as well as body work such as controlling the body in particular ways during diagnosis and treatment (*e.g.* X-rays), and emotional or sentimental labour (Strauss *et al.* 1982).

These changes mean that patients are no longer just supporting characters in a drama where doctors have the undisputed leading role. To continue the analogy, they have gradually moved out of the wings and into the spotlight of research on medical knowledge and medical work. While recent sociologists of medical knowledge and medical work have generally welcomed these changes, they have also pointed out that patient involvement in care is complex and multifaceted. The social constructionist approach has been particularly influential in this respect. From this perspective the greater emphasis that is placed on social factors and patient involvement does not necessarily 'free' the patient from medical control. While once we could look and see power in the hands of medicine, it is now less visible since it is diffused across social relations and practices of health care. Silverman (1987: 195) points out that when everything is to be open between doctor and patient this also means that nothing is to be hidden from the doctor's gaze. Patients are drawn into social and moral discourses – such as what kinds of lifestyle are valued and what counts as quality of life – which are used to justify particular clinical decisions. It can be as, if not more, difficult for patients to resist this more diffuse 'social' kind of control as the technical discourse of biomedicine. Moreover, as the papers in Section 4 of the Reader demonstrate, many patients continue to be relatively powerless to influence the outcome of their interactions with practitioners and judgements about their social worth continue to have a strong influence upon the kind of care that they receive. The operation of power then is complex and multifaceted. Broadly speaking, a decline in the power of medicine and a rise in the power of the patient will not necessarily have the consequence of improving quality of patient care in the way that early researchers envisaged. This has prompted sociologists to rethink the relationship between medicine, the public and the state.

Professional dominance reconsidered

While the early sociology of medical knowledge and medical work argued against the professional power of medicine, it now often points to the negative consequences of declining power. Researchers argue that the changes in the organisation of care described in this Introduction have forced a wedge between doctor and patient, compromising patient care. For example, writing about the USA, Waitzkin opines that while there is no reason to idealise patient-physician relationships of the past, managed care is generating major strains. Doctors' gate-keeper role is intensifying and they are increasingly under pressure from government and insurers to keep the gate closed unless it is absolutely necessary 'for the preservation of life or limb' (Waitzkin 2000: 272). The phrase that appears more and more in both social science and medical literature is a growing *absence of trust* between doctor and patient or nurse and patient. More or less everyone, we are led to believe, now realises that the kind of care that patients receive, or whether they receive any care at all, is motivated as much by economic as it is by clinical concerns. For example, health care rationing which was once largely implicit has been made explicit and rears its head with increasing frequency in the media. Since trust is 'the salient ingredient for sustaining control over one's domain' (Light 2000: 211–12), it is not surprising that lack of trust is linked to defensive practice. In a climate of increasing vigilance by patients, management and other colleagues – much of which is viewed as oppressive – doctors, nurses and other practitioners under- and over-treat, avoiding clinically advisable procedures and undertaking clinical unnecessary procedures for fear of complaints and litigation. A well-known illustration of 'over treatment' is increased intervention in childbirth such as internal fetal monitoring and caesarean sections.

The revitalisation of trust is central to the medical profession's defence of its own professional status. For example, writing in the British context, Ham and Alberti (2002) call for a new compact between government, the public and the medical profession based on 'common goals and trust' between parties. From a sociological perspective, referring to *common* goals seems to jar with growing *individualism* within society. However, it has been argued that individualism does necessarily mean that we live in a me-first society and that cooperation over particular issues at particular times is often essential. Beck and Beck-Gernsheim (2002), for example, argue that a kind of 'social sensitivity' arises from the fact that that people must rely on, and thereby trust, others in the search for self.

Freidson (2001) calls for a revival of the 'ideology of service' that classically defined the professions, such as medicine, teaching, and the law. He outlines three 'professional logics': *bureaucracy*, characterised by managerial control; *the market*, characterised by consumer control; and *professionalism*, characterised by occupational self-control. In his opinion, the consequences of following the logic of bureaucracy or the logic of the market at the expense of professionalism are very detrimental to quality of patient care. He argues that 'the emphasis on consumerism and managerialism has legitimised and advanced the individual pursuit of material self-interest and the standardisation of professional work which are the very vices for which professions have been criticised' (2001: 181). The specific consequences are: loss of discretion in practice which forces patients' individual problems or needs into standardised administrative procedures; the narrowing of knowledge development (since knowledge will be directed by what industry wants or what the public feels it wants); and the loss of the 'spirit of professionalism', that is the professions' independent moral voice in society. In place of this, Freidson argues for the 'third logic' of professionalism. Accepting this logic involves allowing professions to claim 'independence of judgement and freedom of action' (*ibid*: 122) *i.e.* accepting that health practitioners themselves – not patients or managers – determine what work is performed and its relation to the work of others. He argues that, unpalatable though it may seem, the professions need to maintain an economic market shelter, claiming that such monopolies are 'more than modes of exploitation or domination: they are also social devices for supporting the growth and refinement of disciplines and the quality of their practice' (*ibid*: 203). Consequently, professionalism, or the third logic, is self-consciously based on an ideology of 'the profession' as a secular calling with transcendental values such as service to others.

We have suggested that changes in the organisation of health care and new ways of thinking within sociology have led to new research agendas. So far we have explored the ways in which this has influenced conceptualisations of health professions and their work with patients. In the final section of this Introduction we reflect briefly on the increasingly diverse and complex field of medical knowledge and medical work which now goes beyond direct patient care.

New research directions

During the 'early years' the sociology of medical work largely confined itself to the topic of doctor-patient interaction and its implications for patient care. The consequence of this, as Atkinson (1995: 34) remarks, is that all too often the complexities of medical work were 'imploded into this one microcosm', rendering whole tracts of 'backstage' work undertaken in case conferences, in the diagnostic and research laboratory, even in surgery, invisible. The broad reason for this restricted vision lies in the limited conception of what counts as 'social' and therefore the subject matter of sociology. As Timmermans (2000: 310) explains in his review of research on medical technology, there has been an understanding that 'human-related aspects of health care belong to the social sciences, but the technoscientific aspects are the domain of biomedical scientists and engineers.'

This started to change in the mid 1980s when sociologists of science began to stress the need to look at 'science in action' rather than to dismiss science and technology as 'mere tool' on the fringes of medical work. Insofar as medical technologies as wide ranging as thermometers, visual imaging equipment, the laboratory microscope and drugs are the extension of human intentions, they are not simply inanimate objects, they 'have action'. In this sense social actors such as nurses and technologies co-produce working medical science (Latour 1987, Timmermans 2000). Social scientists gradually began to open up the 'black box' of biomedical science to scrutiny.

This move was undoubtedly supported by the new conceptual and theoretical approaches which came to the fore at the time. Certainly by the mid 1980s Freidson's (1970) distinction between the physical/biological and the social – where the former belonged to medicine and the latter to sociology – was seen as outmoded. The social and the biological were now seen as inextricably linked together rather than separate domains. Self-evidently, when biomedical science no longer stood apart from the social, it was amenable to investigation by social scientists (see Elston 1997). Developments in anthropology, cultural and gender studies all fed into the sociology of medical knowledge and medical work giving it an increasingly interdisciplinary character. Theoretically, postmodernism challenged the conventional biomedical view of the body as biologically fixed and given (see Kroker and Kroker 1988). At the same time, scientific developments in areas like genetics, computer-based biotechnology and medical engineering made it possible to deconstruct and reconstruct the body in ways that never would have been thought possible as recently as the 1960s when the sociology of medical knowledge and medical work began. This invites us to re-think the ways in which we view the body in health and in illness. For example, the Visible Human Project is a digital three-dimensional recording of human cadavers which have been dissected, photographed and converted into visual data files which can be manipulated and visualised on the computer screen. The 'real' body, the sentient person, has disappeared in this 'posthuman medicine' (Waldby 2000). But this is still medical work, albeit of a kind way beyond the purview of early sociologists of medical knowledge and medical work. New biotechologies and new ways of thinking have therefore brought new topics to the fore. No longer fixed, the body is viewed as fluid and manipulable and research is as much about the scientists and practitioners who remaster the body, be this in surgery or in the laboratory, as it is patients and their experience. But this does not mean that more traditional research on practitioners and their patients has disappeared. There is still an abiding concern with issues of long-standing concern such as the balance of power between patient and practitioner, and the influence of social, political and economic factors upon medical work. Old blends with new as social scientists and medical practitioners question the suitability of the conventional scientific model for twenty-first century medical work. It has been suggested, for example, that widespread developments such as healthcare rationing are misguided not simply in the sense that they ignore social factors, which is a rather commonplace sociological assertion, but because they are based on fundamentally misguided assumptions about the world and how it works. The assumption that the world is rational, ordered and that the right patient can get the right treatment if only the right formula, protocol or guideline can be found, is challenged by chaos and complexity theory which suggest that rather than being threatened, practitioners should embrace and work with the complexity of patient's problems and not try to introduce false certainty by reducing them into the formulaic boxes that the guidelines industry requires (see Sweeney and Griffiths 2002).

Conclusion

In this Introduction we have explored the changing character of the sociology of medical knowledge and medical work from the 1960s to the present day. The topics sociologists have been interested in have changed over time in response to developments in medical science and in the organisation of health care. The way that sociologists have approached specific topics has changed in response to theoretical developments within sociology and the social sciences more widely. Over time there has been a broadening out from the early focus on doctor-patient interaction to the wider health care division of labour to include patients themselves as health workers and, more recently, to incorporate medical work beyond direct patient care, although the traditional concerns of early research remain central. Many of these developments are reflected in the articles that have been selected for the Reader which is divided into four sections each with a brief introduction to the topic area: Medical Knowledge, Diagnosis and Treatment; Medical Power and the Patient; The Division of Labour in Health Care Work; and Patient-Provider Interaction.

References

Allen, D. (2001) *The Changing Shape of Nursing Practice*. London: Routledge.

Atkinson, P. (1995) *Medical Talk and Medical Work*. London: Sage.

Barrett, M. and Roberts, H. (1978) Doctors and their patients: the social control of women in general practice. In Smart, C. and Smart, B. (eds) *Women's Sexuality and Social Control*. London: Routledge and Kegan Paul.

Beck, U. and Beck-Gernsheim, E. (2002) *Individualization*. London: Sage.

Berg, M. and Mol, A. (1998) Differences in medicine: an introduction. In Berg, M. and Mol, A. (eds) *Differences in Medicine*. London: Duke University Press.

Bird, C., Conrad, P. and Fremont, A. (2000) Medical sociology at the millennium. In Bird, C., Conrad, P. and Fremont, A. (eds) *Handbook of Medical Sociology* (fifth edition). New Jersey: Prentice Hall.

Bloor, M. and Horobin, G. (1975) Conflict and conflict resolution in doctor/patient interactions. In Cox, C. and Mead, A. (eds) *A Sociology of Medical Practice*. London: Collier Macmillan.

Clarke, J. (1983) Sexism, feminism and medicalism: a decade review of literature on gender and illness. *Sociology of Health and Illness*, 5, 853–66.

Davies, C. (2000) Care and the transformation of professionalism. In Davies, C., Finlay, L. and Bullman, A. (eds) *Changing Practice in Health and Social Care*. London: Open University/Sage.

Davis, F. (1960) Uncertainty in medical prognosis: clinical and functional. *American Journal of Sociology*, 66, 41–7.

DHSS (1979) *Patients First*. London: HMSO.

DoH (2001) *Involving Patients and the Public in Healthcare*. London: Stationary Office.

Elston, M. (ed.) (1997) *The Sociology of Medical Science and Technology.* Oxford: Blackwell.

Engel, G.L. (1977) The need for a new medical model: a challenge for biomedicine, *Science,* 196, 129–136.

Fox, R. (1957) Training for uncertainty. In Merton, R.K., Reader, G. and Kendall, P. (eds) *The Student-Physician.* Cambridge: Harvard University Press.

Fox, R. (2001) Medical uncertainty revisited. In Bendelow, G., Carpenter, M., Vautier, C. and Williams, S. (eds) *Gender, Health and Healing.* London: Routledge.

Freidson, E. (1961) Dilemmas in the doctor-patient relationship. In Rose, A.M. (ed.) *Human Behaviour and Social Processes.* London: Routledge and Kegan Paul.

Freidson, E. (1970) *Profession of Medicine.* Chicago: Chicago University Press.

Freidson, E. (1989) *Medical Work in America.* London: Yale University Press.

Freidson, E. (2001) *Professionalism. The Third Logic.* Cambridge: Polity Press.

Giddens, A. (1991) *Modernity and Self Identity.* Cambridge: Polity Press.

Giddens, A. (1998) *Beyond Left and Right. The Future of Radical Politics.* Cambridge: Polity Press.

Graham, H. (1993) Social divisions in caring. *Women's Studies International Forum,* 16, 461–70.

Ham, C. (2001) *The New Politics of the NHS* (4th edition). London: Prentice Hall.

Ham, C. and Alberti, K. (2002) The medical profession, the public and the government. *British Medical Journal,* 324, 838–842.

Harrison, S. and Ahmad, W. (2000) Medical autonomy and the UK state 1975 to 2025. *Sociology,* 34, 129–146.

Kroker, A. and Kroker, M. (1988) *Body Invaders.* London: Macmillan.

Latour, B. (1987) *Science in Action.* Milton Keynes: Open University Press.

Light, D. (2000) The medical profession and organizational change: from professional dominance to countervailing power. In Bird, C., Conrad, P. and Fremont, A. (eds) *Handbook of Medical Sociology* (fifth edition). New Jersey: Prentice Hall.

Lock, M. and Gordon, D. (1988) *Biomedicine Examined.* London: Kulwer Academic Publishers.

McKinlay, J. (1977) The business of good doctoring or doctoring as good business: reflections on Freidson's view of the medical game. *International Journal of Health Services,* 7, 459–483.

Ministry of Health (1944) *A National Health Service.* London: HMSO.

Mishler, E., AmaraSingham, L., Hauser, S. *et al.* (1981) *Social Contexts of Health, Illness and Health Care.* Cambridge: Cambridge University Press.

Olesen, V. (2001) Resisting 'fatal uncluteredness'. Conceptualising the sociology of health and illness into the millennium. In Bendelow, G., Carpenter, M., Vautier, C. and Williams, S. (eds) *Gender, Health and Healing.* London: Routledge.

Parsons, T. (1951) *The Social System.* New York: Free Press.

Parsons, T. (1975) The sick role and the role of the physician reconsidered. *Milbank Memorial Fund Quarterly,* (summer), 257–278.

Porter, S. (1995) *Nursing's Relationship with Medicine.* Aldershot: Avebury.

Roth, J. (1963) *Timetables.* New York: Bobbs-Merrill.

Scheff, T. (1963) Decision rules and types of error, and their consequences in medical diagnosis, *Behavioural Science,* 8, 97–107.

Shaw, N. (1974) *Forced Labour.* New York: Pergamon Press.

Silverman, D. (1987) *Communication and Medical Practice. Social Relations in the Clinic.* London: Sage.

Stacey, M. (1984) Who are the health workers? Patients and other unpaid workers in health care. *Economic and Industrial Democracy*, 5, 157–84.

Stein, L. (1967) The doctor-nurse game, *Archives of General Psychiatry*, 16, 699–703.

Stimson, G. and Webb, B. (1975) *Going to See the Doctor*. London: Routledge and Kegan Paul.

Strauss, A., Fagerhaugh, S., Suczek, B. and Wiener, C. (1982) Sentimental work in the technologized hospital, *Sociology of Health and Illness*, 4, 255–78.

Strauss, A., Fagerhaugh, S., Suczek, B. and Wiener, C. (1984) The work of hospitalized patients. *Social Science and Medicine*, 16, 977–986.

Strong, P. (1979) Sociological imperialism and the profession of medicine: a critical examination of the thesis of medical imperialism, *Social Science and Medicine*, 13a, 199–215.

Svensson, R. (1996) The interplay between doctors and nurses: a negotiated order perspective, *Sociology of Health and Illness*, 18, 379–398.

Sweeney, K. and Griffiths, F. (eds) (2002) *Complexity and Healthcare*. Abingdon: Radcliffe Medical Press.

Timmermans, S. (2000) Technology and medical practice. In Bird, C., Conrad, P. and Fremont, A. (eds) *Handbook of Medical Sociology* (fifth edition). New Jersey: Prentice Hall.

Waitzkin, H. (2000) Changing patient-physician relationships in the changing health-policy environment. In Bird, C., Conrad, P. and Fremont, A. (eds) *Handbook of Medical Sociology* (fifth edition). New Jersey: Prentice Hall.

Waitzkin, H. and Stoeckle, J. (1976) Information control and the micropolitics of health care, *Social Science and Medicine*, 10, 263–76.

Waldby, C. (2000) *The Visible Human Project. Informatic Bodies and Posthuman Medicine*. London: Routledge.

White, S. (1999) Rights and responsibilities: A social democratic perspective. In Gamble, A. and White, S. (eds) *The New Social Democracy*. Oxford: Blackwell.

Wicks, D. (1998) *Nurses and Doctors at Work*. Buckingham: Open University Press.

Wright, P. and Treacher, A. (eds) (1981) *The Problem of Medical Knowledge. Examining the Social Construction of Medicine*. Edinburgh: Edinburgh University Press.

Section 1

Medical Knowledge, Diagnosis and Treatment

Introduction

The activities, investigations and claims of bench, or laboratory-based scientists have been much explored during recent decades (Charlesworth *et al.* 1990, Collins and Pinch 1994, Knorr-Cetina 1983, Latour 1987, Latour and Woolgar 1986, Lynch 1985, Woolgar 1988). Many of these investigations have sought to examine – in various sociological frameworks – the nature of the knowledge claims that scientists make. In a sense they have focused on what 'science' is all about. Naturally, the answers differ in the detail, but one conclusion that runs through most, if not all, of the work is that scientific knowledge is made or manufactured rather than 'discovered'. The exact conditions under which knowledge is made, of course, forms the occasion for empirical sociological investigation. And one consequence of the SSK (sociology of scientific knowledge) stance is that the sociological investigator is required to focus on the situated nature of scientific discussion and inquiry rather than to theorise about such processes from afar.

Naturally, in so far as scientific knowledge is made rather than discovered, it is made in social settings by human beings acting in concert. As such, the 'social' might be said to lay at the heart of science rather than on its sleeve or at the margins. Thus, appeals to facts, or to nature, evidence, data, and proof are, in the end, viewed as involving scientists in the deployment of so many rhetorical devices so as to establish their truth claims one over the other. Scientists themselves, of course, present their investigations and results as the consequence of objective and dispassionate work at the laboratory bench – unaffected by social factors except, perhaps, in trivial ways. In short, they represent themselves as mere conduits for the transmission of facts about a reality that is independent of and external to social relations.

As Latour (1987) has argued – and demonstrated – one way in which we can unravel the claims of the dispassionate scientist is to enter into the 'black box' in which scientific work is executed. That is, to investigate in detail how scientific facts are made in this or that laboratory. Yet, when we do that we discover that the line between the social and the scientific melts away. What then comes into view are numerous and complex inter-relationships between people and things, and Latour and others have talked of such inter-relationships as forming networks. Indeed, they have subsequently sought to advance a form of analysis referred to as actor-network theory or ANT (Law and Hassard 1999). ANT, whatever it might be, is not a theory, but it does offer some very useful concepts and ideas for getting to grips with the nitty-gritty of scientific work. In particular it emphasises the dynamics of 'doing' scientific work. That is to say, it elects to focus on the ways in which scientific networks recruit and manipulate things and other actors in local circumstances so as to advance claims and discoveries. It a related vein, authors such as Mol (1999, 2000), and Law (1994) have focused on the notion of 'performance' to account for the manner in which specific medical conditions – such as anaemia and arteriosclerosis – are produced in the clinic, the laboratory and other settings. Such an emphasis on 'performance' (Law 1994) serves to highlight how the nature of disease entities depend very much on the organizational context in which they are talked about and investigated, and that is a theme that also emerges from the papers that follow this introduction.

The interface between the sociology of science and the sociology of medicine has, of course, formed a special focus of study for readers and contributors of *Sociology of Health and Illness* during recent years. The 1997 Monograph on *The Sociology of Medical Science and Technology* (Elston 1997) offers many examples of the kinds of issues that have been examined in that framework. In addition, the Journal has published a number of papers that were not deliberately or consciously framed in terms of debates pertinent to the sociology of scientific knowledge – and certainly not in terms of ANT – but which nonetheless have much to offer to those debates. Indeed, in the selection that follows we can see a number of parallels between work in the sociology of science and that in medical sociology. For example, we will see how the consideration of 'social' factors, rather than resting at the margins of the clinical decision making process, is absolutely integral to that process. We will also see how operations usually regarded as doing nothing more than reflecting the 'facts of the case' are more often than not responsible for constructing the very facts they claim to represent. And we will see how it is investigation into the situated nature of medical decision making that offers the most productive route to unravelling the multiple processes that occur within the black box of clinical activity.

For example, the paper by Hughes and Griffiths investigates the degree to which decisions about the suitability of patients for cardiac surgery involves much more than a consideration of merely technical or clinical factors about the patient's condition. True enough, the rhetoric of surgeons emphasises technical considerations alone, but when we study surgeons in action (to paraphrase Latour 1987), we discover that the social is brought right into the diagnostic and decision-making process. In fact, it is implicated in such as way as to meld the technical into a much broader organizational mesh. Thus considerations of age, ethnicity and, above all, the lifestyle of patients are routinely called upon to justify or dispute the use of surgical procedures. Consequently, surgeons are adept at constructing a 'moral character' for patients, and it is reflections on that character that are often central to clinical decisions about whether or not to proceed with surgery. The emphasis that is given within the paper to matters of rhetoric, and to the nature of the surgical service as a socio-technical system, resonates of course not merely with SSK, but also with work in the sociology of technology. (See, for example, Bijker, Hughes and Pinch 1990, Lock, Young and Cambrosio 2000).

Silverman's paper likewise examines and highlights the ways in which social and moral considerations impinge on clinical work. We remain in the cardiologist's clinic, but here we are dealing with children – and especially children displaying the signs of Down's syndrome. Silverman argues that cardiac surgeons in the paediatric clinic tend to 'demedicalise' the treatment of Down's syndrome children. That is to say, they tend to elevate social considerations – for example, about the child's quality of life – above medical considerations. In so doing they commonly reverse the order of interpretation in terms of which children are normally dealt with. As Silverman points out in his introduction, his is an essay in the 'mechanics of persuasion', and as with the Hughes and Griffiths paper it serves to illustrate the gap that exists between the standard rhetoric of scientific medicine as dispassionate procedures, and the language of everyday medical practice.

The paper by Bloor and Fonkert focuses on the nature of reality construction in two therapeutic communities. Unlike the previous papers, this one brings the patient into the knowledge creating process, and it does so in a framework that is not too far distanced from ANT – namely, the framework of ethnomethodology. In particular, the authors see the fabrication of knowledge as inevitably ad hoc and pragmatic, and they demonstrate how this is so. Patients do things and then account for them, but they account for them in terms of a rhetoric that is for the most part given to them by professional staff. In consequence, the social structures and social worlds of the treatment settings are progressively established and underpinned as objective realities. No doubt the same kind of analysis could be applied to the reality constructed within clinical consultations in general. Though were that to be done, it would become clear that patients are not always ready and willing to embrace the rhetoric of those who seek to cure them, and often strive to develop an alternative rhetoric of disease and suffering.

Of all the papers in the section, it is Berg's that probably comes closest to the kinds of considerations that are raised in the sociology of science. Berg takes as his point of focus the medical record and examines the various ways such a record shapes the patient trajectory through the treatment process. As far as Berg is concerned, the record, far from being an adjunct to treatment, functions as tool that shapes and determines the things that are done to and for patients. The record may even be said to be responsible for creating the patient's identity. The latter is a claim that Barret (1996) had also advanced – though in his case, with respect to patients expressing elements of serious psychiatric disorder. Within the rhetoric of medicine, of course, the patient record is said to merely mirror the treatment process. However examination of the use of the record in action (and in an organizational network) shows otherwise. Indeed, considering how important the technology of record keeping is in western culture in general and in organisational settings in particular, it is surprising how little is or has been written about the use of documents in medical or other contexts (see, for example, Prior (2003)). Berg's analysis provides an excellent and welcome exception to this generally neglected field by illustrating how documents mediate human relationships and human activities within the clinic. Further, as Berg himself points out, a focus on documents and their use offers sociology a distinctive and novel way of examining 'thinking', decision-making and other supposedly mental activities without any recourse of individual psychology.

The paper by May and Sirur examines the use of homeopathy in general practice. The use of homeopathic remedies touches on issues concerning the efficacy of such treatments and the evidence that can be mustered to support their use. In a world of evidence based medicine (Grayson 1997), of course, such matters are central. As far as methods are concerned, the gold standard of scientific medicine is normally taken to be the randomised controlled trial (RCT). Yet such trials are said to be inapplicable to the analysis of homeopathic remedies. What May and Sirur show, however, is that general practitioners can still call upon 'evidence' relating to the effectiveness of treatments by using different standards and measures of proof. GP's may, for example, question the relevance of scientific standards to patient's problems, or question the appropriateness of RCTs to the assessment of feelings and responses. By so doing the authors both highlight interesting and important features of homeopathic medicine and facts about science. Indeed, parallels between the claims made in this paper and those made in the debates concerning the nature of cold fusion and gravity waves (Collins and Pinch 1993) are, at the very least, instructive.

All in all, then, the worlds of the laboratory scientist and of the clinical scientist are remarkably similar in the procedures and devices that are called upon to support everyday professional activities. These similarities are apparent in the ways in which knowledge is organised and used, the manner in which problems are diagnosed, and the means by which problems are resolved and treated. The selection of materials that follow go some considerable way in demonstrating how those parallels might be studied further. It only remains to emphasise how the papers reprinted here serve to provide excellent illustrative material as to how talk, text, action and technology are ordinarily woven into what Bijker, Hughes and Pinch (1990) have referred to as the 'seamless web' of organisational life. In that respect as Berg shows, they also demonstrate how 'the social' as a pure category is a chimera.

References

Barret, R. (1996) *The Psychiatric Team and the Social Definition of Schizophrenia.* Cambridge: Cambridge University Press.

Bijker, W.E., Hughes, T.R. and Pinch, T.J. (eds) (1990) *The Social Construction of Technological Systems. New Directions in the Sociology of Sociology and History of Technology.* Cambridge, MA: MIT Press.

Charlesworth, M., Farrall, L., Stokes, T. and Turnbuil, D. (1990) Life Among the Scientists. Oxford: Oxford University Press.

Collins, H.M. and Pinch, T. (1994) *The Golem. What Everyone should know about Science.* Cambridge: Cambridge University Press.

Elston, M.A. (ed.) *The Sociology of Medical Science and Technology.* Oxford: Blackwell.

Grayson, L. (1997) *Evidence-based Medicine. An overview and guide to the literature.* London: British Library.

Knorr-Cetina, K.D. (1983) The ethnographic study of scientific work. Towards a constructivist interpretation of science. In Knorr-Cetina, K.D. and Mulkay, M. (eds) *Science Observed.* London: Sage.

Latour, B. (1987) *Science in Action. How to Follow Engineers and Scientists through Society.* Buckingham: Open University Press.

Latour, B. and Woolgar, S. (1986) *Laboratory Life. The Social Construction of Scientific Facts.* 2nd edn. London: Sage.

Law, J. (1994) *Organising Modernity.* Oxford: Blackwell.

Law, J. and Hassard, J. (eds) (1999) *Actor Network Theory and After.* Oxford: Blackwell.

Lock, M., Young, A. and Cambrosio, A. (eds) (2000) *Living and Working with the New Medical technologies.* Cambridge: Cambridge University Press.

Lynch, M. (1985) *Art and Artefact in Laboratory Science. A Study of Shop Work and Shop Talk in a Research Laboratory.* London: Routledge and Kegan Paul.

Mol, A. (1999) Ontological politics. A word and some questions. In Law, J. and Hassard, J. (eds) *Actor Network Theory and After.* Oxford: Blackwell.

Mol, A. (2000) Performing arteriosclerosis. In Lock, M., Young, A. and Cambrosio, A. (eds) *Living and Working with the New Medical technologies.* Cambridge: Cambridge University Press.

Prior, L. (2003) *Using Documents in Social Research.* London: Sage.

Woolgar, S. (1988) *Science. The Very Idea.* London: Tavistock.

Practices of reading and writing: the constitutive role of the patient record in medical work

Marc Berg

Re, the Egyptian sun god, speaks of Thoth, the god of writing who is also the patron of physicians:

I will save him from his enemies, and Thoth shall be his guide, he who lets writing speak and has composed the books; he gives to the skilful, to the physicians who accompany him, skill to cure.

Quoted in Goody (1977: 144)

Introduction

At first sight, the medical record does not seem an interesting topic for medical sociologists. It is commonly perceived as merely representing 'what has taken place': in it, medical personnel record the patient's current condition, his or her medical history, and the diagnostic and therapeutic activities undertaken. As Raffel phrases it, the record is ultimately and ideally a *copy* of an event: it 'repeats the event but is not supposed to be, in any important sense, itself an event' (1979: 18). The notes in the medical record are post-hoc representations of past decisions and investigations – as a 'repository of information' (Dick and Steen 1991), the record merely stores them for possible future reference.

This perception renders the record an uninteresting topic to study – except, perhaps, with regard to the question whether the information in the record provides a *good* representation. Since the representation is seen to be a mirror of what is represented, the former necessarily *follows* the latter in time; sociologically speaking, the representation can never be of direct relevance to what is represented. It is wholly passive: it may *represent* an event more or less adequately, but it does not *affect* the event.

Within (amongst others) ethnomethodology and science studies, however, the concept of 'representation' has been re-evaluated in recent years. No longer willing to restrict debates on representation to the faithfulness of the 'copy' to its 'original', attention has been drawn to the activities of representing, and to the uses to which representations are being put. From this point of view, 'representations' take on a very different life. When the activity of representing is brought into the picture, the relationship between the representation and the represented becomes much more complex. Since the creation of the representation involves the active work of ordering, these authors argue, it *is* in fact involved in the very event it represents. There is no neat temporal succession between the two: rather, the representation and represented are achieved simultaneously. No longer seen as passive mirrors, then, the productive role of representations is now a central concern in analysis (Latour 1987, Haraway 1991, Lynch 1993).

This critique of representational realism should not be misunderstood as a form of sociological determinism. 'Representation' is not the (social) attaching of 'meaning' through which the (natural) world achieves its existence. For one thing, this would merely reverse the direction of the relation between the event and its representation. Rather than showing how they emerge *together*, the latter would then simply constitute the former instead of vice versa. In addition, the argument 'that it is the *social* that is determinant in the last instance', in Law's terms, holds on to 'an impoverished version of the social: warm bodies, selves, their words, their gestures; and maybe their texts' (1994: 129). 'The social', as a pure category, is a chimera: practices always also include artefacts, architectures, paper, machines. An understanding of modern professional and scientific practices requires attention to the fundamentally *heterogeneous* nature of these practices. 'Teasing this heterogeneous and seamless web apart', Law states, simply 'doesn't make much sense' (Law 1994).

This paper draws on these insights in an attempt to reconsider the sociological significance of the medical record[1]. It attempts to demonstrate that the medical record plays an active, constitutive role in current medical work – to show the breadth and depth in which it is implicated in medical practice. It figures prominently, for instance, in the processes of shaping and maintaining a patient's trajectory (Strauss *et al.* 1985, Timmermans 1995). But this is just one of the dimensions that are involved; at the same time, it is part and parcel of the production of hierarchical relations, of the shaping of the doctor–patient encounter, of the processes that constitute the socialisation of interns, and so forth.

Avoiding the Scylla of representational realism and the Charybdis of social constructivism, then, this paper depicts the record as a force in itself, *mediating* the relations that act and work through it (Latour 1994). 'Social interaction' cannot be said to constitute the meaning of the medical record since the record is part and parcel of that interaction; 'social interaction' is *transformed through* it. Yet this does not mean that the medical record determines work processes: the formal demands of medical records, for example, are continually subordinated to the contingent requirements of the actual tasks.

The medical record achieves this role through *practices of reading and writing* (Law and Lynch 1990). These practices, in which the record is turned to, leafed through, read, used for jottings, communicated through, dispatched, form a crucial site in the sociotechnical organisation of medical work[2]. Without these practices, the record would be dead, disconnected, without any relevance. These activities are what bring it to life – and what allow it to have its mediating role in the organisation of medical work. Without the *interrelation* of people and paperwork, in other words, doctors could not be doctors and nurses could not be nurses.

The aim of grasping the multiple ways in which this particular representation is involved in the production of current medical work might be thought too grandiose for a single paper. Yet the breadth and depth of the record's involvement in this production is exactly what this article attempts to bring to the fore. As a way out of this dilemma, I discuss three case vignettes, selected to demonstrate the scope of the record's role. The discussions are not intended as 'definite interpretations' of the material presented: rather, they attempt to illustrate the type of analysis proposed. The vignettes are taken from field notes from two months of participatory observation in the oncology ward and outpatient clinic in an Academic Hospital in the Netherlands. The medical records involved were also studied, and audio recordings were available for the first and last vignette[3].

In the first two sections, I elaborate the claim that the record is an active, constitutive element of current medical work. First, I address the way the record enters into the process of 'medical decision making' during the doctor–patient interaction, and into that interaction itself. Subsequently, I discuss some aspects of how the record mediates medical work as it is performed in the wards, hallways and laboratories of a hospital. Finally, the third vignette is drawn upon to illustrate how the practices of reading and writing tend to produce particular renderings of patients' histories – including notions of how medical work is structured, and of the role of the record itself.

Producing the doctor–patient interaction

It is Thursday morning. Dr. Bear, oncologist, crosses out the name of his previous patient on his schedule for this afternoon's outpatients' clinic. The next line reads 'Ms. Roth 10/02/1928 NP'. 'NP' stands for 'New Patient', which means that the allotted time slot is generous: 45 minutes. He picks up the new record, assembled by the clinic's secretary. It contains the referral letter, an empty 'financial administration' form, and an empty form for the case history (consisting of four preformatted pages on which the current situation is to be outlined, followed by empty, unformatted pages, on which briefer entries are recorded at subsequent patient visits). At a later stage, these pages will be followed by chronologically ordered laboratory results, and by letters to and from colleagues. The secretary has already made copies of two ten-year-old letters written by a general internist, concerning Ms. Roth's diabetes.

Bear scans the general practitioner's referral letter:

Re: Ms. Roth 10/02/1928

Having spoken with you by telephone, I refer above-mentioned patient
concerning carcinomatous pleuritis.
For 1 week, patient has been nauseated and vomiting
Investigation: severe weight loss
                         abdomen: well demarcated lumps
                         pulm: reduced respiratory sounds Right
Previous history: in 1977 breast amputation because of adenoca.
Thorax X-ray: massive amount of pleural fluid in right hemithorax.
Lab: enclosed

Treatment requested.

A separate note contains the laboratory results, requested by the
general practitioner, which show an elevated sedimentation rate of 59
[a non-specific sign of inflammation].

Bear briefly scans the letters, and stands up to get Ms. Roth from the
waiting room. An elderly, thin and fragile looking woman enters and sits
down. Bear smiles reassuringly, picks up his pen, and looks at the referral
letter again. He opens the record at the first page of the case history. At
the entry called *Reason for Referral*, he writes *metastasised breast ca*, while
asking: 'What has your doctor told you?'. He looks at Ms. Roth, who
says: 'Yeah . . . I could not eat well the last couple of days, but I'm doing
a bit better now. It remains inside'. Bear nods, looks down at his papers
again, and asks: 'But he has taken some pictures, hasn't he? X-rays of the
lungs? And he drew some blood?' 'Yes . . . I don't know . . . they gave me
a letter to give to you'. Bear: 'So you haven't seen your doctor any more –
he called and said . . . eh . . . please be at the hospital next Thursday?'
'Yes'. He starts writing in the next section, *(Previous Diseases and
Surgery): 1977. Breast amputation.* 'The breast surgery was in 1977,
wasn't it?' '77, yes'. 'And have you ever had anything else wrong with you?'
'No, thank goodness'. Bear: 'Just a bit of diabetes, right?' (writes this
down). 'Just diabetes, yes . . .'. 'And the breast surgery, what side was that,
left or right?' 'Right'. Bear jots *R* after *breast amputation*, and continues:
'Has that received any radiation after the operation?' 'At the time, yes,
but I haven't had that for years'. 'And no drugs for that operation?'
'No'. 'No', murmurs Bear, writing *follow-up radiation* after the previous
entry. 'No other hospital admissions?' 'Yeah . . . I have . . . once . . . an
inflammation in . . . in my mouth . . . but otherwise . . .'.

Bear ignores this, skips the section *Major Complaint(s)*, and jots down
a circled *1* under the next section, *Anamnesis*. 'And why did you go to see
your doctor this time?' Ms. Roth answers: 'I couldn't eat anything any
more, I hadn't eaten for four days at least, and drink came up also'. Bear
writes *appetite* ↓. 'And you have lost weight?' 'Yeah . . .'. *weight loss* +.
'How much?' 'Well, I don't know, I hardly dared to weigh myself'. *how
much?* 'Do you have any other complaints?' 'Yes, I've got lumps, here'. She

points at her belly. . . . 'And how long have they been there?' 'That must be some months already . . . they are getting larger and larger . . . And there is another one here'. She points at a lump. Bear ignores this, and writes 2. *Has lumps in her abdomen, for some months already.* 'And do you have more complaints?' 'I don't know . . .'. 'You're short of breath, aren't you?' '. . . yes, my right . . . my left foot is swollen somewhat.' 'mm . . . and shortness of breath?' 'yes . . . I tire quickly . . . tired, often . . . weak . . .'. 3. *short of breath. Weak.* 'And do you have a fever?' 'I don't know'. Bear looks at his papers. Ms. Roth rises, and lifts her shirt: 'Here you have the lumps'. 'Yes, we'll look at that in a moment.' He smiles at her, and she sits down again. He writes *Fever -*.

Bear starts writing on a new line (in the same section), and starts with the systems review[4]. 'Have you ever had a heavy feeling on your chest, or pain?' 'No, thanks goodness'. *AP -*. 'And palpitations?' 'No'. *Palp -*. After a couple of questions (including whether she has any children) which are all answered negatively, Bear asks: 'Is there anybody in your family who has had breast cancer?' 'Not that I know of'. Bear moves back up to the earlier section *Previous Diseases*, and adds *family history negative* beneath *1977 breast amputation.*

He skips the sections *Hypersensitivities* and *Family*, moves to *Social Anamnesis*, and asks whether her husband 'is healthy'. 'Yeees . . . he has had a minor stroke a few times . . .'. Bear nods, and writes *husband healthy, no children.* 'Now I would like to take a look at you'. While she undresses, Bear flips through the notes he has written. He examines her, and calls the pathology lab to ask for somebody to take a sample from one of the lumps while she is here. Then he sits back at his desk, and fills in the sections concerning the physical investigation.

When Ms. Roth is dressed again, he tells her that he thinks 'the cancer has returned and has spread'. She reacts calmly, and he proposes to treat her with hormones to 'reduce the lumps' [such treatment might alleviate symptoms in some forms of breast cancer]. He concludes the consultation by writing down: *Concl: metastasised breast ca*, followed by *R/Nolvadex 2 × 20 mg.*

This somewhat conventional portrayal of 'doctor's work', an individual doctor presented with a new patient, offers a fruitful place to start exploring the medical record's role. First, the practices of reading and writing are crucial in the production of the very *possibility* of 'doctoring'. In accounting for the competence of doctors, we tend to focus on their intellectual qualities: the need to study hard and long. Indeed, 'medical decision making' is commonly perceived as being a mental process, located in the individual physician's brain- and a 'good' doctor is someone who (amongst other things) has enough cognitive powers to process rationally all the information that continually floods him or her (Atkinson 1995, Berg 1995). Recent sociological studies of 'thinking-in-action', however, have shown that this image vastly overrates the centrality of the mental realm[5]. What we often consider to be 'intellectual tasks' in fact often appear to be highly embodied activities, in which ongoing interactions with the immediate surroundings play a core role. 'Thinking', as Latour phrases it, is often achieved through our 'eyes and hands' (1986).

One of the ways in which we can assess how 'cognition' is accomplished in practice is by looking at the way the medical record forms an integral part of the process of transforming a patient's problem into a manageable problem. In Dr. Bear's consultation with Ms. Roth, his continuous (re)turning to his paperwork is prominent. He construes an image of 'just what he should do with this patient' through the (re)reading of the letter and the laboratory results and through the (re)reading and writing of his *own* notes. Through his activities of reading and writing, Bear 'channels' the case: he narrows down the plethora of potential tasks and divergent data into a clear notion of 'what to do next'. His first entry, 'metastasised breast ca' as the 'reason for referral', already cuts away a whole range of potential routes to pursue. Denoting Ms. Roth's problem as 'metastasised breast ca' dismisses the option that some other type of cancer is responsible for her current condition (to consider this option would imply invoking a whole spectrum of additional diagnostic tests). This 'summary' distinctively *transforms* the information Bear has at his disposal by assembling it in a specific manner: the referral note does not state that it is the 1977 breast cancer which is now causing the new problem.

In writing down this phrase, Bear sharpens the focus for the current situation; in 'summarising' the 'reason for referral' in this way, he is involved in the *production* of a problem which is manageable for the hospital's working routines (including his own). Writing down short sentences extracted from the multiple resources at hand (the different letters, the questions Bear asks Ms. Roth, her physique, the physical investigation) aids the building of a composite picture of 'just what is to be done'. From the bewildering mass of information, produced for different purposes, the emotionally laden story Ms. Roth produces, and the (equally emotionally laden) cues that her physique and non-verbal reactions provide, Bear construes a 'clear case' in and through filling in the empty sheets before him. He creates an overview, distilling and reconstructing information from different times and places, different relevancies, and different sources into a single frame, in such a way that the bits of information he jots down mutually elaborate each other, and form a clear case of 'relapse of breast cancer for which palliative treatment will be given' (Whalen 1993). Every entry entails the active production of a historical piece of information: the eliciting, interpretation, and subsequent transformation of Ms. Roth's words into a 'symptom' or 'complaint' which fits the medical category of 'metastasised breast ca'. Each entry is a transformation of disparate cues into one which strongly directs the line of action to take. In the next section in the record, 'Previous Diseases and Surgery', Bear immediately writes down those bits of information he (thereby) denotes

relevant to the current situation ('1977. Breast amputation'). He adds
'diabetes mellitus' two lines beneath this, referring to it as a 'bit of diabetes'
– only to further ignore this issue. He pursues his questioning on the treatments she has undergone for the breast cancer, and ignores her final remark
on her mouth problems. (See also how he elicits that the patient is 'short of
breath' and that she has no fever, and how he omits much of what she brings
to the fore).

Bear's paperwork is a crucial feature of this transformation process, then,
in that it affords this iterative channelling process: it affords the creation of
a re-presentation of 'the patient' for him to view at a glance, to ponder, and
to elaborate further[6]. Its value lies in the very fact that it is a highly *selective*,
distanced, abstracted 'representation'. *In* this transformation of multiple
sources of information into some curtailed sentences, the health care worker
gains the opportunity to 'pull' the patient out of the stream of day-to-day
events and into the temporal or anatomical order of, say, a disease's life
span. For example, Bear scans and orders the heterogeneous resources at
hand to construe the temporal progression from the breast cancer's initial
remission to its later relapse. Likewise, he attempts to create an ordered,
anatomical image of just what organs are currently affected. Bear's writing,
here, is not the *recording* of his thought processes: his notes are not a
mere post-hoc, abbreviated recapitulation of his reasoning. His reading and
writing cannot be disentangled from his 'thinking': without the record's
presence, Bear's 'mental processes' would not go very far. The visual overview
that is created on the form, the juxtaposing of terms, the recontextualised
scrutiny that these inscriptions afford, the facticity that is achieved by the
simple but significant phenomenon that Bear's *own* inscriptions become
part of the information resources he has available – all this is inextricably
part of these 'thought processes' *themselves* (Goody 1977, Latour 1986).

Being part and parcel of the process of medical decision making, moreover, the record also affects its *content*. It structures the selections made:
through its set-up, for instance, through its pre-printed forms and categories,
it aids in the process of creating a problem-definition which is 'medically
relevant'. The form lists the questions to ask, and differentiates between
relevant and irrelevant information (by, for example, not mentioning a topic,
or having only a small space for 'social history'). The form Bear has to
complete organises the consultation: he follows the layout of the form in
the organisation of his questioning and the subsequent investigation, letting
himself be 'triggered' by each subsequent heading. Bear's representational
activity, then, shapes the very events he is representing: he sequentially
addresses the different sections, following the logic of the record which thus
co-produces the final definition of the situation[7].

At the same time, however, the record does not determine Bear's behaviour. It is one important resource among those he draws upon to fulfil his
task; in addition to his paperwork, the questions he asks Ms. Roth, her
physique and her reactions to his words all shape the ongoing course of the

consultation. There is no fixed order in which he draws upon these resources. He goes back and forth between them, reacting to cues that happen to be encountered in an ad hoc fashion. The concrete structure of the conversation is accomplished 'on the spot', in continuous interaction with contingent features of the situation that induce a question, an activity, or a new diagnostic option to consider (c.f. Lynch 1985, 247, Luff *et al.* 1992). Bear reacts to the different headings on his form, but he similarly jumps back and forth within the form in response to his patient's replies, and he asks additional questions triggered by the referral note. For example, at the beginning of the consultation Bear is (amongst other things) trying to determine what Ms. Roth knows about her condition. He asks '[your doctor] has taken some pictures, hasn't he?' when looking at the referral note again, now being triggered by its mentioning of an X-ray: this implies that the general practitioner must have told Ms. Roth *something* about why she needed one.

The record's role in the achievement of a 'manageable problem', however, does not stop here. As I have argued elsewhere, medical work is not adequately described by pointing at the way physicians (mentally) combine medical data to make decisions (Berg 1992). Rather, medical work is the active articulation of a wide array of elements (such as time, laboratory data, the support of colleagues, historical information). All these elements shape the ongoing and recurring transformation of patients' problems into manageable problems – and all these elements are (re)constructed in these processes.

The multiplicity of co-occurring tasks is a prominent feature of Bear's consultation with Ms. Roth. Simultaneously, he is trying to find out what she knows about her disease, what exactly her condition is, what type of treatment could be considered, and what information from the general practitioner needs re-checking. 'Has your doctor made X-rays' is not so much a question as to *whether* (s)he did that (the general practitioner's note already mentioned this), although it does help to build Bear's picture of what exactly has taken place. Primarily, the question attempts to find out whether Ms. Roth is aware of her grim prognosis. The same clues are drawn upon to build a picture about Ms. Roth's tumour, to determine the right tone in the consultation, to determine what she needs to be told, and to check what therapeutic options (if any) she has already considered. Likewise, in calling the pathology lab for the results of the biopsy while he examined her, Bear ensures a speedy determination of the type of tumour. At the same time, he avoids delays in his own outpatient's clinic and (by forgoing further diagnostic work) prevents a lengthy and painful hospital episode for Ms. Roth.

The medical record affords the manageability of this plethora of divergent tasks in the same way as depicted above. Writing down one-line summaries on paper – which then take on the existence of 'the current problem' – reduces the complexity of the tasks on hand. Transforming Ms. Roth's remark on her husband ('he has had a minor stroke a few times') into 'husband healthy' effectively allows Bear to delay consideration of her home situation to a later date. With a 'healthy husband', there is as yet no need to worry whether she can handle her deteriorating condition without addi-tional professional help. Likewise, by omitting any mention of her wish (not) to know certain details of her condition, and by writing down 'metastasised breast ca' as the reason for referral, Bear effectively stops wondering about what exactly Ms. Roth does or does not (want to) know. In the remainder of the consultation, he treats her in his routine mode: direct but gentle.

Finally, Bear's reading and writing also enters into the production of a manageable problem through directly mediating the doctor–patient inter-action (Heath 1982). Bear often breaks off an elaboration or an answer by Ms. Roth by looking down at his papers, or, even more effectively, by start-ing to write. His writing and reading *as such* are instrumental in the shaping of the way turns are distributed, 'relevant' issues to pursue are distinguished from 'irrelevant' issues, time to speak is distinguished from time to be silent, and shifts between stages in the consultation (as between 'questions' and 'investigation') are marked. Drawing a line beneath notes written down not only physically separates this entry from the rest: it is also a clear message that the consultation is over (especially when the physician also closes the patient's record). Overall, the fact that Bear is writing and reading, and Ms. Roth is not contributes to the production and mutual recognition of the situation as an 'expert' consulted by a 'client', and of the distribution of duties and rights which come with that (Zimmerman 1969, Silverman 1987).

Organising the clinic

In the previous section, the represented and the representation emerged together within the dyad of the doctor–patient interaction. A compliant, recontextualised and retemporalised body emerged as the outcome of a process in which the physician's recording activity figured centrally. The classic, individual doctor–patient setting, however, is highly circumscribed. Can this same co-production of represented and representation be seen to occur when the scope of the setting investigated is widened? Can the claim that the record is involved in the very production of medical work also be extended to include the myriad of interactions, work trajectories, flows of resources and people that characterise the everyday affairs of hospital-based medical work?

It is Friday, around noon. Matthew, the head nurse of the oncology ward, bumps into Fred, the senior registrar. Matthew has been told that an 'acute leukaemia' is being sent in from a regional hospital. Edward, the junior registrar, joins them; he has spoken to Richards, a senior oncologist who has been involved in the transferring of this case. Edward has made a note of this conversation, and he starts to sum up what is on it. 'Female, 1969, Pearson, acute leukaemia, probably lymphoblastic. Slides, dyed and not dyed'. Fred interrupts: 'Are those bone marrow smears? Or blood smears?' Edward, who does not know, continues the list: '. . . Monday morning: chromosome tests, bone marrow biopsy . . . Vitamin B12 and folic acid . . .'. Fred underlines these last words: 'We must do that now'. '. . . Hickmann catheter [a catheter inserted in the subclavian artery, through which chemotherapy and blood cells can be administered] . . . Peters [a surgeon] preferably Monday morning'. Fred nods. Behind them, a young woman sits on a bench, crying. Matthew looks at her. 'She's here . . .'.

In the registrar's room, they see the carton boxes which contain Ms. Pearson's smears. 'This is bone marrow, see?' says Fred. 'It has little chunks in it. And they're coloured too. Good, then we can confirm the diagnosis this afternoon'. He picks up a sheet of blank paper, and sits down, grabbing Edward's note. 'Monday we'll do the genetics. Can we send stuff to the genetics lab daily?' Matthew nods. 'Fine. I'm going to redo all the blood tests – we need to map her here anyway'. He calls Peters, and tells him that they are not yet sure about Ms. Pearson's clotting function, and that Monday is early enough, since 'we need a diagnosis first anyway'. But Peters prefers to bring the Hickmann in this afternoon: that fits his schedule better. While Fred continues his phone calls to arrange this, he and Edward divide tasks. 'You make sure these blood tests are done. All urgent, and this bleeding time is super urgent. And get a thorax X-ray now – we do not want the surgeon to cut into a tumourous mass'.

Meanwhile, Helen (the ward's secretary) prepares Ms. Pearson's inpatient record[8], and a separate nursing record, containing general checklists (is the patient informed? is the room disinfected?), lists for fluid loss and intake, and so forth. She also prints Ms. Pearson's hospital ID card onto a new order form: an unstructured page, chronologically listing actions requested by physicians which are to be accomplished by nurses (tests to be ordered, medication to be given).

It is 2:00 p.m. The haematology lab phones through Ms. Pearson's bleeding time: 14 minutes. Fred: 'If it's 14, Edward, you have to order extra thrombos [too few thrombocytes – a symptom of leukaemia – causes reduced clotting function]. Fred rises, and walks over to Helen to order this himself. 'Give 8 units to her immediately, and measure the bleeding time again afterwards'. Then he goes to the laboratory where Richards is looking at the slides, and asks whether they have 'a diagnosis yet'. 'Well', Richards says, 'it is not all that clear. You can start hydrating her, but I want to redo the biopsies. I don't trust them when they're not ours'.

In the nursing room, meanwhile, Irene is filling in a temperature list: a preformatted form, included as the first, unfolding page in every inpatient record, where nurses daily enter the pulse and temperature, blood pressure, weight, drugs given, and so forth. Helen comes in, and says that thrombos have been ordered for Ms. Pearson – 'super urgent' she adds wryly. Irene goes looking for John, who is responsible for this patient today. When she returns, she fills in some fluid balance forms – a 'boring chore', she says. It requires checking what a patient has drunk, the amount of fluid 'gone in' through infusions, and the amount of fluid 'gone out' through urine and drains. She calculates how much of an infusion goes in until midnight, and anticipates the remainder on the next day's form. 'The form does not have room for defecation and transpiration. They don't have that here, apparently', she notes ironically.

One hour later, John leaves Ms. Pearson's room. He walks over to Helen, and asks if there is more to be done. She shrugs her shoulders: she hasn't heard anything since Fred last came up to her. John sighs. 'Edward is new. It's always the same'. He goes out and finds Edward in the registrar's room next to Fred, who is copying the list of orders he made earlier (and which Helen has used) onto the order form. 'You have to tell me what's going on, Edward. We can't read your mind . . .'. Edward, hearing the mixture of irritation and playful irony in John's voice, looks up, smiling a bit apologetically. 'Well – we just have to wait and see what happens to the bleeding time after the thrombocytes. And then we can call Peters'. John leaves, and Fred points at the order form. 'This is crucial. This is your memory. Never forget this, or they'll tell you that you never ordered it'. He searches the record of another patient with leukaemia to find the right dosage of a drug. He sighs. It's going to be another long Friday.

Edward's note contains a mishmash of brief phrases: the probable diagnosis, diagnostic and practical information from the hospital Ms. Pearson comes from, and general, shorthand phrases indicating paths of action to be taken. In their interaction, Fred and Edward attempt to elaborate the sense of the items in the list ('are the slides bone marrow smears?'; 'is she on antibiotics?'), and to turn the shorthand phrases into concrete activities ('we have to call the surgeon for the Hickmann'; underlining 'folic acid' to call attention to this laboratory test to be done). They produce a list of actions-to-be-taken which, in turn, sets in motion activities all through the hospital: surgeons arranging the requirements for the insertion of the Hickmann, laboratory workers doing the blood tests, nurses filling in forms, infusion stands being rolled to Ms. Pearson's room.

Here, then, an additional aspect of the record's function becomes apparent. In addition to getting a grasp on 'what is going on', making a list can serve the purpose of initiating a series of organisational routines. The list not only feeds into the activities of individual staff members, it also facilitates their mutual co-ordination. Here again, it is clear that the record's role is not auxiliary. The record does not merely represent this co-ordination of work; it stipulates and mediates it (*c.f.* Simone and Schmidt 1993). It is a material form of semi-public memory: relieving medical personnel's burden of organising and keeping track of the work to be done and its outcomes. The medical record is a structured *distributing and collecting device*, where all tasks concerning a patient's trajectory must begin and end. The simple ticking of a box, or the jotting down of some words set organisational routines in motion. Scribbling 'CBI' [complete blood investigation] will result in the secretary filling in a range of forms, and calling the hospital's blood collecting service. They draw blood in specifically designed tubes, and deliver these to the appropriate labs. These labs process the samples, and send results back to the physician who ordered the tests – results which are copied into the record.

It is this circular motion of inscriptions, yielding tasks, yielding new inscriptions, and the pivotal role of the record within these loops, which afford *action at a distance* (Latour 1987). Writing orders in the record channels a whole range of the hospital's resources around and through Ms. Pearson's body which further transform it into a body manageable for the hospital's routines. Her veins become co-extensive with the plastic tubes of infusions, her blood is drawn periodically and rendered into rows of numbers, her drinks, urine and infusions become equated as 'in-' and 'outgoing fluid'. Drugs are given to prevent bacteria living in her intestines to infect her when the chemotherapy starts to affect her immune system. The transformation of the body, which started above through the production of a 'manageable problem' (including a complaint patient), here acquires new dimensions. The patient's body is rendered transparent through its further disciplining and material rewriting, and through the production of comparable and combinable inscriptions which can be listed on a few sheets of paper. The availability of such an overviewable, durable and moveable set of inscriptions allows physicians the opportunity to extend their gaze across time and space. In other words, the record enables past and distant work – and spaces and time scales otherwise unimaginable – to be brought into the present (*c.f.* Frankenberg 1992, Wood 1992: 1).

Here, represented and representation are wholly interdependent. The former does not predate the latter: rather, the former only exists through the latter, and vice versa. For this organisation's purposes, the reality of a patient's body is assessed *and* transformed through layers of paperwork. The record organises the attachment of the various tubes and measuring devices which, spilling their numbers into the record, construe the documentary reality of a 'fluid balance'. Only through reading the rows of in- and outgoing fluid can Ms. Pearson's state be assessed; only through calculating and writing down new infusion-levels can a perceived imbalance be restored. The practices of reading and writing the record, then, *are* practices of reading and writing the patient's body; the practices of representation are indistinguishable from the activities they supposedly represent. The intertwining of this distributing and collecting device with the hospital's organisational routines is what *allows* physicians to travel through a patient's body from behind their desk, to cross temporal, bodily and professional boundaries, to scrutinise and tinker with Ms. Pearson's digestive system and the composition of her blood.

As in the previous section, the record's constitutive role in the organisation of medical work also affects the content of this work. It mediates *what* and *how* work tasks are distributed and collected. The only information that the nurses enter into the medical record is what needs to be logged on the temperature chart. This form prestructures what data need to be collected, how, and how often. Blood pressure needs to be entered daily, while the temperature and pulse graph divides the 'day' into four eight-hour periods. Similarly, the tabular format requires a highly standardised mode of entry: the effect of 'oversight in a quick glance' which this format affords is only achieved if the nurses stick to reporting the fluid losses in millilitres and the drug dosages in a standard 'frequency times dosage' format.

Unstructured forms can also mediate the distribution and collection of work tasks. The order form, for example, affords the unrestricted ordering of broad ranges of tests: jotting down 'CBI' orders a series of blood tests without the need for some justification, or for some superior's initials. Likewise, the unstructured case history forms leave it up to the physicians constantly to create order, to maintain a focus. From the plethora of other entries in the record and information exchanged during patient meetings and visits, daily 'summaries', and updated 'problem lists' are created which (re)focus attention and (re)define what the trajectory 'really' is about (see also below).

Here we also see how the record feeds into the organisation of the hospital. The unstructured format of the case history forms creates responsibilities for physicians *and* affirms their position as the 'central actor' in the structuring of the patient's trajectory. It is on these pages, which they read and write, that the central course of this trajectory is established. To physicians, this is the central locus of the record; this is where *their* work tasks (including gaining an overview of the current state of affairs) begin and end. The record, then, also mediates the creation and maintenance of *hierarchies* between and within professional groups: the unstructured, central case history pages underwrite the central position of the physician; the unstructured order form underwrites the little constrained hierarchical relationship between physician and nurse; the highly structured 'temperature list' underwrites the disciplined work nurses have to perform in order to *afford* the physician's oversight and reach. The medical record is one of the ways power differences are materially constituted. It regulates the type of access different staff members have, by differentiating who can or must write where, and who can read what. For example, nurses are responsible for the 'lower status' administrative forms, and the only place where they can enter information in the medical record itself is on the temperature chart. It determines whose information is more relevant than others', and whose work is more important: there is only the briefest trace in the record of the nurses' chores (creating the fluid balances, arranging the blood tests) – just the numbers which are produced as the end result of this work (Star 1991, Bowker and Star 1994). In all these ways, the record enters into the (re)production of hierarchical relations at the same time as it affords the creation of a manageable patient's body.

The record's sequential structure also enters into the *temporal* organisation of hospital work (*c.f.* Zerubavel 1979, Atkinson 1981). The eight-hour lines in the temperature list correspond to the nurses' shifts; its graphic and tabular structure calls for a fixed, cyclical execution of circumscribed tasks in order to sustain its ongoing production. Again, the finegrained nature of this temporal organisation (the meticulously detailed structuring of complex chemotherapy schemes, for example) would be impossible *without* the record's central role as distributor and collector of work tasks. The complexity of the hospital's temporal structure can only be maintained through the material infrastructure of lists, planning tables, schedules, and so forth. Moreover, this temporal organisation is interrelated with the hierarchical layout of the organisation: by demanding disciplined, time-intensive chores from nurses, for example, the differential valuation of time between professional groups is built into the structure of the record (Egger and Wagner 1993).

As argued above, however, the record should not be seen as determining the course of action it mediates. It does not impose its structure on those who have to work with it; it is not an uncomplicated intermediary between the 'intentions' of those who order tasks, and the activities of those who perform them. It does not simply explicate itself: the entries made, or the forms used, do not unequivocally determine the way they are to be acted upon. First, most entries are concise and brief. When Fred investigated Ms. Pearson, for example, his only notes in the case history were:

PE: Nodes –
      Spleen –

For an (already knowledgeable) outsider, the only information to be deduced from the record is that, in the *physical examination*, neither enlarged lymph nodes nor an enlarged spleen were felt. An insider, however, knowing this ward's working routines, knowing Fred as a thorough and experienced registrar, and seeing that this is his first entry in the record, *knows* by reading this that Fred has done a brief but thorough physical examination, and has jotted down only those findings that are particularly relevant for the patient's situation at that moment [an enlarged spleen and enlarged nodes are important signs in staging leukaemia]. Paraphrasing Garfinkel, the very *possibility* of understanding the record's entries is based on a shared, practical, and entitled understanding of common tasks, experiences and expectations (1967: 200–1, Rees 1981). The entries' brevity and (seeming) incompleteness 'works' since the reader knows the specifics of the writer's situation, what (s)he is concerned with, or requires. In addition to *allowing* the record to function as it does, then, being brief is a question of economy of effort. Being more complete than necessary for practical purposes wastes both the time of the writer as of those who need to quickly find relevant information in the record (Heath 1982).

However, this feature simultaneously creates trouble: the brevity and conciseness *required* for the record to work at the same time necessitates continuous 'repair work'. The vignette illustrates the ongoing elaboration of just what was or needed to be written down, and what had to be done: what types of slides were sent along? How should 'preferably' be interpreted in the shorthand note 'Peters preferably Monday'?

More generally, there is a continuous toing-and-froing between nurses, registrars and senior physicians, about the very same records that are to structure their communications (*c.f.* Atkinson 1995). What is true for the entries is also true for the structure of the form: the sections do not spell out how they are to be used. Their relevance often needs to be (re)assessed for the situation at hand; the organisational rules inscribed in the forms are constantly reinterpreted or overridden (Lynch 1985, Berg forthcoming). The typical temperature chart on this ward, for example, is replete with omissions and ad hoc modifications. The graphic depiction of the 'breathing rate' is not filled in, the fluid balance rows contain many omissions, comments are written in places where other information should be entered, and so on.

This ongoing process of reworking the form's inscribed procedures is not a symptom of improper use. Quite the contrary: the flexibility these procedures acquire in the processes of reading and writing are essential to their functioning in complex and fluid practices like medical work. Medical personnel continually readjust and tinker with formal procedures in order to get the work done: whenever nurses do not receive an order they expect to receive they call upon the physician involved and make inquiries. In Ms. Pearson's case, for example, nurses went to Edward, pushing him to request the actions that, they knew, needed to be done.

And the active refiguring of formal procedures goes further than this. An ubiquitous feature of the work are the innumerable phone calls and interactions to arrange tests, get the Hickmann catheter, and so on. Because of the urgency of the situation, these matters were informally arranged first, while the formal requests were written afterwards. These formal requests are important: they serve as administrative records for the hospital's financial administration, *and* to 'make evident' that the patient was dealt with in an optimal and rational way (see below). They did *not*, however, function as the 'order' they formally were, since the events they were supposed to trigger had already been set in motion. Likewise, although the blood test form could only be tagged as 'urgent' or 'non urgent', an informal work routine had been established which was referred to as a 'super urgent' request. Such requests had top priority for the nurses. Moreover, Helen would write down the physicians' bleeper number on the form (for which no room was provided either), and she would sometimes repeatedly call the haematological laboratory to speed up the process.

Formal procedures, in other words, are continually 'worked around' to deal with situational exigencies (Gasser 1986): if Irene tinkers with the fluid balance forms to account for the fact that they do not contain a section for defecation and transpiration, she overrules the structure of this form to ensure that a patient's loss of fluid is not forgotten. Finally, staff members often *played upon* formal procedures to achieve ends for which the procedures were not intended. So, physicians often used the order list as a way to ensure that nurses would remind *them* that certain actions needed to be performed. Likewise, nurses would often fill in medication order slips (an activity formally restricted to physicians) and have a physician sign them. In this way, they ensured that drugs or dosage modifications they deemed necessary would be given. Simultaneously, this informal routine reduced their dependency on the physicians' initiative. The latter appreciated these routines, since it took some of the chores of order writing out of their hands (*c.f.* Hughes 1988).

The record's distributing and collecting role, then, should not be seen as a mechanical process. And neither should the work flows and hierarchies it co-produces be seen as strictly delineated and discrete. The continuous back-and-forthing about what is requested, and the informal processes, through which, for example, nurses monitor registrar's activities, render the image much more complex. The formal work flows embedded in the record are constantly superseded by situational exigencies dealt with through informal and ad hoc procedures. But it would be mistaken to conclude from this observation, as it is sometimes done, that it is in fact these ongoing, informal processes that are primary; that 'informal communications' rather than 'formal records' bind complex practices together. That formal procedures stand 'powerless' in the face of the contingent and interactionally achieved nature of the social; that they only hinder the rich, smooth flow of interactions that constitute workplaces. The most promising route towards understanding medical (or other work) practices lies not in opposing the 'formal' to the 'informal', or the complexity of medical work to the record's impoverished representation of it, *but in seeing how the two merge and interlock* (Suchman 1993, Berg forthcoming). The continuous working around and re-interpreting of the record's contents *allows* the record to function – to distribute and collect, and thereby transform, the very work of those who bring it alive.

Reifying the trajectory's history

Mr. Wood has been admitted to the oncology ward with a diagnosis of 'relapsed Hodgkin's Disease': cancer arising from the lymphoid tissues. He had been found eligible for bone marrow transplantation, where bone marrow is collected from the patient's pelvic bone and deep frozen, and the patient is treated with massive doses of chemotherapy [bone marrow cells are predecessors of blood cells and would be killed by the

chemotherapy]. When I met him, he had had his treatment and his
bone marrow had just been reinfused. This is a crucial episode, since
the effects of the chemotherapy on the bone marrow are starting to show,
and the 'reinstalled' bone marrow is as yet only starting to proliferate.
Blood cells are counted daily, and the patient is monitored for signs of
infection or bleeding.

It is Monday. Dr. Howard, head of the department, meets John, the
senior registrar who runs the day-to-day affairs of the ward. '[His
temperature] rose above 38.5 this weekend' says Howard. 'I said that they
should check again two hours later; and if it was above 38.5 again, we
would have to start with antibiotic treatment. But it wasn't. . . . He's got 0
granulocytes [type of white blood cell] at the moment, and that means he's
prone to getting a blood-poisoning [infection of the blood itself], and then
they're dead before you know it'.

During the day Mr. Wood's temperature remains below 38.5 degrees.
John examines him, but cannot find a reason for the fever. That night
his temperature rises again: at 10 p.m. it is 38.8, and at midnight it is 38.6.
Dr. Howard orders that AB [a combination of two antibiotics] should be
started. The next morning, John examines Mr. Wood and finds a small
anal fissure close to a pile. He jots this finding down in the case history
and adds an exclamation mark: this could be the source of the infectious
trouble!

Wednesday, John discusses Mr. Wood's case with Dr. Liston, the
supervising oncologist. 'He's been having a fever for some days', says
John. 'Lately he stabilised above 38.5 degrees, so we started AB. Sunday's
blood culture says that in one out of the four tubes of blood a CNS
[a type of bacteria] has been found for which AB is effective. So we're
on the right track'. 'But the temperature is still rising', replies Dr. Liston
while she points at the temperature curve, 'so we're going to shift to CD
[a different combination of antibiotics]'. John is silent, while she writes
this change on Mr. Wood's order form. 'CD hits that bacterium even
harder', she adds.

Two days later, during the 'paper rounds', John recounts this story to
Dr. Bear, who has taken over supervision duty. That night the temperature
had risen again, but it had been a single peak. 'He has acquired a fever,
since, actually, this weekend. We started with AB, and changed to CD on
Wednesday'. Bear has not heard about this patient for a while, and he
starts by writing a brief summary in the case history: *Relapse Hodgkin* →
BMT [bone marrow therapy]. Fever. He wonders about the quick change
in therapy. He asks the bacteriologist, frequently present at these rounds,
whether he has seen a positive blood culture: 'No'. Bear then sees
that John has written that 'one out of four tubes was positive'. The
bacteriologist shakes his head. 'One out of four means nothing. I would
define that as a contamination, as a skin bacterium which has accidentally
entered the needle when the blood was drawn. That is a negative blood

culture.' John intervenes to defend the shift in antibiotics, which now looks somewhat dubious: 'Since the temperature was high and did not respond to AB, we changed to CD'. The bacteriologist shakes his head: there was no good reason for this shift. Bear now comes to John and Liston's aid: 'Well, we know that, but we had to shift the antibiotic treatment anyway, since the temperature wasn't reacting properly'. He writes: *blood culture: 1/4 CNS. R/CD after no response to AB.* John adds: 'His pile presents a similar problem. Do you have to gear your antibiotics towards that, or towards the positive tube?' The bacteriologist is confident: 'In a situation like this the clinical situation should prevail'. He explains that DE would have been a better choice: that combination would have been targeted more directly against bacteria which may be present in the pile. Bear joins in: '[So] do we change from CD to DE or add something to CD?' The latter is not the most elegant solution: the three agents overlap each other significantly. 'In fact', the bacteriologist remarks, 'you have already made the decision. I think it would be best, now, to add E'. Bear writes in the case history: *also pile problem → add E.*

One month later, the discharge letter summarises this episode as follows:

[Eight days after bone marrow reinfusion] a fever develops. The focus appears to be a . . . pile. Empirically [based on the clinical picture] AB is started. Blood cultures show a CNS, reason to treat patient further with CD. Because the temperature responds insufficiently, E is added. The temperature subsequently normalised only slowly. The anal fissure eventually quieted down. . . . Patient was discharged in a good general condition . . .

At first sight, the medical record seems a mere re-enactment of time: tables listing past measurements; pages and pages of notes of meetings and examinations. The history of the patient's trajectory, it seems, is simply reflected in these pages. Yet it is a mistake, as I have argued, to conceptualise the record as a more or less adequate representation of events. By being part and parcel of the activity of transforming a patient's problem into a manageable problem, by functioning as a structured distributor and collector of work activities, the record is actively involved in shaping the very events it 'represents'.

And there is yet another way in which it would be a mistake to conceptualise the record as a mere 'copy'. In this section, I focus on the way the record is involved in the *reification* (Latour and Woolgar 1986: 174–83) of a trajectory's history. The record allows the interactive, ad hoc character of medical work – including the way it itself mediates this work – to disappear from view. Rather than 'mirroring' the complex, heterogeneous processes that shape a patient's trajectory, the practices of reading and writing produce a streamlined, decontextualised, 'textbook-like' image of 'what has taken place'. Two interrelated features of these practices are involved here.

First, the medical record is always also a source for continual and retrospect inspection of the adequacy of the staff's actions (Whalen 1993). It makes public 'what really happened' – for supervisors, colleagues, and maybe lawyers and government officials (Garfinkel 1967: 197–207, Hunter 1991). In this sense, even an individual writing in a record constitutes a social event, since each entry is made with the awareness that it might be used later to assess the adequacy of the actions 'recorded'. This feature inevitably feeds back into the practices of reading and writing themselves: entries in the record are often explicitly intended to create a post hoc document of the completeness and rationality of the actions undertaken. Registrars were pressed by superiors to 'write something in the record every day' ('no problems' often sufficed), because that created an image of daily surveillance and attention. Likewise, young registrars confronted with a situation they did not feel able to deal with, often resorted to writing down broad depictions, which did not reveal their uncertainty yet would not lead to potentially erroneous interventions.

This feature of the medical record activates the production of entries which together produce a 'rational', 'typical' narrative, in which treatments are 'decided upon' and diagnoses are reached through a systematic approach (Smith 1990). In the case of Mr. Wood, for example, no trace can be found of the fact that John did not agree with Dr. Liston changing the antibiotics: 'they were changed before they could show any effect', he muttered to me afterwards. Likewise, there is no trace of the awareness that CDE is an ad hoc and somewhat superfluous combination of antibiotics. The combination is written down without comment, and the discharge letter depicts the changes in antibiotic treatment as a logical sequence of rational decisions.

The way the record's forms are structured feeds into this predisposition. As Barrett (1988) notes regarding the psychiatric admission form he studied, 'the structure of the record implied that the author's conclusions (Diagnosis and Opinion) be read as a logical (if provisional) sequitur of the data base – as if derived by induction'. The records studied here did not ask for an 'opinion' but for a 'problem list' or a 'conclusion' – but the logical structure of the scientific process of data-gathering and hypothesis-generation is inscribed here just as much.

Second, I have already drawn attention to the ubiquitous phenomena of *summarising*: constantly, information from diverse sources is compressed into short statements of 'what is the case'. In the case history forms, physicians condense the information gathered from tests, nurses, the patient, and previous entries, and create a concise statement of the 'current problem' and its relevant history. When a patient's situation is re-evaluated, the entries made earlier are taken as 'ground' upon which the next evaluation proceeds – stripped of their situational uncertainties and the specific context in which they emerged (Macintyre 1978, Rees 1981). These summaries are created in the light of the problem at hand: every time, the patient's 'medical history' is selectively re-written to underwrite and lead to the current state of affairs.

Detailed descriptions sink back into pages that are no longer 'actual', and are summarised in one sentence, and later in one word – and these ongoing summations construe 'histories' and 'futures' which are continuous with the Now[9].

This ongoing (re)summarising also contributes to the construction of narratives in which the ambiguities, the ad hoc and fluid character of medical work, are lost. At each new patient round, the previous history of the case is briefly summarised and Mr. Woods' story is further stylised. The two peaks above 38.5 degrees first become a 'temperature stabilising above 38.5', which Dr. Bear later summarises as 'fever' – and in the discharge letter, this fever simply 'developed at day eight'. These reconstructions should not be seen as a falsification of history: they are 'needed to produce an account ordered enough to enable action or to communicate what is going on' (Gooding 1992: 76). Ultimately, they create the type of report exemplified in the fragment of the discharge letter, where *almost every sentence* reflects a history of repeated reconstructive work. As is apparent from the vignette, the causal role of the pile in the development of the fever had never been very clear. Similarly, the anal fissure had never been described as 'unquiet'; it was simply the only clue the physicians had.

The medical record, then, is part and parcel of the ongoing *(re)construction* of the present; of an accountably 'adequate' rendering of the Now and its History. The iterative process of summarising aids the emergence of a history which seamlessly and rationally predates, and underpins, the current 'present'. A history emerges in which medical data 'naturally' lead to certain diagnostic conclusions, which then lead to a rational, therapeutic intervention. The interactive processes that shape Mr. Wood's trajectory are replaced by a clear-cut, step-by-step temporal sequence (observation → diagnosis → intervention), matched by a clear-cut causality underlying this sequence, and by a circumscribed and fitting set of 'signs and symptoms'. The multitude of ad hoc articulations made, the wide array of elements involved, the way these elements were (re)constructed: all this is erased in this post hoc reification of a trajectory's history. Also, in this final mediation, the record ultimately deletes itself: it erases all traces of its *own* constitutive role in the production of medical work. It becomes no more than the simple 'carrier' of information, a mere re-enactment of events – a humble object which surely does not merit a sociologist's attention.

Concluding Remarks

Through practices of reading and writing, the medical record functions as a constitutive element of current medical work. It enters into the 'thinking' processes of medical personnel and into their relations with patients and with each other. It helps to shape the form the patient's trajectory takes, and it is actively involved in the transformation of the patient's body into an 'extension' of the hospital's routines.

The record, as a distributor and collector of work tasks, allows a high level of complexity in the organisation of work – yet its own functioning is constantly amended, repaired, and played upon by the same staff members whose work practices it transforms. The 'formal' role of the record is not 'carried' by informal work practices, nor is the 'social practice' determined by the 'technological artefacts' that figure in it. The heterogeneous practices of reading and writing, the interrelation between 'formal' forms and quick phone calls or scribbles in the margins *as a whole* is the sociological unit that requires attention.

One way of focusing this attention is to look at how *different* records mediate medical work in different ways. Especially with the coming of the computer-based patient record, new record systems are being proposed and developed. Going beyond a dichotomy of 'formal' and 'informal', or 'representation' and 'represented', then, we can investigate how various practices of reading and writing will have diverging consequences – consequences much broader than expected when the record is seen as a mere 'repository of information'. I end this paper by proposing how to get a grasp on these repercussions.

To begin with, the record can be seen as a form of 'organisational memory' (Bowker 1994). Enthusiastic supporters of the computer-based record profess a future in which this memory, now 'fragile' and 'messy', becomes 'complete' and 'infinite' (Dick and Steen 1991). No memory, however, can exist without forgetting: selectivity in what ends up in the record (and how) is a prerequisite for the functioning of the record in the first place. The record's 'forgetting' does not hinder medical work – it is what makes it possible. If this is so, however, it makes sense to investigate just what *type* of memory a record embodies, what (links between) data are deemed more relevant than others, and what type of action or intervention it affords and what not. In other words, it makes sense to investigate the *logic* of a record: the specific way it mediates the work that depends on it.

Some records, for example, may restrict the entry of unstructured information, which could limit the type and amount of 'social history' that can be entered. Or a system could make it hard to deduce the source of entries, thereby making the ubiquitous informal judgements on these sources impossible (*c.f.* Cicourel 1990). Simultaneously, these logics include the way the record feeds into the doctor–patient relationship, and the way hierarchies in and between professional groups are affected. Different systems will have different access opportunities, for example, and they might strengthen or rather open up boundaries between nurses and physicians. (Think of a system which would restrict the writing of medication orders to physicians, or, on the contrary, a system which would not differentiate between either nurses or physicians, and thus allow – now virtually absent – equal access opportunities).

These are but pointers to topics that need exploration: this paper has only laid some groundwork for that enterprise. Investigating the logics of different records, the different consequences these representations might yield, is an important challenge.

Acknowledgements

I thank Geoff Bowker, Monica Casper, Emilie Gomart, Annemarie Mol, the anonymous referees and the research group Care, Technology and Culture (University of Limburg) for their helpful remarks and critique on earlier versions of this paper.

Notes

1   Seminal studies in the 'construction of documentary reality' are Zimmerman (1969) and Smith (1990). The medical record has been studied by *e.g.* Rees (1981), Macintyre (1978), Heath (1982), Pettinari (1988), and Hak (1992) – almost invariably from an ethnomethodological perspective. Records are also a topic in Hunter's (1991) study of the narrative structure of medical work.

2   'Sociotechnical' is a term coined to point at the fundamental interrelatedness of the 'social' and the 'technical' (*c.f.* Latour 1994).

3   Names and dates are fictitious; in the usage of first and/or last names, I follow the practices of the setting investigated. Whenever nurses kept a separate 'nursing record', the 'medical record' refers to the record primarily used by physicians.

4   A list of questions regarding the various bodily 'systems' (the respiratory system, the gastrointestinal system).

5   See *e.g.* Lave (1988), Amann and Knorr-Cetina (1989), Cicourel (1990), and Hutchins (1995). Here, I mainly stress how 'thinking' is intertwined with artefacts and in the doctor–patient relation; I do not have the space to discuss the distributed cognition that takes place in interactions between staff members.

6   On the transformation of a patient's problem in the interaction between doctor and patient see *e.g.* Davis (1986) and Silverman (1987). The position of the record is not a central focus in these studies.

7   Physicians do sometimes take histories or perform physical examinations without writing during these activities. This does not invalidate the argument set out here. As Goody has argued, it is only through the emergence of *writing*, through the development of means to organise and catalogue information, that complexly sequenced and branched activities such as the performance of a standardised questionnaire become possible (1977: 108–11). Repeated performance of such activities can subsequently lead to a (partial) *internalisation* of such sequences or lists.

8   This record is different from the outpatient record. The inpatient record, for example, may contain letters written by an outpatient physician, but not that physician's notes themselves; and the outpatient record's only information on periods of hospitalisation are the discharge letters.

9   The avalanche of information that piles up in the pages under the top one can continually be accessed. Their volume and scope allows endless re-modifications of histories that seemed to be closed. Anomalies are easily found; the past is easily rewritten in the light of the unfolding present – and vice versa.

References

Amann, K. and Knorr-Cetina, K. (1989) Thinking through talk: an ethnographic study of a molecular biology laboratory, *Knowledge and Society*, 8, 26.

Atkinson, P. (1981) *The Clinical Experience: The Construction of Medical Reality.* Farnborough: Gower.

Atkinson, P. (1995) *Medical Talk and Medical Work.* London: Sage.

Barrett, R.J. (1988) Clinical writing and the documentary construction of schizophrenia. *Culture, Medicine and Psychiatry*, 12, 3, 265–99.

Berg, M. (1992) The construction of medical disposals. Medical sociology and medical problem solving in clinical practice, *Sociology of Health and Illness*, 14, 2, 151–80.

Berg, M. (1995) Turning a practice into a science: reconceptualizing postwar medical practice, *Social Studies of Science*, 25, 437–76.

Berg, M. (forthcoming) *Rationalizing Medical Work. Decision Support Techniques and Medical Practices.* Cambridge: MIT Press.

Bowker, G. (1994) Dismembering and remembering: classification and organizational memory, *Locating Design, Development and Use*, Oksnoen Symposium, May 13–18.

Bowker, G. and Star, S.L. (1994) Knowledge and infrastructure in international information management: problems of classification and coding. In Bud, L. (ed.) *Information Acumen: The Understanding and Use of Knowledge in Modern Business.* London: Routledge.

Cicourel, A. (1990) The integration of distributed knowledge in collaborative medical diagnosis. In Galegher, J., Kraut, R.E. and Egido, C. (eds) *Intellectual Teamwork. Social and Intellectual Foundations of Cooperative Work.* Hillsdale, NJ: Lawrence Erlbaum.

Davis, K. (1986) The process of problem (re)formulation in psychotherapy, *Sociology of Health and Illness*, 8, 1, 44–74.

Dick, R.S. and Steen, E.B. (eds) (1991) *The Computer-Based Patient Record: An Essential Technology for Health Care.* Washington, D.C.: National Academy Press.

Egger, E. and Wagner, I. (1993) Negotiating temporal orders: the case of collaborative time management in a surgery clinic, *Computer Supported Cooperative Work*, 1, 255–75.

Frankenberg, R. (1992) 'Your time or mine': temporal contradictions of biomedical practice. In *ibid.* (ed.) *Time, Health and Medicine.* London: Sage.

Garfinkel, H. (1967) *Studies in Ethnomethodology.* Englewood-Cliffs: Prentice-Hall.

Gasser, L. (1986) The integration of computing and routine work, *ACM Transactions on Office Information Systems*, 4, 3, 205–25.

Gooding, D. (1992) Putting agency back into experiment. In Pickering, A. (ed.) *Science as Practice and Culture.* Chicago: University of Chicago Press.

Goody, J. (1977) *The Domestication of the Savage Mind*, New York: Cambridge University Press.

Hak, T. (1992) Psychiatric records as transformations of other texts. In Watson, G. and Seiler, R.M. (eds) *Text in Context: Contributions to ethnomethodology*, London: Sage.

Haraway, D.J. (1991) *Simians, Cyborgs, and Women: the Reinvention of Nature*, New York: Routledge.

Heath, C. (1982) Preserving the consultation: medical record cards and professional conduct, *Sociology of Health and Illness*, 4, 56–74.

Hughes, D. (1988) When nurse knows best: some aspects of nurse/doctor interaction in a casualty department, *Sociology of Health and Illness*, 10, 1, 1–22.

Hunter, K.M. (1991) *Doctor's Stories. The Narrative Structure of Medical Knowledge.* Princeton: Princeton University Press.

Hutchins, E. (1995) *Cognition in the Wild.* Cambridge: MIT Press.

Latour, B. (1986) Visualisation and cognition: thinking with eyes and hands, *Knowledge and Society*, 6, 1–40.

Latour, B. (1987) *Science in Action.* Milton Keynes: Open University Press.

Latour, B. (1994) Pramatogonies: a mythical account of how humans and nonhumans swap properties, *American Behavioral Scientist*, 37, 791–808.

Latour, B. and Woolgar, S. (1986) *Laboratory Life. The Construction of Scientific Facts.* Princeton: Princeton University Press.

Lave, J. (1988) *Cognition in Practice.* Cambridge: Cambridge University Press.

Law, J. and Lynch, M. (1990) Lists, field guides, and the descriptive organization of seeing: birdwatching as an exemplary observational activity. In Lynch, M. and Woolgar, S. (eds) *Representation in Scientific Practice.* Cambridge: MIT Press.

Law, J. (1994) *Organising Modernity*, Oxford: Blackwell.

Luff, P., Heath, C. and Greatbatch, D. (1992) Tasks-in-interaction: paper and screen-based documentation in collaborative activity. In Turner, J. and Kraut, R. (eds) *Proceedings of the Conference on Computer Supported Cooperative Work.* New York: ACM Press.

Lynch, M. (1985) *Art and Artifact in Laboratory Science. A Study of Shop Work and Shop Talk in a Research Laboratory.* London: Routledge and Kegan Paul.

Lynch, M. (1993) *Scientific Practice and Ordinary Action: Ethnomethodology and Social Studies of Science.* New York: Cambridge University Press.

Macintyre, S. (1978) Some notes on record taking and making in an antenatal clinic, *Sociological Review*, 26, 595–611.

Pettinari, C.J. (1988) *Task, Talk and Text in the Operating Room: A Study in Medical Discourse.* Norwood, NJ: Ablex.

Raffel, S. (1979) *Matters of Fact: A Sociological Inquiry.* London: Routledge and Kegan Paul.

Rees, C. (1981) Records and hospital routine. In Atkinson, P. and Heath, C. (eds) *Medical Work: Realities and Routines.* Farnborough: Gower.

Silverman, D. (1987) *Communication in Medical Practice.* London: Sage.

Simone, C. and Schmidt, K. (1993) *Computational Mechanisms of Interaction for CSCW.* ESPRIT Report, COMIC Deliverable 3.1.

Smith, D. (1990) *Texts, Facts, and Femininity: Exploring the Relations of Ruling.* London: Routledge.

Star, S.L. (1991) The Sociology of the invisible: the primacy of work in the writings of Anselm Strauss. In Maines, D.R. (ed.) *Social Organization and Social Process: Essays in Honor of Anselm Strauss.* Hawthorne: Aldine de Gruyter.

Strauss, A., Fagerhaugh, S., Suczek, B. and Wieder, C. (1985) *Social Organization of Medical Work.* Chicago: University of Chicago Press.

Suchman, L. (1993) Technologies of accountability. Of lizards and aeroplanes. In Button, G. (ed.) *Technology in Working Order. Studies of Work, Interaction, and Technology.* London: Routledge.

Timmermans, S. (1995) *Saving Lives: A Historical and Ethnographic Study of Resuscitation Techniques*. PhD Thesis, University of Illinois, Champaign, IL.

Whalen, J. (1993) Accounting for 'standard' task performance in the execution of 9-1-1 operations, *Annual Meetings of the American Sociological Association*, Miami, August.

Wood, D. (1992) *The Power of Maps*. New York: Guilford Press.

Zerubavel, E. (1979) *Patterns of Time in Hospital Life*. Chicago: University of Chicago Press.

Zimmerman, D.H. Record-keeping and the intake process in a public welfare agency. In Wheeler, S. (ed.) *On Record: Files and Records in American Life*. New York: Russell Sage.

Reality construction, reality exploration and treatment in two therapeutic communities[1]

M.J. Bloor and J.D. Fonkert

Introduction

In recent years students of what used to be called the socialisation process have been centrally concerned with stressing a symbiotic link between, on the one hand, the learning of accounts and prescriptions for behaviour, and, on the other hand, the processes whereby social reality is constructed, maintained and re-constructed. It is held that members' accounts reflexively constitute the reality to which they refer. Although members typically orient to these accounts and prescriptions as having an unproblematic facticity, they are not, and cannot be, exhaustively elaborated and they are incipiently contradictory: accounts and prescriptions are essentially contingent and defeasible.

The treatment process within therapeutic communities is often described by practitioners as 'social learning'. The data presented below show two apparently contrasting communities to employ similar processes of reality construction as treatment resources. Further, staff conceptions of the constitution of the social realities of the communities corresponded to the sociological accounts paraphrased above. In both communities conscious use was made for treatment purposes of the essentially contingent and defeasible nature of staff prescriptions for patient/resident behaviour.

The term 'therapeutic community' covers a wide variety of treatment facilities catering for a wide variety of disabilities. We will use the term here to refer to locales where all activities and interactions are accounted as having potentially healing and/or rehabilitative and/or supportive properties and where all community members may, consciously or unconsciously, contribute to therapy; social relationships and organisation are not regarded as mere backcloths to professional care but are accounted as forces in a therapeutic milieu. Social relationships and organisation may act as therapeutic agents through the creation of experiences that can be used as learning situations for experiencing and handling behaviour, attitudes and emotions, and which provide staff (and fellow patients) with material upon which they can base therapeutic interventions. In some of these communities therapy can be conceived of as occurring largely through the medium of activities, as in 'Parkneuk' community (described by Bloor[2]), where therapeutic work appeared to centre around the creation of naturalistic, family-like routines which were held to be inherently therapeutic for those with certain disabilities. However, in most therapeutic communities the main medium of therapy is talk (although activities may play an important subsidiary role). This paper examines the issue of what is accounted for as therapy in communities of the latter type.

Data are presented from two contrasting talk-based communities. One community (data collected by Bloor) is a psychiatric day hospital employing professional medical and nursing staff and using group therapy methods pioneered by Maxwell Jones and others[3]; such Maxwell-Jones-type communities are probably the most commonly found therapeutic communities in Britain. The other community (data collected by Fonkert) is a Dutch 'concept house', a residential community for the treatment of drug addicts staffed mainly by ex-addicts and using methods pioneered by the American Synanon Community[4]; such concept houses are probably the most commonly found therapeutic communities in America.

The method of data collection was participant observation. This allowed us not only to observe and monitor events and talk as they occurred in their natural settings, but also to attend to our own experiences as participants, as members of the communities[5].

Our argument will be that treatment in these two communities can be located in an overall process of reality construction. Within this overall process of reality construction we distinguish processes of reality exploration of particular importance for the treatment method. We should emphasise that we are not concerned in this paper with the efficacy of treatment but rather with the sociological description of the treatment process.

By reality construction we refer to patients'/residents' learning of prescriptions for behaviour and accounts of community social relationships and of the community social structure; these accounts reflexively constitute those social relationships, that social structure. More fully, these prescriptions and accounts form a reality description which is furnished by staff and senior patients/residents to new arrivals. The reality description offers a framework for events, experiences, attitudes, behaviour and emotions to be described, interpreted and/or explained, in short to be made accountable. The reality description makes up the commonsense knowledge of the members of the community. In using this commonsense knowledge for making sense of phenomena, the phenomena are reflexively constituted as facts by members. A clear-cut example is the community social structure; staff provide an account of the structure to patients who assimilate that account, use it to explain phenomena, and orient to it in their behaviour; these patient explanations and behaviour reflexively constitute the social structure. The reality description is no neutral accounting framework. It is a moral code invested with piety and supported by social sanctions which distinguishes good from bad, right from wrong – in short, a set of imperatives for attitudes and behaviour.

By reality exploration we refer to patients'/residents' discovery that these learned accounts and rules are inevitably provisional, vague and incipiently contradictory. Through experiment and experience patients/residents are held to discover the limits imposed on behaviour and learn to handle and accept these limits and the essential vagueness of rules and accounts.

Staff believe that these processes provide occasions, resources, and topics for therapy and also opportunities for establishing negotiated compromises with patients, thus inculcating attitudes and perspectives which will equip the patient for life outside the community. In effect, patients are weaned from what the staff view as inappropriate and pathogenic ways of relating to society by the promise of a New World of warm, caring relationships. But once in the New World they find it disturbingly like the Old World, and in struggling to come to terms with the contradiction and accept limits they supposedly develop the ability to relate to outside society.

Reality construction

In contrast to the democratic ethos of the day hospital, the concept house has an elaborate and hierarchical formal structure with a comprehensive set of house-rules, an extensive programme of activities, a hierarchy of statuses through which the resident must progress, and a system of privileges commensurate with progress[6]. Not surprisingly, then, the induction of new patients/residents is a more formalized affair in the concept house than in the day hospital.

After detoxification and an introductory phase, a new resident enters the concept house via an 'intake', a procedure designed to test his motivation. Prior to the intake he/she is 'put on the stool' and given 'The Philosophy' (a short document that describes the object of the concept house and which is also read out, semi-religiously, at each 'morning meeting') to read while the life of the community ebbs and flows around. In the intake he is asked his opinion on the 'The Philosophy', asked to expose himself emotionally (*e.g.* he may be asked to scream 'Help' at the top of his voice), told about the house-rules and that acceptance of these is a pre-condition for entry. After acceptance he or she is introduced to the community, an elder 'brother' and 'sister' are allocated to show him or her the ropes, and he or she is assigned a position in the structure. During the initial period in the community he or she will attend the 'prospect group' for new residents where senior residents will expound the working of the community, and may also attend occasional seminars on the theory of treatment methods.

At the day hospital, on the other hand, a prospective patient first meets the staff to discuss the patient's problem and motivation. At this point the patient learns little about the day hospital other than the fact that all treatment is conducted in groups and he/she will be expected to attend daily. On the first day he/she is given a timetable of activities and introduced to fellow-patients who will give instruction in such matters as the lunchtime routine.

However, in both communities informal induction was of more importance than formal induction. This informal induction has two components. One component is the learning, assimilation and reproduction of accounts – accounts of their problems, accounts of relationships, accounts of the structure and rules of the community, and so on. Thus patients/residents learn to describe, interpret, and explain phenomena after the fashion of their peers. The other component is learning to act in accord with these accounts. The (re-)production of an account is synonymous with reality construction; a rational explanation for an action makes that action rational, makes social life a coherent and comprehensive reality; accounts of relationships and structures reflexively constitute those relationships and structures[7].

Learning to act in accord with accounts does not presuppose the prior learning of accounts. Indeed the reverse is usually the case: patients may learn what constitutes appropriate behaviour in various community settings some time prior to learning how appropriately to account for that behaviour[8]. For example, a patient on his first day at the hospital conducted himself satisfactorily in the encounter group, although while patients were following the group-leader's instructions to move around the room greeting each other he muttered to Bloor 'What the hell's going on?' Similarly, junior residents chatting to Fonkert told him that they did not know the why and the importance of certain activities, but that they did them anyway because, apparently, that was the way things were done in the concept house.

When community accounting practices are subsequently assimilated they may be used for post hoc reinterpretations of previous misconceived and puzzling experiences. The senior day hospital patients could be heard to declare that it was only after some weeks of treatment that they began to 'realize' how the groups worked, what the nature of their difficulties was, and so forth. An illustration of this comes from Bloor's fieldnotes, reporting a pub conversation:

> Harriet was reminiscing about her first day in the group, how she had totally misconceived the purpose of the group. . . . Harriet had assumed, she said, that she could simply throw her problems into the group where they'd be chewed around for a few days and then a magical solution would emerge . . . she went on to say that she now felt a tremendous affection for the day hospital and that she'd really come a long way. All the stuff she'd been spouting in her first few weeks there she now regarded as utter rubbish . . .[9]

Likewise, Fonkert underwent a strong emotional experience in an encounter group which left him in a state of shock, particularly since he found the experience inexplicable at the time. Only later did he begin to 'understand' the experience and the purpose and mechanism of encounter groups in the community[10]. In a conversation with a senior resident about all this he was told: 'First it just happened to me, only later I started to understand.'

Informal induction is accomplished in the course of everyday community activities through the new member's contact with fellow community members. These fellow members live within the moral code of the community and accounts of the structure of the community and of relationships within the community have an objective facticity for them. Their actions and conversation, even the fairly elaborate explanations that may be supplied by the elder brother and sister in the concept house, refer to a wider body of commonsense knowledge about life in the community. What senior community members say (and the way they say it) stand, in Garfinkel's terminology, as a 'document' of this 'supposedly' underlying pattern of shared commonsense knowledge. For example, in the day hospital patients hear senior patients chatting casually about their feelings and motives and quizzing others on how they feel about events. Bloor, in an early fieldnote, recorded his surprise when a patient he hardly knew casually showed in the course of lunch-table conversation that she had intuited what he had felt about a minor incident in one of the morning groups. He was further surprised that she should casually reproduce the incident, and how she thought he had reacted to it, for the benefit of her fellow patients. However, he learned that he was expected to attend to and express his feelings and monitor the feelings of others, and this rapidly became a natural accomplishment. Other patients' conversations about feelings stand as a document to new patients for commonsense knowledge in the day hospital about how extensively and in what manner they should attend to feelings. Coincidentally, an irritated resident criticised Fonkert in his early days at the concept house for 'theorising' about his feelings outside the community and 'explaining' the feelings he had inside the community. He was told to talk about the situations there-and-then in the community and to talk directly about them.

In a similar fashion, patients/residents would rapidly assimilate the argot of the community. Thus, one day a hospital patient jokingly remarked that she had caught herself repeatedly quizzing acquaintances outside the hospital with the formula: 'How do you feel about that?' In-group argot may be used as a gloss: the full meaning of the argot cannot be exhaustively elaborated. In the glossing the speaker appeals to the hearer that his (the speaker's) meaning is sufficiently obvious for the practical purpose at hand[11]. Fonkert noticed an irritated reaction when he sometimes probed to understand the specific meaning of an expression. Thus, argot may come to connote various unexplicated aspects of a community's culture. The assimilation and successful usage of argot by patients/residents therefore involves familiarisation with the shared commonsense knowledge of the community.

The Dutch concept house had inherited much of the argot of the American concept houses; one such term is 'space out'. Thus a resident in a work group who is seen to be constantly staring outside through the window may be told: 'Don't space out so much, or you'll flip to the outside.' Spacing out here connotes running away from a difficult situation, uninvolvement with the community; it glosses the antithesis of the full participation in, and enthusiastic absorption with, the community that is commonsensically expected of residents.

As was implied above, in the concept house learning to act in accord with accounts is facilitated by the fact that any infringement of the rules, any misconception of the structure, is immediately corrected. For example, a new resident in a work group tried to arrange something with an expeditor (one of the more senior members of the status-hierarchy). The expeditor replied that he should do it 'through the structure', that is, he should do it through his immediate superior, the assistant-foreman. This learning of correct behaviour in advance of learning the appropriate account is itself explained (accounted) by the leaders of the community. Thus, Sugarman, writing of an American concept house, explained that it was felt that many new residents were in too much of a mess to listen to explanations – they must be told that they are expected to conform first and look for the reasons later[12]. Indeed, staff told Fonkert: 'Do the community, experience it, explaining and understanding is not so important – that will come later.' Staff were also aware that learning to behave correctly in an imperfectly understood situation may be quite a stressful experience. The resident's handling of this stress may be both an occasion and a topic for therapy.

Induction into the day hospital is a more gentle affair. New patients are allowed to play relatively minor parts in the formal groups while they assimilate the culture of the hospital. While in the concept house acting out behaviour is discouraged (unless it is deferred until the encounter group[13]) by a system of rewards and punishments in line with the principles of behaviour conditioning, in contrast, in the day hospital acting out is encouraged, particularly among new patients, so that their behaviour can be reflected back to them as inappropriate and pathogenic ways of relating to others. Yet despite these, and a wealth of other, important differences between the two treatment facilities, an important principle of treatment remains the same – the induction of the patient into a new social world which the patient comes to take for granted as an objective reality. Bloor recorded his realisation that he had gradually and unobtrusively assimilated one aspect of this new social world:

> I have heard staff especially (but also occasionally patients) refer to
> their concern for 'the group'. Thus I remember Oliver (staff) once called
> the group his family. I couldn't follow this: to feel thus for a group, a
> collective entity, seemed bizarre. In fact I doubted the sincerity of those
> who expressed themselves in this way. But today I realised that I now felt
> the same way. Nichola (patient) was speaking of her good feeling when,
> on a previous occasion, she had led 'the fantasy' (in the weekly encounter
> group) and watched protectively over the huddle of forms as she spoke.
> I realised that I had felt the same as I led the fantasy. I spoke about my
> strong feelings about the group and expressing the thought strengthened
> it further until I actually felt tears pricking my eyes.

Similarly, Fonkert, having assimilated the way that life in the concept house is favourably contrasted with life outside the community, became aware that he was going around defending the community to everybody.

Eventually then, living within this new social world becomes a taken-for-granted practical accomplishment. As was implied in the above field-note extract, one aspect of this new social world is learning recurrently to describe it, to speak about it to the group and to one's fellow patients/residents: transmission of the culture of the institution not only reflexively constitutes the social reality of that institution, but is itself an integral part of reality. In the concept house the requirement that senior residents should transmit the culture to new residents finds formal expression in a variety of institutional arrangements such as the prospect-groups, seminars on the theory of therapy, and the appointment of elder brothers and sisters mentioned previously. One way in which patients/residents learn to transmit the culture is by contrasting unfavourably the lives they used to lead with their new lives. Contrastsets may be employed, such as the equation of life outside the community with a state of non-feeling in contrast to life inside the community where one is put in touch with one's feelings. Similarly, the nature of relationships inside and outside the community might be critically compared. A day hospital patient described the close, caring relationships between patients in this manner:

> . . . before she went into hospital she thought she had a lot of friends, but her experience in hospital . . . has led her to whittle down the numbers of these drastically. In contrast, she's been so close to her fellow-patients that she numbers some of this disparate group her closest friends.

Further, patients/residents learn to present to each other the institution as a setting where new forms of social behaviour can be learned to supplant previous pathogenic behaviour:

> In the . . . group Bill started talking about his failed marriage, his kids, his inability to face his problems, etc. He was eventually cut short by Helen (patient) who told him she was sick and tired of listening to his past history: she'd been a 'useless bastard' in the past too, she wanted to hear about how Bill felt now.

In the concept house the ex-addicts learn to account for their lives in the drug culture as embodying social relationships with others which were exploitative and self-centred, babyish in their unreasoning resistance to all authority; the concept house is portrayed as a place where new and diametrically opposing social relationships can be developed.

While it is not our intention in the paper to attempt to describe formally all aspects of the treatment programmes and treatment ideologies of the two communities, it should nevertheless now be evident that a central feature of treatment in both communities is its reality-constructing character: patients/residents learn to act in accord with accounts and assimilate and reproduce accounts which come reflexively to constitute the social world of patients/

residents. But these accounts and rules of behaviour cannot be supplied unproblematically by community members to make sense of their situation and provide templates for action; members come to recognise these accounts and rules as having a vague, provisional, and incipiently contradictory character. Members' recognition of this character of accounts and rules provides the occasion for a second and complementary central aspect of treatment – reality exploration.

Reality exploration

No rule or prescription for behaviour can exhaustively specify the occasions of its use[14]. No matter how seemingly specific the expression of a rule, there will remain a degree of interdeterminacy in its application to a given context. In effect, any rule contains an 'etcetera clause'[15] which the user must fill in to apply the rule: the user must both interpret the situation at hand to determine which rule may be applicable and elaborate the sense of the rule to cover the situation at hand. Rules are essentially contingent and always in principle defeasible (that is, the appropriateness of a rule to a given situation may be questioned and defeated, another rule always being in principle substitutable). Although members of collectivities normally have a sense of the obvious appropriateness of a given rule to a given situation, this is always potentially disruptable and members can thus become aware of the provisional and possibly conflicting nature of the prescriptions to which they are subject. The same phenomenon is observable with accounts: all learned accounts of structures, relationships, etc. must be elaborated to encompass particular situations; although their applicability may be consensually taken for granted they remain essentially contingent and defeasible and thus potentially open to re-examination as provisional and contradictory.

These processes can be seen in the particular cases of the concept house and the day hospital: patients/residents assimilate and reproduce accounts and prescriptions for behaviour, and these accounts and prescriptions become taken-for-granted resources for everyday living in the two communities. However, as reported previously, these accounts and prescriptions are not (and cannot be) exhaustively elaborated for the new member; they are conveyed by glosses and elicited by the documentary method. Thus any particular assimilated background feature remains potentially open to inspection when its contingent and defeasible nature may be revealed. Elsewhere, Fonkert has illustrated at length how the formal rule in the concept house against violence (the breaking of which was meant to lead to the offender being barred from the house) was in fact contingent and subject to qualification in the light of indexical features[16]. For example:

A boy and a girl are evidently (sexually) attracted to each other. The girl is . . . teasing. She provokes the boy sexually, runs him down and provokes him again. The boy has no defence against it and eventually . . . loses his self-control. He spits in her face and slaps her. Residents write haircut recommendations. Later on that day the head expeditor openly gives him an aggressive haircut[17].

In this instance, although there was general agreement that violence had taken place, the ultimate sanction (barring the boy from the community) was not proceeded with because of a number of indexical features. Firstly, the rule ('Do not use violence or threats of violence') does not specify the notion of violence and consequently has an elaborate etcetera-clause open to reality exploration by community members: apparently there are degrees of violence and the face-slapping was not judged to be extreme violence. Secondly, it was thought that there were extenuating circumstances in that the girl was felt to have provoked the boy. Thirdly, the boy had otherwise been acquitting himself well in the community and was at that time a candidate for 're-entry' (the rehabilitation phase of the concept house programme). Fourthly, it was known that the circumstances of the boy's arrival at the community were such that expulsion from the community would automatically result in the boy being committed to a psychiatric institution.

Similarly, Bloor[18] has described at length the defeasible character of staff prescriptions for patient behaviour in the day hospital: a paradoxical situation occurred whereby any behaviour encouraged by staff as conducive to therapy was always potentially reinterpretable in the opposite light, as detrimental to therapy. Thus, patients were expected to continue the work of the formal groups outside the day hospital programme by taking part in informal discussion, encouraging one another to act to overcome their difficulties, exhibiting concern for fellow-patients and so on. However these activities could also be seen as suspect by the staff: the term 'patient therapist' had negative connotations for staff. Such patients could be seen as interesting themselves in others as a device for avoiding working on their own problems. Or a patient could be seen to be exploring their own predicament in an indirect and manipulative way through the medium of another patient.

In the staff group Dick was talking about the close friendship between Nichola and Eddy (patients). He said Nichola pushes Eddy a lot but she's got just the same problem herself – its as if she's pushing Eddy to test out the water.

Again, it was felt important for patients to provide each other with comfort and support to help each other remain in treatment despite the stresses and strains engendered by the work of the formal groups. Thus, a patient who flees treatment may be coaxed back to the day hospital by a visiting deputation of his fellows, a patient undergoing a crisis may be kept company through the long watches of the night, and so on. However, the provision of comfort and support for fellow-patients could also be seen as anti-therapeutic in the sense of buttressing a patient's resistance to discussing their difficulties in the formal groups. An illustration: during a morning group a staff-member brought back to the group remarks a couple of patients had made to him privately in an attempt to get the patients to examine the feelings that lay behind the remarks:

> None of these attempts to 'bring it back' met with much success:
> Nina denied still feeling angry . . . Rachel got tense and tearful but
> made no reply. In the (following) staff group someone . . . remarked with
> disapproval that at the end of the (formal) group a couple of patients were
> across comforting Rachel while another was closeted with Nina . . . Oliver
> explained that he disapproved because if that concern had been shown
> *during the group* then Rachel might have got it out rather than simply
> bottling it up.

In a similar fashion, staff in the concept house may view emotional outbursts by new residents in a positive light, even if these occur while the resident is working within the structure, since the resident may be held to be getting in touch with his emotions for the first time. Indeed a new resident who does not 'flip out' may get a 'haircut' for his failure so to express himself. However, as the resident becomes more senior he encounters contradictory expectations and will receive a haircut for flipping out within the structure as this contravenes the 'self-discipline' rule.

In sum then, the day hospital and the concept house, like any other organisation, are pervaded with accounts and prescriptions which are essentially contingent and defeasible. However, what differentiates these therapeutic communities from most other treatment institutions is the staff recognition of the contingent and defeasible character of accounts and prescriptions and their self-conscious use of this fact as a treatment resource. Thus, in the concept house the staff speak of the purposeful vagueness[19] of the rules. In the process of interpreting and elaborating the rules (filling in the etcetera-clause) the residents must use their judgment ('they can't keep it safe') and act in ways which can be defeated by staff ('take a risk') and made an occasion and a topic for therapeutic work: the provisional character of the rules leads to reality exploration by residents and reality exploration leads to therapeutic 'haircuts'.

Residents assimilate the therapeutic connotations of reality exploration and orient to it in their behaviour and conversation. For example, a concept house resident had been sent on a shopping expedition; on his return it emerged that he had failed to find some items on the list and so had bought others as substitutes, spending more money than had previously been agreed upon in the process. The expeditor started to make trouble about it but the resident cut him short by saying, 'Well I've taken a risk, haven't I?' The resident had been given an assignment but his instructions had not been exhaustively specified; he had not been told what to do if he could not find all the items on the shopping list. He thus had to elaborate on his instructions to cover the situation at hand: he bought substitute items and spent more money than had been agreed. In so doing he took a risk, which on principle would earn him a reward from his fellows, since he could be held to have faced a problematic situation in an 'adult' manner and not retreated from it, junkie-fashion. He took a risk in so far as he risked getting a haircut for being seen to overstep one of the purposefully vague limits to behaviour, by spending more of the house's money than had been agreed upon. If he had been given a haircut he would have been expected to accept the rebuke even if he still felt that he had made the right decision; he would be expected to contain his anger at the injustice in an adult manner until he could re-raise the issue in the encounter group. Reality exploration is used as both an occasion and a topic for therapy.

In the day hospital staff accepted with equanimity criticism of their prescriptions for patient behaviour as being contradictory:

> We often get accused by patients, and by new staff, of being very self-contradictory, because they don't pick up the essential nature of what we're doing.

Such contradictions are a focus of, and an occasion for, therapeutic work:

> The paradox, the conflict that exists. . . . Without that I don't think we'd be able to do the job we do, or we try to do. It is a copy of, or an image of, reality, because without some kind of conflict you can't end up with a compromise. My feeling is that our aim here is that we come to some kind of compromise with the patient, and the patient comes to some sort of compromise with the setting he lives in.

Staff viewed this part of the treatment process as the induction of the patient into a reality he constructs as consisting of warm, caring relationships where judgments are suspended and a wide range of deviant behaviour is permitted, only to realise slowly that in the day hospital there are contradictions – limits to care, and limits to what is permitted. The staff response to patients discovering the defeasible and incipiently contradictory character of staff prescriptions is to draw the patients' attention to the incipiently contradictory character of all prescriptions: life's like that. When a patient suggested Bloor couldn't really care about her since he only turned up at the hospital three days a week, a staff member intervened to say that Bloor couldn't attend more often and that was the unchangeable reality, 'No one can give you 110 per cent care.' Staff believe that as patients are forced to come to terms with these contradictions and accept these limits, then they are adopting patterns of behaviour which will equip them to deal with life outside the hospital more adequately than formerly, to recognise and accept the contradictions and qualifications of everyday life.

Conclusion

We have taken data from two contrasting therapeutic communities operating in different countries, with a different client group and different organisational forms. Nevertheless, we claim to discern a broad similarity in notions of treatment in both communities. Our argument is that in both treatment structures – the democratic/permissive day hospital and the hierarchical concept house – reality construction occurs in broadly similar ways and is used as a treatment method. Further, that within these processes of reality construction there are inherent processes of reality exploration due to the innately provisional character of accounts and prescriptions, and that staff consciously use these processes as resources, occasions, and topics for therapy[20]. By reality construction we refer to the requirement on patients/residents to learn accounts of the everyday activities of the community in question and to learn to act in accord with those accounts, until those accounts become a taken-for-granted objective facticity, reflexively constituting the reality they purport to describe. By reality exploration we refer to the processes whereby patients/residents come to recognise and inspect the innately and purposefully provisional and defeasible character of accounts and prescriptions for behaviour. The processes of reality construction and reality exploration are symbiotically related: the former provides for the possibility of the latter, and the latter both feeds back into the former and provides an occasion for therapy in that parallels may be drawn with the provisional and defeasible character of life outside the community. These aspects of therapeutic community treatment may be of particular interest to sociologists since they mirror sociological conceptions of reality construction and constitution.

Notes

1   Part of the research reported in this paper was funded by the Medical Research Council whose support we gratefully acknowledge. We wish to thank Bob Harrison, Gordon Horobin, and Neil McKeganey for their comments on an earlier draft.

2   M.J. Bloor, 'The Nature of Therapeutic Work in the Therapeutic Community: some preliminary findings', *International Journal of Therapeutic Communities*, vol. 1, 1980, pp. 80–91.

3   A good description of those treatment methods and their historical development is to be found in J.S. Whitely and J. Gordon, *Group Approaches in Psychiatry*, London, Routledge & Kegan Paul, 1979.

4   See especially L. Yablonsky, *Synanon: The Tunnel Back*, Harmondsworth, Penguin, 1967, and B. Sugarman, *Daytop Village, a Therapeutic Community*, New York, Holt, Rinehart & Winston, 1974.

5   Becoming a member was crucial to our research both epistemologically and logistically. As Mehan and Wood point out:

'if the purpose of the research is to know the reality work of a phenomenon, then the researcher must begin by first becoming the phenomenon. The researcher must become a full-time member of the reality to be studied. . . . To become a member means to do a reality as its members do. . . . Membership cannot be simulated. The researcher must not hold back. The researcher who holds back in the name of objectivity never comes to respect that reality or be respected by its practitioners.' (H. Mehan and H. Wood, *The Reality of Ethnomedology*, New York, Wiley 1975)

Detailed descriptions of the research methods and of the settings in which they were employed are to be found in M.J. Bloor, 'On the relationship between informal patient interaction and the formal treatment programme in a day hospital using therapeutic community methods', *Institute Occasional Paper No. 4*, Aberdeen, Institute of Medical Sociology, 1980, and in J.D. Fonkert, 'Reality Construction in a Therapeutic Community for Ex-Drug-Addicts', The Hague, doctoral dissertation, 1978.

6   For readers ill-acquainted with concept house therapy, staff accounting for the hierarchical structure of the community studied by Fonkert can be briefly summarised as follows. Firstly, the hierarchical structure is a means of putting pressure on a resident so that his behaviour, attitudes, emotions, and ways of relating to others become more visible, since under pressure the resident's normal defence-mechanisms function inadequately. Then in the encounter group his newly visible difficulties can be an object of therapy. Secondly, by working within the hierarchical structure the resident may learn self-discipline and how to work with others. By earning a responsible position he is held to adopt a responsible attitude and to respect others. Thirdly, the structure minimises the possibility of residents isolating themselves since they have to work together. Finally, it gives clarity and organisation in the community.

7   See the discussion in P. Filmer, 'On Harold Garfinkel's Ethnomethodology', in Filmer *et al.*, *New Directions in Sociological Theory*, London, Collier-Macmillan, 1972.

8   There is a parallel here with Garfinkel's analysis of how jurors' decisions predate their assimilation of the 'official rules' of jury decision making, which are only learned in the course of their deliberations (H. Garfinkel, *Studies in Ethnomethodology*, Englewood Cliffs, Prentice-Hall, 1967, pp. 105–15). We are indebted to Neil McKeganey for pointing out this parallel.

9   Where fieldnotes are quoted names of patients and staff have been changed (along with certain background circumstances where necessary) in order to maintain confidentiality.

10   After this experience Fonkert felt he had become a member of the community; he experienced matters in the way that his fellow-members experienced them (see note 5 above).

11   See H. Garfinkel and H. Sacks, 'On the formal structures of practical actions', in McKinney and Tiryakian, *Theoretical Sociology, Perspectives and Developments*, New York, Appleton-Century-Crofts, 1970.

12   Sugarman, op. cit., p. 87.

13   The working out of emotions must take place within the encounter group, the setting especially created for this purpose. Within the structure acting out is normally permitted only in the 'washing tub', the bottom of the status hierarchy.

Elsewhere in the structure residents must learn to cope with stress until the encounter group is convoked.

14   On this point see E.A. Bittner, 'The concept of organisation', *Social Research*, vol. 32, 1965, pp. 239–55; also D. Zimmerman and D.L. Wieder, 'Ethnomethodology and the problem of order: comment on Denzin', in Douglas, *Understanding Everyday Life*, London, Routledge & Kegan Paul, 1971.

15   H. Garfinkel, op. cit.

16   J.D. Fonkert, op. cit.

17   In the argot of the concept house 'haircut' has connotations wider than the merely tonsorial: it refers to a means of correcting behaviour and showing new guidelines to the resident. Best known here is the formalised, lengthy, aggressive, verbal dressing down that a resident may receive for committing a misdemeanour or having the wrong attitude. This may culminate in various measures being taken, one of which may be shaving his or her head. However, other forms of 'haircut' may be simply informational or, indeed, the 'positive haircut' – where the resident is rewarded for appropriate behaviour.

18   M.J. Bloor, op. cit.

19   It may be objected that for staff to speak of the purposeful vagueness of rules is somewhat mystifying in view of their essentially contingent character. However, this objection fails to take into account the fact that while rules are essentially contingent, certain familiar elaborations of rules may come to be seen as the most suitable and desirable in certain familiar contexts. They remain innately defeasible but any change is unlikely because they come to be invested with what Bittner (op. cit.) describes as 'an all-pervading sense of piety . . . a sure-footed conviction of what properly goes with what'. This issue is discussed at length in M.J. Bloor, 'An alternative to the ethnomethodological approach to rule-use? A comment on Zimmerman and Wieder's comment on Denzin', *Scottish Journal of Sociology*, vol. 4, 1980, pp. 249–63. To maintain a purposeful vagueness in institutional rules is thus to combat a natural tendency to routinisation and ritualisation. In the concept house there are a number of institutional mechanisms (such as the rapid shifting of residents between statuses in the hierarchy) which have just this aim in view.

20   While we would contend that the processes of reality construction and reality exploration are broadly similar in both communities and consciously used by both sets of staff as treatment resources, it is not our contention that the manner of their usage is isomorphic between the day hospital and the concept house. As an anonymous reviewer perspicaciously pointed out, staff in the concept house may purposefully engineer situations which elicit reality exploration by residents, while staff in the day hospital more frequently play a comparatively passive role in encouraging patients to recognise the need for, and implications of, reality exploration.

1.3

'But if you look at the coronary anatomy . . .': risk and rationing in cardiac surgery

David Hughes and Lesley Griffiths

Introduction

In recent years the British popular media have become increasingly pre-occupied with the issue of health care rationing, and we have witnessed the beginnings of a public debate about the basis on which rationing decisions are made. Newspaper reports that patients with heart conditions who smoked tobacco were being refused angiography and surgery provoked fierce controversy. On one side were those who argued that smoking and other risk factors affecting prognosis constitute good medical grounds for limiting treatment. From this perspective information on risk factors provides an objective, value-free basis for allocating a scarce resource. On the other side were those who contended that such decisions embody judgements about behaviour that are social rather than medical, that treatment should be given according to clinical need, and that it is wrong for doctors to try to 'police' lifestyle.

The public backlash following the Harry Elphick case[1] has led the medical profession to review its position. Guidelines issued by the British Cardiac Society Council (BCSC) stated that 'Council does not believe it is possible to justify a clinical policy that systematically denies the right of access to treatment to individuals on the basis of a specific risk factor, even if this is self-induced' (British Cardiac Society Newsletter 1993: 395). The BCSC drew attention to an earlier General Medical Council statement, issued in relation to HIV/AIDS, that: 'It is [. . .] unethical for a doctor to withhold treatment for any patient on the basis of a moral judgement that the patient's activities or lifestyle might have contributed to the condition for which treatment is being sought' (British Cardiac Society Newsletter 1993: 395).

Continuing media interest led the British Medical Association to add its voice to the debate. New guidance published in January 1994 stated that: 'Treatment offered must be based on clinical judgement and sound scientific evidence of likely benefit. It is unethical to refuse an available treatment to any patient who might benefit. (. . .) Patients must not be left with the impression that their inability or unwillingness to follow an advised course of action will deprive them of medical attention' (BMA 1994: 11). However, amplifying statements from senior BMA officers suggested that links between lifestyle and prognosis might still be a legitimate consideration in limiting treatment. According to the BMA Secretary: 'This is not a moral stand, or punishing patients who take risks. Doctors simply have an ethical duty not to waste resources'[2].

How plausible are senior doctors' claims that these are purely technical judgements, devoid of moral or social content? In its formative years, medical sociology paid surprisingly little attention to the content of medical work (Berg 1992), implicitly accepting medicine's own characterisation of the scientific basis of clinical judgement. However, that characterisation is coming under challenge from research carried out within a range of theoretical and methodological traditions. Over the years a substantial literature has accumulated which indicates that sociologic and other contextual factors influence clinical decision making (for reviews see: Eisenberg 1979, Hughes *et al.* 1988, Clark *et al.* 1991). This evidence can be set alongside findings from ethnographic studies which describe the subterranean cultures and in-group argots that develop within hospital locales and work groups, and are often openly evaluative of patients (Becker *et al.* 1961, Hafferty 1988, Jeffery 1989, Liederman and Grisso 1985, Mizrahi 1986). More recently – and most interestingly for our purposes – micro-level studies of medical discourse have begun to map out the complex ways in which medical interactions orientate to wider organisational and social environments. The study of discourse in medical settings, particularly collegial discourse, offers a promising route for those who believe that medical work can be productively analysed as social action. As Atkinson (1992, 1994, 1995) shows, medical work in hospitals may be seen as an elaborate round of formal and informal spoken performances. When individual patients become 'cases', their histories are rendered as narratives that are rehearsed and reconstructed in ward rounds and patient conferences. Practitioners are called upon to negotiate and justify proposed courses of action and, in doing so, reveal the vocabularies of justification that are acceptable to, or at least tolerated by, their peers.

Although discourse-based studies rarely touch explicitly on the influence of social factors in clinical decision making, they have drawn attention to ways in which talk in medical settings necessarily builds in references to both 'medical' and 'commonsense' realities. The issue of shifts or transformations between 'social' and 'technical' discourses has generally been linked to the interplay between lay accounts and biomedical knowledge categories in doctor/ patient interaction (Mishler 1984, Silverman 1987, Tannen and Wallat 1987)[3]. However, some authors have attempted to widen this analysis to include collegial discussions, suggesting that doctors, in interactions away from patients, frequently 'break frame' or shift 'footing' as they try to make sense of patient histories (or other aspects of medical work) within wider social and institutional contexts (Frader and Bosk 1981, Griffiths and Hughes 1994).

In this latter respect, medical practitioners may not be very different from colleagues in the wider scientific community[4]. Marc Berg (1992) has commented on the parallels between medical problem solving and the social processes through which knowledge is produced in laboratory science. Ethnographies of laboratory work (Knorr-Cetina 1981, Latour and Woolgar 1986, Fujimura 1987) show that scientists are pragmatic actors, who develop creative solutions to problems encountered in making experiments work.

Typically, these solutions emerge from negotiations between colleagues in which 'cognitive', 'material' and 'social' elements are interwoven in an ad hoc, opportunistic way (Knorr-Cetina 1981). Berg suggests that similar processes occur when doctors set out to transform patients' presenting conditions into soluble problems by re-constructing histories, examination results and other contextual information. He argues that physicians actively seek the information necessary to support the transformation they have in mind, drawing on a range of data sources, and even selecting or omitting examination procedures to prestructure the pathological reality that the favoured intervention will correct.

It is important not to reify the categories discussed here: the 'medico-technical' and 'social' elements that figure in case discussions are constructed rather than given, so that their ultimate status is often contestable. Theorists who employ the concept of medical discourse have generally stressed its fabricated, locally-produced nature. Anspach (1988) draws on transcribed conversational data to show how case presentations use a range of linguistic devices to augment the authority of the medical report as against the inherent subjectivity of doctors' information-gathering practices. She demonstrates how case presentations are organised to de-personalise both patients and practitioners: patients are described in terms of an impersonal vocabulary which often equates the person with the condition label; the active role of doctors' decisions in shaping histories is obscured by omitting these decision-making processes from clinical histories; results from CT scans and other machine data are presented as self-evident facts rather than matters for human interpretation; and the subjective status of patients' accounts is emphasised by doctors' use of 'account markers' which cast doubt on their validity (for example, 'The patient denies that . . .'). These linguistic practices serve to affirm the value of scientific objectivity and diagnostic technology over individual interpretation, so that in effect physicians construct a mode of discourse which fits the model of scientific medicine to which their profession lays claim. However, Anspach also notes that important features of case presentation, such as the mitigation of individual physician responsibility and the enhancement of the factual status of findings, reflect social pressures on the main category of presenters in her data – junior doctors, whose performance is being assessed by superiors.

This last consideration may explain why the medical discourses described by Anspach show little evidence of the frame shifts and incursion of evaluative elements reported by Frader and Bosk (1981). Certainly, the data on cardiac catheterisation conferences (CCCs) that we present in this paper, and comparable observations of neuro-rehabilitation admissions conferences reported by us elsewhere (Griffiths and Hughes 1993, 1994), suggest that doctors are not always willing or able to construct case histories and disposals in these de-personalised terms. In the analysis that follows, we examine data from CCCs to show how case presentations orientate to a range of relevancies with both 'technical' and 'social' content.

Our argument is that narratives are embedded in sequences of social action, directed to bring about outcomes that may be contested by other professionals, and are organised to provide for this latter eventuality. While participants in CCCs agree on a range of grounds that would justify or rule out surgery, there is considerable scope for disagreement in determining disposals for particular patients. The concept of ideological dilemmas (Billig *et al.* 1988) points to the way participants are often faced with multiple discourse-frames, which often suggest conflicting interpretations of events, and sometimes them-selves contain themes and counter-themes that are not easily reconciled. Despite the fact that much talk is about cardiac anatomy and diagnostic technology, doctors often disagree in their portrayal of cases, and produce competing rationales for offering or withholding treatment. To some extent, this reflects a tension between a traditional individualistic treatment ethic of care according to need and a utilitarian standpoint which emphasises the need to achieve the maximum benefit per unit of scarce resource. As we shall see, case discussions which contain references to risk, often move on to touch on issues of patient character and responsibility. The arguments that arise from time to time in catheterisation conferences thus bear a close resemblance to the arguments put forward in the public media debate.

Everyday assessments of risk are a highly salient feature of case talk in CCCs, particularly in relation to selection of patients for surgery, and we also offer some limited comments on the nature of risk formulations. Formal risk analysis, linked to probability theory, has gained much ground in med-ical science in recent years (Royal Society Study Group 1992, Backett *et al.* 1984). While risk calculations are generally based on the health experiences of populations and are largely a public health tool, there have been attempts to incorporate them into clinical decision theory to develop algorithms to inform individual treatment decisions (see: Hughes *et al.* 1988). However, such approaches have rarely, if ever, been applied in clinical practice to date, and those who contend that 'risk factors' are legitimate criteria for limiting treatment decisions say little about how doctors might reach such assess-ments, other than perhaps by imposing blanket exclusions on certain high-risk groups such as smokers. Our data suggest that doctors' formulations of risk in CCC discussions are only loosely linked to formal probability calcula-tions. Risk assessment here (as in some other reported settings) is informed by a 'social rationality', which often depends on 'rule of thumb' judgements or practical heuristics (Perrow 1984, Short 1984), and takes precision only as far as the imperatives of the interaction require.

The Research and its setting

The data we present come from a study of patient selection for coronary artery bypass surgery carried out in 1989–90. The study was conducted in a large teaching hospital, whose single cardiac surgeon had a policy of not operating on tobacco smokers[5]. The research was one of three case studies carried out as constituent elements of a three year study on ethical issues in the allocation of health care resources. A single fieldworker visited the study hospital two to three times per week over a nine months period. Fieldwork involved observation of cardiology outpatient clinics, a two-week period of observation in the operating theatre, informal interviews with key personnel, and observations in the weekly CCCs. This paper draws on these last two data sources. We observed eighteen morning conferences involving discussion of approximately 130 patients. The data extracts included below are based on tape-recordings of CCC interactions, though some of the recorded inter-actions have been elided because of tape quality problems[6]. The resulting transcriptions (together with fieldnotes of some meetings not recorded) were scrutinised for general patterns and coded. Representative extracts were then selected for detailed analysis.

Cardiac services at University Teaching Hospital (UTH) are provided by a single cardiac surgeon, as well as cardiologists attached to three medical firms in the hospital that cover this specialty. Cardiothoracic surgery is a relatively new Regional specialty and in the past most patients were referred for surgery to other centres. At the time of the study an average of eleven major procedures per week[7] were being carried out at UTH. Although the clinicians had plans to increase workload further, the Region and DHA were resisting pressure to exceed agreed activity. The finite supply of ITU beds, theatre sessions and nursing theatre time, was also imposing de facto limits on what could be done. As a result, the waiting list for surgery lengthened significantly. Cardiology also needed to control admissions because of the lack of earmarked cardiology beds and pressure on the single cardiac cath-eter laboratory (used for catheterisation, angioplasty, and valvuloplasty). In the year of the study cardiac surgery activity in Shire Region was running at a level well below Department of Health targets. For example, against a DH target of 500 coronary artery bypass operations per million population per year, Shire, with a population of 1.8 million, set a target of 365 'pump' operations of all kinds. The research thus examined decision-making in a service facing significant resource constraints, where rationing of treatment was a real possibility.

Catheterisation conferences at UTH are held on Tuesday mornings. They are multi-purpose events attended by the cardiac surgeon and consultants, staff and students from the hospital's three medical firms. Most obviously the CCCs focus on the review of angiograms of patients who are being considered for surgery or angioplasty, so as to pool expertise and decide appropriate treatment strategies[8]. They are held in a small lecture theatre, equipped with projection facilities, which is darkened while films are shown. Among other things, the meetings also provide a chance to review mistakes and successes, to discuss the impact of resource constraints, and to educate students. Importantly too, they are the main forum for regular contact between the cardiologists and the surgeon. While many routine referrals are made on standard referral forms, difficult cases are invariably raised at the 'cath conference'. It might be said that the key business of the meeting, if one strips away the niceties of interaction, is that the cardiologists put forward a series of patients for consideration by the surgeon, who must then give some public indication of whether he will accept them for surgery.

'From the technical point of view . . .'

When we asked the study cardiologists what criteria were used in selecting patients for surgery both gave answers which stressed technical suitability.

Extract 1
Cardiologist A: . . . we sit down and look at a film together and find out whether a patient should have surgery on technical grounds and is it technically feasible to operate on this patient. I think largely the decision is made on the technical grounds and not the fact that there is a long waiting list.

Extract 2
Cardiologist B: . . . if we think that somebody needs an operation we put them down for it, we don't sort of put them off and say, well you're not so deserving as the next person.

Certainly the issue of the technical feasibility of surgery comes up repeatedly in the majority of observed conference discussions. It will often be signalled at the outset as the reason why a cardiologist has selected the patient for discussion at the conference:

Extract 3
Cardiologist A: This is a man of fifty-two, a post-infarct case, with unstable angina, and it's really from the technical point of view.

Extract 4
Cardiologist B: On technical grounds I wonder whether you could graft this man?

This preoccupation with technical issues continues to be apparent as cases are discussed. Most CCCs conform to a pattern: a consultant cardiologist introduces the case and summarises the patient history; the group watch the angiography film with the senior clinicians commenting on relevant anatomical features; and there is a discussion of prognosis and appropriate treatment. Where surgery is a possibility there will be a point in this discussion where a direct question is put to the surgeon.

The patient histories presented in CCCs tend to be more compressed than is common in many other hospital settings. The focus of attention is on the angiogram, which gives a direct visual indication of heart anatomy. Much of the talk of the meeting occurs as the film is being shown, with voices raised to carry above the loud clicking of the projector. Where coronary artery disease is involved, the doctors viewing the film will be concerned, among other things, with the extent of narrowing of the coronary arteries, the presence of smaller collateral vessels that may provide a natural bypass around an obstruction, the state of the heart muscle supplied by the diseased artery, and whether the artery is suitable for grafting. They are likely to call attention to all of these features as they become apparent from the film.

There are many examples in our data where inferences made from the film appear to lead on to a decision made with minimal discussion.

Extract 5

Cardiologist A: Now Clive Rees. (. . .) He's a forty-nine-year-old who has limiting angina. And again I was thinking of the possibility of re-grafting from a technical point of view.

[Starts projector]

Cardiologist A: There's the lateral.

Registrar: Got a prominent lateral.

Cardiologist A: There's a lot of plaque in the left main, extending to the LAD. He's really surviving on this large diagonal, I'd say. The LAD is gummed up. A remarkable diagonal actually – goes all the way around the apex.

(. . .)

Cardiologist A: This is the PDA down here.

Surgeon: Again we'll have to find some room. How old is he?

Cardiologist A: Forty-nine.

Surgeon: Ah well, soon then[9].

Extract 5 involves a forty-nine-year-old, a young patient in cardiac surgery terms, with a life threatening condition that is surgically correctable, and the decision appears relatively straightforward. Conversely we observed several cases where difficult coronary anatomy was cited as grounds for a negative decision:

Extract 6

Surgeon: So I don't think we have found anything we can correct anatomically.

Extract 7

Surgeon: I haven't seen anything I can graft.

Extract 8
Surgeon: The difficulty with him is to know what to
                    re-vascularize.

Extract 9
Surgeon: Have you considered angioplasty? I think it's going to be
                    very heroic to take on that LAD without the circumflex.

The technical discourse illustrated in these and similar extracts centres on the feasibility of surgery. Risk sometimes surfaces as an issue, as in the reference to the 'heroic' nature of a technically-difficult procedure in Extract 9, but in most cases long-term prognosis is not discussed. Often the determination of feasibility appears to lead straightforwardly to acceptance for surgery. However, it is important to note that feasibility in itself will not always guarantee surgery. In a minority of cases a broader issue of acceptability arises, which is often linked to longer-term issues of risk and prognosis. Some factors considered to correlate with risk, notably age, are present in the technical discourse, albeit implicitly. But when doctors move on to discuss behaviour and lifestyle, the impression of value-free description becomes harder to sustain. In the two sections that follow we consider how references to age tend to be built implicitly into the stylised language of case presentation, while references to lifestyle tend to lead to discussions about willed behaviour and responsibility difficult to address within a purely technical discourse-frame.

Age

Age is perhaps the best documented of the socio-medical criteria said to affect treatment decisions (Kilner 1990, Hendee 1986, Meissner 1986, Uddo 1986), including priority for cardiac surgery (Naylor *et al.* 1992). North American writers suggest that the age criterion has operated more openly in Britain, with rationing by selective referral and queuing, than in the majority of other developed countries (Haber 1986, Lasagna 1970, Calabresi and Bobbit 1978, Kerr 1967, Veatch 1985). UTH has no official policy excluding older patients, but a number of clinical staff interviewed suggested that they were the prime sufferers under resource constraints. On the basis of the published surgery rates mentioned earlier, we might infer that older patients who would have been candidates in other British Regions are not getting surgery in Shire.

Many commentators believe that the exclusion of older patients has more to do with conservative referral patterns than conscious age rationing. The UTH cardiologists cite GPs' reluctance to refer older patients as one reason for the low Regional surgery rates. However, there is also the obvious possibility of age bias in secondary and tertiary care: notably in selection for cardiac catheterisation, in referral for surgery, in acceptance for surgery, and in priority once on the waiting list. Interviews with the cardiologists, cardiac surgeon and the secretary responsible for managing the waiting list suggest that the latter area is the most significant. The surgeon was blunt in asserting in several informal conversations that 'forty-year-olds deserve priority over eighty-year-olds'. His secretary was explicit about the consequences in waiting list terms:

Extract 10

Secretary: Because of our waiting list um being quite long we have to, in a way, grade it obviously by their condition but also by their age. If it's say for coronaries, [the surgeon] isn't very inclined because of the limited resources, to operate on a seventy-nine-year-old's or an eighty-year-old's coronaries, because he feels it's, you know, maybe it's a thing you come to at the end of your life and you've got 40-year-olds on the waiting list.
But the cardiologists don't always agree with that. They've obviously cath'ed the patient and investigated them so they feel it's warranted. So I think that's sometimes where the discrepancy occurs, they send us old patients, [the surgeon] feels that we shouldn't really be operating on them as soon as they would like, I mean it's a very sad situation.

Examination of the coronary surgery waiting list revealed a clear age gradient. Average ages of patients in the three waiting list categories of 'urgent', 'routine' and 'on hold' were 48.3, 59.7 and 61.5 respectively. This may help explain a rather puzzling feature of our taped data. We have many examples, such as *Extracts 11 and 12*, where age is flagged near to the point of the decision, but no cases where old age alone is used to rule a patient out.

Extract 11

Cardiologist C: Simon what is your feeling about the prospects for surgical re-vascularisation?

Surgeon: Yeah the circumflex marginal's all right. But that's quite a long way out, although it's graftable if grafted to that lesion. Go back again. Stop. Turn around there. The circumflex marginal is graftable. That LAD is very tatty. See, quite small out of the apex.

(film plays)

Surgeon: Yeah

(film plays)

(. . .)

Surgeon: So what age again Bob?

Cardiologist C: Sixty seven.

Surgeon:	And severe angina?
Senior Registrar:	Yeah. Yes I thought about angioplasty, but I didn't see a problem involved in it.
Surgeon:	Well yeah it is graftable Chris. I'll put . . . I'll probably put a mammary on the very badly . . . on the distal LAD.
Cardiologist C:	Grafted to the lesion?
Surgeon:	Grafted to the lesion, because you wouldn't want to go out any further distally than that.
Cardiologist C:	Well it's quite a bit.
Surgeon:	Well . . .
Cardiologist C:	Okay. Thank you.

Extract 12

Surgeon:	That LAD is very tatty and quite small. The origin's narrow. So what age again Colin?
Cardiologist B:	Sixty-seven.
Surgeon:	He needs something done. Well yeah. It's graftable, Colin. I'll put him down.

In instances where older patients are turned down, the reasons for rejection are invariably constructed in technical terms. For example, *Extract 13* involves a seventy-one-year-old woman referred with breathlessness and severe aortic reflux, who had recently suffered a myocardial infarction.

Extract 13

Registrar:	There's a diagonal down there. Stringy LAD!
Cardiologist B:	Very tight circumflex. I was wondering about angioplasty in that circumflex.
Senior Registrar:	It's a bit distal isn't it?
Cardiologist B:	So what do you think is the best approach?
Surgeon:	Shove a catheter down.
Cardiologist B:	She's not a candidate for surgery?

(The surgeon does not respond and discussion moves on to the next case)

Age is a taken-for-granted element of case presentation, often signposted near the point of decision, but its significance generally remains tacit. There is a striking absence of any extended discussion or of any well-developed age typifications. Why is the surgeon so concerned to flag age in some cases if he does not then act upon it? The answer, in our view, is that he does act upon it but not in terms of the acceptance decision. Everybody at the meetings is aware that getting surgery done is a two-stage process, there is the issue of acceptance and then the issue of progress up the waiting list. In signalling to the cardiologists that a patient's age has been registered, the surgeon may also be signalling that the patient will not have a place near the top of the list and thus forestalling any later challenge.

In the cases examined above, age is noted but the linkages to a positive or negative decision are left unstated. Such explicit linkages are more likely to occur in the context of youth than old age. It appears more acceptable to use youth to rule patients in than to use old age to rule patients out.

Extract 14 involves a forty-eight-year-old woman admitted with 'post-diet pain', who was discovered to have suffered a myocardial infarction, and is now a candidate for bypass surgery and ventricular re-section.

Extract 14

Surgeon:	I think I'd want to take a look at her Barry, because if she's grossly obese and with bronchial spasms . . .
Cardiologist A:	From a technical point of view that's a ventricle we could operate on and she's got graftable vessels.
Senior Registrar:	She is well motivated. I think she would get it done.
Cardiologist A:	And she's only forty-eight.

Why should age be signalled as a positive more often than a negative? Apart from a moral inhibition about being seen to use age to disqualify, a possible explanation for this pattern seems to us to lie in the structure of interests in the meeting. The cardiologists are putting forward patients they have preselected as surgical candidates – patients they have already gone to the trouble of catheterising. We are looking at the presentation of cases in a meeting where a majority of participants have an interest in constructing deservingness rather than undeservingness. It is usually the surgeon who signposts age with older candidates, but this is not a factor around which it is easy for him to construct a negative decision. Typically, the agenda for discussion set up by the referring cardiologist as he introduces the patient is technical suitability for surgery. As discussion proceeds the surgeon is being pressed to say whether or not the arteries are graftable. The cardiologists can claim to be as competent in their judgements about prognosis as the surgeon: his special expertise lies in knowing what is technically feasible and, if he wishes to rule out an older candidate, this is the linkage he must make. However, the flagging of age does signal that a difference has been noted, and thus creates a legitimate space for future prioritisation.

Constructing lifestyle

In the majority of case presentations the participants move towards an agreed decision without great drama. Cardiologists are familiar with the decision criteria that the surgeon favours, and it seems likely that cases are selected, or at least presented, to conform to the expected pattern. Where sharp differences do surface, it is usually when discussion moves on to issues of lifestyle – patient behaviours like smoking, drinking or over-eating, which can be constructed as negative indications for treatment. The surgeon at UTH maintains that he operates a 'no smoking' policy and certainly heavy pressure is put on smokers to agree to stop, but there are indications that the rule may sometimes be relaxed.

Extract 15

Cardiologist A: Smoking is one of the main causes of coronary disease. Now if you're not going to deal with the risk factors you're much more likely to have progression of the coronary disease and main graft disease after surgery. The second thing is that the time spent in hospital for a smoker is greater than a non-smoker because they get more chest problems you know, and we've got bed difficulties. But the underlying feeling is, I think, with [the surgeon], you know if we're going to go to all this, you know, do all this to make them better the least they can do is to remove the cause of the problem, which is very often cigarette smoking. I can't actually think of any patients who have not been operated on because they were cigarette smokers, I think the threat is there but it usually works.

Extract 16

Cardiologist B: I do my best to stop people smoking but we have operated on smokers and I don't really have a bar about it, some cardiologists do I know. I've had patients referred to me (. . .) because Professor Harvey in South City will not refer a patient if they continue to smoke. And I've had some of those come to me here, and we, you know, talk to them and generally actually manage to get them to stop. It isn't a total bar. I think that's very cruel to people because they can't always stop smoking. It's a very severe addiction in some people, and you do your best to stop them. But if they won't then you've got to do your best on the symptoms. (. . .) I mean [the surgeon says he won't operate on smokers] as a sort of thing to concentrate their minds and it often does. I would delay . . . he would delay their operation while all this palaver is going on by the way.

Undoubtedly medical practitioners' accounts are shaped by powerful institutional and professional constraints, and the cardiologists here seem careful to be seen to focus on the health implications of the behaviours involved rather than any social or moral dimensions of the cases. But the two extracts nevertheless show that sharply different grounds can be invoked for denying treatment to smokers. As with age, exclusion can be justified in terms of technical feasibility and prognosis. But with lifestyle there is the additional dimension of agency. Whereas ageing affects the body, it can be said that lifestyle has been willed by the person. When cardiologist A talks about 'underlying feelings' he is signalling the relevance of a cultural norm which says that people with self-induced conditions are less deserving of help – that 'the least they can do is remove the cause of the condition'. And in the quote from cardiologist B we see the obvious counterpoint to the agency argument: the contention that some patients should be released from responsibility because, due to addiction or other mitigating circumstances, they are less than full agents of their actions.

When differences of view over the acceptability of patients surface in 'cath conference' discussions, these competing lines of argument are likely to be brought into play. *Extract 17* involved a case where cardiologist and surgeon clash over the suitability of a referral:

Extract 17

Cardiologist C:	The next one's a man of forty-six, with two previous infarcts. (. . .) He runs a golf club, but is about to take over a pub because it will be less stress. He came in 10 days ago with unstable angina – no infarct. He's enormously fat about twenty stones//
Surgeon:	No! What have you done here? You've documented the case of a man who spends his life in an atmosphere of smoke and drink. What am I going to do? Knock him off on the table?
Cardiologist C:	But if you look at the coronary anatomy he's a candidate. He has severe three vessel disease. He is a young man. His activities have been impaired – the kind of case we would be looking to operate on. (. . .) I really think that all things being equal, he is a man who should have surgery,
Surgeon:	But all things aren't equal in this case. Any patient of twenty stones plus is a high risk for any chest surgery
Senior Registrar:	Perhaps the best thing would be to bring him in for three weeks for monitoring and try to get his weight down. (. . .)
Surgeon:	Donald, you've had four years to educate this guy. (. . .) There is no point in operating on this guy if he is going to carry on working in a smoky atmosphere, if he won't modify his lifestyle.

Later after discussing a seventy-six-year-old, valve-replacement patient said to be a 'fearsome risk' the surgeon adds: 'Although you might not agree,

I'd rather do a case like that than a massively obese forty-year-old'. The topic is taken up again at end of clinic:

Surgeon: But the twenty-stone guy, I'm not sure what I'm
                    expected to do there. He has been in and out of
                    hospital for years and not changed his lifestyle.
Cardiologist C: No he hasn't. Give us a break. We've seen him for the
                    first time in four years'.
Surgeon: Well if he isn't willing to modify his lifestyle there is no
                    point in doing anything.
Senior Registrar: The prognosis in a case like this is not good.
(He draws a rough graph on the blackboard illustrating the prognosis for three vessel disease with poor LV function.)
Without surgery mortality is like this (he draws a line) but even if they get surgery it's still like this (the graph is only slightly more encouraging).
Cardiologist C: The most sensible thing would be for us to bring him
                    in for a couple of weeks for monitoring.
Senior Registrar: It's easy enough to put the ball in his court. All we
                    have to do is make clear that unless he changes his
                    lifestyle we can't help him.
Surgeon: What he needs to do is change his job. He needs to
                    stop smoking, and I don't believe that people doing
                    jobs in smoky atmospheres like that can give up
                    smoking.
(The meeting ends with no agreement that surgery will be offered.)

At one level, talk in the foregoing extract is indeed about risk and prognosis – balancing the pros and cons of youth versus obesity, and favourable anatomy versus poor lifestyle. But it is clear that cardiologist and surgeon are also engaged in constructing competing versions of moral character. Right from the start the cardiologist seems to anticipate opposition. In saying that the patient 'is about to take over a pub because it will be less stress', he is putting the best gloss on potentially compromising information. The surgeon's response is constructed to highlight agency. The patient is a man 'who spends his life in an atmosphere of smoke and drink'. 'He has been in and out of hospitals all his life and not changed his lifestyle'. Personal responsibility is underscored by the repeated use of the personal pronoun – 'unless he changes his lifestyle we can't help him' . . . 'he needs to change to change his job. He needs to stop smoking'. Responsibility for lifestyle is sometimes presented as the result of weak will rather than conscious intention, but the surgeon opts for a stronger formulation. The sentence: 'If he isn't willing to modify his lifestyle there is no point in doing anything about it', can be heard as a claim that wilful action rather than negligence is involved. The cardiologist, on the other hand, de-emphasises agency by suggesting that the clinicians can help nullify the effects of lifestyle by bringing the patient in to get his weight down.

These discrepant descriptions of the patient are rhetorically constructed. They are presented in a form which anticipates and allows for likely counter arguments. This also applies to the way risk is formulated. Verbal estimations of risk are nearly always couched in approximate terms: the 46-year-old man is 'high risk for surgery', the patient that follows is a 'fearsome risk'. Even the graph drawn by the senior registrar consists only of two chalk lines without quantified axes – an intimation, rather than a detailed re-citation of results from the technical literature. Colleagues do not come to CCCs with the documentation needed to swap statistics or debate methodology. Precision only goes as far as is necessary to support the practical analysis of the problem being put forward. Actually, in this extract the surgeon offers a highly personalised formulation of risk, highlighting the risk he is being asked by the cardiologist to take: 'What am I going to do? Knock him off on the table?' For the surgeon the short-run risk of surgical mortality has a different significance from the long-term risk of, say, five-year survival – not least because 'kill rate' is a major performance indicator. The surgeon's formulation is a particularly powerful one because it implies that a risk, which will be highly consequential for him, arises because of the cardiologist's inappropriate referral: 'What have you done here?' he says. Far from the missing agent of Anspach's (1988) medical discourse, we have a situation where even colleagues are not exempt from blame attributions.

The cardiologist deals with this problem by directing attention back to the agreed agenda of the meeting. From his standpoint this is the issue of the technical feasibility of surgery – the surgeon's area of special competence. He says that if one looks at the coronary anatomy the patient is the kind of case they ought to take; that on the narrow question of technical feasibility the patient is no more high risk than many others.

Towards the end of the extract the Senior Registrar suggests a compromise – they will put the ball in the patient's court, and make it clear to him that he won't get surgery 'unless he changes his lifestyle'. The seductiveness of this approach lies in the way it allows doctors to sidestep responsibility. They do not need to ration care, rather patients are seen to rule themselves out by their own wilful decisions. By attributing choice to patients, doctors avoid hard choices of their own.

The linguistic constructions used in *Extract 17* demonstrate clearly that a linkage is being made between lifestyle and will. It shows that doctors talking together do not confine their discussions to technical questions of risk and prognosis, but that, as in discourses between lay people, references are made to both technical considerations and issues of personal responsibility.

Bringing in social structure

We have seen that when doctors in CCCs discuss prognosis, they often move on to consider social identities and issues of deservingness, but this is only part of a wider process through which doctors recognise and adjust to the social contexts of medical practice. Structural sociologists would have little difficulty in finding in our data passages of talk they could link to the classic social structural categories of class, gender, and ethnicity. Our own leaning towards interpretive sociology leads us to add the caveat that these are socially-constructed categories, whose power derives largely from the fact that people demonstrably pay attention to them in patterned ways in social interaction. But regardless of this theoretical qualification, what seems clear is that the methods that doctors use to bring 'social structures' into collegial talk are not fundamentally dissimilar from methods employed in everyday lay talk, except with regard to the rules of relevance that apply.

Lay conversationalists generally build in references to social context in an organised way. Talk depends for its coherence on 'contextualization cues' (Gumperz 1982, Drew and Heritage 1992), usually involving lexical, prosodic, phonological, or syntactic choices, used by participants to signal aspects of context relevant in interpreting what they mean. For example, a descriptor such as 'wife' carries a range of connotations for members of our culture in terms of gender roles, as well as interpersonal and family relationships. Depending on what other lexical or other cues co-occur in a strip of talk, participants will orient to relevant cultural knowledge – perhaps, to take just two possibilities, social norms regarding wives as mothers, or wives and marital fidelity. Contextualisation cues are closely bound up with processes of conversational inference by which participants retrieve relevant background knowledge, and thus bring a sense of social structure to the interaction. In terms of our earlier discussion, these cues serve to signal wider discourse frames, and to alert participants to shifts in attentional focus.

The key difference in the CCC setting is that these shifts in focus are affected by professional norms of relevance. The 'ideal' case presentation produced within the medico-technical discourse is cogent, free of superfluous detail, and designed to reflect the assumed relevance-interests of the audience (Atkinson 1994). These institutional norms imply a foreshortened horizon of relevance, which for much of the time restricts what can be introduced.

At the same time, medical practitioners have to cope with the fact that doctor/patient relationships overlap with social relationships, including power and gender relationships, and that these frequently have personal significance and tangible consequences for the parties. Although social identities may be de-emphasised within medical discourse by using the techniques of de-personalisation described by Anspach (1988), they are difficult to shut out completely. The social domain is always likely to surface in real-life contingencies ranging from falling in love to litigation and professional disciplinary proceedings. Against this background, what can legitimately be brought into discourse between medical colleagues is an area of some uncertainty: many things that might be mentioned could be self-discrediting. Professional norms affect where the boundaries of relevance are drawn, and limit the set of interactionally-relevant identities that can be invoked, but still leave scope for situational negotiation.

We can conceptualise this in terms of a gradient of acceptability, where the likelihood of negative reaction from colleagues increases as the linkage between what is mentioned and clinical issues of diagnosis, prognosis and management become more difficult to establish in talk. From our observations, it is the more powerful personnel – the surgeon and the cardiologists – who typically push the boundaries of relevance furthest. Consider, for example, the following case involving a sixty-two-year-old woman said to have poor left ventricular function and some degree of aortic obstruction.

Extract 18

Cardiologist B:	The question is how much good is an aortic valve replacement going to do this lady. She's been told she's having one. Her husband is a judge. And needless to say she is a very high risk case.

(The only possible surgical slot would be the next day. The surgeon says he is apprehensive. There is 'probably' a 'twenty per cent risk'. There remains uncertainty about the detailed diagnosis and there is a prolonged discussion regarding alternative explanations for the poor LV function. Could it be hypertensive heart disease? The coronary arteries appear normal)

Senior Registrar:	Surely we wouldn't lose anything by leaving it for another week?
Registrar:	She's a private patient.
Senior Registrar:	Oh God.
Surgeon:	I think we'd better get hold of the GP and tell him to talk to the family again.
Cardiologist B:	So the consensus is that everybody's a bit doubtful.
Surgeon:	You know quite frankly having decided to do the aortic valve replacement and told the family we're going to do it, we shouldn't be bringing it up again now. That husband – I mean he's a high court judge – is going to think we're a load of idiots. (. . .) It's the wrong time to be talking about this with the family. I think I'm going to have a quiet word with the GP and we'll decide something. (. . .) Poor LV function and twenty per cent risk. But we do a lot of aortic valve replacements with poor ventricular function. It's the old picture.

The significant point about this extract is that a social identity is invoked not because of its implications for medical diagnostic work, but its possible consequences for the medical practitioners doing that work. Here as commonly happens in everyday conversation, the husband's occupation is taken as a proxy for the wife's social status. Such gender-based structuring of talk is evident in our data[10]. We cannot be sure that the identification of the patient as a judge's wife is the crucial factor in inclining the surgeon to go ahead with a high-risk operation, but what the extract does indicate is doctors' sensitivity to contextual factors that can generate trouble for medical practitioners. In this case social identity is not linked to the issue of deservingness or undeservingness but rather to the issue of power. The stated worry is that 'the husband   I mean he's a High Court judge – is going to think we're a load of idiots'; the unstated concern is that any hint of negligence in treating this patient will be punished.

Because Western medical knowledge has developed as part of a broader corpus of cultural knowledge, it makes direct use of certain social categories, particularly in areas such as the epidemiology of morbidity. Ethnicity is one such category which featured in five observed CCC discussions in relation to patients of South Asian origin. *Extract 19* shows that here too technical and social assessments may be interwoven in case presentation talk:

Extract 19

Cardiologist C:	This is a man of forty-two, I'd like some help with as to whether or not he should be offered surgery. He's an Asian from Newtown, which is usually bad news.
Senior Registrar:	An agent?
Cardiologist C:	An Asian. He had a major head injury in 1978, with cerebral contusion and post-traumatic epilepsy, when he was coshed. Ahm and that's slightly, I think, clouded his subsequent management. But he had an infarct four years ago and since then he's been seen on and off in Newtown by his general practitioner with chest pain. And there seems to have been some genuine doubt as to the nature of this chest pain, such that there was an implication among the medical staff that he was making rather more of this chest pain than was reasonable. Be that as it may, he has a cardio-thoracic ratio of over 60 per cent on his chest x-ray, and his ECG shows quite extensive Q waves in the inferior and anterior leads. Attempts to exercise him have never been successful because he says he gets chest pain and just stops walking, or he comes off the mat of the treadmill. So he's never had an exercise-induced tachycardia or an abnormal ECG. His end-diastolic pressure is twenty. [(Angio starts running]
Registrar D:	Oh dear.
Cardiologist C:	Very poor left ventricular function. Akinesis of the whole of the anterior and/
Registrar B:	What medication is he on?

Cardiologist C:	He's on diltiazem.
Registrar C:	Did you say he is diabetic?
Cardiologist C:	No, he isn't diabetic.
Registrar D:	Fortunately.
Registrar B:	It's narrow isn't it?
Registrar C:	Very very narrow
Cardiologist C:	See contractions only there (. . .) and a little bit in the LAD. Very severe indeed, and very poor filling of the distal vessels. There he is coming up there.
Registrar B:	He is yes.
Cardiologist C:	Probably not too bad. (. . .) And there's the circumflex marginal, ghosting.
Registrar B:	Is there a dominant there?
Cardiologist C:	I would think probably not, no. (. . .) This man is now left with . . . complains severely of chest pain. I think one has to say predominantly its angina.
Registrar C:	(. . .) The infarct couldn't have been that bad if he has angina.
Cardiologist C:	Yeah, okay I think that's right. These are the technical questions (. . .) We can't really demonstrate that the vessels are graftable. And a really poor LV. What do you think Simon?
Surgeon:	Well it's . . . I'm sure we can find somewhere to graft. But he's a grim prospect isn't he? Is he still smoking? These Asians smoke like chimneys.
Cardiologist C:	I think he probably is. He certainly has smoked. I can very well find out.
Surgeon:	What's the status after his head injury, Colin?
Cardiologist C:	His superficial conversation is normal I think. His epilepsy is well controlled. He's very bitter about medical staff in general for not taking his chest pain very seriously over the years. And he's talking about litigation and lots of things.
Surgeon:	If you give me the angios I'll have a look.
Cardiologist C:	The next one's a Marcia Blake.
Registrar D:	The mortality of that chap from a surgical point of view is fearsome.
Cardiologist C:	Right. Can I show you an X-ray on a curious girl I saw . . .

Research has shown that patients of South Asian origin living in Britain suffer a higher than average morbidity of coronary artery disease, and present with more severe coronary atheroma than matched European controls (McKeigue 1992, McKeigue *et al.* 1989, Balarajan *et al.* 1991). Although the aetiology remains unclear, these findings are not in dispute.

However, the logic and rigour of the original studies is not necessarily preserved when professionals invoke these 'facts' in everyday work interactions. What seems to be happening in *Extract 19* is that aggregate information on the epidemiology of coronary artery disease in a minority ethnic group forms the basis of a social typification, which structures perception of all patients from that group. The parallel existence of medical and social discourses on a particular population group – 'Asians' – opens up the possibility of shifts between these separate frames of reference, particularly since the doctors themselves see no need to use technical language to refer to the group and its risk profile. Formulations like: 'He's an Asian (. . .) which is usually bad news', and: 'Is he still smoking? These Asians smoke like chimneys', certainly look very much like the social typifications documented in other settings. In this case, assessments of risk overlap with the construction of a particular patient identity. The cardiologist draws attention to the 'genuine doubt' that exists with regard to the chest pain, the feeling of medical staff that the patient was 'making rather more of it than was reasonable', and the failure to co-operate with tests – the stepping off the treadmill. These observations are not entirely negated by evidence from the angiogram and the cardiologist's statement that 'I think one has to say it's predominantly angina'. Finally he notes that the patient 'is talking about litigation and all sorts of things'. The account is constructed to highlight examples of willed behaviour having implications for moral character. What is being signalled to the group is that they are dealing with a difficult patient; a patient whose personal and social characteristics must be considered when decisions about clinical management are made. Again the most powerful actors take the lead in establishing the linguistic premises upon which the legitimacy of accounts will be judged.

Conclusion

We introduced this paper by recalling recent press reports stating that cardiac surgery is being denied to patients on the grounds of moral judgements about lifestyle, and professional counter-claims that medical practice is a technical, value-free activity. Our research suggests that medical practice is a more nuanced, complicated business than either formulation in its extreme form suggests. We found that in a hospital where a surgeon had announced that smokers would not be treated without a prior undertaking to cease smoking, the result was not a blanket exclusion of such patients, but a situation where acceptance for surgery needed to be negotiated by the cardiologist with the surgeon on a case by case basis. However, it was clear that disposal decisions depended not just on technical assessments of feasibility and risk, but also on the interpretation of social information.

Students of doctor-patient interaction have begun to develop a sophisticated account of how the parties use multiple discourse frames to make sense of several, perhaps conflicting, sources of information. Writers like Silverman (1987), Tannen and Wallat (1987) and Cicourel (1982) describe the moment by moment realignments that may be involved as participants move from one frame to another, and how they must sometimes manage tension between frames. They show how these shifts in the social organisation of the participants' experience and awareness of context, are signalled linguistically through the use of cues and markers in speech. We have argued that a parallel analysis can be applied to discourse between medical colleagues, such as that which occurs in CCCs. Here also complex interpretive processes can be seen at work as participants draw on elements of technical and contexual information.

A number of recent studies illustrate how medical case presentations can be productively analysed as social action. Anspach's metaphor of the 'literary rhetoric of medical discourse' draws attention to the stylistic conventions and responsibility-shifting techniques used by junior doctors to persuade superiors of their professional competence. Griffiths and Hughes (1994) describe how doctors, seeking to admit patients to a neuro-rehabilitation facility, support the medical case for admission by providing additional contextual information which establishes deservingness, and is calculated to persuade other admissions conference members of the legitimacy of the referral. Atkinson (1994) has pointed to the skilful ways in which case presentations blend together information from different sources, and how narrators subtly construct 'zones of credibility', so as to align themselves with some sources (and colleagues) and distance themselves from others. This paper offers a further example of the rhetoric of collegial talk by describing how cardiologists referring patients for surgery present the case to the surgeon, and the repertoire of responses used to decline requests or delay acceptance. Within these negotiations, cardiologists and surgeon do their best to construct convincing justifications for the courses of action they are advocating, and in doing so often move between discourse frames. Risk enters these discussions, but almost always through rule-of-thumb assessments, rather than any systematic application of formal probability theory. Overall the standpoints put forward bear a striking similarity to the arguments of the public debate. Although doctors articulate their statements cautiously because of institutional constraints, they engage in a discourse about agency and willed behaviour as well as a technical discourse about prognosis and risk.

Probably, doctors have always talked about these things. What may be changing is that pressures now affecting medical practice lead practitioners to pay more consistent attention to characteristics that differentiate patients. The drive to cut costs, to use resources more efficiently, to view patients as consumers, and to subject professionals to formal performance measurement, all force practitioners to consider the basis of treatment decisions. Economic pressures create a need to ration surgery and exclude some patients who could benefit. Because a majority of candidates have clear clinical need, it becomes difficult to discriminate on purely clinical grounds. There is a tendency to move beyond technical calculations of risk to consider deservingness and an associated moral agenda. Ideas of deservingness are central to medical practice because they provide a language for thinking about patient selection problems which are difficult to resolve in any other way. Ethicists have of course proposed several approaches to the dilemma of rationing, including, for example, medical benefit, and length, quality and likelihood of benefit (Kilner 1990). But technical criteria do not contain any built-in notion of prioritisation: that is assigned afterwards, and always in a particular context.

Because medical practitioners have always been able to talk within both clinical and everyday moral frameworks, there is often ambiguity about which one they are operating in. The overlap between a technical discourse dealing with risk and a moral discourse dealing with character opens the way for unacknowledged shifts between the two. There is the space for doctors to act according to their perceptions of deservingness, while accounting for their actions in terms of medical benefit.

Acknowledgements

The authors are grateful to the Nuffield Provincial Hospitals Trust for funding the study on *Ethical Issues in the Allocation of Health Care Resources*, on which this paper is based. They thank Mick Bloor, Alan Radley and an anonymous referee for providing detailed comments. The paper also benefitted from the responses of participants in staff seminars in the Centre for Philosophy and Health Care, and the Department of Sociology and Anthropology, University of Wales, Swansea.

Notes

1   Harry Elphick was refused tests by a cardiologist at a Manchester hospital, after a heart attack in February 1993, on the grounds that he declined to stop smoking. Mr Elphick died on a second heart attack in August 1993, aged forty-seven. He had been interviewed for a BBC television programme on the hospital's 'no smokers' policy broadcast earlier that year and the case was widely reported in the British press.
2   The quotation is from The Observer, 7th November 1993, p. 1. Dr Stuart Horner has told us in a personal communication that he is unhappy with the overall accuracy of this article. He takes the view that medical care must be based on clinical and not moral criteria. However, patients should only receive treatment that can be shown to be clinically effective. Dr Horner argues that the research evidence indicates that CABG does not improve the prognosis of smokers who carry on smoking, and that it is therefore of less benefit to them than to patients whose prognosis would be improved.
3   For our purposes it is unnecessary to explore the theoretical differences that lead authors to write in varying terms of 'voices', 'discourses', 'frames' or 'footing'.

We use 'discourse' as a general synonym for language in use, while the terms 'frames' or 'discourse frames' refer to the structuring of discourse to orient to a particular system of relevance and background knowledge.

4   In the case of sociologists, too, 'scientific' and 'social' domains are clearly interwoven. For example, Anspach (1988) is only one of many commentators who have suggested that sociology – like medicine – has its distinctive literary rhetorics.

5   That is to say that elective surgery for patients with a history of tobacco smoking, would only be considered if they undertook to cease smoking prior to placement on the waiting list. As we explain in the text, the policy was not always as strictly enforced in practice as the surgeon's interview account suggested.

6   In some instances we have included extracts with inaudible passages omitted and indicated by the symbol '(. . .)'. Since we would be unable consistently to reproduce features of sequential organisation such as overlaps and pauses, we have rendered the transcriptions close to 'standard' speech. This is a limitation of the data, but attention to these detailed conversational features is not necessary in the type of analysis we attempt here.

7   569 major cardiac operations were carried out in the year of the study. The 11 per week is a mean figure and may be slightly misleading given the fluctuations arising with only one surgeon available. Operations completed per week (excluding leave periods) ranged from 2 to 20.

8   Angioplasty involves the use of special catheterisation equipment capable of inflating balloons to open up diseased coronary arteries. It is used as an alternative to bypass surgery, particularly for patients with single-vessel disease. At UTH the work is carried out by cardiologists in a purpose-built catheter laboratory.

9   The abbreviations in the extract refer to the anatomy of the heart. 'PDA' indicates the patent ductus arteriosus. 'LAD' refers to the left anterior descending coronary artery, while the 'circumflex' mentioned in a later extract is the left circumflex coronary artery. 'Marginal', 'lateral' and 'diagonal' refer to branches of the coronary arteries.

10   While we do not have systematic data on the implications for outcomes, studies by Petticrew *et al.* (1993) and Wenger (1990) suggest that there may be a gender bias in selection for bypass surgery.

References

Anspach, R.R. (1988) Notes on the sociology of medical discourse: the language of case presentation, *Journal of Health and Social Behavior*, 29, 357–375.

Atkinson, P.A. (1992) The ethnography of a medical setting: reading, writing and rhetoric, *Qualitative Health Research*, 2, 451–74.

Atkinson, P.A. (1994) Rhetoric as skill in a medical setting. In Bloor, M. and Taraborrelli, P. (eds) *Qualitative Studies in Health and Medicine*. Aldershot: Avebury.

Atkinson, P.A. (1995) *Medical Talk and Medical Work*. London: Sage.

Backett, E.M., Davies, A.M. and Petros-Barvazian, A. (1984) *The Risk Approach in Health Care*. Geneva: World Health Organisation.

Balarajan, R. (1991) Ethnic differences in mortality from ischaemic heart disease and cerebrovascular disease in England and Wales, *British Medical Journal*, 302, 560–64.

Becker, H., Geer, B., Hughes, E.C. and Strauss, A.L. (1961) *Boys in White: Student Culture in Medical School*. Chicago: University of Chicago Press.

Berg, M. (1992) The construction of medical disposals: medical sociology and medical problem solving in clinical practice, *Sociology of Health and Illness*, 14, 151–180.

Billig, M., Condor, S., Edwards, D., Gane, M., Middleton, D. and Radley, A. (1988) *Ideological Dilemmas: A Social Psychology of Everyday Life.* London: Sage.

British Cardiac Society Newsletter (1993) *Heart*, 395.

British Medical Association (BMA) (1994) Annual Report of the Council 1993/4. London: BMA.

Calabresi, G. and Bobbit, P. (1978) *Tragic Choices.* New York: Norton.

Clark, A.C., Potter, D.A. and McKinlay, J.B. (1991) Bringing social structure back into clinical decision making, *Social Science and Medicine*, 32, 853–66.

Cicourel, A.V. (1982) Language and belief in a medical setting. In Byrnes, I. (ed.) *Contemporary Perceptions of Language: Interdisciplinary Dimensions.* Georgetown: Georgetown University Press.

Drew, P. and Heritage, J. (1992) Analysing talk at work: an introduction. In Drew, P. and Heritage, J. (eds) *Talk at Work: Interaction in Institutional Settings.* Cambridge: Cambridge University Press.

Eisenberg, J.M. (1979) Sociologic influences on decision making by clinicians, *Annals of Internal Medicine*, 90, 957–64.

Frader, J.E. and Bosk, C.L. (1981) Parent talk at intensive care unit rounds, *Social Science and Medicine*, 15E: 267–74.

Fujimura, J.H. (1987) Constructing 'do-able' problems in cancer research: articulating alignment, *Social Studies of Science*, 17, 257–93.

Griffiths, L. and Hughes, D. (1993) Typification in a Neuro-Rehabilitation Centre: Scheff Revisited? *The Sociological Review*, 41, 415–445.

Griffiths, L. and Hughes, D. (1994) 'Innocent parties' and 'disheartening' experiences: natural rhetorics in neuro-rehabilitation admissions conferences, *Qualitative Health Research*, 4, 385–410.

Gumperz, J. (1982) *Discourse Strategies.* Cambridge: Cambridge University Press.

Haber, P.A. (1986) Rationing is a reality, *Journal of the American Geriatrics Society*, 14, 761–63.

Hafferty, F.W. (1988) Cadaver stories and the emotional socialization of medical students, *Journal of Health and Social Behavior*, 29, 344–356.

Hendee, W.R. (1986) Rationing health care. In Hamner, J. and Jacobs, B. (eds) *Life and Death Issues.* Memphis: University of Tennessee Press.

Hughes, D., McGuire, A. and McKenzie, L. (1988) *Medical Decision Making: A Bibliography.* Oxford: Centre for Socio-Legal Studies.

Jeffery, R. (1979) Normal rubbish: deviant patients in casualty departments, *Sociology of Health and Illness*, 1, 98–107.

Kerr, D.N.S. (1967) Regular haemodialysis, *Royal Society of Medicine Proceedings*, 60, 195–99.

Kilner, J.F. (1990) *Who Lives? Who Dies?* New Haven: Yale University Press.

Knorr-Cetina, K.D. (1981) *The Manufacture of Knowledge.* Oxford: Pergamon Press.

Lasagna, L. (1970) Physicians' behaviour towards the dying patient. In Brim, O.B. Jr., *et al.* (eds), *The Dying Patient.* New York. Russell Sage Foundation.

Latour, B. and Woolgar, S. (1986) *Laboratory Life: The Construction of Scientific Facts.* Princeton, NJ: Princeton University Press.

Liederman, D.B. and Grisso, J.A. (1985) The gomer phenomenon, *Journal of Health and Social Behavior*, 26, 222–32.

McKeigue, P.M. (1992) Coronary heart disease in Indians, Pakistanis, and Bangladeshis: aetiology and possibilities for prevention (Editorial), *British Heart Journal*, 67, 341–42.

McKeigue, P.M., Miller, G.J. and Marmot, M.G. (1989) Coronary artery disease in South Asians overseas – a review, *Journal of Clinical Epidemiology*, 42, 597–609.

Meissner, J. (1986) Legal services and medical treatment for poor people: a need for advocacy, *Issues in Law and Medicine*, 2, 3–13.

Mishler, E. (1984) *The Discourse of Medicine: Dialectics of Medical Interviews.* Norwood, NJ: Ablex.

Mizrahi, T. (1986) *Getting Rid of Patients: Contradictions in the Socialization of Physicians.* New Brunswick, NJ: Rutgers University Press.

Mukhtar, H.B., Beattie, J.M. and Littler, W.A. (1991) Obesity and coronary risks among South Asians (Letter), *The Lancet*, 137 (April 20), 972.

Naylor, C.D., Levinton, C.M., Baigrie, R.S. and Goldman, B.S. (1992) Placing patients in the queue for coronary surgery: how do age and work status affect consultants' decisions, *Journal of General Internal Medicine*, 7, 492–98.

Perrow, C. (1984) *Normal Accidents: Living with High Risk Technologies.* New York: Basic Books.

Petticrew, M., McKee, M. and Jones, J. (1993) Coronary artery surgery: are women discriminated against? *British Medical Journal*, 306, 1164–66.

Royal Society Study Group (1992) *Risk Analysis, Perception and Management. Report of a Royal Society Study Group.* London: Royal Society.

Short, J. (1984) The social fabric at risk: toward the social transformation of risk analysis, *American Sociological Review*, 49, 711–725.

Silverman, D. (1987) *Communication and Medical Practice: Social Relations in the Clinic.* London: Sage.

Tannen, D. and Wallat, C. (1987) Interactive frames and knowledge schemas in interaction: some examples from a medical examination/interview, *Social Psychology Quarterly*, 50, 205–16.

Uddo, B.J. (1986) The withdrawal or refusal of food and hydration as age discrimination: some possibilities, *Issues in Law and Medicine*, 2, 39–59.

Veatch (1985) *Distributive Justice and the Allocation of Technological Resources to the Elderly, Contract Report Prepared for the Office of Technology Assessment, U.S. Congress.* Washington D.C.: Office of Technology Assessment.

Wenger, N.K. (1990) Gender, coronary artery disease and coronary artery bypass surgery, *Annals of Internal Medicine*, 112, 557–88.

1.4

Art, science and placebo: incorporating homeopathy in general practice

Carl May and Deepak Sirur

Introduction

Lay interest in the use and practice of alternative and complementary therapies has grown rapidly in recent years, and the sociological literature suggests a number of explanations for this. These range from growing concerns about the iatrogenic effects of orthodox medical technologies and treatments, and about the reductionism inherent in modern biomedicine (Lupton 1994); to suggestions that interest in unorthodox therapies represents evidence of the new consumerism that increasingly influences individuals' ideas about health care (Saks 1994). Sociological studies of such therapies have largely focused on lay practitioners and users (*e.g.* Sharma 1992), exploring the ways in which they operationalise their knowledge at points of resistance and engagement with conventional or 'orthodox' biomedicine.

This paper takes a slightly different tack. In it, we explore the ways that a group of general practitioners deploy homeopathy within the context of 'orthodox' biomedicine, or allopathy. The focus of the paper is on how this complementary therapy contributes to their ideas about professional identity and practice, and how this involves them in negotiating the boundaries of conventional medicine and the problem of scientific evidence.

Homeopathy and allopathy in historical context

Although homeopathy is often seen as a reaction to scientific reductionism and the relentless somatisation inherent in 19th century medicine, its origins and continued practice are rather more complex. In fact, it emerged not in opposition to the biosciences, but rather as a humane – and relatively safe – model of medical practice at a time when 'conventional' medicine was both primitive and brutal in form, and frequently lethal for the patient. At the beginning of the 19th century, medical practice relied on the patient's subjective account of her or his symptoms, and on observations of the surface features of the disorder: the appearance of the body; the colour of urine; and so forth. One author describes this model of practice thus:

> For physicians and sufferers alike, a sick person's condition was seen
> to follow from a combination of errors of various sorts, many of
> which were held to be the consequence of self neglect. Faults in

constitution, inheritance, diet, bowel habits, sexual activities, exercise, sleeping patterns and so forth were described as combining to produce disease. Although this disease might have a name . . . what mattered were the symptoms peculiar to the sufferer and the unique disturbance of solids and fluids that produced them. The first of the physician's skills lay in reasoning out what this particular disturbance was, from his knowledge of the sufferer's life and the recent history of the sickness. (Lawrence 1994: 11)

The treatments that followed this kind of diagnostic practice were frequently toxic or traumatic. Growing knowledge about anatomy in no way implied growing knowledge about effective treatment, in part because anatomical investigations were largely confined to the architecture of the dead, but also because adequate theories of disease causation were absent. In this context, treatments – which might involve the application of purgatives, blood letting, or cupping – were barely distinguishable from those that had been applied some hundreds of years previously (Rosenberg 1992). Surgical investigation was impossible in the absence of effective anaesthesia, which did not appear until the 1830s; and the absence of any understanding of the causes of infection or disease transmission meant that physicians and surgeons were quite unable to conceptualise disease except in its surface appearances. Their prestige at the end of the eighteenth century corresponded to their practical success, and was correspondingly low.

Homeopathy, as a system of treatment, was thus developed as an alternative to *brutalism* rather than as a challenge to emergent 'scientific' medicine, which in any case, it preceded[1]. It relies on the principle of *similia similibus curentor*, that 'like is cured by like', in which incredibly dilute quantities of drugs are administered to the patient. What is important about homeopathic practice, however, is not simply its model of therapeutics. Beyond this, it intimately connects psyche with soma through a systematic model of personality, and attempts to apprehend the contribution of psychological factors to the trajectory and experience of illness. While others had used a similar system of therapeutics in a much more limited way, (Jenner's experiments with vaccination, for example, relied exactly on the principle of 'like cures like'), the founding father of homeopathy, Samuel Hahnemann, worked through an extensive repertoire of experimental 'provings' culminating in the publication in 1810 of his *Organon of the Rational Art of Healing* (Hahnemann [1810]1972).

The problem for Hahnemann, and his followers, was that their use of incredibly dilute, and thus 'invisible', drug treatments coincided with the emergence of a 'therapeutic revolution' (Rosenberg 1992) that was founded on the highly visible reactions to be found in the chemistry laboratory. While chemists and anatomists busied themselves with the subjugation of nature in general and the body in particular, developing a taxonomy of visible lesions and disease states (Armstrong 1983), homeopaths, all of whom were medically qualified, continued to concern themselves with individual experiences of illness and with invisible treatments. Without a theoretical foundation for their therapeutics that could compete with the supra-molecular chemistry of the 19th century, they were unable to explain plausibly how and why their treatments worked, and since their 'proofs' were organised through the history of particular cases they were unable to demonstrate that these were in fact 'proofs' in any scientific sense. Homeopathy was thus superseded by an explanatory model of somatic medicine that could be *seen* to work, while its own therapeutic processes remained mysterious – and could only be understood in an era when sub-molecular processes and interactions could be hypothesised. This has haunted homeopathy in the intervening two centuries.

In Britain, homeopathy has remained a minority medical interest throughout this period. Lying outside the accepted bioscientific explanatory framework, it nevertheless retained a degree of popularity amongst the middle classes, and was notably patronised by some members of the Royal Family. Homeopathic hospitals were founded in Liverpool, London, Glasgow and Bristol. Periodic attempts to suppress its practice failed and indeed, a 1932 editorial in the *British Medical Journal* stressed that its use was a matter of autonomous professional practice:

Medicine has no orthodox doctrine . . . once a man has obtained a registerable qualification in the usual way, he was entitled to his own opinion on therapeutics. (cited in Nicholls 1988: 234)

The homeopathic hospitals were incorporated in the National Health Service (NHS) at its inception in 1947, and this was followed in 1951 by the incorporation of the medical Faculty of Homeopaths by statute. While doctors could continue to prescribe homeopathic remedies within the framework of the NHS without having been first examined by the Faculty, they could also obtain a recognised credential and thus secure some further degree of legitimacy for their practice – as a complementary therapy contained within the bounds of conventional medicine.

So homeopathy has always had a limited degree of legitimacy within British medicine, even though it has never been able successfully to compete with allopathic models of practice on the terrain of the orthodox biosciences. The homeopathic hospitals, however, have formed one point of obvious resistance to, and engagement with biomedicine, and from these some work has been undertaken which challenges the allopathic critique of homeopathy as a placebo. These have harnessed the allopathic 'gold standard' of blind randomised controlled trials and have suggested a degree of effectiveness for homeopathic remedies in the treatment of respiratory disorders (Ferley *et al.* 1989) and pollen allergies (Reilly *et al.* 1986), when compared with a placebo. Certainly there was a growth in medical interest in homeopathy during the 1980s and a number of studies have shown both a demand for knowledge about homeopathy amongst junior doctors (Reilly 1983), and pockets of sympathy towards it across the profession of general practice (Anderson and Anderson 1987, Swayne 1989, Wharton and Lewith 1986).

Even though homeopathy sits uncomfortably within a professional framework characterised by conventional or allopathic practice, and although its theoretical framework has been bitterly contested (Coulter 1981), its medically qualified practitioners have been conceded a degree of freedom of manoeuvre by their allopathic counterparts. Swayne (1989) suggests that about 650 were doing so during the second half of the 1980s, and that they were dispensing about 300,000 homeopathic prescriptions annually.

Study group and method

This study was undertaken in a major conurbation in North West England. Through the mailing list of a private homeopathic clinic, we were able to identify ten medically qualified general practitioners, (six males, four females), who employed both homeopathic and allopathic treatments in their NHS practice. Seven of these had qualified for membership of the Faculty of Homeopathy, two were studying for the membership examination, and one had no plans to do so. All agreed to take part in the study. Participants had qualified as medical practitioners between 1959 and 1982, with the majority qualifying towards the latter end of the period.

We used a conventional qualitative method, employing tape-recorded semi-structured interviews which were subsequently transcribed and analysed according to the broad precepts set out by Strauss and Corbin (1990). Interviews were of around 45 minutes duration, and were conducted by DS. Thematic analysis (conducted by DS and CM) revealed a number of broad categories in participants' accounts, and in this paper we shall discuss (i) the ways in which they incorporated homeopathy into conventional practice; (ii) their views about its efficacy; (iii) their concerns about the responses of their 'conventional' colleagues; and (iv) about competing services from lay (*i.e.* non-medically qualified) practitioners of homeopathy.

This paper reports on a study that was limited in scale and focus. The accounts that we discuss in this paper are of a particular kind, quite unusual in the sociology of health and illness. The interviewer (DS) was, at the time the study was undertaken, a final year medical student. He shared a world of discourse – if not experience – with the participants in the study. It is clear from the interview transcripts that some of the latter approached the interview as they would a clinical tutorial with a junior colleague. The construction of evidence and diagnosis are vital parts of such encounters (Good 1994), as are the sharing of ideas about the nature of clinical practice, (and the latter plays a key role in vocational training for general practice). It is important not to overplay this feature of the study, but it does mean that some of the range of possible antagonisms that are inherent in research on clinicians by social scientists (Dowrick 1997) may not have been present in this study.

The homeopathic consultation as an ideal model of general medical practice

The recent history of general practice has been marked by an expansive professional rhetoric that stresses the central place of the interpersonal relationship between doctor and patient. This discourse of holism is a problem for general practitioners (May *et al.* 1996), in part because it sets up such a disparity between professional aspirations and what it is structurally possible to achieve in the context of an encounter that is profoundly limited by the competing demands on the doctor's time. Moreover, there are increasingly fragmented relationships that service users have with those responsible for their care. While the number of patients registered with individual general practitioners has declined by about 20 per cent this is counterbalanced by an increase in the number of doctor-patient encounters of similar proportions, and by the decline in the extent to which service users attribute responsibility for their care to a specific doctor in the practice that they attend (Dowrick 1997). In general terms, the profession of general practice has been forced to make sense of these shifts by directing its attention away from doctor-patient relationships, (marked by continuity of care, treatment and trust); towards more effective consultation techniques, (characterized by a focus on communication skills intended to maximise the content of an interaction and the extent to which the doctor can survey a broad range of topics in conversation with the patient).

In this context, incorporating homeopathy into conventional general practice can be seen in a number of ways. In general terms, it can be seen as a means of recapturing a model of practice that is perceived to be threatened by the ever increasing structural demands of the doctor's work. Nine of the ten respondents in this study took such a view, the tenth had recently retired and now worked part time in a clinic that exclusively offered homeopathic treatment.

> Dr 1: Because of the time constraints on the GP consultation in this country there is never enough time to get to the bottom of problems with patients. Everything is being dealt with at a superficial level and they're just in and out collecting a prescription. There was a feeling of dissatisfaction that I was never starting to deal with what the patient was complaining about. I thought there must be some other way of helping people.

Underpinning this kind of account was the notion that 'conventional' medical practice failed to respond to the deeper problems that each patient presented. This notion that there is a founding 'authentic' self that is lost to the scientific reductionism and objectification of orthodox medical practice is common to much professional discourse about the patient (May 1992), but it also represents in concrete form the very complex nature of much of the sickness encountered by general practitioners. The profession now recognises much minor illness and chronic health problems, (low back pain and other musculoskeletal problems; undifferentiated syndromes and fatigue), in terms of psychological rather than somatic categories. The homeopathic consultation, with its detailed account of the 'personality' of the patient, offered a means of recovering not only the patient's authentic self to medicine, but also detailing more precisely the connections between somatic and psychological problems.

> Dr 10:   The main attraction was to see the holistic side of things for
> the first time really, in its true sense. We're taught all about the
> physical, psychological and social aspects from conventional
> medical training, and that seemed to give you the package for the
> whole person and how to look at them. But really, it's far too
> superficial. And, when you look at things – and you take the sort
> of detail that's required for homeopathic prescribing – it's a lot
> more detailed and really teaches you the types of individuals
> we all are.

The nine respondents who were working in full time NHS general practice all concentrated their attention on 'orthodox' medical practice, and used homeopathy as a complementary technique that gave them purchase upon problems that were intractable in the face of allopathy. While they saw homeopathy as a technique that provided greater depth and detail to their encounters with patients they did not regard it as exclusive in its holism.

> Dr 5:   I think it's important when using the word holistic to remember
> always that most doctors try to practice holistic medicine. We
> don't have to practice homeopathy or any other non-conventional
> medicine to be holistic doctors. It only means viewing the patient
> as a whole and using whatever tools are in your drug range . . . it
> may be that in homeopathy or other non-conventional medicine
> one has the tools to use in a more holistic way rather than
> separating it into drug-based medicine or counselling-based
> medicine.

In other words, homeopathic medicine offered one way to connect the different components – psychological and organic – of the problems that the patient presented in the consultation. The participants in this study found it difficult to deploy homeopathy in their everyday conventional practice, for homeopathic consultations demand significantly greater investment in time, and all limited the extent of their homeopathic practice to particular kinds of problems and patients. We should not therefore regard them as 'medical homeopaths' but rather as doctors who practice homeopathy. They located their homeopathic practice in the context of clinical medicine and allopathic diagnosis.

The professional ideal that marks rhetoric about the doctor-patient relationship, embodied in discourses of holism is just that. To some extent it represents a technique of professional differentiation within medicine, reflected in the notion that the general practitioner is best placed to exercise a biopsychosocial model of medical care – which incorporates a much wider view of the factors that structure the causes and experiences of illness (Neighbour 1987) – than hospital doctors who focus primarily on the underlying pathology that leads the patient to present in the first place (Armstrong 1982). However important ideas about holism or biopsychosocial models of practice are in structuring professional *rhetoric* about practice, the evidence for their practical *application* is rather mixed (Dowrick *et al.* 1995).

Homeopathy as an extension of orthodox medicine that avoids its iatrogenic effects

The participants in this study regarded homeopathy as an effective mode of treatment, and we discuss some aspects of their accounts of the reasons for its efficacy later in this paper. But beyond the personal benefits that they found in homeopathic treatment and prescription they also saw significant benefits for their patients in its application[2]. Chief amongst these, and sitting well with their conceptualisation of homeopathy as a parallel and complementary technique to allopathic practice, was the assertion that it could *do no harm*.

Dr 1: It seemed to be similar to orthodox medicine in that you are actually prescribing medicines, and it was the different therapeutics – in that it is relatively harmless and free of side effects – and the concept of the micro-dose aiding patients to get themselves better. And you realize that experienced practitioners can achieve wonderful therapeutic results.

Just as homeopathy appeared at a time when physicians were conscious of the brutalising effects of their practice, respondents in this study were tremendously aware of the limited effectiveness of some contemporary drug therapies. They stressed the harmlessness of homeopathic remedies, but there was no sense in which they were actively rejecting the therapeutic complex of modern medicine. Instead, they saw homeopathy as an alternative to allopathic treatments in very specific circumstances, often in cases of intractable low level pain and discomfort, or in cases where complex undifferentiated symptoms – for example in the case of post-viral infections or fatigue – were encountered.

Dr 2: It was something I could do in general practice and this appealed to me because I didn't find conventional medicine the whole answer. You couldn't treat some conditions and some you made worse with conventional medicine, so I aimed to use both, which I've since done quite successfully.

Similarly:

Dr 6:   What concerns me most are the side-effects of modern medicines and possibly that we do use drugs inappropriately. It is very difficult when the patient comes in complaining of a condition to actually not offer a medication. It's difficult to decide whether you are not giving them it on grounds of cost, or grounds that it may well be potentially dangerous or not justified . . . Everybody is aware of all the drug disasters and everything.

The key here was their focus on 'experience' as the crucial feature of homeopathic prescription. They had come to define specific situations and disorders as being inappropriate for allopathic treatment. These were rarely major, and in their accounts systems failures – such as heart problems or malignant disease – were specifically discounted as domains of homeopathic practice. So their accounts of experience can be interpreted in terms of professional judgment, not only about where drugs were likely to have iatrogenic effects, but also where not prescribing allopathic remedies was a safe alternative in terms of professional liability, as we shall shortly see.

Dr 8:   After you've been in practice a certain length of time you realize that you often do people more harm than good, because people end up worse off from what you've given them than from their original condition, so as homeopathy is promoted on the basis that it's not going to make you any worse than you are, it's worth looking at.

Placebo effects and professional liability

We have already noted that allopathic medicine is dominated by a model of efficacy that relies on visible or detectable judgements of efficacy across a generalised population. The allopathic 'gold standard' of the randomised controlled trial is difficult to apply to homeopathic remedies unless these are administered in the same way as conventional allopathic treatments, that is without consideration of the wider sociopsychological factors that govern the experience of illness. Where conventional medicines are directed at the objects of clinical procedure – that is, specific organs or lesions – homeopathic remedies are directed at individuals as experiencing subjects. In this context, the gold standard of the randomised trial, which relies on an apparently asocial set of phenomena – the effect of an intervention on the impersonal form of diseased livers, or the functional effects of migraine – provides a body of compelling evidence. This is founded on an intellectually elegant statistical terrain, in which much effort is directed at avoiding chance losses and gains, and assessing efficacy against placebo effects.

Dr 1:   It's never bothered me that much because I don't regard myself as a 'scientific doctor' who will only prescribe if there is scientific evidence of efficacy of treatment. I wouldn't regard myself as an artist either but I'm more interested in the art of general practice than the science of it. I think that most of what GPs do is largely an art than a science.

And in the case of another respondent:

Dr 2:   The point about homeopathy is it turns our scientific paradigm upside down. The concept of more dilute is more powerful just throws people who have been trained in a traditional scientific manner so yes, you know, people think it's a load of mumbo-jumbo. But I just don't accept that. My attitude is that we don't have the means of explaining why it works and that's because we don't have the scientific knowledge to explain it.

Here, personal experience of the success of homeopathic remedies was crucial too, and this was rarely constructed through a rhetoric of scientific validity. Precisely the reverse was true, for although all of the respondents were aware of the limited evidence available from controlled trials, most constructed the motives for using it in terms of anecdote about early experience of particular patients. Here, *visible* recovery was crucial in doctors' attributions of efficacy. This is particularly important in general practice where so much of the symptomology experienced by doctors is ill-defined and undifferentiated, related to broad sociopsychological problems that are mediated through specific, often chronic, disease entities that fit poorly with allopathic management. The greater variety of 'safe' alternatives that the doctor has to hand, the better. But the criticism that homeopathic alternatives acted as placebos was not something that respondents were concerned with.

Dr 6:   I think one of the problems that we all face as doctors these days is the problem of litigation. Most doctors are very well aware that something which is authenticated and taught to them by the establishment is likely to be supported by their colleagues. If they do run into difficulties with any treatment programme they have offered a patient, if they included in that treatment practices that are not authenticated they are going to be much more vulnerable to litigation and subsequent damage to their careers. I think that's where the difficulty arises: homeopathy is validated but it doesn't stand up to the scientific criteria that allopathic medicines stand up to – and as doctors we have to be aware of our own need for support from colleagues, it's very difficult really.

However convinced respondents were about the practical efficacy of homeopathic remedies, they had to place their practice in the context of its wider disciplinary surveillance by professional regulators and the courts. The issue was not so much homeopathy's possible role as a placebo – for this was dealt with by discursively accounting for homeopathy as being a 'science' that lay outside of the realm of the biosciences – but rather the critical judgement of colleagues.

DS: How much of the effect is placebo and does it matter?
Dr 1:   The answer to the second question is that if it is placebo I don't care. If they are getting better and I haven't poisoned them then brilliant. That's the most important thing, that the patient goes away and gets well.

But the question of 'proof' or 'evidence' for efficacy was a problem.

Dr 8:   There's never enough trials to categorically say that there is the undoubted proof because the 'undoubted proof' shoved in front of the general practitioner one year becomes next year's litigation case because of the number of people shown to have died from taking medicines shown to be absolutely effective. No homeopathic drug has been withdrawn from use in two hundred years.

Homeopathy then, was seen to be contested at two distinct levels: first, at the level of 'science' where its effects are explicable only by appeal to ideas about a realm of submolecular activity as yet undiscovered (Schiff 1995); and second, at the level of professional regulation, and ultimately, the courts. At the same time, the safety of homeopathic remedies was an important benefit, all the time tempered by the possibility of adverse judgements by fellow professionals if the treatment failed.

The response of fellow general practitioners

We have already noted that the critical judgements of colleagues were discursively constructed as a constraint on homeopathic practice. In this study respondents organised their accounts around the way in which initial hostility was often gradually displaced by a kind of amused tolerance of personal idiosyncracy, and ultimately by a kind of personal conversion. Once again, accounts of colleagues' responses to homeopathic practice were always organised in counterpoint to the problem of evidence.

Dr 7:   This is the age of the double blind cross over trial and evidence based medicine, which is right[3]. When you do a double blind measuring the effectiveness of an antibiotic you can give the drug, and a placebo; you can measure serum concentrations; and the urinary concentration of it, and draw conclusions – that only applies to 40 per cent of prescribed concentrations. But when you try anti-depressants, you ask them how they *feel*, it's anecdotal, but how else do you measure it?

And this is, in part, the problem of 'science' in general practice. The precepts of conventional bioscience, which give great privilege to 'objective' accounts of pathological mechanisms, are often quite distant from the practical business of treating the patient. Subjective accounts of symptoms and the proximal causes of disease are absolutely vital to the business of general practice, not simply because the problems that face the general practitioner are often undifferentiated and difficult to disentangle, but also because the relationship between doctor and patient is construed as a personal one. As we noted earlier in this paper, notions of 'holism' form a powerful undercurrent in professional discourse about the focus of the doctor's attention. In general practice, diagnostic categories and treatment decisions are often negotiated (May and Mead, in press, Weiss and Fitzpatrick 1997). But the 'relationship' between doctor and patient was never at issue in our respondents' accounts of their colleagues' responses, perhaps because the homeopathic ideal accords so closely with the kinds of practices that are increasingly expected of doctors in the consultation. Instead, the central problem was the mode of treatment, and the evidence available for it.

Dr 3:   Well, they laughed and they think it's funny because actually, of all my colleagues I'm probably the one who goes on about how important it is to have evidence before you treat. . . . I do go on about making sure that we only do things that there is evidence for and then they argue with me and say, 'Why do you practice homeopathy then?' And then they sort of laugh at me saying, 'Isn't it odd, that here I am, at one level I claim to be a scientist and a researcher, and yet I'm using homeopathic medicines'. So I think that my colleagues are amused by it, but what amuses me is that then they come and ask me about it themselves.

The gap here between the kinds of evidence that are privileged in 'scientific' medicine, and those that appeal to the homeopathic practitioner, is dealt with by the respondent pointing either to a generalised change in attitude, or – as we have observed above – to a more gentle conversion by personal example.

Dr 4:   It's much less of a problem now. When I first started [at this practice], some of the patients reported to us that other doctors had said, 'if you go to that [name] you're not staying on my [outpatients] list.' I'd be very surprised to find that attitude now. . . . So attitudes have changed enormously, and sometimes in lecturing [about homeopathy] we do still get audiences of very aggressive doctors who really want to know the scientific mechanisms, but again, most doctors are really interested in learning about the principle of it.

Working in close proximity to each other, doctors in group practices were able to demonstrate to their colleagues the efficacy of homeopathic remedies by example, and persuade them to use it themselves. Once the latter had been done, scepticism could be overcome by practice.

Dr 6:   My partner is actually quite tolerant. She didn't find it threatening at all and was quite happy for me to do it. She used to ask me if it worked! Some of my other colleagues [were] very much in favour of it once they'd done little bits themselves and come into contact with people who use it. I've met people on courses . . . who are openly sceptical, and it's very difficult to convert them.

It is important to be cautious about the extent to which such 'conversions' are an important component of the experience of using homeopathic treatments. Central to the latter is the great autonomy that the general practitioner possesses in prescribing any kind of treatment[4]. Even though there are now greater constraints on prescribing as a result of increasing managerial surveillance and control over individual general practitioners (Calnan and Williams 1995), the act of prescribing remains a key component of the exercise of professional autonomous practice (Weiss and Fitzpatrick 1997). Sceptical peer judgements about utility and efficacy were therefore not necessarily an obstacle to personal preference.

Dr 7:   Most of my friends are doctors and even some of my close friends think I'm wasting my time. My partners when I first joined – who have now retired – one of them didn't not believe in it, but didn't practice it; the other didn't believe in it but let me do what I wanted to do as long as it didn't interfere . . . so long as it didn't increase his workload. . . . The partners I have at the moment are more receptive. One is for it, the other is not against it but not for it.

Even the most sceptical of colleagues could be persuaded, once again through the 'evidence' of personal example.

Dr 8:   My partner, for ten years said he didn't want any of his
        patients to be given that rubbish because if they needed
        an antibiotic then they needed an antibiotic. And after
        ten years he then sat the membership exam himself and
        started using it.

DS: Was that because of the results he saw you getting?

Dr 8:   Well, yeah. After ten years he asked me to treat his son.

Despite this, respondents were unanimous in expressing their own caution
about admitting to homeopathic treatment.

Dr 8:   I think there are pockets of it [scepticism] and pockets of open-
        mindedness. For example, there was a patient who came to me
        with severe facial acne. She didn't want to take the medicine they'd
        given her at the [dermatology outpatients'] clinic, so I treated her
        homeopathically with good results. When she attended the follow
        up clinic, they didn't want to know and told her off for not taking
        the prescribed medication[5]. While on another instance I received a
        phone call from a Registrar at [the same hospital] asking me to see
        a patient with eczema for whom they had had no success. So it
        works both ways. . . . It certainly makes me wary to say at
        meetings that I'd treat someone homeopathically because you're
        never sure what reaction you'd get.

One of the important features of the accounts that we have reviewed so
far in this paper is the extent to which, while they deploy ideas about 'science' and scientific method as a kind of benchmark for 'objective' judgements about the efficacy of treatment, they also permit the respondent to
step into the margins of 'science' in terms of their own preferences about
treatment. Although it is important not to reify science, it is equally important to understand that it forms an extraordinarily powerful total organising
framework for medical practice. In this context, it acts as a secular belief
system that can underpin a quite diverse range of activities. Whether the
doctor is working within an allopathic or a homeopathic framework, it is
differential diagnosis which acts as the principal expression of the monopoly
of knowledge possessed by the doctor. Once diagnosis has been reached, the
treatment decision is autonomous – and whether or not the doctor 'believes'
in it is crucial. In fact, general practitioners quite frequently prescribe treatments that they know to be ineffective: for instance, the treatment of viral
respiratory tract infections with anti-bacterial drugs is frequently held up
as an example (see Weiss and Fitzpatrick 1997). Respondents in this study
seem to be telling us something more, however. Perhaps the key to this is
the extent to which their accounts suggest that their power to persuade, or
'convert' colleagues to this mode of prescription is dependent on the regard
that the latter have for them. Colleagues' responses to our respondents'

decisions to prescribe homeopathically may therefore be as much a function of the confidence that their colleagues have in them as clinicians, as in the 'art' of homeopathic prescribing.

The final appeal in justifying homeopathic treatment was to the finitude of conventional biomedical knowledge.

DS: Do you think that the fact that some medical practitioners regard homeopathy as quackery deters people from taking more of an interest in it?

Dr 2:   I'm sure it has. Medicine is full of very arrogant and opinionated men, mainly, but increasingly women. When I was training, any form of alternative treatment was regarded as quackery. Orthodox medicine was all there was and [it] knew everything and would be able to solve everything. Anyone who practised any other form of medicine was a quack and a charlatan. The majority of the profession now accept that we don't have all of the answers and never will. And, that complementary medicines have a lot to offer in different fields. Now, complementary therapists are working very closely with orthodox medicine, even within the hospital.

DS: Do you find varying degrees of acceptance by different branches of medicine?

Dr 2:   I think so, some are very resistant, but that's an expression of the type that's in that branch. Surgeons, and particularly orthopaedic surgeons think that they're God's gift. They think they know it all, [but] it's just as psychiatry faced antagonism.

In the face of finite medical knowledge, respondents saw no reason to exclude a complementary therapy when it was practised by an autonomous expert. But extending this privileged position to those outside the medical monopoly was the subject of a far greater degree of ambivalence. It is to this that we now turn.

Responses to homeopathy outside of orthodox medicine

All of the subjects in this study implicitly saw themselves as operating in a market place where some groups of patients actively sought a variety of resolutions to their ill-health outside the boundaries of conventional medicine. But for the most part, this was confined to self-medication rather than attraction to practitioners of complementary or alternative therapies.

Dr 3:   Generally, there is a lot of mix-up between homeopathy, naturopathy, aromatherapy . . . and quite often you say to someone that you could try homeopathy and you find that they're already actively doing that. They've been to health food shops and they've been to Boots. So there are a lot of people out there using homeopathy or some other alternative therapy.

In general terms, such self-medication was seen as quite legitimate and as a positive step by the patient. It is certainly a normal part of everyday health care, often organised and undertaken by women within families and wider social networks (Miles 1991). But subjects were ambivalent about non-medically qualified, or lay, homeopaths, (primarily those who have undertaken the programme specified by the lay Society of Homeopaths). This ambivalence was formulated in two quite distinct ways. First, that lay homeopaths lacked the depth of diagnostic knowledge held by medically qualified practitioners; and second, that they might disturb patients' confidence in allopathic medicine. We shall discuss these in turn.

The application of medical knowledge, and thus its scientific authority, turns around the doctor's capacity to offer some kind of definitive diagnosis to the patient. But this is a problem in general practice where much low level self-limiting illness and a good deal of chronic illness is difficult to relate to specific causal mechanisms, and where severity of discomfort or distress experienced by the patient may be difficult to understand. This is, of course, precisely the task that homeopathy sets itself, with its carefully delineated models of character and personality, and its individualised programmes of treatment. Nevertheless, subjects in this study held on to allopathic differential diagnosis as a means of discounting sinister signs and routing those patients into allopathic treatments.

Dr 7:   Well firstly I think it's important to have as accurate a diagnosis as possible when seeing a patient, so whether you're treating them homeopathically or conventionally it's as important to get the background and history and the diagnosis – which involves examination and investigation to no less a standard than you would in conventional practice.

This option is simply not available to lay homeopaths.

Dr 9:   I don't think homeopathy is compatible with lay practitioners treating patients. But some complementary therapies are amenable to lay practitioners . . . but I think homeopathy involves prescribing which means you have got to have the diagnostic skills. It's OK saying that you can go and see your doctor to get the diagnosis and then go out and see the lay practitioner, but things do change and current diseases – in particular – do alter course. And it's not always easy for lay practitioners without the background to pick up the changing signs in a patient that may need early intervention.

It is important to emphasise that respondents in this study were first and foremost orthodox practitioners, schooled in scientific medicine and committed to its practice. They used homeopathy literally as a complementary technique, and constructed this as a benefit to the patient in the degree to which they could choose between therapeutic approaches precisely from the standpoint of medical science.

> Dr 2:   I don't think allopathic medicine is the answer to everything and I don't think that homeopathic medicine is the answer to everything – nor do I think that acupuncture is the answer to everything. . . . I'm not entirely happy about it because I think that mistakes can be made. You might get someone who has a cancer and then go and get homeopathic medicine and it just blatantly won't work for that, and that's my worry . . . I remember one patient who had blatant heart failure and he was trying to convince me that homeopathy was the treatment of choice and he just wouldn't accept it [was not].

Underpinning this is the extent to which subjects were concerned about litigation, and the extent to which scientific disagreement about the efficacy of homeopathic remedies would affect them in a case of professional negligence or misconduct. In this context it is not surprising that, however committed they might be to homeopathy, or any other kind of complementary practice, they confined it to a limited range of patients or problems. The moral nature of medical work is bounded not only by scientific judgements about the effectiveness of treatments, but by a growing awareness that its quality may be adjudicated by the courts (Allsop and Mulcahy 1996).

Beyond this, subjects were concerned about the extent to which lay homeopaths disturbed patients' confidence in conventional medicine. This was organised in terms of the ways that 'evangelical' lay homeopaths rejected some of the basic precepts of orthodox medicine.

> Dr 6:   Some of the non-medically qualified practitioners have a very bad relationship with doctors of medicine and are very critical in a global way of medication that's offered in medical practice and, as such, can create rifts . . . There is an argument at the moment that lay homeopaths are putting people off vaccinating their children. The [medical] Faculty of Homeopathy is in favour of vaccinating children. There is some disquiet [amongst] the medically trained homeopaths that vaccinations may have adverse effects on some people but that is outweighed at present by the long-term big benefits of mass vaccination. . . . Lay homeopaths are dangerous when they say, 'take no vaccinations and stop normal medication at the moment.'

The lay society is no longer opposed to vaccination. Nevertheless, the subjects in this study were medically qualified and they argued that this meant that they alone could best define and organise treatment for patients. All operated from the basis that homeopathy was dangerous where patients were dissuaded from putting their confidence, first and foremost, in orthodox medical knowledge. Only they could define what kinds of iatrogenic effects were unacceptable, and what kinds of procedures and practices ought to engender scepticism. While recognising that lay homeopaths, like other lay therapists, could undermine the patient's confidence in orthodox medicine, some saw those who sought out lay practitioners as already having lost that confidence.

Dr 10:   I think they attract the sort of patients that have an anti-doctor attitude anyway.

Only one subject, however, argued that lay homeopathic practice should not be permitted. This doctor took a view that stressed professional status and the monopoly of scientific knowledge that is externally regulated by the medical profession, but linked this with the need to protect patients.

Dr 9:   I'm very much against it – it's a personal opinion. I spent a long time getting my degree, I cherish it and guard it with intense jealousy. Anyone can learn about homeopathy, but applying it to patients and knowing differential diagnoses is the bit I feel strongly about. People can learn a lot, go on weekend courses . . . and then they are qualified. I resent that very much. I think they do great harm and a disservice. If you were selling a house, you wouldn't go to a butcher who sold the odd house, you'd go to a professional. Until thirty years ago you had to be a qualified doctor and now anyone can put a plaque against their door and call themselves one. People have got to be properly protected [by the] professional standards of people registered with the GMC and properly indemnified against malpractice.

At the root of subjects' accounts of their responses to lay homeopaths was their strong conviction of the value of the depth and breadth of scientific medical training over the highly specialised knowledge of the lay practitioner. Lay homeopaths might undermine the patient's confidence in the range of approaches that the doctor offered by believing too much in the power of their own therapy: here, the absence of a wide scientific training was related by subjects not only to their own professional knowledge, but also, implicitly, to the notion that lay practitioners were insufficiently sceptical about the value of *any* therapy. Lay practitioners were also subject to an insufficient degree of external regulation and control in comparison with their medical counterparts.

Concluding comment

Social scientists have rightly often seen medical responses to alternative and complementary therapies in terms of antagonism between a powerful social institution concerned to protect its authoritative monopoly of knowledge and power to regulate practice, and new bodies of knowledge that threaten the former's technical authority and market control (see Freidson 1970). But homeopathy is in an odd position here. There is some evidence that sections, at least, of the medical profession have growing sympathy for it. The lay sector has responded, in part, by placing less emphasis on 'esoteric, druidic and evangelical' elements of its knowledge base, and embarking on a professionalising strategy that in many ways emulates that of medicine (Cant and Sharma 1995, 1996). The lay Society restricts membership to particular kinds of applicants and places strict controls on their training and practice. The medical profession, on the other hand, permits its members to practice homeopathy on the strength of a conventional medical training, and without further education in its highly specific approach to the art of prescribing[6].

While macro-level contests between lay and medical homeopaths can be conceptualised in terms of professional power to define the limits of complementary therapies, the subjects in this study were primarily concerned with their professional and legal responsibilities to individual patients. This is important, because it is the general practitioner who, in Britain, has clinical responsibility for continuing care of the patient, as well as having absolute responsibility in law for its proper conduct. While patients themselves may choose to seek referral, (or be referred by their general practitioner), to a variety of professionals – both conventional and complementary – it is to their general practitioner that they ultimately return. Subjects in this study saw their role in deploying homeopathy as limited, and were concerned that those limits should also be placed on lay practitioners.

At the centre of participants' accounts of the relationship between homeopathic and allopathic practice in their dealings with patients was the problem posed by scientific medicine as a secular belief system that stresses what Byron Good (1994) characterises as:

> the idea within medicine that disease is fundamentally, even exclusively, biological. Not that experiential or behavioural matters are ignored, certainly not by good clinicians, but that these matters are separate from the real object of medical practice. The fundamental reality is human biology, real medicine, and the relevant knowledge is staggering in scope and complexity. (1994: 70)

The key point to note here is that it was not necessarily the threat of complaint or litigation that led the doctors interviewed for this study to be circumspect about their use of homeopathic remedies. It was rather their accession to a more powerful set of beliefs about the fundaments of medical knowledge. We have emphasised that they did not regard themselves as homeopaths, but rather as medical practitioners. Here, following Kleinman's (1988) distinction between subjective experiences of symptoms, and objective diagnostic categories, it is worth pointing out that their use of homeopathy was limited to particular experiences of illness, rather than categories of disease.

Given the aforegoing, the practice of homeopathy by the general practitioners interviewed in this study can be seen to represent the negotiation of the distinction between illness and disease: the biomedical knowledge base is sometimes insufficient properly to understand the patient's problem; its treatments are potentially harmful to the patient; and its commitment to a particular scientific model closes off possibilities for effective cure or palliation of experiences of illness. Nor, as respondents in this study emphasised, does 'conventional' medicine provide responses to much of the illness experienced by their patients. So one interpretation of our respondents' accounts of homeopathic practice is that it is a *moral* project, intended to remedy the inadequacies of finite knowledge in a sphere of medicine that is full of intractable chronic complexes of illness.

Beyond the professional, moral, project of primary care medicine suggested above, we can also see parallels in these accounts with those given by patients who also negotiate the boundaries of bioscience and choose 'unorthodox' treatments over, or in concert with, those offered by biomedicine. A study by Britten (1996) offers a case in point. Building on Cornwell's (1984) study of lay health knowledge amongst Londoners, she sets out four criteria for classifying accounts of 'unorthodox' treatment regimens (1996: 53):

Self-legitimation: organised through statements about personal beliefs and experiences.

The absence of medical legitimation: where health practices were 'disobedient' to, or implicitly rejected validation by the biosciences.

A conviction that there is no single medical model: where the finite nature of biomedicine opens up the possibility of legitimate alternatives.

An appeal to 'unorthodox' knowledge that legitimises alternative health care practices.

The latter criterion is absent from respondents' accounts: they made it clear that they were first and foremost practitioners of orthodox medicine. But the remainder are deeply embedded in their descriptions of homeopathic practice and of their motives for undertaking it. In fact, it can be argued that they are organising principles that structure these accounts and build into them legitimising conditions. Our respondents were all attracted to practice homeopathy by localised observations of successful treatment, and this experience was crucial in maintaining their interest. Once that interest was established, they had to proceed by way of an explicit critique of the notion of scientific evidence, and this they did by defining their practice in terms of 'art' as much as science. It is important not to view their critique of allopathy too romantically: none of our respondents would have seen themselves as resisting biomedicine as a total organising framework, but all saw themselves as trying to modify its practice.

Acknowledgements

We are grateful to the participants in this study for their time and candour. We are grateful to Mike Crilly, Chris Dowrick, Aneez Esmail, Chris Fleming, Anne Rogers and two anonymous referees for their helpful comments on earlier versions of this paper.

Notes

1   Given this, it might be more accurate to say that homeopathy is a survival of a transitional medical model – lying between humoral and scientific medicine. What is important, is the extent to which contemporary medicine is attempting to recapture the kinds of doctor-patient relationship that underpinned what Jewson (1976) has called 'bedside' medicine, and to define a model of practice that might mitigate against the reductionism of scientific medicine through what Engel (1981) calls a 'biopsychosocial' model of medicine. The tensions between somatic medicine and the broader reach of biopsychosocial medicine have been described elsewhere (*e.g.* Armstrong 1995).

2   Although it is widely contended that 'consumer demand' plays an important part in expanding the field of alternative and complementary therapies, none of the respondents in this study appeared to be greatly motivated by this. Their interest in homeopathy was founded primarily in what they wanted to do, rather than what their patients wanted to receive.

3   The paradox here is that respondents were rightly sceptical about the randomised trial as a means of establishing the effectiveness of many therapeutic interventions. This almost never extended, however, to their evaluation of the utility of randomised trials of homeopathic remedies. Almost all appealed to this form of 'evidence' although the mode of prescribing in homeopathy is completely undermined by the 'blind' administration of a remedy.

4   Homeopathic prescriptions are available as part of National Health Service treatment. Although it was not mentioned by respondents as a key motive for undertaking homeopathic treatment, three respondents pointed to its cost effectiveness at a time when prescribing budgets were under increasing scrutiny. The relatively low cost of routine homeopathic remedies was noted in this respect by Dr 2, who asserted that 'I am aware that it can help, where I don't think they have a serious illness. I say "you're not really that ill, one alternative you could try is homeopathic medicine, you can buy it cheaper" and they're pretty amenable to that'.

Dr 8 observed, 'I have a colleague who, after a year of practising homeopathy, was summoned to the local health authority who wanted to know why his drug bill was at least 10 per cent lower than the rest of his colleagues in the group practice.'

5   In this instance, the reprimand to the patient may not have been so much concerned with the homeopathic mode of treatment, but rather that she sought alternative advice and permitted her GP to interfere with the treatment prescribed by the expert consultant.

6   A very helpful account of the 'professionalisation' of lay homeopathy, and of the general policy context in which this has been situated since the 1970s, may be found in Cant and Sharma (1995). The wider policy context, and the tendency towards the incorporation of complementary therapies in a limited form within the NHS has been set out by Saks (1994).

References

Allsop, J. and Mulcahy, L. (1996) *Regulating Medical Work: Formal and Informal Controls*. Buckingham: Open University Press.

Anderson, E. and Anderson, P. (1987) General practitioners and alternative medicine, *Journal of the Royal College of General Practitioners*, 37, 52–5.

Armstrong, D. (1982) The doctor-patient relationship: 1930–1980. In Wright, A. and Treacher, A. (eds) *The Problem of Medical Knowledge*. Edinburgh: Edinburgh University Press.

Armstrong, D. (1983) *The Political Anatomy of the Body*. Cambridge: Cambridge University Press.

Armstrong, D. (1995) The rise of surveillance medicine, *Sociology of Health and Illness*, 17, 393–404.

Britten, N. (1996) Lay views of drugs and medicines: orthodox and unorthodox accounts. In Williams, S.J. and Calnan, M. (eds) *Modern Medicine: Lay Perspectives and Experiences*. London: UCL Press.

Calnan, M. and Williams, S. (1995) Challenges to professional autonomy in the United Kingdom: perceptions of general practitioners, *International Journal of Health Services*, 25, 219–41.

Cant, S. and Sharma, U. (1995) The reluctant profession – homoeopathy and the search for legitimacy, *Work, Employment and Society*, 9, 743–62.

Cant, S. and Sharma, U. (1996) Demarcation and transformation within homeopathic knowledge, *Social Science and Medicine*, 42, 579–88.

Cornwell, J. (1984) *Hard Earned Lives: Accounts of Health and Illness from East London*. London: Tavistock.

Coulter, H. (1981) *Homeopathic Science and Modern Medicine*. London: North Atlantic Books.

Dowrick, C. (1997) Rethinking the doctor-patient relationship in general practice, *Health and Social Care in the Community*, 5, 11–14.

Dowrick, C., May, C., Richardson, M. and Bundred, P. (1995) The biopsychosocial model of general practice, *British Journal of General Practice*, 46, 105–7.

Engel, G. (1981) The need for a new medical model: a challenge for bio-medicine. In Kaplan, A., Englehardt, H. and MacCartney, J. (eds) *Concepts of Health and Disease: Interdisciplinary Perspectives*, London: Addison-Wesley.

Ferley, J., Zmirou, D., d'Admehar, D. and Balducci, E. (1989) Controlled evaluation of a homeopathic preparation in the treatment of influenza-like syndromes, *British Journal of Clinical Pharmacology*, 27, 329–35.

Freidson, E. (1970) *Professional Dominance: the Social Structure of Medical Care*, Chicago: Aldine.

Good, B. (1994) *Medicine, Rationality and Experience: an Anthropological Perspective*. Cambridge: Cambridge University Press.

Hahnemann, S. ([1810]1972) *Organon of the Art of Rational Healing*. London: Everyman.

Jewson, N. (1976) The disappearance of the sick man from medical cosmology 1770–1870, *Sociology*, 10, 225–44.

Kleinman, A. (1988) *The Illness Narratives: Suffering, Healing and the Human Condition*. New York: Basic Books.

Lawrence, C. (1994) *Medicine in the Making of Modern Britain 1700–1920*. London: Routledge.

Lupton, D. (1994) *Medicine as Culture*. London: Sage.

May, C. (1992) Individual care? Power and subjectivity in therapeutic relationships, *Sociology*, 26, 589–602.

May, C. and Mead, N. (In Press) Patient-centredness: a history. In Frith, L. and Dowrick, C. (eds) *Ethical Issues in General Practice: Uncertainty and Responsibility*. London: Routledge.

May, C., Dowrick, C. and Richardson, M. (1996) The confidential patient: the social construction of therapeutic relationships in general practice, *Sociological Review*, 44, 187–203.

Miles, A. (1991) *Women, Health and Medicine*. Milton Keynes: Open University Press.

Neighbour, R. (1987) *The Inner Consultation*. Lancaster: MTP Press.

Nicholls, P. (1988) *Homeopathy and the Medical Profession*. London: Croon Helm.

Reilly, D. (1983) Young doctors' views on alternative medicine, *British Medical Journal*, 287, 337–9.

Reilly, D., Taylor, M., McSharry, C. and Aitchison, T. (1986) Is homeopathy a placebo response? Controlled trial of homeopathic potency with pollen in hayfever as model, *Lancet*, ii, 881–6.

Rosenberg, C. (1992) *Explaining Epidemics and Other Studies in the History of Medicine*. Cambridge: Cambridge University Press.

Saks, M. (1994) The alternatives to medicine. In Gabe, J., Keelleher, D. and Williams, G. (eds) *Challenging Medicine*. London: Routledge.

Schiff, M. (1995) *The Memory of Water*. London: Thorson.

Sharma, U. (1992) *Complementary Medicine Today: Practitioners and Patients*. London: Routledge.

Strauss, A. and Corbin, J. (1990) *Basics of Qualitative Research: Grounded Theory, Procedures and Techniques*. Thousand Oaks, CA: Sage.

Swayne, J. (1989) Survey of the use of homeopathic medicine in the UK health system, *Journal of the Royal College of General Practitioners*, 39, 503–6.

Wharton, R. and Lewith, G. (1986) Complementary medicine and the general practitioner, *British Medical Journal*, 292, 1498–1515.

Weiss, M. and Fitzpatrick, R. (1997) Challenges to medicine: the case of prescribing, *Sociology of Health and Illness*, 19, 297–327.

1.5

The child as a social object: Down's Syndrome children in a paediatric cardiology clinic

David Silverman

Introduction

This is a study of the execution of a particular medical and surgical policy. It concerns the special treatment accorded to children with Down's Syndrome (once called 'Mongolism') in just one paediatric cardiology clinic. As with all of medicine, different clinics have different policies. In the clinic, this policy was one of non-intervention. Whereas a 'normal' child with suspected congenital heart disease would be put up for catheterisation and, where clinically appropriate, for surgery, a Down's child with an identical cardiac lesion would usually receive neither catheterisation nor surgery. Even conditions which constituted an immediate threat to the life of a Down's child would sometimes be met by non-intervention or delaying tactics.

Such a policy has important social, economic and ethical consequences. These are matters which are not my immediate concern in this paper – though they will be touched on in its conclusion. My interest, rather, arises from the fact that consultations with Down's parents appeared to put a great deal of emphasis upon parents' wishes. Yet the upshot of the often extended discussions between parents and doctors was nearly always fully in line with clinic policy.

I will examine in some detail the various ways in which parents of Down's children were routinely induced to agree with clinic policy and to agree in a relatively smooth and trouble-free fashion. This is, therefore, an essay in the mechanics of persuasion, something in which we all engage but which has rarely been studied in any systematic fashion. As such, this is only a beginning attempt.

In making this beginning, I shall focus on what seems to be three crucial phases in the consultation process: the *elicitation* sequence, the *diagnosis* stage and the *disposal* stage. In each of these, distinctive and fateful talk is initiated by doctors with the parents of Down's children. This talk has, I shall claim, a highly strategic significance.

Methods

The analysis is based on transcripts of tape-recorded consultations which took place over a period of one year at the clinic concerned. The method of analysis combines simple counting procedures with an attempt to depict the construction of subjects within verbal discourse deriving from Silverman and Torode (1980). However, a familiarity with the theoretical issues raised in that work is not required in order to follow the argument[1].

A sample of 12 Down's Syndrome consultations is used here. All were conducted by the same doctor, although, in two cases, another doctor had begun the consultation but withdrew before the examination of the child had taken place. The sample has no claims to random selection. It would have been impossibly time-consuming to have identified the full population of such cases because Down's cases were not the initial focus of the research and, consequently, there was not always a written record of which clinics contained Down's children. Instead, colleagues were asked to consult their clinic notes for any relevant information. On this basis, 12 cases were identified and transcribed. For comparative purposes, a random sample was, however, selected of 22 outpatient consultations carried out by the same doctor.

I have been obliged to deal with small numbers because I am attempting a complicated task: the analysis of different phases in the consultation, each of which has its own complex form. In consequence, analysis is a lengthy business. Nevertheless, the differences between the two groups are so marked that the smallness of the samples is of less consequence than it might have been.

This is principally an hypothesis-generating paper which deals with only a limited number of cases drawn from one clinic. This has two initial consequences. First, there may well be other ways of persuading Down's parents that surgery is inappropriate. Second, it should not be assumed that the policy applied in this clinic is universal. Indeed, my own observations elsewhere suggest variance between clinics. This serves to highlight the chance factors that bring Down's families into contact with a particular clinic and hence a particular policy line – a point to which I will return in the conclusion.

A further consequence of the limited scope of this paper is that it lacks a full comparative analysis of how parents of 'normal' children with congenital heart disease are persuaded *into* surgery and invasive forms of investigation like catheterisation. As I have shown elsewhere (Silverman, 1980), the degree and form of persuasion varies with parents' perception of the child's 'wellness'.

This paper deals, then, with a *deviant* case. As such, it reflects a well-founded preference in sociological research for analysis of deviant cases. This preference goes back at least as far as Lipset's (1962) study of an unexpectedly democratic American labour union. A recent important work on outpatient encounters by Strong (1979), continuing in this vein, has argued that detailed consideration of deviant cases can test and deepen generalisations about 'normal' forms. Here, although the focus is mainly on the intrinsic interest of the deviant form, the mechanisms of persuasion that are revealed have a direct and more general bearing upon the debate about professional dominance and public policy.

The 'stages' of the consultation

I have been suggesting that, compared with other outpatients consultations at the paediatric cardiology unit, Down's Syndrome outpatients take a deviant form. Now, in one sense, this assertion will not hold at all. Looked at from the point of view of the order of formal stages through which a consultation passes, Down's cases do not look any different from others. Indeed, this order is also maintained at a cleft-palate clinic which is being considered in the same research.

As Hilliard (1980) has pointed out, the order of possible stages of the consultation follows this pattern:

1   Greeting exchange
2   Agenda or grounds for consultation
3   Elicitation sequence
4   Examination
5   Talk among doctors
6   Explanation of diagnosis
7   Disposal
8   Question time
9   Social elicitation
10   Ending

I stress *possible* stages because one or more stages may be missed out in any particular consultation. For instance, Stage 5 is dependent on the presence of other doctors, and Stages 8 and 9 may be missed. The overall variability in the presence of certain stages may be dependent on chance factors, such as pressure of time, or may be systematically related to the current position of the consultation in medical career of the patient. What does seem to be relatively invariant, however, is the *order* in which stages succeed one another. For obvious reasons, for instance, explanation and diagnosis comes after the examination. For less obvious and sometimes more contestable reasons, question time comes towards the end of the consultation. At one clinic, for example, where families asked questions before the examination stage, they were given noncommittal answers or met a response like 'Let's see', followed by a commencement of the examination[2].

1 The elicitation sequence
If we return to the order of possible stages in the consultation, I will try to show how, in Down's consultations, the groundwork is laid for what I will call the 'demedicalisation' of the encounter during the elicitation sequence when the doctor seeks information from the parents, prior to his examination of the child. In this clinic, doctors will be concerned to discover any indications of symptoms like breathlessness or blueness which are associated

Table 1 *Initial elicitation question (random sample)*

Is he/she well?	11
From your point of view, a well baby?	2
Do you notice anything wrong with her?	1
From the heart point of view, she's active?	1
How is he/she?	4
Not asked	3
Total	22

Table 2 *Initial elicitation question (Down's Syndrome cases)*

Is he/she well?	0
From your point of view, a well baby?	1
Do you notice anything wrong with her/him?	0
As far as his heart is concerned, does he get breathless?	1
She gets a few chest infections?	1
How is he/she (this little boy or girl/in himself/herself)?	6
None	1
Total	10

with congenital heart disease. However, I am here not concerned with the content of the doctor's questions but with the *form* of his initial question.

In order to establish some picture of the normal form of this question, I examined 22 outpatient consultations selected at random from those carried out by one doctor at this unit during the course of one year but excluded Down's Syndrome cases. The results are set out in Table 1.

Notice here that reference to the child's 'wellness' is made, in two different forms, in a majority of cases (13 out of 22). Now look at the questions asked to Down's Syndrome children (Table 2). Of the twelve cases discussed in this paper, I have used here only the ten who were seen by the same doctor as in Table 1.

Given the small sample with which we are dealing, one clearly would not want to generalise too much from Table 2. None the less, it is interesting to note that the most favoured question to Down's families is no longer 'is he/she well?' but the more ambiguous 'how is he/she?' The latter question is asked in 60 per cent of all such cases and is he/she well is asked only in a variant form and then in just one case out of ten. The comparable figures for the random sample (Table 1) are reversed: 22 per cent for 'how is he/she?' and 60 per cent for 'is he/she well?'.

Moreover, *none* of the questions asked in Table 2 carries any implication that the doctor himself might think that he was dealing with a well child. The variant form of 'From your point of view, a well baby?', used in one case, clearly only enquires about the parents' views, while not implying that the concept of 'wellness' is the doctor's own. Likewise, the other two minority questions that are asked go further and imply that 'illness' rather than 'wellness' is the appropriate frame of reference for thinking about the child (as evidenced in breathlessness and chest infections).

The significance of 'How is he?' lies in its very neutrality. It can be asked about anyone from a healthy child with a runny nose to a dying, elderly person. However, unlike the question 'Is he well?', it carries no implication that a concept of 'wellness' would even be appropriate to such a person. Moreover, it *can* be asked of an acutely sick or chronically handicapped person (or, indeed, in the neuter form, of an object). To enquire whether such a person is 'well' looks wrong in most circumstances (the ordinary-language philosopher, J.L. Austin calls such linguistic errors 'infelicities'). So one significant feature of the use of this form may be that, unlike 'Is he well?', it leaves open the possibility that the person being discussed could not reasonably be thought to be 'well'.

From this, two implications follow. First, because issues of 'wellness' are excluded, a space is created for other criteria to be used in assessing the child. As we will shortly see, social criteria such as 'enjoyment' may play an important part in parent-doctor discourse about Down's children. Second, in medical encounters, like meetings with the Inland Revenue, assessments lead to particular disposals of cases. To assess a child in terms of 'wellness' implies a medical obligation to try to restore the unwell child to a state of health. By avoiding the use of the parameter well/unwell, the doctor helps to prepare the way for an eventual decision not to intervene. An 'unwell' child has to be restored to its normal state of 'wellness'. Handicapped children, like these, cannot be said to have any such normal state. Born imperfect, they are imperfectible. Self-evidently, therefore, the restorative role of medical intervention becomes problematic.

Some of the 'deviant' character of these encounters is becoming clearer. However, we must strengthen the case with more evidence and also attempt to show the way in which parents co-operate with the doctor's strategies to which we have been referring. To do so, let us follow the consultations through their ordered stages.

The elicitation stage is completed by a reply from a parent or other adult accompanying the patient. We have already noticed how the form of the doctor's question precludes the issue of wellness or unwellness which arises in the cases of 'normal' children with episodes of illness. Interestingly enough, Down's parents generally respond to the doctor's question by deepening the sense of the possibly problematic health-status of their child already implied by the form of the question. Their responses make clear their own uncertainty about the present state of their child's health and their limited expectations about its future. Two examples illustrate the point:

(64: 1) M: Well, she's all right today.
(61: 1) M: Well, he's plodding along steadily, you know, he's er (stops).

Indeed in only one case out of the ten was this rule not followed. In this particular case, 'Eric' was constructed not as an ill child who could be made well but simply as a well child. His mother had managed to live with Eric's double handicap by remaining firmly in the present and, despite what she was told by the doctor, trusting in the wonders that the child's innate vitality is supposedly working against all the predictions of medical science.

(Transcript 62: 1–2)

1 D: How is he?
2 M: Oh fine (laughs).
3 D: Good.
4 M: More energy than what I've got.

. . .

5 D: Do you notice any change in his colour?
6 M: No, none at all. I was told, you know, they kept saying to me, does he change colour, does he go blue? I said no. Does he go blue when he's ill? *No*, you know.
7 D: That's lovely, excellent.

. . .

8 M: I think he's more healthy than what I am.

In fact, the sole medical intervention has been a drug which the doctor decides to withdraw at this consultation. Consequently, but only for the moment, Eric's mother is able to live in a world of 'wellness' which can exist side by side with clinical realities[3].

Notwithstanding this sad case, the data suggests that the elicitation stage typically serves to establish Down's children as *outside* the continuum of wellness–unwellness normally applied to ordinary people. Given a shared recognition of the present handicap and limited future of such children, doctors and parents alike can establish for each other the good sense of avoiding invasive forms of medical intervention and of concentrating upon the social functioning of the child.

2 The diagnosis stage

The elicitation stage is followed by the physical examination of the child and, sometimes, by a discussion between the doctors present. The family is present as usually non-participant observers of these stages of the consultation. Since there seems to be no noticeable difference here between consultations with Down's and those with other children, I will move on to the next stage where the doctor explains the likely diagnosis to the family.

Hilliard (1980) has suggested that there are four variables systematically associated with variance in the character of the explanations of diagnosis:

1   The patient's previous treatment history
2   The disposal the doctor intends to propose

3   The doctor's perception of parental competence
4   The extent to which the child's medically-defined condition is matched by symptoms recognised by his parents (the 'patency' of the condition).

The first of these, the child's previous treatment history, will vary from a new patient status to an old customer returning after surgery. The principal stages in the patient's career, as far as the outpatients' doctor is concerned, are as follows: pre-inpatient, post-catheter and post-operative. In turn, the three main disposals available to the doctor are: discharge, routine follow-up and further treatment (*e.g.* catheter, 24-hour ECG, surgery).

Hilliard suggests that treatment history and disposal combine to define the 'site' of the explanation. Perceived parental competence and the 'patency' of the condition are variables whose importance varies with the site but is also partially determined by it. For instance, unless parents of new patients have some kind of medical qualification, they will not be expected to be familiar with the construction of the heart, nor to understand at once that an asymptomatic child may have congenital heart disease or that a 'murmur' may be innocent. Consequently, the explanation of diagnosis that they receive may be extended and may include the drawing of diagrams and the use of helpful analogies: a 'pump' for the work of the ventricles, a blocked 'garden hose' for an understanding of pulmonary hypertension.

However, as already suggested, the character of the explanation proffered is related not only to the stage of the child's hospital career but also the disposal which the doctor intends to propose. In particular, explanation of the diagnosis is usually structured in order to secure the parents' agreement to the doctor's preferred disposal. This is seen most clearly in cases where catheterisation is indicated on an asymptomatic child brought to his first outpatient consultation. Usually what happens here is that parents are reassured that the child is indeed 'well' but that there is a probability that he has a congenital heart condition which, in the long run may cause him problems. Therefore, it is suggested, a catheter test would be sensible. Almost without exception, parents concur.

The form taken by variance at the 'explanation' stage is systematically related to the 'site' of the explanation: the stage of the patient's career and the proposed disposal. Wherever possible, it is preceded by a form of reassurance from the doctor, usually some version of:

D: The first thing to say is that he's very well.

This seems to be a sensible move, given the anxieties parents feel while their child is being examined and the X-ray and ECG data assessed. Whether the doctor is about to propose discharge, a routine follow-up or a catheter, such reassurance, if possible, establishes a secure backdrop for setting out the reasons behind a proposed disposal. For instance, parents of a child with an innocent murmur are, thereby, set on the path towards a forthcoming

Table 3 *Statement of diagnosis (random sample)*

Well/doing splendidly	9
Reassurance	6
Straight diagnosis	7
Total	22

Table 4 *Statement of diagnosis (Down's Syndrome cases)*

Well/doing splendidly	1
Reassurance	2
Straight diagnosis	9
Total	12

discharge. At the other extreme, parents with an asymptomatic child who, none the less, has congenital heart disease can be reassured about his present state but then told later in the consultation that the probable diagnosis is potentially serious and needs investigating by means of a catheter.

Using the same random sample of 22 cases as earlier, three forms of post-examination explanation were found:

1   An immediate reference to the 'wellness' of the child
2   Some other form of 'reassurance' (*e.g.* 'the hole is closed')
3   Bald statements of diagnosis without reference to 'wellness' or reassurance.

The distribution found is presented in Table 3.

When examining Table 3, it should be borne in mind that the statement of diagnosis is always constrained by the clinical facts about the condition concerned. The parents of a seriously ill, blue or breathless baby can hardly be given much reassurance about the diagnosis. Therefore, this distribution may be limited by the range of conditions involved; only a stratified random sample would reveal the full picture. Nevertheless, it is interesting to note that reassurance, in one form or another, occurs in two-thirds of the cases (15 out of 22).

Let us now look at what happens in consultations with Down's Syndrome families. (In Table 4, all twelve such consultations have been used because, in the two consultations excluded earlier, the second doctor withdrew before the examination of the child took place.)

Once again, it must be conceded that the range of conditions involved here may skew the distribution. However, we should remember that, within limits, it is open to the doctor to put a reassuring gloss on a wide range of diagnoses. Many of the children here have few symptoms reported by their parents. Nevertheless, the doctor generally refrains from reassurance and usually offers a blunt statement of the diagnosis. For instance:

D: Our feeling about her was, as you know, she has a hole between the
    two pumping chambers.
D: He does have a hole in the heart.
D: She does have a heart abnormality.
D: She obviously does have a heart abnormality.

Yet in no case do these statements elicit stated doubt or dissent from the
parents. Only with Eric's mother does the doctor offer any obvious reassurance. Presumably in the light of her unrealistic version of Eric's present
condition and future prospects, the doctor plays for time and offers an
initially favourable gloss on his explanation:

D: I think he's doing splendidly.

Overall, less than one-third of the random sample are offered a straight
diagnosis compared to three-quarters of the Down's cases. This treatment of
the diagnosis-statement, with its studious avoidance of any reference to the
'wellness' of the child, fits neatly with the picture presented at the elicitation
stage. As noted earlier, the role of medical intervention becomes very unclear
and limited in a child that is discursively constituted outside of the continuum 'well–unwell'. An unwell child can be restored to health. A child that
seems well at the moment may, none the less, have an underlying disease
which needs to be treated if his apparent wellness is to be preserved. But
a child that is not altogether whole or is imperfect may turn out to be
imperfectible.

There is a curious irony here. At first glance, the bald statement of the
existence of congenital heart disease might seem to be an obvious preface to
the kind of remedial action which, none the less, is not recommended. The
problem, for the moment, is not the lack of action, or its clinical or moral
grounds, but the discursive organisation which allows non-intervention to
follow smoothly from the statement of the diagnosis.

We can understand this organisation best by returning to the dynamics of
the normal outpatients' consultation. The form in which the diagnosis-
statement is couched is designed to secure parental consent to the doctor's
preferred disposal. However, it is the *immediate* disposal that is at issue here,
not the long-term treatment that may be required. Thus, unless the parents
specifically ask for more, the doctor will usually only provide sufficient
information and reassurance to move the child on to the next stage of treatment.
The question of long-term prognosis, for instance, is very rarely raised by a
doctor at a first outpatient consultation leading to a catheter. Not only do
questions of genuine clinical uncertainty arise but also, unless parents specifically ask for more, the doctor may want to avoid too many complicated
issues coming to the fore at one short meeting.

The medical framework for a first outpatient consultation leading to a
further appointment is, then, 'step by step'. Such a developmental frame of

reference fully accords with the medical understanding, supported by this research, that parents' adjustment to their child's health-status is a slow, sometimes painful process (see Baruch 1981). At the same time, it neatly fits into the paediatrician's developmental version of health.

With Down's cases, this symmetry between social and clinical realities seems to work in an opposite direction. The developmental frame of reference is only of limited appropriateness here. A Down's child, as doctors and parents know, has a limited future. In the normal child, all things being equal, it may make sense to plan medical interventions in a step-by-step manner, over many years, related to the child's development (a very good example of this is the work of the cleft palate clinic reported in Silverman 1981). In turn, the parents can gradually adjust to the stresses involved in having a sick child. But parents of Down's children can be assumed already to have made that adjustment before they come to the paediatric cardiology unit.

This foreshortening of the future means that a 'step-by-step' framework would look odd to the latter parents. A brutal frankness is required for parents who, presumably, already know the worst. There is no point in waiting for the situation to unfold gradually as the 'site' of the consultation changes. The situation for them has *already* unfolded.

So a reference to 'wellness' is doubly inappropriate here. First, it implies a diagnostic scheme which is inappropriate in many situations to children with considerable handicaps. Second, it suggests a state of normality to which unwell children can be returned by means of medical interventions which, in this case, appear powerless or counter-productive.

3 The disposal stage

The co-operative production of a child who is neither 'well' nor 'unwell' lays the basis for the discussion at the disposal stage of the consultation. By removing the child from the normal continuum of illness and health, a non-interventionist disposal decision has been prepared which can then be justified by appealing to a non-medicalised version of the child.

The clinical contra-indications to catheterisation and surgery upon Down's children are complex. As before, we shall look at the disposal stage of the consultation in terms of its discursive organisation. How does the doctor present a preferred disposal involving neither catheterisation nor surgery? Non-intervention is defended, it seems, by an appeal to one or more of six grounds:

1   The self-compensating character of the present cardiac abnormality and, hence, the possible dangers of correction.
2   The limited life-expectancy of a Down's child.
3   The technical feasibility of corrective surgery but its doubtful effects, given (1) and (2).
4   The right of the parents actively to decide.

5   The possibility of postponing parental confirmation of a decision for non-intervention.
6   The good sense of intervening medically in other, more minor, complaints.

We can pass speedily over item 1, noting merely that the doctor's account to parents is usually both detailed and clear. The second point, limited life-expectancy, is more interesting. It has already been suggested that, without parental questioning, doctors in the Unit engage in very little discussion of long-term prognosis, especially at the early stages of a child's long medical career. With Down's families, however, the long-term future of the child plays a frequent part in the discussion of the disposal decision.

In the deviant case of Eric, the doctor resisted the implication that he could expect a normal life. Despite an atypical, optimistic mother, he insisted that what was at stake was a normal *childhood*. Elsewhere, he talks very easily in terms of a limited life-expectancy. For instance:

(Transcript 60: 3)
    D: Now, her life-expectancy without doing anything could well be many, many years. All right? I mean certainly childhood and the rest of it.
    M: Yes.

Here, the limited expectations *implied* by the mutual avoidance of reference to 'wellness' earlier in the consultation is openly recognised. This recognition carries the further implication that the disposal decision is centrally related to the limited life-expectancy of the Down's child. Another Down's child, Donald, is discussed in very much these terms. His mother has just heard the diagnosis of an ASD, leaky mitral valve and possible VSD:

(Transcript 56: 3)
    1 D: I think, quite honestly, that I would not be keen long-term on surgery into his heart because if we're correct in our diagnosis, I think it's correct but to be absolutely certain we'd need to do more tests . . . but then it is the sort of condition that if the leak through the valve does not get worse he may be stable for the first thirty to forty years of life and under the circumstances there would be absolutely no indication to do anything because um he might well have, more likely to have other problems before he's fifty than the theoretical possibility . . . (Pause) O.K.?
    2 M: Right, yes.

Notice how the word 'stable' is used about Donald's likely outlook. Once again, as earlier, the word 'well' is avoided. The bleaker long-term future is expressed in the phrase 'other problems'. Despite its vagueness, Donald's mother seems to follow the rationale behind the disposal and to concur immediately with it.

Now an unwillingness to engage in tests or complicated surgery might strike parents as reflecting badly upon the technical skills of the hospital. A third basis for defending non-intervention is, then, to stress that it is not the lack of technical skills but the doubtful consequences of intervention which are the problem. For instance, discussing Fiona, with VSD and pulmonary hypertension:

(Transcript 60: 4)

D: I want to make it absolutely clear it isn't because we can't do the operation, it's because, as a result of the lung factor, to do it, if she comes through, it might decrease not increase her life-expectancy. In fact, one or two children that you see in the papers who go off to other countries for heart operations, they go with this sort of problem because people raise a lot of money for them to go and when they get there of course the operation isn't done or nothing can be done. It isn't that we can't do the operation, it is that it is not in her interests because of the lung problem.

Elsewhere the purely technical feasibility of the operation is stressed in two other consultations involving Down's children. One of these is Gloria, aged $2^3/_4$, with the same diagnosis as Fiona. While Fiona's parents are offered a more or less clear-cut disposal recommendation, the doctor appeals much more to Gloria's mother's right of choice. On three separate occasions, interspersed with a presentation of the risks of surgery, he states that medical intervention ultimately depends on the family:

(Transcript 64: 3–4)

1 D: Um I think what we do now depends a little bit on parents' feelings . . .

2 D: Now it depends, it depends a little bit on what you think . . .

3 D: It depends very much I think on your own personal views as to whether we should proceed.

As in all cases in the sample, the decision about catheterisation is referred to the parents. Yet this reference to consumer-choice is atypical across the run of consultations at the pre-catheter stage. What generally seems to happen is that a clinical decision to catheterise is taken and then justified to the parents, depending upon the patency of the condition. Parental consent still arises but usually only in a formal sense. For example, the doctor may say:

D: What we would like to do, if you agree (with your consent), is a small test . . .

The insistence upon the parents' right to choose in these cases seems to serve three functions. First, it re-emphasises the availability of surgery at the hospital. If the parents take the decision not to intervene, then this can clearly constitute no threat to the status of the Unit's surgical skills. Second, in an area where clinical and moral considerations shade so easily into one another, an emphasis on parental decision-making, backing up with strongly-worded advice against intervention, serves to free doctors from appearing to play God, while making it very likely that the eventual decision will go in the direction which they favour. The third function of parental decision-making relates to the political character of this kind of encounter. Most medical encounters work on the assumption that the doctor can offer some worthwhile service by diagnosing illness and, more importantly, curing it. With Down's children the relevance of this service is limited when doctors are faced with an irreparably 'damaged' child, where even cardiac surgery cannot restore the child to 'normality'. Consequently, the political role of the doctor is weakened.

The situation may be comparable to that in clinics treating handicapped children (Strong 1979) where mothers' assessments and decisions are allowed to displace the central role of the doctor. It may also have a parallel in situations where an operation fails or has unforeseen side-effects (Hilliard 1981). In cases like these, patients or parents may feel that medical science has its limits and may become more assertive of their decision-making 'rights'. By handing over the decision to the family of his own free will, a doctor therefore may pre-empt a later intervention towards this end on territory where his political ground is somewhat weakened.

The unusual emphasis on parents' right to choose is strengthened by the doctor's preparedness to allow them to go away and think about it. Gloria's outpatient consultation is ended, for instance, by the doctor offering the mother the opportunity 'to go away and talk about it with your husband' and even a choice between another appointment or 'to leave it and perhaps telephone' (64: 7). This degree of freedom of choice at the pre-catheter stage seems unique to Down's Syndrome children. Allowing the decision to be taken at home underlines not only the doctor's relatively weakened political position but also the role of social factors in decision-making here.

Once again, a certain symmetry asserts itself. Normal decision-making at the unit is based almost entirely on clinical factors. Here social factors play a much increased role. By implication, it is being asserted that clinical decisions need to be made in a clinical context (the hospital). Social decisions are rightly made in a social context (the home).

The sixth and final ground employed in justifying non-intervention is that medicine is only withdrawing from the problematic issue of cardiac surgery; other, more minor conditions should still be treated if they are making a serious impact on the child's enjoyment of life. Thus the doctor is all in favour of an operation on Donald's 'gluey' ears (56: 3) and the use of drugs on any chest infections that Fiona may experience (60: 4). Medicine still has services to offer; it seeks to withdraw only from those areas where it believes the balance of gains and losses to be uncertain or unfavourable.

Given the detailed statement of this balance-sheet and the frequent appeal to parental decision-making, the disposal stage tends to be much longer with Down's children than with others. Moreover, it does not seem to terminate after the decision is taken or postponed. Both parents and doctor continue to discuss the child but the frame of reference is no longer clinical. While, at earlier stages of the consultation, the ground is prepared for non-intervention, the framework is largely clinical. Now the child suddenly ceases to be a source of clinical data and is constituted as a social subject. Clinically speaking, parents and doctors seem to have no choice but to view the Down's child as irreparably damaged. Yet, because the child is clinically not whole, both parties have a common interest in reconstituting him as socially whole and located within a social whole (the family).

From the parents' side, the social constitution of the child is achieved by stressing his ability to cope with physical symptoms and thus to play a full part in family life. An example of this arises in another sample member whose mother asserted: 'I mean it's not affected 'im really at all' (57: 4). For her, Bill's unfavourable clinical outlook is balanced by his ability to cope. Clinically speaking, Bill may be a lost cause. To her, he is a worthwhile member of the family. It is almost as if, in not being affected by his heart condition, Bill is deliberately trying to do his best to make life easier for his family. 'He seems to cope quite well' his father says (57: 6).

A similar theme of social worth is taken up by Fiona's parents. They tell how her 'resistance to colds' seems to be better. Like Bill, it seems that Fiona is doing her bit and, in doing so, is paying a tribute to what the hospital has done for her.

(Transcript 60: 5)

1 F: Well, I must admit since we saw you . . .
      She's been markedly improved.
2 M: (   )
3 F: Oh yes, much more lively, much more alert. It's marvellous
      improvement . . .
4 F: And she paces herself, you see. If she gets out of breath she stops
      whatever she's doing till she thinks she can do it again.

In more routine cases, where parents offer such social formulations of symptoms which may indicate congenital heart disease, they are persuaded by doctors that things like breathlessness, in conjunction with other clinical evidence, must be taken more seriously. Yet in Down's cases, such social formulations are usually unchallenged and are sometimes, as we shall see in a moment, offered by the doctor himself. The social constitution of such children allows doctors to find immediately understandable grounds for their preferred disposals and permits parents to build a less damaging picture of their child's present and future.

Faced with a patient with a poor outlook, with or without surgery, the doctor too joins in the demedicalisation of the child via an emphasis on a social conception of a normal, happy childhood. For instance the doctor lessens the salience of Anna's heart abnormality by maintaining that it is not 'seriously interfering with her enjoyment of life' (13: 8). The theme of 'enjoyment' and 'happiness' is also central to his depiction of Gloria, in the context of medical non-intervention:

(Transcript 64: 6–7)

   1 D: I mean do you think a happy child of four, playing and growing up with other children and then, perhaps, you know, either late teens or twenties just very peacefully passing away might be . . .

(Compare this to his statement to Fiona's parents):

   D: You should enjoy a happy little girl who plays and does everything normally and could have many happy years ahead of her without doing anything (60: 5).

The doctor is trading off the existence of violently lowered expectations among Down's Syndrome parents. Given a limited future, most parents may feel that a little certain happiness is better than the prospect of none at all. But Gloria's mother is still troubled, not about the early death which she has already accepted but about Gloria's present troubles. The doctor responds to her desire for medical intervention by implying that these troubles are irremediable and, later, by returning to the 'enjoyment' theme:

   2 M: The only (   ), I expect other children are the same, she gets ill so quickly and we were hoping perhaps if something was done she wouldn't be like, um, like that and she's always just been, you know, in and out of hospital since she was born.

   3 D: Well I think that's a little bit related to her having Down's Syndrome independently of the heart.

   4 M: I see. I'll talk it over with my husband / then.

   5 D: /Yes.

   6 M: And he wasn't keen for her to have an / operation.

   7 D: /Yes.

   8 M: really. He said even if it came to it he wasn't keen. (the doctor returns again to the risks of surgery)

   9 D: But I think my own view is if she were my child with Down's Syndrome, I think I would adopt the view well, she's a happy little thing, she's got plenty of years ahead of her, in any case there are going to be problems if she does get to the age of forty or fifty and outlives you and your husband.

 10 M: Yes.

11 D: Maybe the best thing all round is not to distress her with the operation and all the things involved, to enjoy her as she is and to be pleased that you've got a happy little (   ) fits into the family.

12 M: Yes.

13 D: And say O.K. well let's enjoy that and not risk losing you for a rather doubtful gain.

14 M: Yes, yes. Well thank you very much for seeing her and talking to me.

Even here, as already noted, despite the doctor's preparedness to play the role of a moral actor ('if she were my child'), he still leaves the decision to the parents and suggests that it should be postponed. Throughout this concluding passage, the framework is entirely social. Gloria is no longer a 'case', nor data to be clinically defined, but a social subject who derives her significance from her location in the family. Atypically, Down's families are encouraged to appeal to what they know already as family members. They only need to enter the clinical realm to recognise its limits when dealing with what it has to define as an irremediable problem.

Above all, the Down's child has to be reconstituted as simply a child and, therefore, to reflect the intrinsic 'wonderfulness' of all children, handicapped or not. While doctors and parents at this clinic often comment on such wonderfulness at the examination stage of the consultation, only Down's Syndrome children find themselves *essentially* defined in this way throughout the consultation. These two examples, taken from the disposal stage, make the point:

1 D: He's a nice little boy. (57: 7)

2 F: Yeah . . .

1 M: He's very lovable. (63: 8)

2 D: Yes.

3 M: Aren't you?

Conclusions

I earlier referred to the merits of deviant-case analysis. We have seen how consultations with the families of Down's Syndrome children at this paediatric cardiology unit take an unusual, deviant form that I called 'demedicalised'. Progressively, throughout the ordered stages of the consultation, a picture is built up of a damaged child, with a limited future. Such a child can never be fully 'well', with or without medical interventions, but may none the less be viewed within a social framework of happy, family life. Consequently, we usually find an attempt to limit the saliency of medical actions and to relate symptoms of illness to their impact on family life. Faced with an irreparably damaged child, parents and doctor retreat into manageable stereotypes of the essentially 'wonderful' nature of childhood. In this way, doctors ultimately withdraw from their clinical gaze and encourage parents to co-operate in producing a demedicalised, social vision of a tolerable future.

One clear research implication seems to emerge. We have observed here the variability in the character of medical encounters associated with a particular kind of condition. In turn, this analysis has depended upon an understanding of the impact on all doctor-parent relations of the 'site' of the encounter. This suggests that rather than formulating a single typical form of the medical encounter (say 'medical dominance') and a single preferred form (say 'patient-centred medicine') research at the micro-level might properly take up the causes and character of systematic variance in medical encounters. In doing so, it might offer theoretical illumination and the prospect of policy changes with some chance of success if only because they avoid both the polemic of 'medical domination' theory and the psychologism of theories of consulting 'styles'.

Within the constraints of the limited sample, what tentative conclusions may be drawn from the kind of co-operative practices observed here? The first thing to remark is that, curiously, we have discovered here what is, in some respects at least, a fair approximation of the kind of medical encounter favoured by many social science observers. Instead of dwelling in a largely unintelligible, clinical realm, we have seen the doctor move into and encourage social formulations of the child's present and future status. The consequence has been a consultation which is usually longer than most and which seems to allow the family to air their anxieties and hopes. More than most medical encounters, we observe here something close to a family decision-making format, where the consumer is offered considerable information and is allowed to make an informed choice.

However, we should not exaggerate the extent of the 'consumerism' noticed both here and in a cleft-palate clinic offering cosmetic surgery to teenagers (Silverman 1981). In the latter clinic, consumerism seemed to be a specific product of a cultural norm, demanding that only the subject himself could decide whether his appearance should be altered. It was limited by the observed inability of many children to formulate their concerns and desires. Here a consumerist form arises as part of a medical strategy to demedicalise the encounter. Once again, consumerism is limited both by the moral weight of the doctor's advice and by the family's probable prior adjustments to the birth of a Down's child.

However, the limits of 'consumerist' strategies are clearly not the only practical implication of this paper. A more immediate issue arises from evidence that the policy of non-intervention on Down's children with congenital heart disease is part of the 'hidden agenda' in many clinics both in Britain and overseas.

A fascinating recent American study has indicated that medical judgments about the significance of the mental damage sustained by Down's children make doctors predisposed not to intervene on congenital heart disease

Table 5 *Percentage of surgeons prepared to operate according to patient's type of damage*

Severity of cardiac condition	Urogenital	Down's Syndrome parents favourable to surgery	Down's Syndrome parents unfavourable to surgery
Mild (PDA)	93	56	*
Moderate (Tetralogy)	90	59	18
Severe (A–V Canal)	82	50	12

(* figure not available)
(Adapted from Crane, 1975, p. 45)

unless parents are actively favourable. In a study of a number of paediatric cardiology units, Crane (1975) revealed that surgeons presented with case histories said they were much more likely to operate upon a given heart condition where the child has a urogenital anomaly than when it had Down's Syndrome [see Table 5].

Moreover, Crane goes on to point out that what the doctors *said* probably *over-estimated* the actual intervention rate with Down's children. Using a complete 5-year listing of all Down's children catheterised at one teaching hospital and controlling for *type* of heart condition, 39 per cent of Down's cases received surgery, compared to 65 per cent of non-Down's. In A–V canal cases, 29 per cent of Down's children received surgery, compared to 100 per cent of non-Down's. Furthermore, social variables such as being an only child or first-born played a significant part in the extent of surgical intervention with Down's children.

This study has supported Crane's findings within consultations themselves. The practical reality often seems to be the enactment of a clinic's policy hidden from parents and rarely discussed even between medical staff[4]. Variations in clinic policy between hospitals and regions have caused public controversy in both neonatal and renal units (see *The Lancet*, 1981) and illustrate that factors such as geography can have an undesirable impact on the extent and nature of treatment.

One sort of response that I have recently encountered in Brisbane, Australia, is for parents' groups to contact families of Down's Syndrome neonates and to offer advice on which local hospitals are prepared to intervene on associated congenital anomalies (such as congenital heart disease). Although this has merits as a short-term response, consumerism, with all its inherent limits, can hardly serve as a continuing basis for social policy. Moreover, it is possible that parents' groups may serve to press intervention upon some parents who may have reasons for not wanting to intervene. An alternative, more general response has been made in the debate within medical ethics.

Understandably, the issue of the treatment of Down's children has generated a great debate among ethicists, particularly where there has been a suggestion of 'passive euthanasia' (see Robertson and Fost 1976, Waldman 1976, Campbell and Duff 1979). One school of thought (represented by Campbell and Duff) argues that life and death decisions should be left to doctors and parents alone. Crane suggests that 'ethical guidelines' should be erected. Both positions are rejected by Robertson and Fost. Ethical guidelines related to the net social utility of a person's future, they say, would set us on to a 'slippery slope', while the joint doctor-parent decision-making solution, they argue, fails to examine the impact of emotional trauma upon parents' capacities for rational choice. So, instead, Robertson and Fost suggest a committee-based decision-making process relying on an appeal to 'disinterested' persons (see also Waldman).

This debate has the merit of emphasising that the real issue is *not* the final decision itself, since there are no satisfactory *a priori* grounds for arguing that surgical intervention is always right or always wrong for these children. Because the family concerned will have to live with the consequences of any decision, there is a strong argument, however, that the process of decision-making should not involve reference to external standards or to Olympian bodies of 'disinterested' persons.

However, even if decisions are left to doctors and parents, as Campbell and Duff suggest, there remains the strong possibility that parents will continue to be persuaded according to a predetermined clinical policy. What seems to be required is an encounter between doctor and parents where *all* the various options and their consequences are discussed. The child is not simply a social object but equally a clinical, moral, political and legal *subject*. Yet what we have observed here is a formulation of the child which merely *reverses* the interpretation normally found in the clinic *i.e.* by making social formulations prior to clinical formulations. What is required is not a reversal of interpretations but a revolving, or revolution, of discourses[5].

Notes

1   Few of the sophisticated methods of transcription used in conversational analysis are employed here. This is not to deny that such an analysis, based on more detailed transcripts, would pay dividends. I would only argue that the transcripts used here are sufficient for my limited purposes.

2   This is not the place to discuss the detail or significance of this ordering of stages. It seems to reflect medical training, derived from the sound logical principle of an orderly sequence of diagnostic methods based upon the accumulation of data. At the same time, it expresses medical control of the agenda which, especially because it is usually tacit and unnegotiated, lends credence to accounts of 'medical dominance' (*c.f.* Freidson: 1970). Yet a difficulty with some such accounts is that the research direction in which they lead may be quite problematic (see especially Waitzkin: 1979). It is easy, after all, to show that doctors are usually in control of consultations. But the polemical weight of this ever-repeated research 'finding' is limited when we recognise the truism that doctors do possess a specialised

competence to which patients want access and this competence must have an impact on the social organisation of the encounter. Critical energies might better be devoted to analysing the varying bases and sites of doctor-patient consensus and conflict rather than to engage in the hollow spectacle of one profession (social science) 'bashing' another (medicine). Such professional 'mugging' as Strong (1979) has recently implied, is easily, and justifiably, reversible.

3 Likewise, in Strong's (1979) data on seriously handicapped children, a few mothers, but only a few, managed to retreat into the present and to sustain the retreat within consultations over a number of years, despite considerable, although largely indirect, pressure from doctors.

4 For instance, in one Australian unit which I recently observed, the clinic 'line' was to treat Down's children like 'normal' children and so to perform the investigations and operations upon them. It was explained to me that this just happened to be the consultant's own view and that more junior staff applied the line without always agreeing with it.

5 By a circuitous route, I have reached a conclusion similar to the position argued in Silverman and Torode (1980). 'Interpretation', whether it proceeds by constituting the child either socially or clinically, is revealed to be an intrinsically conservative process. An 'interruption' can reveal the discursive possibilities hidden by a unitary interpretive framework.

References

Baruch, G. (1981) 'Moral tales: Parents' stories of encounters with the health professions', Sociology of Health & Illness, 3(3): 275–295.

Campbell, A.G.M. and Duff, R.S. (1979) 'Deciding the Care of Severely Malformed or Dying Infants', *Journal of Medical Ethics*, 5, 65–7.

Crane, D. (1975) *The Sanctity of Social life: Physicians' Treatment of Critically Ill Patients*, New York: Russell Sage.

Freidson, E. (1970) *Profession of Medicine*, New York: Dodd Mead.

Hilliard, R. (1980) 'Analytic Schemes: Outpatient Routines', unpublished MS., Goldsmiths' College.

Hilliard, R. (1981) Unpublished MS., Goldsmiths' College.

Lancet, The (1981) 'Ethics and the Nephrologist', 14 March 1981, 594–6.

Lipset, S.M. *et al.* (1962) *Union Democracy*, New York: Free Press.

Robertson, J.A. and Fost, N. (1976) 'Passive Euthanasia of Defective Newborn Infants: Legal Considerations', *Journal of Pediatrics*, 88, no. 5, 883–9.

Silverman, D. (1980) 'Decision-Making Discourse: The Chauffeur's Model', unpublished MS., Goldsmiths' College.

Silverman, D. (1981) 'The Clinical Subject: Consumerist Medicine in a Cleft palate Clinic', unpublished MS., Goldsmiths' College.

Silverman, D. and Torode, B. (1980) *The Material Word: Some Theories of Language and its Limits*, London: Routledge & Kegan Paul.

Strong, P. (1979) *The Ceremonial Order of the Clinic*, London: Routledge & Kegan Paul.

Waitzkin, H. (1979) 'Medicine Superstructure and Micropolitics', *Social Science & Medicine*, 13A, 601–9.

Waldman, A.M. (1976) 'Medical Ethics and the Hopelessly Ill Child', *Journal of Pediatrics*, 88, 5, 890–2.

Section 2

Medical Power and the Patient

Introduction

Some thirty years ago Eliot Freidson published his *Profession of Medicine* (1970). Freidson opened his study by defining the medical profession mainly in terms of its ability to control and organise to its advantage the social, political and economic relationships that impinge on matters of health and illness. Freedom, and control over the work process were argued to be watchwords of professional action. So Freidson's doctors both defined what illness might be (they were 'experts') and, in an atmosphere of trust and confidence, managed their patients in accordance with their expert judgement. It is not, perhaps, a portrait that would be fully recognisable to present day practitioners.

The issue of medical dominance is still pertinent to medical sociologists of course, and its significance has been duly reflected in contributions to *The Sociology of Health and Illness*. During the intervening years, however, there have been notable changes to the strategic positioning of medicine – as a practice – in that web of influences that affect matters of health and illness. Indeed medicine, in conjunction with most other fields of professional activity, has been subjected to pressures and influences that have eroded the ability of experts to control and define their sphere of operation. The rise of managerialism and new forms of governance, for example, with an emphasis on the standardisation of rules and procedures (as contained in, say, in protocols and guidelines) has notionally reduced the space in which the autonomous professional can exercise personal judgement and individual skill. In addition, control over the ways in which work is evaluated has been wrested out of the hands of professionals and subjected to routine procedures of audit and assessment. Goals and targets are often imposed on professionals by managerial authorities – authorities that are nowadays distanced from occupational control. 'Customers', clients and patients also place pressure on medical professionals to be accountable and to take cognisance of the 'lay' perspective on matters of disease and bodily disorder. What doctors say is no longer taken as gospel, and questions of competence, and of trust in expert judgement commonly arise in everyday work settings. Moreover, we have also to take account of the changing patterns of the division of labour in medical work (investigated in Section Three of this Reader). Patterns that, more often than not, limit even further the terrain in terms of which the specialised professional can operate.

Many of these issues are both reviewed and reported upon in the papers from Lupton and Samson that are included in this Section. Lupton, drawing on qualitative work with Australian doctors, examines the ways in which medical professionals themselves view matters relating to professional status, the impact of consumerism, and the perceived qualities of the 'good' doctor. In so doing she provides clues as to how trust, confidence, expertise and medical dominance are constantly negotiated and re-negotiated through medical encounters in the consultation. In that respect she suggests that arguments about de-professionalisation ought, perhaps, to be reformulated in terms of issues relating to re-professionalisation. The medical consultation is, of course, merely one of numerous arenas in which medical power operates. Thus, Samson, who examines issues of de-professionalisation and proletarianisation in relation to British psychiatry, moves beyond the consultation to take account of the wider policy contexts in which medicine – in this case as psychiatry – operates. Above all, those contexts concern the move from hospital centred to community based forms of psychiatric care. A move that brought in its wake a new ethos of managerialism and consumerism of the kind alluded to above – and with that, the familiar problems of professional control and autonomy.

Whilst both Lupton and Samson defer from adopting a recognisable, and explicit theoretical stance on matters relating to medical power and the patient, the same cannot be said of the remaining papers. For, Armstrong and Arney and Neill adopt a strong Foucauldian approach to the pertinent issues. The writings of Foucault undoubtedly had a major impact on medical sociology in the UK during the 1980s and 1990s, and these two papers provide excellent examples of that influence. In the wake of Monsieur Foucault, Armstrong argues that hospital medicine – centred on the body and the clinic – has been superseded by a surveillance medicine that is centred on populations in the community. In particular, it is a medicine that has focused on risk and risk factors as potential objects for medical study and assessment. Through a consideration of such risk factors, surveillance has, in turn, become embroiled in an assessment and valuation of everyday lifestyles and behaviours. By implication, and most importantly from our point of view, medical power is seen to have extended its jurisdiction over ever larger segments of social life. This Foucauldian theme of surveillance and the disciplining of personal behaviour is also echoed in the paper by Arney and Neill. The latter focus on obstetrics and the ways in which the movement for natural childbirth was interpreted as a threat to medical authority. In order to counter such threats, argue Arney and Neill, medical obstetrics re-positioned itself to incorporate the female subject more fully into its practice. More specifically obstetrics extended its power by redefining its field of practice so as to incorporate a concern with active women and their subjectivity. By creating fields of visibility anew, obstetrics bolstered its own authority.

Clearly, then, these papers contain somewhat contrasting positions on the question of medical dominance in the late twentieth century. The Foucauldians hold to the view that the medical gaze has both extended itself and fortified its position in relation to the late modern world. Those who have picked up on the prevailing themes of postmodernity are more cautious in their assessments, and are more readily inclined to see the empire of medicine somewhat fractured and uncertain of its foundation. They are not, we suspect, positions that are reconcilable, and followers of Foucault would not expect them to be so. In any event, these papers offer the reader not only a variety of fields for analysis – psychiatry, general practice, and obstetrics – but also provide some insight into alternative starting points for those analyses. The papers in that sense touch on a number of themes that medical sociologists in the English speaking world have regarded as central during the last twenty years – the exercise of medical power in modern medical settings.

Whilst the papers say much about the exercise of medical power, they say relatively little about patients and clinics. Indeed, if anything, the patient portrayed herein is seen to play a relatively modest role in modern medical practice, and there is a suggestion that patients and clients as subjects are merely produced through the exercise of power. So, for example, that ubiquitous contemporary figure of the patient 'at risk' is clearly a product of something akin to what Armstrong refers to as surveillance medicine, in particular, perhaps, a product of a population based epidemiology that is forever constructing new statistical figures – in every sense of that last word. Yet, one cannot help but feel that patients are more active than the Foucauldians suggest, and that there is far more to medical practice than textbook and journal based histories of professional practice might indicate. Indeed, when one studies consultations in situ, as it were, it often becomes clear that the power and knowledge of professionals can be matched – blow for blow – by the power and knowledge of patients and clients. This is made apparent in research on GP prescribing decisions. In their paper, Weiss and Fitzpatrick show that GPs perceive patient expectations to be a far more significant threat to their autonomy than greater managerial control one prescribing patterns. Power is therefore not something that stands outside of medical settings, waiting to be recruited by one party or another, but more likely flows through locally contingent interactions. Power, in that sense, is a relational effect rather than a thing. In this light it is work of the kind developed by Ainsworth-Vaughn (1998) rather than Foucault that is more likely to illuminate the power producing process.

However that might be, it is clear that during recent years, there has been considerable impetus to conduct studies on the lay (patient) contribution to definitions of health and illness. Such an impetus is evident, for example, in Arksey's (1998) work on Repetitive Strain Injury, as well as Epstein's (1996) study of AIDS. Whilst on a more restricted level, analysts such as Brown (1992, 1997) have emphasised the virtues of lay thinking in his analysis of 'popular epidemiology', and Davison et al. (1991) have emphasised the significance of 'lay epidemiology'. (For a review of literature relating to lay expertise, see Prior (2003)). One feature that is consistently demonstrated in studies of medical consultations is that professional (medical) and lay parties very often seek to recruit each other's expertise and knowledge so as to advance their individual claims about the nature of ill-health and its treat-ment. In that respect it is clear that medical expertise has been dispersed – and very often to mutual benefit. So modern medical practice is open to various sources of influence. What the content and implications of such influences will be, and how and by whom they are promoted and advanced is, of course, forever a question of empirical (social scientific) inquiry. For the manner in which lay and expert patients combine to construct disease and their treatments is, as Arskey (1998) and Epstein (1996) have shown, always contingent and rarely predictable. What is needed perhaps in medical sociology are analyses of the ways in which broader structural issues that affect clinical practice (such as, say, the financial constraints imposed by managers, or the implementation of professional protocols, or new ways of conceptualising clients) are brought directly into the live and active con-sultation. (Some of these issues are touched upon in a special (2002) issue of *The Sociology of Health and Illness* – see Light and Hughes 2002). With equal fervour, sociologists also need to pay more attention to what clients and patients recruit into such consultations (see, for example, Banks and Prior 2000). For we must never overlook the fact that clients have their own sources and bases of expertise and their own stocks of knowledge. Modern understandings of health and illness are thus forged from many ingredients. That is perhaps why the traditional distinction drawn between biomedically defined 'disease' and socially evaluated 'illness' – a distinction that has proven so useful to medical sociologists – has finally outlived its usefulness.

References

Ainsworth-Vaughn, N. (1998) *Claiming Power in Doctor-Patient Talk*. New York: Oxford University Press.

Arksey, H. (1998) *RSI and the Experts. The Construction of Medical Knowledge*. NY: Oxford University Press.

Banks, J. and Prior, L. (2000) Doing things with illness. The micro-politics of the CFS Clinic. *Social Science and Medicine*, 52, 11–23.

Brown, P. (1992) Popular epidemiology and toxic-waste contamination: lay and professional ways of knowing. *Journal of Health and Social Behavior*, 33, 267–281.

Brown, P. (1997) Popular epidemiology revisited. *Current Sociology*, 45, 137–156.

Davison, C., Davey-Smith, G. and Frankel, S. (1991) Lay epidemiology and the prevention paradox. *Sociology of Health and Illness*, 13, 1–19.

Epstein, S. (1996) *Impure Science. AIDS, Activism and the Politics of Knowledge*. Berkeley: University of California Press.

Freidson, E. (1970) *Profession of Medicine*. NY: Harper & Row.

Light, D. and Hughes, D. (eds) (2002) *Rationing. Constructed Realities and Profes-sional Practices*. Oxford, Blackwell.

Prior, L. (2003) Belief, knowledge and expertise: the emergence of the lay expert in medical sociology. *Sociology of Health and Illness*, 25, 25–37.

2.1

The rise of surveillance medicine

David Armstrong

Introduction

Perhaps the most important contribution for understanding the advent of modern medicine has been the work of the medical historian Ackerknecht (1967), who described the emergence of a number of distinct medical perspectives during the early and late eighteenth century. In brief, he identified an earlier phase of Library Medicine in which the classical learning of the physician seemed more important than any specific knowledge of illness. This gave way to Bedside Medicine when physicians began to address the problems of the practical management of illness, particularly in terms of the classification of the patient's symptoms. In its turn Bedside Medicine was replaced by Hospital Medicine with the advent of hospitals in Paris at the end of the eighteenth century.

Hospital Medicine was clearly an important revolution in medical thinking. Also known as the Clinic, pathological medicine, Western medicine and biomedicine, it has survived and extended itself over the last two centuries to become the dominant model of medicine in the modern world. Even so, a significant alternative model of medicine can be discerned as materialising during the twentieth century around the observation of seemingly healthy populations.

Medical spaces

The commanding medical framework of Hospital Medicine first emerged at the turn of the eighteenth century with the appearance of the now familiar medical procedures of the clinical examination, the post-mortem, and hospitalisation. Foucault (1973) has described these changes in terms of a new 'spatialisation' of illness.

Primary spatialisation referred to the cognitive mapping of the different elements of illness. In the early eighteenth century, under a regime of Bedside Medicine, illness was coterminous with the symptoms that patients experienced and reported. A headache or abdominal pain was the illness. This two-dimensional model of illness in which symptoms were classified as in a table, was replaced by Hospital Medicine in which the relationship of symptoms and illness was reconfigured into a three-dimensional framework involving symptom, sign and pathology. In this new arrangement, the symptom, as of old, was a marker of illness as experienced by the patient, but to this indicator was added the sign – an intimation of disease as elicited by the attentive physician through the clinical examination. For example, the patient's symptom of abdominal pain might be linked to the sign of abdominal tenderness that the physician could discover; but neither symptom nor sign in itself constituted illness: both pointed to an underlying lesion that was the disease. In contrast to the previous regime of Bedside Medicine in which the overt symptom was the illness, the 'clinical picture' as drawn by both symptom and sign enabled the pathology that existed beneath experience to be inferred. This 'clinico-pathological correlation' marked a new relationship between surface and depth. Accordingly, the subtle characteristics of an abdominal pain which in an earlier time would have comprised the illness were now linked with the findings of the clinical examination (the signs), to indicate the presence of a hidden pathological lesion.

Secondary spatialisation referred to the location of the lesion in relation to the body of the patient. The clinician's task under Bedside Medicine was to identify and classify illness through the distinctiveness of clusters of symptoms. Thus, the mobility of illness through the body could be captured by closely monitoring the sequencing of symptoms. In Hospital Medicine, on the other hand, the physician had to infer from symptoms and signs the underlying pathological lesion within the patient's body. In consequence, for the first time, the patient's body as a three-dimensional object became the focus of medical attention. This in turn led to the invention of the classical techniques of the clinical examination – inspection, percussion, palpation and auscultation – that allowed the volume of the human body to be mapped, and to the spread of the postmortem as a procedure to identify incontrovertibly the exact nature of the hidden lesion.

Finally, tertiary spatialisation referred to the locus of illness in the context of health care activity. Under Bedside Medicine, illness was best identified in the natural space of the patient's own home; in Hospital Medicine it required the 'neutral' space of the hospital so that the indicators of the underlying lesion might by properly identified without the contaminants of extraneous 'noise'. This facet of the new medicine was marked by the subsequent dominance of the clinic as the prime centre for health care provision as hospitals were rapidly built throughout Europe.

The novel spatialisation of illness that marked the new pathological alignment of Hospital Medicine came to dominate the nineteenth century and has succeeded in maintaining its ascendancy in the twentieth. To be sure, the techniques for identifying the hidden lesions of the body have grown more sophisticated. Indeed, Jewson (1976) has argued that the addition of laboratory investigations to the repertoire of clinical indicators of disease towards the end of the nineteenth century marked yet another medical model that he called Laboratory Medicine, not least because the body of the patient became even more objectified and the identity of the 'sick man' further lost. But, while clinical investigations in the form of X-rays, pathology reports, blood analyses, etc, marked an extension of the technical apparatus of medical procedures it did not challenge the underlying spatialisation of illness nor the logic of clinical practice: experience and illness were still linked through surface and depth, inference of the true nature of the lesion still dominated medical thinking, and the hospital still – indeed even more so – remained the centre of health care activity.

Despite the clear hegemony of Hospital Medicine over the last two centuries, it is the contention of this paper that a new medicine based on the surveillance of normal populations can be identified as beginning to emerge early in the twentieth century. This new Surveillance Medicine involves a fundamental remapping of the spaces of illness. Not only is the relationship between symptom, sign and illness redrawn but the very nature of illness is reconstrued. And illness begins to leave the three-dimensional confine of the volume of the human body to inhabit a novel extracorporal space.

Problematisation of the normal

Hospital Medicine was only concerned with the ill patient in whom a lesion might be identified, but a cardinal feature of Surveillance Medicine is its targeting of everyone. Surveillance Medicine requires the dissolution of the distinct clinical categories of healthy and ill as it attempts to bring everyone within its network of visibility. Therefore one of the earliest expressions of Surveillance Medicine – and a vital precondition for its continuing proliferation – was the problematisation of the normal.

No doubt there were nineteenth century manifestations of the idea that a person – or more frequently, a population – hung precariously between health and illness (such as the attempts to control the health of prostitutes near military establishments with the Contagious Diseases Acts), but it was the child in the twentieth century that became the first target of the full deployment of the concept. The significance of the child was that it underwent growth and development: there was therefore a constant threat that proper stages might not be negotiated that in its turn justified close medical observation. The establishment and wide provision of antenatal care, birth notification, baby clinics, milk depots, infant welfare clinics, day nurseries, health visiting and nursery schools ensured that the early years of child development could be closely monitored (Armstrong 1983). For example, the School Medical (later Health) Service not only provided a traditional 'treatment' clinic, but also provided an 'inspection' clinic that screened all school children at varying times for both incipient and manifest disease, and enabled visits to children's homes by the school nurse to report on conditions and monitor progress (HMSO 1975).

In parallel with the intensive surveillance of the body of the infant during the early twentieth century, the new medical gaze also turned to focus on the unformed mind of the child. As with physical development, psychological growth was construed as inherently problematic, precariously normal. The initial solution was for psychological well-being to be monitored and its abnormal forms identified. (The contemporary work of Freud that located adult psychopathology in early childhood experience can be seen as part of this approach.) The nervous child, the delicate child, the eneuretic child, the neuropathic child, the maladjusted child, the difficult child, the neurotic child, the over-sensitive child, the unstable child and the solitary child, all emerged as a new way of seeing a potentially hazardous normal childhood (Armstrong 1983, Rose 1985, 1990).

If there is one image that captures the nature of the machinery of observation that surrounded the child in those early decades of the twentieth century, it might well be the height and weight growth chart. Such charts contain a series of gently curving lines, each one representing the growth trajectory of a population of children. Each line marked the 'normal' experience of a child who started his or her development at the beginning of the line. Thus, every child could be assigned a place on the chart and, with successive plots, given a personal trajectory. But the individual trajectory only existed in a context of general population trajectories: the child was unique yet uniqueness could only be read from a composition which summed the unique features of all children. A test of normal growth assumed the possibility of abnormal growth, yet how, from knowledge of other children's growth, could the boundaries of normality be identified? When was a single point on the growth and weight chart, to which the sick child was reduced, to be interpreted as abnormal? Abnormality was a relative phenomenon. A child was abnormal with reference to other children, and even then only by degrees. In effect, the growth charts were significant for distributing the body of the child in a field delineated not by the absolute categories of physiology and pathology, but by the characteristics of the normal population.

The socio-medical survey, first introduced during World War II to assess the perceived health status of the population, represented the recruitment to medicine of an efficient technical tool that both measured and reaffirmed the extensiveness of morbidity. The survey revealed the ubiquity of illness, that health was simply a precarious state. The postwar fascination with the weakening person-patient interface – such as in the notion of the clinical iceberg which revealed that most illness lay outside of health care provision (Last 1963), or of illness behaviour which showed that people experience symptoms most days of their lives yet very few were taken to the doctor (Mechanic and Volkart 1960) – was evidence that the patient was inseparable from the person because all persons were becoming patients.

The survey also demanded alternative ways of measuring illness that would encompass nuances of variation from some community-based idea of the normal. Hence the development of health profile questionnaires, subjective health measures, and other survey instruments with which to identify the proto-illness and its sub-clinical manifestations, and latterly the increasing importance of qualitative methodologies that best capture illness as an experience rather than as a lesion (Fitzpatrick *et al.* 1984).

The results of the socio-medical survey threw into relief the important distinction between the biomedical model's binary separation of health and disease, and the survey's continuous distribution of variables throughout the population. The survey classified bodies on a continuum: there were no inherent distinctions between a body at one end and one at the other, their only differences were the spaces that separated them. (Perhaps the celebrated debate between Pickering and Platt on whether blood pressure was bimodally or continuously distributed in the population was another manifestation of this disharmony between alternative ways of reading the nature of illness (Pickering 1962)). The referent external to the population under study, which had for almost two centuries governed the analysis of bodies, was replaced by the relative positions of all bodies. Surveillance Medicine fixed on these gaps between people to establish that everyone was normal yet no-one was truly healthy.

For a long time, in the past, death came in the shape of a black-cloaked figure to mark the end of life: such deaths were natural in as much as it was nature that came to reclaim her own. The advent of Hospital Medicine two hundred years ago transformed the natural death into the pathological one (Foucault 1973). Death did not come from outside life, but was contained within life from the moment of birth – or, more correctly, conception – as physiological and pathological processes battled for supremacy. (Though it took biomedicine nearly a century to abolish the designation of death from 'natural causes' (Smith 1979)). Since the 1960s, the analysis of death has again shifted. Medical professionals are now encouraged to persuade the dying to speak the truth about their death to the listening ear (Armstrong 1987). The surveillance machinery is trained to hear the anxieties of the dying and through reflection normalise them: the natural death, the pathological death, and now the normal death.

Dissemination of intervention

The blurring of the distinction between health and illness, between the normal and the pathological, meant that health care intervention could no longer focus almost exclusively on the body of the patient in the hospital bed. Medical surveillance would have to leave the hospital and penetrate into the wider population.

The new 'social' diseases of the early twentieth century – tuberculosis, venereal disease, problems of childhood, the neuroses, etc – were the initial targets for novel forms of health care, but the main expansion in the techniques of monitoring occurred after World War II when an emphasis on comprehensive health care, and primary and community care, underpinned the deployment of explicit surveillance services such as screening and health promotion. But these later radiations out into the community were pre-figured by two important inter-war experiments in Britain and the United States that demonstrated the practicality of monitoring precarious normal-ity in a whole population.

The British innovation was the Pioneer Health Centre at Peckham in south London (Pearse and Crocker 1943). The Centre offered ambulatory health care to local families that chose to register – but the care placed special emphasis on continuous observation. From the design of its build-ings that permitted clear lines of sight to its social club that facilitated silent observation of patients' spontaneous activity, every development within the Peckham Centre was a conscious attempt to make visible the web of human relations. Perhaps the Peckham key summarises the dream of this new surveillance apparatus. The key and its accompanying locks were designed (though never fully installed) to give access to the building and its facilities for each individual of every enrolled family. But as well as giving freedom of access, the key enabled a precise record of all movement within the build-ing. 'Suppose the scientist should wish to know what individuals are using the swimming bath or consuming milk, the records made by the use of the key give him this information' (Pearse and Crocker 1943: 76–7).

Only 7 per cent of those attending the Peckham Centre were found to be truly healthy; and if everyone had pathology then everyone would need observing. An important mechanism for operationalising this insight was the introduction of extensive screening programmes in the decades following World War II. However, screening, whether individual, population, multi-phasic, or opportunistic, represented a bid by Hospital Medicine to reach out beyond its confines – with all its accompanying limitations. First, it was too focused on the body. It meant that screening still confronted the local-ised lesion (or, more commonly, proto-lesion) within the body and ignored the newly emerging mobile threats that were insinuated throughout the com-munity, constantly reforming into new dangers. Second, techniques to screen the population have always had to confront points of resistance, particularly the unwillingness of many to participate in these new procedures. The solu-tion to these difficulties had already begun to emerge earlier in the twentieth century with the development of a strategy that involved giving responsib-ility for surveillance to patients themselves. A strategy of health promotion could potentially circumvent the problems inherent in illness screening.

The process through which the older techniques of hygiene were trans-formed into the newer strategy of health promotion occurred over several decades during the twentieth century. But perhaps one of the earliest experi-ments that attempted the transition was the collaborative venture between the city of Fargo in North Dakota and the Commonwealth Fund in 1923. The nominal objective of the project was the incorporation of child health services into the permanent programme of the health department and public school system (Brown 1929) and an essential component of this plan was the introduction of health education in Fargo's schools, supervised by

Maud Brown. Brown's campaign was, she wrote, 'an attempt to secure the instant adoption by every child of a completely adequate program of health behaviour'. (Brown 1929: 19)

Prior to 1923 the state had required that elements of personal hygiene he taught in Fargo's schools 'but there was no other deliberately planned link between the study of physical well-being and the realization of physical well-being'. The Commonwealth Fund project was a two pronged strategy. While the classroom was the focus for a systematic campaign of health behaviour, a periodic medical and dental examination both justified and monitored the educational intervention. In effect 'health teaching, health supervision and their effective coordination' were linked together. In Fargo 'health teaching departed from the hygiene textbook, and after a vitalizing change, found its way back to the textbook'. (Brown 1929: 19) From its insistence on four hours of physical exercises a day – two of them outdoors – to its concern with the mental maturation of the child, Fargo represented the realisation of a new public health dream of surveillance in which everyone is brought into the vision of the benevolent eye of medicine through the medicalisation of everyday life.

After World War II this approach began to be deployed with more vigour in terms of a strategy of health promotion. Concerns with diet, exercise, stress, sex, etc, become the vehicles for encouraging the community to survey itself. The ultimate triumph of Surveillance Medicine would be its internalisation by all the population.

The tactics of Hospital Medicine have been those of exile and enclosure. The lesion marked out those who were different in a great binary system of illness and health, and processed them (in the hospital) in an attempt to rejoin them to the healthy. The tactics of the new Surveillance Medicine, on the other hand, have been pathologisation and vigilance. The techniques of health promotion recognise that health no longer exists in a strict binary relationship to illness, rather health and illness belong to an ordinal scale in which the healthy can become healthier, and health can co-exist with illness; there is now nothing incongruous in having cancer yet believing oneself to be essentially healthy (Kagawa-Singer 1993). But such a trajectory towards the healthy state can only be achieved if the whole population comes within the purview of surveillance: a world in which everything is normal and at the same time precariously abnormal, and in which a future that can be transformed remains a constant possibility.

Spatialisation of risk factors

The extension of a medical eye over all the population is the outward manifestation of the new framework of Surveillance Medicine. But more fundamentally there is a concomitant shift in the primary spatialisation of illness as the relationship between symptom, sign and illness are reconfigured.

From a linkage based on surface and depth, all become components in a more general arrangement of predictive factors.

A symptom or sign for Hospital Medicine was produced by the lesion and consequently could be used to infer the existence and exact nature of the disease. Surveillance Medicine takes these discrete elements of symptom, sign and disease and subsumes them under a more general category of 'factor' that points to, though does not necessarily produce, some future illness. Such inherent contingency is embraced by the novel and pivotal medical concept of *risk*. It is no longer the symptom or sign pointing tantalisingly at the hidden pathological truth of disease, but the risk factor opening up a space of future illness potential.

Symptoms and signs are only important for Surveillance Medicine to the extent that they can be re-read as risk factors. Equally, the illness in the form of the disease or lesion that had been the end-point of clinical inference under Hospital Medicine is also deciphered as a risk factor in as much as one illness becomes a risk factor for another. Symptom, sign, investigation and disease thereby become conflated into an infinite chain of risks. A headache may be a risk factor for high blood pressure (hypertension), but high blood pressure is simply a risk factor for another illness (stroke). And whereas symptoms, signs and diseases were located in the body, the risk factor encompasses any state or event from which a probability of illness can be calculated. This means that Surveillance Medicine turns increasingly to an extracorporal space – often represented by the notion of 'lifestyle' – to identify the precursors of future illness. Lack of exercise and a high fat diet therefore can be joined with angina, high blood cholesterol and diabetes as risk factors for heart disease. Symptoms, signs, illnesses, and health behaviours simply become indicators for yet other symptoms, signs, illnesses and health behaviours. Each illness of Hospital Medicine existed as the discrete endpoint in the chain of clinical discovery: in Surveillance Medicine each illness is simply a nodal point in a network of health status monitoring. The problem is less illness *per se* but the semi-pathological pre-illness at-risk state.

Under Hospital Medicine the symptom indicated the underlying lesion in a static relationship; true, the 'silent' lesion could exist without indicating its presence but eventually the symptomatic manifestations erupted into clinical consciousness. The risk factor, however, has no fixed nor necessary relationship with future illness, it simply opens up a space of possibility. Moreover, the risk factor exists in a mobile relationship with other risks, appearing and disappearing, aggregating and disaggregating, crossing spaces within and without the corporal body.

In terms of secondary spatialisation Hospital Medicine operated within the three-dimensional corporal volume of the sick patient. In contrast, the risk factor network of Surveillance Medicine is read across an extracorporal and temporal space. In part, the new space of illness is the community. Community space incorporates the physical agglomeration of buildings and homes and their concomitant risks to health, though risks from the physical environment reflect more on nineteenth century concerns with sanitation and hygiene (Armstrong 1993). Twentieth century surveillance begins to focus more on the grid of interactions between people in the community. This multifaceted population space encompasses the physical gap between bodies that needs constant monitoring to guard against transmission of contagious diseases, such as tuberculosis, venereal disease and childhood infections. But the space between bodies is also, from the early twentieth century, a psycho-social space which is marked by the shift in the psychiatric/medical gaze from the binary problem of insanity/sanity to the generalised population problems of the neuroses (which affect everyone) (Armstrong 1979), and the crystallisation of individual attitudes, beliefs, cognitions and behaviours, limits to self-efficacy, ecological concerns, and aspects of lifestyle that have become such a preoccupation of progressive health care tactics.

A further important feature of the new population space of illness is its emphasis on a temporal axis. Hospital Medicine contained temporal elements but relied essentially on a cross-sectional nosographic technique: patients had to be classified according to the nature of their internal lesion so that appropriate therapy could be introduced. Diseases, of course, had antecedent causes and they had resulting consequences, but these aspects of illness were analysed from the point of the present: what caused the lesion that presented (better to guide therapy) and what was the future prognosis for the patient? The new medical discourse of the late twentieth century opens up this static model so as to place illness in a wider temporal context. Perhaps this analysis is particularly evident in twentieth century concerns with the problem of development, especially in its relation to children (and recently 'ageing'), but temporal concerns can also clearly be seen in the mid-twentieth century identification of the category of 'chronic illness' as a major medical problem; and it can be identified in the temporal space in which risk factors materialised. Risk factors, above all else, are pointers to a potential, yet unformed, eventuality. For example, the abnormal cells discovered in cervical cytology screening do not in themselves signify the existence of disease, but only indicate its future possibility. The techniques of Surveillance Medicine – screening, surveys, and public health campaigns – would all address this problem in terms of searching for temporal regularities, offering anticipatory care, and attempting to transform the future by changing the health attitudes and health behaviours of the present.

Illness therefore comes to inhabit a temporal space. Illness has a life history: from a series of minor perturbations that indicated its early presence to its 'pre-' forms, from its subtle indicators of being to its overt clinical manifestations, from its first appearance to the medical attempts to alter its natural history. The sub-division of prevention into primary, secondary and tertiary forms summarises the points at which medicine can intervene in the great new cycle of illness. The clinical techniques of the hospital had invested the three-dimensional body of the patient; surveillance analyses a four-dimensional space in which a temporal axis is joined to the living density of corporal volume. Pathology in Hospital Medicine had been a concrete lesion; in Surveillance Medicine illness becomes a point of perpetual becoming.

Reconfiguration of identity

The advent of Hospital Medicine not only signified a new way of thinking about and dealing with illness, it also marked out the three-dimensional outline of the familiar passive and analysable human body. From the primary spatialisation of illness that linked surface and depth, through the techniques of clinical method that celebrated the volume of that body, to its unencumbered observation in the hospital ward, the medicine of the Clinic defined and redefined a discrete corporal space (Foucault 1973). In effect, an identity was forged in the practical anatomy of clinical work.

The integrity of the corporal body co-existed with a form of medicine that kept illness and health separated by a conceptual and practical gesture; the dissolution of the boundary between health and illness under a regime of Surveillance Medicine implies a loss of that anatomical detachment. Identity then begins to crystallise in a novel temporal and multidimensional space whose main axes are the population – within which risk is located and from which risk is calculated – and a temporal space of possibility. The implication is that self and community begin to lose their separateness.

Thus, Surveillance Medicine maps a different form of identity as its monitoring gaze sweeps across innovative spaces of illness potential. The new dimensionality of identity is to be found in the shift from a three-dimensional body as the locus of illness to the four-dimensional space of the time-community. Its boundaries are the permeable lines that separate a precarious normality from a threat of illness. Its experiences are inscribed in the progressive realignments implied by emphases on symptoms in the eighteenth century, signs in the nineteenth and early twentieth, and risk factors in the late twentieth century. Its calculability is given in the never-ending computation of multiple and interrelated risks. Its subject and object is the 'risky self' (Ogden 1995).

The rise of a major new form of medicine during the twentieth century that offers a fundamental reformulation of the epistemological, cognitive and physical map of illness – and, it might be added, its very close alliance with social sciences – merits recognition. But its real significance lies in the way in which a surveillance machinery deployed throughout a population to monitor precarious normality delineates a new temporalised risk identity.

Acknowledgements

I am grateful to Jane Ogden for helpful comments on earlier drafts of this paper.

References

Ackerknecht, E. (1967) *Medicine at the Paris Hospital 1774–1848*. Baltimore: Johns Hopkins.

Armstrong, D. (1979) Madness and coping, *Sociology of Health and Illness*, 2, 293–316.

Armstrong, D. (1983) *Political Anatomy of the Body: Medical Knowledge in Britain the Twentieth Century*. Cambridge: Cambridge University Press.

Armstrong, D. (1987) Silence and truth in death and dying, *Social Science and Medicine*, 24, 651–7.

Armstrong, D. (1993) Public health spaces and the fabrication of identity, *Sociology*, 27, 393–410.

Brown, M.A. (1929) *Teaching Health in Fargo*. New York: Commonwealth Fund.

Fitzpatrick, R. Hinton, J., Newman, S., Scambler, G. and Thompson, J. (1984) *The Experience of Illness*. London: Tavistock.

Foucault, M. (1973) *The Birth of the Clinic: An Archaeology of Medical Perception*. London: Tavistock.

Jewson, N. (1976) The disappearance of the sick-man from medical cosmologies: 1770–1870, *Sociology*, 10, 225–44.

Kagawa-Singer, M. (1993) Redefining health: living with cancer, *Social Science and Medicine*, 37, 295–304.

Last, J.M. (1963) The clinical iceberg, *Lancet*, 2, 28–30.

Mechanic, D. and Volkart, E.H. (1960) Illness behaviour and medical diagnoses, *Journal of Health and Human Behaviour*, 1, 86–90.

Ogden, J. (1995) Psychosocial theory and the creation of the risky self, *Social Science and Medicine*, 40, 3, 409–15.

Pearse, I.H. and Crocker, L.H. (1943) *The Peckham Experiment: A Study in the Living Structure of Society*. London: George Allen and Unwin.

Pickering, G. (1962) Logic and hypertension, *Lancet*, 2, 149.

Rose, N. (1985) *The Psychological Complex*. London: Routledge and Kegan Paul.

Rose, N. (1990) *Governing the Soul: The Shaping of the Private Self*. London: Routledge.

Smith, F.B. (1979) *The People's Health: 1830–1910*. London: Croom Helm.

The School Health Service: *1908–74*. London: HMSO (1975).

The location of pain in childbirth: natural childbirth and the transformation of obstetrics

William Ray Arney and Jane Neill

Introduction

In 1926 J. Whitridge Williams located the pain of childbirth precisely: 'The pain [of contractions] usually begins in the sacral region and then slowly passes to the abdomen and down the thighs. In the early stages of labor it is probably due to pressure upon the nerve-endings between the muscle fibers; but in the later stages it is augmented by the overstretching and dilation of the soft parts, and becomes most marked when the head distends the vulva just before its birth.[1]' The 1976, fifteenth, edition of *Williams Obstetrics*, prefaced several tentative hypotheses about the cause of pain in labour and childbirth with the statement, 'The cause of the pain is not definitely known. . . .[2]' What had happened to pain during the half-century spanned by ten editions of Williams's influential text? Where did it go during the fifty years characterized by the most rapid scientific advances in the history of obstetrics?

During the maturational period of scientific medicine, from its formation during the nineteenth century until roughly World War II, pain, like disease, acquired meaning only within the confines of the body. Under the localizing and circumscribing informed gaze of the physician[3] pain was located at the end of a series of physiological processes and mechanical forces triggered by a stimulus, either a disease which had invaded the body or a force which impinged on it from the outside. After World War II pain derived meaning from its location in the patient's ecology, from its relationships to everything *around* as well as inside the patient. Pain was still experienced within the body, but since locating pain, attributing meaning to it, and understanding its 'causes' were much more complicated tasks under the ecological perspective adopted after 1950, obstetrics was forced to entertain new ways of 'treating' pain. Pain used to exist as an impediment to the obstetrically perfect, mechanically correct birth. It interfered with the work of the obstetrician. For a fleeting moment sometime around World War II women seized their pain and it became for them a signal of their active participation in birth. Very quickly, however, obstetrics reformulated its programme to take into consideration this new, subjective component of birth. Today pain exists between a woman and an experientally optimized birth. Pain is no longer something which necessarily must be obliterated. It is now something to be appreciated, understood, worked through, worked with, and above all *managed* in order to ensure an optimal childbirth experience.

Obstetrics revised its understanding of pain partly in response to the challenge posed by the natural childbirth movement[4]. Reformulating its understanding of pain was, though, only one part of a general transformation of the profession of obstetrics that occurred in the post-World War II period. At its roots the reformulation of obstetrics involved a reconstitution of the patient so that the patient–'object' acquired a peculiar 'subjectivity'. The field of medical power reformed around this new patient.

Early obstetrical work and the challenge of natural childbirth

The history of birth has three stages. Each stage is signified by a change in the location and meaning of pain. Before the rise of modern obstetrics in the nineteenth century pain was a natural and normal part of the momentous event of birth. Birth was a revelatory experience; a woman's pain in childbirth was to be read for what it revealed about her life. Modern medicine arose in opposition to pain and suffering. Obstetrics wrote its own mandate that the pain of birth should be obliterated. In the twentieth century, natural childbirth challenged the obstetrical treatment of birth and argued for the admission of the subjective experience of pain as a dimension of the object of medical ministration.

Prior to the rise of modern obstetrics in the nineteenth century childbirth was a social event and a moral crisis[5]. Women in labour were attended by women from their communities and by midwives whose principal function it was simply to 'be with' women in childbirth. An atmosphere of expectation surrounded birth, but the joy which probably accompanied most births was tempered by a degree of fear, for birth was a crisis, physiological and moral, through which women were destined to pass by virtue of their place in the natural order. Midwives and attendants might try to ease birth using rudimentary interventions to change a foetus's position or to facilitate passage through a contracted pelvis, but they had duties which went beyond the walls of the aborning room. They were there to observe a woman's behaviour for what it might reveal about her character and moral standing. All women suffered pain in childbirth, they knew, because this was the 'curse of Eve', the punishment visited on woman for her part in the original sin. But childbirth pains were signs to be read for other purposes. Unbearable pains might be a sign of especially low standing in the sight of God. If a child were illegitimate a woman might shout out the name of the real father at the acme of a pain. Behaviour under the inevitable pain of birth had to be read for what it revealed about a particular woman's place in the order of things.

For many reasons too numerous and complicated to describe here[6] by 1930 obstetrics had completely eliminated the traditional female midwife and the form of childbirth she represented. The obstetrician replaced the midwife as the primary attendant of childbirth and a new era in childbirth began. The early technology of obstetrics was a technology of domination and control organized around a mechanistic conception of the body. Texts spoke of the 'passages, passenger, and powers' of birth. Birth was a violent event with the forces of nature pushing the baby's head, which Ralph Pomeroy likened to a 'battering ram', against a resisting outlet[7]. It was a process where the foetal 'head has been pounding and grinding the muscle like a piece of steak is pounded by a mallet'[8]. It was a painful process that sent women thrashing about on a bed or around a room in an instinctive attempt to find a comfortable birth position[9]. Obstetrics formulated a technology that met the force and violence of birth with the force and violence of scientific medicine. Episiotomy, an incision in the perineum from the rear of the vagina toward the anus, 'open(ed) the gates and close(d) them after the procession has passed'[10]. Forceps applied prophylactically in the late stages of labour guided a baby down the birth canal following the path prescribed by the engineering-like drawings that originated from the eighteenth-century pelvimetry conducted in France, Britain, and America[11]. The recumbent position exposed the passages and emerging passenger to the view of the obstetrician who sat watchfully before the labouring woman. Obstetrical delivery beds were designed to immobilize patients so that they could not move their obstetrically important parts from the view of the operator[12].

Anaesthesia was one part of the armamentarium with which obstetrics met the violence of birth. Pain interfered with the obstetrician's duty to supervise and conduct childbirth according to the procedures established by early pioneers of the field; against pain obstetrics deployed a full array of techniques for dominating birth to ensure that it proceeded properly. In the middle of the nineteenth century Sir James Simpson used ether and later chloroform to anaesthetize patients during childbirth. In America Dr Walter Channing introduced ether into obstetrical work in 1848. Channing, like Simpson, met resistance from colleagues and clergy and had to argue his case for anaesthesia more on theological than medical grounds: '. . . there are clergymen who say it is a violation of "the curse of God" – if such language be not blasphemy – to mitigate or remove human suffering'[13]. Heated debate continued until 1853 when Queen Victoria delivered having used chloroform. That seemed to silence many critics and allowed medicine to offer pain relief to other women in labour and delivery. By 1926, Williams's text declared, 'except for a few who still believe in following literally the biblical injunction – "in sorrow shalt thou bring forth" – all intelligent women at present demand to be spared as far as possible from the suffering incident to the completion of normal labour'[14].

Obstetrics created birth as one-dimensional. Birth was, to obstetrics, a physiological process delimited in time. The informed gaze of obstetrics carefully dissected out the obstetrical component of women for a very short, obstetrically appropriate, period and submerged all other potentially threatening parts of women beneath a heavy veil of anaesthesia or under delivery table drapes and restraints. By using technologies of control obstetricians made the woman on the delivery table faceless so that women's heads, their psychology and their subjective experiences, never entered into obstetrical decision-making. Early obstetricians had transformed women into simply the vehicle for conveying obstetrical material – the foetus and the machines that would bring the foetus into the world – to obstetrically appropriate places.

Obstetrics tacitly recognized that birth was two-dimensional, that birth had a psychological, subjective, experiential dimension to it. It was just that, to obstetrics, the psychological component of birth had no value in the view of the obstetrician. Perhaps the psychological component of birth had *negative* obstetrical value since uncontrolled, instinctive emotionalism might interfere with obstetrical work that had to be done on the physiological component of birth.

Cast in these terms the challenge of natural childbirth becomes clear. Against obstetrics' position that the psychological side of birth had a negative value, natural childbirth advocates asserted that the psychological component of birth had positive value. They insisted, very simply, that a woman had a face, a psychology and important subjective experiences that deserved to be taken into consideration. Their proposals for the reform of obstetrical practice were often as simple as their suggestion that both dimensions of birth be attributed importance. They claimed, for example, that if women were positioned so that the obstetrical operator could see a woman's face birth would be better, not just in psychological terms, but in physiological terms as well. Grantly Dick-Read, the first major proponent of natural childbirth in Britain, wanted women to give birth in a position which 'allows a woman to see and hear her attendant'. He wanted her face to be seen because 'her wishes must be considered'[15]. The challenge of natural childbirth was simple: that a woman's wishes, her desires, her psychological side, be accorded positive value in the obstetrical encounter, that is, that the obstetrician look the woman in the face.

Grantly Dick-Read, whose book *Childbirth Without Fear* first appeared in 1933[16], argued that the dual dimensions of birth had their basis in the dual dimensions of pain. He felt that the 'mind' pole of the mind–body dichotomy had to be resurrected from the depths to which obstetricians had tried to banish it if the experience of pain in childbirth was to be understood properly and if pain in childbirth was to be treated properly. Pain may have a physiological component but, according to Dick-Read, 'Superstition, civilization, and culture have brought influences to bear upon the minds of women which have introduced justifiable fears and anxieties concerning labour. The more cultured the races of the earth have become, so much more the positive have they been in pronouncing childbirth to be a painful and dangerous ordeal'[17]. Society and culture label childbirth painful and condition women's minds to anticipate pain and then 'fear and anticipation (give) rise to natural protective tensions in the body. . . . Fear inhibits; that is to say, gives rise to resistance at the outlet of the womb'. Resistance causes pain because 'fear, tension, and pain go hand in hand'[18]. He was calling on obstetrics to recognize that the mind, conditioned by culture, played a part in the production of pain.

Dick-Read's view of pain suggested that psychology was causally prior to physiology. This view led some people to think that reducing fear would break the fear–tension–pain chain and that a woman could experience not just 'childbirth without fear' but 'childbirth without pain'. Work in the 1950s concluded that women 'were certainly experiencing pain . . . but they were nevertheless enthusiastic about the regime (of natural childbirth)'[19]. Physicians wondered then how women could give birth using techniques which caused them to experience pain, the old ubiquitous threat to obstetrical work and presumed threat to women's enjoyment of childbirth, and still enthusiastically endorse the techniques they used. Physicians concluded, 'There is a difference between *feeling* and *minding* pain'[20]. The two dimensions of pain were separate from one another. Women might experience pain but physicians had to ask, 'Can she bear the pain?, can she cope with it?[21]' A 1957 review of more than 100 years of research on pain concluded that the experience of pain has two components, the 'original sensation' and the 'psychic reaction component'[22]. Stimuli alone did not *cause* pain, the new view argued. Instead the stimuli had to be processed through the mind and given meaning, either positive or negative. If, but only if, the mind attached a strictly negative meaning to a stimulus would it be experienced as 'painful'. Otherwise, a stimulus might be experienced as pleasurable or as part of an ecstatic experience, or perhaps not even experienced at all. As one study put it, 'Pain and enjoyment emerge as two distinct, though related, dimensions of the birth experience. Social-psychological and medical factors are relatively independent of each other'[23].

Pain that is two-dimensional opens up new avenues to pain management. One-dimensional pain, pain that is the logical and necessary result of physiological responses to physical stimuli, has significance and meaning only within the space of the body. Pain occurs within the body, it can be located there by an informed gaze, and it can be stopped or suppressed there by intervention from the outside. Two-dimensional pain, with its psychological component, achieves meaning because of its location in the patient's socio-psycho-biochemical ecology. A randomized study of the effectiveness of one approach to prepared childbirth concluded, 'the woman's past experiences and present situation influenced her experience of childbirth pain [even more than childbirth education training]. The woman's attitude toward pregnancy and motherhood seemed to be of special importance in this connection'[24]. To understand a woman's pain one must know her location in the world, her relationships to everything else. A woman's past experiences and present situation must be assessed in order to know her present location properly. After all, the mind in the view of medicine articulates with and is influenced by the entire 'exoteric cosmos and its ecological processes'[25]. The woman's location in the cosmos – her relationship to social support, her relationship to her body which is determined in part by her understanding of bodily functions and physiological processes, her relationship to obstetrical attendants, even her relationships with her mother and father as manifest in her present attitudes toward childbirth – determines the significance and meaning of pain and her experience of it.

If, however, the significance of pain is situationally determined, the significance of pain, and thus the experience of it, can be altered by changing the situation, by changing a woman's relationships to everything else. Childbirth education, for example, changes a woman's relationship to her body by making the alien sensations of the contracting uterus familiar; allowing a woman's husband or labour coach to be present at delivery changes her relationship to social supports; delivering at home where medicine is a guest in the house of woman rather than in hospital where woman is a guest in the house of medicine changes her relationship to obstetrical attendants. All of these changes can influence the experience of pain and the experience of childbirth, but furthermore, 'treating' pain by changing a woman's location with respect to other components of the obstetrical care system may be more economical than the rather brutal regimens of care which treat pain as if it were located strictly within the body, as if it were one-dimensional. The dual dimensionality of pain opened up the possibility that childbirth could be treated differently than obstetricians had treated it when they assumed sovereignty over birth, and this was a threat of a very high order to the position and autonomy of the profession. This was the challenge of natural childbirth.

Obstetrics' response

Early obstetrics, like early modern medicine, treated the body as a machine and understood its work as the deployment of force against force. Even the presence of the obstetrician in the delivery suite was cast as a force, a shock to the system, which meets the mechanical forces of the uterus directly, causing them to subside momentarily[26]. Very gradually the profession started to change. During the inter-war years the circumscribing gaze of the physician which located childbirth and its pain in precise anatomical terms expanded to take the environment surrounding birth into consideration. The isolating gaze changed to a gaze of encompassing incorporation until eventually the woman's subjective experience of birth was incorporated into obstetrical decision-making and management. One sees precursors to this change in the period prior to 1950, and then, explosively, the profession transformed itself fundamentally, apparently in response to the challenge of natural childbirth.

Precursors to the transformation of obstetrics included a change in the perspective from which childbirth pain was to be understood, a move away from general anaesthesia to the use of local anaesthesia for pain relief, a developing sensitivity to the childbirth environment, and a change in the images which suffused obstetrical practice. All of these changes took root prior to 1945.

First, the perspective on pain changed. Joseph B. DeLee, in 1914, emphasized the importance of the *obstetrician* seeing the pains of childbirth: 'In the first stage, recurring regularly about fifteen minutes apart, *we notice* the uterine contractions.' He went on to say, 'These are appreciated by the patient as pain,' but that is only because, according to DeLee, all contractions are painful. There was a correspondence between contractions and pain documented by historical and cross-cultural facts, DeLee said, and to note contractions is to see pain[27]. Slowly, the perspective from which pain was viewed changed from that of the obstetrician to that of the woman. The use of scopolamin and morphine to induce an amnesiac state called 'Twilight Sleep' facilitated the shift. Obstetricians noted uterine contractions, but women experienced pain and the question asked of an anaesthetic was no longer simply, 'Does it control a woman?', but was instead 'Does it obliterate a *woman's recollection* of pain?' Williams, in 1926, did not recommend the use of scopolamin highly, but he described it at length. He said the drug should be used to keep the patient 'in a state of relative amnesia' determined 'by showing her some object, which she should promptly forget having seen, if sufficiently under the influence of the drug'. But in 1926, Williams still was tacitly asserting the pre-eminence of the obstetrician's perspective noting that there was no test through which the obstetrician could assure *himself* that the drug had been effective. 'The fact that we cannot promise a satisfactory subjective result to more than three patients out of four makes it apparent that the method is not ideal, and it is my belief that it will gradually fall into desuetude, or at least that its use will be restricted to a small group of neurotic patients, upon whom it is desirable to exert a psychic effect.[28]' Yet, by 1945, in the edition of Williams's text edited by Henricus J. Stander, Twilight Sleep had become more popular and moved ahead of the general anaesthesia in the order of presentation in the text, indicating the emerging importance of the woman's perspective in the experience of pain.

The subjective experience of pain gained even greater importance with the move toward local anaesthesia and analgesia and away from general anaesthesias which Williams and DeLee had both preferred. In summary of its position on pain relief the 1945 edition of *Williams Obstetrics* said, 'During the past decade we have been impressed more and more with the value of local anesthesia. . . . It is our definite opinion that where there is the slightest contraindication to general inhalation anesthesia, local infiltration and pudendal block anesthesia . . . is the method of choice.[29]' Clifford B. Lull and Robert A. Hingson, in a 1945 book called *Control of Pain in Childbirth*, applauded the change from an 'encephalic' approach to the relief of pain to an 'anatomic' approach, from obliteration of pain in the brain to the blocking of pain pathways near the site of stimulation. They maintained an interest in conducting a controlled delivery in which the patient did not interfere with the work of her obstetrician, but they recommended a psychological instead of primarily pharmacological approach to establishing obstetrical control: 'The patient in whom fear is completely controlled is the ideal one for the use of the anatomic approach. The one in whom fear is uncontrolled can be relieved usually more satisfactorily by one of the forms of general anesthesia or amnesia.' According to them fear could be controlled only by 'establishment of the patient's confidence in her physician and by the maintenance of comfort in her surroundings'[30], a principally psychological approach.

As a woman's consciousness, her subjective self, was released from the restraint of general anaesthesia, obstetrics' concern for the environment, that which influences a patient's mind and thereby her experience of birth, emerged. In 1945, for the first time, texts registered a concern for the effects of pain relief on the foetus's environment and on foetal outcome. This concern was part of a more general 'discovery of the foetus' as obstetrics' second patient that occurred during the 1940s[31]. Drugs passed out of the maternal organism into the now conceptually separate foetal environment and on into the foetus where they might have a depressing effect which could be augmented by maternal respiratory depression and decreased oxygenation[32]. Obstetrics also developed a concern for the external environment. Obstetricians were instructed to manage the environment and not just the patient: 'In the management of a patient who is conscious, much can and should be done to give her mental tranquility without fear of the outcome of her labor. This can be accomplished by a cheerful atmosphere in the labor room, which should be furnished much like the patient's own comfortable room at home'[33]. Texts instructed staff members concerning their deportment. Nurses and physicians were to talk to the patient 'along lines that have nothing to do with her present ordeal'. They must not speak or laugh in the presence of even unconscious women for 'oftentimes under the influence of these drugs statements are confused and are remembered after the drugs have been eliminated'[34], and 'laughter is frequently interpreted as directed toward her', the patient[35].

It is a minor point by comparison, but it is only after 1945 that obstetricians became concerned with the explosiveness of gaseous anaesthesias that had been so popular earlier. For the first time, obstetricians voiced concern over *their* environment. Even gaseous anaesthetics that were otherwise attractive received low marks in the 15th edition of *Williams Obstetrics* if they were explosive. Furthermore, texts expressed concern over the long-term effects of anaesthetic gases on pregnant women (and their foetuses) whose jobs required them to work in delivery rooms[36]. This collage of changes shows how obstetrics began to shift to an environmental-ecological orientation to its approach to birth.

Even the 'images in practice', the metaphoric terms used to describe obstetrical work, began to change. Using Twilight Sleep or gases, patients were to be kept in darkness and silence: 'the patient should be kept in a dimly lighted room, from which all noise is excluded, her ears should be plugged with cotton and her eyes shaded by colored glasses'[37]. As techniques of pain relief changed, as the patient's subjectivity began to emerge into the obstetrical setting, the patient was subjected to greater illumination and surveillance. The 1945 edition of *Williams Obstetrics* said it was 'essential . . . that the patient be attended constantly by a trained professional attendant throughout labor'[38], and by 1976 the same text, while not recommending that all births be electronically monitored, said, 'It is mandatory . . . that for a good pregnancy outcome a well-defined program be established that provides careful surveillance of the well-being of both the mother and fetus.[39]' The imagery of illumination, light, and watchfulness replaced the imagery of darkness and complemented the establishment of a 'cheerful atmosphere' in 'comfortable surroundings'.

Technical changes (changing from general to local anaesthesia), changing to an environmental orientation to childbirth management, and the concomitant change in the imagery of the profession, allowed a woman's subjective side to enter the obstetrical encounter. Subjectivity acquired expression, escaping from the confines in which obstetrics had been able to contain it previously. All of these changes created a highly pressurized situation in which natural childbirth provided a spark that demolished old approaches to obstetrical work. In the midst of the debris obstetrics had to reconstruct its approach to birth. In obstetrics' response to the emergence of natural childbirth we see the reconstruction begin to take shape.

Obstetrics, the profession, accepted natural childbirth surprisingly quickly[40]. Early studies done by the profession showed that women trained in psychoprophylactic techniques had shorter labours and a lower incidence of operative intervention in labour than untrained women, that trained women required less anaesthesia and less analgesia, that they experienced less blood loss, and that they had a lower incidence of gestational hypertension. They tended to experience more perineal tears, but they had no more serious complications of pregnancy than their untrained counterparts. Trained women's reactions to their deliveries, both psychological in terms of satisfaction and happiness and physiological in terms of convalescence, were better than untrained women's reactions. Babies produced by women using natural childbirth techniques were happier and healthier, too[41]. The early research insisted that women prepared under one of the natural childbirth regimens not only had a better time in childbirth, but also that they were better patients, obstetrically speaking. Prepared women just *did better* overall.

Critics were equally quick to rise as were those who endorsed the new procedures. Doctors, hospitals, and even nurses – the team member generally thought responsible for the 'caring' side of the medical care/cure complex – all erected barriers to the widespread implementation of natural childbirth practices. Reid and Cohen, for example, reviewed the obstetrical literature and concluded that there was no reliable and valid evidence that uterine contractions were painless, that there was no evidence to indicate that pain in labour is psychologically desirable, and that on the basis of the available evidence '. . . one cannot draw any conclusion regarding the soundness of the obstetrics of "natural" childbirth.[42]' They were right of course. As a 1978 review of the obstetrical literature on natural childbirth showed, most studies – even those done in the 1970s – suffered from major methodological flaws. Typically investigators did not randomly assign subjects to treatment and control groups, did not control the effects of professional attention given to treatment groups which might, itself, have placebo effects on pain relief, did not employ experimentally blind assessors to rate outcomes of treatment programmes, did not specify treatment schemes in sufficient detail to permit adequate outside evaluation of the work, and did not use appropriate measures of pain and anxiety[43]. But obstetrics has always accepted innovation on the most meagre scientific-looking evidence when it has been to its advantage to do so. This is exactly what happened with natural childbirth preparation. Just as with episiotomies, prophylactic forceps operations, and other innovations earlier, the profession embraced the innovation offered by psychoprophylaxis and natural childbirth, the critics had their say, and then the profession reformed itself to incorporate the new development.

The end of the old obstetrical regime was in sight once obstetricians accepted two-dimensional childbirth as a reasonable conceptual basis for speaking about birth and once critics realized that they could no longer use the archaic language of one-dimensional childbirth. Reid and Cohen were critics of natural childbirth to be sure, but essentially they wanted to work out a compromise in which obstetrical safety could be ensured while the psychological component of birth was given its due. 'Scientific psychology and scientific obstetrics are not incompatible,' they declared. For the time being, though, they had to be kept separate and scientific obstetrics had to be accorded more importance, but eventually, they conceded, 'Certain techniques may be developed which appear to abolish fear and readily establish confidence'[44]. Other critics of the period even started working out treaties that would divide up the obstetrical territory as the need for compromise became imminent. Clyde Randall, in a 1959 paper called 'Childbirth Without Fear of Interference', saw the possibility of a truce and said: 'Let us hope that the proponents of natural childbirth will eventually be willing to see their philosophic approach revolutionize our former conduct of the first stage of labor, and accept the evidence that actual delivery, even of the normal case, can be most safely accomplished by the prophylactic measures recommended by DeLee two generations ago.[45]' Women could have part of childbirth and obstetricians could retain another part, Randall said, in laying his proposal on the table. The antagonist's terms in the struggle – natural childbirth's two-dimensional birth – had been accepted by obstetrics and the only possible avenue left open to the profession was to accommodate the challenge of natural childbirth by working out a plan that met the demands of women while still preserving the obstetrical project for obstetricians.

Reforming a field of power

Developments in obstetrics permitted women's subjectivity to seep out of the confines in which early obstetrics had tried to place it. Natural childbirth, a development which straddled the border of obstetrics, provided the impetus which gave the subjectivity of women a voice, a very loud, assertive voice. Obstetrics was faced with a problem. Its field of power, constituted by the circumscribing, localizing informed gaze and characterized by practices of domination and control, had ruptured and had been rendered relatively ineffective. Obstetrics had to reformulate its field of power, which meant reforming its work to accommodate the challenge of natural childbirth and the self-assertiveness of women generally. By reformulating its field of power around a new patient-object, obstetrics would reconstitute its patient-object. The reformulation could occur because there was an important conjunction between the demands of natural childbirth and obstetrics' interests in maintaining control over birth. In fact, natural childbirth would be made a component of obstetrics' new modality of control.

Women wanted a sense of mastery and control over birth in addition to having a safe birth[46]. This is the message implicit in natural childbirth's reconceptualization of pain. Two-dimensional pain is pain that women can experience as their own pain, the pain that accompanies active participation in attempts to master a challenge. Just like Virginia Woolf's character Lily Briscoe, a woman artist who lifts her brush only to have it 'for a moment [stay] trembling in a painful but exciting ecstasy in the air'[47] before she could make the first brush stroke, a woman can now experience that painful but exciting *ecstasy* that signals to her that she is actively participating in the delivery of her child.

With natural childbirth women can achieve a sense of mastery and can, in fact, control many of the physical aspects of birth which had hitherto been strictly under the control of obstetricians. Obstetricians' initial hostility to natural childbirth and their frustration with women who wanted to use it arose from a sense of alienation from what had been their work.

> Obstetricians felt threatened in their authority. They were suddenly asked to relinquish a most rewarding role, namely, that of being not only the expert, but also of being the wise father figure, the all-knowing, benevolent friend, or even the lucky chap who was allowed to kiss and certainly be kissed by grateful young women, to whom he had just delivered a healthy baby. He was now asked to become a member of the team, to share his knowledge, and above all to become involved in a very emotional and significant event in a young couple's life, where *he* was not kissed at the birth of the child, but the husband was. And he did not like it. The great scientist became emotional and said louder and louder that he would not sacrifice his great skill to some emotional nonsense, such as keeping the family unit together[48].

Even members of the profession critical of their colleagues' reluctance to accept natural childbirth techniques realized that loss of obstetrical authority to the pregnant woman was at the heart of the profession's resistance. As a group of obstetrical specialists wrote in 1952, 'We believe that the few people who are criticizing the method have not given it a fair trial, or else may have had a deflation of the ego when they saw how successfully a patient could accomplish, with proper preliminary training, what a physician has been trained for years to do with all sorts of specialized drugs and instruments.[49]' In this criticism of their colleagues these obstetricians were calling on obstetrics to change by incorporating the demands of women into a newly fashioned field of medical power.

The task of the profession was to exploit the conjunction of interests that existed between women and obstetricians. Women wanted controlled births without intolerable pain; so did obstetrics. Women's methods of control differed from obstetricians' methods and women's demands were clouded (from obstetrics' view) by a veil of emotionalism and talk of subjective experiences which had never had a place in scientific obstetrics, but at the roots of natural childbirth appeared to be a set of interests consistent with those held by obstetrics since its earliest days. Women wanted a flexible system of obstetrical alternatives in which women's experiences of birth could achieve prominence[50]. But even this was not inconsistent with the ends obstetrics had in mind. For example, the Interprofessional Task Force on Health Care of Women and Children, founded in 1976 by five American professional societies, issued in 1978 a Joint Statement on the Development of Family Centered Maternity/Newborn Care in Hospitals that used language indistinguishable from language used by critics of obstetrics[51].

Obstetrics replaced the field of power characterized by domineering control with a field of power characterized by pervasive visibility that has the power (a) to extract from patient-objects those inner, subjective feelings, fears, and desires that might interfere with the achievement of an optimal childbirth experience and (b) to normalize patient-objects according to an optimizing, normalizing scheme laid out for them. Obstetrics reformulated its field of power to incorporate considerations of subjectivity into its management of patient-objects. Obstetrics used natural childbirth to create fields of visibility which Foucault has described as having this effect: 'He who is subjected to a field of visibility, and who knows it, assumes responsibility for the constraints of power; he makes them play spontaneously upon himself; he inscribes in himself the power relation in which he simultaneously plays both roles; he becomes the principle of his own subjection.[52]' Change the pronoun and you have an accurate description of what happened to women under the control of natural childbirth techniques.

Natural childbirth knows 'subjecting women to a constant field of visibility' as 'providing women with social support during labour and delivery.' Obstetrics recognized early the value of having women constantly visible and realized natural childbirth provided this service. Herbert Thoms said in

1951, for example, '"support" during active labor is the most important single factor in our program.[53]' 'Support' meant then as it does now letting a woman have as much privacy during labour as she wants, but making sure that that privacy is constantly monitored: 'As nearly as possible, we try to have someone with the patient during her entire labor, whether it be friend, nurse, husband, or intern.[54]' The woman remains in a field of visibility but it is a calm field in which 'activity and busyness on the part of those attending [the woman] are kept to a minimum.[55]' The guard, one pole of the power relation, need not be present constantly for, 'In a normal labor, the prepared couple are in control and can manage for long periods with intermittent professional supervision. They do what is normal and will call for help if they suspect anything is amiss.[56]' If the field of visibility (the provision of adequate support) breaks down, control dissipates and delivery becomes painful: 'A feeling of inadequate support from the midwives correlated with the experience of delivery as painful,' in one recent study[57]. Control can be reinstituted efficiently and without resorting to old regimes of control, though, by simply fortifying the field of visibility:

> We have on many occasions been called to a patient who has lost control
> toward the end of labor. She was crying out with her contractions,
> thrashing around on the table in the intervals, thoroughly out of control.
> But after talking with her for a few minutes, sitting with her through a
> couple of contractions, reassuring her about the progress of labor, we have
> been amazed to see this woman regain control, become relaxed and free of
> tension during the intervals, and bear down with her contractions with
> little evidence of the pain that had previously seemed so severe[58].

Subjecting women to constant visibility brings about the control of birth in the first place and re-establishes control if it is ever lost.

Making women aware of the field of visibility and placing them, in their own minds and for others to see, on what Foucault called 'normalizing grids of observation' are the tasks of childbirth education classes. Childbirth preparation classes are constructed in the form of a confessional: 'Classes encourage women and their partners to *air their concerns* ahead of time, and teach pregnant women and their partners many techniques that will help during childbirth.[59]' The 'work of worrying'[60] drives couples to classes and incites them to speak about their concerns so that they might find out where they fit on the distributions of possible experiences known to childbirth educators and so that they might find out what can be done, either by them or for or to them with their consent and participation, to optimize the experience of birth. Ideally groups can be tailored to the characteristics of participants. Just as the priest must tailor the penance to the person and not just to the sin, 'it would sometimes be desirable to educate separately certain women.[61]' Women who are less developed intellectually, who might be on the verge of neuroses, or simply women who have had one baby previously all need special instruction and special attention[62]. Ideally, as in the confessional, education and preparation programmes would be designed for the individual, and all of her individual concerns could be aired, accommodated, monitored, and controlled.

Natural childbirth controls women, but it acts reflexively to reform hospitals and change staffs as well. Usually, social institutions which provide services try to lay blame for failure at the feet of clients; they try to blame the victim. In the case of natural childbirth, however, members of the profession have attributed failure to the 'impatient doctor'[63] or to 'poor communication of the obstetric team' and 'lack of adequate and honest feedback between consumers and teachers.[64]' The profession attributed failure to the structure of hospitals and the care system:

> We have found the hospital the most difficult part of our natural
> childbirth technique. To make sure that nothing happens to the woman in
> the hospital to increase her fears or anxieties, to have someone with her or
> at her call throughout the entire labor, to arrange the hospital physically
> so that she does not have to be in close proximity to the delivery rooms
> until she needs to go there, to protect her from the behavior of the less
> disciplined woman who is making outcry, to instill into the hospital
> personnel the philosophy necessary, all these things are not easy of
> achievement and take a great deal of time and attention[65].

The hospital had to be reformed to accommodate natural childbirth, even if it meant rebuilding the entire physical space to include birthing rooms or to relocate labour suites.

Just as natural childbirth was powerful enough to move walls it was powerful enough to command reformulation of relationships among health professionals: 'Natural childbirth, with its emphasis on the normal and natural, on teaching, and on the development of good relationships brings together the specialists in the various departments of the hospital and helps to focus their skills and knowledge on the mother, her baby, and her family.[66]' Physicians and staff must change their attitudes to achieve Dick-Read's cardinal requisites for the obstetrician and midwife: patience, peacefulness, personal interest, confidence, concentrated observation, and cheerfulness[67]. To achieve this state requires that physicians and staff enter the confessional as the penitent as well: 'Teaching physicians to *become conscious* of their sexual biases and to *talk* about sexuality in a relaxed manner should ideally begin at the medical school level.[68]' 'The future doctor must have some understanding of the dynamic determinants of his own personality and especially of his *unconscious*.[69]' Medical schools must be made into instruments which incite doctors-to-be to air their feelings and desires and to subject themselves to normalizing distributions and technologies. If medical schools fail, regional perinatal programmes' evaluations of cases referred to regional medical centre hospitals or analyses of perinatal deaths in the region become the material of the confessional with the sins of the penitent known before his arrival. Perinatal programmes thus create an incitement to discourse, but they also constitute a technology for extracting confessions if other aspects of the system fail to work. The staff at all levels are encouraged to confess what they have done well and what they have done poorly, and they must pledge themselves to reform. Hospital staffs must be trained, educated, and subjected to systems of surveillance, just as women must be trained, educated, and subjected to systems of surveillance, in order to assume their proper places in the new system of obstetrical alternatives.

The new order of obstetrical power subjects women and staffs to its control, extracts information as necessary, and subjects all to analysis, location, and normalization for one purpose: that childbirth and family-centred care is seen to benefit all:

> For the woman herself, through education [natural childbirth] reduces anxiety due to lack of knowledge about the birth process. . . . For the married couple, it gives the husband ways of helping his wife and allows both to share in the birth experience. Furthermore, medical benefits including shorter labors, lower levels of medication and anesthesia in labor and delivery, and fewer operative deliveries have been claimed for the psychoprophylactic method[70].

All of the subjective aspects of birth and beyond become subjects of scientific inquiry. Maternal–infant bonding[71] and whether or not a woman should be attended by a 'supportive companion'[72] are elevated to the level of the scientifically important and medically real. No longer are they 'alternatives', the desirability of which arises from a woman's experience and her own desires concerning her child's birth, but they are scientifically indicated means for achieving the optimal birth experience. Even conceptualizing birth as a psychosexual experience is done with the goal of management in mind: 'In the *management* of reproductive behavior, the underlying similarities of all three [behaviours, *i.e.*, coitus, birth, and lactation] should be kept in mind.[73]' The psychosexual aspects of birth are fitted into schemes of utility at the psychosexual level, the economic aspects of birth are optimized at the same time, and all attention is focused through natural childbirth and family-centred care on the optimization of the obstetrical project at many levels.

Discussion

When pain was one-dimensional and birth likewise, surrendering pain to obstetrical relief from it meant surrendering childbirth to obstetrics. With two-dimensional pain and two-dimensional childbirth, submitting to pain management schemes in order to optimize and control childbirth means surrendering not just childbirth but the woman's mind, the woman's experiences, her subjective self, to the regimen of control. Women had not surrendered their lives to old-time obstetrics; they had just given up childbirth. Under the new order, women do, in fact, surrender their lives, the possibility of making themselves their own point of reference for the assessment of their own experiences. They surrender to an external order, an order in the construction of which women have participated. Yet beyond this key issue, this analysis of the transformation of obstetrics in the post-war period instructs us concerning the dynamics of change of fields of power.

David Armstrong, in his paper 'The doctor–patient relationship, 1930–1980' outlines the transformation of medical discourse which occurred around the time of the transformation of obstetrics under consideration here. Prior to 1950, Armstrong says, 'the body was held in and constituted by a field of surveillance from which it could not escape.' After 1950, however, the problem of 'compliance' and the idea of the patient as 'potential defaulter', a person who contains a 'germ of idiosyncrasy', entered the medical vocabulary. As Armstrong puts it 'the element of choice [stood] in contrast to the docility of the patient as conceived in traditional medical discourse.' Post-war medicine created a new patient, 'a "subject" imbued with personal meanings, constructs, feeling, subjectivity, etc.' Medicine has, according to Armstrong, created the subjective patient. He ends his paper with a quote from Foucault to the effect, 'power produces; it produces reality; it produces domains of objects and rituals of truth. The individual [the idiosyncratic, choiceladen, "subjective" patient in this case] and the knowledge that may be gained of him belong to this production.[74'

Armstrong's description of the reappearance and recreation of the sick-man, the subjective patient, is accurate and aligns exactly with the appearance of the subjective woman delivering a child. What is left wanting in Armstrong's paper, however, is some sense of why the transformation of medical discourse occurred, and why it occurred when it did. This is not a terribly damning fault since Foucault himself only gives hints as to what might be *causing* or facilitating the transformations in other fields which he so richly describes. In a description of a course he gave in 1970–71 he says, however,

[Discursive practices] possess specific modes of transformation. These transformations cannot be reduced to precise and individual discoveries; and yet we cannot characterize them as a general change of mentality, collective attitudes, or change of mind. The transformation of discursive practices is linked to a whole range of usually complex modifications that can occur outside of its domain (in the forms of production, in social relationships, in political institutions), inside it (in its techniques for determining its object, in the adjustment and refinement of its concepts, in its accumulation of facts), or to the side of it (in other discursive practices)[75].

This is a point of departure for considering the emergence of subjectivity in medical discourse.

Many changes occurred in and around obstetrics around World War II. The state threatened the franchise of medicine; the war itself affected birth rates and thus the pool of obstetrical material; war-time advances in technology and electronics improved monitoring devices and provided access to the foetus such as obstetrics had not enjoyed before; the place of women changed before and during and then again after the war; third-party payers emerged in the United States and the government established the National Health Service in Britain; the 'staged' conceptualization of pregnancy changed and a 'calculus' of pregnancy emerged; local anaesthetics replaced general anaesthesia as the pain relief method of choice[76]. In short, the medico-political ecology of birth changed dramatically over a short period of time. These changes had one notable effect: it *allowed* the subjectivity of women *to assert itself*; it created a void which could, momentarily, be flooded with the experiential aspects of pregnancy. Women seized pain from obstetricians and, for a short moment, made it their own. But then with extraordinary rapidity obstetrics mobilized a 'rush to knowledge' to analyse this new aspect of childbirth. Joined by social scientists who modelled the quality of childbirth experiences[77] obstetrics recaptured pain, relocated it so that it stood outside women, in between them and the optimal childbirth experience which could be achieved only with obstetrics' managerial assistance.

Instead of being purely productive, power, in this instance at least, was reconstitutive. Power does not produce *de novo* or according to some preordained plan; it produces reactively as previous fields of power begin to fail, and fields of power begin to fail when the wilful individual asserts herself/ himself against power. But, as this analysis of obstetrics has shown[78], power is *rapidly* reactive; it sees and moves quickly to reconstitute its object – the 'subjective' patient in this instance – in order to preserve the set of social relations in which it gains expression.

Acknowledgements

Much of the research for this paper was done on the senior author's sabbatical leave. Thanks to the Whiting Foundation, Guy's Hospital Medical School, London, and the Department of Community Medicine, University of Edinburgh, for support during that leave. David Armstrong and Bernard Bergen have made important contributions to this work.

Notes

1   J. Whitridge Williams, *Obstetrics: A Text-Book for the Use of Students and Practitioners*, 5th edn., New York: Appleton, 1926, p. 254.

2 Jack A. Pritchard and Paul C. MacDonald, *Williams Obstetrics*, 15th edn., New York: Appleton-Century-Crofts, 1976, p. 300.

3 Michel Foucault, *The Birth of the Clinic: An Archaeology of Medical Perception*, New York: Vintage Books, 1973.

4 As with most 'movements' there was no natural childbirth movement *per se*. A movement is a sociological invention used to describe, in this case, diverse strands of alternative approaches to childbirth that arose in Russia, Western Europe and Britain during the 1930s and 1940s. I use the term to cover both the psychoprophylactic school of obstetrics that has its bases in the experiments of Pavlov and in the hypnotic approach to birth first systematically developed in Russia and the romantic, educative approach to birth proffered by Grantly Dick-Read in Britain.

5 The best overview of social childbirth can be found in Richard W. Wertz and Dorothy C. Wertz, *Lying-In: A History of Childbirth in America*, New York: Free Press, 1977.

6 For this history see Jane B. Donegan, *Women and Men Midwives: Medicine, Morality, and Misogyny in Early America*, Westport, CT: Greenview Press, 1978; Judy Barrett Litoff, *American Midwives: 1860 to the Present*, Westview, CT: Greenview Press, 1978; Jean Donnison, *Midwives and Medical Men: A History of Inter-Professional Rivalries and Women's Rights*, London: Heinemann, 1977; Barbara Ehrenreich and Deirdre English, *For Her Own Good: 150 Years of the Experts' Advice to Women*, New York: Doubleday, 1978; Francis E. Kobrin, 'The American midwife controversy: A crisis in professionalization', *Bulletin of the History of Medicine*, 40 (1966): 350–63.

7 Ralph H. Pomeroy, 'Shall we cut and reconstruct the perineum for every primapara?' *American Journal of Obstetrics and the Diseases of Women and Children*, 78 (1918): 211–20.

8 Joseph B. DeLee, 'The prophylactic forceps operation', *American Journal of Obstetrics and Gynecology*, 1 (1920): 33–44, p. 43.

9 Edward A. Schumann, *A Textbook of Obstetrics*, Philadelphia: W.B. Saunders, 1936, pp. 206, 216; J. Whitridge Williams, *Obstetrics: A Text-Book for the Use of Students and Practitioners*, 6th edn., New York: Appleton-Century 1930, p. 377.

10 Pomeroy, 1918, p. 213.

11 DeLee, 1920.

12 William George Lee, *Childbirth, An Outline of Its Essential Features and the Art of Its Management*, University of Chicago Press, 1928, p. 275.

13 Walter Channing, 'A treatise on etherization in childbirth', Boston, 1848, quoted in Wertz and Wertz, 1977, p. 109.

14 Williams, 1926, p. 359.

15 Grantly Dick-Read, 'Letter: Position for delivery', *British Medical Journal*, 2 (1955): 850–1, pp. 850, 851.

16 Grantly Dick-Read, *Childbirth Without Fear*, 1st edn., London: Heinemann, 1933.

17 Grantly Dick-Read, *Childbirth Without Fear: The Principles and Practice of Natural Childbirth*, 3rd edn., London: Heinemann, 1956, p. 10.

18 Dick-Read, 1956, p. 10.

19 Carl Tupper, 'Conditioning for childbirth', *American Journal of Obstetrics and Gynecology*, 71 (1956): 733–40, p. 734.

20 Ibid., p. 735.

21   'Coping' with pain is a relatively new term. The literature of the 1950s spoke of women being able to *bear* pain. The physicians asked, 'Can women *tolerate* pain?' 'Bearing' pain connotes that pain has a life of its own, that it is still somewhat independent of the woman and her psychology. 'Coping' with pain seems more sensitive to the fact that stimuli are processed psychologically before something becomes painful. Women who 'cope' with pain may either 'bear' it, 'suppress' it, 'transform' it, 'transcend' it, or do any number of things to it. Coping recognizes the psychically internal character of pain. So during the 1970s papers appeared which had titles like that of Susan G. Doering and Doris R. Entwisle's paper, 'Preparation during pregnancy and ability to *cope* with labor and delivery', *American Journal of Orthopsychiatry*, 45 (1975): 825–37, italics added.

22   Henry K. Beecher, 'The measurement of pain: Prototype for the quantitative study of subjective responses', *Pharmacological Reviews*, 9 (1957): 59–209.

23   Kathleen L. Norr, Carolyn R. Block, Allan Charles, Suzanne Meyering, and Ellen Meyers, 'Explaining pain and enjoyment in childbirth', *Journal of Health and Social Behavior*, 18 (1977): 260–75, p. 270.

24   Per Nettelbladt, Carl-Fredrick Fagerstrom, and Nils Uddenberg, 'The significance of reported childbirth pain', *Journal of Psychosomatic Research*, 20 (1976): 215–21, p. 220.

25   N. Destounis, 'On teaching psychosomatic medicine to medical students', pp. 68–70 in *Psychosomatic Medicine in Obstetrics and Gynaecology, Third International Congress, London, 1971*, Basel: Karger, 1972, p. 68.

26   Williams, 1926, p. 253.

27   Joseph B. DeLee, *The Principles and Practice of Obstetrics*, 1st edn., Philadelphia: W.B. Saunders, 1914, p. 117, italics added.

28   Williams, 1926, pp. 362–4.

29   Henricus J. Stander, *Textbook of Obstetrics Designed for the Use of Students and Practitioners*, 9th edn. (of *Williams Obstetrics*), New York: D. Appleton-Century, 1945, p. 430.

30   Clifford B. Lull and Robert A. Hingson, *Control of Pain in Childbirth*, 2nd edn., Philadelphia: J.B. Lippincott, 1945, p. 114.

31   William Ray Arney, *Preserving Childbirth: Power and the Profession of Obstetrics*, Chicago UP, forthcoming, chapter 4. In the 1940s, for the first time, obstetrics used the term '*foetal* distress' to describe foetal bradycardia and hypoxia. The foetus became the second patient, new tools for monitoring the foetus *in utero* were developed, obstetricians became foetal advocates, and the field of 'foetal ecology' took shape. (See, for example, Pritchard and MacDonald, 1976.)

32   Stander, 1945, p. 430.

33   Lull and Hingson, 1945, p. 116.

34   Ibid.

35   Pritchard and MacDonald, 1976, p. 323.

36   Ibid., pp. 355–6, 358.

37   Williams, 1926, p. 363.

38   Stander, 1945, p. 411.

39   Pritchard and MacDonald, 1976, p. 328.

40   We do not mean to imply that all obstetricians endorsed natural childbirth and encouraged their patients to use the method, or even that all obstetricians allowed patients the opportunity to use the method of their choice. As illustrated

by the case of a friend seeking obstetrical care in Macon, Georgia, there is still open hostility to patient's desires to practise the Lamaze technique or other procedures recommended by childbirth educators. My (WRA) friend was so humiliated and infuriated by her obstetrician's reaction to her questions and requests that she changed physicians. She secured obstetrical care from a person who would accommodate her needs and desires, but she could do so only by driving one and one-half hours from her home.

Everyone has her or his horror story about mistreatment at the hands of modern obstetricians. But the statement still means what it says: 'Obstetrics – the profession – accepted natural childbirth, quickly.' Opinion leaders endorsed the techniques in journals, scientific investigations approved the techniques, and the small band of critics, some of whose opinions are discussed in the text, were shouted down and forced to retire to their private and clinic practices to deliver care in ways inconsistent with the direction the profession was trying to take.

41 See Michael J. Hughey, Thomas W. McElin, and Todd Young, 'Maternal and fetal outcomes of Lamaze-prepared patients', *Obstetrics and Gynecology*, 51 (1978): 643–7, or Niels C. Beck, 'Natural childbirth: A review and analysis', *Obstetrics and Gynecology*, 52 (1978): 371–9, for reviews of this literature.

42 Duncan E. Reid and Mandel E. Cohen, 'Evaluation of present trends in obstetrics', *Journal of the American Medical Association*, 142 (1950): 615–23, pp. 618, 619, 622.

43 Beck, 1978.

44 Reid and Cohen, 1950, pp. 622, 623.

45 Clyde L. Randall, 'Childbirth without fear of interference', *Clinical Obstetrics and Gynecology*, 2 (1959): 360–6, p. 366.

46 Anne M. Seiden, 'The sense of mastery in the childbirth experience', pp. 87–105 in Malkah T. Nortman and Carol C. Nadelson (eds), *The Woman Patient: Medical and Psychological Interfaces*, Vol. 1, New York: Plenum, 1978, p. 92.

47 Virginia Woolf, *To the Lighthouse*, New York: Harcourt, Brace & World, 1927, p. 235.

48 Elizabeth D. Bing, 'Psychoprophylaxis and family-centered maternity', pp. 71–73 in *Psychosomatic Medicine in Obstetrics and Gynaecology, Third International Congress, London, 1971*, Basel: Karger, 1972, p. 72.

49 H. Lloyd Miller, Francis E. Flannery, and Dorothy Bell, 'Education for childbirth in private practice: 450 consecutive cases', *American Journal of Obstetrics and Gynecology*, 63 (1952): 792–9, p. 798.

50 See the article by Seiden, 1978, for example.

51 Interprofessional Task Force on Health Care of Women and Children, *Joint Position Statement on the Development of Family-Centered Maternity/Newborn Care in Hospitals*, Chicago: American College of Obstetricians and Gynecologists, June, 1978, p. 3.

52 Michel Foucault, *Discipline and Punish: Birth of the Prison*, London: Allen Lane, 1977, p. 203. See also Michel Foucault, *The History of Sexuality, Volume 1: An Introduction*, New York: Pantheon, 1978.

53 Herbert Thoms and Robert H. Wyatt, 'One thousand consecutive deliveries under a training for childbirth program', *American Journal of Obstetrics and Gynecology*, 61 (1951): 205–9, p. 206.

54 Tupper, 1956, p. 739.

55   Thoms and Wyatt, 1951, p. 206.
56   Jeanette L. Samsor, 'The role of the father in labor and delivery', pp. 277–80 in *Psychosomatic Medicine in Obstetrics and Gynaecology, Third International Congress, London, 1971*, Basel: Karger, 1972, p. 279.
57   Nettelbladt, Fagerstrom, and Uddenberg, 1976, p. 220.
58   Tupper, 1956, p. 735.
59   Susan G. Doering, Doris R. Entwisle, and Daniel Quinlan, 'Modeling the quality of women's birth experience', *Journal of Health and Social Behavior*, 21 (1980): 12–21, p. 13, italics mine.
60   Doering, Entwisle, and Quinlan, 1980, p. 18.
61   J.-P. Clerk, 'Fifteen years of obstetrical prophylaxis in private practice', pp. 74–7 in *Psychosomatic Medicine in Obstetrics and Gynaecology, Third International Congress, London, 1971*, Basel: Karger, 1972, p. 76.
62   See Clerc, 1972, but also see H.A. Brant, 'Preparation of multigravid patients', pp. 78–80 in *Psychosomatic Medicine in Obstetrics and Gynaecology, Third International Congress, London, 1971*, Basel: Karger, 1972.
63   Tupper, 1956, p. 739.
64   A. Blankfield, 'Conflicts created by childbirth methodologies'; pp. 87–9 in *Psychosomatic Medicine in Obstetrics and Gynaecology, Third International Congress, London, 1971*, Basel: Karger, 1972, p. 89.
65   Tupper, 1956, p. 739.
66   Marion D. Laird and Margaret Hogan, 'An elective program on preparation for childbirth at the Sloane Hospital for Women, May, 1951, to June, 1953', *American Journal of Obstetrics and Gynecology*, 72 (1956): 641–7, p. 646.
67   Dick-Read, 1956, pp. 140ff.
68   Weiss and Meadow, 1979, p. 113, italics mine.
69   Destounis, 1972, p. 69.
70   Allan G. Charles, Kathleen L. Norr, Carolyn R. Block, Suzanne Meyering, and Ellen Meyers, 'Obstetric and psychologic effects of psychoprophylactic preparation for childbirth', *American Journal of Obstetrics and Gynecology*, 131 (1978): 44–52, p. 44.
71   See Marshall H. Klaus and John H. Kennell, *Maternal–Infant Bonding: The Impact of Early Separation or Loss on Family Development*, St Louis: C.V. Mosby, 1976, for a review of the scientific studies of bonding and William Ray Arney, 'Maternal–infant bonding: The politics of falling in love with your child', *Feminist Studies*, 6 (1980): 547–70, for a critique.
72   Roberto Sousa, John Kennell, Marshall Klaus, Steven Robertson, and Juan Urrutia, 'The effect of a supportive companion on perinatal problems, length of labor, and mother infant interaction', *New England Journal of Medicine*, 303 (1980): 597–600. Many of the same criticisms, methodological and political, of the bonding literature developed in Arney, 1980, apply to this recent research.
73   Niles Newton, 'Interrelationships between sexual responsiveness, birth and breast feeding', pp. 77–98 in Joseph Zubin and John Money (eds), *Contemporary Sexual Behavior: Critical Issues in the 1970s*, Baltimore: Johns Hopkins University Press, 1973, p. 96, emphasis added.
74   David Armstrong, 'The doctor–patient relationship, 1930–1980', in A. Treacher and P. Wright (eds), *The Problem of Medical Knowledge: Towards a Social Constructivist View of Medicine*, Edinburgh University Press. Quotes are from the unpublished manuscript. Final quote is from Foucault, 1977, 194.

75 Michel Foucault, 'History of systems of thought: Summary of a course given at Collège de France – 1970–1971', pp. 199–204 in Donald F. Bouchard (ed.), *Language, Counter-Memory, Practice: Selected Essays and Interviews by Michel Foucault*, Ithaca, NY: Cornell University Press, 1977, p. 200.

76 See Arney, *Preserving Childbirth*, for a fuller description of these changes.

77 See, for example, Doering, Entwisle, and Quinlan, 1980, or Norr, Block, *et al.*, 1977. These papers present path analytic models of the childbirth experience. Even though the models are constructed from cross-sectional data, they have a temporal, processual character to them. Some analysts, the authors of these two articles included, use path analytic models to develop dynamic explanations of behaviour that can be used to design behavioural management and experience optimizing schemes.

78 Again, we must add this caveat for this is a study of obstetrics. The 'modes of transformation' of discursive practices must be discovered in individual empirical studies and generalization must proceed only with utmost caution.

2.3

Doctors on the medical profession
Deborah Lupton

Introduction

> When I was young, we were as poor as church mice and we were living in a country town. And there was a sort of a holy trinity: there was the headmaster of the school and the bank manager and the local GP – 'God almighty', you know! And it would not matter what sort of clod he was, he was 'Doctor'. When I was a very small child, if my grandparents, for example, had cause to call 'Doctor', the thing to do was to put out a fresh towel and a fresh cake of soap and a basin and bring in water for 'Doctor'. (Joan, 63-year-old medical practitioner)

Over the past two to three decades, there has been a continuing debate in the sociological literature over whether or not medical practitioners are becoming 'deprofessionalised' or 'proletarianised' and therefore losing their privileged social status and political power. Writers such as Haug (1976, 1988), McKinlay and Arches (1985) and McKinlay and Stoeckle (1988) have contended that there is a trend towards the deskilling of doctors, associated with the growth of bureaucratic organisation limiting their autonomy, the provision of salaries to medical staff and the fragmentation of the profession because of the increasing number of sub-specialty societies. These factors, they argued, combined with a continuing over-supply of medical practitioners, the emergence of the patient consumerist movement and better education among lay people, have contributed to the erosion of the traditional power of doctors and an increase in their economic vulnerability and alienation in the workforce.

These writers are commenting on medicine in the United States, where the medical care system has undergone certain changes that are not necessarily shared by other western countries, at least to the same extent. Indeed, not all sociologists have agreed with their diagnoses even in relation to the American situation. Other commentators (see, e.g. Freidson 1993, Light 1993) have preferred to retain the 'medical dominance' thesis, arguing that despite evidence of changes in the working conditions of doctors, these have not been substantial enough to support the thesis that doctors' status and authority have significantly diminished.

In Britain, the questioning of medical authority and expertise has increased markedly since the early 1980s, intensifying as debates over the future of the National Health Service (NHS) gain momentum (Armstrong 1990, Larkin 1993). There has been a dramatic increase of late in malpractice litigation (Annandale 1989) and patient complaints (Nettleton and Harding 1994). So too, there is evidence of increasing media coverage challenging medical knowledge and technology (Kelleher *et al.* 1994: xvi, Bury and Gabe 1994), and cases of sexual misconduct perpetrated by doctors on their patients are gleefully reported in lurid detail by the British tabloid press (Bradbury *et al.* 1955). Elston (1991) points out that doctors in Britain currently have less economic autonomy under the NHS than those in the United States. Despite this, she argues, British doctors have enjoyed a high level of some aspects of professional autonomy and dominance. Further, there is little evidence that British patients are relinquishing notions of faith and confidence in their doctors (see also Calnan 1988, Calnan and Gabe 1991).

In Australia, as in other western countries, there is evidence of an increasing cynicism towards the expert knowledge of medicine. As in the United States and Britain, media representations of the medical profession in Australia have veered from portraying doctors as the saint-like saviour of lives or restorer of good health (particularly if they are surgeons), to criticising doctors for medical negligence, avarice and sexual harassment (Lupton and Chapman 1991, Chapman and Lupton 1994). It is a moot point, however, to what extent the status of medical practitioners in Australia has been diminished, or lay people's attitudes have changed towards the profession. The Australian health-care system is currently partially funded by the government under the national health insurance scheme Medicare, which partially refunds patients for medical consultations and hospital treatment. Within this system, the medical profession is still characterised by a high level of personal autonomy over members' working conditions, authority bestowed by scientific knowledge and a position as 'experts' on medical matters, and political lobbying power through organisations such as the Australian Medical Association (Willis 1988, 1993).

Sociological research has suggested that while some Australians, particularly those who are themselves from professional occupations or are tertiary-educated, have become more demanding and 'consumeristic', many prefer to retain a sense of trust and faith in the expertise and integrity of their doctors (Lupton *et al.* 1991, Lupton 1997a). While there is evidence that complaints about doctors are rising (Willis 1993: 113) and that Australians are turning in greater numbers towards alternative therapists for health care, they are likely to combine this treatment with orthodox biomedical consultations (Australian Bureau of Statistics 1992, Lloyd *et al.* 1993, Lupton 1997a). Public opinion polls conducted in Australia still suggest that medical practitioners receive the highest ranking of any other occupation in terms of public esteem and social status (Willis 1993: 109).

What do doctors themselves make of these debates? Do they feel as if their status has fallen in recent times and that patients are becoming more confrontational? While there is a plethora of research currently directed at measuring 'patient satisfaction' with medical care (see Buetow 1995, Meredith 1993) and numerous insightful ethnographies of medical work have been published (see, *e.g.* recent book-length studies by Fox 1992, Atkinson 1995), surprisingly little sociological research has sought to investigate directly the 'satisfaction' of medical practitioners, or their opinions about their working lives and social status. To address these issues in greater detail and depth, using qualitative research methods, a multi-dimensional study exploring the status of medical practitioners in contemporary Australian society was conducted in 1994–95. The study combined analysis of media representations of the medical profession with one-to-one interviews with 60 lay people and 20 medical practitioners living in Sydney. The present discussion focuses on the data from interviews with the medical practitioners (see Lupton 1996, 1997a for detailed discussion of findings from the lay people's interview data).

The study

The doctors were recruited into the study by a combination of methods, which included use of a university department in which they were undertaking post-graduate study, and of doctors' societies. Limited snowball sampling was also employed. The decision was made to limit the doctor group to 20 because of resource constraints, but the eventual participants were, by design, a diverse group. Their practices were in areas of Sydney ranging from highly socio-economically disadvantaged, including a high proportion of clientele from non-English-speaking backgrounds and the long-term unemployed, to the most wealthy suburbs. The younger doctors had been practising medicine for a matter of months or years; the older doctors had been in practice for decades (two had been practising for at least 40 years). They ranged in age from 24 to 63 years: four of the doctors were aged 30 or less, 10 were aged between 31 and 49 and six were aged 50 or older. Half were Australian born of Anglo–Celtic ethnicity, a further four doctors were of non-English-speaking European ethnicity, three had been born in England, two were of Asian ethnicity and one reported mixed Asian and European parentage. (See the Appendix for socio-demographic details of the participants.)

The participants were asked a series of questions in a semi-structured individual interview that was audio-taped and later transcribed in full. The interviews were carried out in early to mid-1995. They ranged in length from about 30 minutes to well over an hour, with most lasting approximately 45 minutes. The interview questions were designed to be reasonably open-ended and general, allowing the participants to expand upon their opinions and experiences. Amongst other issues, the participants were asked to comment on what the general public currently thought of doctors, whether in their own experience patients are more demanding now than in the past (giving examples from their practice), whether the status of members of the medical profession had changed in recent times and the ways in which the participants would characterise a 'good' and a 'bad' doctor.

The interview transcripts were analysed for recurring discourses and themes, or patterned ways of articulating experiences and points of view and conveying meaning, as well as contradictions in the ways that the participants discussed these issues. The present discussion focuses on three major aspects relating to the social position and professional experiences of doctors in contemporary Australian society: the participants' views on changes in the status of the medical profession, the impact of consumerism on their work and their notions of what is a good doctor.

Changes in the status of the medical profession

Most of the doctors who were interviewed, particularly the general practitioners (GPs), stated their opinion that the status of the medical profession had diminished in recent years and that patients had become more demanding and more likely to want a second opinion. The participants commonly made references to the notion of doctors as 'god-like' and 'on a pedestal' to refer to the public's view in previous times:

I remember when I was a little kid, you know, when my parents would take us to the doctor's, it was always 'We're going to see "Dr So and So"'. And 'Dr So and So' was always a man, usually an older man. Nowadays my mother calls her general practitioner Suzanne, she refers to her as Suzanne, she never calls her Dr Ramsay. And I think people are starting to see doctors more as just people that have specific skills rather than as being like some pedestal-like authoritarian figure (Rebecca).

I think there has been a change, probably a general change, where (inappropriately, I feel), doctors were once put up on some sort of pedestal or thought to be some sort of demi gods. And as our society becomes more accountable, I think that image of doctors and doctors' fallibility has come out more. And I think doctors have been removed to a great degree from that pedestal, appropriately I feel (Meg).

The major reasons put forward by the participants for these changes were better education levels on the part of the general public, a broad tendency of less respect towards professionals in general and more attention given to medical and health forums such as the mass media, including coverage of the failings of medicine and the mistakes made by doctors.

Some doctors had found the diminishing of the status of doctors so great that they were embarrassed to reveal their occupation to strangers. As Sean recounted:

I suppose for a period there, through most of the '80s, I felt embarrassed to be a doctor. I mean, you would go out socially and people would say

'What sort of work do you do?' And I seriously used to think to myself, 'Better not say I am a doctor'. You know, you would say something else, like 'health worker'.

There was by no means general agreement, however, among the participants that patients' attitudes had significantly changed towards the medical profession. A number of the doctors interviewed commented that they had not noticed a major change in their own patients' attitudes. A common comment made by these people was that while lay people's estimation of the medical profession as a whole may have diminished somewhat, they still tended to hold great faith in their own doctors. As Joan, who is currently working in palliative care, noted:

I think that if the man or woman has a reasonable degree of competence and a reasonably civilised manner I think 'my doctor' – in inverted commas – is regarded as a good doctor, but I think that doctors in general are regarded unfavourably. I think that they are regarded as possibly uncaring, don't listen enough, yes – perhaps unfeeling. But 'my doctor' – in inverted commas again – is usually [seen as] a good doctor, provided that he or she delivers, in the sense of produces, if not a cure, at least an alleviation of symptoms and has a reasonably pleasant manner.

Nigel, who is a rheumatologist working in a major Sydney hospital, agreed:

Well, I think that people still have a high regard for [doctors'] scientific skills and their integrity and probably expect a great deal of them. I mean there is some negative feeling from people thinking that their doctors just want money as well, but my impression has been that people don't usually think that their own doctor is like that. They think, 'Oh yes, there might be some money-grabbing doctors, but not my own particular one.' Because I don't hear many people complain about their own general practitioner. They might complain about someone that they didn't like or they thought only wanted their money. But most of them seem quite happy with their GP.

Nick, a young doctor who has worked as a locum in several areas, including rural regions, commented that he has noticed that patients' demeanour towards him is usually very respectful, demonstrating their awe of doctors. This is despite his own attempts to reduce the social distance between himself and his patients by being friendly and informal:

I think that patients are generally quite reverent, if that is the word. They are quite polite and show you a fair amount of respect . . . Just the way that they talk to you and the way they refer to you, you know, 'Doctor' this and 'Doctor' that, when I am probably trying to say, 'G'day, how are you going?', to kind of, maybe break that down a bit. But they seem to try, most of the time, to maintain that, that distance. I think they like that professional distance [laughter]! Well, when I try to break it down by telling a few jokes or something like that, they take a step back and try to maintain the formality.

Thus, while according to these doctors the general image of the medical profession as a whole may have become tarnished, few had noticed that their own patients were displaying less respect or even reverence towards them. Doctors may have been removed from their pedestals to some extent, but they still find that at the individual, interpersonal level patients often want and expect them to retain an air of authority and formality. The doctors' observations were borne out in the interviews with the lay people, where most participants agreed that they respected doctors' knowledge, expertise and capacity to cure illness and save lives, and did not necessarily want to have a very informal relationship with them (see Lupton 1996, 1997a).

The impact of consumerism

Notwithstanding the above statements on patients' continuing respect for their own doctors, the discourse of consumerism was commonly employed by the doctors to describe changes they had noticed in patients' attitudes. Several doctors who had been in practice for many years referred to somewhat of an 'evolutionary' change they had observed in their patients. For example, Sally, a GP and gynaecologist who has been practising medicine for 27 years, said that she had noticed over that time that her patients, particularly women, were becoming more assertive and knowledgeable, and more willing to challenge doctors:

Certainly yes, I think people don't see the doctor as the god, I don't think as much now, and they are prepared to challenge and question. And I think that is really healthy and I think doctors are having to answer to that and be less patronising and less domineering and less powerful. I hope that it is changing, I think there are trends towards that, particularly, I think, in the feminist movement and women are starting to stand up and say, 'No, that is not good enough.' It comes in then, into my practice, where women – I am really pleased – can say 'No, I am not going to take that, I am going to get another second opinion.' So I think there is more equality coming into the service and doctors are having to provide a better service and be accountable.

As the above comments suggest, this fall from 'god-like' status was not necessarily a negative phenomenon for the doctors, for it allowed them to encourage patients to see themselves as more responsible for their own health care and to avoid patients' unrealistic expectations of what medicine could offer.

It was observed by several participants, however, that not all patients were embracing consumerist approaches to the medical encounter. Some doctors compared patients and made comments on their responses in relation to the patients' socio-economic characteristics. For example, Meg, who said she had worked in both upper-middle-class and working-class areas of Sydney, remarked upon the differences she noticed between patients coming from different areas. The middle-class patients, she said, were far more demanding of both her time and information, asking many questions, while the working-class patients tended to rely far more on her judgement as a doctor and would say, 'Whatever *you* think, Doctor' if asked to make a choice: 'They want you to tell them, they want you to be didactic – it is quite different'. Clive, a doctor who emigrated to Australia from England some two decades ago, described how his first practice in Sydney's wealthy eastern suburbs largely comprised patients who made more demands of him than had other patients he had previously treated: 'Oh they just, well they expect everything even before you can begin to think about it, they expect it. You know, they expect you to jump and they phone up and all sorts of things, they expect an awful lot'.

Age was also identified as an important factor in the ways that patients responded to their doctors. Sally, for example, remarked upon the age difference she noted in her female patients, in terms of younger patients generally demonstrating greater knowledge about their medical treatment compared with the older women she sees:

Well, I see older women who are just typical and a very common question is – they have had an operation, a gynaecological operation – and they say, 'Oh, I had it all out.' And I will say, 'Well, what did you have out?' And they would say, 'Oh, I don't know.' So I would say, 'Well, did you have your uterus out?' 'Oh, I think so.' 'Well, did they take the ovaries?' 'Goodness knows!' They would not have a clue! And yet young women today, if you ask them what operation they had had, they can at least tell you what they had removed! [laughter].

A similar comment was made by Sarah: 'Older people have or still hold doctors in that still, same sort of esteemed position. Younger people are much more – probably more reality based about it all, but then a bit cynical as well.'

Nigel and Gerald, who are both specialists, commented that their own patients seemed not to be particularly demanding, usually allowing them to make the decisions. Given that they are specialists, they said, they find that many of the patients they deal with simply do not have the resources to attempt to 'take charge' of their condition. Rather, the patients most often would prefer to defer judgement and decision-making to them as the specialist, even if they tried to include the patients in the process. As Nigel commented:

> You know, a great deal gets written about informal consent and explaining options to people and so on. And I often set out for people what could be done. But I usually tell them what I think is the best thing, and if I didn't they would usually ask me, 'What do you think is the best thing?' And nine times out of ten they would take the option of what I thought was the best thing for them . . . But if it was serious rheumatoid arthritis, usually I tell people what I think is the best thing to do – partly because I think it is terribly hard for a person who is not a specialist in a particular field to weigh up all the pros and cons. And I think it is not, sometimes I think it is artificial to pretend that, you know, just a man off the street – say a fireman – can weigh up what might happen to him without treatment, versus two or three courses of action with different side effects and different degrees of difficulty. And I think a lot of people go to the doctor because they want the doctor to tell them what is the right thing to do, so I usually do that. And there would be one or two patients who would say, 'Oh look, what else could I do?'. But most don't.

Rebecca also pointed to the differences she had observed across patients. She had found that many patients still wished unquestioningly to invest their trust and faith in her as their doctor, while others appeared to want more information:

> There's some people that you just say 'You've got this – take this' and they're happy. And if you try and tell them anything else they sort of get that glazed look in their eyes. And there's some people that want to know lots and lots. There's a big spectrum. I find it very variable.

Rebecca went on to say that she noticed differences in patients' attitudes according to their illness. She has worked extensively with patients who have chronic renal failure and also with patients who have HIV/AIDS. She said that she found members of the latter group to be much more motivated and interested in their condition: they tended to understand the medical terminology and to ask questions far more often, whereas the renal patients tended not to engage in these 'consumerist' types of behaviours.

The doctors' views of patients, therefore, were articulated drawing mainly upon two competing dominant discourses. There was the 'consumerist' discourse, used most often to refer to specific groups: younger patients, middle-class or wealthy patients, patients with HIV/AIDS or consulting a GP for a relatively minor problem. On the other hand, the doctors also frequently drew upon the 'dependent patient' discourse, particularly in relation to those patients consulting specialists for serious or complicated health problems, and older and working-class patients. Here again, these patterns of identification of patient 'types' are consonant with the views articulated by lay people themselves in this study in relation to their experiences with and opinions of doctors (Lupton 1996, 1997a).

Qualities of a 'good' doctor

In the interviews both members of the lay public and medical practitioners were asked to provide their opinion of what qualities characterised a 'good' and 'bad' doctor. These 'templates' are employed by patients to shape their expectations and evaluations of the medical encounter and by doctors in formulating their own ways of approaching interactions with patients.

Like the lay people (see Lupton 1996), the doctors commonly drew upon the discourse of 'communication' to describe ideal professional behaviour, commenting that doctors should be able to draw patients out, to listen to their concerns and to translate medical jargon into terms that patients can easily understand:

> I think one of the most important things is to be able to explain in simple terms what is happening to someone and what they are to expect or watch out for. And of course, it is all about communication. You know, you always want someone who is technically good if they are a surgeon, and know their stuff, I mean that goes without saying. But in terms of a person living with their illness or getting on and managing life with whatever they can with whatever it is, understanding is just so important! (Sarah)

Associated with the notion that good doctors are also good communicators was the notion that they should also be empathetic, able to understand the patient's perspective:

> You have to think, well, this is a person just like me and they are going to be feeling pain . . . they are complaining and that might be annoying me, but they are complaining because they are in pain or because they are worried about the outcome of their illness (Nick).

> I think good doctors are good listeners and they genuinely are interested in people and their welfare. I think a good doctor has to be older than, say 30, because you haven't lived any part of your life. I mean, I grew up in a reasonably sheltered life, so I didn't really have any hassles and worries of general life. And I think unless you have seen those, and had a few heartbreaks and losses, you can't really be empathetic (Kristin).

'Bad doctors', in contrast, were described by the participants as dishonest, failing to listen carefully, unable to communicate properly with patients and being 'in it for the money' rather than to provide assistance to people. As Angela put it, a 'bad' doctor is:

> One that doesn't listen to his [sic] patients. One that can't be bothered to listen, basically. One that doesn't have a good medical knowledge. One that doesn't explain things to his patients properly, yes. One that doesn't gain a rapport with his patients, basically.

Other participants also commented that doctors should attempt to avoid patronising their patients, approaching them with a superior manner and not recognising them as individuals. John, for example, contended that 'you can't be forever didactic to patients. The worst doctor is the one who preaches to patients and has a prepared routine that they are forever giving to this patient and that patient'.

One noticeable difference in the ways that the doctors described their understanding of a 'good' doctor compared with lay descriptions was in relation to possessing current knowledge and equipment. The doctors tended to stress this quality more than did the lay participants, making such comments as:

> Well, I mean, a good doctor has got to have obviously a good level of education and being up to date. I mean you have got to be up to date to be a good doctor. You have got to be computerised these days (Clive).

> I think success in being a good doctor depends on your ability to keep acquiring and absorbing new information, new knowledge (Sean).

The doctors also referred more often than did the lay people to issues relating to the importance of being able to make difficult decisions in relation to medical care:

> In clinical medicine you need to be a judge of risk because all the things that occur carrying some risk. Doing nothing carries a risk, having an operation carries a risk, suggesting some other form of treatment all carries a risk. And therefore you have got to be well informed, and moreover, you have got to have that sense of risk. You have got to have confidence that you have assessed it properly. And yet you can't be impervious to new evidence or the fact that you may be wrong, you have got to have a backstop in place (John).

As Warwick observed, good medical practice involves not just medical knowledge but good judgement: 'it is still an art, despite all the whiz bang things that patients want . . . it is a skill, it is an art that you either do or you don't [have]'. So too, the doctors were more likely to make mention of the importance of follow-up care of patients: 'A good doctor has to be somewhat obsessional and follow all the steps of the treating process' (Nick).

The doctors' responses suggest that members of the medical profession generally hold the same kind of assumptions as do their patients about what is important in providing medical care, or what are the 'templates' of appropriate professional behaviour. While they may also have emphasised expert knowledge and judgement of uncertainties as important, the doctors typically articulated the importance of practising a medicine that was empathetic and involved good communication between patient and doctor, including the doctor being able to listen to the patient and being genuinely interested in the patient's feelings and symptoms.

Discussion

The findings from this study suggest that doctors are highly aware of and sensitive to changes that they feel have taken place in the public perception of their profession. Most of the participants in the study agreed that doctors were not considered quite as omnipotent as perhaps once they were. However, there were a range of opinions articulated by the participants as to how this had affected their own practice or how widespread or extreme patient disaffection with their own medical practitioners might be. There was little evidence of hostility towards the notion of greater consumerism on the part of patients among these doctors. Instead, their comments suggested that overall they supported a diminishing of the 'god-like doctor' image for more realistic expectations of what they could offer their patients. Several participants, indeed, were highly supportive of patients who wanted more information and had attempted to render the medical encounter less formal, sometimes in the face of patient resistance.

The female and younger practitioners were particularly positive about changes they believed had occurred in relation to patients' attitudes to their doctors. The type of medicine the doctors practised also appeared to influence their views. Those participants who were specialists (and who were also invariably older and often male), noted that they had found their patients to be still willing to invest faith in their medical expertise and knowledge, demonstrating little desire to question the doctor's judgement and authority. These differences may be attributed to a number of factors. Female and younger doctors, particularly if they are GPs, may present a less authoritarian 'front' to patients than older or male doctors and therefore find their patients more willing to act assertively. Specialists, male doctors, and older doctors, by the same token, may be considered more authoritarian and knowledgeable by their patients. Those doctors who deal with more serious, life-threatening or complex conditions may also find their patients less willing to challenge their expertise.

The findings of this study suggest that the 'deprofessionalisation' and 'proletarianisation' debate needs to move beyond its primary focus on macro-structural and policy issues, the relationship of doctors as a professional group to the state, to the micro-sociological aspects of the everyday experiences of medical practitioners at work. The range of responses expressed by the doctors in the present analysis suggests a level of complexity relating to their professional position that goes beyond notions of their autonomy as a professional group, the ways they receive payment and so on (although these factors clearly shape the micro-level of interaction and experience). So too, the data from the interviews with lay people suggests that there is by no means a general, unproblematic taking up of a consumerist or a more hostile position on the part of patients towards doctors. Again, the situation is more complex than this, involving ambivalence and paradox, a continual tension between seeking dependency and wanting autonomy, in terms of how patients think and feel about doctors (Lupton 1996, 1997a).

Developing a Foucauldian rather than a structural analysis of power relations to explore the 'deprofessionalisation' debate may provide a fresh view that goes beyond the notion of the doctors 'possessing' more or less power as a social group to an understanding of power as shared, negotiated, relational, situational and a resource for action: that is, the notion of 'power to' as well as 'power over' (Law 1991). Foucault's analysis of the medical encounter moves from examining the conscious, centralised forms of power at the state level to locating the largely unconscious techniques of power which are located in 'banal' institutions, such as the clinic, the prison, the school, and in the micro level of interaction within these institutions.

One major area of interest in relation to the 'deprofessionalisation' debate is the nature of the doctor–patient interaction and doctors' understandings both of what their patients want from them and how they conceptualise appropriate medical practice. An emphasis on 'good communication', empathy and the need to give the patient an opportunity to have greater 'responsibility' by sharing uncertainty has been a central discourse in both the medical and patient advocacy literature since the 1970s, particularly in writings informed by the psychotherapist Michael Balint's work (Balint 1957). It draws upon the neo-liberal humanist perspective towards the professions; that is, avoiding authoritarian and coercive approaches for a notion of 'person-centred medicine' and shared responsibility (Osborne 1994). More pragmatically, this approach has been a central feature of medical writing on preventing malpractice suits (Annandale 1989: 10–11).

Under contemporary understandings of what constitutes appropriate professional practice, doctors, as well as patients, are expected to be 'reflexive' actors in the medical encounter. Doctors are called upon to see each patient as different, as individuals with personalised biographies, and to shape their interactions with them accordingly. This involves not only the application of expert biomedical knowledge but working to draw patients into collaborative relationships, and eliciting and 'managing' patients' emotions as a therapeutic strategy (May et al. 1996). Under the new ethic of 'person-centred' or 'empathetic' medicine, doctors are called upon to exercise self-surveillance, to 'know themselves better' so that they might better relate to patients

(Osborne 1994). These actions are not generally undertaken in a deliberate attempt to maintain or exert power over patients, or alternatively to give 'more power' to patients, but rather as an ethic of professionalism that is seen to benefit both doctor and patient.

This suggests that the micro-politics and power dimensions of medical practice is somewhat more complicated than some of the 'deprofessionalisation' literature would have it. For example, does the notion of the doctor 'sharing responsibility' with patients and treating each patient 'as an individual' detract from or enhance their professional standing, status and job satisfaction? Who holds the upper hand in this new conceptualisation of the medical encounter? Some of those taking up a Foucauldian analysis have suggested that this new focus on communication, collaboration and the 'whole' patient is an ever more subtle operation of the 'clinical gaze' upon patients, reaching further and further into their thoughts, feelings and everyday lives in unprecedented ways (Arney and Neill 1982, Armstrong 1984). However, while the ethic of 'person-centred' medicine may support the need for patients to reveal more of their private lives to doctors, to know more about their condition and have more 'control' over their treatment and health status, patients themselves do not always want to do this (as some of the doctors in this study themselves noted). Even when doctors encourage patients to speak, patients may choose to remain silent, effectively 'paralysing' the doctor's capacity to act. So too, doctors may find the type of information elicited from patients (e.g. details of sexual abuse), difficult to deal with or beyond their scope of action (May et al. 1996). In other words, contemporary notions of professional practice tend to complicate the power dynamics in doctors' relationships with their patients in ways that do not necessarily involve a loss of professional status or authority but sometimes test the limits of doctors' ability to act, despite the best efforts of both patient and doctor.

The embracing of the 'communication' and 'person-centred' discourses, therefore, may be problematic for doctors' practice, even while they themselves may strongly support the principles underlying them. What is more, patients' own ambivalence about wanting to invest their trust in doctors, at the same time as being highly aware of the risks and uncertainties attendant upon contemporary medical care (Lupton 1996), presents a difficult situation for doctors to negotiate successfully and sensitively. As the present study suggests, doctors are highly aware that their patients' trust is now no longer necessarily won by virtue of their occupying the role of 'Doctor', but must be earned and worked at continually. It is rather too simplistic, thus, to argue that patients and doctors have contradictory interests or are engaged in a struggle over who may hold the most power. Changes in the medical encounter and the status of doctors are not just a matter of the state, patients or other groups 'gaining' or 'taking' more power from doctors, or vice versa, but involve a series of dynamic and interpersonal negotiations of power centred on the ethic of professional practice (Lupton 1997b).

It appears evident that doctors still understand themselves, and are perceived by the general public, as 'professionals', albeit bearing different meanings and responsibilities from previous notions of professional practice. As such, perhaps the debate could be reoriented, moving from examining '*de*professionalisation' to '*re*professionalisation', bearing in mind that professional power is constantly negotiated at the level of everyday practice as well as at the level of policy and organisational structure. Questions to be further explored might include how doctors are encouraged through their training and their experiences in practice to 'act upon themselves' reflexively, how they develop knowledge of and deal with patients' individual needs and expectations, how they seek to order a complex and heterogeneous set of practices, strategies and relationships with others as part of professional practice, and how aspects of medical training and practice are shaped and experienced in different spatial, geographic, economic, political and cultural contexts (for instance, in the hospital versus the private surgery, or in the Australian compared with the British or American health care systems).

Acknowledgements

Thanks are due to the Australian Research Council for funding this research by awarding a large grant for 1994–95, to the project's research assistant, Jane McLean, for her expertise in arranging and carrying out the interviews, and to the interview participants themselves.

Appendix

Socio-demographic details of the participants interviewed for the study are as follows (all names are pseudonyms):

Joan, aged 63, Anglo–Celtic Australian, practising for 40 years in Australia and Britain, currently in palliative care

Sean, aged 36, Anglo–Celtic Australian, practising for 12 years in Australia, currently a GP and politician

Rebecca, aged 27, Anglo–Celtic Australian, practising for two years in Australia, currently resident in a public hospital

Meg, aged 38, Anglo–Celtic Australian, practising for 12 years in Australia, currently a GP

Sally, aged 50, Anglo–Celtic Australian, practising for 26 years in Australia and Britain, currently a GP

Nigel, aged 40, Anglo–Celtic Australian, practising for 18 years in Australia, currently a rheumatologist at a public hospital

Nick, aged 29, Anglo–Celtic Australian, practising for six years in Australia, currently a GP

Clive, aged 57, Anglo–Celtic Briton, practising for 23 years in Australia and Britain, currently a GP

Sarah, aged 30, Anglo–Celtic Australian, practising for eight years in Australia, currently a nuclear medicine physician in private practice

Gerald, aged 42, Anglo–Celtic Briton, practising for 18 years in Australia and Britain, currently a colo-rectal surgeon at a public hospital

Kristin, aged 35, Japanese–Polish Australian, practising for 11 years in Australia, currently a GP

Angela, aged 24, Greek Australian, practising for six months in Australia, currently an intern in a public hospital

John, aged 64, Hungarian Australian, practising for 28 years in Australia, currently a GP

Warwick, aged 55, Anglo–Celtic Australian, practising for 32 years in Australia, currently a GP and dermatologist

Jill, aged 41, Anglo–Celtic Australian, practising for 17 years in Australia, currently an obstetrician and gynaecologist

Eric, aged 37, Jewish South African, practising for 13 years in Australia, currently a nuclear medicine physician

Felix, aged 46, Filipino Australian, practising for 16 years in Australia, currently a GP

Peter, aged 45, Chinese Australian, practising for 17 years in Australia, currently a GP

Bronwyn, aged 40, Anglo–Celtic Briton, practising for 15 years in Australia, currently a staff specialist in a GP training programme

Jennifer, aged 51, Hungarian Australian, practising for 28 years in Australia, currently a GP.

References

Annandale, E. (1989) The malpractice crisis and the doctor–patient relationship, *Sociology of Health and Illness*, 11, 1, 1–23.

Armstrong, D. (1984) The patient's view, *Social Science and Medicine*, 18, 9, 737–44.

Armstrong, D. (1990) Medicine as a profession: times of change, *British Medical Journal*, 301, 691–3.

Arney, W. and Neill, J. (1982) The location of pain in childbirth: natural childbirth and the transformation of obstetrics, *Sociology of Health and Illness*, 4, 1, 1–24.

Atkinson, P. (1995) *Medical Talk and Medical Work*. London: Sage.

Australian Bureau of Statistics (1992) *1989–90 National Health Survey: Consultations with Health Professionals, Australia* (Catalogue No. 4376.0). Canberra: Australian Government Printing Service.

Balint, M. (1957) *The Doctor, His Patient and the Illness*. New York: International Universities Press.

Bradby, H., Gabe, J. and Bury, M. (1995) 'Sexy docs' and 'busty blondes': press coverage of professional misconduct cases brought before the General Medical Council, *Sociology of Health and Illness*, 17, 4, 458–76.

Buetow, S. (1995) What do general practitioners and their patients want from general practice and are they receiving it? A framework, *Social Science and Medicine*, 40, 2, 213–21.

Bury, M. and Gabe, J. (1994) Television and medicine: medical dominance or trial by media? In Gabe, J., Kelleher, D. and Williams, G. (eds) *Challenging Medicine*. London: Routledge.

Calnan, M. (1988) Lay evaluation of medicine and medical practice: report of a pilot study, *International Journal of Health Services*, 18, 2, 311–22.

Calnan, M. and Gabe, J. (1991) Recent developments in general practice: a sociological analysis. In Gabe, J., Calnan, M. and Bury, M. (eds) *The Sociology of the Health Service*. London: Routledge.

Chapman, S. and Lupton, D. (1994) Freaks, moral tales and medical marvels: health and medical stories on Australian television, *Media Information Australia*, 72, 94–103.

Elston, M.-A. (1991) The politics of professional power: medicine in a changing health service. In Gabe, J., Calnan, M. and Bury, M. (eds) *The Sociology of the Health Service*. London: Routledge.

Fox, N. (1992) *The Social Meaning of Surgery*. Milton Keynes: Open University Press.

Freidson, E. (1993) How dominant are the professions? In Hafferty, F. and McKinlay, J. (eds) *The Changing Medical Profession: an International Perspective*. New York: Oxford University Press.

Haug, M. (1976) The erosion of professional authority: a cross-cultural enquiry in the case of the physician, *Milbank Memorial Fund Quarterly*, 54, 83–106.

Haug, M. (1988) A re-examination of the hypothesis of physician deprofessionalization, *Milbank Quarterly*, 66, supp. 2, 48–56.

Kelleher, D., Gabe, J. and Williams, G. (1994) Understanding medical dominance in the modern world. In Gabe, J., Kelleher, D. and Williams, G. (eds) *Challenging Medicine*. London: Routledge.

Larkin, G. (1993) Continuity in change: medical dominance in the United Kingdom. In Hafferty, F. and McKinlay, J. (eds) *The Changing Medical Profession: an International Perspective*. New York and Oxford: Oxford University Press.

Law, J. (1991) Power, discretion and strategy. In Law, J. (ed) *A Sociology of Monsters: Essays on Power, Technology and Domination*. London and New York: Routledge.

Light, D. (1993) Countervailing power: the changing character of the medical profession in the United States. In Hafferty, F. and McKinlay, J. (eds) *The Changing Medical Profession: an International Perspective*. New York and Oxford: Oxford University Press.

Lloyd, P., Lupton, D., Wiesner, D. and Hasleton, S. (1993) Socio-demographic characteristics and reasons for choosing natural therapy: an exploratory study of patients resident in Sydney, *Australian Journal of Public Health*, 17, 2, 135–44.

Lupton, D. (1996) 'Your life in their hands': trust in the medical encounter. In Gabe, J. and James, V. (eds) *Health and the Sociology of Emotion* (*Sociology of Health and Illness* Monograph Series). Oxford: Blackwell Publishers.

Lupton, D. (1997a) Consumerism, reflexivity and the medical encounter, *Social Science and Medicine*, in press.

Lupton, D. (1997b) Foucault and the medicalization critique. In Petersen, A. and Bunton, R. (eds) *Foucault, Health and Medicine*. London: Routledge.

Lupton, D. and Chapman, S. (1991) Death of a heart surgeon: reflections on press accounts of the murder of Victor Chang, *British Medical Journal*, 303, 1583–6.

Lupton, D., Donaldson, C. and Lloyd, P. (1991) Caveat emptor or blissful ignorance? Patients and the consumerist ethos, *Social Science and Medicine*, 33, 5, 559–68.

McKinlay, J. and Arches, J. (1985) Towards the proletarianization of physicians, *International Journal of Health Services*, 15, 2, 161–95.

McKinlay, J. and Stoeckle, J. (1988) Corporatization and the social transformation of doctoring, *International Journal of Health Services*, 18, 2, 191–205.

May, C., Dowrick, C. and Richardson, M. (1996) The confidential patient: the social construction of therapeutic relationships in general medical practice, *The Sociological Review*, 44, 2, 187–203.

Meredith, P. (1993) Patient satisfaction with communication in general surgery: problems of measurement and improvement, *Social Science and Medicine*, 37, 5, 591–602.

Nettleton, S. and Harding, G. (1994) Protesting patients: a study of complaints submitted to a Family Health Service Authority, *Sociology of Health and Illness*, 16, 1, 38–61.

Osborne, T. (1994) Power and persons: on ethical stylisation and person-centred medicine, *Sociology of Health and Illness*, 16, 4, 515–35.

Willis, E. (1988) Doctoring in Australia: a view at the bicentenary, *Milbank Quarterly*, 66, supp. 2, 167–81.

Willis, E. (1993) The medical profession in Australia. In Hafferty, F. and McKinlay, J. (eds) *The Changing Medical Profession: an International Perspective*. New York and Oxford: Oxford University Press.

2.4

The fracturing of medical dominance in British psychiatry?

Colin Samson

Introduction

The health service reforms instituted by the Thatcher government signalled a fundamental realignment of professional power and influence within the health and mental health services in Britain. Both the clinical base of psychiatry, the mental hospital, and the clinical autonomy of psychiatrists, have been assailed by these reforms which were systematised with the White Paper, *Caring for People* (Department of Health 1989) and culminated in the National Health Service (NHS) and Community Care Act of 1990. Although policy moves and professional ideological stances towards community care were made previously, this legislation confirmed a major government-led switch towards community, rather than hospital, provision which was sealed by the implementation of a political and economic structure – privatisation and contracting out. As part of this general process, a reorientation towards managerial, rather than medical, control over the organisation of mental health services was signalled. This latter is significant because the NHS had, until the advent of the 'managerial revolution', ushered in by the first Griffiths report, (Department of Health and Social Services 1983) institutionalised a dominant position for the medical profession. The end result of the extensive compromises made by the Labour government of 1946 in order to elicit the agreement of the medical profession was a privileging of medical status, knowledge and power within the health services (Abel-Smith 1964, Forsyth 1973, Klein 1983).

The concept of medical dominance, as originally formulated by Freidson (1970) and hinted at earlier by Parsons (1951), pivots around a number of observations as to the peculiarly favourable status of physicians within the health care system and the internal medical division of labour. The feature identified by Freidson (1970) as a chief distinguishing mark of a profession, autonomy, the right to control its own work, has enabled medicine, and psychiatry as a 'branch' of this, an extensive power base protected by the professional associations, the British Medical Association (BMA) and the Royal Colleges. Physicians have had great license to determine the time, character, and even emotional tone of their interactions with patients (see Strong 1979: 141). While they are evaluated by others, the skilled and esoteric character of medical work has traditionally sheltered doctors from lay interference. Besides this, the medical profession's presentation of its own role as being that of a public service has helped to make questioning of the privileges granted to it appear uncharitable and grudging. Finally, physicians are seen to be 'dominant' in another sense; they have been organisers, supervisors and regulators of other paraprofessional groups within the hospital and community health systems.

These features of medical dominance, I argue, do not necessarily apply to British psychiatry in the context of the reorganisation of health services. Community care, as a conduit for the shift from NHS provision to private, voluntary and local authority provision through the contracting out process, presents fundamental dilemmas for the profession of psychiatry since its status, power and pre-eminent role in treatment has been so closely tied to the authority structures of the NHS. Although never unquestioned within the mental health services, psychiatrists have been the most powerful group in defining illness, deciding which patients ought to be admitted to hospital and, if admitted, under which administrative and legal powers. Psychiatrists have also presided hierarchically over the professions of nursing, social work and psychology. Community care, by contracting outside the NHS, by bringing questions of resource allocation into play, and by imposing a base of knowledge which is in many respects non-medical, poses a potential threat to the traditional leadership and autonomy of the psychiatrist, and, by extension, to the continued utilisation of biomedical discourse upon which the legitimacy of the profession has been constructed. Biomedical discourse in psychiatry has been further threatened by the overtures to consumer choice and patient satisfaction which have been a part of the Conservative welfare reform package (see Pilgrim and Rogers 1993: 165–166) and which have been fought for by the mental health users movement (Rogers and Pilgrim 1991). The attention to 'consumer choice', if only in rhetoric, challenges the legitimacy of both the legal powers of psychiatry, which are premised on the belief that many mental patients are not capable of making decisions in their own best interests and the diagnostic formulae which both tacitly and overtly assume a lack of self-knowledge on the part of the patient.

The medical dominance expressed in British psychiatry has depended on both the legitimation of the state, via the structural support of the NHS, and on the assertion of specialist scientific knowledge of the origins and treatments of mental illness. These latter ideological claims have involved the making of a public image and a self-perception of operating eclectically, even holistically. In this paper I outline the development and features of medical dominance in psychiatrists' professional self-perceptions and the concommitant biomedical emphasis on drugs and electrical treatments. Threats to the continuation of medical dominance, it will be argued, are posed by the rise of alternative therapeutic approaches and managerial power. In conclusion, I will examine the proletarianisation thesis and the potential sources of resistance to an erosion in psychiatric power and status. Data from an ethnography and in-depth interview study (see Samson 1990) of psychiatrists and managers in the Bristol area in 1989–90, as well as examples from the psychiatric press will be used to illustrate these processes.

The world view of medico-eclecticism

While there has been a clear shift of emphasis in American psychiatry since the mid-1970s towards the 'new biologism' (Brown 1985) and away from social and psychoanalytic models, few changes of theoretical direction appear to have affected its British counterpart. This is partly a result of a more constant, although not entirely unquestioned, allegiance to the assumptions and methods of the natural sciences. While it has had some interests and involvement in community rehabilitation and psycho-social models of mental health, British psychiatry has not made any serious excursions as a profession into non-biomedical approaches analogous to, for example, the community mental health movement of the 1960s in the US (see Caplan 1964).

Ever since the co-option, then disappearance, of moral treatment in the 19th century (see Scull 1993), British psychiatry has been predominantly biological in its aetiological theories, medical in its professional organization and political allegiances, and yet 'eclectic' in its self-perception. That is, while biological medicine has provided the main source of knowledge for theory and practice, members of the profession have represented their enterprise as one engaging in wider domains within the social sciences. Although social theories of mental ill health have been forwarded, these have been present only on the margins of the profession. The therapeutic community and social psychiatry innovations, for example, at the Cassell, Dingleton and Henderson Hospitals (see Busfield 1986: 336) were not widely practiced outside these institutions. The psychoanalytically-oriented Tavistock Clinic was largely ignored for much of its history (Ramon 1985: 173) and the Philadelphia and Arbours Associations, although influenced by philosophically and psychoanalytically inclined psychiatrists, have taken an oppositional path from the mainstream of the profession (see Cooper *et al.* 1989).

The eclectic outlook has been given public expression over the last two decades by Anthony Clare in his practice, teaching, broadcasting and books. The medical model presented by Clare (1976) in his original formulation is an amalgam of a variety of factors – the physical, the social, the psychological, the environment, the organism. Ten years later, Roth and Kroll (1986: 59) presented what was almost an identical depiction of the medical model, as a broad, holistic, and humanitarian approach – a 'biopsychosocial' fusion. The theoretical work of John Wing (1978) and others at the Institute of Psychiatry made similar representations. More recently, Elaine Murphy, a professor of psychogeriatrics at Guy's Hospital, London, has stated:

> The all-embracing concept of mental disorder as 'illness' can . . . lead
> to a mechanistic approach to diagnosis and treatment which focuses on
> symptoms. These often respond best to drugs and physical treatments, but
> often are the least troublesome problem the sufferer has to cope with.

Emphasizing the medical problem and ignoring the social difficulties which may result from it are a result of trying to treat a mental disorder as if it were no different from a broken leg. (1991: 86–7)

Ironically, while the language suggests that Murphy advocates a more liberal approach than a 'mechanistic' medical model, another determinism is concealed; that social problems are of interest only insofar as they result from underlying medical abnormalities, not as causes. A recent article on the relationship between psychiatry and sociology in the *British Journal of Psychiatry* underlines a similar point:

> If problems of labelling and case definition can be resolved so that
> the sociologist can accept and work comfortably with psychiatric
> diagnostic rubrics, the way is open to a fruitful collaboration in which
> the occurrence, course and outcome of mental disorder serve as the
> dependent variables of inquiry, while social characteristics are numbered
> among the independent variables (Cooper 1991: 595).

The author here is not saying that social problems are an offshoot of medical abnormalities; in fact he appears to be saying the opposite. Nonetheless, the point is that researchers who study social phenomena must first construe diagnostic categories within the medical framework as objective in order to assist with correlational studies. The 'diagnostic rubrics' are, of course, based on symptom patterns which assume an essential pathology. Consequently, sociologists are expected, eventually at least, to be able to see the process of diagnosis as a non-social event, and mental illness as a fact that may have demographic variations.

Some of the clinicians I interviewed in Bristol repeated variations on the premises of eclecticism illustrated above. For example, a child psychiatrist:

> . . . I've tried to avoid becoming a therapist, a practitioner with too
> limited a tool bag. I've tended to deliberately stay eclectic . . . But, yes,
> I do have a philosophy behind it which is developmental and systemic.
> Seeing a child within its developmental and systemic context, as a
> developing organism, psychologically, within family and cultural
> contexts.

and a psychiatrist involved in the treatment of alcoholism:

> Our essential concept is that alcoholism and addiction are diseases . . .
> The illness has a medical, *i.e.* biological/genetic factor, a psychological
> factor, as well as a socio-environmental factor. I feel that they are all
> intertwined. To take one in isolation is perhaps totally fallacious because
> we're not going to get anywhere with that, but to look at it in an overall
> context is perhaps more helpful.

and a general adult psychiatrist:

> I always think of looking at three dimensions of treatment: biological,
> psychological in the sense of what one does for that individual, and social
> in terms of looking at the setting in which they begin and the setting to
> which they'll return and the setting in which they live in hospital.

These psychiatrists were putting forward similar conceptualisations of the
medical model to Clare. Various non-physical, environmental factors were
believed to be important to the understanding of mental illness. Nonetheless, the manifestation of these factors in the illness was still held to occur
in the human organism. Illness and disease were not principally understood
as social or psychological processes. Rather, social and psychological 'factors'
simply gave the disease its individual stamp. Consistent with this eclectic
vision, psychiatrists employed a multitude of approaches to treatment. The
following psychiatrist at a large hospital described the range of treatment
interventions that he was able to enlist:

> One of my beliefs is that you've got to work with enthusiasms. So, we
> have someone on the staff who is keen on massage, and we tend to use
> massage on people, and for instance, for quite a few years we had
> somebody working here as a nursing assistant who was training to be
> an acupuncturist, so we tended to use quite a lot of acupuncture. At the
> moment we have a visiting aromatherapist who comes to give us a free
> session once a week . . . Drugs and ECT [Electro-convulsive therapy] –
> ECT has sort of got a bad press and I don't like it myself because it
> is something completely out of the patient's control . . . Mostly, ECT
> nowadays, at least on this ward, tends to be given to people who have had
> ECT in the past.

Here we have the gamut of techniques on a single ward, ranging from
massage to electricity, depending, according to the account, on the psychiatrist's perceptions of the multiple interests and abilities of the staff under
his authority. Similarly, a community psychiatric nurse (CPN) described her
treatment approach as a 'mish-mash'. The chameleon-like nature of treatments was underlined by a psychiatrist who maintained:

> My own inclinations? Well, working with all colours, I have to be
> prepared to work in as many models as necessary. Sometimes I'm an
> organic, traditional psychiatrist talking in terms of disease entities etc.
> But wherever possible, I try to work in a more dynamic model,
> intra-psychic processes.

Another consultant psychiatrist, whose specialism was alcohol treatment,
referred to the 'supermarket model':

> We run a fairly eclectic programme, the name for it would be the supermarket model . . . Somebody might need a lot of individual work because they have very complicated personality difficulties; somebody else might need ECT because they're severely depressed and the drinking's part of that; somebody else might need some social skills training because they just don't know how to say no to a drink etc.

The emphasis in the supermarket model was not on deploying idiosyncratic staff skills because a more precise matching of treatments to patients was thought possible. Different treatments were employed on different patients because the configuration of symptoms varied. In turn, the treatments may have been more or less physical. It is likely, then, that in therapeutic practice medico-eclecticism has varied widely, relying to a certain extent on trial and error, shelving the classifactory systems if certain treatments are seen to 'work' on particular patients. The various component parts – the psychological, the social and the biological – are called upon at different times according to a host of contingencies relating to the theoretical biases of the psychiatrist, clinical perceptions of patients, and available ward resources.

However, as some interviewees claimed, the eclectic approach to treatment contains a more specific grounding in scientific medicine than other fields that have developed knowledge and experience in mental health. Other ways of looking at mental illness were often entertained, but the non-medical treatment that might be implied by an alternative was often discarded. Alternatives were used if they happened to be available, but would not be the dominant treatment modalities on any NHS ward. A psychiatrist at a secure unit argued the case for various modalities to be oriented around a medical corpus:

> Eclectic. We really have to be . . . We've got to try and come up with the goods for everybody who comes our way . . . The treatment the patients get is standard, orthodox, British psychiatric treatment so they're going to get the works. Generally that involves medical treatment because of the kind of people we get here, so there is the full range of medical treatment. Maybe some patients aren't on some form of medication but they're few and far between. Most of them will be on some form of medication. In cases where there's major affective disorder, then we'll use ECT. I have no qualms about it.

The adoption of an eclectic belief system may be seen as contributing to the maintenance of medical dominance. The presentation of eclecticism connotes a particular authority, an intellectual and therapeutic flexibility which enables the psychiatrist to handle the wide range of mental conditions encountered by the mental health services. However, eclecticism does suffer from certain weaknesses. Its unsystematic linkage to treatment modalities and lack of specificity to medicine gives it a certain diffuse quality, expressed in metaphors such as getting the 'works', working with 'all colours', and the 'supermarket model'. It is vital, therefore, that the eclectic practices do not become overly generalised because other professional and paraprofessional groups that also claim expertise over mental illness may demand certain jurisdictional rights which have been denied them within the NHS. An ideology which may have helped to counter this possibility is the claim of the superiority of the doctor, which is advanced by many psychiatrists and their professional organisations.

The superiority of the doctor

The notion of a medical core to the eclectic belief system was supported by a popular view among some of the psychiatrists interviewed in this study that the doctor, as physician, is both intellectually and clinically superior to other professionals. The doctor, so the view goes, not only possesses special capacities to diagnose and treat mental illness, but understands the wide range of associated problems. The psychiatrist's background and training is seen to embrace social and psychological knowledge in addition to medicine. Therefore, those trained outside medical schools, such as social workers and clinical psychologists, were construed as having less wide-ranging skills than the psychiatrist. This belief was expressed aptly by a consultant psychiatrist:

> I think the role of the psychiatrist is that he can look at the biological as well as the psychological and the interpersonal. The social worker may well feel that he can only look at the interpersonal. The psychologist may only look at the intra-psychic approaches – he cannot actually examine somebody's tummy if they say they've got belly ache as well as depression. I can do both. Now, it's not to diminish the role of those other people, but I think the psychiatrist has a very special role in being able to straddle several approaches and disciplines.

This is an important point. Psychiatrists claim they are absolutely vital to the mental health team because they have professional expertise over both body and mind. The psychiatrist is represented as a holistic healer, capable of transcending the philosophy of mind/body dualism which biomedicine is so often depicted as basing itself upon (see Capra 1982, Turner 1987: 214). However, this has been accomplished at the theoretical level primarily by materialising the mind as biological matter. An example of this appears in the recent book by psychiatrist, David Healy (1990: 29), who considers mind, psyche and brain to be material elements – '[o]nly physical elements can ever exist in minds. There is no other mental ingredient, no immaterial ghost . . .'. A 'psychiatric' or 'psychological' illness in standard British psychiatric usage usually means that some hypothesised material element has malfunctioned to produce socially, psychologically or functionally adverse consequences for the patient. Although the initial impetus may be thought to be socially derived – bereavement, for example – this is held to trigger a physiological response which drives the illness. Therefore, lacking specialised training in neurology, physiology, pharmacology and anatomy, the psychologist, nurse or social worker are considered less effective than the psychiatrist.

The argument for the superiority of the doctor can sometimes incorporate the self-perception that the medical practitioner possesses ecumenical and polymath qualities. A child psychiatrist, for example, maintained that the doctor, has '. . . a greater range of experience of the child's world, with all the facets that go into making a child an individual'. Another consultant psychiatrist spoke of the doctor in the team having 'the broadest base of background'. A prominent academic psychiatrist at the University of Bristol, Professor Morgan, outlined the components of the 'unique skills' of psychiatrists in a local psychiatric journal. According to Morgan (1990), the psychiatrist has an unmatched breadth of approach in the mental health field, is unchallenged in the use of physical treatments, has 'all inclusive' training which imparts a 'unique skill in seeing psychopathology as a whole', and has a key contribution to make in the assessment and management of risk. However, these are not sufficient without the personal qualities of maturity, empathy and objectivity which are 'most developed' in the psychiatrist.

Psychiatrists and physicians in general, especially those in the senior ranks, have traditionally been recruited from a narrow social band of the British population and are predominantly male, white and upper middle class (Littlewood and Lipsedge 1982: 21). Women, for example, account for only 26.5 per cent of hospital doctors, 15 per cent of consultants and 21 per cent of consultant psychiatrists in general mental illness (Department of Health 1991: 20–2). Nonetheless, there is a popular belief in the profession that medical education provides the basis for a capacity on the part of those trained to transcend social divisions as well as their own social background. Such a belief approximates to Mannheim's (1936: 157) conceptions of the intelligentsia and liberal professions as subsuming 'all those interests with which social life is permeated'. Specialised training in less prestigious fields such as psychology, nursing or social work is seen as being less 'broad' and not as non-partisan as medical training. These observations are underpinned by some of the interview responses which will follow.

It would seem that within treatment teams, both in hospital and community settings, the potential for considerable conflict between the consultant psychiatrist and other mental health staff exists if this attitude of superiority becomes widely vented. One mechanism for conflict resolution has been the imposition of the statutory authority of the consultant psychiatrist as the member of the hospital staff legally responsible for actions taken under his or her authority.

In the psychiatric literature, Andrew Sims (1989) has argued for medical superiority to extend outside the mental hospital. Sims uses the feminine pronoun to refer to the consultant psychiatrist and summarises why she must assume the leadership role in the community:

(a) her very broad and comprehensive training, and even her initial selection for training, in general best fits her for this role;
(b) other professional disciplines, other medical referrers, and patients will assume her and prefer her to be in this role;
(c) she is paid for taking this responsibility;
(d) legally she will be considered to be the responsible medical officer;
(e) her specialist training in the use of diagnosis with precision and economy, and in the broad aspects of treatment methods equip her for this role;
(f) she is most likely to be in the best position for innovation in treatment methods, service, and advocacy for the individual patient;
(g) in practice she is very often the longest serving person with that individual patient . . . ;
(h) if the consultant is not in this role, usually anarchy ensues rather than an alternative form of clinical care (Sims 1989: 286).

In this paradoxically gendered pose, Sims encapsulates a representation of professional psychiatric superiority. This view, while common among the psychiatrists interviewed, may not be unanimous within the profession. The Bristol consultant, Bennet (1988: 274–5), for example, has argued for the necessity of more democratic teams. However, the felt need among some psychiatrists in the recent past to strenuously assert the credentials of the doctor suggests some degree of occupational insecurity.

A further source of conflict, which is discussed in more depth below, is that between the biomedical orientation of psychiatry and the more practical, psychotherapeutic orientation of the voluntary sector. Drawing upon the Darwinian metaphor, a recent article in the *Bulletin of the Royal College of Psychiatrists* took seriously the notion that psychiatrists were a 'species' under threat. The perceived competition with other professionals and managers was seen as a matter of particular alarm: 'the encroachment of other species who are hungry for the psychiatrists' territory still goes on and, if unchecked, loss of habitat could reach the stage of other threatened species who survive as bygone curiosities in zoos' (Harrington 1988: 169).

Certainly, psychologists, as well as psychotherapists, have attempted to occupy terrain granted to psychiatry by the state. In the 1970s, Eysenck (1975) suggested a division of labour by which psychology would treat neurotic disorders, while the psychoses would be left to psychiatry. In the 1980s clinical psychology as a profession became more independent from psychiatry and medicine, but at the same time became subject to the destabilisation incurred on all NHS professionals as a result of the health service reforms (Pilgrim and Treacher 1992: 175). Nevertheless, clinical psychologists have maintained pressure on psychiatry by continuing to publish research evidence pointing to a positive contribution of psychology in the treatment of mental illness. A recent collected volume on schizophrenia (Bentall 1990) for example, includes claims that cognitive, clinical and behaviourist psychology could be profitably employed in the treatment of schizophrenia.

The superiority of drugs and ECT

The idea of the superiority of the doctor was based not only on a presumed ecumenical, professional and personal background, but also on a monopoly control over the varieties of medical treatment. Physical methods have remained central to the treatment of particular categories of patient within British psychiatry. Johnstone (1989: 215), a psychologist working within the NHS mental health services in Bristol in the late 1980s, suggested that polypharmacy, the prescription of 'cocktails' of drugs, has probably been the norm within psychiatric hospitals for large numbers of patients, and not unknown in outpatient settings. A longitudinal study of prescribing practices for outpatient schizophrenics showed that despite some reductions in the 1970s, polypharmacy has grown since 1983, especially at non-teaching hospitals (Johnson and Wright 1990). Another study of the long acting major tranquillisers, depot injections, showed that up to half of patients in a large sample were additionally prescribed anti-Parkinsonian drugs, laxatives and other psychotropics to combat the side effects of the primary prescription (Crammer and Eccleston 1989). The 1989 MIND/Roehampton Institute study of mental health service users found that 76 per cent of a sample of 516 mental health users were prescribed minor tranquillisers, while 80 per cent had been treated with antipsychotic medication (Rogers et al. 1993: 122–3).

As long as drugs remain in high profile as a treatment modality in mental health services, the continued involvement of the profession of psychiatry is ensured since only physicians can prescribe drugs. The use of drugs in community mental health care is justified by the belief that they prevent inpatient admission and that they are beneficial in relieving symptoms. A consultant psychiatrist described the importance of the depot injection to patients living in the community:

> So my CPN probably deals with about half the patients that I look after who are chronic patients who, if they didn't have that kind of resource, would be inpatients. So the development of tranquillisers by injections means that the patient's been dosed up – in addition to the fortnightly/three weekly visit, – the two have to go together. I think these are preventative measures. The quality of life of the patient, the length that they remain well is longer; they establish themselves better, therefore they stay out of hospital longer, the population at large is able to contain them better so the pressure on beds is less. You get a sort of ripple effect from that. We have hundreds of patients on that kind of follow up whereas before long stay patients were wheeling in and out of hospital.

This conviction is, of course, part of the older notion, accepted as a *sine qua non* among psychiatrists (Murphy 1991: 47) and the pharmaceutical industry (Office of Health Economics 1989: 4), that the development of major tranquillisers made community care possible from the mid 1950s onwards. Advertisements for psychotropic drugs in British psychiatric journals of the late 1980s traded on the role of drugs in facilitating the bridge from hospital to community. An advertisement for Clopixol which was issued in the late 1980s in psychiatric journals is headed 'From Clinic to Community'. It features two pieces of a jigsaw puzzle being put together; one piece depicts a 19th century asylum and the other a suburban house. What allows the two pieces to be snapped together, it is visually suggested, is the neuroleptic Clopixol. The pharmaceutical industry must therefore be considered an important force in the generation and perpetuation of these beliefs. The industry spends vast amounts on advertising and influencing doctors to prescribe their products. 'Drug lunches' featuring films, promotional material and gifts to doctors are common elements in hospital culture. It has been argued that the drug company representatives' accounts – stressing the therapeutic benefits and downplaying side effects – of the medications is the primary information that some doctors make decisions upon (Johnstone 1989: 191–7).

Another factor cited in the continued use of drugs and somatic treatments was rapidity of effect. Drugs and ECT were believed to improve the condition of patients much faster than non-physical alternatives. Obviously, with the cost consciousness, emphasis on efficiency and effectiveness and managerial pressures for shorter lengths of stay in in-patient units, which have become a part of the health service culture, the speed with which patients can be treated is highly valued. As the following consultant psychiatrist indicated, 'when the symptoms are very crippling, you can't afford much else [than drugs] . . . you have to correct their symptoms quickly in order to get on with all sorts of other things. Also, if you've got a very few beds, there must be very rapid recoveries'.

ECT was also justified in this way by a consultant psychiatrist, drawing upon an anecdote about the organicist psychiatrist William Sargant:

There's a harsh saying by that well known psychiatrist with an organic bias, Dr. William Sargant, very much a pioneer, dedicated to his patients, very sceptical of the value of psychotherapy, very prone to push physical treatment. He used to say 'they think I push the ECT too far, but what's the alternative? psychotherapy and free straw.' Meaning that they could stay on the ward for as long as it took, but it would take a very long time.

Contrary to popular belief and despite the widespread public unease over its use, ECT has not become marginalised as a treatment procedure. In 1990 an alliance of mental health workers and users, Bristol Action for Mental Health, initiated a campaign against it. The previous year, another group,

Table 1 *Usage of ECT at Barrow and Glenside Hospitals 1982–1989*

	No. of Courses[#] of ECT	No. of Admissions	Courses of ECT per Admission
BARROW			
1982	154	1044	0.15
1983	130	1085	0.12
1984	117	1213	0.10
1985	160	1174	0.14
1986	129	1136	0.11
1987*	134	1148	0.12
1988*	148	1055	0.14
1989*	172	1078	0.16
Average	143	1117	0.13
GLENSIDE			
1982	53	823	0.06
1983	34	839	0.04
1984	44	793	0.06
1985	51	667	0.08
1986	47	660	0.07
1987*	43	718	0.06
1988*	33	706	0.05
1989*	31	742	0.04
Average	42	744	0.06

[#] A course is a sequence of one or more ECT treatments given to a single patient until a medical decision to stop the sequence is implemented.
* Fiscal years, 1987/8, 1988/9, 1989/90.

Sources: Information Department, South Western Regional Health Authority, Bristol; Office of Information Technology, Bristol and Weston Health Authority; Statistics Department, Frenchay Health Authority; Medical Records Departments, Barrow Hospital and Glenside Hospital, United Bristol Healthcare Trust.

the Avon Mental Health Alliance (1989), published a report of the views of service users on drugs, ECT and mental health services. The Alliance called for an end to 'disinformation' about the effects of ECT and drugs and criticised the practice of staff coercing patients to consent to ECT.

Table 1 shows the extent of ECT usage over time at the two largest psychiatric hospitals in Bristol in 1989–90 – Barrow and Glenside. By taking the number of patients to have undergone courses of ECT as a proportion of the annual admissions, a rate of ECT usage per admission has been calculated. The figures show considerable variation over the years within and between the two hospitals. The average rate of use at Barrow (13 per cent of admissions from 1982 to 1989) is more than double that of Glenside (6 per cent of admissions from 1982 to 1989). No overall downward trend is discernable as the rates fluctuate and do not differ substantially from year to year. The variation between the two hospitals, however, is in line with national figures indicating broad disparities in the use of ECT between regions. The MIND Roehampton survey of 464 users found the considerably higher rate of 48.5 per cent who had experienced ECT in psychiatric custody over their hospital careers (Rogers *et al.* 1993: 143).

Few doubts were expressed among the professionals interviewed in Bristol as to the linkage between biological aetiology of mental illness and the efficacy of physical treatments. The reasoning implied that pharmaceutical and electrical treatments which alter biochemistry or brain activity *must* validate the biological aetiological hypothesis. The question of aetiology was raised in interviews, and among some clinical workers the notion of biological origins was put forward almost as a faith:

> I've got past the stage of reading about mental illness and wondering why people are the way they are. The only conclusion I've drawn is that the group of illnesses labelled schizophrenia is a biochemical abnormality. It's insidious, destructive. I think ex-patients have helped me to understand. I think with some of the schizophrenias, it has to be something wrong chemically. It has to be some sort of problem in the biochemistry.

And by others as something which scientific research in the future would validate:

> Certainly there's a great resurgence in neuropsychiatry, psychopharmacology, all these biological approaches to mental illness. I think the pendulum has swung back a very long way in that direction, which is fine and it's exciting. I think that the time is coming, dare one say it, that there will be breakthroughs. The geneticists seem to be getting close. The psychopharmacologists, the neuro-endocrinologists, are making great strides.

Reversing the causal arrows

The 1980s was a period of continued, even intensified, use of physical treatments and biomedical aetiological theories in psychiatry, accompanied by calls from within the profession for continued medical leadership. At the same time, the promotion of alternative treatment approaches and theories of mental illness was fuelled by both the Conservative emphasis on 'consumerism' and the mental health users' movement.

Although not unknown within psychiatric practice, alternative treatment approaches were more commonly represented in Bristol outside the statutory services, particularly in the voluntary sector. They drew upon a broad range of philosophies including humanistic psychology, psychoanalysis, spiritualism, the New Age movement, user empowerment and simple pragmatism.

An important point of difference between the 'holism' of these approaches and that proclaimed by biomedical psychiatry is that the alternative eclecticism is not aligned to a privileging of medical knowledge. There is no attempt to materialise the mind. Techniques of healing which are more self-consciously intuitive may come into play. For example, a private psychotherapist in Bath elucidated his humanistic approach as having five components:

1. Client centred and a belief in the self-healing power of the individual, releasing the self-healing power. With that goes self-responsibility.
2. There's a place in the therapy for authentic relationship as well as transference relationship; you're working towards an authenticity of meeting which means that the therapist isn't just a blank screen.
3. A holistic approach which values the body, mind and spirit. You're attending to the body and soul.
4. A belief that the importance of catharsis as well as insight, the emotional release often precedes insight. So people would use work with cushions, talking to somebody directly.
5. Utilising the here and now. Bringing it into the present, into this relationship.

Proponents of alternative therapies did not share the enthusiasm of many consultant psychiatrists for biomedical treatments. They invoked a different aetiological stance, preferring to argue for the social roots of mental ill health in poverty, unemployment, marital discord, loneliness and homelessness. While avowedly anti-psychiatry attitudes were rare, they did surface in some interviews, such as the following with a clinical psychologist who was employed on an NHS in-patient unit:

> I'm very anti- the medical model approach, myself. I don't believe in it at all. I suppose I see most problems as being a social or marital or group problem or political problems. I don't see patients with illness. I try to help people understand their problems in their own terms. I work in a psychotherapeutic model . . . I think my approach is much more valid, and I don't find the medical model to be particularly scientific or true or objective.

And reflecting a pragmatic perspective, a development worker with a voluntary organisation:

> . . . We don't use the word mental illness here. It'll come up and we might use it because of what we need to do because of jargon. We see that people experience distress . . . We think that through enough pressure and stress and strain and misery and unhappiness people can escape reality in lots of ways or they can internalise anger and they can become depressed. So we think we have to be very accessible to people on a

human level which just means sitting down, holding somebody's hand and saying 'What's up?' . . . Whilst accepting that some people are on medication and we would not say to them that you must stop it, we give people information about the choices that they have, we don't see it as the only alternative.

According to these mental health workers, the psychotherapeutic approach was more useful and valid than biomedical psychiatry as the latter did not recognise the need for empathy, information and consequently the full consideration of extra-biological causes of mental health problems. As a result, mental and emotional problems, it was argued by alternative therapists, needed to be addressed at a social or psychological level – 'in their own terms'. A similar position was taken by a voluntary sector worker who argued that 'homelessness causes and exacerbates mental health problems', thus reversing the causal arrows often drawn by psychiatrists and others who principally blame community care policies for the observed mental health problems of the homeless.

The treatment modalities that flow from reversing the causal arrows dramatically differ from those endorsed by medico-eclecticism. Rather than the psychiatric mixture of physically-based treatments, voluntary sector mental health workers favoured counselling, psychotherapy, practical help and therapeutic communities. Underlining the belief in the social aetiology of mental illness, assisting patients or clients in the practicalities of their everyday lives, was given a high priority. A voluntary sector worker put it as follows:

My philosophy is very much to work on practical problems first – to get people into accommodation, to get their rights and benefits, get them decently clothed and fed and then to look at other problems. Once you've done that a lot of people's mental health problems disappear.

In support of this, the interviewee described the case of a homeless woman who had exhibited bizarre behaviour, being both angry and mute. But once accommodation had been secured, the aberrant conduct abated and the woman eventually went on to a government employment training scheme.

An administrator with a local association of MIND reasoned that the formal psychiatric (biomedical) component of a community patient's circumstances was largely inconsequential, although it might be amplified in terms of the stigma attached to having experienced psychiatric treatment. As a result, the statutory medical or social work help was seen as being tangential compared to the longer term difficulties that people incur just getting by in life:

What we are trying to get the world out there, professionals, and more especially, politicians to recognise is that if you look at somebody's life as a whole, the time spent in hospital, the time the community nurse comes, and your social worker comes is infinitesimal compared with your life as a whole. And nobody is putting resources into their life as a whole, which is the long term social support staff, having somebody to actually help you into more normal life, special forms of employment with a reasonable income, the right sort of supported housing. Things like that we feel are as important, if not more important, than things that are about the illness state.

Again, the social milieu was seen as the most important influence over mental ill-health. Life situation changes were viewed as the most appropriate and effective. The biomedical model, emphasising drugs, ECT, notions of illness, and doctor leadership, was considered to detract from the practical difficulties that many users of mental health services encountered. In an era of increased social inequality and material hardships for those at the bottom, the severity of some social problems was such that all professional mental health approaches could sometimes be rejected. A CPN attached to an inner city mental health team argued 'if a guy's sleeping rough and he's got a gammy leg, he's not going to want to talk to you about how depressed he's feeling'. What was needed was attention to physical health, accommodation and financial problems.

Although both medico-eclectic psychiatry and most participants in the voluntary sector in mental health broadly agree on the 'reality' of the suffering and mental anguish of individual patients, there obviously is a contestation of knowledge and practice at stake. Some voluntary sector workers in Bristol conveyed an implicit criticism of the philosophical assumptions of psychiatry when describing their own approach:

I think it's about empowering people to take the next step. It's about focussing on what people can do rather than on what they can't do. It's about remembering old skills and learning new ones. It's about believing people. We notice that when we believe people and listen to people they can make sense of their lives and move forward. We notice that helps them change.

The point was that in conventional psychiatric practice, patients are not always 'believed'. Their conduct and speech is scrutinised for symptoms of mental illness and placed within a taxonomic scheme, rather than being seen, at least in part, as occurring in the context of particular, especially adverse, circumstances. The alternative approach of the voluntary sector was perceived by its members as being 'planets' away from the treatment given patients in the NHS. Psychiatric professionals were sometimes regarded with pity among those working closely with ex-patients in the community, as this community administrator with a women's mental health housing association implies:

Obviously there's a lot of education that needs to happen in the Health
Service; there's also a lot of protection for professionals inside the
Health Service to outside organisations, particularly with consultants.
Isolationism and arrogance on their part – they don't really know what
our expertise is. It's hard . . . The resources in hospital are very limited,
they resort to drug therapy because that's the only way in which they
can manage. The resources to deal with some really deep problems are
not around.

Efficiency and psychiatry

If the voluntary sector represents one challenge to the theoretical and treatment basis of medical dominance, the private sector and rationalisation,
as further incorporated in the health service reforms, present organisational
and occupational threats. The increasing emphasis on multidisciplinary
teams in the community effects autonomy since a consultant's status in
British medicine has been tied to the number of beds and subordinate staff
commanded. Continued leadership in a bedless community care system is,
therefore, jeopardised. Increasingly, psychiatrists' work has been monitored
by managers with a central government mandate to promote 'efficiency' and
allocate resources within mental health services.

Certainly, there has been some fear of professional management expressed
from psychiatrists, which is further provoked by the increasing potentiality
of negative managerial evaluations of the work of consultants. Often, however, medical opposition to management is justified by a belief that the drive
for efficiency is not serving patients well (Flannery 1988) and is driven by a
cost-cutting agenda. While doubtless being informed by perceptions of the
ambitions of the neo-liberal Conservative governments to destabilise public
services, such an opposition on the part of consultants may also reflect a
fear of outside scrutiny into what has hitherto been highly self-regulating
work.

Before the NHS reforms, it was largely assumed by successive governments that doctors could police themselves. Empowered by the reforms,
Health and Social Service managers around the country have been given a
state mandate to evaluate the extent to which psychiatrists and other professionals could be more rationally deployed within the 'internal market'.
As one manager expressed it:

There's a move within Social Services to consider within every job
whether there really is a need for professionals. A lot of it is just support.
So I need to tackle the issue of how would we bring to the benefit of the
service, support workers into the community . . . Next year is when we
start talking about whether we want specific professionals, or do we want
a generic community worker. That's really going to come into play.

Psychiatrists' opposition to rationalisation, while obviously related to a fear of a loss of clinical autonomy, or even unemployment, was also associated with the widespread belief in some quarters that psychiatric services, in contrast to other medical services, were not as readily amenable to the economic analysis of efficiency because they were held to lack measures of outcome (Wilkinson and Pelosi 1989: 63). The success of a heart transplant, so the argument goes, can be crudely monitored by the length of time a person lives after the operation, but the success of ECT for a depressed elderly person is less easily measurable.

Nonetheless, the research prescribed by the health service reforms in relation to the imposition of community care is unlikely to consider methodological subtleties in its instrumental focus on needs assessment and efficiency. In looking for expertise, both psychiatrists and sociologist have been bypassed as individuals from management and economics backgrounds (such as David King 1988) are called upon to supervise and undertake the ground research made necessary by *Caring for People*. Within this context research assuming certain rationalistic behaviours of health consumers and employing complex econometric models has provided the intellectual stimulus to the reforms (Ashmore *et al.* 1989). This has resulted in the replacement of the positivist epidemiology of the psychiatrist – concerned with validating psychiatric diagnostic taxonomy and legitimating *medical* planning – with the positivist epidemiology of health service managers and economists – concerned to rationalise resource allocations and legitimate *economic* grounds for planning health services. The conflict between the two types of research is illuminated by recent research carried out from the latter perspectives, working towards the implementation of the reforms, rather than from within NHS psychiatry, which argued, for example, that measures of outcome in mental health *are* possible (Reed 1991: 399).

A psychiatrist employed at a secure unit in Bristol demonstrated his opposition to rationalisation and the difficulty of applying the management principles to psychiatric services in the following comment:

It's difficult to go about measuring for a start. All of my patients don't want to be here in the secure unit, they'd rather be elsewhere. So, in terms of consumer satisfaction, they're all dissatisfied. Half of them, at least, don't recognise that they're ill so they're non-consumers for a start. It's me who goes out and says you, you and you are sick, come to hospital. So I create the demand and I supply that demand.

Not only was efficiency measurement considered problematic, but also the application of consumer metaphors. Symbolic either of ignorance of or resistance to managerial encroachments, this psychiatrist assumed that it is the physician who creates the supply of patients. The imperatives of the drive to rationalise the NHS problematise this prerogative and open up the possibility of more economically cost effective actors, such as nurses, social workers, psychologists, or some tier of management, making such decisions within a more strictly resourced and managed organisational setting. Some cost-benefit studies have already shown that for certain classes of patients community psychiatric nursing is more cost-effective than an out-patient psychiatrist (Mangen *et al.* 1983).

Additionally, the rise of private health provision, which has been encouraged by the Conservative government and directly relates to the community care reforms through the contracting out mechanisms, may adversely affect the clinical autonomy of psychiatrists. Contracts specify particular economic parameters for treatment which directly challenge professional discretion. Private insurance-based schemes, as practiced in the United States, constrain services to certain treatment modalities which are generally more easily quantified, measurable, physical, speedy and create incentives to 'cream skim' the least expensive patients (see Dougherty 1988, Seltzer 1988). Private mental health care in Britain contains pressures to tailor treatment towards acceptable reimbursing conditions. A medical director of a private clinic outside Bristol tacitly accepted this when he said of his patients, 'we know what their insurance policies will pay for, so we make sure we come within that'. As in the US, British insurers were by the late 1980s gradually becoming suspicious of long-stay psychiatric treatment, and starting to promote reimbursement for short term provision. The following administrator who directed a private alcohol and addiction clinic acknowledged the power of insurance companies to dictate the length of a therapeutic programme:

> From the insurance companies we have the startings of very much a desire to move into the American system of a 28 day programme. Currently, as I said, we have a 6–8 week programme And the health insurance schemes would be very, very amenable to funding 28 day programmes for very obvious financial reasons. Now we are rebelling against that at the moment and they are not actually turning round and saying 'we will not pay you' but they are making noises of 'we would really like you to do this'. And it may happen in time that they will actually turn round and say that only 28 day programmes will be paid for. So we may have to do a 28 day programme.

Conclusion: the proletarianisation of psychiatry?

A series of political and economic impediments to medical dominance has been identified. The strident and confident assertions of medical power embodied in eclecticism must be counterposed with the ominous threats to any continued leadership, autonomy and status of the psychiatrist within British mental health services. Whether these new limits to clinical autonomy amount to a proletarianisation of the doctor is a matter of some debate (Elston 1991). However, many of the processes involved in proletarianisation, identified by Turner (1987: 138) in his review, increasingly apply to British psychiatrists. These include; (1) an extension of the division of labour, (2) the conditions of work and the nature of the workplace are set by a higher authority, and (3) wages are determined by the marketplace rather than individual negotiation.

The evidence presented here would suggest that the first two conditions of proletarianisation are in place. Braverman's (1974) famous exposition of de-skilling, which attributes prime importance to the sequestering of traditional esoteric knowledge by management and its reduction to rules and formulae, has a contemporary ring to it. While the physical treatments may prove to be vital to the economic and control requirements of the health service reforms, discretion over their deployment and regulation may increasingly be prized from psychiatry for the purposes of rapid patient turnover. As for the third of Turner's conditions; although doctors' salaries within the NHS are still established by negotiation with the government, further moves towards market liberalisation could easily erode this privilege.

However, if we take the proletarianisation thesis literally, it does seem implausible at present that psychiatrists are descending to a working class status. There may even be some signs of a partial reversal of the trends emphasised in this article. I cite here three possibilities. Firstly, it is possible that psychiatrists may develop strategies to gain advantage from the 'internal market'. Already, in some locations their expertise and knowledge has been turned to the planning and administration of NHS trusts and to participating in private sector initiatives.

Second, and relatedly, by the 1980s the language and logic of business efficiency and Taylorism had become so pervasive as a characterisation of virtue in the health services, that it had become incorporated in psychiatric research and thinking. This is apparent in the current vogue for psychiatric research into 'outcome' and the discourse on 'evaluation' and 'appraisal' (see for example, Watt 1989, Tansella 1989). Therefore, the comment by one (retiring) consultant at a large mental hospital in my interview study that 'a lot of what consultant psychiatrists do, doesn't bear critical evaluation', could perhaps be addressed by some form of self-policing. This would incorporate the ideology of neo-liberal efficiency, distance itself from absolute clinical autonomy, and thereby stabilise medico-eclecticism.

Thirdly, community care has begun to lose its glow, as problems of social order have been linked, especially in the mass media, to inadequate community care. In particular, homelessness and public incidents of violence and self-destruction involving former hospital patients in the community have served to re-direct thinking back to the advantages of the mental hospital – biomedical knowledge, legal custody, and 'safety'. Interestingly, it is in this grey area between public safety and social control that psychiatrists have been able to retain authority. Little has been done in Britain in recent years to attenuate the psychiatric power to compulsorily detain patients and the *extension* of these powers into the community via Community Treatment

Orders has been advocated by both the Royal College of Psychiatrists (1987) and the current Health Secretary.

Clearly, British psychiatry is at a pivotal juncture. The political economy of managerialism and contracting out, and the ideology of consumerism, give a clear counter-direction to the mental health services which appears to weaken the position and contradict the eclecticism of psychiatry. However, as with Braverman's analysis of de-skilling and Taylorism which provided the basis for proletarianisation of craft workers, there are resistances also with psychiatric professionals. But, against the power of the state, these have taken the form of adjustment and flexibility. What can be said, then, is that if medical dominance is retained by these strategies, it is likely to be in a fractured form, marking out a new landscape of collaboration with managerialism in which aetiological theories, treatment modalities and power alignments increasingly bend to political and economic directive.

Acknowledgements

This article is based on a paper presented at the Festschrift for Eliot Freidson at the American Sociological Association Conference, Miami Beach, 15 August 1993 and a lively seminar in the Sociology Department at the University of Leicester on 27 October 1993. I would like to thank Professor Joan Busfield for providing some very thoughtful observations on a previous draft, and two anonymous referees. Help with statistical information on ECTs in Bristol was provided by Joyce Fisher of the South West Regional Health Authority and Barbara Stephens of the United Bristol Healthcare Trust.

References

Abel-Smith, B. (1964) *The Hospitals, 1800–1948*, London: Heineman.
Ashmore, M. *et al.* (1989) *Health and Efficiency*, Milton Keynes: Open University Press.
Avon Mental Health Alliance (1989) *The Reality Within*, Bristol: South West MIND.
Bennet, G. (1988) What should psychiatry be doing in the 1990s?, *British Medical J.*, 296, 274–5.
Bentall, R. (ed.) (1990) *Reconstructing Schizophrenia*, London: Routledge.
Braverman, H. (1974) *Labor and Monopoly Capital*. New York: Monthly Review Press.
Brown, P. (1985) *The Transfer of Care*. Boston: Routledge and Kegan Paul.
Busfield, J. (1986) *Managing Madness*. London: Hutchinson.
Caplan, G. (1964) *Principles of Preventive Psychiatry*, New York: Basic.
Capra, F. (1982) *The Turning Point*, London: Flamingo.
Clare, A. (1976) *Psychiatry in Dissent*, London: Tavistock.
Cooper, B. (1992) Sociology in the context of social psychiatry, *British J. Psychiatry*, 161, 594–8.
Cooper, R. *et al.* (1989) Beginnings, in R. Cooper (ed.), *Thresholds Between Philosophy*

and Psychoanalysis: Papers from the Philadelphia Association. London: Free Association.

Crammer, J. and Eccleston, D. (1989) A survey of the use of depot neuroleptics in a whole region, *Bulletin of the Royal College of Psychiatrists*, 13, 517–20.

Department of Health (1989) *Caring for People: Community Care in the Next Decade and Beyond* (Cm 849), London: HMSO.

Department of Health (1991) *Women Doctors and their Careers*. London: HMSO.

Department of Health and Social Services (1983) *Report of the National Health Service Management Committee*. London: HMSO.

Dougherty, C. (1988) Mind, money and morality: ethical dimensions of economic change in American psychiatry, *Hastings Center Report*, 18, 3, 15–20.

Elston, M.A. (1991) The politics of professional power: medicine in a changing health service. In Gabe, J. *et al. The Sociology of the Health Service*. London: Routledge, 58–88.

Eysenck, H. (1975) *The Future of Psychiatry*, London: Methuen.

Flannery, D. (1988) Phenomenology and the price of beans, *Bulletin of the Royal College of Psychiatrists*, 12, 320–2.

Forsyth, G. (1973) *Doctors and State Medicine*. London: Pitman Medical.

Freidson, E. (1970) *Profession of Medicine*. New York: Dodd, Mead.

Harrington, J. (1988) Psychiatrists – an endangered species?, *Bulletin of the Royal College of Psychiatrists*, 12, 169–74.

Healy, D. (1990) *The Suspended Revolution*, London: Faber and Faber.

Johnson, D.A.W. and Wright, N.F. (1990) Drug prescribing for schizophrenic out-patients on depot injections, *British J. Psychiatry*, 156, 827–34.

Johnstone, L. (1989) *Users and Abusers of Psychiatry*, London: Routledge.

King, D. (1988) Replacing mental hospitals with better services. In Ramon S. and Giannichedda M. (eds), *Psychiatry in Transition*. London: Pluto, 191–98.

Klein, R. (1983) *The Politics of the National Health Service*. London: Longman.

Littlewood, R. and Lipsedge, M. (1982) *Aliens and Alienists*. London: Pelican.

Mangen, S.P. *et al.* (1983) Cost-effectiveness of community psychiatric nurse or out-patient psychiatrist care of neurotic patients. *Psychological Medicine*, 13, 407–16.

Mannheim, K. (1936) *Ideology and Utopia*, translated by Louis Wirth and Edward Shils. New York: Harvest.

Morgan, H.G. (1990) Psychiatric education: the way forward, *South West Psychiatry*, Spring, 23–29.

Murphy, E. (1991) *After the Asylums*. London: Faber and Faber.

Office of Health Economics (1989) *Mental Health in the 1990s: From Custody to Care?*, London: Office of Health Economics.

Parsons, T. (1951) *The Social System*. Glencoe, Il.: Free Press.

Pilgrim, D. and Treacher, A. (1992) *Clinical Psychology Observed*. London. Routledge.

Pilgrim, D. and Rogers, A. (1993) *A Sociology of Mental Health and Illness*. Buckingham: Open University Press.

Ramon, S. (1985) *Psychiatry in Britain*. London: Croom Helm.

Reed, J. (1991) The future for psychiatry, *Psychiatric Bulletin*, 15, 396–401.

Rogers, A. and Pilgrim, D. (1991) 'Pulling Down Churches': accounting for the British mental health users movement, *Sociology of Health and Illness*, 13, 129–48.

Rogers, A. *et al.* (1993) *Experiencing Psychiatry*. London: Macmillan and MIND.

Roth, M. and Kroll, J. (1986) *The Reality of Mental Illness.* Cambridge: Cambridge University Press.

Royal College of Psychiatrists (1987) *Community Treatment Orders: A Discussion Document.* London: RCP.

Samson, C. (1990) *The Privatization of Mental Health: Political and Ideological Influences in Psychiatric Care in the United States and Great Britain, 1979–1989,* Ph.D. Dissertation, Department of Sociology, University of California, Berkeley.

Scull, A. (1993) *The Most Solitary of Afflictions: Madness and Society in Britain, 1700–1900.* New Haven: Yale University Press.

Seltzer, D. (1988) Limitations on HMO services and the emerging redefinition of chronic mental illness, *Hospital and Community Psychiatry,* 39, 137–9.

Sims, A. (1989) What is the role of the consultant in the community?, *Psychiatric Bulletin,* 13, 285–7.

Strong, P.M. (1979) *The Ceremonial Order of the Clinic.* London: Routledge and Kegan Paul.

Tansella, M. (1989) Evaluating community psychiatric services, in Williams, P. *et al.* (eds), *The Scope of Epidemiological Psychiatry.* London: Routledge, 386–403.

Turner, B. (1987) *Medical Power and Social Knowledge.* London: Sage.

Watt, D. (1989) Appraisal of institutional psychiatry, in Williams, P. *et al.* (eds), *The Scope of Epidemiological Psychiatry.* London: Routledge, 375–85.

Wilkinson, G. and Pelosi, A. (1989) Economic appraisal, in Williams, P. *et al.* (eds), *The Scope of Epidemiological Psychiatry.* London: Routledge, 63–73.

Wing, J. (1978) *Reasoning About Madness.* Oxford: Oxford University Press.

2.5

Challenges to medicine: the case of prescribing
Marjorie Weiss and Ray Fitzpatrick

Introduction

Sociological literature during the 1960s and 1970s emphasised the professional dominance of medicine. Medicine was the model for a profession: a publicly mandated and state supported monopolistic supplier of a valued service, exercising autonomy in the workplace and collegiate control over recruitment, training and the regulation of members' conduct (Freidson 1970, Johnson 1972). However, more recently, professional power and autonomy have been viewed as under threat (Gabe et al. 1994). Two distinct processes pose challenges to medical dominance: deprofessionalisation and proletarianisation (Elston 1991). Deprofessionalisation is seen as part of the more general social trend of the demystification of expert knowledge rendering it more amenable to lay scrutiny. Conversely, proletarianisation refers to a process in which occupations are divested of control over their work (McKinlay and Stoekle 1988). Recent developments in health care, particularly the increasing managerial control of the health service, are thought to contribute to this process of proletarianisation (Elston 1991).

While these themes have been most frequently examined in relation to recent developments in the American health care system, there have been parallel developments within the British health care system. A number of challenges to UK doctors have been identified, including the growth of managerial systems such as the introduction of an 'internal market' within the National Health Service and the development of fundholding (Hunter 1994). More general challenges include the occupational development of the nursing profession, the growth in complementary or alternative medicine and the trend towards greater questioning of medical decision-making through increased litigation, greater media attention to medical issues and the growth of self-help organisations (Gabe et al. 1994).

With a few recent exceptions (Flynn 1992, Gabe et al. 1994, Calnan and Gabe 1991), sociological analyses of the trends impacting upon medical dominance have focused upon evidence from the United States. This is understandable given the specific circumstances in the United States where the dominance of the medical profession in the health care system could be dramatically reduced (Relman 1987, Elston 1991). Specifically, the push to control costs in a pluralistic, competitive environment and the spread of managed care create strong pressures to reduce medical autonomy in clinical decision-making, one of the core supports of medical dominance (Starr 1982, Derber 1984). The hold over the sociological literature of the American case, in which primary care is less salient, may also be responsible for the tendency for debates to focus on the process of proletarianisation with regard to hospital medicine. It is in the hospital arena, whether in Europe or the United States, that contests for control between managerial and professional groups have been most vivid and analyses the most insightful (Feinglass and Salmon 1990, Hunter 1994).

This paper argues that primary care in the United Kingdom provides a distinctive and important arena in which professional dominance is currently being challenged. Early insights regarding the relevance of the deprofessionalisation and proletarianisation arguments for general practice were provided by Calnan and Gabe (1991). More recently, sociologists have examined this sector and have argued that, whilst concepts such as deprofessionalisation and proletarianisation are relevant to the general practitioner (GP) in the National Health Service (NHS), the distinctive context of primary care requires analysts to be cautious in their use of such concepts (Calnan and Williams 1995). For example, general practitioners have traditionally enjoyed very high levels of freedom from managerial control compared with their hospital counterparts in the NHS. This may, at least partly, be explained by the relative lack of development of administrative resources and expertise in the primary care sector compared with hospital managerial systems (Butler 1992).

At the heart of the GP's clinical autonomy is the ability to prescribe without external influence. It is one of the largest contributions that the GP makes to the overall pattern of health care and is certainly the biggest component of primary care costs (Chew 1992). The Limited List, introduced in 1985, limited the range of drugs that could be prescribed under the National Health Service and was an early attempt to control prescribing expenditure (Anonymous 1984). Within the last decade, the government has introduced further initiatives, both direct and indirect, to influence GPs' prescribing as a means of containing escalating drug costs. In April 1990, in accordance with the provisions laid down in *Working for Patients*, the first wave of practices became fundholders (Secretaries of State for Health 1989). This is a voluntary scheme whereby money saved on prescribing can be used for other aspects of patient care. In fundholding practices, GPs are now responsible for budgets which enable them to purchase hospital care and allow them greater control over their practice's prescribing costs. Any savings made on either of these budgets can be used by the practice. Should there be a shortfall in one budget, any savings from the other budget can be used towards that shortfall. In essence, fundholding has become an elaborate financial incentive (Iliffe and Munro 1993). A relatively easy source of cost savings is prescribing. Less potent financial incentives are available under the indicative prescribing scheme for non-fundholders in which practices are able to keep a small proportion of financial savings made on their allocated drugs' bill (Bradlow and Coulter 1993). Indirectly, a variety of micro-mechanisms have been introduced to inform GPs about the cost and volume of their prescribing relative to their colleagues and to educate them about therapeutic appropriateness (Audit Commission 1994).

Family Health Services Authorities (FHSAs) are responsible for the administration of primary care. They have been transformed from medically dominated bodies passively administering the GP's contract into more managerial entities with a smaller GP representation (Klein 1995). This more proactive role will be enhanced as a result of the merger with health authorities and is dramatically reflected in their role in GP prescribing, where FHSAs are expected to become far more interventionist. The FHSAs employ medically trained medical advisers with specific responsibilities to pursue the FHSA's objectives in relation to controlling prescribing costs. They are responsible, amongst other things, for advising and influencing individual GPs whose drug costs or appropriateness is deemed problematic. From the point of view of this paper, they represent an important and, to date, sociologically neglected factor in the debate about challenges to professional dominance.

In the United States, a new cadre of physician manager has emerged that, whilst medically trained, is employed by hospital corporations to pursue management objectives. This trend has produced 'vertical stratification' within the profession of medicine (Freidson 1989). If physician administrators increasingly identify with managerial rather than medical professional values and objectives, such trends may speed up the processes of proletarianisation, since this new cadre is better equipped scientifically to understand and, therefore, to control medical decision-making (Wolinsky 1993). For these reasons, the appearance in any health care system of a role requiring medical qualifications within the administrative system with managerial responsibilities is a potential threat to medical dominance (Hunter 1992).

This paper therefore examines developments in primary care prescribing in the UK in relation to the broader sociological debate about challenges to medicine from deprofessionalisation and proletarianisation. The paper draws on qualitative interviews with FHSA medical advisors describing their efforts to influence GPs' prescribing and with GPs who describe perceived constraints on prescribing. The focus of the interviews was upon external constraints and pressures on prescribing. These external factors are then interpreted in terms of the concepts of proletarianisation and deprofessionalisation.

Following the original formulation of the concept by McKinlay and Arches (1985) in relation to American medicine, proletarianisation is here considered as any trend towards greater control over professional activities by the organisation which principally administers primary care at the local level in the NHS, the FHSA. Instances of such control in the field of prescribing would be the imposition of protocols, guidelines or other techniques of influencing clinical decisions by applying formal, externally-derived rules. Rizer and Walczak (1988) refer to the threats to professional dominance as challenges by 'formal rationality' to 'substantive rationality'. Formal rationality is a Weberian concept that refers to the growing emphasis upon universally applied rules, regulations and laws, especially promoted by the large-scale structures of modern bureaucracies. Substantive rationality refers to the pursuit of social values such as the good of the client in the case of professional work. Ritzer and Walczak see the formal rationality of modern bureaucracies as in opposition to the substantive rationality of professions.

Deprofessionalisation is here considered to be any trend towards diminished respect for professional activities on the part of the public. According to Haug (1973), greater access to and understanding of medical knowledge will result in a decline in respect for medical expertise and greater readiness by patients and consumers to challenge medical decisions. In the field of prescribing, this would be evidenced by increased tendencies for patients specifically to ask for particular drugs and to challenge the rationale of prescribing decisions. At least in private and 'unofficial' accounts, evidence already exists of such challenges to medical authority in lay views about medical prescriptions (Britten 1996).

More general evidence already exists which suggests that British general practice is undergoing adverse changes in work experience. Recent research has noted a decrease in general practitioners' job satisfaction since the introduction of the new contract with GP respondents experiencing high levels of stress, anxiety and depression (Sutherland and Cooper 1992, Chambers and Belcher 1993, Caplan 1994). Young doctors have reported increased disillusionment with medical practice, with concern being expressed about the declining popularity of general practice as a career (Dillner 1994, Grey 1990). Low morale in general practice has been compounded by an increased workload and an increasing number of complaints about the health service (Beecham 1993, Handysides 1994, GP Workload Survey 1994, Department of Health 1991). Within prescribing, general practitioners have expressed a high level of concern regarding current pressures that could affect prescribing (Weiss *et al.* 1996). Perceived pressures examined include an increased burden for providing health care and a greater sense of pressure from demanding patients. While this evidence may not provide direct proof for either the proletarianisation or deprofessionalisation thesis, it does suggest a need for research which, as will be discussed here, will explore the extent to which recent developments in health care can be viewed as possible forces for the deprofessionalisation or proletarianisation of medicine. The particular arena chosen for this investigation is primary care prescribing.

Methods

Five FHSA medical advisers and twenty-three general practitioners were interviewed using an unstructured interview format between October 1993 and January 1994. In an effort to contextualise the broader effects of changes in health care policy on prescribing, several other interviews and field observations were conducted within the FHSA, at region, and the NHS

Management Executive. The results of this group of interviews and observations provided background information on prescribing but will not be discussed further. The FHSA advisors were selected non-randomly based upon geographical location. To obtain the interview sample for the general practitioners, 25 GPs were randomly selected from 49 respondents who had earlier completed a questionnaire as part of a previous study (Weiss 1995). The 49 respondents from the earlier study represented a response rate of 36 per cent to a questionnaire of 30 case vignettes examining GPs' decision-making. Out of the 25 GPs selected for interview, 17 (68 per cent) participated. It was anticipated that physicians from fund-holding practices could have different perceptions of prescribing than those from non-fundholding practices. With the bias in the sample group towards non-fundholders, nine additional fundholding GPs within the two FHSAs were also contacted for interview so that a greater diversity of opinion could be obtained. These fundholding GPs included GPs who were in their preparatory year prior to becoming fundholders in April 1994 at the time of the interview. Five of the nine (56 per cent) fundholding GPs agreed to be interviewed. The secretary of the relevant Local Medical Committee[1] was also selected for interview. The total sample of 23 GPs included 8 fundholders, 14 non-fundholders and one Secretary of the Local Medical Committee who was non-practising.

The general practitioners in the interview sample were between the ages of 34 and 58 with a mean age of 45 years. Twelve respondents were Members of the Royal College of General Practitioners. Twenty of the 23 general practitioners and all of the medical advisers interviewed were male. In the interests of confidentiality and simplicity, the pronouns 'he' and 'his' will be used to describe the interviewees.

During the interviews, GP respondents were encouraged to discuss the factors most influencing their prescribing, to express their perceptions of their role as prescribers and to discuss how this role had been affected by the changing nature of health care. FHSA advisers were asked about their role in prescribing, their objectives or targets for prescribing, how they influenced the prescribing of GPs and any difficulties they had experienced in trying to change GP prescribing behaviour. The interviews were conducted by one of the authors (MCW) who had professional training in pharmacy and social science; all the respondents were informed of the interviewer's background. It was also made clear that interviews were to contribute to a research study, with no direct involvement from the Department of Health or the FHSA. All the interviews were transcribed. The data were analysed using the principles for the analysis of qualitative research as described by Becker and Geer (1982). Initially, broad, preliminary distinctions were made between quotations that discussed different subject areas. Quotations were then grouped together into categories which discussed similar themes. At this point, some categorical distinctions were refined through a process of sub-categorisation. Other categories were linked and integrated with different categories by defining the nature of the relationship between related quotations. Once the categories were fully elaborated, several core categories and related themes emerged from the data.

Results

The paper proceeds by considering, first, the views of FHSA advisers, followed by those of general practitioners.

FHSA advisors and prescribing

A primary source of FHSA influence on general practitioners' prescribing is through the medical adviser. However, in some FHSAs, a prescribing team has evolved which might include one or two pharmaceutical advisers or a designated Prescribing Adviser (usually a pharmacist) in addition to the medical adviser. As well as prescribing, this team has responsibility for community pharmacists', opticians' and dentists' remuneration, the community pharmacy-GP interface, the primary-secondary care interface and other medical concerns such as the deputising service[2]. These interviews focused solely on the role of the medical adviser in prescribing.

FHSA medical advisers saw their main responsibility as being to serve as the main link between general practitioners and the FHSA. This included advising GPs on initiatives from the authority and, likewise, bringing back any comments or complaints from general practitioners to the FHSA. They described a variety of activities which might be considered to have potential 'proletarianising' consequences for the GP. This included setting the drug budgets for both fundholding and non-fundholding practices and the more general strategic objectives raising GPs' awareness of cost without detriment to patient care:

> I think we do have a role to see that they are paying attention to costs and they don't regard prescribing as a totally open cheque book . . . We also have a responsibility . . . to make sure that they don't let quality suffer (FHSA Interview 1).

> I think the FHSA role is to advise and to be a resource both for drug information . . . and also for prescribing information. And advising GPs within that profile . . . where they can make cost savings (FHSA Interview 4).

In this respect, these FHSA advisers had developed a delicate role in influencing prescribing. They recognised the need to foster rationality and cost-effectiveness in prescribing, in line with their more managerial agenda yet did not want to be too overtly challenging to general practitioners' autonomy. To accommodate this managerial agenda, these respondents had also undertaken specific initiatives in line with regional or FHSA targets for prescribing. These initiatives included increasing the overall rate of generic prescribing, increasing generic prescribing within specific therapeutic areas, decreasing a practice's range of drugs prescribed or encouraging therapeutic substitution (changing the types of drugs prescribed within a broad therapeutic area).

In this respect, the advisers' backgrounds as former practising GPs gave them an advantage in fostering greater rationality in prescribing. They were all in their mid-forties to fifties and, as the medical adviser role had been created with the health care changes begun in 1990, no one had been in post longer than 3 years at the time of interview. Although concerned with rational prescribing, they frequently focused on the need to decrease prescribing costs. Since they were now employed by the FHSA, there was a potential for them to feel some degree of conflict between their role as FHSA adviser and their allegiance to their professional colleagues. Some advisers aligned themselves more with their former colleagues than with their current employer:

> Most GPs do want to prescribe cost-effectively actually, I don't think they get any pleasure out of spending more money than necessary in prescribing . . . I was actually quite a high cost prescriber (laughter). I know why . . . So it gives me a particular sympathy with GPs who have high costs . . . (FHSA Interview 1).

Another respondent was similarly sympathetic to GPs but had adopted a more confrontational approach with his FHSA managers:

> I get into trouble with the managers but it does mean that I can at least face the GPs . . . We have GPs ring up about all manner of things say 'I knew you'd understand' . . . They find they have an ally here who knows some of the problems (FHSA Interview 3).

These quotations suggest that good relationships with the GPs were quite important to these advisers. They prided themselves on the way in which GPs looked upon the medical advisor as one of their own. To achieve a balance between their natural sympathies towards GPs and their FHSA responsibilities did not need to be particularly problematic, but it may have required a little ingenuity:

> I think they [FHSA managers] realise we are acting with a professional viewpoint. If we can find a form of words whereby we're happy that the professional aspects are taken care of and region is happy that costs are taken care of. I mean, life is just a question of putting words in the right order, really . . . and getting one's point across (FHSA Interview 3).

Indeed, should the FHSA have wished to adopt a stronger role in achieving changes in general practitioners' prescribing, it is unlikely that this group of advisors would have supported such a development:

You've got to respect the fact that no administration has got the patient
in front of them . . . Therefore the GP has got to be allowed to
prescribe . . . without having to feel totally constrained by cost . . . if
anything goes wrong, they've got the problem (FHSA Interview 4).

These advisors apparently understood their role as agents of the government's agenda by encouraging rationality and cost-effectiveness in prescribing but also needed to recognise and make accommodations to the reality
of prescribing for general practitioners. Indeed, some respondents were
openly critical of some of the current health care policies. One respondent
voiced grave concerns over fundholding, in complete contradiction to his
FHSA role, whereby doctors may be tempted to withhold drugs should their
budget be overspent. Another respondent was critical of the effect of policies
which raise patient expectations of medical care, while applying pressure on
GPs to keep costs down:

They [GPs] feel they have been victimised anyway all along . . . they've
been whipped in a way to do things to bail the government out of what
. . . was the government's fault in the first place (FHSA Interview 4).

However, it was also possible to be equally critical of some of the government's policies without expressing sympathy with the front-line practitioner.
Indeed, one respondent suggested an alternative solution whereby the power
to influence the prescribing of certain intransigent general practitioners was
concentrated within the FHSA itself:

I think there is scope to have some sort of stick . . . I would like the power
to make a withholding from a practice that over-spends on their IPA
[drugs' budget] and uses drugs that are not on [an] NHS approved
list . . . any overexpenditure that you [a high cost GP] make as a result of
not making these changes will come out of your pocket. And I guarantee
that however high his principles were, he would make the changes
(FHSA Interview 5).

This respondent was careful to emphasise that he did not want the Regional
Health Authority to give advice to the FHSA as to how to use this stick,
but felt it to be a discretionary power within the FHSA. This adviser saw
himself as distinct from government or regional doctrine, and was openly
suspicious of governmental motives for health care policies.

In contrast to his colleagues, there was one respondent who allied himself
more closely with the ethos of health care policies and was enthusiastic to
make prescribing changes. His role as FHSA adviser was unproblematic.
Difficulties with GPs who were reticent to make prescribing changes were
viewed as solvable problems:

> One of the big lessons of fundholding is that there are savings to be made in the area of prescribing . . . I'm always at pains to point out that we are going to be just as concerned . . . [about] underprescribing, we'll be just as keen to point that out and encourage more prescribing . . . [but] there are probably more issues of where there is potential over-prescribing than there are under-prescribing (FHSA Interview 2).

Regardless of whether the advisors aligned themselves with general practitioners or health policy objectives, all the respondents mentioned the importance of emphasising quality, not just cost, in their messages to GPs. This could be because quality initiatives make the FHSA role more palatable to GPs, increasing the likelihood that other messages involving cost will also be taken on board. In addition, some respondents felt they had a professional obligation to encourage good quality prescribing and improve patient care irrespective of any governmental initiatives on quality. This higher professional calling may have made their own, potentially conflicting, role as FHSA adviser more palatable to themselves. Finally, for the advisors who aligned themselves with 'ordinary' general practitioners, there appeared to be a desire to demonstrate an *esprit de corps* with their professional colleagues. By emphasising the importance of quality in prescribing, they were showing that they recognised the wider concerns of their professional group.

It was not only an emphasis on quality in prescribing that could be used as a strategy to influence the prescribing behaviour of GPs in line with the government's agenda for achieving rationality in prescribing. Several respondents mentioned the 'one cake' argument and used this to try to influence GPs:

> . . . Making sure that every GP is aware that if he is profligate with his use of drugs, then that is only going to come off the health service somewhere else. And that he owes it to the rest of the health service to be careful of what he does or she does (FHSA Interview 2).

Another potent method of influencing the prescribing of general practitioners was the use of peer pressure through comparative prescribing data. This could be used at the practice level, whereby one practice's prescribing was compared to other practices within the FHSA, or among partners in a practice. If a GP saw his prescribing as being vastly different from his peers, it could be a powerful influence:

> If a doctor was prescribing a drug, appetite suppressants, we can say, 'well, you're the only practice that's actually prescribing these' . . . One can perhaps sometimes shame them into changing. Get a little question mark every time they're about to write something . . .
> (FHSA Interview 3).

This respondent suggested that, not only did GPs dislike being radically different from their colleagues, they also liked to be liked by their FHSA. Advisors would use this need to be liked in their interactions with GPs:

> Practices like to be liked by us. If they are good at their prescribing, they are liked by us . . . We've [the FHSA] been a bit more gentle in our approach [to increase generic prescribing] . . . Appealing to their professional integrity. What we call bullying a little (FHSA Interview 3).

This approach could be used to emphasise general practitioners' wider professional responsibility to good medical practice where a professional should always be looking for ways to improve the quality of care provided. By stimulating discussion and debate within a practice, the adviser could develop GP partners' ownership in an idea in order to change their prescribing behaviour:

> 'If you can . . . sow the seeds in their minds of an idea, that they during a discussion then develop . . . sort of nurture and they think it's their idea . . . it's ownership of the idea. I think some flattery is important to tell them that they're good at prescribing . . . Have you thought of applying your good practices in this area in other areas? (FHSA Interview 3).

While the advisers agreed that one of the best methods of influencing prescribing was as a catalyst to practice debate using comparative prescribing data, it was recognised that it was appropriate to tailor the method to the individual. Other methods of influence included FHSA newsletters, the use of local consultants or financial incentives including fundholding. One advisor was able to distribute FHSA prescribing information through the Local Medical Committee (LMC), recognising that the LMC gave greater credibility to the prescribing data in the eyes of the GPs. Another advisor used a service to test the quality of generic drugs so that, should a GP query the efficacy of a generic product, this could be countered immediately.

With such a range of methods at their disposal and a keen insight into the most successful strategies to take when approaching GPs, the advisers still experienced some difficulties in influencing GP prescribing. Among non-fundholders, the most common difficulty was indifference:

> One of our biggest problems is that we still get the 'so what' response. So you're going to be on a massive overspend, so what? Our answer is well, people may not get operations done next year but that doesn't come home on a personal basis. They can't relate it to their own individual patients (FHSA Interview 2).

Advisers believed some GPs to have a philosophical stance against current health care policies:

> I think one of them called it, it's government blackmail – the threat that if you overspend on your IPA [drugs' budget], the money will be lopped off hospital and community services . . . 'I'm not going to subject myself to blackmail so I'm not going to do it' (FHSA Interview 5).

As medical advisers were viewed as the front-line for government health care policies, many GPs were considered distrustful of the FHSA's motives for concentrating on prescribing:

> For quite a long time there was a lot of antagonism to the new contract and anything that the government wanted to do was greeted with suspicion by the doctors . . . they saw cutting prescribing costs as just another example of the government trying to make economies that they shouldn't be making in the health service (FHSA Interview 1).

There were few incentives for non-fundholding doctors to change their prescribing habits, particularly in the area of generic substitution. To change a patient's medication to the generic equivalent meant providing a detailed explanation to the patient. Doctors also perceived patient resistance to generic substitution on the basis of decreased efficacy of the generic drug. Advisers recognised that the general benefit of the national economy was frequently not a strong enough incentive to motivate GPs to alter their prescribing. Compounding this difficulty were differences in clinical opinion, particularly problematic in clinical areas which lacked a clear treatment choice. From the advisor's view, a GP might prefer a drug which, while not clinically irrational, is more expensive:

> It's a bit like going to work in your Bentley when you could have gone in your Metro . . . [If a high cost prescriber says] 'We think ACE inhibitors are the best treatment for mild hypertension.' It's difficult to argue against that. And one just goes on by saying, well, the majority of practices in the county find that they are quite happy using so-and-so . . . there's no way that one can say that a doctor who prescribes on that basis is doing anything wrong (FHSA Interview 3).

While the GP might not be clinically wrong, the adviser was concerned that he might be equating the best with the most expensive:

> They just assume that you get what you pay for in this world and if it's more expensive, it must be better (FHSA Interview 2).

Indeed, there was a sense that clinical freedom and professional independence was what attracted many GPs into general practice in the first place:

> They just don't like the thought of outsiders going in and telling them what to do . . . many are in general practice rather than anything else

because they like the independence of it. They like to be able to make their own decisions (FHSA Interview 1).

Advisers sympathised with some of the practical difficulties in trying to make prescribing changes. Pressures from patients, the power of the pharmaceutical industry, the ease with which existing computer systems adapt to change and the difficulties in modifying long-standing habits were all cited as disincentives to change. The personality of the GP also played an important part:

If they're the sort of doctor who likes to wear belt and braces and to be doubly sure, then he's probably going to prescribe more than a doctor who has a more happy go lucky attitude and is more prepared to live with a bit of risk (FHSA Interview 1).

The medical advisers interviewed had carefully considered a range of methods by which to influence general practitioners' prescribing and to communicate the principles of rational prescribing. They were aware of the limitations to different methods and had developed an eclectic approach by adapting the method to suit an individual GP. Respondents were able to describe a number of problems in influencing the prescribing of GPs but were able to concentrate their efforts on problems that could be overcome through their influencing skills. Most noticeable were the intricacies of the relationship between medical advisors and GPs, and the extent to which these intricacies had been appreciated by the advisors.

In terms of the hypothesis of proletarianisation, it is clearly the intention of FHSAs to promote a wider application of the formal rationality to which Ritzer and Walczak (1988) refer. GPs are expected, increasingly, to adopt approaches to prescribing generated by the FHSA's views of appropriateness and cost-effectiveness. The FHSA adviser currently attempts to promote such formal rationality by the micro-management of attitudes rather than more confrontational methods. This approach is in stark contrast to the direct imposition of rules, where adherence is routinely monitored, that is described by McKinlay and Arches's (1985) in relation to doctors in American hospitals.

General practitioners' views of managerial influences on prescribing
Beginning in the 1980s, the government introduced a series of health care reforms that targeted, amongst other issues, primary care prescribing. Documents such as *Promoting Better Health* (Secretaries of State for Social Services 1987) and the 1989 GP contract (Department of Health and the Welsh Office 1989), brought major changes to primary care by increasing consumer choice, by placing a greater emphasis on health promotion and disease prevention and by supporting greater management and budgetary control (Hannay 1992). In terms of prescribing, the most significant document

was the white paper, *Working for Patients* (Secretaries of State for Health 1989). This document initiated the development of GP fundholding and indicative prescribing amounts (IPA), or notional drug budgets, for non-fundholding practices.

All of these health care developments, by implication or design, advocated more rational prescribing in primary care. However, none of the general practitioners in this sample found the trend towards more rational prescribing to be particularly problematic at a general level. The FHSA's more proactive role in prescribing was similarly perceived to be wholly appropriate. In none of the interviews did a GP cite any experience of undue or inappropriate pressure from the FHSA generally or from medical advisers specifically. One general practitioner explained his perceptions of rational prescribing and the logical wisdom of approaching prescribing in this manner:

> In other words, if there is a well-established clinical indication, we should prescribe something that is safe and effective. Having said all of that, I think it's reasonable to choose the most cost-effective [drug] (GP 14).

Within the general conceptions of rational prescribing, it was always cost considerations that were, potentially, of most concern to these GPs. However, these general practitioners were amenable to incorporating cost into their prescribing decisions, on the proviso that patient care should not be adversely affected:

> I think the doctor has still got to have the freedom to prescribe what he feels is in the best interest of that patient. But I think the doctor also has a responsibility to try and keep the cost down to a minimum (GP 21).

This general practitioner suggested that his role as a physician acting in the patient's best interest was compatible with his social responsibility to maximise the limited financial resource available for health care. In this respect, the trend towards a greater cost awareness in prescribing was fairly unproblematic. Indeed, one non-fundholder felt that the pressure to reduce expenditure was not unreasonable:

> There is constant pressure to prescribe cheaper which isn't necessarily a bad thing. I think unless you get pressure from prescribing, you all tend to prescribe expensively – often for no benefit (GP 18, non-fundholder).

It is perhaps unsurprising that a greater cost awareness was acceptable to these GPs provided they retained control over prescribing. They saw themselves as retaining the ability to decide the extent to which they incorporated cost into individual patient decisions. Indeed, most respondents recognised that it was important to try to achieve a balance between clinical freedom and some standardisation of treatment:

I don't believe that one should necessarily say that everybody should be like peas in a pod and prescribing in exactly the same fashion. I do believe there's to be a certain amount of freedom. But, having said that, there must be certain norms, certain criteria that are generally accepted for certain conditions (GP 5).

For these general practitioners rational prescribing was about achieving a balance: between clinical freedom and standardisation of treatment and between prescribing costs and quality.

Indeed, the general acceptance of the principles of cost effectiveness extended to the much larger and more contentious issue of fundholding. While respondents were generally amenable to incorporating cost into their decision-making, some respondents felt that fundholding emphasised cost disproportionately within the framework of rational prescribing. Their belief was that cost, as opposed to quality, was the main focus of fundholding. Within the context of rational prescribing, appropriateness of care meant that patients had a right to advice not unduly influenced by cost:

The person who is giving the advice and is making an unbiased opinion . . . (should give that) unbiased opinion regardless of what the cost implications are. Patients have to have the right to get advice from their doctor that doesn't take those sort of factors into account (GP 20, non-fundholder).

The underlying assumption of this statement is that fundholders, by taking cost into account may be swayed into giving advice which is not in the patient's best interest. This emphasis on cost, in preference to quality, became a source of conflict for prescribing as non-fundholders speculated how patient care decisions could be affected, should a practice go fundholding:

What concerns me is that when it comes to the crunch . . . is the decision as to who has the operation dealt with financially or is it dealt with by the need of the patient? (GP 8, non-fundholder).

Another non-fundholder more bluntly stated his ultimate fear:

So it's all very well saying, bring the price down but then the cheapest patients are undoubtedly dead ones (GP 17, non-fundholder).

These non-fundholders had theoretical concerns about the effect of fund-holding on clinical autonomy. However, these speculative concerns were not supported by fundholders. Fundholders maintained that cost and quality received equal weight within their conceptions of rational decision-making:

If we are going to use a drug, we will use it because we think it's going to
be efficient. We will choose it because we think it's going to be free from
side effects and then we will use it – as opposed to another drug – because
we think it's more economical. In that order. Not the reverse order
(GP 19, fundholder).

According to this respondent, fundholders' ethical standards would keep
costs in perspective and this would guide them through their clinical decisions. These fundholders viewed their control over prescribing as being
unaffected by any external pressure to reduce cost as implied by fundholding. In addition, these fundholders felt they could realise patient benefits
through the development of formularies and therapeutic guidelines. The
process of developing these guidelines was said to make their prescribing
more rational:

I think we're going to be trying to streamline that a little bit so that we're
using fewer and a more rigorously thought-out range of drugs rather than
whatever the rep's been to talk about the previous week (GP 15,
fundholder).

Ultimately, it was believed that a more rationally-selected group of drugs
should also improve patient care. In addition, any cost savings generated
from the development of formularies and guidelines could be used on developing and improving patient services. Indeed, it was not only that these
fundholders could improve the quality of their prescribing, but that their
greater control over resources would mean they could make their provision
of patient services more rational overall:

To have more control over our own resources . . . To not have to put up
with long waits for our patients to get treatment. To be able to target
resources where we think it's appropriate (GP 7, fundholder).

In this general practitioner's view, fundholders' ability to target financial
resources meant that issues relating to quality, including efficacy, safety
and appropriateness, could be addressed through fundholding. While non-
fundholders could similarly target their resources, fundholders felt they had
the incentive to target resources and reap the financial and professional
rewards of greater financial control. Through the provision of cost and
outcome information, these fundholders argued that they were able to target
certain disease states, examine drug choice within a therapeutic area or
compare the cost and outcomes of a drug treatment versus surgery:

Before [fundholding] we just bumbled a lot – we sent patients out, we
didn't know how many we were sending out 'cause we never bothered
to look. You didn't really look at the outcomes of referrals as, you

know . . . how are [we] sending our stuff that needs referring? . . . You actually start to account, to see what you're doing and see where you can do better, where things are falling down (GP 21, fundholder).

This fundholder discussed some of the features of fundholding: greater accountability, an increased emphasis on audit and the monitoring of expenditure in relation to the services provided. Fundholders asserted that these developments have improved patient care:

Some of the [prescribing] data [that] comes through demonstrates that there are extraordinary differences in prescribing habits . . . and the providing of good information about costs and our comparative performance allows us to behave appropriately (GP 19, fundholder).

Increased cost information and comparative data made these general practitioners feel they were being more rational in their approach to prescribing and in their consideration of how to allocate their limited resources. In this manner, through a realisation of the cost benefits of fundholding, these respondents were able to adhere to the principles of rational prescribing. In their opinion, the end result of fundholding was to encourage a more considered approach to decision-making which would ultimately improve patient care.

What may appear to be processes of rationalisation consistent with the thesis of proletarianisation, for example pressures to adopt prescribing protocols and cost containment considerations that limit clinical freedom, were generally not viewed in this way by GPs. This is in contrast to an ethnographic study of American hospital doctors' responses to bureaucratisation which showed that doctors made direct connections between hospital management initiatives to control costs and threats to their professional autonomy (Fielding 1990). Many GPs viewed current policy initiatives as actually enhancing their control. Those who were opposed to developments such as fundholding held such views more because of ethical concerns about the scheme being used to ration resources for health care as a whole than because of threats to individual clinical autonomy.

Prescribing as a coping strategy
While the managerial influence was not perceived as an overt challenge, interviews with the GPs underlined the importance of clinical autonomy at the level of the individual consultation. Indeed, the main concern about government and FHSA objectives in controlling prescribing was less about external impositions on their clinical autonomy, as such, and more a concern that too inflexible an approach would limit their use of prescribing as a pragmatic problem-solving device. While these GPs may have accepted the general principles of rational prescribing, they recognised that there were circumstances in the context of everyday patient situations in which rational

prescribing was impracticable. In this manner, these general practitioners resisted complete rationality in their decision-making by retaining the discretion to prescribe in an 'irrational' way to cope with their work. In common with previous research, general practitioners in this sample described situations in which they used a prescription to conclude a consultation and forestall lengthy discussion (Hall 1980, Comaroff 1976). One respondent discussed how the prescription assisted in coping with the demands of a busy clinic:

> [A prescription is] the fastest way to get the patient out the door. It's probably the worst way to get the patient out the door but it's the fastest way. It's rather short-termism because they come right back . . . But when you're engulfed by minor ailments because there's a bug going round or there's flu going round, then it's sometimes the only sane way out of a busy clinic (GP 4).

This respondent acknowledged the use of prescribing as a coping strategy while recognising that the outcome was counter-productive to longer-term patient management and the principles of rational prescribing. The chief advantage seen by these general practitioners in opting for the short-term alternative was that it allowed them greater control over their time. These respondents viewed the benefits of prescribing as a method of coping to be particularly important when there was the added pressure of an increased workload:

> There have been studies which suggest . . . the shorter the length of consultation, the greater is the likelihood of a prescription being produced. So, if you say that our workload is increasing, and by God it is . . . then it may be in fact . . . that the aim of the consultation is to get the blighter out as quickly as possible. And the quickest way to get somebody out the door, traditionally, is to scrawl something on a piece of paper and open the door for them (GP 23).

It was not only time constraints and practice pressures which were alleviated through prescribing. The GPs used the prescription to cope with, or diffuse, potentially demanding or difficult patient situations:

> If you were in a confrontational situation with a patient, then I think it's often easier to give a prescription than to actually sit and discuss (GP 6).

However, patients were not the only potential source of irrational prescribing. Greater control over prescribing could also help general practitioners cope on a more personal level. These respondents acknowledged that prescribing gave them the flexibility to cope with their own perceived levels of stress:

In practice, I would probably prescribe more towards the end of the day than earlier in the day, more in busy surgery than in a quiet surgery, more if I'm running behind than if I'm running on time. In other words, it relates to my levels of stress as much as it may do to what is wrong with the patient (GP 11).

Another GP perceived the psychological benefits of prescribing slightly differently:

Sometimes you feel more in a prescribing mode and sometimes you try and be more into an explaining and let's withhold the prescription [mode] – and so I'm sure how I'm feeling can make a difference (GP 12).

These respondents described prescribing as a mechanism for coping with practice, patient and personal needs. However, general practitioners also gained a sense of their professional effectiveness through the process of prescribing. Comparable to the findings of Stimson and Webb (1975), a prescription could be used to reduce the uncertainty inherent in general practice. This may have been particularly important in situations where there was no obvious rational prescribing treatment option:

I have a suspicion that I might be more responsive to the more social factors and be persuaded to prescribe when my medical persona would be saying 'well, perhaps you shouldn't'. I think, with sore throat in particular, that's the one thing where all doctors know there really isn't any truly, logical way of deciding who needs antibiotics and who doesn't (GP 5).

Comaroff (1976) also explains how the prescription can give both the doctor and the patient the feeling that an unambiguous diagnosis, with an appropriately straightforward therapy, has been found to explain the patient's illness. Prescribing as a method of reducing medical uncertainty can also offer medicolegal benefits by allowing the doctor to 'err on the side of caution.' As described by Scheff (1963), prescribing can result from the fear of overlooking serious illness and may decrease the likelihood of litigation:

And you want a safeguard . . . You see a child with an infection . . . I've seen complaints where the doctor hasn't given a prescription and the mother's carted the child off to the hospital 3 hours later and the casualty officer – who actually probably knows less than the GP – has given a prescription. And they've used that as grounds for a complaint. You know, the hospital thought it was necessary to give an antibiotic, why didn't the doctor? (GP 6).

Given the ambiguity inherent in general medical practice, prescribing can reduce the general practitioner's own sense of uncertainty surrounding medical practice and can convey the impression of a clear choice of treatment. A prescription also offers medico-legal benefits as it frequently represents the cautious treatment option. In particular, antibiotic prescriptions can be seen as decreasing the possibility of a deterioration in the patient's condition and the chance of rare complications.

Comaroff (1976) suggests that the prescription can benefit the general practitioner by communicating his or her concern for the patient and their willingness to provide a cure. It is an economical means to demonstrate symbolically the physician's concern for the patient's well-being. The prescription is a sign of action by the doctor (Hall 1980), showing that s/he is 'doing something' concrete to help the patient (Stimson and Webb 1975, Comaroff 1976). This theme of 'doing something' can be seen in the following extract:

> A patient came to me . . . who has cancer and was waiting for
> chemotherapy. She got a sore throat. I knew that she was terrified that her
> chemotherapy would be cancelled . . . she was convinced she would never
> get better from the sore throat and it was some other sort of cancer.
> And I gave her antibiotics more or less without even bothering to look at
> it. I mean, I did look at it but I was going to give her antibiotics anyway
> because she'd got herself into such a tiz – but they were entirely to calm
> her down (GP 17).

In this instance this general practitioner felt the need to prescribe as a way of managing the patient's distress. Whether or not the prescription was clinically necessary was of secondary concern. It can be speculated that the action of prescribing enabled the physician to feel as if he had done something to help the patient and demonstrated his concern for the patient's general medical condition.

As noted by another author (Harris 1980), several general practitioners in this sample discussed circumstances where prescribing could serve an important function in maintaining and developing doctor-patient relationships. One doctor described a consultation where prescribing was more likely to occur because of the specific features of the relationship:

> Whilst clinically I would put it in the same trivial category as another
> person who I would not prescribe for, because, perhaps, our particular
> doctor-patient relationship would be a more paternalistic one: or, you
> know, 'I'll take over, take command, I've got broad shoulders, I'll give you
> an antibiotic because that will make you feel better' even though maybe
> it would be completely and utterly inappropriate. But it might be more
> appropriate in the context of that relationship rather than in the context
> of that illness (GP 4).

This general practitioner may have had more egalitarian relationships with other patients but felt that, at this patient's behest, he was being placed in a more paternalistic relationship. By acceding to the patient's wishes for a prescription, this general practitioner was fulfilling the patient's expectations of him as a physician irrespective of any clinical rationale for the prescription. In a similar vein, another general practitioner used a prescription to build up his relationships with patients:

> I use the antibiotic prescribing as a bargaining chip. So if the chip
> goes in there – I point out to the patient I don't think it is necessary.
> That gives me a bargaining point for next time . . . hopefully, at a
> later date you get up your bargaining points and you say, 'What are
> the real issues, why do you keep attending? What's going on?'
> (GP 1).

By giving the patient a prescription and acknowledging their concerns, he was building up his credibility with the patient so that underlying issues for a patient's frequent surgery attendance could be addressed at a later date. For both these general practitioners, the prescription was being used as a device to endorse or enhance the doctor's relationship with the patient irrespective of the clinical necessity of the prescription.

These findings reinforce previous research which has identified a range of circumstances in which a prescription could be used 'irrationally'. To this end, all the respondents were aware of the interviewer's background as a pharmacist. This was an advantage when clinical issues were discussed and rationales and influences on prescribing could be followed-up closely. Equally, this could have had a detrimental effect upon the respondents' willingness to admit to 'irrational' prescribing strategies with another health professional who may have been perceived to be judging the rationality of the respondents' prescribing. However, given the respondents' candour and the diverse range of 'irrational' prescribing strategies mentioned, respondent bias did not appear to be problematic. Respondents in this study described situations where they would use a prescription to cope with personal, patient and practice demands and as a method of reinforcing their sense of professional effectiveness. While it might be anticipated that the current emphasis on rational prescribing might make physicians less likely to use, or admit to using, a prescription in this manner, the findings of this study suggest that GPs, perhaps more than ever, need prescribing as a method of coping with their workload pressures.

The effect of consumerism on prescribing
GPs did, therefore, experience external pressures on their work but, in the terms of this analysis, they derived more from processes akin to deprofessionalisation than proletarianisation. The greater challenge to professional control over prescribing was felt to come from patients. In common with the findings of Bradley (1992a), general practitioners identified patient expectations as an important influence on their prescribing:

My own belief is that these things should be a shared decision between doctor and patient . . . But I think one has to accept that . . . one's patient's decision will be the one that actually wins the day (GP 13).

Acceding to the wishes of patients was also felt to have certain advantages:

I am susceptible to patient pressure or I'm certainly very willing to negotiate with patients about what they feel they want to do with the treatment. I think that . . . if you cooperate and the patient gets what they want then there's certainly a lot of psychological (benefit) (GP 12).

However, taking into account patients' expectations of drug therapy may also have created some conflict between patients' expectations of drug therapy and the GP's desire to prescribe rationally:

(MW: What influences your decision whether or not to prescribe?) I think patient demand. I think it is very important to try and determine what the individual wants and what their expectations are. And if I'm faced with a patient or a mother who very much wants some treatment for their sore throat, then I'm more inclined to prescribe it, to be honest (GP 9).

The patient's expectations would certainly play a role and so there are occasions where one might end up prescribing maybe even against one's better judgment (GP 5).

Increased patient demand in conflict with the doctor's desire to prescribe more rationally may be compounded by historical prescribing patterns, placing the prescribing GP in a difficult situation with respect to his professional colleagues, should s/he try to alter patients' misconceptions of drug therapy:

'My previous doctor always gives me penicillin, I get better in 48 hours' – you then have to take a decision on the spot. Are you going to argue the toss about the viral origins of most of these and destroy that which your colleague or other doctor has done over the years? . . . or, believing you are not going to do any great harm, prescribe . . . (GP 19).

It was the recent trend towards greater consumerism, aided by initiatives such as the Patient's Charter, which could make the possibility of conflict, between demanding patients and the doctor's desire to prescribe more rationally, particularly problematic. Patient demand, and raised societal expectations of health care, had the potential to limit the doctor's clinical freedom to decide appropriate patient management:

There is an increasing group of society that's less willing to accept a non-interventional policy (GP 6).

Interventions in this context included 'positive actions' taken by the physician and may have included prescribing, referral to another clinician or further investigation of the patient's condition. As suggested by the previous respondent, other potential outcomes for a patient consultation such as general health advice or a sympathetic ear, may have been less acceptable.

While the Patient's Charter may have fostered the shift towards a more demanding public, other sources have also contributed to this change. Pressures from the media, particularly women's magazines, and the activities of certain high-profile medical elites favouring the decision to prescribe, make the possibility of not prescribing the more difficult option:

> The number of women that come along and demand, as of right, HRT [hormone replacement therapy] now because Dr. Kindness in *Women's Own* has said . . . go along and see your male chauvinist pig of a doctor and tell him that it's your right to have HRT (GP 6).

> There's always somebody with a hobby horse on radio or television on their own particular subject saying 'Oh my goodness, if you've got low back pain for two minutes, you must see your doctor 'cause it could be ankylosing spondylitis' (GP 10).

These passages suggest that the increased demand for services has placed general practitioners under pressure to address more complaints, many of them trivial. The preceding respondent intimates that he was aggrieved at being at the behest of demanding patients and being bothered by trivial medical complaints. While the doctor may desire to prescribe rationally, it may become an ideal which is increasingly difficult to attain. This sense of being at the behest of demanding patients can be exacerbated in situations where the patient has knowledge of the general practitioner's terms and conditions of service:

> The Patient's Charter has made no end to patient demand. Encouraged the patients to demand things and many of our patients seem well informed about their rights (GP 17).

> I've actually had patients come in and say, 'oh, you recommend so and so. If I find I can have this on prescription and you suggested that I buy it over the counter, I'm going to report you' (GP 20).

A few respondents felt aggrieved at the GP having to meet the raised societal expectations and increasing patient demand for health care. In this view, resources to meet these expectations have not been forthcoming:

> . . . the government in its utter stupidity produces Patient's Charters and raises patient expectation massively . . . and the resources to match what

the government has done in increasing patient expectations have not been provided (GP 19).

Some general practitioners felt themselves particularly compromised by this situation in which the GP represented the first stage in addressing any health care problem. This devolvement of responsibility for health care to the level of the general practitioner was felt acutely by one respondent:

> The GP is the lowest common denominator of any health-related issue. You know, *Woman's Own* 'if in doubt go and see your GP' at the end of every problem letter . . . and that means that a lot of our workload is in response to fairly unimportant issues that are generally caused by raised expectations of what the GP can do – be that by government, or by *Woman's Own*, or whatever. The emphasis, to my mind, should be placed on the individual's shoulder not on the medical profession's shoulders (GP 4).

As noted by another respondent:

> I feel certainly that general practice is sometimes a dumping ground for other things that other people don't want to do or can't do or haven't got the money to do. We're left to sort out the patient (GP 12).

These respondents felt a sense of undue pressure on their prescribing, resulting from overt patient demands and the need to address a range of health-related complaints from raised societal expectations. This pressure has been exacerbated by recent developments in health care and the trend towards greater patient advocacy. It is, of course, important to stress that this sense of being overwhelmed by demanding patients is only one view of the dynamics of consulting behaviour. Social research has consistently indicated how infrequently overt demands are made of GPs (Boulton *et al.* 1986). Previous research has found that up to a fifth of patients leave consultations with a prescription they do not expect (Britten 1995, Webb and Lloyd 1994). Britten recommended that doctors address patient expectations explicitly and, where appropriate, ask patients if they were hoping for a prescription (Britten 1994). In contrast to the work of Britten, this study solely addresses the general practitioner's view of demanding patients without examining the patient's perspective. The comments from these GP respondents reflected perceived demand which might well be different from actual patient demand. Nonetheless, the comments do identify the extent to which these general practitioners felt threatened by demanding patients. This threat to medicine's authority was perceived as coming more from challenges from patients and the public at large. This challenge is closer to Haug's (1973) sense of deprofessionalisation arising from greater access to medical knowledge, the declining awe and trust towards doctors' expertise and an increasingly consumerist public.

Conclusion

Rational prescribing is one of the shared objectives of primary care on which all parties, in principle, can agree. It is prescribing that is appropriate, safe, effective and economic (Parish 1973). In reality, GPs' prescribing decisions are influenced by a wide range of pragmatic and contingent factors (Bradley 1992a). While it is recognised that there are wide variations in GPs' prescribing, the explanations for such variation are limited (McGavock 1988, Forster and Frost 1991). Because of such variation, and the uncontrolled escalation of drug expenditure, FHSAs have been encouraged to play a more proactive role in influencing GPs' decision-making (Audit Commission 1994). Compared with their American counterparts, the British medical profession has not previously experienced the effect of substantial external efforts to scrutinize and influence clinical decisions in this way (Schultz and Harrison 1986, Klein 1995). Primary care prescribing in the NHS is therefore an important subject for the sociology of the professions.

Management has always been potentially constrained in their attempts to control medical professional decisions by the inherent complexity of medical knowledge. For this reason, the emergence of doctors acting in pursuit of management objectives and values represents an important challenge to medical autonomy (Hunter 1992). The involvement of doctors in administration provides for vertical stratification of the medical profession that may result in greater external control of clinical behaviour (Derber 1984, Freidson 1989). The FHSA medical advisors in the current study found their role as agents of government policy, on the one hand, and professional colleagues of GPs on the other, to be a delicate balancing act. Whilst GPs accepted overall health policies, advisors were constantly made aware of the 'realities' of patient care and the professional values of their GP colleagues. As a result, their strategies for modifying colleagues' prescribing were subtle and non-confrontational.

Although it is not possible accurately to assess the effectiveness of such strategies, two observations are striking. Firstly, GPs did not experience the influence of FHSAs as obtrusive or constraining. No GP reported undue or inappropriate interference with their prescribing from FHSAs. Secondly, the objectives of FHSAs to balance prescribing costs and quality were, on the whole, perceived as legitimate. This acceptance may be because of a long-standing recognition by the British medical profession of the need to work within substantial resource constraints in health care (Aaron and Schwartz 1984). However, recent evidence suggests that American primary care physicians also make positive and pragmatic adjustments to the increased economic and managerial controls encountered in managed care (Hoff and McAffrey 1996).

Freidson (1984) has argued against the proletarianisation thesis in relation to the medical profession, partly on the grounds that it is not non-professional managers and bureaucrats but an elite group within the medical profession who increasingly exert control over their medical colleagues. In this way medical dominance is maintained, albeit with the emergence of stratification within the medical profession. The accuracy of this prediction turns entirely on whether this new elite view their role as managers primarily representing the goals of the organisation (formal rationality) or as professionals defending traditional values such as clinical autonomy (substantive rationality). In the context of American hospitals, there are a variety of medico-legal, financial, technological and other mechanisms that operate, contra Freidson, to incorporate the medical elite into the values and mores of hospital bureaucracies and away from their professional colleagues (Burns *et al.* 1990). Sophisticated management information systems also increase the power of the new medical elite to change clinicians' behaviour (Feinglass and Salmon 1990). In the context of British general practice, FHSA medical advisers clearly did not act as the simple expression of NHS organisational objectives. They felt in a contradictory position vis à vis FHSA and medical professional values. They did not appear to have any more powerful techniques or resources than subtle persuasion to promote organisational objectives of value rationality. GPs did not experience the influence of FHSAs and medical advisers as constraining their professional autonomy. It may be argued that the failure for GPs' work to be proletarianised in the sense used here is merely temporary and will change as FHSAs become more experienced in their new proactive role.

Ritzer (1975) makes the important point that professional and bureaucratic rationality need not be in conflict. GPs appeared to accept the external formal rationality of the FHSA in many respects, and only one issue may be of concern in the future interactions between FHSAs and the medical profession. Within the field of prescribing, the only serious managerial threat to GPs' clinical autonomy, their professional subjective rationality, was the possibility that 'irrational' prescribing might be curtailed. 'Irrational' is here used as a short-hand term for prescribing that is not primarily determined by considerations of therapeutic effectiveness, safety and appropriateness in a narrow sense, but is used for short-term problem-solving such as reassuring or satisfying the patient and terminating difficult consultations. This broader role of the prescription in primary care has been noted in previous studies (Comaroff 1976, Bradley 1992b). Cost constraints and practice protocols potentially jeopardise this essential resource in day-to-day practice. However, provided FHSAs only constrain the global resources available for prescribing, GPs retain the flexibility at the level of the individual consultation to prescribe pragmatically. This is an instance of the larger and long-term 'stand-off' between medicine and the state in the NHS with constrained global budgets but considerable discretion in individual clinical decisions (Klein 1995).

The bold organisational initiative of fundholding has changed clinical behaviour. It has substantially reduced prescribing costs and promoted generic prescribing in fundholding practices (Bradlow and Coulter 1993,

Wilson *et al.* 1995). Yet the scheme is voluntary, albeit with financial incentives to participate. Respondents in this study viewed such initiatives as increasing control over many aspects of their work. By 1996, one-third of GPs had entered the scheme. Ritzer (1975), following Weber, argued that it was wrong for sociology to view the growth of complex bureaucracies as inevitably inimical to professional autonomy. Clinical autonomy within capped budgets for the GP in the UK is a very different resolution of the conflict between formal and substantive rationality from that of the detailed monitoring and control over individual clinical decisions experienced by American hospital doctors and may postpone those aspects of proletarianisation that most distress American medicine. The rather general and informal methods of persuasion described by FHSA advisers contrast dramatically with the elaborate information systems that can be employed to influence and alter individual clinical decisions in American hospitals (Feinglass and Salmon 1990).

GPs felt more concerned by growing demands and expectations of patients, fuelled, as they saw it, by government policies focusing upon consumerism. Our study is consistent with the evidence of Bradley (1992a and b) who found that aggressive, demanding or manipulative patients gave rise to the greatest discomfort in GPs' prescribing decisions, as did those decisions brought about by patients' expectations rather than clearly defined therapeutic objectives. Such studies emphasise the effect of psychological responses on the part of the GP to difficult prescribing decisions. We would want to re-frame such evidence within a sociological perspective. To the extent that GPs feel the burden for increasing patient demand for specific drugs or more non-specific expectations for therapies, and feel discomfort by such experiences, then such responses may be related to threats to clinical autonomy with patients constraining medical decision-making. The greater perceived challenge to clinical autonomy comes, not from proletarianisation in the sense of managerial controls over the content of work, but from deprofessionalisation through lay challenges to professional expertise.

Acknowledgements

The authors would like to thank Dr. David Scott for his helpful comments in reviewing the draft of this paper. The authors gratefully acknowledge the assistance of the Department of Health for the funding of this DPhil project at the University of Oxford under the Pharmacy Practice Research Enterprise Scheme. The views expressed in this article are those of the authors and do not necessarily represent the views of the Department of Health.

Notes

1   The Local Medical Committee represents the views of general practitioners within the locality. Activities it is involved with include offering advice to the

FHSA on government initiatives, representing GPs within the complaint's procedure and supporting GPs in negotiating service contracts.
2   The deputising service is an on-call service which provides medical cover at nights
or on the weekend. The FHSA has a responsibility for monitoring the quality of
this service.

References

Aaron, H. and Schwartz, W. (1984) *The Painful Prescription: Rationing Hospital Care*. Washington: Brookings Studies in Social Economics.
Anonymous (1984) Prescribing limit for benzodiazepines and drugs for minor ailments, *The Pharmaceutical Journal*, 233, 595–6.
Audit Commission (1994) *A Prescription for Improvement – Towards More Rational Prescribing in General Practice*. London: HMSO.
Becker, H. and Geer, B. (1982) Participant observation: the analysis of qualitative field data. In Burgess, R. (ed.) *Field Research: A Sourcebook and Field Manual*. London: Allen and Unwin.
Beecham, L. (1993) Powerlessness in general practice is causing low morale, *British Medical Journal*, 307, 806.
Boulton, M., Tuckett, D., Olson, C. and Williams, A. (1986) Social class and the general practice consultation, *Sociology of Health and Illness*, 8, 325–50.
Bradley, C. (1992a) Uncomfortable prescribing decisions: a critical incident study, *British Medical Journal*, 304, 293–6.
Bradley, C. (1992b) Factors which influence the decision whether or not to prescribe: the dilemma facing general practitioners, *British Journal of General Practice*, 42, 454–8.
Bradlow, J. and Coulter, A. (1993) Effect of fundholding and indicative prescribing schemes on general practitioners' prescribing costs, *British Medical Journal*, 307, 1186–9.
Britten, N. (1994) Patient demand for prescriptions: a view from the other side, *Family Practice*, 11, 62–6.
Britten, N. (1995) Patients' demands for prescriptions in primary care, *British Medical Journal*, 310, 1084–5.
Britten, N. (1996) Lay views of drugs and medicines: orthodox and unorthodox accounts. In Williams, S. and Calnan, M. (eds) *Modern Medicine: Lay Perspectives and Experiences*. London: UCL Press.
Burns, L., Andersen, R. and Shortell, S. (1990) The effect of hospital control strategies on physician satisfaction and physician-hospital conflict, *Health Services Research*, 25, 527–60.
Butler, J. (1992) *Patients, Policies and Politics*. Buckingham: Open University Press.
Calnan, M. and Gabe, J. (1991) Recent developments in general practice: a sociological analysis. In Gabe, J., Calnan, M. and Bury, N. (eds) *The Sociology of the Health Service*, London: Routledge.
Calnan, M. and Williams, S. (1995) Challenges to professional autonomy in the United Kingdom? The perceptions of general practitioners, *International Journal of Health Services*, 25, 219–41.
Caplan, R. (1994) Stress, anxiety, and depression in hospital consultants, general practitioners, and senior health service managers, *British Medical Journal*, 309, 1261–3.

Chambers, R. and Belcher, J. (1993) Work patterns of general practitioners before and after the introduction of the 1990 contract, *British Journal of General Practice*, 43, 410–12.

Chew, R. (1992) *Compendium of Health Statistics, Eighth Edition*. London: Office of Health Economics.

Comaroff, J. (1976) A bitter pill to swallow: placebo therapy in general practice, *Sociological Review*, 24, 79–96.

Department of Health and the Welsh Office. (1989) *General Practice in the National Health Service. A New Contract*. London: HMSO.

Department of Health. (1991) *Return of Written Complaints by or on Behalf of Patients in England – Financial Year 1989/90*. Government Statistical Service and Management of Information Division Branch SM12.

Derber, C. (1984) Physicians and their sponsors: the new medical relations of production. In McKinlay, J. (ed.) *Issues in the Political Economy of Health Care*. New York: Tavistock.

Dillner, L. (1994) Doctors are more miserable than ever, says report, *British Medical Journal*, 309, 1529.

Elston, M.A. (1991) The politics of professional power: medicine in a changing health service. In Gabe, J., Calnan, M. and Bury, M. (eds) *The Sociology of the Health Service*. London: Routledge.

Feinglass, J. and Salmon, W. (1990) Corporatisation of medicine: the use of medical management information systems to increase the clinical productivity of physicians, *International Journal of Health Services*, 20, 233–52.

Fielding, S. (1990) Physician reactions to malpractice suits and cost containment in Massachusetts, *Work and Occupations*, 17, 302–19.

Flynn, R. (1992) *Structures of Control in Health Management*. London: Routledge.

Forster, D. and Frost, C. (1991) Use of regression analysis to explain the variation in prescribing rates and costs between family practitioner committees, *British Journal of General Practice*, 41, 67–71.

Freidson, E. (1970) *The Profession of Medicine*. New York: Dodd, Mead and Company.

Freidson, E. (1984) The changing nature of professional control, *Annual Review of Sociology*, 10, 1–20.

Freidson, E. (1989) *Medical Work in America: Essays on Health Care*. New Haven: Yale University Press.

Gabe, J., Kelleher, D. and Williams, G. (eds) (1994) *Challenging Medicine*. London: Routledge.

General Medical Practitioners' Workload Survey 1992–93. *Interim Report. Review Body on Doctors' and Dentists' Remuneration*, London, HMSO.

Grey, D. (1990) Recruitment in general practice, *Practitioner*, 234, 1011.

Hall, D. (1980) Prescribing as social exchange. In Mapes, R.E. (ed.) *Prescribing Practice and Drug Usage*. London: Croom Helm.

Handysides, S. (1994) Morale in general practice: is change the problem or the solution? *British Medical Journal*, 308, 32–4.

Hannay, D.R. (1992) General practitioners' contract: the good, the bad and the slippery slope, *British Journal of General Practice*, 42: 178–9.

Harris, C.M. (1980) Personal view, *British Medical Journal*, 281, 57.

Haug, M. (1973) Deprofessionalisation: an alternative hypothesis for the future. In Halmos, P. (ed.) *Professionalisation and Social Change*. Keele: University of Keele.

Hoff, T. and McAffrey, D. (1996) Adapting, resisting and negotiating: how physicians cope with organisational and economic change, *Work and Occupations*, 23, 165–89.

Hunter, D. (1992) Doctors as managers: poachers turned gamekeepers? *Social Science and Medicine*, 35, 557–66.

Hunter, D. (1994) From tribalism to corporatism: the managerial challenge to medical dominance. In Gabe, J., Kelleher, D. and Williams, G. (eds) *Challenging Medicine*. London: Routledge.

Illife, S. and Munro, J. (1993) General practitioners and incentives, *British Medical Journal*, 307, 1156–7.

Johnson, T.J. (1972) *Professions and Power*. London: Macmillan.

Klein, R. (1995) *The New Politics of the NHS*. London: Longman.

McGavock, H. (1988) Some patterns of prescribing by urban general practitioners, *British Medical Journal*, 296, 900–2.

McKinlay, J. and Arches, J. (1985) Towards the proletarianisation of physicians, *International Journal of Health Services*, 15, 161–95.

McKinlay, J. and Stoeckle, J. (1988) Corporatization and the social transformation of doctoring, *International Journal of Health Services*, 18, 191–205.

Parish, P. (1973) Drug prescribing – the concern of us all, *Royal Society of Health Journal*, 93, 213–7.

Relman, A. (1987) Practicing medicine in the new business climate, *New England Journal of Medicine*, 316, 1150–1.

Ritzer, G. (1975) Professionalization, bureaucratization and rationalization: the views of Max Weber, *Social Forces*, 53, 627–34.

Ritzer, G. and Walczak, D. (1988) Rationalization and the deprofessionalization of physicians, *Social Forces*, 67, 1–22.

Scheff, T.J. (1963) Decision rules, types of error, and their consequences in medical diagnosis, *Behavioural Science*, 8, 97–107.

Schultz, R. and Harrison, S. (1986) Physician autonomy in the Federal Republic of Germany, Great Britain and the United States, *International Journal of Health Planning and Management*, 2, 335–55.

Secretaries of State for Health, Wales, Northern Ireland and Scotland. (1989) *Working for Patients (Cmnd 555)*. London: HMSO.

Secretaries of State for Social Services, Wales, Northern Ireland and Scotland (1987) *Promoting Better Health. The Government's Programme for Improving Primary Health Care (Cmnd 249)*. London: HMSO.

Starr, P. (1982) *The Social Transformation of American Medicine*. New York: Basic Books.

Stimson, G. and Webb, B. (1975) *Going to see the Doctor*. London: Routledge and Kegan Paul.

Sutherland, V.J. and Cooper, C.L. (1992) Job stress, satisfaction, and mental health among general practitioners before and after introduction of new contract, *British Medical Journal*, 304, 1545–8.

Webb, S. and Lloyd, M. (1994) Prescribing and referral in general practice: a study of patients' expectations and doctors' actions, *British Journal of General Practice*, 44, 165–9.

Weiss, M. (1995) *Factors Influencing the Prescribing Decisions of General Practitioners* [DPhil Thesis]. Oxford University.

Weiss, M., Fitzpatrick, R., Scott, D.K. and Goldacre, M.J. (1996) Pressures on the general practitioner and decisions to prescribe, *Family Practice*, 13, 432–8.

Wilson, R., Buchan, I. and Walley, T. (1995) Alterations in prescribing by general practitioner fundholders: an observational study, *British Medical Journal*, 311, 1347–50.

Wolinsky, F. (1993) The professional dominance, deprofessionalisation, proletarianisation and corporatisation perspectives: an overview and synthesis. In Hafferty, F. and McKinlay, J. (eds) *The Changing Medical Profession*. Oxford: Oxford University Press.

Section 3

The Division of Labour in Health Care Work

Introduction

This Section contains a selection of papers all of which are concerned with the division of labour in the direct provision of health care. Taken together, they illuminate the complexity and diversity of contemporary health care work. They also illustrate how, over the past twenty-five years, sociological research on the division of labour in health care has, to a large extent, shifted away from a focus on the work of particular occupations – above all, of medicine – towards studying the inter-relationship between different occupational groups, and the interactions between individuals from different occupations within particular work arenas. It has been increasingly recognised that occupational roles and the boundaries between different occupations' areas of 'jurisdiction' (Abbott 1988) are not determined solely by technological considerations. Rather, these are the outcomes of specific social and political processes. Inter-occupational boundaries and task allocation are not inexorably fixed, any more than are the divisions into specialties within a single profession.

This shift in sociological attention is, in part, a response, to current developments in health care systems. As noted in the Introduction to the Reader, at the start of the twenty-first century, health care policy concerns in many countries have led to a new emphasis on professional boundaries, or rather on their alleged outdatedness for efficient and effective health care delivery. Health care work is not immune from more general changes in labour organisation, for example those often characterised as 'post-Fordist' (Walby et al. 1994). Through such measures as 'flexible working' arrangements, competence-based task allocation, team-work, and multi-professional training, there are moves to change the division of health care labour from the 'top down'. This is particularly apparent with respect to questioning of traditional task demarcations between nurses and doctors, or between qualified nurses and nursing aides, and in calls to extend or expand nursing duties (Allen 2001).

However, one of the contributions of sociological studies of specific work settings has been to show how when people come together in work settings they do not simply follow officially sanctioned role descriptions and role demarcations. Rather the social order in the workplace is developed through interaction and negotiation over time. Official role demarcations may be sustained, but also sometimes may be ignored or changed at the 'patient's bedside' as it were. The first article in this Section, by Allen, re-examines this idea of a negotiated order, first put forward by Strauss et al. (1963). Her study focused on role boundaries and interaction between doctors and nurses in light of the moves to extend nursing duties in the United Kingdom's National Health Service. During her ethnographic observation of work in two acute hospital wards, she found that overt, face-to-face negotiation over nursing-medical boundaries was rare. Rather, nurses managed many competing demands, including those from doctors, through boundary-blurring strategies. These were generally tacitly accepted by all parties, despite sometimes being counter to formal hospital rules, at least where relationships of interpersonal trust were established. Allen also uses her findings to reflect on the significance of choice of research design in sociological studies of the relationships between medicine and nursing.

The health care division of labour is a social division in another sense. That there are persistent patterns of occupational segregation in the health care workforce by gender, class and ethnicity has been widely noted in recent years. There is now a substantial body of sociological research examining the implications of this social patterning, not just for professionals' careers, but also for the way health care and its division of labour are constituted. In particular, Davies (1995) has argued that, rather than regarding gender as an attribute individuals bring to the workplace, sociologists should focus on how gendered assumptions are embedded in the construction of work roles and, indeed, in the very conception of the autonomous professional. Both her work and Allen's have drawn attention to the ways in which the fleeting encounters patients have with autonomous medical professionals in hospitals are generally underpinned by the more sustained interactional work of nurses, work in which feminine competence in caring is tacitly presumed.

James's paper on emotional labour takes these insights further. In her analysis of task allocation and boundaries in hospice work, she shows how the work organisation draws on gendered assumptions about caring skills. But she also shows how it cannot be assumed that caring is (and is seen to be) the particular province of the qualified nursing profession. Rather, she shows that, in hospice settings, despite the centrality of emotion work with dying patients to nursing and palliative care professionals' ideology, in practice, such work is mainly done by non-qualified auxiliary staff. Because this intangible person-focused work is not easily amenable to official recording and monitoring, qualified hospice staff tend to give precedence, in the face of organisational pressures, to other, relatively visible and recordable activities. Yet, as Strauss and colleagues (1982) have argued, largely invisible sentimental work, such as that done by auxiliaries in James's study, plays a vital part in maintaining social order and facilitating smooth working routines in stressful healthcare settings.

The maintenance of social order is also a theme in Fox's study of intra-occupational boundaries and the situational negotiation of medical authority in the face of divergent intra-professional opinion. His analysis of interactions between surgeons and anaesthetists in the operating theatre and its immediate vicinity is one of the few sociological studies of surgery, a key area of clinical practice. Fox notes the potential tension between surgeons' concern with effective resection of disease and anaesthetists' paramount goal of patients' continuing survival, a tension expressed in the different discourses about 'illness' and 'fitness' used by surgeons and anaesthetists respectively to describe patients. He shows how the authority relationship between anaesthetists and surgeons can shift quite sharply in the course of an operation. By drawing on his or her specialist knowledge claims, the anaesthetist may challenge the conventional dominance of the surgeon through claims about patients' compromised fitness for surgery.

Given the multiple tasks and personnel involved, modern surgery might be regarded as a form of team-work, but the term is usually applied to a specific form of complex work groups: to multi- or inter-disciplinary groups where an avowedly egalitarian structure and ethos of sharing knowledge prevails. That such an approach is desirable, particularly for the care of those with long-term dependencies, is widely claimed. For example, it is often suggested that this mode of working promotes a high-quality, holistic and client-centred approach. However, as Opie's paper shows, the research evidence on how such teams work and for their effectiveness is thin. Drawing on a study of a team caring for adults with severe disabilities in New Zealand, Opie examines the way team members discussed with each other their work in relation to specific clients. What she found was the preponderance of task- and occupational-specific representations of work to be done, rather than holistic, team-based representations. Opie argues that the latter is only likely to emerge if team-members can and do spend time (and therefore resources) together, reviewing and mutually problematising their various ways of representing clients and their needs. However, as Opie notes, resource constraints and heavy case loads are not conducive to this type of standing back from immediate practical considerations.

The relative invisibility of some forms of health work and, gendered assumptions about who is competent to do it, and negotiation over task allocation and role responsibility are all themes addressed in the final paper in Section 3 by Mayall. Until relatively recently, those who actually undertake the bulk of health care work were virtually ignored in both social research and health policy. However, one of the major conceptual developments in the sociological analysis of the health care division of labour over the past twenty-five years, is the explicit recognition of lay and informal health care. This development was strongly influenced by the recognition of the gendered character of health care work and feminist analyses of domestic labour and by increased policy emphasis on patients (or healthy lay persons) as consumers and producers of health care. The first influence has led to a substantial body of research on informal care for those with long-term health needs, and on the emergence of the 'carer' in policy discourse (Heaton 1999). The second has stimulated sociological interest in self-care and preventive health practices, as the latter have been increasingly identified in policy-making as the responsibility of individuals and families rather than professional health services.

Mayall's paper is a contribution to this relatively new body of research on individuals' preventive health work. But it also stands as an example of the burgeoning interest in children as social actors within medical sociology and sociology more generally. She provides an account of how schoolchildren move from dependency to independence in relation to the task of preserving and promoting their own health, and of how their moves are shaped but not wholly determined by the actions of more powerful parents and teachers. In many respects, her emphasis on the children's action and negotiation in relation to health promotion tasks provides an illuminative contrast to the more Foucauldian approach to health promotion exemplified in Section 2. She has developed these ideas in more depth in subsequent publications (*e.g.* Mayall 1996). Her research illustrates how the health care division of labour needs to be understood as a complex and multi-faceted one: spanning home, and, in this instance, school as well as formally designated health care settings, and incorporating lay people as providers as well as recipients of healthcare work.

References

Abbott, A. (1988) *The System of Professions: An Essay on the Division of Expert Labour*. Chicago; University of Chicago Press.

Allen, D. (2001) *The Changing Shape of Nursing Practice*. London: Routledge.

Davies, C. (1995) *Gender and the Professional Predicament in Nursing*. Buckingham: Open University Press.

Heaton, J. (1999) The gaze and the visibility of the carer, *Sociology of Health and Illness*, 26, 759–777.

Mayall, B. (1996) *Children, Health and the Social Order*. Buckingham: Open University Press.

Strauss, A., Fagerhaugh, S., Suczek, B. and Wiener, C. (1982) Sentimental work in the technologized hospital, *Sociology of Health and Illness*, 4, 254–278.

Strauss, A., Schatzman, L., Bucher, R., Ehrlich, D. and Sabshin, M. (1963) The hospital and its negotiated order. In Freidson, E. *The Hospital in Modern Society*. New York & London: Free Press.

Walby, S., Greenwell, J., Mackay, L. and Soothill, K. (1994) *Medicine and Nursing in a Changing Health Service*. London: Sage.

3.1

The nursing–medical boundary: a negotiated order?

Davina Allen

Introduction

Over the past thirty years, sociologists have moved away from simplistic models of medical dominance (Freidson 1970) to underline the subtle and situated character of doctor–nurse relations (Rushing 1965, Stein 1967, Devine 1978, Hughes 1988, Stein *et al.* 1990, Porter 1991, Porter 1995, Mackay 1993). A number of studies have demonstrated that nurses often influence patient care and medical decision-making in ways that belie their place in formal organisational hierarchies (Rushing 1965, Stein 1967, Devine 1978, Hughes 1988, Porter 1995). Nevertheless for the most part, the role of negotiations has remained a sub-text in these analyses. In a recent paper in *Sociology of Health and Illness* however, Svensson (1996) has explicitly made the case for adopting the negotiated order perspective as the most appropriate theoretical framework for understanding patterns of doctor–nurse interaction.

The negotiated order perspective

Strauss *et al.* (1963, 1964) first introduced the term 'negotiated order' into the literature as a way of conceptualising the ordered flux they found in their study of two North American psychiatric hospitals between 1958 and 1962 (Maines 1982). In order to address the question of how social order was maintained in the face of change, negotiated order theorists attempted to show how, on the one hand, negotiation contributes to the constitution of social orders and, on the other, how social orders give form to interaction processes, including negotiations (Maines 1982). Strauss *et al.* (1963) argued that hitherto, students of formal organisations had tended to overemphasise stable structures and rules at the expense of internal change. It was suggested that a more fruitful approach would be to conceptualise the social order as in process, reconstituted continually.

The negotiated order perspective was an important attempt to transcend the micro–macro distinction (*c.f.* Berger and Luckman 1967, Giddens 1984) which underpins the structure-agency debates within sociological theory (see, for example, Dawe 1970). It is not surprising therefore, that a key issue in the development of the paradigm has been the relationship between stable social orders and negotiation processes. For example, a frequent charge is that the approach assumes everything is indefinitely negotiable and is thus unable to deal with limiting factors in negotiation settings (Benson 1977a, Benson 1977b, Benson 1978, Day and Day 1977, Day and Day 1978, Dingwall and Strong 1985). It is certainly possible to find passages in Strauss's early writings to support such a criticism:

> The realm of rules could then be usefully pictured as a tiny island of structured stability around which swirled and beat a vast ocean of negotiation. But we could push the metaphor further and assert what is already implicit in our discussion: that there is only vast ocean (Strauss *et al.* 1964: 313).

Closer inspection of the early texts, however, suggests that Strauss *et al.* did not discard the notion of constraint as unequivocally as their critics claim. For example, Strauss and his colleagues refer to the organisational hierarchy shaping patterns of negotiation (1964: 304) and the constraining effects of formal organisational policies and rules (1964: 313). In later work moreover, Strauss (1978) clearly backtracks from the radical position implied in the earlier texts. He introduces the concepts of negotiation context and structural context to sensitise researchers to the relationship between negotiation processes and extra-situational constraint arguing that:

> not everything is either equally negotiable or – at any given time or period of time – negotiable at all. One of the researcher's main tasks, as it is that of the negotiating parties themselves, is to discover just what is negotiable at any given time (Strauss 1978: 252).

A number of studies have subsequently attempted to examine the dialectic between structural constraints and negotiation processes (*c.f. Urban Life* Special Edition – October 1982). Busch's (1982) analysis shows the historical processes through which structural conditions are produced by negotiations and, once produced, shape subsequent negotiations. Hall and Spencer-Hall's (1982) comparison of two North American public school systems suggests ways in which different organisational arrangements suppress or encourage negotiations. The relationship between extra-situational contexts and negotiations is a theme taken up by Svensson in his study of the interplay between doctors and nurses.

Svensson: the interplay between doctors and nurses – changing negotiation contexts

Svensson (1996) begins by arguing that traditional models of medical dominance are deterministic and provide an inappropriate basis for understanding doctor–nurse relationships on contemporary hospital wards. He suggests that the negotiated order perspective is a more appropriate theoretical framework for studying patterns of nurse–doctor interaction. Drawing on interview data with nursing staff on medical and surgical wards in five Swedish hospitals, Svensson claims that the conditions for inter-occupational negotiation have altered fundamentally over the past decade, augmenting the influence of nurses vis-à-vis doctors. He argues that viewed in historical terms, the relationship between doctors and nurses has 'changed dramatically'.

Svensson attributes this shift in the doctor–nurse relationship to three key changes in the negotiation context which have given nurses 'space' for directly influencing patient care decisions and interpreting organisational rules. First, he argues that the increased prevalence of chronic illness has resulted in a shift of emphasis from preventing death to handling life, introducing a social dimension into health care. According to Svensson, nurses are powerfully placed to contribute to patient management given the centrality of 'the social' to holistic care. Second, Svensson maintains that the shift from a system of task allocation to team nursing has fundamentally altered the nurse–doctor relationship. Team-nursing facilitates a closer nurse–patient relationship because the nurse is responsible for fewer patients. Moreover, the nurse's knowledge of the patient is no longer exchanged in a two-step process via the ward sister, but presented directly to the doctor. Third, Svensson argues that the introduction on many wards of the sitting round, where the doctor and nurse discuss their patients before the 'walking' round, offers an arena in which nurses feel more able to converse with the doctor and influence patient management decisions.

Svensson's work is an important contribution to sociological understanding of contemporary doctor–nurse interaction and also to the relationship between negotiation processes and social orders. Unfortunately, as Svensson himself concedes, the analysis is hamstrung by its reliance on interview data which cannot necessarily be read as literal descriptions of an external reality (Scott and Lyman 1968, Silverman 1993: 90–114). Moreover, although Svensson is concerned with the patterns of interaction between doctors *and* nurses, the interviews were undertaken with nurses only, and thus we are given only a partial view. This raises the question as to whether nurses' position has shifted as radically as Svensson claims. Acknowledging some of the shortcomings of his data, Svensson suggests that one way in which sociological analysis of the ward as a negotiated order could be further developed, is through the utilisation of systematic observational methods.

In this paper I shall be drawing on ethnographic data generated on a medical ward and a surgical ward in a single, UK Trust[1] hospital. The focus of the original study was on nurses' day-to-day accomplishment of occupational jurisdiction; nursing work was examined through the analysis of five nursing boundaries: nurse–doctor; nurse–patient/relative; nurse–nurse; nurse–support worker and nurse–management (Allen 1996). For current purposes however, I am going to concentrate on data relating to the boundary between nursing and medicine. My aim is to build on Svensson's analysis: I shall be exploring some features of nurses' and doctors' work in a hospital setting that *inhibited* inter-occupational negotiations but which nevertheless resulted in the modification of the medical–nursing division of labour. The implications of these findings for the negotiated order perspective are considered, and the question is raised as to what researchers working within this tradition understand by 'negotiation' and how it can be studied.

Method

The study was undertaken in a 900-bedded District General Hospital[2] in the middle of England which provided general, acute, obstetric and elderly services to a local population of 254,000. At the time of the study the hospital had an annual budget of £60 million and employed about 2,800 staff.

For ten months I observed and participated in the working worlds of doctors, nurses, health care assistants, auxiliaries and clinical managers. Although myself a nurse, I was not employed as such during the fieldwork. Nevertheless, I was open about my nursing background, and my role ranged from observer to participant depending on the situation. 57 tape-recorded, semi-focused interviews were carried out with ward nurses (n = 29), doctors (n = 8), auxiliaries (n = 5), health care assistants (n = 3) and clinical managers (n = 11)[3]. Interviews lasted between an hour and an hour-and-a-half. Spontaneous extended conversations were undertaken; these were not taperecorded, but they had a different feel to the briefer discussions held with staff while they worked. Data were also generated through the analysis of organisational documents and attendance at nursing and management meetings and in-service study days.

A holistic approach to data analysis was employed; material from different sources was compared in order to make judgements as to how each piece should be interpreted. Individual data extracts were related to the larger picture in order to evaluate their meaning and, on the basis of the analysis of these different snippets, the meaning of the whole would itself be modified. *'FolioViews Infobase Production Kit version 3.1'* was used to facilitate data handling. A more extensive description of the research methodology and the fieldwork process can be found in Allen (1996).

Background and guiding assumptions

The starting point for the study was the observation that recent developments in the UK in nursing and medical education (DHSS 1987, GMC 1993, UKCC 1987) and health policy (DH 1989) had created the impetus for shifts in the hospital division of labour, rekindling deep-rooted historical tensions between professional and service versions of nursing. The Project 2000 reforms of nurse education and its underlying patient-centred ideologies may be read, in part, as a professionalising strategy aimed at carving out an area of functional autonomy in order to augment the status and material rewards of nurses. The contemporary nursing ideologies, which have come to be termed 'New Nursing' (Beardshaw and Robinson 1990), reject the old system of hierarchical task allocation and assert that nursing practice should be the jurisdiction of trained staff. This is a vision of nursing that is clearly at odds with that of many UK health service managers however, concerned to cut labour costs and faced with a Government imperative to reduce junior doctors' hours[4]:

Nurses are locking themselves in too tight a definition. What's a doctor and what's a nurse [. . .] you get the work done by people who are best qualified to do it [. . .] Hands-on care is below nurses' level of competence [. . .] A higher quality, cheaper service, with a competitive edge will be achieved by those who make the most improvements in their labour costs (Naish 1990, quoting Eric Caines[5]).

These debates, however, were not confined to policy-makers. Practitioners also seemed to experience strains over inter-occupational boundaries. For example, in an extensive interview study of doctors and nurses in the UK, Walby and Greenwell et al. (1994) devote a whole chapter to exploring boundary conflicts between nursing and medicine. Moreover, a survey study of nurses', junior doctors', and support workers' views of the potential for nursing role developments in the context of the initiative to reduce junior doctors' hours (NHSME 1991) revealed considerable uncertainty and ambivalence amongst rank-and-file staff (Allen and Hughes 1993, Allen et al. 1993).

Drawing on the ideas of Abbott (1988), Strauss and colleagues (Strauss et al. 1963, Strauss et al. 1964, Strauss 1978, Strauss et al. 1985) and Hughes (1984), the aim of the research was to move on from the policy debates to examine the ways in which nurses accomplished occupational jurisdiction in the course of their everyday work. The research was framed by a perspective in which the division of labour was conceptualised in dynamic terms. Occupational roles, in this view, are not self-evident but have to be actively negotiated within a system of work or, to put it in Abbott's (1988) terms, jurisdiction has to be claimed and sustained in the work arena.

I began the study anticipating an increased need for negotiation and associated inter-occupational tension at the nursing–medical boundary. The research was based on the premise that the policy changes taking place, and the debates they had precipitated, would throw the processes through which occupational boundaries were shaped into sharp relief. Abbott (1988) argues that inter-professional competition is a fundamental fact of professional life. Furthermore, proponents of the negotiated order perspective suggest that negotiations are encouraged by ambiguity and uncertainty (see for example, Strauss 1978, Hall and Spencer-Hall 1982, Maines and Charlton 1985):

Negotiations occur when rules and policies are not inclusive, when there are disagreements, when there is uncertainty, and when changes are introduced (Maines and Charlton 1985: 278).

The aim of the research was to undertake a fine-grained analysis of negotiation processes in the workplace. As Mellinger (1994) has pointed out, although the negotiated order perspective has significantly enhanced our understanding of occupational and organisational settings, little attention has been addressed to the structure of real-world negotiations. Accordingly, I planned to pay particular attention to members' talk. The concept of negotiation was thus employed in a fairly restrictive sense to refer to face-to-face interaction between the respective parties to the work boundary.

The changing division of labour in health care – the view from the wards

The nurses in this study were being encouraged by hospital managers to develop the scope of their practice in order to meet the requirements of the junior doctors' hours initiative. The main areas where nurses were extending their skills were: administration of intravenous antibiotics, venepuncture, ECGs, male catheterisation, and intravenous cannulation. From my conversations and interviews with medical and nursing staff it was clear that there was uncertainty and disagreement about their changing work boundaries.

Most ward nurses were equivocal about doctor-devolved work. They saw potential advantages for patient care but were also concerned that, in the absence of additional resources, an expanded jurisdiction would make it harder for them to undertake 'hands-on' work:

> I think that sometimes it takes us away from the simple idea of what a nurse is for and what the patient thinks we're for. I think it's a good idea when you haven't got the doctor and there's an IV to be given and you can't get one and the nurse can give it on time (Interview – Staff Nurse).

Doctors were happy for nurses to take-over what they regarded as low status menial activities: intravenous antibiotic administration, venepuncture, ECGs and cannulation. Nevertheless, many felt these were essential medical skills which they were loathe to lose:

> Taking blood and putting in cannulas. Especially putting in cannulas. I think that's very important. I think it is a vital skill that doctors should have really (Interview – PRHO).

Doctors were less clear, however, about those activities – such as patient clerking and diagnostic investigations – which came closer to the focal tasks of medicine. Some believed nurses could undertake this work provided they worked within clearly defined protocols. Others felt this was moving too far towards nurses making diagnoses, and this was a responsibility that most doctors (and also nurses) believed should remain with the doctor. Doctors were also divided on whether expanded role activities should be shared with nursing staff or permanently devolved. Most of the nurses believed tasks should be negotiated with medical staff according to the exigencies of the work.

As the above extract make clear, there were divergent perspectives concerning changing inter-occupational boundaries. Furthermore, in my conversations and interviews with staff many recounted instances of contested boundaries. Nevertheless, my field observations revealed that on the wards, nursing, medical and support staff carried out their work activities with minimal inter-occupational negotiation and little explicit conflict. These findings clearly raise important methodological and empirical questions as to why the uncertainty and disagreement in both the literature and in actors' accounts were so little in evidence on the wards.

The nurse–doctor boundary – a non-negotiated order?

When I asked them how they managed the boundaries of their work in daily practice, the nurses emphasised their jurisdictional control. They insisted that their priority was nursing care; if busy, they expected to negotiate the allocation of work with medical staff:

DA: When do you decide whether you will do these things
              rather than the doctor?
Staff Nurse: Whether I'm busy or not. Nursing comes first and it's my
              registration on the line. I'm here to do nursing and the
              patients perceive that to be my role (Fieldnotes).

These accounts are consistent with the new professional guidance on UK nurses' scope of practice (UKCC 1992) which places the onus for decisions about the boundaries of nursing firmly in the hands of individual practitioners. 'The Scope of Professional Practice' (UKCC 1992) supports role expansion providing it does not result in unnecessary fragmentation of patient care or lead to the inappropriate delegation of work. Nevertheless, despite their commitment to nursing care activities and, contrary to the UKCC guidelines and their own accounts of their working practice, those nurses who could undertake doctor-devolved work did so regardless of their other work pressures.

I read this discrepancy between nurses' accounts of their work and their daily practice, as a reflection of the staff's efforts to demonstrate their continuing control over their work boundaries. Contemporary nursing ideology emphasises nurses' autonomous practitioner status. By insisting they had choices about whether to undertake doctor-devolved work, the nurses in this study may have been attempting to resist the charge that they were being 'dumped on' by the medical profession wishing to discard their 'dirty work'. However, although it may have jarred with nurses' professional identities, carrying out doctor-devolved activities clearly made sense within the constraints of the work context.

To understand why nurses constituted the boundaries of their work in the shape that they did, and thus how the changing division of labour between nurses and doctors was accomplished with minimal negotiation and little explicit conflict, we need to focus our sights on key features of the work context. These were features which constrained the routine accomplishment of nursing jurisdiction in important ways, and led to non-negotiated blurring of the nursing and medical boundary. I suggest that when it is recognised that non-negotiated boundary-blurring is a taken-for-granted feature of normal nursing practice, then the lack of inter-occupational negotiation and overt conflict relating to policy-driven shifts in the hospital division of labour becomes understandable.

The work context

Hospital wards constitute 'turbulent' (Melia 1979) work environments. At one level, this turbulence reflects the centrality of the patient, which as Strauss *et al.* (1985) point out, makes medical work fundamentally non-rationalisable. Health care takes place against the backdrop of highly variable fluctuations in the pace of work where an emergency is always possible. At another level, hospitals are complex, internally segmented organisations and patient care has to be co-ordinated around the clock, throughout the year, with numerous internal and external timetables which are often in conflict (Zerubavel 1979). Staff at the point of service delivery have to manage unpredictable patient needs with the complex temporal structures of the hospital. Finally, hospitals are staffed by diverse occupational groups, each with their own cultures, career structures, internal divisions and hierarchies. This internal segmentation poses numerous difficulties of co-ordination, illustrating the centrifugal tendencies of an excessive division of labour that were identified by Durkheim (1933). I suggest, that taken together, these features form the fundamental dilemma of work in hospital wards. Within the contemporary UK health context however, these elements are further exacerbated by resource limitations.

Organisational turbulence has important implications for the ways in which the work is managed at the point of service delivery. In order to function as competent team members, not only did the nurses on the ward have to be competent clinicians, but they also had to have the skills to manage the turbulence of the work environment. Observing the nurses on the ward, the juggling analogy, so often applied to women's domestic work, seemed equally fitting. Organisational turbulence also has important implications for the management of role boundaries, making a rigid division of labour extremely difficult to sustain. In this study there were three key features of the organisational turbulence which had particular implications for the boundary between medical and nursing work: the respective transience and permanence of nursing and medical staff, the fragmented temporal-spatial organisation of medical and nursing work, and the dysjuncture arising out of status hierarchies and the flow of work.

Transience and permanence

The hospital drew heavily on the immediate community for its non-medical staff. Most of the nurses had trained locally and staff turnover was low. Nurses were typically permanent employees, although there was evidence of an increasing number of nursing staff being employed on short-term contracts. Compared to the nurses, junior doctors were transient members of the ward team. PRHOs (pre-registration house officer) rotated as frequently as every three months, SHOs (senior house officer) every six months, with registrars staying in post for up to a year.

In contrast to the nursing staff, few of the junior doctors were local; many had come from overseas and, like the doctors in Hughes's (1988) study of Casualty work, their transient status was exacerbated by cultural difference and lack of familiarity with the UK health system.

Weber (1970) has indicated the extent to which bureaucrats may have considerable power over political incumbents, as a result, in part, of their permanence within the political bureaucracy, contrasted to public officials, who are replaced more frequently. Low ranking officials become familiar with the organisation, its rules and operation, which gives them power over the new political incumbent (Lipsky 1980). The ethnographic literature suggests that the relative permanency of nursing staff can augment their influence vis-à-vis doctors (Haas and Shaffir 1987, Mumford 1970, Myers 1979, Hughes 1988, Roth and Douglas 1983, Bucher and Stelling 1977). Where turnover of nurses is rapid relative to medical staff however, the influence of non-medical personnel is likely to be significantly compromised (Dingwall et al. 1983).

In this study, the permanence of nursing relative to medical staff, created discontinuities of experience and status. Nurses wielded considerable influence. Doctors relied on them for guidance on details of local protocols and aspects of ward practice as well as for the location of materials and equipment:

Doctor:	What do I have to write on here?
Staff Nurse:	Just write 'Dextrose powder for glucose tolerance'.
Doctor:	Do I need to fill in a special form or do you just carry it out?
Staff Nurse:	We just do it.
Doctor:	(to DA) I don't think I am the best candidate to study because I am new to the NHS and I ask more questions than I should (Fieldnotes).

Nurses often volunteered advice on various aspects of hospital practice, which was particularly important when medical staff changed over.

Many nurses were often more knowledgeable than doctors about the ward speciality. Nurses exerted an important influence over treatment decisions. It was commonplace for doctors to seek nursing advice about drug dosages, for example:

PRHO: Rachel? The Becotide inhaler is fifty milligrams isn't it?
Sister: Micrograms.
PRHO: Fifty micrograms.
Sister: Yes fifty or a hundred (Fieldnotes).

Nurses frequently questioned junior doctors' drug prescriptions if they differed from the standard medication regimes with which they were familiar:

Staff Nurse: This has been written as a PRN (as required) MST.
PRHO: It seems fair enough?
Staff Nurse: It's a bit silly isn't it? Can't it be Oromorph instead. It's only for – she's having debridement of her shoulder tomorrow.
The house officer alters the kardex (Fieldnotes).

Staff Nurse: (to PRHO) I just want to query this Erythromycin. Do you want it just once a day? It's usually twice a day.
PRHO changes the prescription (Fieldnotes).

Nurses routinely requested specific drug prescriptions for patients and were rarely questioned by medical staff. The informal prescribing power of nursing staff is revealed by the observation that nurses referred to doctors as 'writing up' drugs rather than prescribing them.

For their part, doctors freely acknowledged the skills and influence of nursing staff:

[A] nursing sister who's been on a unit for years knows far more than I do. We learn molecules and chemical biology in our training. You don't get the clinical feel until much later (Interview – Registrar).

To be realistic about it, most of it is what they [PRHOs] learn themselves from the nursing staff by being told 'This is what happens on the ward. This is how to do things. This is what the consultant expects. This is what is required' (Interview Consultant).

These findings are consistent with those of Svensson (1996) and other recent ethnographic studies (Hughes 1988, Porter 1991, Porter 1995, Stein et al. 1990), which indicate that much contemporary nurse–doctor interaction goes beyond the passive influence attempts described by Stein (1967) in his account of the doctor–nurse game. Moreover, it is clear that the relative permanence of nurses augmented their influence over key aspects of medical practice and education which resulted in the negotiated modification of the nursing and medical boundary. In order to understand how this contributed to the non-negotiated blurring of other aspects of the nursing and medical division of labour, we need to analyse its interactive effects with a second feature of medical and nursing work: its fragmented temporal-spatial organisation.

The temporal-spatial organisation of nursing and medical work
24-hour medical and nursing coverage was provided 365 days a year but accomplished in rather different ways. Patient care was provided by nursing and support staff via a three-shift system, whereas junior doctors routinely worked office hours, Monday to Friday. Outside normal working hours medical cover was provided by the on-call team. Medical and nursing work also had a different spatial organisation. Nurses were ward-based but the work of junior doctors took them to other wards and departments.

The difference in the temporal-spatial organisation of medical and nursing work was most marked outside normal hours when doctors were on-call. The on-call period ran from 9am until 9am the following morning. The on-call team were responsible for all admissions in their particular directorate[6] and emergency ward cover. On weekdays, ward cover did not begin until 5pm, but at the weekend and on public holidays the on-call team were responsible for ward work for the full 24-hour period. The introduction of an admissions unit[7] meant that doctors spent little sustained time on the wards during the on-call period.

The different temporal-spatial organisation of medical and nursing work created rather different perspectives and priorities which were a source of strain. Nurses' sights were focused on the needs of the patients on their wards, whereas doctors were concerned with the whole directorate and new admissions. Doctors tried to organise their work systematically so that they were not expending unnecessary 'leg-work' moving between the wards. At the same time, however, they had to attend to patients in order of clinical priority. Nurses were ever-conscious of the constraints of external organisational timetables; considerable nursing effort went into co-ordinating patient care activities and ensuring that treatments were carried out to schedule. Moreover, it was nurses who were faced with the distress of patients and/or relatives.

Organisational hierarchies and the flow of work
The temporal-spatial ordering of medical and nursing work creates a second, related tension, which mirrors those described by Whyte (1979) in his study of restaurant work. Whyte argues that a central problem of the large restaurant is to tie together its line of authority with the relations that arise along its flow of work. In a restaurant, the flow of work usually originates with

the customer and is passed to the waitresses who then have to initiate the work of higher status countermen or barmen. Whyte proposes that relations among individuals along the flow of work will run more smoothly when those of higher status are in a position to initiate work for those of lower status in the organisation, and conversely, that frictions will be observed more often when lower status individuals seek to initiate the work of those with higher status. According to Whyte, a number of strategies are developed in restaurants – either consciously or unconsciously – to cut down waitresses' origination of action for higher status staff. For example, the rule that orders must be written cuts down interaction, although not always enough to eliminate friction.

Similar problems arise in relation to doctors and nurses. Although nurses were able to influence medical staff in important ways, within the formal organisational hierarchy doctors had higher status. This created strains because, owing to the temporal-spatial ordering of their respective activities, it was nurses who initiated much of medical work.

Managing the strains – blurring the nurse–doctor boundary

In their study of nursing and medicine in the UK, Walby and Greenwell *et al.* (1994) argue that nearly half the points of conflict they identified between doctors and nurses could be traced to the different spatial and geographic organisation of nursing and medical work. These strains are often reflected in tensions over the bleep system. A common nursing complaint in this study, was of the difficulties in getting doctors to come to the ward. Because of their proximity to the patient, nurses have a key role in coordinating patient care and protecting them from the organisational turbulence. When doctors were unavailable this greatly increased the burdens on nursing staff. Equally however, on-call doctors frequently worked under immense pressures and quickly became irritated when their work was constantly interrupted by the bleep. The junior doctors felt that other members of the health care team did not understand the on-call experience. Interestingly, nurses' frustrations with the fragmented temporal-spatial organisation of medical and nursing work, were intermingled with a sympathetic acknowledgement of the burdens medical staff faced.

Staff at the point of service delivery employed a number of strategies to manage these strains. For example, nurses expended considerable effort organising doctors' work; tasks were saved up, rather than the doctor being bleeped for every single problem as it occurred. Another tactic was to anticipate patient requirements and ensure that doctors had prescribed 'PRN' [as required] medications so that nurses could respond to patient need without having to contact the doctor. One PRHO had developed the practice of signing blank dietitian referral forms so that they were available when nurses required them.

By far the most important way in which the strains created by the differ-ential temporal-spatial ordering of nursing and medical work were managed, however, was by nurses routinely undertaking a whole range of activities that fell outside their formal jurisdiction. The difficulties nurses experienced in getting medical staff to come to the ward, coupled with their acknowledge-ment of doctors' situation, led nursing staff routinely to violate organisa-tional policies by undertaking medical work.

Nurses' Boundary-Blurring Work

There is a sense in which some blurring of the nurse-medical boundary is unavoidable. This reflects the impossibility of sustaining a formal division of labour in which doctors diagnose and nurses merely observe. I have called this *de facto* boundary-blurring.

Formally, medical diagnosis is the responsibility of the doctor. This is one reason for nursing's inferior status in the hospital division of labour, since without diagnosis there is no patient and hence no need for nursing inter-vention. In everyday practice however, the line between nursing observations and medical diagnosis is almost impossible to sustain. At a fairly mundane level, out of the wealth of information nurses gather about their patients they have to decide what is medically relevant (Gamarnikow 1991). As Gamarnikow points out, the medical 'gaze' (Foucault 1976) is articulated through and mediated by nursing practice. At another level, because of the temporal-spatial organisation of medical and nursing work, nurses have little choice but to make diagnostic decisions, although most nurses and doctors did not see them as such. In addition to *de facto* boundary-blurring, nurses also intentionally undertook medical tasks. I have called this *purposive* boundary-blurring of which there are five sub-types.

Nurses did doctors' work in order to maintain continuity of patient treatment. The most common example of this *continuity-oriented* boundary-blurring was the 'prescription' of additional intravenous fluids. They also informally blurred the nurse-medical boundary to ensure co-ordination of the work. This *articulation-oriented* boundary-blurring occurred when nurses requested stand-ard blood tests so they were ready for the phlebotomist, and tests were carried out on time. Nurses frequently initiated tests and referrals on the basis of their own judgement. An example of *judgemental* boundary-blurring was when nurses requested blood tests if they thought patients looked anaemic. *Rule-oriented* boundary-blurring occurred when nurses worked in the spirit of one rule even if this meant breaking another. Nurses routinely gave saline flushes after the administration of intravenous antibiotics, although nurses were pro-hibited from prescribing drugs. It was also relatively common practice for nurses to administer unprescribed drugs and request the doctor to prescribe them later. Nurses justified this *lay-oriented* boundary-blurring on the basis of the action the patient would have taken, had they been at home.

Nurses, however, had not simply incorporated this work into their every-day practice; rather, they undertook informal boundary-blurring work when the doctor was unavailable. When doctors were physically present on the ward, nursing staff adhered to hospital policy and asked the doctor to carry out these tasks. It was also more common for experienced nurses to blur occupational boundaries than junior staff. Indeed I observed junior nurses asking more senior staff to do their boundary-blurring work for them. More-over, nurses were more likely to break the rules for doctors they trusted:

> If you were going to break the rules you'd always do it for someone that you trusted than someone you didn't (Interview – Staff Nurse).

Interestingly, there was little informal purposive boundary-blurring at night. This was surprising: the ethnographic literature (Roth and Douglas 1983, Porter 1995) indicates that during the night-shift nurses carry out many duties they do not do during the day in order to give the on-call physician a rest. There seemed to be a number of possible explanations for the dearth of informal boundary-blurring on the night-shift in this study. First, the working environment at night was not as 'turbulent' (Melia 1979) as it was during the day and ward nurses were less preoccupied with coordination activities. Secondly, night staff did not have established relationships with medical staff. With the opening of the admissions unit, doctors only attended to jobs as they arose, whereas in the past they could be on the ward for pro-longed periods dealing with new patient admissions. Thirdly, nursing care at night was provided by a separate night staff which had its own moral order. All of the night nurses I spoke to were quite clear that they would not give unprescribed drugs to patients. Many justified their position by recount-ing the same 'moral tale':

> I heard on the grapevine. She gave Temazepam and asked the doctor to write it up later, which she would have done, but somebody told a tale and she was sacked for prescribing (Interview – Staff Nurse).

Making sense of nurses' non-negotiated boundary-blurring

Nurses' boundary-blurring may have been against the hospital rules, but it undoubtedly benefited patients. As a consequence, patients received symp-tom relief when they needed it, tests were carried out on time, and treatment was continued without interruption. Doctors recognised the skills of nursing staff and were grateful when nurses were prepared to employ those skills in ways that eased their burden of work:

PRHO: Diane on geriatrics is brill. She really sticks her neck out. She's really good.

DA: In what sense?
PRHO: Well, she prescribes things say like Maxolon. I get there
                  and she says she's done it (Fieldnotes).
Staff Nurse: She's had some indigestion, burning pain and I gave her
                  some Malox.
PRHO: Thank you for being so keen. I was once bleeped at six in
                  the morning to give some Malox! (Fieldnotes).

As far as nurses were concerned, given the informal influence they wielded
over treatment decisions, it was only a small step to take this further and do
the work themselves when the situation demanded it. Furthermore, given
the strains arising from the fragmented temporal organisation of their work
and the dysjuncture between the flow of work and formal organisational
hierarchies, it was easier and less time-consuming for nurses to undertake
work themselves than it was to try and get the doctor to do it:

[I]n the time it would take you to get a doctor to re-site a cannula you
could have done it yourself (Interview – Senior Nurse).

You can bleep the doctor and wait for six hours or do it yourself!
(Fieldnotes – Staff Nurse).

It was nurses who were in the firing line if patients were waiting on doctors.

Staff Nurse: The thing is, this is really the doctors' work but if we didn't
                  do this then the doctors wouldn't do it and TTOs aren't
                  written up and then it comes back on us doesn't it when
                  the patients get cross and they can't go home (Fieldnotes).

This illustrates the point made by Strauss (1978), that members' perceived
options are important in understanding the decision of whether to embark
upon negotiations or not.

Critics have suggested that extended roles undermine nurses' claim to
autonomous practitioner status by bringing the occupation under medical
control (Tomich 1978). On the wards, however, nurses' boundary-blurring
actually gave them greater local autonomy over their work, improved patient
care, and had the additional advantage of avoiding inter-personal tension.
Nurses' non-negotiated boundary-blurring clearly made sense within the
work context. Nevertheless, these findings raise important questions about
the constraints within which nurses worked which made non-negotiated
boundary-blurring their easiest option and the implications that this had for
their professional identities. This is clearly a complex issue. In this paper I
have emphasised the influence of the work environment and the ways in
which this interacted with status hierarchies in order to draw out the organisational logic of nurses' non-negotiated boundary-blurring practices. Other

issues – such as contemporary nursing ideologies, resource constraints, gender ideologies and workload considerations – are also clearly relevant, but beyond the scope of this paper. A further discussion of these issues may be found in Allen (1996, Chapter 9).

Discussion

This study raises several methodological and theoretical issues in relation to the negotiated order perspective that warrant further discussion.

First, there is the question of which method of enquiry can provide an adequate basis on which to build sociological understanding of negotiation processes and social orders. To recap briefly, I began this research with what I considered to be good reasons for anticipating an increased need for negotiation of the nursing and medical boundary and also associated inter-occupational conflict. These expectations appeared to be confirmed by my interview data which revealed uncertainty and disagreement about the changing division of labour in health care. As we have seen, however, my field observations revealed little evidence of this ambiguity in the day-to-day interactions between doctors and nurses on the wards. The discrepancy between nurses' accounts of their work and their observed daily practice, illustrates the dangers that were raised, in relation to Svensson's work, of an unquestioning reliance on interview accounts. Arguably it would be methodologically more fruitful to treat interview data as displays of perspectives or moral forms (Silverman 1993: 107), rather than as literal representations of reality. Interpreted in this way, we can understand the interviewees' accounts in this study as reflecting real conflicts of interest and perspective, but this should not necessarily lead us to expect these tensions to be manifested in their daily interactions. Furthermore, if we want to develop sociological understanding of the negotiation of social orders then, as Svensson points out, systematic observational methods are clearly essential.

Second, these findings raise broader issues relating to the clarity of the concept of negotiation. As we have seen, the negotiated order perspective originated in a context of a growing disillusionment with the traditional rational-bureaucratic model of organisations and was developed as a way of addressing the question of how social order was maintained in the face of change. In this view, negotiation contributes to the constitution of social orders and, social orders give form to interaction processes. According to Strauss *et al.* (1963), negotiations are the key to understanding how order and change fit together (Maines and Charlton 1985). The findings of this study, however, reveal that formal organisational structures can be modified in the absence of face-to-face negotiations. This raises the question as to what researchers working within the negotiated order perspective actually mean by the concept of negotiation.

Reviewing the literature one finds that negotiation can refer to 'bargaining, compromising, brokering, mediating or collusion' (Maines 1977), 'making a deal (an explicit compromise), trading off, reaching a formal agreement (say with respect to each others' turf), or reaching more formal agreements signified by contracts and other signed arrangements' (Strauss 1978). Negotiations can range from tacit understandings (Strauss *et al.* 1964) to explicit contracts. They can be one-shot, sequential, repeated, serial, multiple or linked and their time scale can vary from immediate transactions to ones occurring over a period of time (Strauss 1978). Indeed some appear to use the concept of negotiation and social interaction interchangeably (*cf.* Freidson 1976).

In arguing that shifts in the division of labour between nurses and doctors were virtually non-negotiated I have employed the concept of negotiation in a fairly restricted sense to refer to face-to-face negotiation between the respective parties either side of the work boundary. As we have seen, however, the day-to-day constitution of the nursing and medical boundary was clearly the product of the meaningful actions (if not interactions) of the field actors. Which raises the question whether the concept of negotiation is simply a convenient shorthand for diverse processes of social interaction or whether its meaning is more restricted? This lack of conceptual clarity is problematic, particularly if the research aim is to compare the extent of negotiation in different settings or make generalisations about the types of conditions that encourage or inhibit negotiations – an issue which was clearly of relevance to this study. One possible route forward would be to consider social order as continuously accomplished rather than negotiated. Such an approach would retain the underlying assumptions of the negotiated order perspective – that social order is the product of the meaningful interaction (or non-interaction) of actors – but would employ a broader approach to reality construction. From this perspective, then, negotiation becomes one of a number of possible processes through which social reality is routinely constituted.

Finally, there is also an issue in relation to where researchers look for negotiations. Although there was little face-to-face negotiation of the division of labour between nursing and medicine on the ward, that is not to say these boundaries were wholly un-negotiated. Often negotiations had taken place in other arenas – such as hospital management meetings. In assessing negotiative activity then, it is clearly important to identify the various arenas in which negotiations might take place. Of particular interest are the ways in which different negotiative arenas shape negotiation processes (see, for example, Holstein and Miller 1994).

Summary and Conclusion

In this paper I have attempted to build on Svensson's analysis of the interplay between doctors and nurses by analysing some features of nursing and medical work that inhibited inter-occupational negotiations but nevertheless led to the blurring of the nursing-medical division of labour. I have described how my reading of the professional and sociological literature has led me to anticipate that as a result of recent policy developments there would be an increased need for inter-occupational negotiations and associated tensions at the boundary between nursing and medical work. Although these expectations appeared to be confirmed by my interview data they were not supported by my observations, which revealed little evidence of negotiations or inter-occupational strains on the wards. In attempting to explain these findings, I have suggested that the strategies staff developed in order to manage the tensions associated with the social organisation of hospital work, meant that non-negotiated informal boundary-blurring was a taken-for-granted feature of normal nursing practice. When this is recognised, then the absence of negotiations and lack of conflict associated with policy-driven shifts in the hospital division of labour can be better understood.

In exploring these substantive findings I have also raised some methodological issues relating to the clarity of the concept of negotiation and how 'negotiated orders' can be best studied. Pointing to the discrepancies between the interview accounts and my field observations in this study, I have underlined the need for observational methods in order to develop understanding of social orders as negotiated orders. I have highlighted the need for researchers to consider the different arenas in which given aspects of the social order are negotiated. I have also identified some problems relating to the imprecision and ambiguity of the concept of negotiation. I have suggested that one possible route forward would be to consider negotiation as one of a number of possible social processes through which social order is accomplished; the challenge for sociologists will be to develop further conceptual categories in order to facilitate their rigorous analysis.

Acknowledgements

The research on which this paper is based was supported by a Department of Health Nursing and Therapists Research Training Studentship. The views expressed here are the author's own and do not represent those of the Department of Health. I am grateful to the anonymous SHI referees for comments on earlier drafts of this paper.

Notes

1 Trust hospitals were established in the UK as a result of the *1990 National Health Service and Community Care Act*. Hospitals and Community Units that were able to satisfy specified management criteria were allowed to apply for self-governing status.
2 A District General Hospital is a non-teaching hospital which provides a range of services to a local population.
3 These figures do not add up because one person was interviewed more than once and two auxiliaries were interviewed together.

4 The *'New Deal'* (NHSME 1991) sets firm limits on junior doctors' contracted hours (72 per week or less in most hospital posts) and working hours (56 hours per week) to be achieved in all hospitals. As a means to this end the *'New Deal'* calls for an increase in the number of career grade posts and encourages new ways of organising junior doctors' work such as shifts, partial shifts and cross-cover between specialties. It also suggests the 'sharing' of key clinical tasks by nurses and midwives. *'Working For Patients'* (DH, 1989) also raised the issue of occupational boundaries and in recent years 'skill-mix' and 're-profiling' have become vogue phrases in the search for efficiency savings within the NHS.

5 At this time Eric Caines was the Personnel Director of the NHS.

6 A directorate is a unit of management within the Trust. In this hospital the medical and surgical services were separate directorates.

7 The admissions unit was created primarily with the needs of junior doctors in mind. The unit acted as a 'buffer' for medical emergencies admitted to the hospital. Patients could stay on the unit for up to 48 hours where their condition could be assessed, and if deemed necessary, an appropriate bed found on one of the wards. The admissions unit concentrated on the efficient processing and disposal of patients; it increased the efficiency of on-call doctors by concentrating all acute medical admissions in one area rather than placing them in different wards around the hospital.

References

Abbott, A. (1988) *The System of Professions: an Essay on the Division of Expert Labour.* Chicago: University of Chicago Press.

Allen, D. (1996) The shape of general hospital nursing: the division of labour at work. Unpublished PhD thesis, University of Nottingham.

Allen, D. and Hughes, D. (1993) Going for growth, *The Health Service Journal*, 103, 5372, 33–4.

Allen, D., Hughes, D. and Pickersgill, F. (1993) *Receptivity to Expanded Nursing Roles: the Views of Junior Doctors, Nurses and Health Care Assistants*, Paper presented at Nurse Practitioners: the UK/USA experience conference, The Cafe Royal, London.

Beardshaw, V. and Robinson, R. (1990) *New for Old? Prospects for Nursing in the 1990s.* London: Kings Fund Institute.

Berger, P. and Luckman, T. (1967) *The Social Construction of Reality.* London: Allen Lane.

Benson, J.K. (1977a) Organisations: a dialectic view, *Administrative Science Quarterly*, 22, 1–21.

Benson, J.K. (1977b) Innovation and crisis in organizational analysis, *The Sociological Quarterly*, 18, 5–18.

Benson, J.K. (1978) Reply to Maines, *The Sociological Quarterly*, 19, 497–501.

Bucher, R. and Stelling, J. (1977) *Becoming Professional.* Beverly Hills: Sage.

Busch, L. (1982) History, negotiation and structure in agricultural research, *Urban Life*, 11, 368–84.

Dawe, A. (1970) The two sociologies, *British Journal of Sociology*, 21, 207–18.

Day, R.A. and Day, J.V. (1977) A review of the current state of negotiated order theory: an appreciation and critique, *The Sociological Quarterly*, 18, 126–42.

Day, R.A. and Day, J.V. (1978) Reply to Maines, *The Sociological Quarterly*, 19, 499–501.

Devine, B.A. (1978) Nurse–physician interaction: status and social structure within two hospital wards, *Journal of Advanced Nursing*, 3, 287–95.

Department of Health (1989) *Working for Patients: the Health Service Caring for the 1990s*. London: HMSO.

Department of Health and Social Security (1987) *Hospital Medical Staffing (Achieving a Balance) – Plan for Action*. Health Circular, 87, 25, London: HMSO.

Dingwall, R. and Strong, P. (1985) The interactional study of organization: a critique and reformulation, *Urban Life*, 14, 205–31.

Dingwall, R., Eekelaar, J. and Murray, T. (1983) *The Protection of Children: State Intervention and Family Life*. London: Basil Blackwell.

Durkheim, E. (1933) *The Division of Labour in Society*. London: Collier-MacMillan Ltd.

Foucault, M. (1976) *The Birth of the Clinic*. London: Tavistock.

Freidson, E. (1970) *Professional Dominance*. New York: Atherton Press Inc.

Freidson, E. (1976) The division of labour as social interaction, *Social Problems*, 23, 304–13.

Gamarnikow, E. (1991) Nurse or woman: gender and professionalism in reformed nursing 1860–1923. In Holden, P. and Littleworth, J. (eds) *Anthropology and Nursing*. London: Routledge.

Giddens, A. (1984) *The Constitution of Society*. Cambridge: Policy Press.

General Medical Council (1993) *Tomorrow's Doctors*. London: GMC.

Haas, J. and Shaffir, W. (1987) *Becoming Doctors: the Adoption of the Cloak of Competence*. London: JAI Press.

Hall, P.M. and Spencer-Hall, D.A. (1982) The social conditions of the negotiated order, *Urban Life*, 11, 328–49.

Holstein, J. and Miller, G. (1994) Settling disputes: negotiation processes in welfare agencies. In Dietz, M.L., Prus, R. and Shaffir, W. (eds) *Doing Everyday Life*. Ontario: Copp Clark Longman Ltd.

Hughes, D. (1988) When nurse knows best: some aspects of nurse–doctor interaction in a casualty department, *Sociology of Health and Illness*, 10, 1–22.

Hughes, E.C. (1984) *The Sociological Eye*. New Brunswick and London: Transaction Books.

Lipsky, M. (1980) *Street-Level Bureaucracy: Dilemmas of the Individual in Public and Services*. New York: Russell Sage Publications.

Mackay, L. (1993) *Conflicts in Care: Medicine and Nursing*. London: Chapman and Hall.

Maines, D. (1977) Social organization and social structure in symbolic interactionist thought, *Annual Review of Sociology*, 3, 235–59.

Maines, D.R. (1982) In search of mesostructure: studies in the negotiated order, *Urban Life*, 11, 278–9.

Maines, D. and Charlton, J.C. (1985) The negotiated order approach to the analysis of social organisation. In Faberman, H.A. and Perinbanayagam, R.S. (eds) *Foundations of Interpretative Sociology: Original Essays in Symbolic Interaction. Studies in Symbolic Interaction*. Supplement 1, 271–308. Greenwich, Connecticut: JAI Press Inc.

Melia, K. (1979) A sociological approach to the analysis of nursing work, *Journal of Advanced Nursing*, 4, 57–67.

Mellinger, W.M. (1994) Negotiated orders: the negotiation of directives in para-medic–nurse interaction, *Symbolic Interaction*, 17, 165–85.

Mumford, E. (1970) *Interns: from Students to Physicians*. Cambridge, Massachusetts: Harvard University Press.

Myers, L.C. (1979) *The Socialization of Neophyte Nurses*. Michigan: UMI Research Press.

Naish, J. (1990) Vision or nightmare? *Nursing Standard*, 12, 18–19.

National Health Service Management Executive (1991) *Junior Doctors: the New Deal*. London: NHSME.

Porter, S. (1991) A participant observation study of power relations between nurses and doctors in a general hospital, *Journal of Advanced Nursing*, 16, 728–35.

Porter, S. (1995) *Nursing's Relationship with Medicine: a Critical Realist Ethnography*. Aldershot: Avesbury.

Roth, J. and Douglas, D. (1983) *No Appointment Necessary: the Hospital Emergency Department in the Medical Services World*. New York: Irving Publishers.

Rushing, W.A. (1965) Social influence and the social psychological function of deference: a study of psychiatric nursing. In Skipper, J.K. and Leonard, R.C. (eds) *Social Interaction and Patient Care*. Oxford and Edinburgh: Blackwell Scientific Publications.

Scott, M.B. and Lyman, S.M. (1968) Accounts, *American Sociological Review*, 33, 46–62.

Silverman, D. (1993) *Interpreting Qualitative Data: Methods for Analysing Talk, Text and Interaction*. London: Sage Publications.

Stein, L. (1967) The doctor–nurse game, *Archives of General Psychiatry*, 16, 699–703.

Stein, L., Watts, D.T. and Howell, T. (1990) The doctor–nurse game revisited, *Nursing Outlook* 36, 264–8.

Strauss, A.L. (1978) *Negotiations: Varieties, Contexts, Processes and Social Order*. London: Jossey-Bass.

Strauss, A., Schatzman, L., Ehrlich, D., Bucher, R. and Sabshin, M. (1963) The hospital and it's negotiated order. In Freidson, E. (ed.) *The Hospital in Modern Society*. New York: Free Press.

Strauss, A.L., Schatzman, L., Bucher, R., Ehrlich, D. and Sabshin, M. (1964) *Psychiatric Ideologies and Institutions*. London: The Free Press.

Strauss, A., Fagerhaugh, S. and Suczet, B. (1985) *Social Organisation of Medical Work*. Chicago: University of Chicago Press.

Svensson, R. (1996) The interplay between doctors and nurses – a negotiated order perspective, *Sociology of Health and Illness*, 18, 379–98.

Tomich, J.H. (1978) The expanded role of the nurse: current status and future prospects. In Chaska, N. (ed.) *The Nursing Profession: Views Through the Mist*. New York: McGraw-Hill Inc.

United Kingdom Central Council for Nursing, Midwifery and Health Visiting (1987) *Project 2000: the Final Proposals*. London: UKCC.

United Kingdom Central Council for Nursing, Midwifery and Health Visiting (1992) *The Scope of Professional Practice*. London: UKCC.

Walby, S. and Greenwell, J. with MacKay, L. and Soothill, K. (1994) *Medicine and Nursing: Professions in a Changing Health Service*. London: Sage.

Weber, M. (1970) *From Max Weber: Essays in Sociology*. London: Routledge and Kegan Paul.

Whyte, W.F. (1979) The social structure of the restaurant. In Robboy, H., Greenblatt, S.L. and Clark, C. (eds) *Social Interaction: Introductory Readings in Sociology*. New York: St Martin's Press.

Zerubavel, E. (1979) *Patterns of Time in Hospital Life*. Chicago: Chicago University Press.

Care = organisation + physical labour + emotional labour

Nicky James

Introduction

The formula 'care = organisation + physical labour + emotional labour' identifies component parts of carework as they were observed in a study of a British Continuing Care Unit, the National Health Service form of hospice (James 1986). However, 'care' in the sense of 'caring for' has many different meanings and associations. Though the primary purpose of the paper is to explore the balance of the component parts of in-patient hospice care, such 'carework' can usefully be compared and contrasted with the 'family' care which has been used as a model for in-patient hospice services.

In the first section I sketch the contexts within which care arises and present ideal types of domestic care and in-patient hospice care. In the following three sections components of care are identified and similarities and differences between domestic and in-patient settings are noted in order to highlight difficulties in hospice aspirations to offer individualised, 'total patient care'. In the second section, 'organisation' is discussed both in the sense of 'an organisation' and in the sense of 'organising' – the day-to-day decision making which is carried out by non-managers as well as managers in paid employment. In the third section I suggest that physical labour is both 'work' and 'framework' and shapes the form in which care is given. My discussion of emotional labour, the fourth section, is an attempt to establish emotional labour as a key factor in domestic and workplace carework, but one which is often invisible. Finally I speculate on the future of emotional labour in workplace health care.

Ideologies of care

A confusion of rhetorics have accumulated around the notion of care as it is used to include nurture (Oakley 1974), treatment (James 1991), protection for children 'in care' (Packman 1986), overseeing in private or state accommodation for the frail or disabled (Audit Commission 1986), containment for elderly confused people (Evers 1981), and custody for the disturbed criminal (Rowett and Vaughan 1981). Politicians on both sides of the Atlantic vie to appear more 'caring' than their rivals and 'caring' is also big business (Hochschild 1983, Gray 1986, Griffith, Iliffe and Raynor 1987).

As the notion of 'care' is problematic, so too is the label 'carer'. With paid professionals, paid non-professionals, volunteers and the care which arises from unpaid domestic work, a variety of relations evolve between carer and cared for (Leat and Gray 1987, Dalley 1988, Goldberg 1969). Carers are likely to combine at least two carer roles since the majority of paid carework is carried out by women in addition to domestic duties (Brook and Davis 1985, Lewis and Meredith 1988). Furthermore, if we accept that many people are 'cared for' as well as being carers and that being 'cared for' involves an active role, the picture becomes more complex and we recognise that care relations are culturally and politically shaped (Graham 1983, Roth 1984, Ungerson 1987a,b, Stacey 1988, Dalley 1988). For the purposes of this essay, a carer is defined as someone who gives sustained, close, direct mental and physical attention to the person being cared for.

Despite the pervasiveness of 'care', social science concepts of 'the family', 'work' and 'organisation' failed to consider the social relationships through which ideologies of care are produced and reproduced until feminist writers began to look at women's contribution to social production and reproduction (Finch and Groves 1983). For the most part interdisciplinary divisions within the social sciences obscured rather than illuminated our understanding of care, whether in the privacy of home or in the public and commercial sectors. It is within this context of care as a cross-subject issue that I give more detailed accounts of the ideology and practice of two different traditions of care, firstly, unpaid domestic care, and secondly, paid in-patient care.

Domestic care
Women, in their capacity of 'homemakers' are held responsible for not just the care of their children but for the care, in its broadest sense, of their family – the needs of their husband and the nursing of dependent relatives. Though 58 per cent of married couples with dependent children both work (FPSC 1991), and despite discussion of the role of male carers (Bytheway 1987, Ungerson 1987a,b, Arber, Gilbert and Evandrous 1988), both the ideology and the practice of women as carers remain strong (Morris 1990, Wheelock 1990, Kiernan and Wicks 1990). In her essay, 'Caring: a labour of love', Graham (1983) usefully highlights the complex nature of care within families and explores how caring is simultaneously about women's 'material existence' and their 'consciousness'. Domestic care combines 'caring for' with 'caring about' and caring is part of women's activity and identity in a way which differentiates them from men, affecting how women enter the social world and the social relations of employment.

Family care emerges as being characteristically women's work, unpaid, but usually in addition to paid work, and based in the home where it becomes a 24 hour, 'on-call' responsibility. Carer and cared for are familiar with each other and the care is an integral part of the intimacy of the family, so that 'caring for' is assumed from a relationship of 'caring about'. Poorly documented, hidden from public scrutiny and usually from public consciousness, the processes through which domestic care is carried out merge with cultural expectations of private family life.

Workplace health care

Twentieth century Western health services emphasise illness and cure rather than, as in domestic care, maintenance care and caring attention to the young, disabled and sick. In addition, the organisation of health care has its own imperatives and depends on paid labour; inter- and intra-professional divisions; hospital-led funding priorities; and, until recently, overall direction from doctors who constitute 4 per cent of the healthcare workforce. Under these circumstances, attempts to alter the philosophy of health care confront a tradition of a scientific, biophysical, quantitative, workplace, approach to illness. The ideals of a planned balance of care components are therefore likely to be challenged by the longstanding expectations and traditions of health care staff and patients, as well as structural obstacles and constraints. If domestic care can best be located and understood in terms of family, hospital and hospice care can best be understood in terms of the workplace.

From the examples of health services and domestic care, I have drawn out two, contrasting ideologies. Formal, health service ideology involves paid professionals, trained in a form of 'scientific' knowledge, skilled in the use of specialist tools and requiring specialist buildings in which to use those tools. It is about 'doing', and treating with physical interventions. In this tradition of health care, the aims are highly specific, diagnosis and cure, and if cure is not possible, the alleviation of gross symptoms. The guiding ideology is a particular view of illness.

The ideology of family care comes from a quite different historical background based on familiarity and closeness. Though subject to changes in political policy and financial imperatives, it comes from an older system of organising life with a much broader remit and no particular end. The carework is unpaid, unspecific and usually unspecified, but provided by individually identifiable kin and friends. Family health care, for the most part, is not differentiated from other types of maintenance care. Yet the assumed superiority of family carework begs the question of differences between domestic and workplace care – an important differentiation with growing numbers of people without a family, together with those who never married or had children reliant on 'public' care.

It could be argued that hospices should be exempt from the workplace model of care because they were deliberately developed outwith mainstream health services to counter the depersonalised, institutional care available (Taylor 1983). As an alternative, 'family' care was an influential model drawn on by hospice staff and in hospice literature, particularly in the early phases of hospice development (James 1988). 'Family' was both a means of explaining the warmth and essence of caring involvement which hospices hoped to convey, and an implicit critique of health services in which the imperatives of organisation overpowered individual requirements for care. By combining a model of family care with post war developments of 'total care' (Arney and Bergen 1983) hospices built organisational structures in which 'teamwork', devoid of inter-professional rivalries, would deliver 'individual patient care'. This holistic model of care is an emulation of what is deemed important in, and integrated into, family life – that is social, spiritual, psychological and financial as well as physical care.

Yet while research on hospices in the United States and Britain shows there is a wide variation in services, the organisational pressures they face suggest that they are best understood within the ideal-type of workplace health care, rather than on the model of 'family' care to which they aspired (Kastenbaum 1982, Abel 1986, Johnson *et al.* 1990, Seale 1989, 1991, James and Field 1992). Contrasting findings from an ethnographic study of nursing in one hospice (James 1984, 1986) with domestic care highlights the tensions of attempting to transfer a family model of care into the workplace.

Organisation

Making organisation the first component of a care formula is a moot decision. It makes analytic sense because it sets the context within which care is carried out, but to the daily givers and receivers of care it is probably the least obvious of the three components. Although for the sake of consistency this component of care might be referred to as a form of 'mental labour' it would be inappropriate to ally it with Marxist distinctions between mental and manual labour, or to imply it has a 'rationality' in direct, but inappropriate contrast with emotional labour (Waerness 1987, James 1989).

A distinction needs to be drawn between organisations and organising, and the tensions between them explored. It is in an effort to emphasise the latter, a vital but under-rated aspect of the daily labour of care, that organisation was included within the formula. However when analysing hospice care, and in particular when the balance of the components of care is being questioned, the effects of the organisation cannot be left out. This section is divided into two. In the first part, the division of labour is emphasised, paying specific attention to 'organisation', and in the second part, organising care, the emphasis is on the organisational and managerial skills demanded in daily carework.

Divisions of labour
The family has been described as a 'unit' (Mann 1983), an 'institution' (Porter 1982), and a 'group' (Webster's Collegiate Dictionary 1939), but does not come under the rubric of 'organisation' since it does not have the following four, key, organisational features as outlined by Mann: 1) being consciously established to marshal social power; 2) possessing relatively explicit aims; 3) composed of functional positions and roles distinct from the individuals occupying them; and 4) having explicit rules governing the relations between

the roles (Mann 1983). However a significant similarity between workplace and domestic care is the gender division of labour. It is the gender division of labour which predicts that women provide the greater part of direct care, and it is the gender division of labour which structures the value attributed to physical and emotional labour. Yet while some domestic gender divisions of labour are replicated in health care services, the connection is not direct. Certain types of organisation and planning which are carried out by women in the family (Oakley 1974, Sharpe 1984) when carried out in a hospital setting are mainly allocated to male doctors, administrators and managers (Lorber 1984, Strong and Robinson 1990, Witz 1992).

Oakley (1983) points out that the doctor/male nurse/female distinction is relatively recent and occurred with the professionalisation of medicine and the introduction of institutions to care for the sick away from home. Nevertheless she and others have noted its pervasiveness and its reflection of gender differentiation in society at large (Leason and Gray 1978, Hearn 1987). An analogy between the domestic triumvirate of father/mother/child with the hospital doctor/nurse/patient has been drawn in order to highlight the patriarchal relations of hospital care and the diminished power of patients (Gamarnikow 1978, Holden and Littlewood 1991). Graves (1984) uses the same patriarchal, family analogy in a management analysis of hospice care. However in his model the administrator becomes father, and the doctor is relegated to the role of benevolent uncle or aunt. So the analogy between family and health care staff is limited by the inability to take account of how health services divide the labour force to meet the demands of a large organisation processing large numbers of people. In hospitals and hospices distinctions between housekeeping functions (food preparation and delivery, laundry, cleaning), administration, management, maintenance (of buildings), medical treatment and nursing help affect the forms in which 'care' is given (Holden and Littlewood 1991). In the family all these functions are carried out within the one unit for its own internal benefit, but in the hospice the division of this labour separates diagnosticians from domestics, and clerks from carers. Further, the new managerialism increasingly emphasises the efficient financial management of services with business plans dictating the type and quality of health services available, in preference to principles of effectiveness and equality (Flynn 1990, Strong and Robinson 1990). Health service managers who have a remit over hospices as well as hospitals are part of a division whereby responsibility for broader overall organisational objectives is separated from responsibilities for organising care, despite the impact of their organisation decisions on the day-to-day management of care. As the tools for audit and monitoring are inadequate so will the information on which to plan policies be (Spitzer 1987, Birch and Maynard 1988, Carr-Hill 1988a). In health care, unlike domestic care, the division of labour between managers, medics and nurses, between purchasers, providers and practitioners, means that each have a quite different role to play in balancing the components of care (Sheaff 1990, Uttley 1991, Lawler 1991).

Organising care

The term 'organising' is used in this section primarily to convey the immediacy and purposefulness of the organisational and managerial skills integrated within direct day to day care by carers. It does not require a major leap of imagination to agree with Sharpe that:

> It is ironic that the organisation involved in combining home,
> childcare and job would qualify many women for a management
> diploma, yet it goes unrecognised outside the home.
> (Sharpe 1984, 233)

Necessary both for the givers and receivers of care, planning and organising gives order to effective care. Organisation in this sense is the link between how the balance of physical to emotional labour is developed and maintained. Negotiating day-to-day care is both a matter of organisations and organising. In the domestic domain, negotiations for care centre first round the duties and responsibilities of kin (Ungerson 1987a,b), but qualified by the availability of other forms of collective provision (Dalley 1988) such as nurseries, day centres, hospital beds, and people to whom care is delegated (Sharpe 1984).

The domestic carer can be characterised as being responsible both for overall organisation, and for the details of an individual's care. The person cared for may be able to negotiate their requirements – even if it is displayed by throwing food they do not like back at the carer – but responsibility for planning the menus, shopping, cooking, cleaning and coordinating this with other requirements remains with the carer. In some circumstances this can create a tension as no decision is the right one (Ungerson 1987a).

It is a truism to note that you do not need to be sick to be cared for in the domestic domain. However, domestic arrangements have to be sufficiently flexible to cope with sudden illness. Women tend to arrange their paid work so that it fits round family work (Cornwell 1984) and can accommodate family crisis, though carers also have to be flexible enough to adjust to children becoming less dependent as they grow older while the elderly grow more dependent. The responsibility for care does not necessarily bring domestic carers commensurate power. Not only are carers subject to the comings and goings of others, but they may be coerced into a 'caring relationship' over which there is little agreement and which holds little satisfaction (Ungerson 1987a).

During the hospice study (James 1986) differences between workplace and domestic organisation of day to day care began to emerge which suggest that the model of family care cannot be directly transferred to an institutional setting. The main carers, the trained and auxiliary nurses, faced the conundrum of attempting to apply their principles of 'individual' care to a hierarchically organised place of employment. Theoretically they believed in letting the patients choose what they wanted:

I think most of the staff at Byresfold do regard patients as individuals, and don't try to mould their patients into the routine. They do, most of us try to assess what their needs are, rather than what the nurses' needs are because of the lack of time or whatever.

Yet within this statement is an acknowledgement of the power of organisational demands over those of the patient. This was stated even more clearly by the Sister during one particularly busy phase:

We're having to think of our routines before our patient. But then, what is this hospital system? This is what happens. We've got to have a routine.

However, even within this dominant hospital-type system, the nurses had some power in organising details of patient care. Their organising skills do not fit into neat schemas, but may make considerable difference to the quality of life and perceptions of the people being cared for. One ill person was washed first because he liked to be able to get out of the unit into the grounds as soon as possible, though this became more of a problem when a second person with the same views arrived. There was a nurse who as part of his planning of care would find out the strength each patient liked their orange squash because he believed that when someone was eating and drinking very little it was important that they had exactly what they wanted. On night duty one auxiliary nurse always made time to go and sit with a patient who liked her company for the last cigarette of the night.

Unlike domestic care where familiarity is assumed, in the hospice the good organisation of an individual's daily care involved learning enough about each patient and their family to be able to judge when routines should be interrupted and individual requirements attended to. It also required a system that was flexible enough to be responsive to such individually made decisions to break routines. One of the problems facing nursing staff was that tensions between organisational priorities and organising individual patient care may appear insurmountable even when staff actively seek to give 'good patient care':

Mr Orton asked me to wash his hair, and I thought, as soon as we had finished the back round I would easily go and do it. 10 minutes. I never got time to do it, so he washed it himself. And he said the water was cold, because the shower wasn't working properly. I would have washed it in the sink for him. And I felt guilty because I never got back to him.

In this example, the nurse's eagerness to deliver an individual the care they needed at an appropriate time was thwarted by the routines which governed the overall running of the unit and which she was unable to change. In effect the hospice care exemplified that of an organisation with the high status policy-making and decision making of managers, doctors and senior nurses separated from the low status 'organising' required in individual patient care.

In the family, unpaid carers work with little recognition of the range of organisational skills involved, though they mirror skills in the workplace care in type if not in scale. The overall organisation of family as a unit is combined with school and work routines and the negotiation of individual requirements, but in the hospice the employed carers may have the skills and knowledge necessary for organising day-to-day care while being prevented from applying them by the hierarchically ordered, task divided requirements of the 'organisation'. In terms of people being cared for, it is the minutiae of daily living, the quality and type of food, being able to choose what to wear and when to get up and go to bed, that is likely to play a major part in determining quality of life. Domestic and workplace care differ in the flexibility with which individualised responses can be made. In the workplace the numbers of staff, patients and relatives involved, combined with a task oriented division of labour, compounds inflexibility of decision-making.

Physical labour

A major difficulty in recognising and taking account of the components of care is their invisibility, but of all the components of care, physical labour is the most readily identified. In this section I suggest that physical tasks provide a timetable, a framework, for care. In hospitals, and the hospice studied, the organisation of nursing work is crucially about the provision of physical care, but the physical tasks also have an additional meaning since they are the principal component of 'work' in the sense of paid labour.

Physical tasks as work and framework

Although I have suggested that physical labour is the most visible aspect of carework, there are discrepancies of visibility, flexibility, range of tasks, timetables and accountability between physical labour in the domestic domain and that in in-patient care. Compared with the domestic domain, the hospice had a single, clear aim – to facilitate death with dignity. The physical labour of the nursing care was focused round the mundane tasks associated with daily living requirements for food, hygiene, activity and rest, and treatments where necessary. What is required of hospice services is increasingly written down in policies and standards, and staff are accountable for its completion (*Help the Hospices* 1991). In contrast, families fulfil multiple functions and this is reflected in the physical tasks associated with family life and with domestic carework. In comparison with the hospice, domestic physical labour is broad in its remit, largely invisible to the outside world and with unclear boundaries. 'Housework' is not synonymous with 'caring' for others and whether house redecoration is included as a form of caring work depends on perspective (Oakley 1974, Bytheway 1987, Morris 1990, Wheelock 1990). Nevertheless if the definition of carer as someone giving 'sustained, close, direct mental and physical attention' is applied, much of the physical labour of domestic work where it is for others is likely to be included – the provision of food and clothing and the ordering and maintenance of the domestic environment.

Though physical labour provides a timetable for both domestic and hospice care, at home it is a timetable which can be altered and negotiated to fit round individual comings and goings. The hospice aimed to provide a 'home' environment of a similarly flexible nature but there was minimal let-up in the routine. Meals were delivered at a particular time, drugs were given four hourly, admissions were arranged for particular times and though efforts were made to organise an individual's care, the good of the unit as a whole came first. The result was that the framework of physical labour also became the justification and explanation of paid work. Having been sitting talking to a patient a nurse would say 'I must go and do some work now', meaning it was time to do some physical tasks.

Accounts of domestic labour suggest that the tasks involved are notable chiefly if they are incomplete, if the meal is not ready, the beds unmade, the clothes left dirty (Rowbotham 1973). Together with the many other physical tasks which are unlikely to be observed such as taking and collecting children, routine cleaning and mending, these tasks form a framework for domestic carework (Oakley 1974, Sharpe 1984). So both in the family and in the hospice, listing and timetabling the tasks, formally or informally, is a way of ordering the work to be done and of explaining the framework of the day (Oakley 1974, James 1986).

If one of the characteristics of domestic carework is that one person does most of it, precisely the opposite is true of workplace care. Part of the impersonality of hospital care arose through the increasing division of labour and so the symbolic value, standards and personal contact of certain physical tasks were lost. Even in the hospice the division of labour through which food is prepared in one area of a complex, laundry in another, specialist treatments in another, and by which 'clean' and 'dirty' work were separated highlights differences between domestic care which can be responsive to the family movements and the hospice system which demanded a predictable continuity of staffing to cover ever-present patients.

The hospice movement made efforts to build interdisciplinary teams to overcome the impersonality and poor communication caused by the workplace division of labour (Hull et al. 1989). At the hospice studied the domestics were included in preliminary training, and would take distressed relatives a cup of tea if the nurses were busy. Allocations of food meant that on occasion a light meal might be cooked for a patient with little appetite rather than relying on the food sent from the main kitchens. Yet despite the commitment to 'holistic' care, physical labour was the priority. At times there was a reversion to health service emphasis on physical tasks and routinisation (Davies 1976, 1977). It was the physical labour which explained the framework within which the social relations of the hospice developed and also explained why there were more nurses on 'early' shifts when the baths and bedmaking were done and two meals served. Though familiarity with the unit and the patients affected the quality of the carework, learning the physical work was the first priority. The comings and goings of nurses and patients were fitted round the routines, rather than vice-versa. Different physical tasks were allocated to different status staff – trained staff, auxiliaries and domestics – and guiding timetables were provided throughout. With physical tasks dominant any individual nurse's ability to 'organise' an individual patient's care was proscribed, albeit unwittingly, and at times the 'total care' the staff were so anxious to give became expendable and had to be dropped to deal with what were seen as the more immediate, physical needs:

> Last night, if people weren't sick, for dressings, catheterised, or needed something, they weren't seen.

In family care, such concentration on the physical occurs within preceding experiences of familiarity, attention and companionship and so can be absorbed within the broader history of the relationship. In the hospice though, where there was often minimal past intimacy upon which to draw or empathise, concentration on the physical was more likely to be depersonalising.

Despite a philosophy that looks well beyond the task orientation, failure to stick to routines was a disruption to the social order of the hospice. Though Rowbotham and Oakley have noted a sense of disorder when housework tasks are not completed, in the hospice such personally imposed pressure was in addition to the organisational pressure:

> I came on the other day at 3.30 pm, and I said to Lisa, 'Have you done the laundry?'. And she says 'Oh, what laundry?'. So I put out the laundry through for dirty and I said, 'Have you done the clean linen? Have you done the bread and feed?'. She said, 'Oh, do you do that now?'. And I said, 'Is the sluice tidy?'. This is at 3.30 pm. Now all those things should have been done by that time.

At the hospice, an additional force behind physical labour was that, at one level, nurses relied on the common-sense understanding of 'work', paid work, as physical labour or 'doing' something. As one nurse said:

> If you're sitting on someone's bed talking, you keep looking round, expecting someone to tell you to do something.

The sense of physical tasks as 'work' held advantages for the nurses as well as having the disadvantage of colluding with the view that nursing is unskilled labour. From a nursing perspective one of the effects of embracing an ideology of 'total care' is that, as in domestic care your job is never complete. As the hospice Sister described it:

You could say that you do your routines and your work and that's the patient done. But here it is never really done. You're pretty constant doing various things for them all the time.

Physical tasks could be seen to have been finished, moreover they could be seen to have been done well. If the patient looked neat and comfortable, if the sluice was shining clean and if the drug trolley was tidy, the ordering complete, the work was well done. The sense of control which could be gained from doing physical tasks contrasted with the sense of inadequacy that could so easily be generated when patients or their families were unhappy – a not unusual occurrence when someone is dying.

Additionally, the sense of paid work and physical tasks helped explain variations in status, the territorial divisions of labour and differences in salary. It was also a means by which nurses could limit what was expected of them. No nurse would have felt happy about complaining that a patient wanted too much 'care', but it was legitimate to complain about an overload of physical tasks, or tasks inadequately carried out.

The nurses' sense of 'work' in the sense of paid labour, reflected not only a common-sense use of the work (Dex 1988) but also management analyses of nursing work, where 'workload' is measured by physical work (Gibson *et al.* 1986). Thus care of an ill person in hospices as well as hospitals could easily become transposed to physical work. Even the illness itself could be used as an incentive to *do* things:

I mean they will always think about their illness, but if you keep them busy . . . I think you'd feel better. I would if I was busy doing something. It would keep your mind at rest.

Although there are similarities between the domestic and hospice tasks associated with carework, the differences suggest an inflexibility in the system within which hospices operate. In the family it is the departures and arrivals of the family, including the carer when they are in paid work, which shape the timetable for tasks. The content of the work varies depending on household interpretations of the standards to be achieved, the combinations of tasks to be carried out, the division of labour, and the capabilities of those being cared for, but the 'basic' human requirements are ordered.

When a crisis occurs in the family, ordinary maintenance routines may be abandoned. Despite cultural and self-imposed pressures to carry out domestic tasks, in some families there is a degree of flexibility and choice. The order of routines and tasks in domestic carework vary enormously. In comparison in hospices the majority of physical tasks are carried out at roughly the same time in nearly the same way and, unlike care in the domestic domain, the physical labour of care is taken account of and negotiated over to raise or diminish staffing levels and skillmix.

In contrast with the physical labour of hospice carework, domestic care is relatively invisible, unaccountable and flexible. Although in the hospice there was a greater opportunity to adjust to individual patients than on many hospital wards (Field 1989) there was still a pressure to conform to the organisation's routines. As an explanation of paid 'work', and by providing a framework for 'care', physical labour in the hospice had primacy over both emotional labour and 'organising' – a primacy that the philosophies of 'teamwork' and 'total care' were unable to erode.

Emotional labour

The emotional component of care, like the physical component, is labour in the sense of hard work. Unlike physical labour, emotional labour has no well-developed history in analyses of work, labour or organisations and although anthropologists and psychologists profitably analyse 'normal' emotions (Schweder and Levine 1985, Harre 1986), they shed little light on emotion in relation to the labour process. As Stacey wrote in 1981:

> The emotional component of human service has been ignored by classical theories but is critical in all human service work.

Emotional labour has been explored in detail elsewhere and explained as involving the regulation and management of feeling (Hochschild 1983, James 1989, Smith 1992). Emotional labour is about action and reaction, doing and being, and can be demanding and skilled work. The labourer is expected to respond to another person in a way which is personal to both of them but like other aspects of care it develops from the social relations of carer and cared-for and is shaped by the labour process.

Since emotional labour is a personal exchange, it could be argued that it depends on 'caring about' before it can be effective. However, Hochschild's work on flight attendants has shown that emotional labour can be appropriated for competitive, commercial purposes. Under these circumstances the response may not be 'genuinely' personal but has the appearance of being so as the staff are trained to respond to the clients' perceived emotional needs, though Wouters (1989) disputes this element of 'pretence'.

For the most part the emotional labour of care consists of day-to-day responses to common situations. This does not mean that it is any less demanding than repetitive physical tasks, though like much physical labour the outcomes of emotional labour are likely to depend on how skillfully each situation is managed. Shouting at a crying baby is as inappropriate as telling someone with Alzheimer's disease that they are confused. However, domestic and workplace emotional labour may also involve dealing with major life crisis. For example, domestically a husband may have to decide how best to support his wife recently diagnosed as having cancer of the breast. He might have to decide whether to talk about it openly or bear the burden himself, how to respond to the distress of others, as well as coping with his own worries. Emotional labour in this sense is common even though to the individuals concerned it may be exceptional.

Like other aspects of care, emotional labour is subject to gender division. An historian gave a highly selective view of the effect on the family of the migration of work outside the home during the industrial revolution when he wrote that it left the family:

> . . . free to concentrate on its more fundamental function of home-making, child-bearing and rearing, and the emotional satisfaction of affection and companionship. (Perkin 1974)

By leaving 'the family' free Perkin meant women. The social relations through which women are ideologically associated with home-making, child-bearing and rearing and men with the workplace also ideologically associate women with emotion and men with rationality (James 1989). It has meant not only that women are deemed to be emotional, but also that they are the best people to deal with others' emotions. This imperative to deal with others' emotions may render women less able than men to control the pace and content of their work as Rowbotham (1973) notes in *Women's Consciousness, Men's World*.

Expressions of emotion appear to be legitimate in the domestic domain but anathema in the workplace (Anthony 1977). As the domestic domain remains the ideological base of emotion and emotional labour it has been assumed that 'family care' is necessarily better than 'substitute' care because of the 'commitment and affection' which characterises family care (Graham 1983). This misconstruction of 'caring work' is pessimistic and oversimplified. The pessimism is that 'substitute' carers are necessarily inadequate, a point which can be challenged (Dalley 1988). The oversimplification is two-fold. Firstly there is the assumption that the affection of family transforms 'caring-work into life-work' whereas research on family violence shows how romanticised this can be and Ungerson's interviews showed how 'caring-work' can transform affection into resentment (Feminist Review 1988, Ungerson 1987a). Secondly there is the assumption that skills learned as 'family' carers, including the ability to empathise and the capacity to be committed to other people, have no real place outwith family care. Yet as Graham and others (Stacey 1981, Beechey and Whitelegg 1986) have pointed out it is largely unpaid domestic carers who are employed for workplace care.

The emotional labour of working with patients
Although Armstrong (1983) observed that the 'caring' nurse is a relatively recent development, the hospice nurses' domestic caring skills were applied rather than abandoned in the workplace. Depending on their training, and building on the philosophy of the unit, the nurses were able to make use of

their skills in the management of emotion at work, both formally and informally. This connection between domestic caring skills and patient care was made by one hospice auxiliary nurse commenting on her friend:

> Poor Meg. She seems to be getting all the patients that pour their hearts out to her. And her daughters don't want to get married. I said, 'you're too good for them Meg. They all want to stay at home.'

Hospice staff work from within mainstream medicine even as they try to offer an alternative to it. The nurses' descriptions of 'good care' included 'spending time', 'involvement', 'listening,' 'being there', and 'family care' denoted the quality of care they aimed to give (James 1988). Although this quality of care was vulnerable to the dominant emphasis on physical tasks, genuine efforts were made, at personal cost to the carer. The staff were aware that their efforts were not always sufficient, and also that there are times when no amount of care can be sufficient. An auxiliary was talking about a woman with cancer of the bronchus, who, despite all medical efforts, was struggling to breathe:

> Last night I took Mrs McIntosh through for a cigarette. And she says, 'oh just sit down'. And she was telling me all her deaths. Her brothers and sister. And her husband. He died on Christmas Eve, and someone took money out of his pocket. And I said, 'You've got three lovely grandchildren'. And she said, 'I know. But I don't like them seeing me like this'. Of course it gets you more involved if you start a conversation with people. Listening to their lives. And when they die you miss them more.

Like the other components of care, emotional labour is subject to the professional division of labour. Hospice attempts to overcome the difficulties caused by professional demarcations, through teamwork, have met with varying degrees of success. Habits learned during training are difficult to overcome (Hull *et al.* 1989). Traditionally it is doctors who give patients information about their illness, and alterations to this order require an active and concerted effort from all those involved. In the following quotation the staff nurse touches on several significant points, the difficulty of identifying occupational responsibilities; the difference between knowledge, attitude and behaviour; the need for guidance; and one of the genuine dilemmas of emotional labour, knowing what is right for each individual person being cared for:

> One of the things we're supposed to be good at is talking to the patients about their inevitable death, and I think the times we actually do that are very small. Partly it's very difficult for anybody to do it. Partly because we're not always with the same patient all the time. We're afraid . . . we don't, maybe we don't think it's our place. And by and large because there's nobody in a leadership position is helping us to do it.

Policies which depend on emotional labourers must not only take account of the gender division of the work but also the relative importance of different cultures, life experience, training, status and the familiarity of those involved. It is arguable that the knowledge, skills and techniques of emotional labour require training in exactly the same way that physical labour does and that for the most part this apprenticeship takes places in the home rather than through workplace education.

At the hospice, at the time of the study there was almost an inverse law of status and skill in emotional labour. The temporary medical director explained that he was 'no good at that kind of thing' (*i.e.* disclosure), and the better-paid, higher status, but young staff-nurses relied on the four older auxiliaries who were described as being the 'backbone' of the unit. A proficient staff nurse described one incident:

> At that time I just didn't know how to cope. And luckily with having the older auxiliaries here – if Maggie hadn't been on that day I don't know what would have happened. I just didn't know what to do with this poor woman. She just completely broke down and collapsed in front of me. I went to get Maggie and said 'Come and help me, please'. And Maggie was very firm with her, but very sympathetic at the same time.

Reasons that so much of the emotional labour lay with the auxiliaries were that emotional labour takes time and requires considerable knowledge of the patient as a person. Doctors are least likely to have access to the time or the information, which is why auxiliaries, particularly older auxiliaries with experience of life, played the same nurturant role in the hospice that women do at home. Their ready availability and their close physical contact with patients offered a regular opportunity for effective emotional labour.

Although the study drawn on here was about hospices, the emotional labour which takes place generally within health services is recognised (Davis and Rosser 1986, Strauss *et al.* 1985, Field 1989, Smith 1992). The most significant similarity between domestic emotional labour and that in the health services is that, as with physical labour, the key practitioners, those who are most closely involved with patients, are of low status and deemed to be unskilled or semi-skilled. The most significant differences between health service and domestic emotional labour are that health service staff and patients and relatives cannot assume a shared culture or shared expectations; familiarity has to have time to grow; unequal status and power may obstruct closeness; but perhaps most important of all, the sheer numbers of staff involved in shiftwork covering 24 hours/day, seven days/week for twenty patients and their relatives and friends mitigates against a sense of continuity.

In the family, it is 'caring about' which is assumed to lead to 'caring for', and so ideologically family relationships provide the guiding framework. In hospital care though, and in some hospices, the needs of the organisation and physical care come first while the emotional labour remains largely informal and grafted on to the dominant biomedical, physical system.

Balancing the components of care?

In this essay I have suggested that each of the component parts of care deserves consideration. The physical elements of care can be observed relatively easily, though the skills involved may be undervalued. Management level 'organisation', with decisions about staffing, patient numbers and unit functions, is easier to explain than small scale day-to-day 'organising'. Yet the lack of sophistication in our methods of accounting for health services (Hunt 1987, Norman 1988, Ashmore *et al.* 1989, Packard 1991) with its physical labour, management and financial techniques only serves to highlight the major difficulties which are likely to arise when we try to explain the more complex 'emotional labour'. As expectations of adequate social and psychological care are raised by growing emphasis on 'individual care', and the adequacy of health services are measured by quality as well as quantity, planning and accountability for emotional labour is likely to become more overt. Government policies and managerialism demand measures of health service activity and outcome (Strong and Robinson 1990, Sheaff 1990, Uttley 1991, Common 1992). Yet how this 'work' should be measured, and who should have responsibility for legitimating the value of the measures to patients is a matter of dispute. The following quotation shows a remarkable optimism about clinicians' ability to measure the quality of life, as it advocates an index which appears to exclude the need for 'emotional labour':

> I maintain that indices can be designed so that clinicians can score the patient's quality of life or health status after observing or examining a patient even without eliciting information from the patient about how he or she feels at a given point in time. (Spitzer 1987)

The invisibility of emotional labour and its associations with family care mean it has ambivalent status. While the ideological values of family care may be attractive, the low status and unacknowledged transferability of the skills mean that they do not fit effectively with professional strategies. Yet however informally and incoherently, emotional labour has long been part of public health care through the work of chaplains, the support of friends and family, the work of clerical officers, the 'subjective' relationships of health care workers and patients, and the friendliness of domestic staff. Within a limited and highly partial sense some skills required for emotional labour are being formally adopted within the health care services as there is new emphasis on care for families as well as adopting 'family care' as a model.

The real challenge is not just to recognise emotional labour and its significance as a component of care, but to build upon the emotional labour which is already part of our health care system without destroying or 'commercialising' the social fabric upon which it depends. Taking account of emotional labour, its purpose, its application, its labourers, and its outcome is in its infancy compared with physical labour and organisation, and therein lies the opportunity. It is possible that critiques of health care provision will be given credence and help circumvent the specialist, gender divided, territoriality of our present treatment-oriented approach to health so that components of care can be balanced appropriately for different circumstances.

Contrasts between the two caring ideologies of family and workplace illustrate how workplace organisation and priorities act to limit individual care, responding instead to the demands of the dominant group or of the community as a whole (see also Baron 1984). The small group familiarity which is characteristic of domestic care makes it unlikely that hospices or health services more generally can provide an exact match, despite their deliberate and 'careful' attempts to emulate 'family' quality care. The question also arises of whether aiming for 'total care' is appropriate in public health care, and if so, what it would mean, or whether it is an unwarranted intrusion.

A major shift in the balance of care components in workplace health services is likely to be double-edged, bringing both benefits and harm. If health care services have been imperialist in the post-war period (Strong 1979, Arney and Bergen 1983), the formal extension of emotional labour into public health care structures will expand medicine's territory further. Not only will this alter the social relations of health care, but as Western health care exports its methods so opportunity for creating further 'expertise' is developed for sale abroad.

Acknowledgements

I would like to thank Nickie Charles, Alice Lovell and Jane Robinson for their comments on this paper.

References

Abel, J.M. (1986) The hospice movement: institutionalising innovation, *International Journal of Health Services*, 116, 71–85.

Anthony, P.D. (1977) *The Ideology of Work*, London: Tavistock.

Arber, S., Gilbert, N., Evandrous, M. (1988) Gender, household composition and receipt of domiciliary services by elderly disabled people, *Journal of Social Policy*, 17, 153–7.

Armstrong, D. (1983) The fabrication of nurse-patient relationships, *Social Science and Medicine*, 17, 457–60.

Arney, W. and Bergen, B. (1983) The anomaly, the chronic patient and the play of medical power, *Sociology of Health and Illness*, 5, 1–24.

Ashmore, M., Mulkay, M., Pinch, T. (1989) *Health and Efficiency*. Milton Keynes: Open University.

Audit Commission for Local Authorities in England and Wales (1986) *Making a Reality of Community Care*. London: HMSO.

Baron, C. (1984) The Paddington Day Hospital: crisis and control in a therapeutic institution, *International Journal of Therapeutic Communities*, 5, 157–70.

Beechey, V. and Whitelegg, E. (1986) *Women in Britain Today*. Milton Keynes: Open University.

Birch, S. and Maynard, C. (1988) Performance indicators, in Maxwell, R. (ed.), *Reshaping the NHS*. London: Policy Journals.

Brook, E. and Davis, A. (eds) (1985) *Women, the Family and Social Work*. London: Tavistock.

Bytheway, W. (1987) Male carers: questions of intervention. Conference paper at 'Evaluating Carer Support', York.

Carr-Hill, R. (1988a) Quality control: a sensitivity analysis of QALYSs. Centre for Health Economics, University of York.

Carr-Hill, R. (1988b) The QUALY industry: can and should we combine morbidity and mortality into a single index? Centre for Health Economics, University of York.

Common, R., Flynn, N., Mellon, E. (1992) *Managing Public Services; competition and decentralization*. Oxford: Butterworth-Heinemann.

Cornwell, J. (1984) *Hard-Earned Lives*. London: Tavistock.

Dalley, G. (1988) *Ideologies of Caring: rethinking community and collectivism*. London: Macmillan.

Davies, C. (1976) Experience of dependency and control in work: the case of nurses, *Journal of Advanced Nursing*, 1, 273–82.

Davies, C. (1977) Continuities in the development of nursing in Britain, *Journal of Advanced Nursing*, 2, 479–93.

Davies, C. and Rosser, J. (1986) *Gendered jobs in the health service: a problem for labour process*. Hampshire: Gower.

Dex, S. (1988) *Women's Attitudes Towards Work*. London: Macmillan.

Evers, H. (1981) Women patients in long-stay geriatric wards. In Hutter, B. and Williams, G. (eds), *Controlling Women: the normal and the deviant*. Beckenham: Croom Helm.

Family Policy Studies Centre (1991) *The Family Today, Fact Sheet 1*, London.

Feminist Review (1988) *Family Secrets: Child Sexual Abuse*, No. 28, Spring.

Field, D. (1989) *Nursing the Dying*. London: Tavistock.

Finch, J. and Groves, D. (eds) (1983) *A Labour of Love: women, work and caring*. London: RKP.

Flynn, N. (1990) *Public Sector Management*. London: Wheatsheaf.

Gamarnikow, E. (1978) Sexual division of labour: the case of nursing. In Kuhn, A. and Wolpe, A. (eds), *Feminism and Materialism*. London: RKP.

Gibson, S., Buxton, M., Caine, N., O'Brien, B. (1986) Measuring Patient Dependency, *Nursing Times*, 82, 36–40.

Goldberg, G. (1969) Nonprofessionals in human services. In Grosser, C., Henry, W., Kelly, J. (eds), *Nonprofessionals in the Human Services*. San Francisco: Jossey-Bass.

Graham, H. (1983) Caring: a labour of love. In Finch, J. and Groves, D. (eds), *A Labour of Love: women, work and caring*. London: RKP.

Graves, D. (1984) Models of hospice management. St. Christopher's Hospice, Sydenham, London.

Gray, B. (ed.) (1986) *For-Profit Enterprise in Health Care*. Washington: National Academy Press.

Griffith, B., Iliffe, S., Raynor, G. (1987) *Banking on Sickness*. London: Lawrence and Wishart.

Harre, R. (ed.) (1986) *The Social Construction of Emotions*. Oxford: Blackwell.

Harrison, S. (1988) The workforce and the managerialism. In Maxwell, R. (ed.), *Reshaping the NHS*. Policy Journals.

Hearn, J. (1987) *The Gender of Oppression: Men, masculinity and the critique of Marxism*. London: Wheatsheaf.

Help the Hospices. *A Guide to Good Standards and Practice*, 34–44 Britannia Street, London W1X 9JG.

Hochschild, A. (1983) *The Managed Heart*. Berkeley: University of California Press.

Holden, P. and Littlewood, J. (1991) *Anthropology and Nursing*. London: Routledge.

Hunt, S. (1987) *Measuring Health Status*. London: Croom Helm.

Hull, R., Ellis, M., Sargent, V. *Teamwork in Palliative Care*. Oxford: Radcliffe Medical Press.

James, N. (1984) A Postcript to Nursing. In Bell, C. and Roberts, H. (eds), *Social Researching: Politics, Problems, Practice*. London: RKP.

James, V. (1986) *Care and work in nursing the dying*. Unpublished PhD thesis, University of Aberdeen.

James, N. (1988) A family and a team. In Gilmore, A. and Gilmore, S. (eds), *A Safer Death*. New York: Plenum.

James, N. (1989) Emotional labour, *Sociological Review*, 37, 15–42.

James, N. (1991) Care, work and carework – a synthesis? In Robinson, J., Gray, A., Elkan, R. (eds), *Policy Issues for Nursing*. Milton Keynes: Open University.

James, N. and Field, D. (1992) Routinisation of hospice: charisma and bureaucracy. *Social Science and Medicine* 34, 1363–75.

Johnson, I., Rogers, C., Biswas, B., and Ahmedzai, S. (1990) What do hospices do? a survey of hospices in the United Kingdom and Republic of Ireland, *British Medical Journal*, 300, 791–3.

Kastenbaum, R. (1982) New Death Fantasies. *Death Education*, 6, 2.

Kiernan, K., Wicks, M. (1990) *Family Change and Future Policy*, Family Policy Studies Centre.

Langman, M. (1985) The unitary approach: a feminist critique. In Brook, E. and Davis, A. (eds), *Women, the Family and Social Work*. London: Tavistock.

Lawler, J. (1991) *Behind the Screens: Nursing, Somology and the Problem of the Body*. Edinburgh: Churchill Livingstone.

Leat, D. and Gray, P. (1987) *Paying for Care: a study of policy and practice in paid care schemes*. Research Report No. 661, Policy Studies Institute, London.

Leason, J. and Gray, J. (1978) *Women and Medicine*. London: Tavistock.

Lewis, J. and Meredith, B. (1988) *Daughters Who Care*. London: Routledge.

Lorber, J. (1984) *Women Physicians*. London: Tavistock.

Mann, M. (1983) *Sociology: Macmillan Student Encyclopedia*. London: Macmillan.

Morris, L. (1990) *The Workings of the Household: a US–UK Comparison*. Cambridge: Polity.

Norman, S. (1988) *The Resource Management Initiative and Ward Nursing Management Information Systems: a Review of Issues and Progress*. Department of Health, Nursing Division.

Oakley, A. (1974) *Housewife*. Middlesex: Penguin.

Oakley, A. (1983) Women and health policy. In Lewis, J. (ed.), *Women's Welfare, Women's Rights*. London: Croom Helm.

Packard, J. (1991) *Hospitals in Transition.* Milton Keynes: Open University.

Packman, J. (1986) *Who Needs Love?.* Oxford: Blackwell.

Perkin, H. (1974) *The Origins of Modern English Society.* London: RKP.

Porter, R. (1982) *English Society in the Eighteenth Century.* Harmondsworth: Penguin.

Roth, J. (1984) Staff-inmate bargaining tactics in long-term treatment institutions, *Sociology of Health and Illness,* 6, 111–31.

Rowbotham, S. (1973) *Women's Consciousness, Man's World.* Harmondsworth: Penguin.

Rowett, C. and Vaughan, P. (1981) Women and Broadmoor: treatment and control in a special hospital. In Hutter, B. and Williams, G. (eds), *Controlling Women: the normal and the deviant.* Beckenham: Croom Helm.

Seale, C. (1989) What happens in hospices: a review of research evidence, *Social Science and Medicine,* 28, 551–9.

Seale, C. (1991) A comparison of hospice and conventional care, *Social Science and Medicine,* 32, 147–52.

Sharpe, S. (1984) *Double Identity.* Harmondsworth: Penguin.

Sheaff, R. (1991) *Marketing for Health Services.* Milton Keynes: Open University.

Shweder, R. and Levine, R. (eds) (1984) *Culture Theory; essays on mind, self and emotion.* Cambridge: CUP.

Smith, P. (1992) *The Emotional Labour of Nursing.* Basingstoke: Macmillan.

Spitzer, W. (1987) State of Science 1986: Quality of Life and functional status as target variables for research. *Journal of Chronic Disease,* 40, 465–71.

Stacey, M. (1981) The division of labour revisited or overcoming the two Adams. In Abrams, P. and Deem, R. (eds), *Practice and Progress: British Sociology 1950–1980.* London: Allen and Unwin.

Stacey, M. (1988) *The Sociology of Health and Healing.* London: Unwin Hyman.

Strauss, A., Fagerhaugh, S., Suczek, B., Wiener, C. (1985) *Social Organization of Medical Work.* Chicago: University of Chicago Press.

Strong, P. (1979) Sociological imperialism and the profession of medicine: a critical examination of the thesis of medical imperialism, *Social Science and Medicine,* 13A, 199–215.

Strong, P. and Robinson, J. (1990) *The NHS Under New Management.* Milton Keynes: Open University.

Taylor, H. (1983) *The Hospice Movement in Britain: its role and functions.* London: Centre for Policy on Aging.

Ungerson, C. (1987a) *Policy is Personal.* London: Tavistock.

Ungerson, C. (1987b) The Life Course and Informal Caring: towards a typology. In Cohen, G. (ed.), *Social Change and the Life Course.* London: Tavistock.

Uttley, S. (1991) *Technology and the Welfare State: Developments of Health Care in Britain and America.* London: Unwin Hyman.

Waerness, K. (1987) On the Rationality of Caring. In Showstack Sassoon, A. (ed.), *Women and the State: the Shifting Boundaries of Public and Private.* London: Hutchinson.

Wheelock, J. (1990) *Husbands at Home: the Domestic Economy and Post-industrial Society.* London: Routledge.

Witz, A. (1992) *Professionals and Patriarchy.* London: Routledge.

Wouters, C. (1989) The Sociology of Emotions and Flight Attendants: Hochschild's Managed Heart. *Theory, Culture and Society,* 6, 95–123.

3.3

Anaesthetists, the discourse on patient fitness and the organisation of surgery

Nicholas J. Fox

Introduction

The subject-matter of this paper is the organisation of a care setting – unusual in Western health care – in which two clinicians share responsibility for a patient under their care, and in which there is potential for an extreme divergence of opinion as to how that patient should be treated. This situation, which is also extremely frequent, is the surgical operation, where a patient is dependent not only upon a surgeon (who will undertake the procedure), but also on an anaesthetist (who will govern her/his consciousness and sustain her/his life during the operation).

I am interested in exploring here some of the strategies used by anaesthetists to extend their input to the clinical management of surgical cases. Although surgeons and anaesthetists share many positions: both take a biomedical model as the framework for understanding disease, they collaborate clinically and professionally, they may associate within the same collegial structure – from the point of view of the organisation of their work, I wish to suggest that there is a conflict of interests between these clinical specialisms. While surgeons wish to undertake the most effective resection of disease, despite the traumatic effects this may have upon a patient, for an anaesthetist, a patient's continuing survival is paramount, and surgery – as a stressor upon the patient's vital capacity, is potentially more harmful (during the operation) than the disease itself.

In this paper I focus specifically on this conflict, and wish to show by recourse to ethnographic and interview material[1] how it is managed on a day-to-day basis, and how surgeon and anaesthetist actively engage in *fabricating* their own versions of the reality of the patient in order to achieve their differing objectives, while – of course – sustaining the necessary collaboration without which there could be no surgery. In particular, I shall focus on an anaesthetic discourse on *fitness*, which serves to define the perspective of the specialism on the surgical patient, as counterpoint to a perspective on *disease* or *illness* which organises the surgeon's perspective. Finally, I will document cases in which this conflict has deleterious effects on patients, in particular when one specialist succeeds in achieving discursive superiority over her/his 'opponent'.

Within the sociology of organization there has been a recent interest in post-structuralist and postmodern analysis (Clegg 1990, Cooper and Burrell 1988, Cooper 1989, Reed 1989). Such approaches are summed up by Cooper and Burrell (1988: 92) as

a shift away from a prevailing definition of organization as a
circumscribed administrative-economic function (the organization)
to its formative role in the production of systems of rationality . . .
Weber made us see modern organization as a process which emblematized
the rationalisation and objectification of social life, and it is to this
process that the current debate returns us, but with a fresh twist
which directs our attention to the concept of discourse . . . (by
which is achieved) the continuing mastery of the social and physical
environment.

The distinctive character of such an approach is perhaps worth exploring.
Structuralist, both functionalist and Marxist, perspectives reify 'organisations' as things, treating the structures they uncover as *sui generis* realities
(Silverman 1985). For the post-structuralist, so to do is to confuse the
model or method of social analysis with organisation itself: if you look for
a system, you will find one (Parker 1990).

While symbolic interactionism has supplied the notion that the meanings attached to the social world are constructed, and ethnomethodological
approaches have been fruitful in exploring the micro-processes of the
negotiation of these meanings so that social life is carried off successfully
(Silverman 1985, Rosenau 1992: 13), post-structuralist or postmodern perspectives add to these positions a primary concern with power and control
as processes achieved – not through coercion or through monolithic structures – but through continual strategies, such as surveillance or assessment
of individuals. Importantly, the position emphasises that these strategies of
power and control work through the fabrication of discourses of *knowledge*
(Game 1991: 34–5).

Within the sociology of health and illness, Foucauldian analyses adopting this perspective on power as a 'micropolitics' have contributed to an
understanding of the relationship between medical knowledge and medical
power (Armstrong 1983, Arney and Bergen 1983, Nettleton 1992). Foucault
rejected the idea that power could ever be won finally and absolutely or
'held' by a class or a state, and argued (1979, 1988) that techniques of power
could never resolve struggles for control and domination. Resistance to techniques of power are continuous, and demonstrate the necessity for similarly
continual responses, in an effort to produce docile bodies, subjected to, and
subjects of, this micro-politics of power.

From a postmodern perspective, organisation is the response to these
challenges or threats to power and the strategic claims to 'knowledge',
'expertise' or 'professionalism' by which power is retained and resistance
quashed. Rationality and rationalisation are processes which obscure the
contradictions within a social situation, the call to organise is motivated by
the desire to privilege unity, identity and immediacy over difference, absence
and separation (Cooper and Burrell 1988: 99–100). Unlike structuralist
approaches, which start from the position that organisation is possible, and

moreover is there for all to see, the assumption which the postmodern theorist begins with is the opposite: that *organisation is impossible*, that it is continually subject to resistance or challenge, and consequently is in a continual state of fragmentation and crisis, perpetually patched and augmented, to respond to the next onslaught on its integrity. It should be noted that, while not ignoring the impact of such factors as class, gender, age, seniority or race considered in structuralist accounts, the postmodern perspective would see these as discursive elements available to be used strategically in the prosecution of struggles for control, but never in themselves final arbiters of such struggles.

I have shown elsewhere (Fox 1991, 1993a) how this kind of analysis provides an interesting starting point in situations where there are conflicting perspectives on a situation. For example, clinicians and managers take very different views of how surgical services should be organized, with each group trying to fabricate and sustain its own discursive framework concerning what surgical healing is. On a surgical ward round, surgeons use a range of discursive strategies in order to head off challenges from patients concerning the 'success' of surgical interventions.

In this paper, I shall explore the organisational (or discursive) strategies used by anaesthetists to challenge the activities of surgeons in the operating theatre, and the counter-challenge mounted by surgeons. I will seek to demonstrate that these organisational strategies are grounded in rival discourses which *fabricate* the surgical patient in radically differing ways. Surgical discourse concerns itself with the patient as *carrier of disease or illness* and with the removal or reduction of this disease. On the other hand, the anaesthetic discourse sees a patient as *possessor of a complement of fitness* which it is the task of the anaesthetist to maintain.

I begin by outlining some of the organizational features of everyday activity in the operating theatre, in particular the privileging of the surgeon's authority within this setting. I then explore the organisational challenges to this authority fabricated in anaesthetists' discourse. Two case studies demonstrate some of the more dramatic consequences of these differing fabrications of the patient.

The division of labour within the operating theatre

Some of the organisational strategies by which surgeons and anaesthetists sustain their claims to clinical judgement in the operating theatre (OT) are constituted via the physical arrangements for surgery. Within the OT, the two clinical specialisms of surgery and anaesthetics necessarily come into intimate contact, both have rights to inhabit this space, to regard it as the focus of their work. However, the division of labour and spatial organization within the OT contribute discursively to mark the different responsibilities, interests and objectives of the two specialisms.

1. Anaesthetists and surgeons often use different modes of access to the OT: the anaesthetist through the anaesthetic room, the surgeon through the scrub area. Anaesthetists first contact patients in the anaesthetic room, and stay with them throughout the operation, and then go with them to the recovery area; surgeons come into contact only with an anaesthetised or induced patient in the OT itself, and leave when the resection is complete.

2. The patient's head will normally be the domain of the anaesthetist. However, this arena of anaesthetic control is transgressed in situations when a surgeon requires access to the head of the patient, for bronchoscopies or during neurosurgery. (See the second case study in this paper for an example.)

3. Monitors and other instrumentation are the province of the anaesthetist, and the surgeon does not normally comment on the readings, indeed s/he is assumed not to be able to decipher them. In this way, technology supplies a discourse by which anaesthetists define themselves:

> Anaesthetist *B*:   The surgeon is a technical person trained to do carpentry, with some background knowledge of how the system works. At some point there is a need for the technical knowledge of the anaesthetist; it's a technical field with use of equipment which anaesthetists understand because of their interest. Surgeons do not understand the machinery. We are applied physiologists and pharmacologists as well as physicians.

The anaesthetist will inform the surgeon if any monitor indicates deviation from a norm, for instance low blood pressure. The anaesthetist in effect 'interprets' the technical data for the benefit of the surgeon, who is then expected to act upon it. Similarly, a surgeon will advise the anaesthetist of the progress of surgery: it would be inappropriate for the latter to comment on what surgeons are doing during an operation.

These organisational arrangements enable a *modus vivendi* within the OT, with both specialisms using such strategies to define their rights to clinical autonomy. Despite such strategies, interviews with anaesthetists during fieldwork demonstrate that they perceive their position as threatened by surgeons' efforts to define the activity within the OT. The extent to which anaesthetists fabricate a different and distinctive version of what is happening in 'surgery' can be seen in their discourses on surgeons and their actions.

One continuing source of irritation for anaesthetists concerns the organisational strategy adopted by surgeons in admitting patients for elective surgery, whereby referrals from GPs to surgeons do not concurrently lead to an anaesthetic consultation prior to administration:

> Anaesthetist *B*:   A patient goes to the GP, who identifies a problem and refers the patient to the surgeon of his preference, most

likely as a result of the old-boy network rather than any thoughts about waiting lists. How patients are sent for (from the waiting list) is up to the surgeon. Sometimes, rarely, a date will be fixed at the out-patient appointment and put in the diary, but at the other end of the spectrum, the surgeon's secretary determines who comes in off the waiting list. Or a consultant may plan lists at the beginning of the week, and state which cases he wants to see. Then when a patient is admitted, he is seen by nurses, then a junior doctor who will do investigations, but rarely any which they think the anaesthetist will need.

Patients may thus be admitted who are quite unsuited to surgery because of their being at high risk from general anaesthesia, or may be put on a list without recognition of the long induction time associated with non-general techniques such as epidural anaesthesia:

Anaesthetist *B*: Surgeons assume that there is nothing wrong with a patient apart from what they are having the operation for. But this may not be the case, and must be identified. There may be consequences of the treatment for the anaesthetist, because while a surgeon is interested in the patient in terms of the abnormality, the rest of the patient is of interest to the anaesthetist. Two to three per cent of patients will have a problem which cannot be sorted out in advance, and in these cases your choices are either to hope for the best, or to cancel the operation, or initiate further investigations. But some of these could have been done by the GP, or by the surgeon, or could have been done if an earlier admission had been arranged.

A second source of irritation concerns the way surgical lists are made out — usually by a surgeon. Oral surgeon *P* saw nothing problematic in this:

Surgeon *P*: At the moment, I make up the list. With day case surgery, the administrators pull patients off a waiting list which will then be vetted by me to ensure it is appropriate. At out-patients I make an assessment.

This did not satisfy an anaesthetist informant:

Anaesthetist *B*: An anaesthetist should see the patient, or should at least be informed about the patient by the house doctor. The

anaesthetist can contact the surgical departmental
secretary to find out who is on the list, or wait till five-
thirty on the day previous to a list, when it is pinned
up, but some surgical firms will not have been able to
concoct a list till the morning of the schedule, and its
very difficult to get details of the list which may indicate
problems.

These lists are not only constructed at the last minute, but can be (from an
anaesthetist's perspective) totally unrealistic:

Anaesthetist *C*:   The surgeons don't consider the anaesthesia to be anything
other than time wasted, and do not seem to calculate for
it when they make up a list. They don't take any interest
in the anaesthetic, even though they depend on it.
We have to have the patient ready when they want it.

Anaesthetist *J*:   However a list is made up, directly or from a waiting
list, it is a real problem for the smooth running of
surgery that surgeons will think of the operating time,
but will forget the anaesthetic and induction time.

Observations during the fieldwork suggested that surgeons and anaesthetists
used the organization of anaesthetic induction time as a point of contest,
often at the expense of the patient:

Anaesthetist Dr *D* had induced the patient and he was ready for the
operation to begin. However the surgeons were in their office. Dr *D* went
to the scrub room door and shouted 'Surgeons!' to call them. On a
subsequent case, having induced the patient for a very minor procedure,
the surgeons were not scrubbed and ready. By the time they were ready,
the anaesthetist had been forced to attach monitors because a longer
period of unconsciousness was required than originally anticipated.
(Field Notes)

The exasperation with this privileging of their own perspective by surgeons
was summed up by one respondent:

Anaesthetist *C*:   The surgeons regard the theatre as their own, they say
what will go on.

The anaesthetist's challenge

Faced with surgeons' organisational strategies to control activity in the OT,
anaesthetists look elsewhere for a means to organise to challenge this

privilege. The field work suggests that this challenge concerns *the suitability of patients for surgery*. In the rest of this paper I will consider how this leads to patients becoming the principal arena of contestation between surgeons and anaesthetists in this organisational struggle.

The decision to admit a patient for a particular elective surgical procedure will be taken by a surgeon in out-patient clinic, based on clinical judgement of diagnosis and prognosis, severity of condition and history. Patients will therefore be admitted for surgery principally on an assessment of the particular problem presenting, as the earlier quotation from surgeon *P* indicated.

However, while surgeons diagnose and plan the detail of case management, surgical procedures etc., anaesthetists potentially have a considerable input into the detail of treatment. The focus of anaesthetists' decisions concerning a patient is the kind of anaesthesia and the choice of type of anaesthetic agent to be used in a particular surgical circumstance. Their technical knowledge is employed to ensure that, in their opinion, an appropriate method of anaesthesia is utilised. In interviews, anaesthetists suggested that such choices are based on three criteria:

1. The nature of the surgical procedure.
2. The physiological status and history of the surgical subject.
3. The social circumstances of the surgical subject.

Anaesthetists seek to make clinical judgements about patients by an assessment of these criteria, and the consequences in terms of the kind of surgical procedure which can be undertaken can be very significant. In some cases, an anaesthetists' clinical judgement concerning a patient may prevent surgery being considered as an option altogether, or require a far less drastic procedure to be substituted.

Decisions concerning anaesthesia are usually taken only after the patient has been admitted, and this may in itself be a source of tension between surgeons and anaesthetists. For any surgical procedure, there will be ground rules which define appropriate anaesthetic technique, such that a range of procedures would be conducted under general anaesthesia, others under blocks and so on (category 1 above). However, the physiology and social circumstances of particular patients may necessitate deviation from these ground rules, and it is in these areas (categories 2 and 3) that anaesthetists claim their right to exercise control over patient passage through surgery.

Informants provided the researcher with many examples of how these deviations are assessed. For example, young patients are often intractable during surgery except under general anaesthesia; patients over 70 years have increased risk of cardiac or respiratory complications and may be considered unsuitable cases for general anaesthetics. Decisions as to what anaesthetic is to be employed in these cases are made by an anaesthetist, usually as a result of a visit to the ward the evening previous to surgery. Consultation with the patient's consultant surgeon, who from experience will know a good deal about the kind of patient who may require non-standard anaesthesia, may also have taken place, as may other interventions:

> A patient Mr *H* who had been called for surgery for inguinal hernia and fistula was informed by a housedoctor, on admission, that he might have to have his operation under spinal anaesthesia, a possibility he confided to the researcher he anticipated with considerable anxiety. Two conflicting pieces of information were contributing to uncertainty: a history of ischaemic heart disease (IHD) had led to his GP suggesting he was unsuitable for general anaesthetic, while a consultant anaesthetist six years previously had used a general, and no further IHD symptoms had subsequently presented. The final decision was to be made by a consultant anaesthetist who was to visit the patient and take a history and examination the evening before the operation. (Field Notes)

Social circumstances also affect choice of agent, principally in relation to recovery from anaesthesia. Patients who can be made comfortable at home, or have familial commitments may be selected for anaesthetic blocks more readily. These 'niceties' of anaesthetic technique may be seen as part of the professional discourse which enhances the anaesthetist's status in the OT. The anaesthetist's decision thus has great potential to constrain the opportunities for surgeons to unilaterally organise their work. The interviews and observations suggest that anaesthetists organize their decisions within a discourse which fabricates their patients in a way which is quite distinct from the surgical discourse on disease, and which constitutes a perspective which cannot be reduced to that of the surgeon. In short, they focus not on disease, but upon *fitness*.

The patient as both ill and fit

The inscription of the surgical patient within a discourse specific to the discipline of anaesthetics, and opposed to the surgical discourse, was suggested by various comments during fieldwork. One suggested that an anaesthetist was naturally 'watchful', while another claimed a more 'holistic' approach than the surgeon's simple concern with a lesion or dysfunction, which might consequently place a patient in her/his appropriate context. As was documented above, one informant, anaesthetist *B*, argued that 'while a surgeon is interested in the patient in terms of the abnormality, the rest of the patient is of interest to the anaesthetist'. On another occasion this informant expanded this position:

> *B*:   Assessment for anaesthesia goes hand-in-hand with surgical assessment. Usually an anaesthetist has to do a separate

work-up (case-history, examination etc. to assess a patient's condition), because while surgery, and medicine in general is concerned with *disease*, the anaesthetist is concerned with a patient's *fitness*. A patient will be assessed as unfit by an anaesthetist if the disturbance to the system caused by anaesthesia, and aggravated by surgery would threaten survival. That is a different concern to that of the surgeon.

Researcher: Does that affect the questions in your work-up?

B: Yes, we have to ask questions in relation to health, rather than about the condition to be treated in surgery. (my emphasis)

This suggests contrary and in some senses contradictory definitions of the areas of concern of surgeon ('Disease') and anaesthetist ('Fitness'). The Fitness of a patient to undergo surgery is the concern of the anaesthetist, in opposition or in dialogue with the surgeon's concern with the patient's Disease or Illness – the deviation which has led him/her to the surgical setting. For both parties, a patient possesses both Illness and Fitness. Only the virtually moribund is entirely Ill; all other patients will possess balances of Illness and Fitness, contingent upon the relative severity of their condition, their personal characteristics and their previous history. The Fitness of the patient is a measure of her/his history. The Fitness of the patient is a measure of her/his ability to survive the stress of the operation, and is therefore of concern to the anaesthetist, who is designated not only the task of rendering the patient suitable for surgery (unconscious or locally anaesthetised), but also the maintenance of the vital functions during surgery. If s/he is not convinced that these vital functions can be maintained, s/he will declare the patient 'Un-fit' for surgery.

If this discourse is being used by anaesthetists to organize their activities concerning surgical patients, then the conflict between the anaesthetist's and the surgeon's definition of the patient is very significant. The surgeon is interested primarily in the 'Illness' of the patient, her/his deviation from a norm of structure or function. By definition the patient is 'Unfit', but in a different sense to that employed by the anaesthetist, here to be Ill or unfit is to make a patient suitable for surgery. For the surgeon:

1. The patient presents with a deviation from a norm, an Illness.
2. The surgeon alters the Illness of the patient, by resection, excision or reconstruction of the deviant tissue.
3. The patient's Illness is thereby removed or reduced (if the operation is 'successful').

On the other hand, for the anaesthetist, there is a quite different perspective:

1. The patient presents with a complement of Fitness, or capacity to withstand physical stressors.

2. The anaesthetist submits the patient to stressors (surgical shock, anaesthesia) within the limits the patient can tolerate, and monitors the response to ensure these limits are not surpassed.
3. The patient's Fitness is thereby (temporarily) removed or reduced.

An operation represents for the surgeon, the *desirable reduction in Illness* of a patient. For the anaesthetist it represents the *undesirable reduction in Fitness* of the patient. In any surgical procedure there will be a trade-off between reduction in Illness and reduction in Fitness.

Co-operation and conflict over the Ill/Fit patient

This discussion of a patient as Ill and Fit suggests that, despite their common biomedical discourse, surgeons and anaesthetists hold different perspectives concerning their patients, and their responsibilities toward them. From this it may be expected that the patient is potentially at the focus of organisational contestation, with each specialism attempting to impose its own discursive position at the expense of the other, to establish a position of power and control over proceedings. In situations where there are arguments over selection of cases and time devoted to appropriate anaesthesia, as documented earlier, these might be understood as grounded in such a conflict of discourses: skirmishes in a continual and continuing struggle.

To explore this rivalry and its effect upon patient care during surgery, Fig. 1 sets out four possible combinations of Illness and Fitness outcomes following surgery. In the top left-hand quadrant (cell *A*), the outcome of

		Illness	
		Reduced/Removed	Not Reduced/Increased
	Reduced within tolerable limits	**Operation successful** Patient condition improves, health enhanced A	**Condition un-responsive** Patient does not improve, but fitness retained B
Fitness		C	D
	Reduced beyond limits	**Operation 'successful'** Patient's fitness temporarily or permanently compromised In ITU or dead	**Operation a failure** Patient more ill and with little reserve of fitness

Figure 1 *Interaction of outcomes of surgery in terms of Fitness and Illness*

surgery can be perceived as successful by both specialisms, in that the deviance is removed or reconstructed, and that the effect of the operation does not itself lead to mortality or further morbidity.

In cell *B*, patient Fitness is not compromised by the anaesthesia and surgical shock, but the surgical intervention does not resolve the deviance, and may in fact increase the Illness. Surgery, from a surgeon's perspective has not been successful.

In cell *C*, 'the operation was a success but the patient died' – the lesion was successfully resolved, but the compromise to the patient's Fitness was very great, although in some cases not permanent or fatal. From an anaesthetist's position, the operation was unsuccessful.

Surgery on patients in cell *D* is unsuccessful from both perspectives. The resection has failed, and the effect of the operation on Fitness leads to deterioration or death.

While in many cases, the differing perspectives will not lead to conflict over care, this diagram suggests where conflicts may arise during surgical procedures. Surgeons will try to make patient outcome fall in cells *A* or *C*, while for anaesthetists, successful outcomes fall in cells *A* and *B*. Where an outcome in *A* is fairly certain (a young, not very ill patient) conflict will be minimal, but where outcome may fall outside *A*, the specialists will pull in different directions. The risk, as will be seen in the case studies which follow, is that the conflict will lead to the worst-case scenario, an outcome for the patient in cell *D*.

What I have suggested is that the anaesthetist's organisational strategy within the OT is constituted in a continual effort to define the distinctive character of a patient in terms of her/his fitness. As will be seen in the first case study, this definition is precarious and can be countered by a challenge which once again privileges the surgical definition. In the second case, however, the discourse on fitness is spectacularly victorious over its rival.

Two case-studies of organisational conflict

In these case studies I am concerned to illustrate how the organisational strategies in surgeons' and anaesthetists' practices in the OT are constituted in their conflicting perspectives on their patients. In the first case, a patient faces a relatively straightforward procedure for a prostate condition, but with a fairly low reserve of fitness due to his age and previous history. Surgeon and anaesthetist have different objectives: the former wishes to complete the procedure successfully, while the latter is concerned to minimise the risk of anaesthesia on this old man.

Case Study 1
The patient was an 80-year-old male with a history of angina. The procedure was the trans-urethral resection of the prostate (TURP), which removes

prostate hypertrophy by means of instruments inserted via the urethra from the exterior, using diathermy (electrical cutting and scarring) to resect tissue blocking the urethra.

The patient had been pre-medicated on the ward, and was brought to the anaesthetic room in a very drowsy state. Dr Z was unwilling to give a general anaesthetic to this frail patient, and instead used a spinal anaesthetic. This is a difficult procedure, requiring the anaesthetist to introduce a catheter successfully into the sub-arachnoid space, within the outer two meninges (membranes around the cord), taking care not to damage the spinal cord. With this old patient, calcification between the vertebrae made this very tricky, and Z abandoned his first attempt and had to use a second spinal anaesthetic set before he was satisfied. Once in place, the catheter was taped to the patient, and a syringe attached by means of which measured doses of anaesthetic could be infused. The patient was taken into the theatre and prepared for the operative procedure (lithotomy position, with legs in slings attached to the end of the table), with standard blood pressure and heart rate monitors. This induction took thirty minutes, and organisationally, the anaesthetist was able to control the timing of the procedure, to ensure a safe operation. When Dr Z was ready, he asked the nurse to call the surgeon, who was in fact already hovering over the operating table.

Surgeon Mr X began the TURP, but it soon became apparent that the patient was experiencing some sensation or pain. Dr Z was also aware of this, and continued to administer anaesthetic via the catheter. Some fifteen minutes into the procedure there was the following exchange

Mr X: It's no good, whenever I use the diathermy he moves.
Dr Z: Well I have given the patient all the anaesthetic which he can safely receive.
Mr X: I cannot carry on with the procedure when he is moving.
Dr Z: I don't think the spinal can be working. I had better put him under (Field Notes).

While it was in principle feasible to abandon the surgery at this point, Mr X indicated that he was unwilling to do so. Dr Z was forced to compromise his earlier decision not to risk the patient with a general anaesthesia. The procedure was concluded with the patient unconscious, and following the operation, Dr Z spent a long time in the recovery area with the patient, ensuring that he was recovering from the trauma of the surgery and the anaesthesia.

The moment at which the surgeon seized the initiative in this procedure was when it became clear that despite his extended induction, the anaesthetic had not provided adequate analgesia, presumably due to a failure by the anaesthetist to position the catheter correctly inside the meninges. Mr X pressurised Dr Z to compromise the patient's fitness by a general anaesthetic, against his earlier judgement, and consequently a minor surgical procedure (low or medium illness) was transformed from having little effect on fitness to having a greater effect. Patient outcome, which should have been in cell *A* was forced into cell *C*, an undesirable outcome for the anaesthetist.

The alternative – of abandoning surgery – which would have led to an outcome in cell *B*, was not entertained by the surgeon, and the anaesthetist had no choice but to acquiesce, and administer general anaesthesia. The consequence was that the anaesthetist was unable to fulfil his role of proxy for the patient's fitness during the operation. The conflict between surgeon and anaesthetist thus also meant an undesirable outcome for the patient.

It might be contended that in such situations of conflict, the surgeon (being the more powerful specialist) will automatically take control. The position which I wish to argue here, following the postmodern analysis of power and expertise, is that this is to see things in reverse. Power and control are the *outcomes* of successful discursive (organisation) strategies. In this case, the anaesthetist failed to supply a demonstration of his expertise, and could no longer sustain the organisational position he had established in the face of an implicit challenge as to his capacity to serve the patient's interests.

The second case illustrates the situation in which a surgeon failed to demonstrate that his organisational strategy for treating a patient, based within a discourse on disease or illness, was sufficient to ensure a satisfactory outcome. In this case, the rival discourse on fitness placed the anaesthetist – unusually – at centre-stage.

Case Study 2
The patient was a 63-year-old female, admitted as an urgent case. The procedure was the resection of a meningioma (a tumour of the meninges covering the cerebral cortex), causing life-threatening pressure on the brain.

Neurosurgery – it appeared throughout fieldwork – was the subspecialism in which the surgical discourse was most strongly privileged, and this was reflected in many aspects of the organization of work in neurosurgery OT. The patient was brought to the anaesthetic room, and together anaesthetist *A* and surgeon *C* looked at brain scans indicating the position of the tumour and discussed the patient's history, and the anaesthesia to be administered. Surgeon *C* stood and watched during anaesthesia: once unconscious, the patient was transferred to the operating table, which had been brought into the anaesthetic room, and her head clamped rigidly. The anaesthetist connected leads for the various monitoring equipment, the patient was then draped and wheeled into theatre.

The operation proceeded smoothly, although after the removal of the meningioma there was considerable haemorrhage. With this stemmed to the satisfaction of the surgeon, the meninges were sutured, the portion of skull-bone replaced. The patient was brought to consciousness, and taken to recovery. Throughout the surgeon was dominant, and the anaesthetist's concern with the fitness of the patient was deemed secondary to her illness, as a consequence of the severity of the condition. Compromise to fitness was seen as a necessary trade-off against reduction in illness, which if untreated would quickly kill the patient.

Ninety minutes later, during a procedure on a subsequent patient, anaesthetist *A* was summoned to the recovery room to look at the former patient. She had an EEG trace which indicates unconsciousness as opposed to sleep. After conducting tests, Dr *A* returned to theatre:

> Dr *A*:   Mrs *X* seems to be a bit flat. She's displaying a (technical detail of brain wave pattern). I wonder if you would like to have a look.
>
> Mr *C*:   She's unconscious? (Dr *A* assents) Yes I'll come in. (They go together to the recovery room, Mr *C* leaving his assistant to continue the current operation.) (Field Notes)

Dr *A* diagnosed a sub-arachnoid haemorrhage, which had caused pressure on the brain, and a consequent lapse into unconsciousness. Without emergency surgery, the patient would rapidly deteriorate and die. He arranged for a third neuro-theatre to be opened to receive the patient, and he coordinated the emergency operation on the patient, with Mr *C*'s assistant doing the surgery, and a house officer to assist.

It is impossible to give anything other than a flavour of the ensuing activity: to try to evoke (Tyler 1986) the character of the proceedings. Mr *C*'s theatre was suddenly empty of personnel, while the tiny third neuro-theatre was packed as the drama attracted attention. When Mr *C* finished his procedure, he slipped quietly into the back of the third theatre to watch the emergency operation to painstakingly remove clotted blood which had haemorrhaged from the site of the operation earlier in the day. With the pressure removed, the patient has a better prognosis, but there has been considerable shock to the patient's system, and Dr *A* was concerned about low blood pressure and abnormal electrocardiograph trace. The emergency operation completed, the patient was taken to recovery in a very poor condition, under the care of anaesthetist *A*.

As was noted previously, neurosurgery is characterised by a balance of control heavily weighted in favour of surgeons' definitions of the patient. One discursive strategy which appeared to be used in neuro-surgery was to re-define patients such that illness outweighed any concern with fitness, by emphasizing urgency and life and death situations:

> Surgeon *C*:   We do not really have a concept of elective surgery in neuro. Most of the patients we see in out-patients are admitted as urgent cases, in that if they are not operated on their condition will deteriorate. There is no choice but surgery in most cases.

All the organisational arrangements supported this discourse, and closed down the possibilities of challenges based on alternative positions. What the postmodern perspective on organisation – as a precarious strategic manoeuvre mediated and sustained discursively – suggests is an explanation of the shift in authority from surgeon to anaesthetist after the diagnosis of the bleed in surgeon C's patient. Previously the surgeon's definition of his patient as possessing illness which outweighed any concern with residual fitness was accepted by the anaesthetist, enabling surgeon C to organize the procedure according to his claim of precedence. When it became clear that C had not only compromised fitness, but failed to reduce illness: heading the patient towards the very undesirable cell D (fitness reduced, illness not reduced), and that he had had his chance to organize an outcome in at least cell C (illness reduced with fitness also reduced) and failed, it was possible for anaesthetist A to take the initiative. With the anaesthetist (and his discourse on fitness) as the agency by which the patient might be delivered out of cell D, and into cell B (some fitness retained), he was able authoritatively to define the patient in his terms.

I am not suggesting that in this situation there was any disagreement as to the need for a second operation, only that its significance served, discursively, to shift the balance of control from surgeon to anaesthetist. Of course, in this situation, the surgeon does not acquiesce totally. Having been challenged, he may well try to organise the situation further, to respond to the challenge. It is extremely unlikely that when the next case came along, that the power balance would have shifted irrevocably. Indeed, I am arguing that such irrevocable shifts cannot happen: there is always potential for resistance, for a re-definition of reality. What the case illustrates is the *undecidability* in organization, the potential for the meaning of events to be re-constructed in a way which no longer favours the (currently) powerful. Only in such extreme cases as the one recounted here, is there so radical a re-alignment.

Discussion

The suggestion that surgeons' and anaesthetists' discourses are organised around different definitions of their patients, emphasising illness and fitness respectively, supplies a way of addressing the peculiar situation in which these two specialisms find themselves. At once, they are dependent upon each other, while at the same time, they have interests which may conflict. It might no doubt be possible to speculate upon the ways in which the two groupings have collaborated while sustaining individual identities and career structures. Further, the differing patterns of anaesthetic staffing in various countries might also supply researchers with interesting data: in some European countries, most anaesthesia is carried out by non-medical staff.

In this paper I am not concerned to link the micropolitics of the encounter I have described to such structural arrangements. Instead I shall confine myself to a brief consideration of the implications of the organisational strategies adopted by surgeons and anaesthetists, and in particular how this may affect patient care.

Firstly, it would appear that in most cases, the objective of reducing illness (the surgical discourse) takes precedence over sustaining fitness. This is hardly surprising, as if this were not the case then no surgery but the most inconsequential would be conducted. However, this means that the balance between surgeon and anaesthetist is inherently unbalanced from the outset. As the patient's proxy during surgery, the anaesthetist has a responsibility to sustain her/his patient's life against the assault of surgery. One needs to ask whether this activity is compromised by the inherent bias in favour of illness-reduction over fitness-maintenance?

Secondly, does this imbalance in control in the OT mean that anaesthetists will turn their attentions to other domains, where they can be more influential? One example, is their increased involvement in Intensive Care Units[2], while I have documented an enthusiasm shown by some anaesthetists for managerial roles in the reformed National Health Service (Fox 1991): such posts provide a new discourse and a new set of organisational strategies by which to challenge surgical authority. As one anaesthetist who had become a part-time clinical manager told me:

> *F*:   Surgeons will only change the way they work if they are forced to by re-organisation.

While this may provide anaesthetists with a new source of authority, it does not contribute to rectifying the power imbalance in the situation of the operation itself, in which the anaesthetist is the patient's proxy. A fascination with technology among many anaesthetists – on the other hand – may not only be used to challenge surgical definitions of what is happening during an operation, but could assist anaesthetists to act on behalf of patient fitness, by providing an additional claim to authority over-and-above 'experience' or clinical judgement.

Finally, is there an opportunity for a further discursive voice in the OT? While surgeons and anaesthetists engage in their collaborative/conflictual struggle, perhaps an alternative advocacy could be devised. Of course, within the perspective of postmodernism, any such new grouping – say health economists, management or even medical sociologists – would fabricate its patient-subject in its own particular image (Ashmore *et al.* 1989, Fox 1993b). There is no such thing, in this position, as the essential patient.

I want to take up this point in my concluding remarks. The sociology of health and illness has shown many times how patients and health professionals hold differing perspectives on health and illness (Calnan 1987, Currer and Stacey 1986), how differing explanatory models provide cultural meanings for the experience of pain and suffering and how these may be important in determining compliance with regimes of treatment (Kleinman 1988). Indeed it has been suggested (Armstrong 1987, Nettleton 1992) that in supplying such demonstrations, sociology has contributed to a new biopsychosocial model for medicine, in which psychological and social aspects of patients are observed and accounted for, alongside physical pathology.

The postmodern approach to organisational analysis suggests how such discourses on the patient's body constitute the link between knowledge and power. The organisational strategies adopted by a group, and the resistances which this engenders among those who are to be organised, signify both the differing bodies of knowledge or expertise held by these groups, and the site of struggle for control of a situation or setting. I have tried in this paper to show how some details of the organisation of surgery reflect differing discourses on patients held by surgeons and anaesthetists concerning notions of 'fitness' and 'illness', and that possibilities for control of the surgical setting inhere in such discourses. The analysis presented here is just one partial account, and the postmodern position would distance itself from claiming the over-arching truth of one position. But what the postmodern perspective supplies is a way of understanding conflict and uncertainty, control and resistance, as the failed outcome of efforts to organise – efforts which continually fragment and founder in the undecidability of discourses inscribed in language. For the surgical patient, this continual struggle may often protect from the extremes of surgical discourse, but on occasions may be very serious indeed.

Notes

1 The field work which is reported here was carried out at three English hospitals during the late 1980s, and formed the basis of a doctoral thesis for the University of Warwick, and a monograph (Fox 1992). The comments of referees have been valuable in the preparation of this paper.
2 I am grateful to an anonymous referee for pointing this out.

References

Armstrong, D. (1983) *The Political Anatomy of the Body.* Cambridge: Cambridge University Press.

Armstrong, D. (1987) Theoretical tensions in biopsychosocial medicine, *Social Science and Medicine,* 25, 1213–8.

Arney, W.R. and Bergen, B.J. (1983) The anomaly, the chronic patient and the play of medical power, *Sociology of Health and Illness,* 5, 1–24.

Ashmore, M., Mulkay, M. and Pinch, T. (1989) *Health and efficiency.* Milton Keynes: Open University Press.

Calnan, M. (1987) *Health and Illness: the lay perspective.* London: Tavistock.

Clegg, S.R. (1990) *Modern Organizations.* London: Sage.

Cooper, R. and Burrell, G. (1988) Modernism, postmodernism and organisational analysis: an introduction, *Organisation Studies,* 9, 91–112.

Cooper, R. (1989) Modernism, post-modernism and organisational analysis 3. The contribution of Jacques Derrida, *Organisation Studies*, 10, 479–502.

Currer, C. and Stacey, M. (eds) (1986) *Concepts of Health, Illness and Disease*. Leamington Spa: Berg.

Foucault, M. (1979) *Discipline and punish*. Harmondsworth: Peregrine.

Foucault, M. (1988) Technologies of the self. In Martin, L.H. *et al.* (eds) *Technologies of the Self*. London: Tavistock.

Fox, N.J. (1991) Postmodernism, rationality and the evaluation of health care, *Sociological Review*, 39, 709–44.

Fox, N.J. (1992) *The Social Meaning of Surgery*. Buckingham: Open University Press.

Fox, N.J. (1993a) Discourse, organisation and the surgical ward round, *Sociology of Health and Illness*, 15, 16–42.

Fox, N.J. (1993b) *Postmodernism, Sociology and Health*. Buckingham: Open University Press.

Kleinman, A. (1988) *The Illness Narratives*. New York: Basic Books.

Nettleton, S. (1992) *Power, Pain and Dentistry*. Buckingham: Open University Press.

Parker, M. (1990) Postmodernism and organisational analysis: a contradiction in terms? Paper presented at the British Sociological Association Conference, Guildford, April 1990.

Reed, M. (1989) *The Sociology of Management*. Hemel Hempstead: Harvester Wheatsheaf.

Silverman, D. (1985) *Qualitative Methodology and Sociology*. Aldershot: Gower.

3.4

Thinking teams thinking clients: issues of discourse and representation in the work of health care teams

Anne Opie

Introduction

The use of inter-disciplinary teams has become an increasingly familiar part of health care services in Western countries; indeed under some health care regulations in the United States such teams are mandatory (Mellor and Solomon 1992); this is also the case in New Zealand[1]. While it could be expected that the introduction of such teams into health organisations has been based on clear evidence of effective practices within teams, a survey of the research literature demonstrates that this is not the case. Much of the literature on teamwork in health care has been described as anecdotal, exhortatory and prescriptive (Mizrahi and Abramson 1994, Sheppard 1992). There is an absence of research describing and analysing teams in action (Sands 1993), and Atkinson's (1994: 118) comment on the under-development of 'analysis of spoken collegial discourse in medical settings' is apposite in light of what appears to be a similar absence of analysis of health teams' discourses.

The first section of the article presents some of the main themes in current research on health care teams; the second section concentrates on an analysis of a discussion of one client in a case conference. This conference was taped in the process of gathering qualitative data on the work and practices of multi-disciplinary teams working with clients in the hospital and in the community in three of New Zealand's Crown Health Enterprises (CHEs: formerly 'hospitals'). The fieldwork involved observation and taping of team conferences about clients and discussions to which the client and family were invited to contribute, taping of individual interviews with team members, and analysis of relevant team and policy documentation. My purpose in this analysis is to concentrate not on process in terms of interpersonal dynamics, which is the preoccupation of much literature on team work in the organisational and health field, but to attend to the conceptual work performed by teams in the course of discussing their clients. To this end, I will focus particularly on the team's representational practices and the implications of those practices.

There is an issue to be noted about the focus of the analysis. As has been remarked elsewhere (Opie 1995, Youssef and Silverman 1992) the practices of health professionals are intimately affected by the organisational and policy environment in which those professionals operate. The underdevelopment of this dimension here does not reflect a desire to construct idealist notions of practice. Rather it reflects my decision to highlight representational issues in team work because of the relationship between representation and dimensions of effective team work. The fuller discussion of the interaction between effective team work and organisational structures and policies is, however, the work of a later paper.

My interpretation of the data provided by the case conference is conducted within the theoretical framework provided by Michel Foucault's work on discourse, power and governmentality. Foucault has argued that particular disciplines or discursive practices are shown to be privileged in institutional and other social contexts with the effect of disempowering other disciplines and discursive practices present in the same institutional or social space (Foucault 1978, 1991, Gordon 1986, Kritzman 1988). Dominant discourses both define reality through the representations of it which they offer and result in the construction of social practices, behaviours and truth effects embodying the realities they have defined. There is, though, nothing deterministic about this state of affairs; given that many discourses are simultaneously active in a society, the dominance of a particular discourse can be challenged and modified by other discourses with their different representations of reality.

The distinctive features of a representation of an event or situation point directly to the discourse or discourses used to produce that representation. As recent commentators on textuality (for example, Atkinson 1990, Clifford 1983, 1986, Clifford and Marcus 1986, Said 1978, 1989, Smith 1990) have emphasised, language can no longer be understood as a transparent or neutral medium through which meaning can be grasped. Because language mediates between the event and its representation, no account can ever be complete. There are always other accounts which, as a result of emphasising constituent factors differently, make for alternative interpretations. Said's (1989: 216) remark on the absence of a vantage point 'outside the actuality of relationships' emphasises the affiliation (complicity) between representation, power and discourse. Language, as one mode by which representations of events are constituted, is inextricably embedded in relations of power. As a corollary to the above, it follows that I cannot claim a definitive reading for my representation of the case conference discussed below – what is offered is one representation of that event, and other representations could be generated from different theoretical positions.

Research perspectives on team work

The current literature on health teams reveals a significant group of issues and preoccupations about (1) the efficacy of health care teams; (2) the problems associated with defining 'effective' work, and (3) the nature and extent of organisational resourcing required to assist in the production of effective work.

The efficacy of team work
Although the international literature on team work in health care suggests that team work may offer substantial benefits, the same literature also makes extensive reference to the problems such work generates (see, for example, Abramson and Rosenthal 1995, Clark 1994, de Silva *et al.* 1992, Fox 1994, Gubrium 1975, Gilgun 1988, McClelland and Sands 1993, Mellor and Solomon 1992, Paxton 1995, Roberts *et al.* 1994, Saltz 1992, Specht 1985, Toseland *et al.* 1986, Webb and Hobdell 1980).

Much of the rationale for establishing teams in health care draws on assumptions about the benefits to be gained from multi-disciplinary work. These are commonly identified as: the development of quality care for clients through the achievement of coordination and collaboration of inputs from different disciplines; the development of joint initiatives; the achievement of better, because more fully informed, care plans; the provision, therefore of holistic care; a higher level of productivity; increased staff satisfaction and professional stimulation and, consequently, a more effective use of resources.

Equally, as the authors cited above have commented, the putative benefits of team work are offset by the identification of significant problems. These include: inadequate, or an absence of, organisational support; the absence of training in team work; the absence of orientation programmes for new members joining the team; lack of interprofessional trust resulting in complicated power relations between professions; an over-abundance of or, alternatively, an absence of conflict; lack of clear structures and directions; unclear goals; the dominance of particular discourses resulting in the exclusion of others; the existence of tensions between professional discourses resulting in potentially unsafe practices; lack of continuity of members; difficulty of definition of key terms; the production of client discussions which, far from addressing client goals, marginalise them and contribute to clients' disempowerment; and an absence of teams' examination of their processes.

Further, as some recent writing on teams in non-health organisations suggests, the concept 'team' may have been inadequately defined and, consequently, groups of people who work together have been too easily labelled a 'team' (Katzenback and Smith 1993). These authors also comment that teams in many organisations frequently lack a purpose and may well 'accept goals that are neither demanding, precise, realistic, nor actually held *in common*' (1993: 21), and, despite the emphasis in the organisational literature on the benefits of team work, they note that high performance teams in the business world are rare.

Measuring effectiveness
Measurement of teams' effectiveness using other than quantitative measurements (the value position of which may well not be acknowledged (Fox 1991)) has not been extensively discussed in relation to health teams. However, the research discussed below highlights the complexity of evaluating effective

team work given the range and interdependence of factors necessary for its achievement. Antoniadis and Videlock (1991: 158) quote research done by Shea and Guzzo who have defined group effectiveness as mediated by three interrelated factors: (a) 'task interdependence', *i.e.* the extent of cooperation required to manage tasks. Acquiring such interdependence requires members to have multiple opportunities to interact in order to build a team consensus through delineation of norms and clarification of roles; equally, consensus about client issues by way of problem definition is achieved through information pooling and brainstorming[2]; (b) 'outcome interdependence', *i.e.* the extent to which rewards are linked to group performance; and (c) 'potency', *i.e.* access to the necessary skills and environmental supports to perform the task, including feedback, so enabling the team to evaluate its work. Antoniadis and Videlock (1991: 162) postulate further that effective transdisciplinary team work is mediated by both individual and environmental factors. They define the factors in the clinical environment productive of effective work as comprising: a strong theoretical base; clear intervention targets; appropriate clinical tools; effective procedures and policies; feedback; prescriptive supervision; and training and validation of members. Relevant clinical factors include: role release; the possession of a common knowledge base; the presence of trust and respect; risk taking; and clinical competence.

Guzzo (1986) has conceptualised effectiveness as referring to two dimensions: 'ultimate effectiveness', which refers to group outputs, the overall satisfaction of members and 'healthy social interaction'; and 'intermediate effectiveness', which refers to the 'quality of the group interaction process as it performs the task at hand'. Evaluating the effectiveness of the group interaction process requires, therefore, 'assessments of the level of member effort, the extent to which resources are applied toward task accomplishment, and the appropriateness of strategies used by a group to accomplish its task' (Guzzo 1986: 46).

In addition to these issues, an evaluation of the effectiveness of the work of a health care team has to be contextualised in relation to the level of integration of work and performance that a particular type of team can be expected to display. Multi-disciplinary teams are defined as teams where members, operating out of their disciplinary bases, work parallel to each other, their primary objective being that of coordination. Interdisciplinary teams are those where members continue to work from particular disciplinary orientations but undertake some joint collaborative work. Transdisciplinary teams are those where a significantly higher level of integration of work is achieved and where, as a result of opening professional values and terminology to scrutiny, the team is able to develop a common language (Clark 1994, Rosenfield 1992, Sands 1993).

Organisational resourcing
While not all of the nine factors Roberts *et al.* (1994) identified as contributing to the success of an interdisciplinary gerontological programme are relevant

to developing team work those that have clear organisational relevance to such developments are:

1. the achievement of common goals;
2. the existence of institutional support and support from key people;
3. availability of sufficient expertise in order to develop [practices];
4. the breadth of the concept encouraging the participation of multiple partners;
5. attention to team building;
6. [members] having staying power and high commitment to the [team]; and
7. sufficient financial resources.

These multiple, interacting factors suggest that effective, sustained inter-disciplinary work requires a nurturing organisational environment (Webb and Hobdell 1980, Miller 1993). Further, it is likely that establishing and maintaining well-functioning teams in settings with strong hierarchical tra-ditions, no tradition of multi-professional team work, and an absence of a legitimating ideology, may well be difficult.

Team functioning may also be determined by the way it is organisationally conceptualised. Mellor and Solomon (1992: 205) have described teams as comprising 'representatives of the various identified disciplines [who] meet together to assess, treat and order the health and social service care needs of the individual older person'; and Saltz, citing Ducanis and Golin, has defined teams as '*a functioning unit, composed of individuals with varied and specialized training, who coordinate their activities to provide services to a client or group of clients*' (Saltz 1992: 134; her emphasis). These definitions highlight function and output, issues of increasing concern in the achieve-ment of economically efficient health care. However, Kane (quoted in Sands 1993: 546), introduces a significant additional dimension when she writes of teams as requiring a 'common purpose, separate skills or professional con-tributions, and some process of communication, coordination, cooperation, or *joint thinking*' (my italics).

Enabling these different processes and members' skills to come together productively is complicated. Time is typically at a premium in health care organisations and the conduct of case conferences may well preclude atten-tion to such details as Good's (1994) evaluation of the practices of routine medical practices in the United States suggests:

Case presentations represent disease as the object of medical practice. The 'story' presented is of a disease process as the object of medical practice. . . . The person, the subject of suffering, is represented as the site of disease rather than as a narrative agent. The patient is formulated as a medical project and given the extreme pressures of time, case presentations are designed to exclude all except that which will assist in diagnostic and therapeutic decisions. . . . One result is the inattention to the lifeworld of the patient . . . (Good 1994: 80).

Nor, as Gubrium's analysis of case discussions in a rest home (1975) has demonstrated, is it sufficient simply to build in a more extensive discussion about clients. Attention to the discourses which shape that information, and to the resultant representations of clients, is also necessary.

The focus, then, in this article is on team work as *reflexive* or 'thinking' work, requiring identification of the discourses accessed by the team and of the representations of clients occasioned by those discourses. My argument will be that this process of standing back, or *thinking through* such issues, of attending to how the team goes about its work of 'joint thinking' contributes to the development of reflexive practice in team work; and that it is this reflexivity which is a critical dimension in effective practice in making manifest the endemic imbalances in power between clients and health professionals, and seeing to redress these. Myerhoff and Ruby (1982: 1–2) have defined reflexivity 'as consciousness about being conscious; thinking about thinking . . . the capacity of any system of signification to turn back upon itself, to make itself its own object by referring to itself . . .'

I am using 'reflexivity' to refer to the metaprocess involving a conscious critique of the way members *think about* the process of their work. This, I will argue, requires a focus going beyond attention to interpersonal dynamics among team members, to address members' training to assist them to foreground, in their routine activities the way in which they think about and assess their performance and 'product' (*i.e.* their case conferences, care plans, and related documentation). If teams are, however, to address the conceptual basis of their work and the representations which their accounts of clients produce, they require some regular time to think about and critique their performance. That teams require time to review, not just the clients, but also the quality of the team's 'products' is clearly a critical but overlooked factor in determining effectiveness.

Such conditions are not currently easily attained in the New Zealand health service where the organisational environment is perceived by many health professionals to be inimical to good practice. Witten (1993) has commented on the way organisational stories reflect an organisational ethos – in the health teams participating in the research project the organisational stories were substantially of mismanagement, lack of interest by management in staff work and conditions, corruptness, incompetence, selling out, the increasing dominance of managerialist discourses, an increasing reductivist practice for some professionals (Opie 1995) and failure to stem the departure of experienced and qualified staff. Members of the team whose work I have drawn on for this paper commented on the way in which work with people with disability was regarded as the Cinderella of the health service. The ward was very crowded, noisy and in need of upgrading and efforts to control budgets had resulted in cuts in nursing staff to levels considered by some team members to be dangerous at key points of the day. While space precludes a detailed discussion of the re-structuring of the New Zealand health system (Salmond *et al.* 1994), it is pertinent to note that there have been constant internal re-structuring within the CHEs over the last decade in addition to two major re-structurings of the health service and, for a number of years, a reduction in the health budget[3]. These have resulted in significant staff redundancies, loss of expertise, uncertainties about security of positions and morale loss; within two-and-a-half years, thirteen of the Chief Executive Officers in the 23 CHEs have resigned or not sought to renew their contracts; this particular CHE was heavily in debt and its future was uncertain.

A team at work

Much of the work of the 3 multi-disciplinary teams which to date have participated in my research can be described as routine and focused on the workers' accountability to the clients, the team and the organisation. Members were expected to briefly report on work undertaken for or with clients since the previous meeting; to outline where necessary further work to be undertaken, sometimes within timeframes; and to co-ordinate arrangements for clients within or across agencies. However, the teams also engaged from time to time in lengthy discussions about some clients whose situations were complex and were seen to require work across psychological, medical, nursing, physiological and social issues, and where there was team disagreement or uncertainty about how to proceed. I have chosen the discussion of Patient 22 because, as an example of non-routine work, it makes very visible the strategies which could enable the team to move beyond impasse and frustration when working with a complex situation. It is *not* a unique instance; the significant features of this particular discussion have been repeated frequently in the many team case conferences I have attended as a researcher (Opie 1995), and as a clinician.

The team discussion occurred during a weekly case conference held by a multi-disciplinary team working with people with chronic and severe physical disabilities. Those present at the conference were a rehabilitation specialist (RS), a staff nurse (N), a doctor attached to the ward (WD), two occupational therapists (OT1 and OT2), a speech language therapist (SLT), a social worker (SW), and a locum physiotherapist (PT). The meeting was chaired by one of the OTs as in this team, non-medical staff rotated the chairpersonship. The clinical nurse specialist (CNS), who was also the team leader, was absent.

P22 was a middle aged, married man living apart from his wife who was considering divorce. He had been admitted to the ward for assessment and rehabilitation from a community residential facility. The team defined the primary purpose of the admission as stabilising a medical problem with his bowels to prevent the breakdown of his placement in the residential facility which lacked the facilities to manage heavier care residents. Because of a lack of more appropriate alternatives, breakdown would result in his placement in a geriatric home, which the team considered was highly undesirable. Although the initial expectation was that he would be discharged back to the community quite quickly, the team regarded P22 as 'at risk' because of the medical, social and psychological complexities of his situation (one factor was that he had not accepted that his illness was degenerative, although he had been ill for more than a decade). Under the circumstances, it might be expected that the team would have emphasised their client's perceptions of his situation to assist their development of effective strategies for working with him. There was, however, no discussion in the first case conference of what the team thought the client understood about the reasons for his admission or what he expected to be its outcome, an omission commented on by P22 when he and his wife met the team shortly after the case conference to discuss progress and plans for his future. Despite P22's anger about this lack of consultation and the team's delineation of client consultation as one of their goals, the team continued not to address these issues.

Similarly, although the meeting with P22 and his wife had gone disastrously and had left the team members distressed and angry, their sense of competence threatened by this 'uncooperative' patient, there was only passing reference (the fact of its occurrence) to that meeting in the beginning of the discussion on which I am focusing (the team's second case conference on this client). Their distress notwithstanding, the team never attempted to examine how they as a group might have contributed to this difficult event.

The team allocated an hour-and-a-half to discuss the 16 patients on the ward. This particular discussion of P22 lasted about 25 minutes, as had the discussion the previous week following his admission. The team continued to discuss this client at some length over the next three conferences at which I was present (by which stage I had completed the fieldwork at this site). The time given to discuss P22's situation thus represents a considerable amount of team time to devote to one client, yet despite these extensive discussions the team believed that it was not making progress with this client and felt somewhat demoralised. In Guzzo's (1986: 48) terms, one dimension of the team's 'ultimate effectiveness' was compromised.

Although Sands (1993), in an analysis of an interdisciplinary team's assessment meeting, did not comment on the quality of that team's extensive discussion or the ensuing representation(s) of the client, her outline of the structure of the conference described what would appear to be a logical, coherent process, albeit a very time-consuming one. The discussion involved: a detailed case presentation (20 minutes); questions from team members (5 minutes); creation of a problem list by the group (20 minutes); discussion and editing of problems (3 minutes); identification of objectives to be met in the assessment process (13 minutes); further discussion and completion of the plan (6 minutes) (Sands 1993: 551).

In contrast, the discussion about P22 launched immediately into a variety of team members' concerns[4]: P22's on-going medical problems, identification of tasks to have been discharged by different team members over the previous week; and an outline of the team's 'attitude' to their client, and delineation of further 'goals'

OT2:   ... P22 ... ah, very hard to manage, self medicating and not managing well to care for himself, seems to have unrealistic expectations ... still having accidents with his bowels, threatening to discharge himself. Um, the team felt it was very important that he was consulted every step of the way about any treatment that is going to happen and it seems they are going slowly and his tests have been done and they're waiting for the results and we had seven goals for P22: um the first one was cognitive testing from OT1 and self assessing from OT1, um, there was need to get the manager from um . . . the residential home on board and the SNT {a senior nurse who worked in the community} was going to look after that. The rehab specialist was going to get heavy on Thursday with P22 and –

RS: – not successful.

WD: I mean strong, a pep talk.

OT2:   and there was a suggestion that there should be a mini family meeting as soon as possible and I understand that happened. Um, continue to reinforce a bowel pattern and um perhaps look at using the urodrome.

OT1:   I spoke with CNS just a couple of days ago, just going through the goals and working out what progress has been made and um like we both feel that P22's, just his adjustment to his condition and also from personality features mean that it's actually really difficult to um make as much progress as we would like and what the residential placement would like, um, so goals have been set with P22 but often there is, often he will come up with an excuse, um, and CNS has also said that she'd like to eliminate the possibility of a problem in his bowels because there's not a great amount of progress being made there so I –

WD: – we need to go ahead with something else (lines 1222–1249).

The transcript of the remainder of the discussion on P22 shows the team taking up the following issues:

1. (lines 1262–1279): team reviewed P22's need for assistance in self cares (dressing, showering, toileting etc.); a request from the residential placement for cognitive testing was noted; and concern that employment may affect his beneficiary status was mentioned.
2. (lines 1289–1407): extensive discussion about his working as a financial consultant; whether the team should be actively discouraging him from doing this; and the possible need for more complex memory tests than had been used to date.

3. (lines 1392–1416): *i.e.*, slight overlap with above) need for P22 to have hobbies.
4. (lines 1418–1443): question asked about whether P22's goals had been identified or whether team goals had predominated.
5. (lines 1445–1460): discussion with emphasised P22's obligation to cooperate with team.
6. (lines 1462–1470): discussion focusing on team tasks and bowel management.
7. (lines 1412–1526): discussion about pressure sores.
8. (lines 1530–1548): point raised about multiple issues affecting P22 and how these may affect his returning to the community-based residential home.
9. (lines 1550–1638): discussion whether the home could provide the necessary assistance; the need for clear advice to the home about P22's medical condition because the team was reliant on it as a scarce community resource (*i.e.* they could not 'fudge' his problems to the home even if this meant that he might become a so-called 'bed-blocker'); and the extent to which P22 'covers up' his disabilities.
10. (lines 1643–1671): team set tasks for following week: discussion with P22 about leisure pursuits, work to maintain skin integrity, work on developing transfers, bowel management.

The structure of the team discussion described by Sands (1993) implies that such discussions:

*   allowed for the detailed presentation of the issues;
*   were exploratory (this would suggest there was time for members to raise possibilities or seek clarification, hence allowing for expansion of information and conceptualisation of that information);
*   enabled the identification of the range of relevant problems or issues;
*   enabled the team to narrow down the issues it wished to address;
*   identified tasks and objectives for team members; and
*   confirmed the allocation of tasks.

This list, when placed against the range of issues outlined above which were addressed by the New Zealand team, could support a positive interpretation of their work. The team discussion could be represented to be effective for the following reasons: members had had a detailed discussion about their concerns; sought clarification of a number of issues between themselves; had identified relevant issues; narrowed down tasks; and had allocated these to different members.

An alternative representation, and the one I want to pursue, is that the discussion, although wide-ranging, maintained a persistent emphasis on what the team was to do for P22. Apart from the long exchange about whether P22 should be allowed by the team to practice as a financial adviser, much of the discussion was dominated by medical and physiological concerns: bowel management, skin integrity, and transferring (*i.e.* his ability to move from bed to chair etc.). These were very necessary issues to consider in relation to the client's functioning but they were not the only ones. The team defined its mode of operation as client-centred and empowering. Members saw part of their role as working as client advocates and as involving clients in the development and implementation of goals. They sought to develop a holistic approach to client care (so taking up issues of addressing the person's 'life world' to which Good (1994) refers). However, putting such objectives into practice requires some defined procedures (such as the clear identification of which team member *is* the client advocate) and the need to ask different questions which in themselves would refer the team back to seeking the client's understanding of his position. While a few comments did point to the team's concern with other than medical issues and tasks to be accomplished, these comments were easily marginalised:

WD: very very tricky. I mean bowels is not the only thing. There are so many other issues. (Right, that's right) I don't think he, it doesn't look as if he can go back to to the residential placement.
OT2:   Did the community OT get the um head rest for him?
OT1:   Yes but she cannot go ahead with that because it's not certain that he will be returning there but he –
SW: – What I've got for the review are bowels, hip pain, heel, skin integrity, transfers . . . (team talk over each other for 3 seconds)
WD: Very tricky/everything is . . . one of them is bad enough. There's the combination of them that is –
RS: – Yeah well [   ] you know um um unless he can hoist himself ah, ah, ah which I think his chances are zero (lines 1530–1540).

Given the fact that much of the discussion circled around issues aired the previous week and the fact that P22 was seen as 'difficult', the team's practical orientation was understandable; equally it was problematic because of the absence of reference to the client's concerns and perspectives. Questions which could have assisted the team's focus on these could include: 'What does this man hope for?' 'Why does he think he was admitted to the ward?' 'What does he see as the problems?' 'Does he know of, and if so how does he explain, the team's concerns about his future?' 'How does he envisage his future?' Instead, the team stuck to its familiar mode of operation even when it was patently not working. Each member contributed to the narrative developing around this man but without the team as a whole adopting a methodical procedure that enabled them to bring out the client's understandings of his position, and to think reflexively about the information they possessed.

There was, though, one critical moment when a team member (SLT) questioned the appropriateness of the team's processes, the extent to which their work was empowering their clients, and challenged the representation of the client which the team was developing. Her suggestion, that the team needed to move beyond their familiar pattern of working, was not only quite strongly rejected but resulted in others' developing a representation of the client as greedy and as making untoward demands on CNS. This representation went unchallenged.

SLT: The other thing is that right at the start about his resistance to some of the goals and him making excuses: one of the things I found very useful was sort of paradoxing where you actually go with the resistance and say things like, 'Yeah I can see how hard that would be' (mm) and just keep going with that resistance and often the client comes back two or three days later and says, 'You know when we were talking about such and such' and that suddenly the very intrinsic motivation –

OT1: – I think for CNS though it's just got incredibly frustrating and I don't know if she always has the time to work through that process.

WD: Going with that –

SLT: – *I think it is important that we look at that because we have a lot of clients that do this and whether it's because we haven't goal set with them on board right from the start I mean that that it could come at an earlier stage that we've got problems in our system and set our goals rather than their goals – perhaps that's the issue – but quite often we have clients who just quite happily set goals with us and then they throw all sorts of spanners in the works and part of our job is really to deal with that.* (my emphasis) (all talk at once)

OT1: I think yeah – if you feel strongly about that . . . talk to CNS about that.

SLT: Well, I was just wondering whether that as a team we should be talking about it because it's how we manage our clients in general.

N: But the thing is that his, he, does he want to go back to his residential placement? If he does so he actually has to go, to *cooperate with the um the goals that have been set for him* (my emphasis) but the things that are –

WD: – maybe we should actually –

N: – actually, like he has to be at a certain standard to be actually living there. He has to cooperate with us more.

OT1: (overlapping) What CNS thought we'd do is see what's happening in a week's time because if it's looking as if he can't go back to the residential placement, um we're not even sure what our options are, if there are any.

Apart from SLT's marginalised critique, there was no other point where the team identified the problematic nature of its discussion. The discussion remained descriptive, rather than analytical. There was no attention paid to the nature of the representation of the client which was developing; how this representation positioned the client *vis à vis* the team; or how it affected the possible orientation and prioritising of the work to be undertaken.

From my reading of the transcript it highlights how the team's representation of P22 failed to address the relationship between the structural and the personal. OT2's description of P22 as 'unrealistic' powerfully suppresses who defines 'reality' and locates the problem in the individual, rather than addressing systemic problems. It is not unrealistic for adults to wish to go to bed at 11.00 pm (which was what P22 had requested) instead of 8.30 pm but as a result of an absence of resources for home support services, a systemic and resource issue (over which the team had no control) became transformed into a personal pathology. A desire to go to bed at an 'adult' time can be organisationally complex for a person with a disability dependent on assistance from a home aide but for P22 to be seen as difficult and manipulative because of such desires was to relocate him in the very systems of dependency which the team's work was intended to avoid. The team's anxiety about his expectations over his bedtime was not only that this would further complicate his returning to the community but that he could become a 'bed blocker' of scarce assessment and rehabilitation beds. P22 had come to the ward without a 'sale or return' clause[5]. He would therefore have to stay on the ward until a place was found for him, should the community placement refuse to accept him back. Such an outcome could compromise the organisational evaluation of the unit's efficient use of resources.

Control issues also surfaced in these competing representations. The patient was to be 'consulted' (which implies some sharing of power) yet one of the medical staff was to 'get heavy' with him; other representations defined him as deviant, unco-operative, ungracious. This, it should be noted, produces the binary of 'proper' patients as grateful, docile and, above all, rational, able to make choices which complement the team's understanding of its role and its work.

My intention is neither to assert that working with this man would have been easy nor that faecal incontinence is other than extremely unpleasant to cope with; it *is* to propose that attention to and analysis of the implications of their representations could have enabled the team, rather than persistently returning to the (contested) actions they were intending to take on their patient's behalf or in relation to his body, to question their own modes of working; and that this would have been possible within the time spent discussing this client. Such a focus could have produced questions which moved beyond the medicalisation of the problem (*i.e.* the focus on bowel management) to those which enabled the team to incorporate a structural and psychosocial focus which legitimated rather than pathologised their client's reaction to his condition and which could have allowed them to attend to their responses to P22.

Such questions may also have highlighted the presence of competing representations of the concept 'adult'. The team's representation drew on a discourse in which adulthood was equated with the production of logical and rational behaviour, including acceptance of dependency and its consequences; the client referred to a discourse of adulthood emphasising independence and choice. Neither representation is 'wrong' in itself, but in this context each was based on quite different conceptions of desirable behaviours.

Instead of being positioned supportively alongside their client (which the team intended) they and their client were glaring angrily at each other across a no-man's land of shit (metaphorical and literal) and mutual rejection. The more difficulties the team experienced in this contact with P22, the more they concentrated on actions to be performed with the consequence that they were unable to attend to their representation of the client and the material effects of that representation. It is not, then, just a question of setting up new structures or proposing new modes of client-professional relationships (for example, 'client-centred' work) as antidotes to the problems of differential power. Working reflexively includes acknowledging the inevitability of differential power relations between clients and health professionals and the development, and on-going critique, of modes of interaction which seek explicitly to minimize that difference. It also includes acknowledging the client's reality – a critical dimension, especially in the provision of chronic and aged care (Hunter 1991).

Producing effective work

I wish to conclude this essay in two ways: first, by commenting further on the sociological significance of developing an analysis of the representational practices of health care teams, and how these practices make an impact on effective team work; and secondly by offering some tentative conclusions about some of the conditions required for effective team processes. Discussion of these conditions emphasises the importance of the commitment of organisational resources to the development of teamwork.

1. I argued at the beginning of this essay that representational practices contribute powerfully to the discourses which inform the work of the team and therefore their approach to clients; moreover, the ways in which events or clients are represented have material effects in the social world. The breadth or richness of a representation of an event, situation, or client can restrict or expand the team's field of play and its perceived options for action[6], thus highlighting the sociological significance of ongoing work on representations generated in multi-disciplinary team discussions. Marks (1993: 138–9) has highlighted the value of attending to the nature of team discourses in discussing a process of analysis of case conferences in the educational field when she writes:

In addition to the critical impulse *vis-à-vis* challenging professional practices, we were also concerned with the liberatory goal of empowering the subject of the case conference. Critical reflection on language would expose the dominant ways of seeing in the meeting which we felt had served to regulate him. . . . By exposing the way in which he was positioned in and through language, it was hoped that the feedback meeting would open a space for challenging discursive practices and for enabling Mike [the subject of the conference] to resist being positioned as the 'problem'.

Analysis of the nature of representations and their positioning of the client (albeit difficult), and the generation of alternative questions in order to explore parameters of change and development for the client and the team is, I suggest, of mutual interests to sociologists and professionals.

My argument is, therefore, that effective work by health teams, especially with patients whose situations are very complex and where the team strikes an impasse, depends upon the team's moving beyond that account of clients' needs which is generated by the necessary and practical question, 'What does this person need'? To make this move depends upon their developing an analysis of the client's situation *with the full participation of that person*. Alternative questions could be: 'What are the issues confronting this person and how does s/he understand them?'; 'what are the issues for the team in developing care plans for this client?'; and, at a meta-level, 'how does the team, in its discussions, conceptualise its activity?'; 'what are its representational practices?'; 'how do these position the client?'; and 'how do they affect team/client interaction?' *Different* questions are needed to enable the development of a *different* representation of the client and of the work the team needs to undertake.

This process of standing back, or *thinking jointly* through such issues, as well as attending to the very necessary practicalities, contributes to the development of reflexive, and therefore effective, practice in team work[7]. What I want to emphasise here, however, is that questions such as those outlined above are not put forward in the belief that they will produce the 'truth' about the client – they too inevitably exist within the domains of representational practices and power relations. Yet conceptualising the work differently allows previously repressed, excluded or erased issues both about the client and about the team's concept of its work to be addressed.

From this perspective, alertness to and focus on its range of discourses and their resultant modes of producing the client becomes a hallmark of an effective team. The effect of attending to issues like autonomy, loss, change, grief, and dependence which confront the older client or a person with physical disabilities and their relatives, in conjunction with them, is very different from focusing primarily on needs, *i.e.* the need for a particular type of mattress, wheelchair, bowel management, financial advice or placement in a rest home.

The more analytic mode of discourse reaches towards the representation of a client which incorporates emotionality, relationships of self with self and self with other, irrationality, bodily and psychological disjunctions and physical degeneration. It seeks to attend to those issues as well as their practical manifestations; in contrast, a 'needs related' discourse can too easily produce a representation of a technologised, physiologically (mal)functioning body, divorced from its social and psychological expressions.

Further, I suggest that attending to its discursive modes of production and analysis (the results of its 'thinking jointly') offers the team an opportunity to make a critique of that production. This has significant organisational ramifications, in particular the organisational recognition of the importance of a team having time to review and critique their performance, and the inclusion of such practices in team training and development programmes. The importance of such an organisational commitment is further emphasised by Nontaka and Takeuchi (1995). In their discussion of organisations as knowledge creators rather than dealers in information, these writers have defined the critical organisational role to be identifying what constitutes knowledge relevant to the organisation and ensuring that the management systems enable its development.

2. The definitions of multidisciplinarity, interdisciplinarity and trans-disciplinarity offered at the beginning of this paper defined increasingly complex team processes and interactions, although in practice teams, by dint of association and interaction, may well be located between different modes of team type (perhaps particularly between multi- and inter-disciplinary). Given the intricacy of situations to which multi-disciplinary teams must respond, the actual effectiveness of such teams may be questionable. The objective of such teams – to achieve coordinated work – is problematic. Does 'coordination' refer primarily to the coordination of administrative issues?; i.e. the team knows that this person is to be discharged and will ensure that they have carried out their contribution to that discharge by the requisite date? Or does it mean bringing together knowledge from different professionals and from clients in order to allow these differently sited knowledges to interrogate each other, so setting in train a much more complex process, which suggests a more complex level of functioning? Each level of integration of work suggests changing or different access among disciplines to power in decision-making, different team processes and modes of operation, different ways of conceptualising and working with the co-ordinated information and the development of means of empowerment for clients. Development of more co-ordinated work points, therefore, to the need for organisational support.

Shea and Guzzo's concept of organisational 'potency' (Antoniadis and Videlock 1991) has a double reference – to skills and environmental (i.e. organisational) support. The team members participating in this research were skilful; their individual knowledges about their areas of responsibility were impressive and were almost always thoughtfully displayed in a situation where, as noted earlier, conditions of work were often stressful and where the work itself was often very emotionally demanding. My representation of the team's mode of operation, however, derives from focusing not on issues of individual skilfulness but on assessing how it permitted its members to manage stressful and difficult work. Faced with substantial organisational demands and uncertainties, and client distress and deterioration, team members focused on *what they could do* to confront, address and hopefully ameliorate clients' difficulties. Focusing on practical actions was in this sense purposive.

Yet for the team to move beyond its repetitious modes of interaction, the familiarity of which reinforces their value, requires an awareness of the different discourses spoken by the team and of the resulting representations of clients. Attending to the nature of representations generated by professional discourses, and to the analytic processes of team discussions (the inclusion of conceptualisation, rather than a predominant focus on task-orientation) requires training, time and opportunities provided by the organisation to think reflexively. Mohrman and Mohrman (1993: 93) have suggested that innovation relies on the 'availability of slack resources, redundancy of effort, trial and error, experimentation, freedom from constraints . . . , autonomy, and the ability to be playful'. These conditions, which clearly require organisational commitment and resourcing, are those also required for fostering reflexive team work. However, the implementation of managerialist principles in the health sector in New Zealand, intended to result in allocative and productive efficiency, has meant in practice a predominant concern with outputs, continued restructuring, the loss of clinical expertise, professional uncertainty, high staff mobility[8], shrinking resources, and a reduction of training opportunities for many staff. In the day-to-day experiences of many health professionals in New Zealand there is a distinct absence of organisational conditions which would enable the development of reflexive team work.

Acknowledgements

The research on which this article reports is funded by the Health Research Council of New Zealand. The original paper from which this article was developed was presented at the New Zealand Sociological Association Annual Conference, Akaroa, December 1–3, 1995. That paper has been published as 'Thinking teams, thinking clients' in Norris, P. (ed.) *Health-Related Papers from the Sociological Association of Aetearoa Annual Conference*, Akaroa, December, 1995: Working Paper 16: Christchurch, Dept. of Sociology in collaboration with the Health Services Research Centre. I would like to thank Brian for his valuable commentary on the various drafts of this article.

Notes

1 In New Zealand, assessment by multi-disciplinary teams governs access by older people to services; by 1997 people with a disability will be required to have their needs for services assessed by multi-disciplinary teams.
2 However, this leaves unquestioned the nature of the achieved consensus.
3 More recently, there have been injections of funding into the health system. These have been largely directed at the politically sensitive areas of waiting lists and mental health. The 1991 re-structuring promised a reduction in waiting lists for operations – instead, waiting lists have grown exponentially. Mental health has also been promised increased funding following the highly critical Mason Report (1996). However, because some of this increase is to be funded by the re-direction of funds within the 4 Regional Health Authorities rather than by 'new' money, this commitment has been greeted with public cynicism.
4 The team typically began reviews of patients by reading the tasks members were to have discharged over the previous week. In introducing P22 the chairperson said:

> P22: um, changeable in history giving, on fat free diet, query cognitive impairment. Has an iron deficiency and a significant disability. He's got swollen ankles. The goals are regularised bowel management [   ] cause of anaemia, cognitive testing and that was OT(1), and review medication on the doctor's ward round please . . . so how did you all get on with this challenging guy?
>
> CNS: (slowly and with emphasis) Look this guy is really very very hard to manage; we are having a terrible time with him and he's telling me he's going out today, he won't stay any longer.

Transcription conventions
word-   indication of interruption
-word   indicated that speaker had interrupted
[ ]   inaudible passage
word . . . word   pause (each period indicates approximately 1 second)

5 Such a phrase nicely illustrates the dominant managerialist discourse within the New Zealand health system.
6 In his study of social work practice, Pithouse (1987) quoted from a supervision session where the father of a client was represented by the social worker (in very imprecise language and drawing on highly stereotypic images) as a latent homosexual and as ineffectual as 'head of the household'. These unchallenged representations not only positioned the father in a very weak position in relation to the very powerful social worker (whose problematic representation had organisational and legal status which it is likely the father would have found difficult to challenge) but also closed off alternative representations of the 'dysfunctional' family which might have enabled the identification of different modes or foci of engagement, and discussion of the social worker's representational practices and their material effects on clients.
7 This process appears to be very similar to Elias' concept of a 'detour *via* detachment' (Dopson and Waddington 1996: 545) where Elias is referring to the importance of being able to stand back to develop an analysis of one's own action, despite one's involvement in the situation. As is also noted, this is not easily done.

8 Development of reflexive teamwork also requires organisational commitment to continuity of staff. Within 6 months of completing the fieldwork at one site, one team had been substantially re-structured; at another, several key staff had left.

References

Abramson, J. and Rosenthal, B. (1995) Collaboration: interdisciplinary and inter-organizational applications. In Edwards, D. and Hopps, J.G. (eds) *The Encyclopedia of Social Work*. 19th edn. Washington DC: NASW Press.

Antoniadis, A. and Videlock, J. (1991) In search of teamwork: a transactional approach to team functioning, *The Transdisciplinary Journal*, 1, 2, 157–67.

Atkinson, P. (1990) *The Ethnographic Imagination: Textual Constructions of Reality*. London and New York: Routledge.

Atkinson, P. (1994) Rhetoric as skill in a medical setting. In Bloor, M. and Taraborelli, P. (eds) *Qualitative Studies in Health and Medicine*. Aldershot: Avebury.

Clark, P. (1994) Social, professional and educational values on the interdisciplinary team: implications for gerontological and geriatric education, *Educational Gerontology*, 20, 53–61.

Clifford, J. (1983) On ethnographic authority, *Representations 1*, 2, Spring, 118–46.

Clifford, J. (1986) Introduction: partial truths. In Clifford, J. and Marcus, G. (eds) *Writing Culture: The Poetics and Politics of Ethnography*. Berkeley: University of California Press.

Clifford, J. and Marcus, G. (1986) (eds) *Writing Culture: The Poetics and Politics of Ethnography*. Berkeley: University of California Press.

de Silva, P., Dodds, P., Rainey, J. and Clayton, J. (1992) Management and the multidisciplinary team. In Bugra, D. and Burns, A. (eds) *Management Training for Psychiatrists*. London: Royal College of Psychiatrists.

Dopson, S. and Waddington, I. (1996) Managing social change: a process-sociological approach to understanding organisational change within the National Health Service, *Sociology of Health and Illness*, 18, 4, 525–550.

Foucault, M. (1978). *The History of Sexuality. Volume 1. An Introduction*. London: Penguin.

Foucault, M. (1991). Governmentality. In Burchell, C., Gordon, C. and Miller, Peter (eds) *The Foucault Effect: Studies in Governmentality*. Harvester: London.

Fox, N. (1991) Postmodernism, rationality and the evaluation of health care, *Sociological Review*, 39, 907–44.

Fox, N. (1994) Anaesthetists, the discourse on patient fitness and the organisation of surgery, *Sociology of Health and Illness*, 16, 1, 1–18.

Gilgun, J. (1988) Decision-making in interdisciplinary treatment teams, *Child Abuse and Neglect*, 12, 231–9.

Good, B. (1994) *Medicine, Rationality and Experience: An Anthropological Perspective*. New York: Cambridge University Press.

Gordon, C. (ed.) (1986: 2nd edition) *Michel Foucault Power/Knowledge: Selected Interviews and other Writings 1972–1977*. Bury St Edmund: Harvester Press.

Gubrium, J. (1975) *Living and Dying at Murray Manor*. New York: St Martin's Press.

Gubrium, J. (1980) Doing care plans in patient conferences, *Social Science and Medicine*, 14A, 659–67.

Guzzo, R. (1986) Group decision making and effectiveness in organizations. In Goodman, P. and Associates (eds) *Designing Effective Work Groups*. San Francisco and London: Jossey-Bass.

Hunter, K. (1991) *Doctors' Stories: The Narrative Structure of Medical Knowledge*. Princeton: Princeton University Press.

Katzenback, J. and Smith, D. (1993) *The Wisdom of Teams: Creating the High Performance Organization*. Boston: Harvard Business School Press.

Kritzman, L. (ed.) (1988) *Michel Foucault: Politics, Philosophy, Culture: Interviews and other Writings 1977–1984*. London and New York: Routledge.

Marks, D. (1993) Case-conference analysis and action research. In Burman, R. and Parker, I. (eds) *Discourse Analysis Research*. London: Routledge.

The Mason Report (1996) *Inquiry under Section 47 of the Health and Disability Act 1993 in respect of certain Mental Health Services: Report of the Ministerial Inquiry to the Minister of Health, Hon. Jenny Shipley*. Wellington: Parliament Buildings.

McClelland, M. and Sands, R. (1993) The missing voice in interdisciplinary communication, *Qualitative Health Research*, 3, 1, 74–90.

Mellor, M.J. and Solomon, R. (1992) The Interdisciplinary geriatric/gerontological team in the academic setting: hot air or energiser? *Geriatric Social Work Education*, 18, 3–4, 203–15.

Miller, R. (1993) *From Dependency to Autonomy: Studies in Organization and Change*. London: Free Association Books.

Mizrahi, T. and Abramson, J. (1994) Collaboration between social workers and physicians: an emerging typology. In Sherman, E. and Reid, W.J. (eds) *Qualitative Methods in Social Work Practice Research*. New York: Columbia University press.

Mohrman, S. and Mohrman, A. (1993) Organizational change and learning. In Galbraith, J., Lawler, R. and Associates (eds) *Organizing for the Future: The New Logic for Managing Complex Organizations*. San Francisco: Jossey Bass.

Myerhoff, B. and Ruby, J. (1982) Introduction. In Ruby, J. (ed.) *A Crack in the Mirror: Reflexive Perspectives in Anthropology*. Philadelphia: University of Pennsylvania Press.

Nonaka, I. and Takeuchi, H. (1995) *The Knowledge-Creating Company: How Japanese Companies Create the Dynamics of Innovation*. New York: Oxford University Press.

Opie, A. (1995) *Beyond Good Intentions: Support Work with Older People*. Wellington: Institute of Policy Studies, Victoria University of Wellington.

Paxton, R. (1995) Goodbye community health mental health teams – at last, *Journal of Mental Health*, 4, 331–4.

Pithouse, Andrew (1987) *Social Work: The Organisation of an Invisible Trade*. London; Gower.

Roberts, K., Wright, J., Thibault, J., Stewart, A.V. and Knapp, K. (1994) Geriatric partnerships in health and care: the life span model, *Educational Gerontology*, 20, 2, 115–28.

Rosenfield, P. (1992) The potential of transdisciplinary research for sustaining and extending linkages between the health and social sciences, *Social Science and Medicine*, 35, 11, 1343–57.

Said, Edward (1978) *Orientalism*. London: Penguin.

Said, Edward (1989) Representing the colonized: Anthropology's interlocuters, *Critical Inquiry, 15*, Winter, 205–25.

Salmond, G., Mooney, G. and Laugeson, M. (eds) (1994) Health care reform in New Zealand. *Special Issue: Health Policy, 29*, 1 and 2, 1–182.

Saltz, C. (1992) The interdisciplinary team in geriatric rehabilitation, *Geriatric Social Work Education*, 18, 3–4, 133–43.

Sands, R. (1993) 'Can you overlap here?' a question for an interdisciplinary team, *Discourse Processes*, 16, 4, 545–64.

Sheppard, Michael (1992) Contact and collaboration with general practitioners: a comparison of social workers and psychiatric nurses, *British Journal of Social Work*, 22, 4, 419–36.

Smith, Dorothy (1990) *Texts, Facts and Femininity: Exploring the Relations of Ruling*. London and Canada: Routledge.

Specht, H. (1985) Managing professional interpersonal interactions, *Social Work*, 30, 225–30.

Toseland, R., Palmer-Ganeles, J. and Chapman, D. (1986) Teamwork in psychiatric settings, *Social Work*, 31, 46–52.

Webb, A. and Hobdell, M. (1980) Co-ordination and teamwork in the health and personal social services. In Longsdale, S., Webb, A. and Briggs, T. (eds) *Teamwork in the Personal Social Services and Health Care*. London: Croom Helm.

Witten, M. (1993) Narrative and the culture of obedience at the workplace. In Mumby, D. (ed.) *Narrative and Social Control: Critical Perspectives*. Newbury Park and London: Sage.

Youssef, V. and Silverman, D. (1992) Normative expectations for medical talk, *Language and Communication*, 12, 2, 123–31.

3.5

Keeping healthy at home and school: 'it's my body, so it's my job'

Berry Mayall

Introduction

Children in Western European societies are increasingly restricted both ideo-logically and in practice to the supervision of adults in the home and the school (together with pre-school and out-of-school institutions) (Skolnick 1975, Liljestrom 1981). This restriction has been explained in terms of adult demands for the controlled socialisation of children (Alanen 1987, Dencik 1989, Cunningham 1991). Children as the objects of socialisation by adults are commonly conceptualised as incompetent, vulnerable, incomplete per-sons, and thus as projects requiring induction under adult supervision and care into adult norms. Along the way they need protection from adult social worlds and exclusion from their dangers (Engelbert and Buhr 1991). They are excluded from public places, from streets and workplaces and from many social events. In between and beyond the home and the school, so adults say, lie the dangers of activity without competence, child-unfriendly conditions, adult-oriented planning and specialised structures and institutions which children are incompetent to handle.

The home as private domain has been contrasted with the public domain: where paid work, dominated by men, commands high status, reinforced by the development of knowledges legitimated by the establishment of profes-sional bodies (Stacey 1981). In the home, women carry out low status unpaid work, informed and shaped by 'lay' experiential knowledge. As regards the reproduction of citizens, the labour is split between the private and public domains, and, notably, between the mother, whose principal ascribed func-tions are health care and social and moral education; and the teacher, who, as servant of the public education system, is required to educate children for their place in adult social and work worlds.

This conceptualisation increases our understanding of the low status of women's knowledge and women's work both inside and outside the private domain. However, as Stacey (op cit) notes, it excludes from consideration children as a social group, with distinctive knowledge and experience. Adequate understanding of the division of labour requires questioning the 'natural' social positioning of children as subordinate socialisation projects at home and at school; and reconceptualising them as active participants in and contributors to the social events of these settings. This redressing of the status of children is appropriate in its own right. It also has the important function of requiring a shift from simplistic patriarchal models of women's primary responsibility for children's health care. It will be necessary to consider children's own contributions, and to study in more detail the processes by which the transfer of responsibility takes place from mother to child. Such considerations may lead to more complex models, incorporating notions of shared and negotiated responsibility.

The idea of children as a social group allows the observer to separate children out conceptually from the social contexts in which they spend much of their time. It allows for the possibility that for them, as for women or for men, their interests may only partially intersect with those of the home and the school (Oldman forthcoming). And the points of intersection may well differ for each setting: for instance, it will be suggested in this paper that children find the home a relatively more coherent moral and social frame, within which they negotiate their daily activities, as compared to the school, where academic and caring agendas have conflicting aims and together provide a relatively difficult arena in which to work out an acceptable daily life. However, children's accounts indicate that in both settings their daily life is achieved and constantly renegotiated, rather than 'natural', and unproblematic. Some parts of children's energies go to the making and sustaining of their own social worlds, separate from but related to the adult-controlled worlds of home and school.

This paper focusses on how children understand the division of health care labour between themselves and others in the contexts of the home and the school. It uses data collected from children, mothers and teachers to contribute to knowledge of children's social positioning within these two settings. It is relevant here to note that whilst the home can undoubtedly be conceptualised as more private than the school, the person-work of women (*c.f.* Stacey 1981) in caring for children goes on in both. Primary school teachers, who are mainly women, not only deliver the curriculum and maintain the moral order of the school, but see it as essential to their work that they care for the children; as Steedman (1988) describes, they are mothers made conscious. This caring work comprises monitoring children's well-being, referring them for treatment, and informal health education, based on lay health knowledge. If, then, we study children's understanding of the social and moral order of the school, we may ask whether and in what circumstances they do appeal to the teacher as carer; and how the teacher responds to such appeals. The aim is to consider the implications for the health care order of the school of conceptualising children as active participants in learning about health and doing health care work.

The study reported on here has developed out of earlier work on the health care of pre-school children by mothers, minders, nurseries and health professionals (Mayall and Petrie 1983, Mayall 1986, Mayall and Foster 1989); here, as in those studies, the focus was on ordinary day-to-day health maintenance and health promotion: what people think are relevant factors, actions, procedures and avoidances; how they divide up the tasks and negotiate the division of labour and responsibility. In moving up the age-range and studying the care of school-age children, I was particularly interested in what children perceive as their own part in self-care, now they go to school and move daily between two domains: the private and the public; and between two social contexts: the family and the school.

Though there are studies of children's understanding of school (Davies 1982, Cullingford 1991), there are few on their understanding of their social positions in the various contexts of their daily lives. Goodnow and Burns' 1985 Australian survey provides some provocative points. There are, as far as I know, few studies exploring through open-ended methods children's ideas on health care (*c.f.* James 1990, Backett and Alexander 1991) and none on the division of labour. A large-scale survey of children's health beliefs, using a 'draw and write' technique (Williams, Wetton and Moon 1989), provides useful outline data. In general, whilst there has been intense policy and some research interest on the health care of under-fives (Blaxter and Paterson 1982, Stacey and Davies 1983, Boulton 1983, Currer 1986) and whilst interest revives once those children as adolescents are perceived to engage in risky practices (Harding 1988, Nutbeam, Aaro and Catford 1989, Brannen *et al.* forthcoming), the years between have provoked relatively little interest among policy-makers and researchers.

Children's experiences are increasingly a focus for consideration, but most research and services strongly support both the division of social worlds into private and public, and understanding of children's experience according to age. Thus research demarcates and focusses on sites of learning according to age: for under-fives the private domain of home, complemented by pre-school; for over-fives, the school (cf Dunn 1984); even the comprehensive investigation by Newson and Newson (1976, 1977), reports on seven-year-olds' home and school lives separately. Similarly, preventive health services focus on the mother for under-fives and on the child in school for over-fives. Furthermore, research, through its emphasis on public domain medical consultations (*e.g.* Strong 1979, Silverman 1987), encourages acceptance of the notion that people think of these as the most important consultations. Perhaps so, yet these form a tiny proportion of discussions on health matters that people have – with relatives, friends, neighbours and colleagues (Cornwell 1984). Just as children move physically from the private to the public (from home to school) and assess the relative value of interactions and negotiations in each, so research may usefully follow them and attempt to record their assessments.

Methods

The paper draws on data from a small-scale study carried out by the author, in one primary school in inner North London. It is housed in post-war buildings, and is an oversubscribed school, mixed in social class, with about a quarter of the children in some sense from ethnic minority backgrounds.

In the classes studied, about half the children lived in council flats and half in privately owned flats or houses. The area has many inner city character-istics: varied but mainly cramped housing, litter-strewn streets, noisy com-petitive traffic dominating the street environment, some good local amenities (parks, sports centres, libraries, swimming pools). The school operates an 'integrated day', and teaches core topics mainly through project work.

The study's main aim was to consider the division of labour in health care between children, parents, teachers, and other staff at school (the 'helpers', the school secretary, the school nurse). I spent two days a week over two terms in 1991, as a helper with the reception class (22 five-year-olds) and with the fifth year class (30 nine-year-olds). Data were collected through a range of methods. Observation and informal discussion with teachers, helpers and children took place throughout the fieldwork period. As regards the children specifically, discussions were held with the whole class, and taped discussions with children in twos and threes; food diaries, drawings and writing were collected; some individual interviews were carried out at home, with another child present. Taped semi-structured interviews, were conducted in school with class teachers (6), the head teacher, the four helpers[1], the school secretary, the school nurse; and at home with mothers of five- and nine-year-olds (12 and 10 mothers respectively, selected randomly, but so that mothers of boys and girls were equally represented).

During the study, data were collected from children on the following: what factors keep them healthy; which aspects of their lives they enjoy and why; their experience of and views on home, school and the neigh-bourhood as health-promoting environments; how the work and respons-ibility for health care is divided up between themselves, their parents and school staff.

An important aim of the study was to do the research for rather than on the children; the aim was reflected in the methods used. It was necessary to describe how ordinary daily life was experienced by children; but collecting data from people on topics which are the stuff of ordinary daily life is difficult, because it requires reflection on and analysis of what one takes for granted (Smith 1988). I asked the children to talk about recent events, and to compare the home and the school, and to describe their daily lives. I then identified common issues within their accounts and built on one set of data to structure the next session with the children. I presented to them my version of their agenda for verification and for further discussion and story-telling. For instance, a theme which emerged early in children's accounts of their daily lives was the importance of having control over their activities. I followed this up by asking them to describe what they liked and disliked about time at home as compared to school life, and why. Another example: a word that cropped up endlessly in nine-year olds' accounts was 'boring'. In a later session, I reported this point back to the children and encouraged analysis of the word and its uses. At a more general level, it was productive to follow up the agenda provided by the five-year-olds in order to explore how well it matched the concerns of the nine-year-olds. For instance, the younger children's emphasis on access to food and on peer relationships at school as means of making school days acceptable was followed up with the older children.

The aim of identifying and promoting children's viewpoints also entailed trying to shift the balance of power from the adult (researcher) to the children (c.f. Wilkinson 1988). For this reason discussions were held with two or more children present. This social situation encouraged the children to talk with each other, rather than answer questions: to spark off ideas, to argue, to develop and refine points.

The exploratory and accumulative method outlined here (c.f. Hammersley and Atkinson 1983, Silverman 1985) offers considerable advantages in developing research for children. It may be objected that adult interpretation distorts children's accounts. However, this may equally be so when adult researchers interpret adult accounts. Perhaps the principal methodological interest in studying children's accounts is that it forces recognition of the many assumptions (cultural, political, economic) researchers commonly make when analysing and reporting on data from respondents. Questioning one's assumptions is particularly important where there are marked power inequalities between researcher and researched.

Finally here, a note on analysis. The aim of contributing to understanding of children's social positioning requires in the first instance, as Qvortrup suggests (1990), adopting the generational perspective – including consideration of structural relationships between children and adults, before going on to consider how far children are distinguished by gender, social class and ethnicity in their views and their social position. One would expect these factors to distinguish between children's accounts, and they did in this study, but the aim here is to focus on the underlying generality of their accounts. However, age differences are considered, since it seemed likely at the outset, and it did prove so, that there would be critical differences in children's understanding of their social positioning as they move out of the private domain into school at five and four years later.

Children's agenda

It has been suggested earlier that children's relationships and activities are profoundly influenced by adult understanding of their status: how far adults view them as socialisation projects or as participating actors. Children's accounts suggest they aim to engage with adults in the home and the school via three main activities: negotiating an acceptable position; establishing independence; and constructing a domain for themselves: a child domain. These are on-going activities throughout childhood, constantly re-appraised and re-opened as issues. In this section of the paper, these activities are briefly introduced.

Negotiating an acceptable social position

The evidence from the five- and nine-year-olds is that they were constantly negotiating and re-negotiating with adults – parents and teachers – a social position acceptable to themselves, within the home and the school. The areas for such negotiation include: what are desirable and permitted activities, including health care activities; what are and should be children's duties and tasks; what are allowable and allowed pleasures; what division of time between various activities is desirable and allowable. Explicit in many of these accounts, as regards their place in the home, was children's concern for their own sense of well-being: to feel in control; not to feel coerced; to have a good time. As regards their place at school, children aimed towards negotiating a tolerable daily life, within a regime which offered some important gains (learning) and enjoyment but which was essentially too heavily controlled by teachers and school norms and routines to be entirely comfortable for children.

Establishing independence

Secondly, children emphasised their desire for and their moves towards a measure of independence in their daily lives. Important dimensions were time, space and bodily control. Children stressed that home scored over school here, since adult social control was lighter: especially as regards use of time. Children disliked school-imposed time-tabling: having to get up at a certain time, be there on time, obey the teacher-controlled time-regime, all day and every day.

Establishing independence covers metaphorical and physical aspects of space. It includes questioning the power or authority of institutions and structures. It also includes establishing the right and the practice of playing out in certain places that you make your own, getting about on the streets (to and from school, and for other purposes), going on public transport.

Taking control of their own bodies was important to children. In describing daily life, they, like adults, described themselves as actors (not objects of socialisation); they assumed the desirability of being in charge of their bodies, and of having space (and time) to do this. As James (1991) has suggested, running through children's food traditions (such as choice of sweets) are two parallel themes: control of the body and control of identity.

Constructing a child domain

Children's accounts suggest a third desired enterprise: that of constructing a domain for themselves: a domain not ordered in adult interests but established and promoted by and for the social group children. Both younger and older children, boys and girls, indicated their enthusiasm for their own social groupings and for developing their own activities, in, across and outside the 'official' social contexts of home and school.

Children's play has been widely researched (*e.g.* Bruner *et al.* 1976, Roberts 1980) but the focus, as James and Prout (1990) point out, has been mainly

on play as a socially isolated phenomenon or on its developmental significance. There has been little research on relationships between children's
social worlds and adult worlds. Pioneering work has been done here by
Ward (1990) and Moore (1986), who have focussed specifically on children's
own activities in response to the hostile urban environments they grow up in.

These three sets of policies and strategies: negotiating an acceptable position, establishing independence and constructing a separate child domain;
comprise children's attempts to come to terms with the structures they must
live within, to make a claim for themselves as people both within and
beyond those structures, and to set up structures that run in parallel. This
paper considers how health care by and for these children is structured and
worked out in the context of these sets of policies and strategies in the home
and the school, and outside these social settings.

Health maintenance at home

The home is the primary health care domain; and health care is one of
mothers' principal functions (*c.f.* Graham 1984). These well attested adult
propositions were strongly shared by the children. In class discussion, the
nine-year-olds pointed to the home as the first and main site. After encouragement to suggest other sites, they suggested parks and sports centres; and
health services. School was not mentioned. As they described it, home was
where you were cared for, taught the principal health beliefs and behaviours.
Though, like other people, children referred to 'parents' as authorities and
teachers, in detailed story-telling they identified their mother as the main
actor in health care. It was also clear that children saw behaviours as the
outcomes of negotiations, or even conflict, in which actions that people are
told are good may give way before other pressures or priorities (*c.f.* Kalnins
et al. 1992). This was true for parents as well as for themselves. They commented that parents sat about reading the paper, smoking and drinking,
'after a hard day at the office', as one nine-year-old ironically put it; parents
bought them sweets, under pressure after school, while arguing that sugar
was bad for teeth.

These children's identifications of health promotive factors, like those
adults make (Blaxter 1990), ranged beyond the physical and included mental
and psychological well-being. Asked directly what keeps you healthy, all the
children talked about food; the older ones talked about exercise, fresh air
and hygiene (just as their mothers do!). They noted that being ordered
around, being bored or tired by adult demands reduced their well-being,
freedom to exercise, and their control over their lives.

The children's accounts showed that they perceived themselves as carrying
out many basic daily health-related activities. According to the five-year-
olds, they routinely washed and dressed themselves, cleaned their teeth, got
drinks from the fridge, chose what and how much to eat, remembered their

apple to take to school, put on their coats (but had some help with shoe-laces). In their accounts, the child was actor and achiever, but happy to be helped and to have the necessaries of life provided by Mum, the organiser and provider for the family. These five-year-olds thus proposed themselves. as actors within the moral and practical framework provided by their mothers. They took for granted that she ran the home, was the authority on health care, and was the main health educator.

Both five-year-olds and their mothers indicated that children were negotiating their own duties and what were permissible activities and the appropriate division of health care[2].

A: (In the morning) I wash me first.

I: Yourself?

A: Yes. I get dressed. I have my breakfast. I put my shoes on, on my own. Get ready for school. I get my book. I remember it, to bring it back. Then we go to school. With my Mummy.

M: She reminds me about giving her vitamins in the morning. And that she's supposed to do her teeth.

B: I brush my teeth, but sometimes my Mum helps me, and when the toothpaste's stiff and I can't get it out, she helps.

Children were also considering the moral order of the home. A mother described her child's rethinking of her mother's authority and personal relationships:

M: Whereas before I was her Mummy, now I'm her bossy Mummy. She kind of would do anything for me before. Now she realises she has this personality that's confronted by mine. It manifests itself in arguments about how things should be done. She has her own views now.

The children accepted in principle, if not always in practice, that they should contribute to the running of the home. They negotiated which jobs they should and would do, what contribution they made to maintaining the order of the home:

M: She said she would do a job, because her (elder) sister did one. It was clearing the table, but they both wanted to do that one, so I ended up doing it myself.

M: He's more mature now. More willing to take his share. For instance, we were out shopping and he started by saying, 'I'm only little' but in the end, size for size, he did, he carried some bags. And he was running home with them at the end, so he could carry them.

Both children and mothers reported on children's developing wishes and activities as regards establishing some time and space of their own. Children emphasised the relative advantage of home in providing some freedom to choose what they did and when: activities which were theirs rather than family activities, for instance, playing on their own or with friends, having time away from family, organising their own time. Mothers agreed, and added that children were beginning to propose the standard of peers in opposition to those of home: being cheeky and rude, using swear words and slang from school.

A:　(on school) I don't like having to get up in the morning and get there on time. I always love the holidays where you don't have to rush out in the mornings.

I:　What are the best things about being at home?

A:　That I don't have to do anything I don't wanna and I don't have to write anything I don't want to when I'm writing. I don't have to play anything I don't wanna.

A:　I like school because it's fun. It's not all fun because sometimes we do boring work.

B:　Sometimes we have to do really boring things and –

A:　Sometimes we have to do really hard things that we can't even do.

B:　And sometimes when we don't want to do something, the teachers won't let us not do it.

I:　So you have to do things at school?

A:　Yeah. Sometimes we don't have to.

I:　Do you have to do things at home?

A:　No, not really.

B:　Well, my mum tells me to put my stuff away. I don't really.

A:　I don't really either.

The nine-year-olds' picture of their life at home has some continuities with the five-year-olds'. But the division of health care labour and responsibility shows marked shifts as the children negotiated an acceptable position, sought control and attempted to establish their own domain.

Nine-year-olds reported their moves on negotiating a position in the household acceptable to them and others. They helped with some household chores, negotiated which, when and how much. They recognised their part in maintaining and promoting the home as a comfortable, enabling social environment (girls more than boys). They described their mother as overseer and checker of routine health maintenance work, with a more distant role than for younger children (a point confirmed by mothers).

As regards self-care (washing, teeth-cleaning, choice of clothes, preparation and choice of food), nine-year-olds identified the division of labour as a discussion point; they recognised that they share it with parents.

I:　Whose job is it to keep you healthy?

A:　Our Mum.

B:　Our Dad.

C: It's mainly our job.

B: Mainly.

C: Because we're the ones . . .

D: We're the ones that have to take care of ourselves. Like, when we live by ourselves we will.

C: So we should, like, do that. We're keeping ourselves healthy by doing things ourselves. It's my body, so it's my job.

D: It's us mainly. We do it. Sometimes!

And establishing their own domain (in terms of space, time and social life) was an important feature of their accounts. The children put high value on having space they could call their own, for their own activities at home: the well-off ones described their own room; the disadvantaged, being crowded and harassed. They valued having time out and about, with or without friends, when they decided what to do, using hitherto proscribed public spaces, such as waste land, streets, buses, shops. Friendships constituted the forum for making up games and playing established games, forming clubs, buying illicit sweets and drinks common to the group:

A: I like playing tennis and being with friends.

I: Do you prefer being with friends to parents?

A: Easily! You can do what you like, go where you like. Buy crisps. Where, with parents, they go: No! It's true, isn't it?

I: Last week (half-term holiday), did you enjoy that?

A: Yes, really good. I went out every day with my friends. My parents just picked me up at the end of the day.

Parents, like this one, confirmed these points:

M: I mean, a lot of the time, they're better off being with their friends. It takes them away from hassles and Mum telling them what to do all the time. And they have more fun, with each other.

How shall we best understand these values and negotiations proposed by children? From various traditional adult points of view, they can be seen as aspects of developmental stages, or as accommodations to benevolent parental socialisation, or as a counter culture, set up in opposition to the children's natural environment: the home. From the children's point of view, whilst these points have some validity, these activities may be understood as normal human responses to social institutions; activities comparable to adult carving out of space, time and social groups separate from the home and the workplace. Whilst the home may have advantages, the child domain offers relief from adult demands and more freedom of choice.

The children's accounts indicate their understanding that the important health-related activities take place at home. Health care there is an enterprise lightly undertaken by them as actors, within the accepted context of maternal authority. It is, above all, an interactive enterprise, where the division of labour is constantly negotiated. Children are beginning by age nine to understand that health-related behaviours result not from the simple application of belief, but from a complex of factors, within a broad, flexible framework encompassing not only beliefs and family customs but social constraints and opportunities. The processes whereby children learn critical appraisal of all these needs detailed investigation.

Health maintenance at school

Health care has a lower overt profile at school, where teachers, officially, are principally concerned with the curriculum and with socialising the children into acceptance of school routines and customs (Ashton 1975, Sharp and Green 1975, Cullingford 1985) in the interests of moulding the good schoolchild, with qualities and behaviours suitable for adult social worlds (Pollard 1985).

As noted earlier, the teacher operates a dual role as carer and teacher. In a sense, caring is an assumed not official activity; none of the teachers interviewed recalled caring as a topic for discussion during their training. Yet all the teachers assumed that they should look to the children's well-being, both as an essential component of responsibility for them during the school day, and, more instrumentally, so that they were fit to learn. However, caring activities operated much more for the youngest children than for older ones. The teacher combined care of her class, responsive (sometimes, in some cases) to individual need, with management of the group and moulding of the children into a good class of school children. As regards older children, the teachers were more urgently conscious of the need to deliver the curriculum, and less concerned with children's physical and psychological ability to profit from it.

The observational data indicate that children in both the age-groups studied negotiated their social position at school, through reaching a compromise between conforming with the formal school regime and remaining themselves. Conforming involved, notably, carrying out prescribed work tasks; limiting peer interaction in class; meeting teachers' norms for tidiness and orderliness. But classroom organisation encouraged the children to sit and work with their friends, and the teacher allowed them (within time and noise limits) to chat about other topics, plan games, tell stories, gossip. Through these activities, children maintained their sense of having their own agenda in parallel with the official agenda and some control over life at school (*c.f.* Davies 1982).

But children's accounts strongly point to their low control over their daily life at school, as compared to home. Children at school, even in a 'child-centred' 'progressive' regime, have restricted opportunity to take the many actions and make the many adjustments that promote well-being and obviate stress: such as getting a drink or a snack, having a break from an activity, taking some exercise. Observation confirmed teachers' increasing control over older children: frustration and boredom commonly showed in the nine-year-olds' expressions, comments and movements but less commonly in the five-year-olds' – who had greater control over the pacing of their activities.

In particular the school can be described as not recognising children's competence and knowledge about health maintenance. This is shown in the way ordinary health care activities were managed and controlled. Whilst a child at home is encouraged to get on with the jobs of washing, going to the toilet, fetching drinks, making food choices, helping prepare food, pacing their day to include sessions of rest and activity, all of these were controlled by rules and customs at school. The children were required to behave as a group, rather than as individuals. Movement itself was restricted and routinised; spontaneous and creative movement was frowned on. For instance, lining up had certain prescribed characteristics: children should move in an orderly way, not too fast or slow, should not push, should line up behind the next person, not next to them, might talk but not shout, laugh but not too loudly; and must move only when the teacher said, Now! (*c.f.* Waksler 1991). Here a five-year-old describes (to her mother and the researcher) the school's control over urination and water consumption:

I: And what about if you want to go to the lavatory?
A: Well, you have to ask Miss X.
I: And does she let you go?
A: Sometimes.
I: Why does she sometimes not?
M: Do you think sometimes if you've just come back from play, or if you're just going to be going to play in a couple of minutes?
A: No, if you've just come back from play and you want to get a drink or you need to go to the toilet, she says No, because you had all that time to get it in the playground.
I: So can you go and get a drink when you want one?
A: Well, you have to ask the teacher first and if she says, No, you can't. Then if she says, Yes, you can.
I: Sometimes she says, No?
A: Yeah, sometimes.
I: Do you know why that is?
A: Because she wants you to get your work done.

Children's accounts of food and friendships at school indicate their importance in helping children feel in control. Two-thirds of the nine-year-olds brought a packed lunch. In addition to half-joking rhetoric about yucky school meals, these children described how they chose what food to bring, and put it together themselves. It commonly included crisps, a sandwich, a chocolate bar and a drink. Observation of the school hall at dinner time indicated that whereas school dinner children had to line up (quietly) and have their choices and behaviour monitored by the dinner ladies, the packed lunch children sat, unsupervised, at the other end of the hall. All in all, bringing a packed lunch seemed to offer more autonomy.

Similarly friendship may be seen as important not just in itself but as a bulwark against school regimes. Almost every child, in both age-groups, asked what she liked about school, talked about friendships. For the younger ones, friendships and alliances were still being negotiated, in the context of the social worlds of the classroom and playground. Having friends meant having social support and something to do in the playground; friends meant the pleasure of inventing and playing games. Bad social relationships were a threat to these five-year-olds: they hated standing about feeling cold and lonely, being pushed over, fights, people crying.

The play after dinner: it's too long, I get cold and bored, because nobody plays with me.

I like playing with people, but Jack wouldn't let me. We was making an engine, and Jack came and made a muddle.

Amongst the nine-year-olds, friendships were mostly well established, and their importance was shown by children's distress if a friendship broke down. Asked what they saw as the value of school, most of the children talked about the usefulness of the three Rs and the opportunities for making friends and being with them. Friendships may be seen as a response to the general tendency of a school to devalue individuality in favour of group conformity. Indeed some children consistently refused to obey, were cheeky, bent the rules, and, in sum, behaved as individuals rather than as group members.

Thus at school, children in a range of ways tried to establish a child domain, separate from, sometimes parallel to the official school agenda. This domain occupied not only the temporal and spatial areas of playtime in the playground; it took place also in the classroom, when and where children could (often under the teacher's tolerant eye) seize time and space for their own activities. Lunch time offered more control for those who brought their own food, and this, rather than the quality of the school meal, may be a reason why some children prefer to bring their own. It should be stressed that the importance of the child domain lies not in children's rejection of the central functions of the school (imparting knowledge and skills); on the contrary they endorsed and welcomed these. Its functions at school appear rather to lie in promoting valued social activity and in counteracting school routines, norms and practices.

Most of these points hold broadly across the two age-groups studied, but five-year-olds indicated greater acceptance of school as presented to them; to some extent and most of the time, they seemed to enjoy learning the rules of the game. Nine-year-olds were more sceptical and critical of school imposition, and more instrumental as regards the curriculum: they valued the basic 3Rs above other official school areas of work; and they understood that much of teacher activity was childminding. They were experienced and constructively critical on the relative virtues of teachers, and on the value of school rules and routines.

The data indicate the increasing subordination of health interests to school interests as the children moved up the school. In the reception class, the teacher was teacher and socialiser, also carer: an important job was negotiation with mothers on health maintenance and health care. The teacher ran a carefully paced day, which encouraged play and recreation interspersing short work sessions. 'They're too young to work all day; and they need to play.' Even so, the teacher gave high priority to socialising the children, even at the expense of caring for them. For instance, a child in great distress, having cut her lip in the playground, was told not to fuss, but to carry on taking part with her class: to eat dinner and participate in the afternoon session; only half way through that, when her distress did not abate, and her lip looked very swollen, did the teachers jointly decide to phone her mother.

School priorities – getting through the curriculum, enforcing social norms – acquire even greater prominence as children move up the school. Thus the teacher of first year juniors (age eight) reported that when children complained the morning (an extra half hour now) was too long and asked when they could stop work and play, she had to tell them that 'we don't really play in the juniors'. Several of the older children noted that the amounts of work and play were better balanced at age five than at age nine: then it was recognised that children wanted to play; now this recognition was dimmed or rejected by the school:

A: In the infants it was more fun. Because you weren't sat down all the time, you were doing things, like painting.

B: Now you don't do painting. In Class 6 we built the Great Wall of China. We made it go right round the room. With the big bricks.

I: You liked doing that?

B: We did then! We're not allowed to do it now. We did this big thing: we made a big catapult, across both classrooms and –

A: – we made it, it (joint laughter), it didn't work in the end!

I: Whereas now?

B: We're doing more of: sit down, write down, write up!

A: The teacher reckons we're too big to do running around, because we hardly ever do. We hardly ever go out. We usually work.

And another child:

I: What do you like doing?

C: Swimming. I go nearly every day after school. It's fun and it gives you exercise, more than at school, where you don't get any exercise, except in the playground. They make you sit down all the time.

But as children moved up the school they were expected to accept the increasing proportion of work to play, and the limitation of play to playtime. The nine-year old's class teacher reported thus on children's sickness bids – and her assumption that children should be comfortable with class routines and work:

T: I mean, there's two or four children in the class who tell me regularly that they feel unwell, I mean nearly on a daily basis.
I: Three or four?
T: Urn, not on a daily basis for three or four, but urn, regularly, one or two on a daily basis.
I: What sort of illness?
T: Tummy ache, sore throat. I mean, it's really sad, because it's definitely either a matter of drawing attention to themselves, which one of them most definitely it is, and the other one, it's an avoidance tactic.
I: So what do you do about it?
T: It depends really. Normally not, I'm not very sympathetic. I mean I've got to the point that I'm so used to it, that it's you know, hard not to be sarcastic sometimes.

Two of the children reflected on connections between school work and health:

A: School – it's not good and it's not bad for you.
B: If you're working all the time you're in school, your brain gets a bit annoyed and you get a headache and that's bad.
A: But it's exercise for your brain, and it gives you a good education.

As regards health care, children are faced with a prescriptive lay health care system, whose authority derives from school norms. Teachers implement a complex of functions. Through their management of the group of children they control washing, excretion and nutrition, rest and exercise; they assess sickness bids (*c.f.* Prout 1986); they teach 'health education' as part of the curriculum; they propose health behaviours opportunistically, in connection with projects, stories, outings, events at school. Their knowledge here is essentially lay knowledge, transmitted within the context of their authority as teacher[3].

Not only were the health-related prescriptions seen by the children as in some cases arbitrary, and often in conflict with what they have learned at home, but we may speculate that the school's division of labour in health care may structure children's understanding of their teacher, for children explained that it was the helpers who cared for you in case of accident or illness. Mothers, by contrast, fulfilled all functions: management, education, care and cure[4].

The child domain

Whilst (as noted at the outset) Western European children are increasingly controlled within adult-constructed institutions, children's accounts given above suggest that they wish to promote a domain of time, space and social relationships: a child domain, running concurrently with their lives in the official domains of home and school. In a physical sense the child domain occupies the time and space between: before school, between home and school, after school; going on expeditions, playing out in the street, in the park, on chosen bits of land between housing estates and roads. Above all, it is a domain where friendships are promoted.

I have suggested that both parents and teachers recognise children's wish to engage with the social world of their peers, and take steps to facilitate this. But the hostile environment of inner London, where the children lived, made parents unwilling to allow their five-year-olds much independence; most were accompanied to and from school, and few allowed to play out unsupervised in the neighbourhood. What children may have perceived as autonomy or control, looked to some mothers like supervised entitlement:

M: She's allowed to play on the street, but only to the corner, so I can see her (five-year-old).
M: Just this last few months, she can go round the corner, up the street, when it's light, to the shop. But with a time limit on it (nine-year-old).

At school children's daily lives can be seen as routinised from the start but there are paradoxes here as regards the balance of adult control and child control. The reception class teacher put heavy stress on inducting the children into school routines and the children seemed keen to conform; the teacher also allowed some freedom for children in class to develop their own spaces, activities and friendships, but friendships were as yet not constant or reliable. The older children were required to work for longer sustained periods in class and some expressed boredom and irritation about the imposed length and character of playtime; but with more firmly established friendships and greater savoir-faire in using the possibilities presented within school routines for promoting their own enterprises, the nine-year-olds may also have experienced greater feeling of control over their time in school than the five-year-olds.

By age nine, some children went alone or with friends to school, and many were allowed to play out, in certain designated spaces. Children ascribed importance to the space between home and school: gave detailed accounts of the journey to school; buying sweets, being with friends, negotiating roads. Also important was the space beyond. Those children who travelled about London, described their trips with pride, as representing independence and adventure. So did those who earned money of their own. They also valued free time on their own, to determine and shape as they wished. This separate domain, constructed by themselves at least in their minds, however limited it may look from adult view points, seemed to provide an important source of children's well-being by allowing them to develop their own interests and increase their sense of control over their lives. The adult vision of an idyllic child domain evident in many late Victorian novelists' creations (*c.f.* Ward 1988) was reflected in this child's account of den-building:

> *A*:   Sometimes, we go up the park, with my friends. There's a, by the road, there, we're building a tree-house up there. It's for us.

But another grimly noted the dominance of mass culture over creative play:

> *B*:   If you go out to play, they always want to play football. Football, football every day. If you don't, no-one plays with you.

Evidently too parental rulings that children must always be accompanied had sunk in: children recounted incidents when they protected each other, against dogs, against fear. But they also noted how being with a friend could mean taking responsibility, and (implicitly) could mean you realised you could do so.

> *A*:   I was with my friend, he fell and cut his leg on a bit of glass. There was no-one around. So I ran round the corner and met someone, and said, scuse me, my friend's hurt himself and she took us – not far – to where they, and they put a plaster on it.

As noted earlier, some children indicated that their ability to lead a health-promoting life at school reduced as they got older; observation suggested there was an increasing disjunction between their competence and their having insufficient control over how they spent the day. At home, too, whilst they might be encouraged to take responsibility for their own health care, this was within the norms and customs of the home, and under the eye of parents. Thus the domain between – a child domain – has importance in children's lives – not so much for age five, but certainly for age nine. As regards gender, girls may be early and forcefully socialised into accepting home-making responsibilities (*e.g.* Steedman 1982, Walkerdine and Lucey 1989) and may be more involved in these than boys, as many studies, like this one, indicate (*e.g.* Morrow 1992); but girls, like boys, constructed a domain of time, space and social groupings apart from the official ones of the home and the school.

Discussion

Children's accounts of their daily lives in the school and the home point to interesting paradoxes in both. The ideology of the child-centred school (still in force in the one studied) runs in parallel with the adult-defined aims of education and socialisation. This combination seems to present barriers to child autonomy and responsibility. Teachers argue that they aim to relate to each child as an individual and to encourage independence. But they also explicitly value socialising children into group norms. In addition, they propose their own moral codes, including those relating to health behaviour, prescriptively to children. Interactive learning on morality hardly featured at school. The home, proposed ideally as the context where concern for the health and welfare of the child should be paramount, but often denigrated as in practice insufficiently caring towards children, may indeed have competing interests and goals at work, since adults do have other commitments and interests and they are multiply constrained. In practice, these competing priorities give more space, time and encouragement to children to look after themselves. Health learning at home has an interactive character. This is based on the child's insistence, on adult respect for the child as a person, and on the perceived seriousness, in the eyes of both adults and children, of the enterprise of enabling children to take on the labour and responsibility for their own care. Thus the relative freedom of the home and the character of teaching provide contexts likely to promote in children the health care knowledge and values (whether 'good', 'right' or not) dominant in their family.

This analysis squares with children's designation of the home as the principal site for health care and for learning health knowledge and behaviour. This was a judgment not of quality but of substance. Children understood that health issues are complex moral issues, set in the contexts of human relationships. Whilst therefore the home may have a range of functions and competing interests, it can be seen as providing holistic health care: as having health and welfare goals at its centre. By comparison, they did not identify school as offering health care or knowledge. Indeed the school had other goals, which to some extent conflicted with health care goals. Thus children's accounts indicate a conceptualisation of health care as deeply contextualised; its value and the effectiveness of health education may depend on the consistency of the message with the social context.

The data indicate that the teacher's functions are seen to derive from the formal curriculum; her authority and prescriptions as regards health knowledge and behaviour are arbitrary and linked to the social norms of the school. There are possible implications here as regards health education; the optimal setting may be the home rather than the school. The evidence suggests that school health education programmes commonly fail to change behaviour (Tones *et al.* 1990). It has been widely suggested that health promotion must involve empowering people, and therefore must address problems people regard as important, must include participation by those people, and must be in harmony with wider health policies (Kalnins *et al.* 1992). If this argument holds, it can be argued that schools will be well ordered for health promotion, only if they address children's concerns, regard them as active participants and operate regimes designed to promote health.

At present we can only speculate what balance children construct, as they grow to adulthood, between what they learn first at home and later both there and in the public domain. But including children as a social group into our analysis of the division of labour in health care may enable us to challenge traditional sociological formulations on the high status of public domain male knowledge and the low status of private domain female knowledge. For children remind us of the bases of health knowledge in family relationships and activities. Study of the experiences of children, to add to those of women, may help to upgrade the status of lay knowledge in the division of health care labour. Indeed study of the sources of people's knowledge, in childhood and the home, may deepen understanding of lay-professional encounters, where lay people appear to accord high status to medical knowledge but implement their own.

Children's (and mothers') accounts show that children are active participators in health care learning and health care activity. The unsurprising point that children both work and are worked on has implications for division of labour theory. Feminists have directed attention to the importance of women's person work in and across the public and private domains (Stacey and Davies 1983, Graham 1984); it is important to recognise children too as unpaid workers in health care. What professionals do paid in the public domain, women and children do unpaid at home, and in negotiations across the private and public. Furthermore, whilst women in general and mothers in particular have been schooled (by health educators and health professionals) to downplay the value of their health work at home, children give home-based health work high value. They imply the desirability of upgrading the status of the private domain as compared to the public. Indeed the work of women and children provides a suitable basis for conceptualising public domain work, rather than the other way round. Their work comes first in time in everyone's life and forms the basis for later activity and learning. Thus concepts of work derived from the public domain may be more appropriately replaced by concepts comprising an evaluation of human activity, that is, people's input into those actions that are seen as necessary and valuable in a given society. Judging children's, women's and men's activity under the heading 'socially valuable activity' may allow us to reassess the traditional high evaluation of paid over unpaid, and public over private.

Finally, the data indicate the relevance of considering relationships between children's own social worlds and adult worlds. It seems that children see the child domain as providing escape from the adult power latent and expressed in the home and the school; perhaps it can provide children with a sense of control and group solidarity which strengthen them or their daily experience in those institutions. In addition the data suggest that learning goes on when children are alone and with their friends, through inventing and modifying game rules, discussing moral and social issues, establishing social conventions, interacting with computers and TV programmes (*c.f.* Roberts 1980). Potentially, the child domain, cross-cutting private and public, may provide children with some of the strength, skills and knowledge needed to cope with adult worlds. If so, then relationships of children's own social worlds to adult worlds as well as their activity in adult-controlled institutions must be taken into account, in the division of labour.

Children's experience is shaped by adult perceptions of them. Whilst schools and teachers may be comfortable with the child as project, mothers conceptualise their children as people with a strong drive towards independence, and with a contribution to make to the social world of the family, from their earliest months (*c.f.* Hallden 1991). These distinctive views, it has been argued, are critical in structuring the home and school as social contexts for children's daily health care activity and experience, including their part in the division of health care labour. Understanding of the division of labour in health care, whether in the private or public domains, is sharpened by recognition of children's active participation and negotiation; and of the key role of the personal: the individual relationships and interactions that provide a firm basis for learning and behaviour. Recognition of the importance of 'lay' work in the private domain suggests the appropriateness of reconsidering concepts of work derived from the public domain. And children's own social worlds too provide a context for learning to live with and in adult worlds.

Notes

1 The helpers are employed as supervisors at dinner-times and in the playground. They also help the teacher in the classroom, with managing the children and their activities.
2 In reporting direct speech, the following conventions are used: $A, B, C \ldots$ = child; M = mother; T = teacher; I = interviewer.
3 Though 'health education' is offered in most teacher training colleges, only a quarter of students on initial training courses 'did' it as a core component of their course in 1981 (Williams 1985).
4 This speculation will be pursued in a further paper focussing on adult divisions of health care labour across the home and the school, including the care of ill children.

References

Alanen, L. (1987) Re-thinking socialisation, the family and childhood. In *Growing into a Modern World*, proceedings of an International Inter-disciplinary conference on the life and development of children in modern society. Trondheim, 6, 10–13.

Ashton, P.M. (1981) Primary teachers' aims 1969–77. In Simon, B. and Willcocks, J. (eds) *Research and Practice in the Primary Classroom*. London: RKP.

Backett, K. and Alexander, H. (1991) Talking to young children about health: methods and findings, *Health Education Journal*, 50, 34–7.

Blaxter, M. (1990) *Health and Lifestyles*, London: Routledge.

Blaxter, M. and Peterson, E. (1982) *Mothers and Daughters: A Three-generational Study of Health Attitudes and Behaviour*. London: Heinemann Educational Books.

Boulton, M.G. (1983) *On Being a Mother*. London: Tavistock Publications.

Brannen, J., Dodd, K., Oakley, A. and Storey, P. (forthcoming) *Young People, Health and Family Life*. Milton Keynes: Open University Press.

Bruner, J., Jolly, A. and Sylva, K. (eds) (1976) *Play: Its Role in Development and Evolution*. Harmondsworth: Penguin.

Currer, C. (1986) Concepts of mental well- and ill-being: the case of Pathan mothers in Britain. In Currer, C. and Stacey, M. (eds) *Concepts of Health, Illness and Disease: A Comparative Perspective*. Leamington Spa: Berg.

Cornwell, J. (1984) *Hard Earned Lives: Accounts of Health and Illness from East London*. London: Tavistock.

Cullingford, C. (1985) *Parents, Teachers and Schools*. London: Robert Royce.

Cullingford, C. (1991) *The Inner World of the School: Children's Ideas about School*. London: Cassell.

Cunningham, H. (1991) *The Children of the Poor: Representatives of Childhood since the Seventeenth Century*. Oxford: Blackwell.

Davies, B. (1982) *Life in the Classroom and Playground: The Accounts of Primary School Children*. London: RKP.

Dencik, L. (1989) Growing up in the post-modern age: On the child's situation in the modern family and on the position of the family in the modern welfare state, *Acta Sociologica*. 32, 155–80.

Dunn, J. (1984) *Sisters and Brothers*. London: Fontana Books.

Engelbert, A. and Buhr, P. (1991) *Childhood as a Social Phenomenon: National Report, Federal Republic of Germany*. Eurosocial Report 36/10, European Centre, Berggasse 17, 1090 Vienna, Austria.

Goodnow, J. and Bums, A. (1985) *Home and School: A Child's Eye View*. Australia, Sydney: Alien and Unwin.

Graham, H. (1984) *Women, Health and the Family*. Brighton: Wheatsheaf Books.

Hallden, G. (1991) The child as project and the child as being: parents' ideas as frames of reference, *Children and Society*, 5, 225–38.

Hammersley, M. and Atkinson, P. (1983) *Ethnography: Principles in Practice*. London: Tavistock Publications.

Harding, G. (1988) Adolescence and health: a literature review. In *Health Education and Young People*. TCRU Occasional Paper No. 9. Thomas Coram Research Unit, 41 Brunswick, Square, London, WCIN IAZ.

Inner London Education Authority (1985) *Improving Primary Schools*. Report of the Committee on Primary Education. London: ILEA.

James, A. (1991) Children, food and identity. Paper given at conference organised by the International Commission on the Anthropology of Food and Food Problems. Oxford.

James, A. and Prout, A. (1990) Time and transition in the study of childhood. In James, A. and Prout, A. (eds) *Constructing and Reconstructing Childhood: Contemporary Issues in the Sociological Study of Childhood*. London: Falmer Press.

Kalnins, I., McQueen, D.V., Backett, K.C., Curtice, L. and Currie, C.E. (1992) Children, empowerment and health promotion: some new directions in research and practice, *Health Promotion International*, 7, 53–9.

Liljestrom, R. (1981) The public child, the commercial child, and our child. In Kessel, F.S. and Siegel, A.W. (eds) *The Child and other Cultural Inventions.* New York: Praeger.

Mayall, B. and Petrie, P. (1983) *Childminding and Day Nurseries: What Kind of Care?* London: Heinemann Educational Books.

Mayall, B. (1986) *Keeping Children Healthy.* London: Alien and Unwin.

Mayall, B. and Foster, M.-C. (1989) *Child Health Care: Living with Children, Working for Children.* Oxford: Heinemann Professional Publications.

Mayall, B. (1990) Childcare and childhood, *Children and Society*, 4, 374–85.

Moore, R.C. (1986) *Childhood's Domain: Play and Place in Child Development* London: Croom Helm.

Morrow, V. (1991) Children's Work at Home. Paper given at Resources in Households Study Group, Institute of Education, London.

Newson, J. and Newson, E. (1976) *Seven Years Old in the Home Environment.* London: George Alien and Unwin.

Newson, J., Newson, E. and Barnes, P. (1977) *Perspectives on School at Seven Years Old.* London: George Alien and Unwin.

Nutbeam, D., Aaro, L. and Catford, J. (1989) Understanding children's health behaviour: the implications for health promotion for young people, *Social Science and Medicine*, 29, 317–25.

Oldman, D. (forthcoming) Adult-child relations as class relations. In Qvortrup, J. (ed.) *Childhood Matters.* (publisher unknown).

Pollard, A. (1985) *The Social World of the Primary School.* London: Cassell Education.

Prout, A. (1986) 'Wet children' and 'little actresses': going sick in primary school, *Sociology of Health and Illness*, 8, 11–36.

Qvortrup, J. (1990) *Childhood as a Social Phenomenon: An Introduction to a Series of National Reports.* Eurosocial Report, 36/1990, European Centre, Berggasse 17, 1070 Vienna, Austria.

Roberts, A. (1980) *Out to Play: The Middle Years of Childhood.* Aberdeen: Aberdeen University Press.

Sharp, R. and Green, A. (1975) *Education and Social Control: A Study of progressive Primary Education.* London: RKP.

Silverman, D. (1985) *Qualitative Methodology and Sociology.* Aldershot: Gower Publishing Co. Ltd.

Silverman, D. (1987) *Communication and Medical Practice: Social Relations in the Clinic.* London: Sage.

Skolnick, A. (1975) The limits of childhood: conceptions of child development and social context, *Law and Contemporary Problems*, 39, 38–77.

Smith, D.E. (1988) *The Everyday World as Problematic: A Feminist Sociology*, Milton Keynes: Open University Press.

Stacey, M. (1981) The division of labour revisited or overcoming the two Adams. In Abrams, P., Deem, R., Finch, J. and Roch, P. (eds) *Practice and Progress in British Sociology 1950–1980.* London: Alien and Unwin.

Stacey, M. and Davies, C. (1983) *Division of Labour in Child Health Care: Final Report to SSRC.* Sociology Dept., Warwick University.

Steedman, C. (1982) *The Tidy House.* London: Virago.

Steedman, C. (1988) The mother made conscious: the historical development of a primary school pedagogy. In Woodhead, M. and McGrath, A. (eds) *Family, School and Society: A Reader*. London: Open University Press.

Strong, P.M. (1979) *The Ceremonial Order of the Clinic*. London: Routledge.

Tones, K., Tilford, S. and Robinson, Y. (1990) *Health Education: Effectiveness and Efficiency*. London: Chapman and Hall.

Walkerdine, V. and Lucey, H. (1989) *Democracy in the Kitchen: Regulating Mothers and Socialising Daughters*. London: Virago.

Waksler, F.C. (1991) Dancing when the music is over: a study of deviance in a kindergarten classroom. In Waksler, (ed.) *Studying the Social Worlds of Children: Sociological Readings*. London: Fahner Press.

Ward, C. (1990) *The Child in the City*. New edition. London: Bedford Square Press.

Ward, C. (1988) *The Child in the Country*. London: Robert Hale.

Wilkinson, S.R. (1988) *The Child's World of Illness: The Development of Health and Illness Behaviour*. Cambridge: Cambridge University Press.

Williams, T. (1985) Health education and initial teacher training in England and Wales. In Campbell, G. (ed.) *New Directions in Health Education*. London: Falmer Press.

William, T., Wetton, N. and Moon, A. (1989) A *Picture of Health: What do you do that makes you healthy and keeps you healthy?* Health Education Authority, Hamilton House, Mabledon Place, WC1H 9TX.

Section 4

Patient-Provider Interaction

Introduction

As noted in the Introduction, the 'doctor–patient relationship' was, for many years, a, if not *the* core topic in courses in the sociology of health and illness. Discussion of the work of Talcott Parsons (1951), was, and often still is, a starting point. The Parsonsian model of the doctor–patient relationship in industrialised societies depicted an encounter framed by normative expectations about morally neutral, scientifically trained experts interacting with lay persons who accepted the authority of professionals. Much subsequent sociological research has been concerned with examining the extent to which these normative expectations are sustained in practice; with analysing patients' relationships with the wider range of health care occupations which constitute modern formal health care; and with the extent to which Parsons' model, first put forward in the 1950s, is still appropriate in an era of more active patients. For example, it is often suggested that a more contractual relationship between professionals and their clientele may be emerging in place of implicit trust in professionalism (Bury 1997). At the same time, professional practice may be changing in the face of patients' increased propensity to resort to malpractice litigation and formal complaint (Annandale 1996).

However, as Freidson (1988) has argued, any moves to ostensibly less professionally-dominated forms of patient-professional relationship might not, in practice, empower patients. In highly bureaucratised health care systems, managerial rationality and risk assessment rather than direct consumer control may be replacing professional discretion and judgement, especially if, as may be happening in the United Kingdom and elsewhere, public entitlement to health care based on citizenship rights is being replaced by greater emphasis on individual users' responsibilities as well as on their rights (Higgs 1998). Moreover, an emphasis on patient and public agency and consumerism should not lead us to overlook the positive functions of trust in professionals as a means of coping with complexity and uncertainty, and problems of co-operation (Scambler and Britten 2001). And not all patients are (or are regarded as being) equally equipped to be active contractors of care. The articles included in this Section demonstrate the ways in which patients' social identities and clinical diagnoses together frame patient-provider interactions, complementing the emphasis on how social considerations shape knowledge construction in Section 1. Thus, we have included papers analysing how social characteristics of patients, or the expectations of professionals about particular social groups, *e.g.* children, the elderly or the indigent, structure professional discourse and patient experience.

Taken together, the articles reprinted in this Section illustrate the impressive range and depth of sociological work on patient-professional interaction. We have chosen studies of different settings, different countries, and different occupations, which exemplify the range of different methodologies that have been used to study patient-provider interaction: including ethnographic observation of clinical settings, detailed analysis of audio-recordings of consultations, in-depth interviews with professionals, and structured questionnaires obtaining retrospective assessments by patients of their interactions with professionals.

Our first selection addresses the classic topic, the doctor–patient relationship. Hak's paper is concerned with the extent to which and how medical dominance over patients is reproduced at the micro-social level. He provides readers with a very detailed analysis of the form of doctor–patient conversations, thus connecting the sociological tradition of conversational analysis with more general questions about how power and authority might be conceptualised and investigated. He asks whether we should seek evidence for professional dominance (or, indeed, the lack of it) in explicit verbal exchanges, or whether such dominance is tacit, part of the background expectancies that shape such conversations?

Pilnick's paper also uses conversational analysis to examine a situation in which professional dominance seems less clearly a part of background expectations than in the consultations studied by Hak. In her study of pharmacists' interactions with adults collecting medicines prescribed for the treatment of children's leukaemia, Pilnick demonstrates how the lay expertise and competence of those with long-term experience of cancer drug therapy is asserted by these lay persons and sometimes recognised by professionals. At the same time, however, interactional asymmetry between professionals and even these relatively expert members of the public is still sometimes observable. Consumer agency is constrained even in this context.

Two of the papers reprinted here analyse situations where professionals make more negative assessments of patients' moral worth and social competence than in Pilnick's study. The extent to which persons who are HIV positive perceive themselves to be stigmatised by health care professionals is the theme of Green and Platt's research. This paper complements studies of professionals' response to such allegedly 'high-risk' patients (*e.g.* Bosk and Frader 1991) and serves as a reminder of the diversity of groups affected by HIV/AIDS. In her paper, Bowler examines professionals' interactions with patients from minority ethnic backgrounds, through an observational and interview study of UK midwives working with women of South Asian descent. She notes how generalised stereotypes held by the midwives about all South Asian women sometimes operated to these women's disadvantage, even when contradicted by evidence in specific cases. It would seem that the construction of professionals' 'common-sense' as well as their scientific knowledge warrants sociological attention.

The final two selections also show how, in some settings, social and political considerations, as well as clinical ones, enter into the professional-client interaction, but in more complex ways than some early, uni-dimensional sociological models of professional dominance in professional-client interaction indicated. The paper by Fisher and Groce dates from the period when the feminist critique of medical power was at its most forceful, but they eschew a simple, monolithic account of patriarchal medicine at work. Through a detailed analysis of the consultations by two different women with the same doctor, they show the ways in which cultural assumptions about femininity and the proper role of women served to structure face-to-face interaction and treatment. But these have very different consequences for the two women. While some of the particular assumptions about women's role and doctors' behaviour revealed might have changed, were the study to be repeated today, the general point Fisher and Groce stress, the reflexive relationship between cultural assumptions and communicational work, still holds.

The article by Dodier and Camus explicitly encourages comparison between professional-patient relationships in the 1990s and the 1970s, and between national health care systems. In the inaugural issue of *Sociology of Health and Illness*, Jeffrey (1979) showed how, in the Accident and Emergency Department of a British NHS hospital, negative assessment of patients, particularly in terms of their social worth, led to staff stigmatisation and equivocal service provision. In the emergency room of the French specialist teaching hospital studied by Dodier and Camus, staff also typified patients but in terms of gradations, rather than dichotomies, of service 'mobilising worth', using multiple criteria including the intellectual interest or professional challenge posed by patients' conditions. But apparently negative assessments, or patients presenting with social rather than appropriate clinical demands, were not routinely accompanied by unwillingness to offer such patients' assistance. Rather, staff drew on the hospital's historical tradition of open access, depicted as particularly important for those who had difficulty accessing other, theoretically more suitable, healthcare services. In drawing attention to the complex ways in which patients were categorised and responded to, Dodier and Camus bring out the highly contextualised nature of decisions about patients, noting the differences in response between individual members of staff and according to the pressure of work. Their detailed and perceptive analysis illustrates how illuminating and exciting a topic the sociological study of professional-patient interaction continues to be.

References

Annandale, E. (1996) Working on the front line: risk culture and nursing in the new NHS, *The Sociological Review*, 44, 416–451.
Bosk, C.L. and Frader, J.E. (1991) AIDS and its impact on medical work: the culture and politics of the shop floor. In Nelkin, D., Willis, D.P. and Parris, S.V. (eds) *A*

Disease of Society: Cultural and Institutional Responses to AIDS. Cambridge: Cambridge University Press.

Bury, M. (1997) *Health and Illness in a Changing Society.* London: Routledge.

Freidson, E. (1988) *Medical Work in America: Essays on Health Care.* New Haven: Yale University Press.

Higgs, P. (1998) Risk, governmentality and the reconceptualization of citizenship. In Scambler, G. and Higgs, P. (eds) *Modernity, Medicine and Health: Medical Sociology towards 2000.* London: Routledge.

Jeffrey, R. (1979) Normal rubbish: deviant patients in casualty departments, *Sociology of Health and Illness*, 1, 90–107.

Parsons, T. (1951) *The Social System.* New York: Free Press.

Scambler, G. and Britten, N. (2001) System, life-world and doctor–patient interaction: issues of trust in a changing world. In Scambler, G. (ed.) *Habermas, Critical Theory and Health.* London: Routledge.

The interactional form of professional dominance

Tony Hak

Introduction

Since Freidson (1970) analysed the structural concept of 'professional dominance', many studies have been published on the verbal strategies used by doctors in order to control the medical encounter. These studies portray particular conversational phenomena, such as interruptions and specific types of questions, as effective means by which doctors inhibit patients from getting the floor. Eglin and Wideman (1986) have called these studies 'the interactional form of professional dominance'. Criticising a British volume of several studies of this kind (Wadsworth and Robinson 1976), Sharrock (1979) argued that such strategies depend on the patient's cooperation and, hence, cannot assure the doctor's dominance. He concluded

> that we (as sociologists) are quite a long way from having answers to the (simple?) question 'what does go on between doctor and patient?' and that studies which are intended to provide answers can give exaggerated, rather perverse, interpretations of the nature of the medical consultation (Sharrock 1979: 144).

Many studies have been published since, which give similar 'exaggerated' and 'perverse' interpretations of the nature of the medical encounter (*e.g.* Fisher 1984, Mishler 1984, West 1984). Other authors, ethnomethodologists in particular, have presented opposite descriptions of the nature of the doctor–patient encounter. Hughes (1982), for instance, describes the absence of patients' initiatives in the encounter rather as indicating reluctance on the part of the patient than as the effect of doctors' cutting off patients' utterances. He suggests that this reluctance has to do with difficulties that patients have in recognising relevance and in offering organised descriptions of their conditions (1982: 364). And Eglin and Wideman (1986), in developing Sharrock's and Hughes' viewpoint, picture the conversational form of the professional encounter as derived from the parties' mutual orientation to the performance of a set of tasks, which establish a characteristic distribution of speakers' rights to turns, turn types and turn sizes (1986: 355).

In this paper I argue that the Freidsonian concept of 'professional dominance' does not in the first place refer to the asymmetrical distribution of *interactional tasks* but rather to the asymmetrical distribution of specialised, *professional knowledge*. Hence an 'interactional form of professional dominance' should not be sought in strategies for controlling turns (whether these are conceived as being imposed by the doctors' verbal strategies or derived from the parties' mutual orientation) but rather in other features of the conversation – not of the turn-distribution type – which secure doctors' objectives.

The paper consists of three parts. First, the concept of 'professional dominance' is discussed. Freidson (1970) described the 'structural' dominance of the professional perspective over the layman's perspective, *i.e.* doctors' authority over services requested by the patient, but he did not study the contents nor the interactional structure of medical encounters. Next, I will discuss examples of studies of the medical encounter which represent the 'interactional form of the professional dominance thesis'. Although these studies portray the encounter as an unequal transaction, following a course determined by the doctor rather than the patient, they fall short in explaining why and how this asymmetry could be seen as a form of professional dominance. Eglin and Wideman's claim, however, that the interactional shape of medical encounters should rather be seen as a joint production of the doctor and the patient, raises the question of what the interactional form of professional dominance then could be. In the third part of the paper I will propose another operationalisation of this concept: as the unequal distribution of parties' access to each other's objectives. I will illustrate this proposal with some data from Dutch mental health care encounters[1].

The structural form of professional dominance

Although Freidson (1970) does not provide a definition of the concept of professional dominance, it can be reconstructed from his discussion of the relationship between the client and the professional. First, he notes that professionals and clients bring different perspectives to the encounter. This difference is described both as a function of the professional's occupational experience (which leads him or her to take a more routine view of the problem than the sufferer's) and as a function of the specialised knowledge acquired both by occupational experience and by the formal training that professionals provide for their members (1970: 106).

Clients, as lay people, are by definition lacking the educational or experiential prerequisites that would allow them to decide, on grounds shared with the professional, whether to accept any particular piece of professional advice or not. Hence the professional's grounds for persuading clients to obey are 'inherently problematic':

Any expert whose work characteristically requires the cooperation of laymen is handicapped because laymen know neither the occupational rules of evidence nor the basic content of his skill. What *distinguishes the professional from all other consulting experts is his capacity to solve some of these problems of authority by formal, institutional means. His solution*

minimizes the role of persuasive evidence in his interaction with his clientele
(Freidson 1970: 109–10; stress in the original).

According to Freidson, the profession's solution to this problem lies both in
its capture of exclusive control over the exercise of particular skills, and in
its capture of the exclusive right of access to goods and services the layman
needs in order to manage his own problems independently of expert advice.
In short, the profession's solution to the problem of authority consists of its
capture of the formal position of gatekeeper. Thus, a twofold definition of
'professional dominance' can be deduced: first, that, particularly in matters
of health, the opinions of laymen are subordinated to the opinions of professional experts; second, the profession's legally guaranteed exclusive right
of access to goods and services the layman needs.

As is clear in the above quotation, Freidson contends that the professional's formal status as a gatekeeper will minimise the role of persuasive
evidence in the interaction. On theoretical, not empirical, grounds, he distinguishes four 'practical alternatives' for the interaction, of which persuasion
is only one (1970: 119):

(1) If the practitioner's advice or service does not correspond to the desires
     of the client, clients may merely withdraw from the situation when they
     realise that they cannot get the practitioner to conform to their desires.
     According to Freidson, no authority of any kind is exercised in this case.
(2) If the client desires some resource which can be obtained only by at
     least temporarily accepting what the practitioner 'suggests', the client
     may give in and do what the practitioner advises. The client's conformity
     is obtained because of command over accessory resources by the prac-
     titioner. It does not mean that the client accepts the value of the prac-
     titioner's competence.
(3) In some cases the practitioner's advice happens to correspond to what
     the client expects or desires, whether or not the grounds for the client's
     expectations are the same as they are for the practitioner.
(4) In some cases clients will be persuaded in the course of the interaction
     that the practitioner's advice is in their best interest, whether or not it
     happens to conform with what they initially believed they needed.

Freidson emphasises the necessity of faith or trust in the practitioner, *i.e.*
imputed competence (1970: 119). It is assumed that the doctrine of 'free
choice' allows the professional to put the burden of compliance on the
client. This allows the professional 'to rest on the authority of his professional
status without having to try to present persuasive evidence to the client that
his findings and advice are correct' (1970: 120–1). Thus, in Freidson's view,
the typical form of professional dominance in medical encounters is the
exclusion of alternatives for the client with the effect that he or she has little
choice but to accept the practitioner's opinion (1970: 122).

Freidson's description of the client–professional relationship lacks any (explicit) empirical grounding. It seems to depend completely on the profession's self-image. This may be an explanation also for the fact that Freidson does not mention the other two (logically available) alternatives:

(5)   The practitioner may do what the client expects, without accepting the client's competence.
(6)   The practitioner is persuaded in the course of the interaction that the client's request is in the client's best interest, whether or not it happens to conform with what the practitioner initially believed the client needed.

Freidson does not present any empirical evidence from which it could be concluded that it is legitimate to exclude these two alternatives from the discussion, or for the claim that professional service-providers avoid persuasion. It is not my claim that professionals do *not* avoid persuasion, but the point is that Freidson has not provided sufficient data for judging whether or not this is the case. He explicitly excludes the content of interaction between the client and the professional from his discussion:

> I shall not concern myself in any significant detail with the content of interaction between doctor and patient, or among doctors and other health workers. Instead, I shall focus on the significance of the way that interaction is organized by the formal, indeed often legal, relationships that establish the limits of legitimate behavior, and by the way in which the pattern of relationships exercises influence on the content of interaction independently of the individual characteristics of the participants. (Freidson 1970: 32)

Freidson apparently assumes that a study of the content of interaction would imply importing individual characteristics of the participants into the analysis. This, however, is not necessarily the case. It is not clear why we could not ask how doctors and patients typically accomplish their interaction in order to (re)produce 'professional dominance'. This question is addressed by the studies of the 'interactional form of professional dominance'.

The interactional form of professional dominance

One of the first studies addressing the problem of how professional dominance is (re)produced in the medical encounter is Bloor's study (1976) of consultations in ENT (ear, nose and throat) clinics. In contrast to Freidson, who emphasises that the medical encounter is organised by 'structural' professional dominance (*i.e.* the formal or legal relationships that establish the limits of legitimate behaviour), Bloor claims to have found empirical evidence that 'routine work practices' determine the degree of professional authority. A specialist's routines are, according to Bloor, related to professional authority and dominance in two analytically distinct ways. In the first place:

> there is a sense in which their sum is the *embodiment* of his functional autonomy. They serve to orchestrate consultations according to specialists', not parents', purpose. They may have the effect of excluding the parent from effective participation in the decision simply through their structuring of the consultation without regard for the parent's purposes. Thus, while the doctor may have a diffuse, culturally approved 'right' to legislate by fiat in health and illness, the totality of his routines are the practical embodiment of his dominance in the medical encounter. (Bloor 1976: 54).

'Embodiment' is the immediate translation of structural professional dominance into interactional forms. This is, however, not the case with the second way in which Bloor describes the relation between the doctors' routines and professional dominance:

> Yet in addition to the above general sense in which routines embody specialists' functional autonomy they also, in a more particular sense, *facilitate* specialists' autonomy. Routines can be seen not as just simply excluding parents by structuring consultations according to specialists' purposes, but as actively denying parents any potential influence. (Bloor 1976: 54).

Thus, according to Bloor, routines 'facilitate' professional dominance when they are seen as *actively* denying patients influence on the outcome of the encounter, whereas routines 'embody' professional dominance when they are seen as merely giving shape to other mechanisms of exclusion. As with most studies of the interactional form of professional dominance, Bloor claims to document routines which facilitate professional dominance rather than embody it. The doctor is seen as being concerned with asserting and sustaining his dominance over the patient at each and every turn, excluding any possibility that the patient might take any part in determining the outcome of the encounter. In order to enforce his dominance, the doctor is assumed to employ various verbal strategies for controlling the encounter, among which the use of interruptions and questions are prominent. The patient, for his or her part, is seen as being continuously involved in trying to challenge the doctor's control over the encounter. In other words, the 'interactional form of professional dominance' is conceived of as located in the observable concern of parties to assert their perspective in the encounter.

One routine, which according to Bloor has the consequence of denying patients influence, is framing questions 'in forms that demand specific rather than elaborated replies, and so provide little in the way of a conversational opening for parents' (Bloor 1976: 61). The following extract exemplifies this routine:

> *Extract 1* (from Bloor 1976: 61)
> (D = ENT specialist; M = mother of patient)
> D1:   How old is he?
> M1:   Nineteen months.
> D2:   He's had two bad attacks?
> M2:   Yes.
> D3:   He's fevered?
> M3:   Yes.
> D4:   And he came into hospital with one of them?
> M4:   Yes.
> D5:   In between times he's all right?
> M5:   Yes.
> D6v He eats his food?
> M6:   Yes, fine.
> D7:   He hasn't had ear trouble?
> M7:   No.

According to Bloor, the doctor's questions 'demand' specific answers and hence inhibit the mother to raise a topic of her own interest. In this way the doctor is said not only to secure his professional autonomy but rather to establish it actively. However, a remarkable feature of this example, and in fact of most of the other examples in the literature, is the *absence* of what is supposed to be there, namely observable concern of parties to assert their own perspective. Therefore, Sharrock has argued that Extract 1 documents, rather, *the absence of an interactional form of professional dominance*, at least of the 'facilitating' type. He presents the following hypothetical variant to Bloor's fragment:

> *Extract 2* (from Sharrock 1979: 142)
> (D = ENT specialist; M = mother of patient)
> D2:   He's had two bad attacks?
> M2:   I'm not sure really. I mean the first time I didn't know what it was
>   . . . etc.

Sharrock concludes from this hypothetical example that the format of the answer is:

> in answerer's control and constrained not by the form of the question, but by answerer's sense of what the answer is and of the relevances that dictate the question. Similarly, with the problem of topic [. . .]. There is nothing in the *formal* structure of an exchange of questions and answers which prevents people introducing topics. [. . .] If the medical professional is

reliant upon the way in which he structures his talk with the patient (in this sense) for his control, then he is indeed dependent upon the very weakest constraints which could not contain or control anyone who genuinely wanted to raise the topic and was willing to try to get answers to their questions. (1979: 142)

The interactional structure consisting of 'restricted' questions and 'specific' replies, 'embodies' rather than 'facilitates' professional dominance. There are constraints imposed upon the patient but, apparently, these are imposed by patients upon themselves rather than by doctors (Sharrock 1979: 143).

Interruption is another routine which has been accorded particular significance in the literature on the interactional form of professional dominance. By means of interruptions, the doctor is said to cut off the patient's attempts to give a full and complete story which tells it from the patient's point of view. Mishler (1984), for example, presents the following fragment as an example of interruption:

Extract 3 (from Mishler 1984: 129–30)[2]
(D = physician; P = patient)
D1:   You had an ulcer at age *nine*?
P1:   Um about – between nine – nine and eleven I had the first one.
D2:   The first one?
P2:   And then – uh the two years later I developed a second one.
D3:   (0.4) That was about thirteen or so.
P3:   Between – between nine – nine and thirteen. (0.8) The only thing –
D4:   That's when you had your second one.
P4:   Yes. The only thing I can remember is that my doctor was shocked to death because he never knew a girl my – my age that had two ulcers.
D5:   And how did – how did the ulcers present. What uh – what happened? (0.6) Just pain or uh
P5:   It's a well – yeah, pa – lot – lots and lots of pain sour stomach.

In Extract 3 a pattern of 'restrictive' questions and 'specific' answers is observable that is similar to Extract 1. The difference is that the patient at P3 does what Sharrock (hypothetically) did in Extract 2. This example shows that the format of the answer is in answerer's control indeed and that it is not completely constrained by the form of the question. But what the patient starts to tell (P3–P4: 'The only thing I can remember is that my doctor was shocked to death because he never knew a girl my age that had two ulcers') seems to be unwelcome. First it is interrupted (P3/D4), and consequently the doctor does not acknowledge it in any sense but instead changes topic (P4/D5). According to Mishler, this fragment documents the 'struggle' between the patient's attempts to give a full and complete story which tells it from the patient's point of view and the doctor's attempts to dominate the encounter.

Not only Mishler, but many other researchers have also claimed that doctors 'may interrupt the patient almost at his or her liking' (Lacoste 1981: 170). Whereas patient's talk typically is seen as a form of storytelling (*i.e.* the description of the illness or problem is wrapped up in stories that refer to the everyday lifeworld of the patient), the physician is said to attempt to stop this story-telling by various means. The frequent occurrence of interruptions is evidence indeed that the encounter is an unequal transaction following a course determined by the doctor rather than the patient. But does it imply that the doctor needs interruptions in order to 'facilitate' professional dominance? Or is it rather a mere 'embodiment' of structural professional dominance? It is remarkable that Mishler himself observes that interruption (such as in Extract 3) is not seen by the patient as strange:

> As members of this culture we, as observers, and the patient, are likely to assume that the physician has 'reasons' for his questions. It is somewhat remarkable, but understandable on the basis of this shared assumption, that the patient does not reject any of his questions as inappropriate, however disjunctive they are with previous content, but makes an effort to answer them. (Mishler, 1984: 120)

Thus, according to Mishler, the patient's assumption that the doctor has good reasons for his or her questions, however disjunctive they are with previous content, explains the patient's compliance (D4 and D5) in Extract 3. But it is precisely this compliance that makes it very difficult to read this extract as a document of a 'struggle' between the patient's attempts to give a full and complete story and the doctor's attempts to dominate the encounter. It is rather the absence of 'struggle' that is documented by Extract 3. The assumption that the doctors' questions are reasonable is something that the patient brings to the encounter. It is not produced interactionally. As such it documents the relevance of the structural – not the interactional – form of professional dominance.

Discussing other examples of interruption, such as presented by Lacoste (1981) and West (1984), Eglin and Wideman also conclude that interruptions in medical encounters, if to be found at all, typically are 'joint productions', characterised by the patient's compliance (1986: 345). It can be concluded that the interactional form of professional dominance, as presented by authors such as Bloor (1976), Lacoste (1981), Mishler (1984) and West (1984), in which professional dominance is seen as something which the doctor actively imposes upon the patient, cannot be sustained. This conclusion confirms Freidson's assumption that the problematic nature of authority in the doctor–patient relationship has been resolved by structural means.

Eglin and Wideman (1986) go even further in claiming that an 'interactional form of professional dominance' does not exist. They view the particular interactional shape of medical encounters not as an 'embodiment of professional dominance' but rather as derived from 'the parties' mutual orientation to the occasion of the encounter as one directed to the performance of a set of technical tasks, which establish the relevance of co-identification in terms of a particular set of identities ('doctor'/ 'patient') and a characteristic distribution of speakers' rights to turns, turn types and turn sizes' (1986: 355). However, although Eglin and Wideman convincingly describe the interactional shape of the medical encounter as jointly produced by the doctor and the patient (which justifies their rejection of the version of the interactional form of professional dominance as found in the literature), this does not justify their rejection of any interactional form of professional dominance. This wrong conclusion originates from their restricting the inquiry to the unequal distribution of turn types and turn sizes, which is only one possible interactional form of professional dominance.

Freidson (1970) described professional dominance as the phenomenon of subordination of the laymen's perspective to the professional perspective. The proposal of Bloor and others to describe verbal strategies for controlling the encounter, such as interruptions and particular types of questions, explicitly addressed the problem of the control of the patients' perspective, not of the patients' turn types or turn sizes. It was assumed that doctors deny the relevance of patient perspectives by discouraging them from voicing their concerns. The finding that interruptions and particular types of questions are not effective as a means of controlling patient talk does not imply that there are no other means of controlling patients' opinions. On the other hand, even if interruptions and questions were effective in controlling patients' talk, this would not establish the operation of the interactional form of professional dominance. The repression of patients' talk (*i.e.* inhibiting patients from expressing their opinion) does not necessarily coincide with the subordination of patients' opinions. It is quite possible that patients' opinions play a role in the encounter without being expressed, and the reverse may be true also. It follows that

> [i]f we do want to isolate 'tactics' that doctors and patients use to assert or challenge each other's autonomy we shall only be leaping to premature conclusions if we do single out episodes of interaction without a clear awareness of the way in which those episodes are engaged in doing medical work. (Sharrock 1979: 144)

In the next section I will present an approach which takes this into account.

Another approach to interactional dominance

Extract 4 is a fragment from a transcript of an encounter between a social psychiatric nurse who is working in the Emergency Psychiatry Department of a Dutch Regional Institution for Ambulatory Mental Health Care (RIAGG) and a patient. The encounter takes place in the living room of a sheltered home, where the man now lives after having stayed, off and on, in a psychiatric hospital for some years. The patient has asked to be re-admitted to a psychiatric hospital[3].

Extract 4
(N = social psychiatric nurse; P = patient)

P1:   Well, I find it rather unpleasant to to uh well to to to go uh to go to sleep in my own room.

N1:   Why? What is wrong with that room?

P2:   This traffic, it is going on the whole night through.

N2:   Mmmm.

P3:   It troubles me. An uh in the morning at six o'clock the birds start whistling and uh that troubles me terribly. Because then I know that I cannot uh rest in a normal way.

N3:   Yeah, yeah.

P4:   It is irritating to me.

N4:   Yes, they deprive you of your rest.

P5:   Yes.

N5:   And in the psychiatric hospital?

P6:   And this is this is terribly annoying. I have nothing against birds but I mean in the way it is I mean it awfully annoys me.

[data omitted]

      I absolutely do not want to stay here.

N6:   And the birds are anywhere. You will find them particularly everywhere in the countryside.

P7:   Hihi yeah yeah that is true. Yeah.

N7:   Isn't it?

P8:   Yes, that's right.

N8:   Even more than here I guess.

P9:   That's right yes.

N9:   Than in the city.

P10: But uh I mean this this pain in my my my head I I I do not know what it is.

There is no doubt structural professional dominance in the relationship between this nurse and his client. The nurse is a gatekeeper. It is he who decides on the admission into a psychiatric hospital. But how can this dominant position be read in the transcript? To begin with, *not* by a characteristic distribution of speakers' rights to turns, turn types or turn sizes. There is an asymmetrical distribution of interactional roles: the patient providing information and the nurse evaluating this, but this distribution is not in any sense 'characteristic' for this encounter. It is a distribution that is characteristic for any conversation in which one party is the teller of a story and the other party is its recipient. Furthermore, the nurse's questions are not 'disjunctive to previous content'. Rather, these questions, however 'restrictive' they may be (*e.g.* N7: 'Isn't it?'), explore and evaluate previous content. This extract resembles the type of exchange that has been described by Jefferson and Lee (1981) as a 'problematic convergence of a "troubles telling" and a "service encounter"'. Compare, for example, the next fragment:

> *Extract 5* (From Jefferson and Lee 1981: 405–6)[4]
> (J = James; V = Vic)
> J1:   The next time you see me I'm gonna be looking like hell you know
>   why, (0.7) Cause every damn one of these teeth coming out, bottom
>   and top. (0.7)
> V1:   Doesn't matter you still be you won't you James,
> J2:   s-uh, yeh I guess so – *maybe* ( ) *when* I see that dentist (come at me)
>   with that damn needle I'm ready to run like hell. I don't mind eh
>   pulling them but he coming at me that needle's what I can't stand.
> V2:   Tell him gas.
> J3:   hh huh?
> V3:   Tell him gas. (0.4)
> J4:   Uh – No I don't (want no gas, no) I will take it. You know.
> V4:   Let me ask you one question.
> J5:   Yeh.
> V5:   Are you getting toothaches? (0.4)
> J6:   *No!* (0.2) But I got cavities!

Extract 5 is a fragment of an everyday encounter, not a service encounter. In Extract 4 as well as Extract 5, one person (the 'troubles teller') is complaining about certain circumstances. In both cases, the other party introduces some thoughts ('advice') which he invites the first (complaining) party to align with. Finally, in both cases, the complainer attempts to avoid the adviser's conclusion ('But I . . .'). It can be concluded from this resemblance that there is no interactional form to be discovered in Extract 4 that could be called 'characteristic' for medical or psychiatric diagnostic encounters. But where then could the interactional form of professional dominance be found?

In everyday 'troubles telling' and 'advice giving', acceptance and rejection of advice is in great part an interactional matter, produced by reference to the current talk, and more or less independent of intention to use it or of actual subsequent use (Jefferson and Lee 1981: 408). In Extract 5, neither James' rejection nor his acceptance of Vic's advice will have real life consequences. However, in Extract 4, for parties it is clear that one party (the nurse) subsequently will make a judgement on the relevance of the patient's complaints in order to assess the necessity of an admission into a psychiatric hospital. For this reason, the patient's 'But uh I mean this this pain in my my my head' and James' 'But I got cavities!' will differ in subsequent effects, although they seem to have the same properties interactionally. James can reject Vic's advice, because the advice and its rejection do not have significance outside the interaction in which they are produced. On the other hand, the client needs the nurse's consent for getting the service he desires, an admission into a psychiatric hospital. The structural position of the nurse as a gatekeeper 'demands' that the client makes a new attempt to present problems which may convince the nurse. The distinctive difference between Extracts 4 and 5, thus, is not in interactional form but rather in the parties' interests and purposes. Whereas James and Vic only have to deal with what is available to them interactionally, the nurse and the client have to deal with much more, i.e. each other's position and perspective.

It is certainly possible that institutional encounters differ from everyday encounters in systematic, describable ways and that these differences could be found by comparing 'genres' (Ten Have 1989, Maynard 1991). Such differences, however, cannot be considered as 'embodiments' of professional dominance in the Freidsonian sense, i.e. as strategies used for subjecting the patient's perspective to the professional perspective. The differences, for instance, that Maynard (1991: 473–83) has described in the way 'perspective display series' occur in 'bad news' interviews in comparison to everyday conversations[5] can be explained by parties' mutual orientation to the doctor's obligation to provide information irrespective of its accordance with the patient's expectations. Expressing a different viewpoint is quite a different thing from dominating the encounter. My contention is that dominance can occur in interactions even in cases where the interactional form cannot be discerned from an everyday encounter. This implies, of course, that (professional, ideological, political or whatever) dominance can occur in everyday encounters. And there is no reason, indeed, why this could not be the case.

It follows that the interactional form of professional dominance only can be described by importing knowledge of the parties' perspectives, particularly knowledge of parties' unequal access to each other's perspective, into the analysis. In Extract 4, the patient knows that the nurse has the 'power' to decide on an admission into a psychiatric hospital but he does not know how the nurse should be convinced. By trial and error he attempts to find a complaint that is convincing for the nurse. This explains why the nurse does not show any inclination to 'control' the situation. He can simply wait for what the client offers him. The following fragments (Extract 6) of the report, written after the visit by the nurse, document this:

Extract 6
He tries to give all kinds of reasons for an admission into a psychiatric hospital. For instance, he pretends that he is not well. The traffic bothers him, but the birds also.
[data omitted]
When he notices that he is not successful in his arguments about being admitted into a psychiatric hospital, his behaviour changes to somewhat more normal conduct, it becomes less pitiful.

The nurse interprets the patient's utterances as 'giving all kind of reasons for an admission into a psychiatric hospital'. It cannot be said that the nurse really 'knows' what the patient was doing – there is no way of looking into the mind of the patient – but the important point is that the nurse does not have to know more for practical purposes. In this sense, he knows everything he needs to know about the patient's objectives and strategies. The patient, in contrast, by knowing in general terms what the nurse is doing – judging whether hospitalisation is necessary – does not know enough, because he does not know what the professional criteria are which the nurse uses in judging his complaints. He does not know what he must say or must not say in order to avoid the judgment that he 'pretends that he is not well'. Thus, professional dominance is 'embodied' in this encounter by the parties' unequal access to each other's perspective[6].

This inequality can be illustrated also with the following fragment. The social psychiatric nurse of this extract is working at the same Emergency Psychiatry Department as the nurse of Extract 4. The patient is a woman being visited at home by the nurse, after she had been referred to the department by a cardiologist at a public hospital to which the woman had presented cardiac complaints. The cardiologist could not find any serious cardiac problem and asked the Emergency Psychiatry Department to assess her case. During this home visit, the patient repeatedly attempts to convince the nurse that she needs cardiological help. The nurse repeatedly replies that the cardiologist could not find anything, but that he perhaps can provide another kind of help.

Extract 7[7]
(N = social psychiatric nurse; P = patient)
P1:   Someone made me feel a little bit nervous. Yes.
N1:   Yes? Who made you feel nervous?
P2:   My father.
N2:   And then . . . you have got those cardiac complaints?
P3:   I don't know suddenly.
N3:   Umm? ((pause))
P4:   Suddenly I got a couple of stupors and I started to shiver like mad and then suddenly it stopped. I was frightened and I thought keep breathing. And I would like to stay alive another while for I did not live yet.
N4:   Yes.
[data omitted]
        What is on your program yet? Do you mean something in particular when you say I like to stay alive another while?
P5:   Well, I wanted to see everything. I have seen everything. I've been used all my life.
        ((pause, then very softly:))
        (what I had already ( ) the whole country)

N5:   Sorry.
P6:   The whole country knew that.
N6:   What did the whole country know?
P7:   What I just said.
N7:   I don't understand. I just don't get it.
P8:   I've just been used all my life.
N8:   By whom?
P9:   By boys.
N9:   Yes. And how does the whole country know about this?
P10:   It was broadcast.
N10:   It was broadcast. On radio or something?
P11:   And on TV.
N11:   That you're being used?
P12:   No uh with whom I went to bed.
N12:   Strange.

Although the nurse is not formally a gatekeeper of cardiological services, the patient is perceiving him as someone who can provide some help with regard to her cardiac problems. In this respect there is structural professional dominance here. Extract 7 also shows evidence of interactional asymmetry. It is the nurse who is doing the questioning, whereas the patient is giving answers. But it has to be noted that there is no sign of 'restrictive' questions or questions that are 'disjunctive to previous content'. On the contrary, the nurse allows the patient to tell her story, and does not make use of pauses to interrupt her and to change the topic. It is the hesitations of the patient that might be atypical for an everyday conversation in which the story-teller probably would elaborate upon her story in a more fluent way.

However, it also occurs in everyday conversations that one party makes use of a series of questions in order to get a clearer picture of what the other party is saying. Similarly, in this extract, the nurse makes use of everyday conversational means in order to reach an understanding of the patient's account. The fact that it appears to be difficult (for the nurse but also for us) to understand the patient, is not a problem of an interactional kind. Note that there is no sign that one of the parties breaches mutual 'trust' (Garfinkel 1967). Questions and answers are chained without any apparent problem in terms of the mechanisms of the 'interactional machinery'. The asymmetry of Extract 7, thus, does not document professional (or any other kind of) dominance, but rather the nurse's difficulty in understanding the patient.

But the nurse and the patient are not mere everyday conversationalists. For both the client and the nurse it is clear that at the end of the day the latter will assess the patient's complaints. This implies that the patient's talk has a different meaning for the nurse than it would have had in an everyday conversation. However, the patient does not know exactly what this other meaning is. Therefore, the nurse, similarly to the nurse in Extract 4, does not need to 'control' the situation and can merely wait for what the client has to offer him. Yet, the nurse apparently attempts actively to gain a better understanding. What does he want to understand better? This question can be answered by inspection of the nurse's assessment of the patient's complaints, as reported to his colleagues.

At the end of the encounter, of which Extract 7 is a fragment, the nurse advises the patient to go to an emergency centre, to which she decides to go. Later on the same day, the nurse visits her again at the emergency centre and uses this opportunity to inform his colleague at this centre about his findings. Extract 8 is a fragment from the nurse's report to the colleague of the emergency centre. Finally the nurse writes a report on the case. Extract 9 is a fragment from the report.

Extract 8
(N = social psychiatric nurse)
N1:   She clearly has delusional ideas as well.
[data omitted]
Her sexual life, things that happened in it, appears to her as if they were broadcast on the radio, or at least that somehow happened. So in that sense she has quite clear circumscribed delusional ideas.

Extract 9
There are clear delusional ideas. She fancies her sexual past being disclosed on the radio.

These extracts show *post hoc* the psychiatric relevance of the statement 'It was broadcast on radio with whom I went to bed'. Note that the patient has not said in so many words that her sexual past has been disclosed on the radio, but that it is rather the gist of the whole sequence of (the nurse's) questions and (the patient's) answers. This information, that is jointly produced by the patient and the nurse in their talk, figures in the nurse's report as a symptom of a particular psychiatric 'reality', i.e. 'delusion'. This is not to say that we know for sure that the nurse was consciously involved in conversationally eliciting the symptom by asking the appropriate questions. But it is likely that the nurse was oriented to the potential psychiatric relevance of this talk during its unfolding.

Note that we, as analysts, now 'know' the psychiatric relevance of the nurse's questions in Extract 7, *not* by means of consulting a general body of knowledge about what an emergency psychiatric nurse is normally aiming at (his generally assumed tasks and competences) but rather by consulting the nurse's own 'analysis' of what was said. This implies that we do not need any assumption about the parties' mutual orientation and co-identification as Eglin and Wideman do. Thus, whereas I do not want to dispute Eglin and Wideman's claim that in a medical encounter doctor and patient mutually orient to the conversational tasks at hand, i.e. that they jointly and concertedly accomplish a *conversation*, I do dispute the claim that parties mutually orient to tasks which are specific for the *medical encounter*. In other words, parties in medical encounters co-identify in terms of conversational identities (that is as turn-takers), not in terms of institutional identities. The patient and the nurse mutually orient to conversational tasks, but they do not have the opportunity to orient mutually to each other's interests. Whereas the nurse is able to recognise the patient's relevancies, the patient is not able to recognise the nurse's relevancies nor how these inform the nurse's utterances.

Conclusion

Although patients' knowledge of professional standards and objectives will vary considerably with the kind of service (*e.g.* the public knows more about procedures and standards of general practice than of psychiatry) and patients' characteristics (*e.g.* class, gender and education), it is a characteristic feature of medical encounters that professionals (*i.e.* doctors and nurses) have a relatively complete understanding of what the patient attempts to achieve in the encounter. On the other hand, patients cannot understand doctors' objectives and, hence, strategy, completely. This difference constitutes my interactional version of the professional dominance thesis. The approach in which the interactional form of professional dominance is confined to particular turn types or to the overall interactional shape of the encounter are bound to fail, because professional dominance has to be conceived of as a relationship between perspectives in the first place, not between turns.

Acknowledgements

A draft version of this paper was presented at the Annual Conference of the British Sociological Association, University of Manchester, March 1991. The present version has benefited from comments of Fijgje de Boer, Joke Haafkens, David Hughes and two anonymous reviewers.

Notes

1   The discussion in this paper is restricted to encounters (or those parts of encounters) in which the professional solicits information from the client in order to assess the problem. I do not discuss how professionals communicate their diagnostic conclusions and their proposals for treatment.
2   See Appendix for details of transcription symbols. Mishler's very detailed transcript has been reduced (particularly by eliminating indications of overlap, intake

of breath, and the like) because this detail is not necessary for my present purpose).

3 See Appendix for details of transcription symbols. This data was collected in the frame of a research project on decision-making in psychiatry (see De Boer and Hak 1986). This data has not been collected for the purpose of discussing the interactional form of professional dominance. It can be asked to what degree the extant discussion in the literature has been shaped by the more or less accidental fact that certain data from a particular setting was at hand. The most extreme case is Eglin and Wideman's (1986) who present data from telephone calls to the police in order to criticise interpretations other researchers made of data from medical encounters. I consider it positive that many contributions to this discussion refer to data of doctor–*parent* conversation, because this makes it easier to make the necessary distinction between the mere application by professionals of professional procedures to an object (the patient as a body, here represented by the child) and the articulation of its practical implications in a dialogue with other parties and their perspectives (the patient as a person, here represented by the parents), of which only the latter is the field in which professional 'dominance' matters (see Strong 1979: 132). Because in psychiatry the patient as a person is the object of professional assessment as well, it is more difficult to maintain the distinction between 'pure' professional work and its articulation to the patient's perspective. The latter perspective itself can become an object of professional assessment. Professional 'dominance' is therefore a less distinct and more pervasive feature of mental health encounters.

It can be asked as well to what degree the discussion in the following part of this paper has been shaped by the fact that it takes as data an encounter between a social psychiatric nurse, not a psychiatrist, and a patient. However, the aim of this paper is not to describe how professional dominance looks like in specific settings or with different kinds of professionals but rather to discuss how it can be 'discovered' and described in conversational data.

4 See Appendix for details of transcription symbols. Jefferson and Lee's very detailed transcript has been reduced because this detail is not necessary for my present purpose.

5 For the purpose of this discussion I take it for granted that differences could be found. I would like to point out, however, that differences found between 'institutional' and 'everyday' encounters do not necessarily reflect the effects of the 'institutional' setting. There are many other concurrent differences between the compared settings than the mere difference between 'institutional' and 'everyday'. Most of the comparisons between doctor–patient encounters on the one hand and everyday conversations between, say, friends on the other hand, for instance, ignore the fact that the medical encounter takes place in an environment in which the doctor is 'at home' and the patient is a 'guest'. Comparing the doctor–patient interview with, *e.g.*, 'everyday' talk between a boy and the parents of his girlfriend at the occasion of his first visit to her parents' home will reveal that so-called 'institutional' characteristics of talk can be found in that kind of situation as well. The same applies, for that matter, to nonverbal characteristics such as that the guest does not take his coat off before being invited by the host to do so, that the guest does not move freely in the room, etcetera (see for more examples: Strong 1979: 130).

6   This is a good example of Freidsonian 'dominance' because there is no disagreement between the nurse and the client on the client's diagnosis or therapy, *i.e.* on matters that could be considered as entirely within the professional's competence. The client's problem at hand is to convince the nurse that his complaints about housing be considered a part of the professionally acknowledged (psychiatric) problem. It is left entirely to the professional's discretion to decide whether a complaint is relevant in his perspective or not. In other words, it is not a matter of 'dominance' whether an *acknowledged* complaint is considered a symptom of, say, schizophrenia or another kind of psychotic disturbance. But it is a matter of professional dominance that the professional is in the position to judge a complaint as 'serious' or just 'pretending'. This is an additional reason why conversational 'asymmetries' such as described by Maynard (1991), which may be correct descriptions of how professionals make use of conversational devices in a particular way, are not always relevant for a study of 'dominance' (in a Freidsonian sense). It is not the professional assessment of the client's problems as such (the diagnosis), nor its telling, that is the issue for the study of professional dominance. The issue rather is the decision on what counts as a 'symptom' to be diagnosed. In other words, *applying* a professional perspective cannot be 'dominant' in itself, but deciding on what is taken as a relevant thing to be diagnosed is contestable and hence a matter of dominance.

7   This data has been collected as part of the same research project as Extract 4. See for further analyses of this data: De Boer and Hak (1986), Hak (1989) and Hak (1992).

Appendix

Symbols used in data transcription.

(0.5)	pause of 0.5 seconds
(word)	word(s) unclear but 'retrieved' as far as possible by transcriber
( )	utterance produced but its sense could not be discerned
((sobbing))	transcriber's comments
nine	underlining indicates emphasis on that word or part of word

References

Bloor, M. (1976) Professional autonomy and client exclusion: a study in ENT clinics. In Wadsworth, M. and Robinson, D. (eds) *Studies in Everyday Medical Life*. London: Martin Robertson, 52–68.

de Boer, F. and Hak, T. (1986) *Besluitvorming in de acute psychiatrie* (Decision-making in emergency psychiatry). Rotterdam: Erasmus University, Institute for Preventive and Social Psychiatry (Konteksten series no. 7).

Eglin, P. and Wideman, D. (1986) Inequality in professional service encounters: verbal strategies of control versus task performance in calls to the police, *Zeitschrift für Soziologie*, 15, 341–62.

Fisher, S. (1984) Doctor–patient communication: a social and micro-political performance, *Sociology of Health and Illness*, 6, 1–29.

Freidson, E. (1970) *Professional Dominance*. New York: Atherton Press.
Garfinkel, H. (1967) Studies in Ethnomethodology. Englewood Cliffs (NJ): Prentice-Hall.
Hak, T. (1989) Constructing a psychiatric case. In Torode, B. (ed.) (1989) *Text and talk as social practice*. Dordrecht: Foris Publications, 72–92.
Hak, T. (1992) Psychiatric records as transformations of other texts. In Watson, G. and Seiler R.M. (eds) (1992) *Text in Context: Contributions to Ethnomethodology*. Newbury Park (CA): Sage Publications, 138–55.
Hughes, D. (1982) Control in the medical consultation: organizing talk in a situation where co-participants have differential competence, *Sociology*, 16, 359–76.
Jefferson, G. and Lee, J.R.E. (1981) The rejection of advice, *Journal of Pragmatics*, 5, 399–422.
Lacoste, M. (1981) The old woman and the doctor, *Journal of Pragmatics*, 5, 169–80.
Maynard, D. (1991) Interaction and asymmetry in clinical discourse, *American Journal of Sociology*, 97, 448–95.
Mishler, E. (1984) *The Discourse of Medicine*. Norwood (NJ): Ablex Publishing Company.
Sharrock, W.W. (1979) Portraying the professional relationship. In Anderson, D.C. (ed.) *Health Education in Practice*. London: Croom Helm, 125–46.
Strong, P. (1979) *The Ceremonial Order of the Clinic*. London: Routledge and Kegan Paul.
Ten Have, P. (1989) The consultation as a genre. In Torode, B. (ed.) (1989) Text *and Talk as Social Practice*. Dordrecht: Foris Publications, 115–35.
Wadsworth, M. and Robinson, D. (eds) (1976) *Studies in Everyday Medical Life*. London: Martin Robertson.
West, C. (1984) *Routine Complications*. Bloomington: Indiana University Press.

4.2

'Why didn't you say just that?' Dealing with issues of asymmetry, knowledge and competence in the pharmacist/client encounter

Alison Pilnick

Introduction

The existence of asymmetry in medical encounters has been discussed many times in previous research, beginning with Parsons' influential function-alist view of socially prescribed roles for physician and patient. However, as Bogoch (1994) points out, the underlying assumption of this traditional Parsonian model is one of 'a disinterested professional acting on the basis of complex theoretical knowledge and the interests of the client, and a client who cannot understand or appreciate professional opinions, accepting and complying with professional diagnosis and treatment recommendations' (Bogoch 1994: 66). Two distinct issues relating to asymmetry are raised by this Parsonsian perspective; the first is the ancillary question of whether this 'mystical' professional expertise has now become more routine and access-ible to an increasingly educated, 'consumerist' public. Secondly, and more fundamentally, as Maynard (1991) describes, these descriptions of the mani-festations of institutional power and authority largely fail to consider how participants organise interaction in the first place. The end result is thus that communication has often been considered only as a by-product of these over-arching societal structures of power and authority. However, as Maynard contends, asymmetry in the form of physician control cannot be considered as an automatic effect of institutional processes; analysis of consultations shows that *both* parties to the consultation constitute and enact this asym-metry throughout the interaction. In part, he suggests, these patterns develop as a way of handling the interactional difficulties the doctor/patient encounter creates.

Bloor and Horobin (1975) describe these difficulties as a 'double-bind' situation for patients, in that they are expected to use their own judgement as to when it is appropriate to seek medical advice, but later to defer to the doctor's judgement when undergoing treatment. As Heath notes, consider-ing the process of diagnosis, 'patients' accounts of their illness or behaviour, and in particular the ways in which they attempt to justify having sought professional medical help, reveal a deep sensitivity to the asymmetries in the relationship between patient and doctor' (Heath 1992: 261). He goes on to consider how, by describing their own subjective experience of the illness, or by qualifying their version of a particular episode, patients systematically preserve, through their talk, the differential status between their own under-standing of the complaint and its professional assessment, and between medical expertise and lay opinion. In conclusion, he suggests that patients display a 'central concern to avoid any response which could serve to imply that the participants' versions and assessment of the condition had an equi-valent status' (Heath 1992: 262). Any response to diagnosis which challenges this asymmetry inevitably undermines the patient's grounds for seeking pro-fessional medical help in the first place.

The complex nature of the doctor/patient encounter suggested here by Heath is also the central argument used by Sharrock (1979) in his considera-tion of the lay/professional nature of the relationship. He criticises sociology for acting as an indictment, in the sense that by describing the professional/client relationship as 'oppressive', it is both finding fault and apportioning blame. By constituting the doctor/patient relationship as a *struggle* for dom-inance, the implication is that each and every meeting between doctors and patients is a struggle, and that patients would have much more to say *if* they were allowed to. Subsequently then, 'if the medical professional is reliant upon the way in which he structures his talk with the patient . . . for his control, then he is indeed dependent on the very weakest constraints which could not contain or control anyone who genuinely wanted to raise the topic' (Sharrock 1979: 142). The conclusion implicit in this evaluation then is that, rather than struggling for dominance and losing, patients do not in actual fact really try to contest the authority of the doctor.

These notions of 'interactional submission' by the patient are also found in ten Have's (1991) consideration of the doctor/patient encounter. He high-lights the twofold nature of asymmetry in such interactions, suggesting that there is first an asymmetry of topic, in the sense that it is the patient's condition that is under review rather than the doctor's, which leads to a secondary, associated asymmetry in terms of task distribution within the encounter. Thus, although the initiative for the encounter is likely to be the patient's, the distribution of tasks in terms of an ultimate goal of diagnosis involves quite 'natural' interactional dominance by the doctor, which is enacted through questioning, investigating and decision-making behaviour, and is complied with by the patient. The implication then, is that it takes specific and deliberate effort on the part of the patient to counter the inter-actional contingencies leading to asymmetry, and that this is rarely seen in practice.

Frankel observes that 'in its modern guise, the [medical] interview is treated more as a *technique* used by one person to obtain information from another' (Frankel 1995: 233). Defining interviews in general, he suggests that they are 'an instance of the division of labour: The interviewee supplies the matter, the interviewer supplies the form' (1995: 234). Where clinical inter-views unfold largely through Question and Answer exchanges, the focus 'is organized around solving one or more problems. As such, much of the questioning that occurs in a clinical encounter is designed to elicit information that is complete and accurate enough for the physician to arrive at a conclusion' (Frankel 1995: 248–9). Like ten Have, then, he suggests that the various phases that make up a clinical encounter are regulated in terms of larger organisational tasks. However, he points out that there are particular moments in clinical encounters which represent 'windows of opportunity' for patients' talk, for example their expression of affect. In conclusion, he observes that the 'act of caring and being cared for' is also a fundamental dynamic feature of clinical encounters, and that this necessarily has an effect on the patterns of talk which emerge.

Hutchby (1996), discussing power in discourse in relation to data collected from talk radio, describes how an approach informed by conversation analysis (CA) can provide an account of power as an integral feature of talk-in-interaction, so that 'through focusing on such issues as how participants orient to features of a setting by designing their turns in specialised ways (e.g. restricting themselves either to asking questions or to giving answers) [this] can be used to address how power is produced through oriented-to features of talk' (Hutchby 1996: 482). Thus, he suggests that the ways in which participants design their interaction can, in effect, place them in relationships where 'discourse strategies' of power are differentially available to each of them. Power can in this way be viewed as an 'emergent feature of the oriented-to discourse practices in given settings' (1996: 482).

In discussing this approach, he draws on Davis's (1988) study of power in doctor/patient encounters, which suggests that whilst CA may be used to address power in this setting, it requires a more detailed theoretical underpinning. Hutchby rejects this argument, and goes on to illustrate, with reference to the talk radio data, *how* power can be seen as a feature of the unfolding of talk in a particular setting. Specifically, he describes how power may be seen as a 'shifting distribution of resources which enable some participants locally to achieve interactional effects not available to others' (Hutchby 1996: 481). In this setting, the distribution has to do with both the organisation of activities within a call, and the asymmetrical distribution of argument resources provided by a participant's position within that argument. Second position in an argument, he suggests, represents a more powerful position, in that the second speaker is only required to attack the first speaker's contribution to produce an appropriate response, rather than setting out their own stance. It is easy to see, then, how these principles may also be applied to the question-answer format noted in doctor-patient interaction, where the instigation of new topics is largely undertaken by doctors, and patients are required to respond to this.

The overwhelming conclusion from this and other studies then, is that asymmetry, rather than being imposed, may be interactively achieved by both participants to an interaction, and specifically to the doctor/patient encounter. However, it is important to note that most of this literature is based on episodic, as opposed to long term relationships. Conversation analysts, in particular, have not tended to focus on long term interactional sequences.

Nevertheless, it would seem plausible that such encounters with long term patients are likely to contain significant differences, centred on the issue of knowledgeability. As Macintyre and Oldman state in their work on migraine:

> Those who suffer from chronic illnesses, particularly ones that doctors can do little about, develop a special knowledge of their condition. This knowledge is of a rather different order from that held by doctors, and from the point of view of the patient, it is subtly superior (Macintyre and Oldman 1977: 55).

This superiority arises, they argue, because the patient's knowledge is personal and forged from direct experience; it is 'what I know' about an ailment rather than 'what is known', and is therefore constructed rather than received. These two sorts of knowledge are not, however, independent of each other, and may therefore be subject to negotiation within the interaction.

In a similar vein, West's (1976) work on the management of childhood epilepsy also deals with interaction between doctors and 'experienced' patients or carers. In his analysis he suggests that, where these carers perceive that information is not being volunteered, or even withheld, this 'leads parents to initiate challenges to the doctor, opening up the agenda and creating the situation where the doctor has to "work" to construct his claim to competence' (West 1976: 28). Such actions are explained by one father as necessary because of doctors' reluctance to reveal 'the secrets of their profession'. Likewise, Silverman's (1987) interactional analysis of encounters occurring in paediatric clinics traces the impact of experience on outpatient interviews, concluding that this experience has a significant effect on the interactions observed in terms of the way issues are initiated and discussed.

There are other suggestions in the wider sociological literature that patients with chronic illnesses are of a different order from episodic patients in their interactions with the health care system. As Freidson (1973) notes, in terms of Parsons' description of the sick role, the sick person's exemption from the duties of everyday life 'is temporary, and its legitimacy conditional on trying to get well' (Freidson 1973: 234). This kind of temporary exception, however, is applicable only to acute illnesses; in chronic illnesses such as cancer and leukaemia, legitimacy is not conditional on trying to get well. Indeed, as Freidson indicates, it is generally believed impossible to recover from most chronic ailments. Secondary to this, the behaviour of the sick person 'comes to assume a more definite pattern when he is thought to have a chronic illness requiring long term and sustained contact with a practitioner' (Freidson 1973: 311) in the sense that chronic patients develop some kind of organisation in their lives which is related to the (professionally defined) demands of their treatment. In other words, rather than a person's life being organised by the disease and any associated incapacity, it is organised instead by 'professional conceptions of the disease and what is needed to treat it; the disease becomes a professionally organised illness' (Freidson

1973: 311–2). Within this organisation, however, there is still the opportunity for the patient to backslide, by for example missing appointments or failing to comply with the prescribed medication regimen.

Methodological background

The data presented throughout this paper are drawn from a paediatric oncology outpatient clinic, which deals with long term cancer and leuk-aemia patients under the age of 16. These patients and their carers make regular visits to the clinic, often over a period of several years, and as such are an unusual group with respect to their knowledge of particular condi-tions and treatments. The data are also unusual in terms of the wider liter-ature in that they involve pharmacist/patient, as opposed to doctor/patient, consultations. Interesting questions of status and expertise are raised by this, as in a professional sense there is some degree of separation between know-ledge and status: pharmacists have claim to a specialised body of knowledge but are not generally seen as having the same status as that of a doctor. Whilst there are some studies that have explicitly considered pharmacist patient/communication, these are largely informed by a fairly simple quan-titative social psychology paradigm. This approach, as can be seen in stud-ies such as those by Morrow *et al.* (1993) and Smith and Salkind (1990), depends on developing a categorisation system, and then coding and count-ing occurrences of a particular type. Communication is broken down into discrete components, and in the results such variables as 'number of ques-tions asked by the pharmacist per minute' are discussed. In this manner, the two-way nature of the interaction process is ignored, and these studies shed little light on the factors that may be affecting this process.

There are also distinctions to be made between these encounters and other (non physician) health professional/client interactions; where for example health visitors may need to establish with their clients 'What their visits are about', in this setting both parties to the interaction have a clear idea of why they are there. Heritage and Sefi's (1992) work on visits made by health visitors to first-time mothers reveals that this 'establishing the purpose of the visit' is a fundamental component of these interactions. How-ever, in this case the patients and carers involved will already have had regular contact with a pharmacist during their initial inpatient admission following diagnosis, and the role of the clinic is to monitor *maintenance* therapy. As might be expected, then, a fairly well-defined agenda appears to exist for the encounters. In addition, visits to the clinic pharmacist take place immediately after a consultation with the clinic doctors, so the pos-sibility exists that there are details arising from the former which the phar-macist has not yet been made party to. All of these factors have implications for the interactions which occur, and particularly for the ways in which issues of expertise and/or knowledgeability are managed or pre-empted.

Tape-recorded consultations between pharmacists, patients and their carers were collected from the clinic over a two-month period, in the presence of the researcher. Ethnography, combined with conversation analysis was used as the primary methodology in order to analyse the encounters which took place. The collected audio tapes (43 in total) were thus transcribed in detail, and the analysis itself was carried out on a turn-by-turn basis. Field notes collected by the researcher during the consultations have been used alongside the CA analysis, in an attempt further to illuminate some activities and interactional references. The pre-existing CA and ethnographic literature concerned with issues of asymmetry, largely in the doctor/patient encounter, provides the background against which this analysis is set.

For the purposes of the analysis presented here, a variety of extracts have been chosen in order to illustrate the range of influences that may result from having an 'experienced' patient or carer as one party to the interaction. The initial plan, to follow a series of encounters between one patient or carer and the clinic doctors, was eventually dismissed as restrictive in terms of both length and the exclusion of apparently relevant and related occurrences which could be seen in other encounters. However, since, as has been stated, this is a maintenance clinic, all the data presented here have been drawn from encounters in a series.

Analysis

How competence is asserted at the beginning of the encounters
The issue of patient knowledgeability, and the way in which it frames the consultations, is evident even in the opening sequences of the encounters. As I have already indicated, both parties to the interaction have a clear idea of why they are there, and so the consultations routinely move from a greetings and/or identification sequence straight into the 'business' of the encounter, without any of the 'pre-beginning' type exchanges described by Zimmerman (1992), which are common in institutional talk. In this situation, the 'business' consists of advice or information about prescribed medication, in terms of dosages, administration, etc. The move into this 'informing' component of the encounter is frequently framed by the pharmacist in terms of patient expectations, as below:

37:sk/nc/op (simplified transcript)
1 Ph: Right (.) Two weeks' worth (.) Is that what you were expecting?
2 M: Yeah =
3 Ph: = Coming back in two weeks' time
4 M: Yeah

and

43:nq/nc/op (simplified transcript)

```
1 Ph:   Right (.) now is it what we expect (.) 100% (.) Two weeks (.)
        Y[es?
2 M:     [yeah (.) yeah
3 Ph:   4mg (.) He's had the vincristine (.) ((begins to dispense tablets))
```

In both cases the patient or carer is constituted by the pharmacist as someone who *has* an expectation about their medication and its dosage, and any
advice which is then given in the encounters is framed within these terms
(for example, 'Are you giving 5mls?' rather than 'The dose is 5mls', etc). In
the second extract, the pharmacist's pursuit of an answer from the mother
of the patient after the question 'Is it what we expect?' reinforces the notion
that she is included in this 'we', and thus serves to place both parties on a
more equal footing in terms of their expectations of the patient's therapy.
The mother's (repeated) affirmative response to this direct question confirms
that '100 per cent' for 'two weeks' is indeed what she had been expecting,
and the pharmacist then proceeds to dispense the medication. The use of
medication records or drug cards is also an important factor in these interactions; in both cases the pharmacist refers to the card before producing the
treatment summary. In fact, the pharmacist would be able to tell from these
cards whether any alteration had been made to the planned treatment, and
in this knowledge-seeking sense the opening questions are redundant[1]. However, they also serve to topicalise dosage information in a manner which
explicitly constitutes patient competence. In addition, the fact that these
statements are quoted from a document perhaps serves to give them some
kind of objectivity, in the sense that the card becomes the representation of
the organisation to which 'we' (pharmacists and patients or carers) belong.

   This deferral to perceived patient knowledge or competence as an opening
strategy for the encounter is perhaps one method by which the pharmacist
can ensure that redundant or unnecessary advice is not delivered to the patient.
Contrastingly, where pharmacists try to proceed directly to the 'informing'
segment of the encounter without first establishing some sort of shared
footing for their advice, this may be badly received, as can be seen below:

```
7: dc/op/be (simplified transcript)
1 Ph:   (name)? (.) OK (.) [I'll go through it all with you
2 M:                       [Yes
3       (0.6)
4       It's alright (.) I know [it anyway
5 Ph:                           [Oh yeah
```

Here, the pharmacist's statement 'I'll go through it all with you' allows for
little or no knowledge on the part of the mother, and is immediately countered
with what can be heard as a rather defensive response. Interactional difficulties
such as this highlight the somewhat delicate position pharmacists dealing
with long term patients such as these are placed in, in the sense that their

Code of Ethics requires them to ensure that patients are familiar with the dosage instructions for their medications. This creates the obvious difficulty of either attempting to give advice to already knowledgeable patients, thereby running the risk of undermining their competence, as above, or else assuming knowledge on the part of the patient, as in the prior two extracts, and attempting to tailor any advice around this. Heritage and Sefi's (1992) work on health visiting, discussed briefly in the previous section, considers the difficulties of attempting to give unsolicited advice to a party who may neither want nor need this, concluding that it is likely to be badly received, or at best that its usefulness will be interactionally minimised. Whilst this latter strategy of assuming knowledge may then seem preferable, and is used quite successfully in the examples above, it too, as the following extract shows, can create difficulties:

```
30:nq/nc/op (simplified transcript)
1 Ph:    ((Indicating tape recorder)) It's a bit official in't it (.) hh: (.) I'm
2        not going to say anything to you really because you've had it all
         before haven't you?
3        (0.5)
4 F:     No (.) the missus usually does it =
5 Ph:    = Oh right (.) It's what we were expecting 50%
```

Interestingly, although the assumption the pharmacist makes in this case is proved to be wrong, and the father of the patient states that 'the missus' usually attends the clinic, the pharmacist does not proceed into any kind of explanation or information for the father. Instead, the utterance in line 5, 'It's what we were expecting 50 per cent' seems to provide for the fact that 'the missus' will have anticipated this dosage regimen and will be competent to deal with it, making any further explanation unnecessary.

Perceived differences between mothers' and fathers' competencies
This last extract, taken from a consultation where only the father is present with the child, is particularly interesting in the light of Strong's notion of 'the loving but incompetent father'. Also considering interaction within a paediatric clinic, he suggests that within the clinic, fathers' qualities as regards their children are 'strictly limited- or so they were treated' (Strong 1979: 60). He notes that when mothers attended clinics by themselves, little or no reference was ever made to their partners. Conversely, when fathers attended clinics alone with their offspring this was treated as a matter of interest, and often a source of problems, by the staff. In short, 'whereas mothers' competence was never openly questioned, this was almost a matter of routine for fathers. They might not be the ideal representative for a child, but it was also made explicit that this was not a duty to be expected of a father' (1979: 63). This perhaps sheds some light on why the pharmacist in the extract above is content to allow the absent mother's presumed competence

with her child's medication to stand in the way of any further explanation to the father.

There are a small number of consultations within the body of data collected here where a father is the sole representative of the patient; as in Strong's data the consultations which take place under those circumstances appear to be of a different order to those where a mother is present. In the extract below, for example, no information is given to the father about the child's medication.

Transcript 32:- ml/nc/op (simplified transcript)
```
 1  Ph:   Right
 2        (0.6)
 3  Ph:   Coming back in a week's time (0.3) Right (0.2) have you got
 4        plenty of Septrin at home? (.) or (.) [uhhh
 5  F:                                          [We have (.) uhhh better
           take some more
 6  Ph:   There's your blister =
 7  F:    = Ta
 8        (1.0)
 9  Ph:   There you go (.) There's another bottle for you
10  F:    Oh alright (.) thank you
11  Ph:   Have fun (.) See you
```

Interestingly, in answer to the pharmacist's question at line 3, 'Have you got plenty of Septrin at home?', the father answers 'We have', thus giving the impression that his child's medication regime is not something for which he has sole responsibility or control. In general, the consultations involving fathers alone tend to follow this pattern; little or no advice is given by the pharmacist to the father, and the expertise of the mother is invoked by both parties to facilitate this. As Strong puts it, it seems that the medical audience have 'tacitly validated mothers' authority' (Strong 1979: 61).

This pattern does not hold true, however, for the one occasion in the data where a child is brought to clinic not by either parent, but by an elder brother. In this consultation (see below), information is sought from the sibling (e.g. in line 8), and dosage information is offered by the pharmacist (lines 15-17).

Transcript 25:- sc/nc/op (simplified transcript)
```
 1  Ph:   ((Taking drug card from patient)) Thanks
 2        (2.4)
 3  Ph:    Great (.) I don't have to change anything
 4  B:     Yeah (.) I don't think so
 5  Ph:   No (.) the count's fine
 6  B:    Mmmhmm
 7        (0.7)
 8  Ph:   And you're coming back in a week?
```

9   B: Monday
10 Ph: Alright yeah (.) I've given you seven days anyway
11 B: Yeah
12 Ph: Because it's-
          – it it works out easier (0.2) but you'll get a new lot on
          Monday ( )
13 Ph: D'you want some of the Septrin (0.4)
14 B: Yeah (.) better take some just in case
15 Ph: Yeah (.) well there's that one and that's 7.5ml =
16 B: = Mmmhmm
17 Ph: twice a day on Monday Wednesday and Friday (.) is that
          alright
18   (.) Do you want a bag (Child's name)
19 C: No thank you
20 Ph: No [OK
21 B: [Alright then ((laughs))
22 Ph: ((Laughs))
23 B: Bye
24 Ph: Bye

Throughout the course of this encounter, then, the sibling is treated as someone with a degree of knowledge, able to comprehend the significance of blood counts (line 5), and to decide whether any further antibiotic supplies are needed (lines 13–14). Interestingly, at the conclusion of the clinic on this particular afternoon, the attending nurse enters into a discussion with the pharmacist about what a 'sensible boy' the patient's elder sibling (who is aged 16) is, and how fond he is of his brother. It also transpires that he is a frequent representative for his brother at the clinic, making it highly plausible that his treatment as a competent and knowledgeable party is a phenomenon which has been negotiated and achieved over a period of time (and a period of evaluation!) by the clinic staff.

Returning to Strong's data, one of his other major observations concerning the representation of children at clinics is that 'not only did staff treat mothers as entirely competent to answer their questions, but mothers typically answered in the same fashion' (Strong 1979: 61). Thus:

> when a couple did attend a clinic together, staff placed fathers in a subordinate position to their spouses. Questions were asked directly to the mothers, and, though fathers sometimes added their own comments to which staff might reply, they normally returned to the mother for their next question (Strong 1979: 61).

In the data from the oncology clinic, however, there is only one instance of a child who attends with both parents (see below). In contrast to Strong's model, the father here is very much the dominant party, answering the large majority of the pharmacist's questions (*e.g.* in line 16), and initiating topics for discussion (line 23).

Transcript 36:- sr/nc/op (basic transcript)
1 M: Have we only got one this time?
2 Ph: Yeah ( ) Hi [(child's name)
3 M: [They did it wrong
4 F: Can I have another patch?
5 Ph: Yeah sure
6 F: Last time they couldn't get a vein (.) on that hand so they had to
7   transfer it to ( ) [to where ( ) on the other hand ( ) I know ( )
8 Ph: [Oh right
9 Ph: There you go ( ) a spare one
10 C: What's that for Mummy?
11 F: Injection darling =
12 M: = For your ( ) for your magic cream
13 C: Have we got some Mom?
14 M: We've got some magic cream
15 Ph: Coming back next week then aren't you?
16 F: Yeah
17 Ph: Just a week's worth here
18 F: Yeah ( ) yeah
19   ( )
20 Ph: ((to child who is watching him prepare blister)) You've got lovely
         eyes you know
21 F: Come back Thursday
22   ( )
23 F: It's much better now than pharmacy before ( ) I used to hate
         doing that
24 Ph: Waiting outside you mean ( ) Yeah ( ) Most people have said they
25   like it much better [this way
26 F: [It's a lot quicker isn't it and nearer ( ) no
27   point in waiting around there ( ) hours
28 Ph: Are you OK for Septrin ( ) or could you do [with some more
29 F: [No ( ) we need
         some more (.) want
30   some more =
31 M: = Please
32 Ph: No problems (.) tablets then
33 F: Thank you
34 Ph: Here we go =
35 M: = What's that one
36 Ph: This is the ( ) [aniseed one
37 F: [aniseed

```
38 M:    aniseed ( ) that's the [one
39 F:                          [That's the one
40 Ph:   Two and a half mls of this one yeah
41 M:    Yeah
42 Ph:   Yeah ( ) That's it
43 M:    She doesn't like the other [one does she?
44 F:                               [No
45 Ph:                               [Thank you (name) ((to doctor who
         has brought in a drug card))
47 Ph:   Yeah (.) OK
48       ( )
49 M:    Come on then
50 Ph:   See you then
51 M:    Bye
```

In this context, the father's use of 'I' in 'Can I have another patch' (line 4) is interesting; it is also the father who answers the child's question in line 10, despite the fact that it is explicitly addressed to 'Mummy'. From line 15 onwards, when the pharmacist begins to ask questions and check arrangements, it is also the father who provides answers or confirmations to these utterances. It subsequently becomes clear that he has been a regular attender at clinic for a long period; in line 23 his statement 'It's much better now than pharmacy before, I used to hate doing that' is a reference to the new clinic consulting room arrangements (where the pharmacist and doctor occupy adjacent rooms) brought in some months previously. The mother's first contribution to the encounter since the opening (apart from speaking to her child) comes at line 31, and serves merely to emphasise the request for more Septrin made in the prior turn by her husband. As the pharmacist begins to hand over the medication (line 32), the mother fails to recognise one of the bottles and asks 'What's that one' (line 35): she is answered by both the pharmacist and her husband in unison. The overall impression gained from this consultation then, is that the father has a greater degree of competence with (and familiarity regarding) his daughter's medication than does the mother. Even the knowledge which the mother does display about her child is confirmed by her husband, as in line 43. In contrast to what might be expected from Strong's findings, this division of expertise does not appear to be problematic for any of the participants in the encounter. However, it is difficult to draw any conclusions from this since it is the only instance in the data where both parents are present and there are thus no other consultations for comparison. Nevertheless, it is interesting to note that in both this consultation and the previous one, both the father and the elder brother are clearly regular representatives for the respective patients at the clinic. It seems at least plausible that this may account for at least some of the deviation from the pattern that might be expected.

The use of jargon by patients and carers
The consultations also raise interesting issues around the use of jargon; in this case medical, technical terms. Meehan (1981), in his consideration of the use of medical terms by doctors and patients, draws on Barnlund's (1976) suggestion that the use of jargon between members of a group can increase efficiency of communication, cultivate a rapport amongst members and provide a sense of common identity. Moreover, the use of jargon in communication with outsiders is most often characterised as having *negative* effects, so that in a technical, medical sense, to assume professional ownership of such a language precludes the possibility of patient understanding. However, as is clear from these data, in this setting patients and/or carers themselves commonly use technical terms, and pharmacists appear to treat this body of knowledge as something which the patient has access to. There is little use of mitigators, qualifiers or questioning intonation around the terms, or any other interactional contingencies which might serve to suggest that the patient has limited access to this language, as the extract below clearly illustrates.

```
38: jb/nc/op (simplified transcript)
1 Ph:    50 per cent then (.) for a week
2        (0.3)
3 M:     Yeah
4 Ph:    Count's up again is it?
5        (0.2)
6 M:     No (.) it's down (.) He was on 150 last week
```

Here the participants are discussing the tailoring of medication dosage to the patient's white blood cell count, but considering this extract in isolation there is perhaps little to suggest it is a professional/client encounter as opposed to a discussion between two professionals. Since jargon may be seen in this way as a claim to knowledge, this use of technical as opposed to vernacular vocabulary by both parties is one sense in which the 'knowledge-based asymmetry' of the model professional/client encounter may be eroded. Significantly, on the occasions where pharmacists refrain from using technical terms, this is often countered somewhat by the patient or carer, as below:

```
Transcript 38: jb/nc/op (simplified transcript)
57 Ph:   Does he take the (.) medicines OK?
58 M:    He doesn't like the methotrexate
59 Ph:   Oh the (.) once a week one
60 M:    Mmmmm (.) He doesn't like that very much
61 Ph:   Does it taste significantly different?
62 M:    I don't know (.) I've no [idea (.) he doesn't like steroids
63 Ph:                            [He must know though
64       (0.7)
```

65 M: He doesn't like [steroids either that is (.)
66 Ph: [Oh yeah
67 M: but I have tried [that (.) that's horrible
68 Ph: [That's (.) looking at this he's OK with the one he
69   has to take every day then isn't it?
70 M: Yeah (.) Yeah (.) and the Septrin he's alright with that as well

In this extract the pharmacist continually uses 'lay' terms to describe the patient's chemotherapy regime to the mother, for example 'medicines' (line 57), 'the once a week one' (line 59) and 'the one he has to take every day' (lines 68–69). The mother responds to this by using the names of the actual drug or class of drug in response; 'methotrexate' in line 58, 'steroids' in line 62, and 'Septrin' in line 70. Thus, although she does not actually contradict the pharmacist's terminology at any point, her utterances serve to make it perfectly clear that the use of jargon is not in any way problematic for her. In this instance then, any criticism of the pharmacist is implicit; on occasion it can become more explicit, as below. (although here the criticism is not so much related to the terminology which is used in the course of the explanation, but rather to the more general form in which the explanation is provided):

Transcript 12:-gg/op/be (simplified transcript)
23 Ph: Right (0.5) Uh:hm (.) do you want me to explain your tablets cos
        they're not
24   [in blisters to you
25 C: [No:o I know what to do
26   (0.5)
27 Ph: You know what to do with them all (1.2) Right so you've got all
        those for your mercaptopurine (1.1) [Two of them
29 C: [What do I do take (0.5)
        two of them and what d' ya call it
30   one of them each?
31   (0.6)
32 Ph: Hold on (.) you take two of the 10mg each morn[ing (0.2) =
33 C: [Yeah
34 Ph: = that's two of the little ones [(0.5) two of the 50mg =
35 C: [yeah
36 Ph: =(0.7) 't's two of those (.) and one of the half tablets it's already
37   halved (1.5) o[kay?
38 C: [Yeah yeah = yeah = ye'
39 Ph: so that makes you a total of 145mg
40   (0.2)
41 C: Oh (0.4) Why didn't you just say that
42   (1.0)
43 Ph: Pardon?

44 C: Why didn't you just say that I would have remembered that
45 Ph: OK Right (.) Well (1.0) and you've got your methotrex[ate
46 C: [Yeah

In this case then, the patient is explicitly critical of the way his dosage details
are presented to him by the pharmacist ('Why didn't you just say that' in
line 41 is his immediate response to the conclusion of her first segment of
information). In this way the patient manages to provide for the fact that his
apparent ignorance (which is ostensibly assumed by his lack of response at
the pause in line 27 and demonstrated by his utterance in line 29) is related
to the way in which the details that have been presented to him, rather than
existing as a phenomenon in itself. The pharmacist acknowledges his complaint, albeit minimally, in line 45, and then begins to proceed with the next
segment of the dosage details, concerning the methotrexate.

The continual negotiation of knowledge claims

It is thus becoming evident that a collaborative process of sustaining an
apparently common body of knowledge does not necessarily hold firm
throughout the encounters. Instead, it is continually established and reestab-
lished according to local contingencies, underlining the nature of asymmetry
as an interactional achievement. The following (complete) encounter serves
to illustrate more fully the ways in which pharmacists and their clinic clients
move into and out of a shared footing of knowledge, or a shared orientation
to the activity of the here and now.

13:-lc/op/ be
1 Ph: Prescription for (name)?(1.6)(Name)? Anyone else down
          there(.)
2   No? (to other non-clinic patient) Are you being seen to by the
3   way? (Response unclear) (.)
4   Prescription for (name)? (2.1) Excuse me sniffing (.)
5 Ph: I've [just had a burst of the sneezes
6 M: [It's alright (laughs)
7 Ph: Now first of all I've got to apologise we haven't got any blisters at
8   the moment =
9 M: [That's alright
10 Ph: = [They're somewhere between here and America
11   (0.2)
12 M: Oh right!
13 Ph: I'd love to know where [(laughs) hopefully they'll be in for
14 M: [(laughs)
15 Ph: next time you come back =
16 M: = Right
17 Ph: (name)'s coming back in a week that's [right isn't it
18 M: [Yeah (.) Yeah (. . .)

19 Ph: Yeah and she's had her vincristine hasn't she
20   (.)
21 M: yes
22 Ph: today(.) so she's got her prednisolone to go with her
        vincristine (.)
23 M: Yeah
24   (0.7)
25 Ph: It's just 25mg tablets (0.6) one to be taken each morning and
26   = [night
27 M: [night yeah
28 Ph: Right that's just for 4 days (0.7) a:and (.) she's got her mercaptop
29   urine here (.) 2 of the 50mgs each morning starting tomorrow
30   (0.5)
31 M: Yeah
32   (0.7)
33 Ph: and one of the halved (.)
34   [they've already been halved for you
35 M: [Oh right yeah(.)oh right yeah(.)good yeah two and a
        [half each morning =
36 Ph: [so that makes your 125
37   = hundred and twenty five
38 M: Right
39   (0.5)
40 Ph: Uhh (.) What's next oh the methotrexate (.) two to be taken on
        Wednesday
41 Ph: the thirteenth of the sixth the 10s ( ) and two of the 2.5s =
42 M: = Right so that doesn't go up then it's only the
43   (0.2)
44 Ph: No (.) once you get to 100% your methotrexate doesn't increase
45   (0.2)
46 M: Right
47 Ph: You only increase your mercaptopurine (0.5) OK?
48 M: Right (.) yeah
49   (0.4)
50   As I say it's the first time she's got =
51 Ph: = Is it the first time she's gone up that high (.) Oh right
52   that must be a good sign =
53 M: = (I don't need) the uhhh dropper for Septrin she is must be
        about
54   uhhh *three* months now (I think)
55 Ph: *Oh* right
56 M: She's having uhh (.) pentamidine (.)
57 Ph: instead of Septrin 'cos she didn't respond very
        [well to it?
58 M: [Well no we was just

```
59        forever going (.) right down off treatment altogether and going =
60        = [back to 50 again
61 Ph:    [right
62 M:     and definitely (.) well this certainly does seem to be working
63        [better
64 Ph:    [seems to be working (.) excellent (unclear . . .)
65 Ph:    Well that's a good sign anyway isn't it?
66 M:     That's right
67 Ph:    OK well I'll see you next week then
68 M:     OK (. . [ . . .)
69 Ph:         [Right (.) bye bye
70 M:     Thank you
```

In the first part of this consultation (down to line 42), there is little interactional contribution from the mother. However, a range of technical, medical terms are used by the pharmacist, none of which are treated (by either participant) as problematic; instead they are seemingly treated as common knowledge. Although there is little in the way of asymmetry in this 'knowledge-based' sense apparent in the opening of this encounter, there are nevertheless the manifestations of a different kind of asymmetry in evidence, in the sense of interactional dominance. In this particular encounter, the pharmacist begins by explaining (in lines 7–8) that the patient's medication will be presented in a different form from usual; in individual bottles rather than in a 'blister' pack which contains each day's dosages already counted out and compartmentalised into the appropriate section for day, date and time of day. The packaging of the tablets in bottles in this instance renders the mother's knowledge and/or competence of administration using the blister packs redundant. Having accounted for a reason why dosage details are necessary on this occasion, the pharmacist is then able to proceed with this information, beginning at line 22. Even this informing segment, however, is framed in terms of the mother's knowledge of other events, such as when the child is next due to attend clinic (line 17), and the injection she has just been given (line 19). The pharmacist then displays each individual bottle to the mother in turn, describing the instructions for each, and the mother acknowledges each component of these instructions, for example by resummarising the pharmacist's utterance, as in line 35. This section of the encounter then, from lines 22–41, appears to proceed along the 'standard' lines of a typical lay/professional encounter, in that the talk is dominated by the pharmacist, the mother's utterances are limited to responses or reactions to the pharmacist's talk, and there are clear distinctions between the professional and non-professional party. The interactional dominance (and submission on the part of the mother) that is apparent here manifests itself in the way in which the pharmacist initiates the topics for discussion, and thus sets the 'agenda' for the initial stages of this encounter. Interestingly, this agenda is itself explicitly invoked in the talk by the use of the statement 'first of all' at line 7; this leads into the topicalisation of item-by-item instructions for the medication.

In line 42, however, the mother begins to demonstrate her knowledge, by picking up on the fact that although the rest of the dosage regimen has changed, the dose of one drug (methotrexate) has remained the same. Having solicited an explanation from the pharmacist for this (lines 42–47), she begins to account for her question, by beginning to state that this is the first time that the child has received full strength chemotherapy. She then goes on to inform the pharmacist that a dropper for Septrin (an antibiotic syrup) is not necessary, as her daughter is receiving a different (nebulised) antibiotic. The pharmacist's utterance 'Oh right' in line 55 marks this as newsworthy, and she then questions the mother further about this; the explanation (line 58–60) provided by the mother is couched in technical terms and is followed by an assessment of the new therapy ('Well this certainly does seem to be working better'). This second section of the interaction, then, proceeds in a much more collaborative manner. Not only is the mother displaying knowledge that the pharmacist does not appear to be party to, but the interactional dominance by the pharmacist which characterised the first segment of the interaction has largely been eroded. Significantly, it is the mother's initial *demonstration*[2] of knowledge in line 42 which heralds the move towards this more symmetrical *interactional* alignment.

Conclusions

This last encounter underlines the ways in which interactional manifestations of knowledge and competence are continually negotiated by the participants in this setting in ways that tend to minimise the asymmetry that is commonly seen in the doctor/patient encounter, or indeed in other lay/professional encounters. This is evident both in the interactional dominance sense (related as this appears to be to the 'task' of the encounter for the pharmacist) and in the knowledge-based sense. Although features of knowledge-based asymmetry are sometimes evident in the data, they are rarely sustained for any length of time; even when 'new' information is imparted by the pharmacist, the ability of the patient or carer to relate this to the knowledge they already have has a minimising effect. This body of knowledge which the patient is party to in turn has an effect on the interactional dominance commonly exhibited by the professional party in lay/professional encounters. Thus, Heath's (1992) assertion that, through talk, patients preserve the differential status between their own and professional understandings of their complaint, in order to prevent an undermining of their grounds for seeking help, does not appear to apply entirely to these data. Patients' descriptions of their conditions or treatment in this setting are frequently couched in the same terms as those used by pharmacists, and they are not hesitant to draw their own conclusions or make their own assessments as to how a particular treatment is working or how the use of a particular drug should be tailored to their circumstances. It seems, for a variety of reasons, that the 'ownership' of a long term disease such as leukaemia is greater for patients or carers than that of an episodic illness, and that this in turn has an effect on the differential status between 'lay' and 'professional' understandings.

The issue of 'interactional submission'

Much consideration has been given in these data to the ways in which patients and carers display their knowledge, and the ways in which pharmacists appear to defer to this. However, whilst patients and/or carers appear to demonstrate their knowledge and competence freely throughout the encounter, even in instances where pharmacists do not appear to be responding to this, the notion of 'interactional submission' would still seem to have some relevance. As ten Have (1991) suggests of the doctor/patient interaction, and as has been suggested briefly here, to some extent this may be due to task distribution; the pharmacist may need to establish certain facts, such as the date for the next clinic attendance, any medication received that day etc, or more generally to give instructions and hand over medication, which necessitates periods of interactional dominance. The interactional dominance on the part of the pharmacist which occurs in this setting, in terms of both initiation and agenda, is thus often clearly 'justified' in the talk (through its reference to future arrangements, changes to therapy etc) and by the physical task (since the handing over of bottles is used to facilitate information sequences). The actual interactional task (advising or informing) is less clearly justified in this way because of the issues of knowledge and competence it invokes. Despite their (often apparent) knowledge, patients or carers seem prepared to accept this 'control' of the encounter by the pharmacist, to the extent that they are sometimes prepared to accept a whole package of partly unnecessary details on the initiative of the pharmacist, rather than raising specific questions themselves.

Returning to a consideration of knowledge, the access to the medical technical language of the clinic that is continually demonstrated by the clients appears to play a key role in achieving the more broadly symmetrical footing that appears to exist. This in turn raises the question of what can actually be seen to count as 'jargon' in a particular setting, since neither of the parties in the majority of these interactions appears to treat medical, technical terms as part of a specialised vocabulary. In the context of repeated visits to institutions such as hospitals, terminology that is initially unknown to lay participants gradually becomes known, and thus ceases to become jargon in the exclusive sense. Patients and carers also become gradually familiarised with clinic procedures and how these are organised, and use this knowledge to inform their encounters with clinic personnel. Professionals in these settings, as here, respond to this, and the use of technical terms thus becomes a means by which patients or carers can display their knowledge. It would be interesting to discover whether consultations between doctors and long term patients exhibit similar features in terms of this displayed knowledge or expertise, and if so, how this is constituted within the interaction.

The extent to which this diminished interactional asymmetry may be accounted for by differential professional status (*i.e.* pharmacists as opposed to clinicians) is also worth further consideration. It has been suggested earlier that asymmetrical interaction is in part a result of the contingencies of the doctor/patient encounter, arising as a way of handling the interactional difficulties the encounter presents. In the sense of Bloor and Horobin's (1975) 'double-bind' situation, however, long term patients on return clinic visits have not used their own judgement as to when it is appropriate to seek medical advice, although they are still expected to defer to the doctor's judgement when undergoing treatment. Long term patients' encounters with pharmacists differ further, in that the pharmacist is in a sense the facilitator of the doctor's judgement regarding medication; whilst it is the patient's condition under review, it is not in any substantial sense the pharmacist who reviews it. Since pharmacists (in hospitals at least) are not required to diagnose illnesses, but instead provide drug therapy for patients who have already received an assessment of their condition, the 'double-bind' situation as described by Bloor and Horobin (1975) as existing in doctor/patient consultations is largely irrelevant here. The input of the pharmacist is mainly concerned with assisting the patient in carrying out the doctor's medication instructions; any 'review' occurs in relation to reported difficulties in so doing. What remains, however, is the asymmetry of task distribution seen in medical encounters, although here it is related to dispensing rather than diagnosis. It is asymmetry in this task-related sense that is most apparent in these oncology clinic encounters; the suggested interactional dominance of the pharmacist in the initial phase of the extract above is strongly related to dispensing contingencies. Thus, since the pharmacist has a particular task to accomplish (handing over the medications) and the patient or carer has visited the pharmacist primarily to receive this medication, for the pharmacists to direct or 'dominate' the encounter is perhaps the easiest method to ensure that this is brought about swiftly and successfully for both parties. Whilst the physical component of this task, the dispensing, is clearly in the domain of the pharmacist alone, the interactional component of advising or informing, drawing as it does on potentially mutual knowledge, is less sharply defined. Asymmetries of knowledge in this setting are both less evident, and much more fluid, reflecting the shared body of experience and competence with chemotherapy medication that exists between the pharmacist and the long term oncology patient.

Acknowledgements

The author would like to extend her grateful thanks to Robert Dingwall and Anssi Perakyla for their insightful comments on the theory and the data of this paper respectively, and to the two anonymous referees whose suggestions helped to shape the final version. This paper uses data collected for a study funded by the Department of Health Enterprise Scheme.

Notes

1   The drug card contains a week by week description of the planned regime for a particular condition, and is therefore subject to alteration as a result of the patient's white blood cell count, nausea, general well being etc. Any such alterations are made by the doctor at the clinic visit and marked on the card. Thus, the pharmacist can tell by looking at the card if this has occurred. Additionally, it is entirely possible that a carer, because of previous experience and a firsthand knowledge of a child's condition over the previous week, may be 'expecting' a change in therapy on arrival at the clinic.
2   A demonstration of knowledge is not presumed to be the only purpose, or even the intended purpose of this utterance. However, just as it partly characterises a lack of knowledge, it also characterises some degree of knowledge on which the query is based.

References

Barnlund, D.C. (1976) The mystification of meaning: doctor-patient encounters, *Journal of Medical Education*, 51, 716–27.

Bloor, M.J. and Horobin, G.W. (1975) Conflict and conflict resolution in doctor/patient interaction. In Cox, C. and Mead, A. (eds) *A Sociology of Medical Practice*. London: Collier-MacMillan.

Bogoch, B. (1994) Power, distance and solidarity-models of professional client interaction in an Israeli legal aid setting, *Discourse and Society*, 5, 1, 65–88.

Davis, K. (1988) *Power under the Microscope*. Dordrecht: Foris.

Frankel, R. (1995) Some answers about questions in clinical interviews. In Morris, G.H. and Chenail, R.J. (eds) *The Talk of the Clinic: Explorations in the Analysis of Medical and Therapeutic Discourse*. Hove: Lawrence Erlbaum Associates.

Freidson, E. (1973) *Profession of Medicine: A Study of the Sociology of Applied Knowledge*. New York: Dodd, Mead and Company.

Heath, C. (1992) The delivery and reception of diagnosis in the general-practice consultation. In Drew, P. and Heritage, J. (eds) *Talk at Work: Interaction in Institutional Settings*. Cambridge: Cambridge University Press.

Heritage, J. and Sefi, S. (1992) Dilemmas of advice: aspects of the delivery and reception of advice between health visitors and first time mothers. In Drew, P. and Heritage, J. (eds) *Talk at Work: Interaction in Institutional Settings*. Cambridge: Cambridge University Press.

Hutchby, I. (1996) Power in discourse: the case of arguments on a British talk radio show, *Discourse and Society*, 7, 4, 481–97.

Macintyre, S. and Oldman, D. (1977) Coping with migraine. In Davis, A. and Horobin, G. (eds) *Medical Encounters: the Experience of Illness and Treatment*. London: Croom Helm.

Maynard, D. (1991) Interaction and asymmetry in clinical discourse, *American Journal of Sociology*, 97, 2, 448–95.

Meehan, A.J. (1981) Some conversational features of the use of medical terms by doctors and patients. In Atkinson, P. and Heath, C. (eds) *Medical Work: Realities and Routines,* Westmead: Gower Ltd.

Morrow, N., Hargie, O., Donnelly, H. *et al.* (1993) 'Why do you ask?' A study of questioning behaviour in community pharmacist-client consultations, *International Journal of Pharmacy Practice*, 2, 90–4.

Sharrock, W. (1979) Portraying the professional relationship. In Anderson, D.C. (ed.) *Health Education in Practice*. London: Croom Helm.

Silverman, D. (1987) *Communication and Medical Practice*. London: Sage.

Smith, F.J. and Salkind, M.R. (1990) Presentation of clinical symptoms to community pharmacists in London, *Journal of Social and Administrative Pharmacy*, 7, 4, 221–4.

Strong, P. (1979) *The Ceremonial Order of the Clinic*. London: Routledge.

ten Have, P. (1991) Talk and institution: a reconsideration of the 'asymmetry' of doctor-patient interaction. In Boden, D. and Zimmerman, D. (eds) *Talk and Social Structure: Studies in Ethnomethodology and Conversation Analysis*. Cambridge: Polity Press.

West, P. (1976) The physician and the management of childhood epilepsy. In Wadsworth, M. and Robinson, D. (eds) *Studies in Everyday Medical Life*. London: Martin Robertson.

Zimmerman, D. (1992) The interactional organization of calls for emergency assistance. In Drew, P. and Heritage, J. (eds) *Talk at Work: Interaction in Institutional Settings*. Cambridge: Cambridge University Press.

4.3

Fear and loathing in health care settings reported by people with HIV

Gill Green and Stephen Platt

Introduction

Stigma, or rather the degree to which an identity is spoiled as a result of having an illness, is a key variable in the social construction of illness. It functions independently of the biophysical reality of illness and is an important aspect of the social experience of illness (Williams 1987). Many people with stigmatising conditions try to conceal or 'pass' to avoid being discredited. In health care settings where they are receiving treatment this is usually neither possible nor desirable as the condition is normally noted in patient files in order that carers may provide the most suitable treatment. Health care workers (HCWs) are therefore privy to potentially discrediting information about their clients and may be among the very few, possibly the only, people who know of their stigmatising illness. The onus this places on HCWs to maintain client confidentiality has been recognised. What is less well understood is that their reaction to the patient is an important aspect of the patient's social experience of illness.

A stigmatising reaction by HCWs is potentially socially very damaging as HCWs are supposed to be knowledgeable about and familiar with illness and to care for people who are ill. They are expected to be among those whom Goffman (1963: 41) has called the 'wise', namely persons 'whose special situation has made them intimately privy to the life of the stigmatized individual and sympathetic with it.' Yet health policy and practice are deeply embedded in general cultural values and medical models and attitudes reflect lay values, beliefs and attitudes (Scambler 1984). HCWs are individuals who share societal norms and attitudes and may not be 'wise' about all stigmatised conditions. There is evidence that HCWs may have limited understanding about the psychological and social complexities of many conditions (*e.g.* dwarfism, see Ablon 1981), and social interactions between 'normal' HCWs and 'spoiled' patients with a stigmatising illness will be as marked by social disruption as they are in other settings.

Negative reactions or tactless comments from HCWs have been identified as a potential source of trauma. For example, the most traumatic aspects of the birth and development of dwarf children may be related to doctors' ill-advised statements to the family (Ablon 1981), a mother of a girl with neurofibromatosis fainted when a doctor told her her daughter had 'Elephant Man's' disease (Ablon 1995), and people with epilepsy reported that the doctor's diagnosis and pronouncement on the disease labelled them and 'made them into epileptics' (Scambler 1984:213). HCWs thus not only treat the physical manifestations of disease but also may be instrumental in shaping the social adaptation of patients who have a stigmatising disease, a task for which they are given very limited training.

Goffman (1963) has described how stigmatised persons incorporate and internalise standards from wider society and discredit themselves. Self hatred and shame develop from internalising negative values. The discrepancy between what is expected in a normal individual and what is actual in a stigmatised individual 'spoils' the social identity and isolates the stigmatised individual from self as well as social acceptance (Alonzo and Reynolds 1995). Negative attitudes among the general public towards stigmatised people are thus important sources of stigma, and serve to pattern the individual's self-conception in a self-fulfilling manner (Williams 1987).

In the late twentieth century, seropositivity is one of the most stigmatised health conditions. The negative symbolism of AIDS is a result of cultural processes whereby boundaries are drawn between the 'healthy self' and the 'unhealthy other' who is diseased, contagious, sexually deviant and addicted (Crawford 1994). Seropositives (i.e. people with HIV) are stigmatised because the illness is associated with deviant behaviour, is viewed as the responsibility of the individual, tainted with immorality, perceived as contagious and associated with unaesthetic death. It is not well understood and is viewed negatively by health care providers (Alonzo and Reynolds 1995). Whilst these traits may be associated with many illnesses, the fact that HIV has been most prevalent in Europe and North America among gay men and drug users who were already targets of prejudice (Herek and Glunt 1989) means that people with HIV are linked with 'deviant' behaviour and are 'doubly stigmatised' (Kowalewski 1988). Stigma has also been shown in general to be greater where the stigmatised have a contagious disease which poses a danger to others (Jones et al. 1984), and where blame may be attached to a person's condition (Jones et al. 1984, De Jong 1980). People with HIV who have been infected sexually or through sharing needles to inject drugs are thus particularly vulnerable to 'victim-blaming'. Stigma may be 'felt' or 'enacted', a distinction which was first recognised among people with epilepsy (Scambler and Hopkins 1986). Enacted stigma refers to sanctions that are individually or collectively applied to people with a condition, while felt stigma relates to feelings of shame and an oppressive fear of enacted stigma. Both enacted and felt stigma have been reported among people with HIV (see Green 1995b).

Drawing upon interviews with seropositives in Scotland, three sources of stigma among people with HIV have been identified (Green 1995a), which broadly conform to the biomedical and metaphorical meanings of HIV/ AIDS identified by Crawford (1994). They include 'cognitive aspects' (a belief that seropositives are intrinsically 'bad' or at least different from others), 'blame aspects' (a belief that seropositives are responsible for their condition), and 'treatment or restriction aspects' (a belief that seropositives should have their behaviour restricted so that they do not threaten others with HIV transmission). Although the majority of the general population does not subscribe to such beliefs, attitude surveys report that there is a small minority that holds very hostile views towards seropositives and such views are occasionally widely publicised in sections of the media. As a result, hostile attitudes are perceived by seropositives and the general population to be widely held (Green 1995a).

There are several studies about the knowledge and behaviour of HCWs in treating seropositives. Throughout the world concerns have been reported across all health care professions about treating people with HIV/AIDS (e.g. hospital physicians, nurses and social workers in Chicago (Dworkin et al. 1991), GPs in Marseilles (Morin et al. 1995), dental and medical students in Pittsburgh (Weyant et al. 1994), physicians, nurses and technologists in Ontario (Taerk et al. 1993), undertakers in the East End of London (Howard 1993)). Such studies consistently report that a major barrier to the treatment of people with HIV among HCWs is fear of infection. This is found to have a greater effect than other identified barriers such as homophobia, dislike of drug users, economic factors related to the cost of treatment seropositives, or AIDS being a terminal illness (Taerk et al. 1993, Weyant et al. 1994, Dworkin et al. 1991, Ross and Hunter 1991). In Britain, the Hospital Infection Society and the Surgical Study Infection Group (1992) were sufficiently concerned to convene a workshop and issue guidelines to minimise the occupational risk of infection from HIV and hepatitis. Fear of infection is largely related to the procedures involved in the care of patients with HIV, and HCWs who practise the most invasive procedures, report the highest level of concern (Dworkin et al. 1991, Weyant et al. 1994, Ross and Hunter 1991). The level of fear is thus very dependent upon the situational context, and perception of risk is related to actual risk. Counteracting this trend, however, is the fact that familiarity with a practice makes it routine and less likely to be considered a risk. Thus HCWs who have most experience in treating seropositives and who therefore have a higher actual risk tend to have a diminished perception of risk (Kunzel and Sadowsky 1993) and less fear of infection (Gallop et al. 1991). Studies of HCWs tend to be cross-sectional, making it difficult to assess changes over time. However, the most recent literature reports less fear from HCWs and the issuing of standard guidelines has doubtless led to a greater standardisation of practice and less stigmatising behaviour. It is therefore likely that stigma towards people with HIV has decreased over time.

Testimonies from people with HIV and their informal carers cite instances of stigmatisation from HCWs; for example, the doctor who wrote without his patient's knowledge or consent to 'warn her employers' (anon 1992), being in hospital and made to use a separate toilet with 'control of infection' on it (Richardson and Bolle 1992). Such experiences, or even just hearing about them, may deter seropositives from consulting HCWs. Gay men in London for example showed a degree of reluctance to register or consult a

GP (Wandsworth and McCann 1992). Many specialist units for seropositives have arisen largely to avoid stigmatising behaviour from HCWs, and satisfaction of patients utilising such units tends to be high. For example, seropositives attending a dedicated dental clinic were as satisfied as seronegatives attending a general dental practice staffed by the same personnel (Robinson and Croucher 1994, see also Cleary *et al*. 1992). There is concern, however, that specialist units are themselves stigmatised which may deter seropositives from attending.

HIV-related stigma has to be addressed by people with HIV in all their social relationships, including those with health professionals with whom they come into contact. There is concern that stigma may have a negative effect upon the relationship between seropositives and their care-givers in health care settings, and deter people with HIV from seeking health care. This paper aims to examine how stigma affects the relationship between people with HIV and HCWs and to identify the mechanisms through which it operates in health care settings in Scotland. What constitutes stigmatising behaviour and what forms does it take? How does this relate to the wider theoretical background about processes of stigmatisation?

Methods

Given the extreme difficulty of recruiting people with HIV into this type of study, we deliberately decided to use a theoretical or 'purposive' sample. Although respondents were not selected at random, considerable care was taken to include all transmission groups and recruit from a variety of settings, thus maximising the representativeness of the group. Recruitment was carried out in a number of diverse settings, including outpatient clinics, prisons, drug rehabilitation units, general practices, self-help and voluntary support organisations. The recruitment procedure varied in each setting according to the advice and requirements of the 'gate-keepers' in each organisation who controlled access. In some settings we were able to recruit directly. More often, however, the gate-keeper arranged a meeting after having obtained verbal consent from the respondent. All respondents gave written consent to participate in the study before being interviewed. They were interviewed twice at annual intervals between 1991 and 1992 (N = 61 in the first interview, N = 40 in the second). The high rate of attrition is accounted for by deaths between interviews (N = 7) and the number of respondents who either could not be contacted or did not wish to be interviewed again (N = 14). This latter group included 9 of the men who had been recruited in prison, 6 of whom had been released between interviews. For reason of confidentiality, the follow-up of non-respondents was sometimes less stringent than reported for other studies. For example, if respondents failed to respond to letters and/or phone calls requesting another interview, we considered it unethical to call round uninvited. Characteristics of the sample at

Table 1 *Description of the sample at both points of contact (1991/92 and 92/93)*

	1991/92		1992/93	
	n	%	*n*	%
Sex				
Male	50	82	31	78
Female	11	18	9	22
Age	32		32	
(mean and range)	(21–49)		(21–49)	
Transmission group				
Gay men	12	20	10	25
Drug users	29	48	13	33
Haemophiliac	10	16	10	25
Other	10	16	7	17
Stage of illness				
Asymptomatic	47	77	32	80
Symptomatic	6	10	4	10
AIDS	8	13	4	10
Year of diagnosis	1987		1987	
(mean and range)	(1983–1991)		(1983–1991)	
Total	61		40	

time of first and second contact are shown in Table 1 and discussed in the next section. The data presented in this paper are based on both the first and second interviews.

Respondents were interviewed at home, in the researchers' office, or recruitment centre by one of two researchers (the authors). Interviewer consistency and reliability were checked frequently in meetings between the two researchers and by exchanging interview schedules, transcripts and notes. The section on health care was part of a longer interview about the psychosocial impact of living with HIV. In the first interview semi-structured questions were used to ask about contact with health services in the previous year: which services had been consulted, how often, and the overall impression of the treatment they received. We encouraged respondents to elaborate upon their answers. Using these responses we devised an instrument to use in the follow-up interview to measure satisfaction with health services following diagnosis. We asked respondents to list all hospitals and hospital departments where they had received treatment since diagnosis, and all general practitioners and dentists that they had consulted. They were asked to rate satisfaction (on a 5-point Likert scale: very satisfied, satisfied, mixed feelings, dissatisfied, very dissatisfied) with each institution about four aspects of care: satisfaction with overall treatment, knowledge and understanding of

HIV, the quality and amount of information they had been given about HIV, and the measures taken to ensure confidentiality. These responses were condensed using the Multiple Response facility in SPSS (Norusis 1993).

Respondents were also asked whether any GP or dentist had ever refused to treat them. After each series of questions, *i.e.* about in-patient, out-patient, GP and dental care, respondents were asked if they had experienced any problems with any aspect of their care, and were asked to elaborate. This combination of data-collection techniques (set questions leading to an open-ended discussion) facilitated recall on the part of the respondents and provided useful prompts for the interviewer to initiate a more open discussion. As a result of the information we had gathered in the first interview about the individuals and their collective experience of health care, the data gathered in the second interviews tended to be of greater depth. In both the first and second interviews the semi-structured questioning was either tape-recorded or extensive notes were taken and these were entered onto a software computer programme for qualitative data analysis (Ethnograph, see Seidel *et al.* 1988).

In general a grounded theory approach guided data collection and analysis. In particular we would emphasise our use of theoretical sampling and the development of theory in intimate relationship with the data (see Glaser and Strauss 1968). Stigma was rapidly identified as a core variable in interactions between people with HIV and HCWs. Subsequent categories emerged and were elaborated in systematic examination and re-examination of the data. Data relating to HCWs' fear of treating people with HIV were most prevalent (44 specific instances cited). These data were then re-examined to identify the various dimensions of this concept, *e.g.* HCWs dressed as spacemen, barrier nursing, refusal to give treatment. A second category (20 specific instances cited) related solely to the social stigma of HIV in that it appeared to be unrelated to its infectivity. Important features were the double stigma of HIV (because of its association with gay men and injecting drug users) and the subsequent stigmatisation of all people with HIV and places where they were treated, particularly those centres that specialised exclusively in HIV. A third important category (25 specific incidents cited) related to issues of confidentiality and further analysis linked this to health care practice concerning patient care. The best 'fit' of the data was achieved by the use of these three categories which form the framework for the discussion of qualitative results below. Other categories, identified in the analysis but unrelated to HIV, are mentioned below but not discussed in detail. Examples of *all* categories are to be found in the accounts of members of *all* transmission groups in all health care settings, although some variation was noted (see below).

Many of the key concepts are illustrated through the use of quotations from respondents. These are important since the empirical focus of this paper is the perceptions of people with HIV. They should not, however, be accepted uncritically; they may not necessarily given an 'objectively' accurate account. Many respondents were reporting retrospectively on incidents which happened long ago. As such their reliability is only as good as respondents' memory, which is likely to retain selectively the less pleasant experiences. The impact of felt stigma upon people with HIV and the fear of enacted stigma which accompanies it also have to be considered. Negative incidents may well be wrongly attributed by respondents to their HIV status.

The sample

Respondents were all living in the central belt of Scotland and were white. The majority were male although about one-fifth were female at both interviews. They were mostly in their late twenties and early thirties (mean age 32). Representatives of all the main transmission groups were included (gay men, injecting drug users, people with haemophilia and people who believed they had been infected heterosexually). Initially, almost one-half of the sample were current or ex-injecting drug users, but due to a higher rate of attrition among drug users, the proportion fell to less than one-third in the second interview. About 10 per cent of the sample had experienced symptoms of HIV disease and about 10 per cent had an AIDS diagnosis. The mean year of diagnosis of seropositivity was 1987 (range 1983–91), and most respondents had been living with HIV for a few years. Some, however, had been diagnosed only a few months prior to the first interview (Table 1).

Satisfaction rating

Much dissatisfaction in all health care settings was reported by respondents about various aspects of treatment (Table 2). (Those labelled dissatisfied in this table do not include those who reported they had 'mixed feelings', although their subsequent reasons for having 'mixed feelings' were included in the qualitative analysis.) With the exception of confidentiality procedures, where the level of dissatisfaction was somewhat lower, respondents were dissatisfied with about one-third of hospitals where they had been in-patients, about one-sixth of out-patient departments and about one-quarter of GPs and dentists whom they had consulted. Dissatisfaction with health visitors was much lower. The underlying cause of dissatisfaction was investigated, using semi-structured techniques in both the first and second interviews. In the course of the two interviews, 127 specific causes of dissatisfaction were reported by 47 people in the sample. The level of dissatisfaction expressed is considerably greater than that generated by most studies of satisfaction with care where the answers tend to be generally approving. It should, however, be noted that negative results are in the minority. Because of the focus upon problems and difficulties which had been experienced, the negative results are (over)emphasised. Positive aspects of care are not discussed in detail,

Table 2 *Proportion of health care contacts with which respondents were dissatisfied*

	Proportion of health care contacts for which respondents dissatisfied with overall treatment		Proportion of health care contacts for which respondents rate carers' knowledge of HIV to be poor		Proportion of health care contacts for which respondents dissatisfied with quality of info given about HIV		Proportion of health care contacts for which respondents unhappy with confidentiality procedures	
	n*	%	n*	%	n*	%	n*	%
Hospital in-patient care	74	36.5	64	31.2	39	30.8	72	20.8
Hospital out-patient care	110	16.4	95	16.9	60	15	102	12.7
Health visitor	26	7.7	24	8.3	13	15.4	24	4.2
GP	83	25.3	68	27.9	18	22.3	83	12
Dentist	19	26.4	13	23.1	NA		13	7.7

* The 'n' figure = all the health care contacts which respondents reported having received treatment since diagnosis

although many respondents were positive about the health care they were receiving and were sometimes enthusiastic about certain aspects of their care or about individual HCWs. It should also be stated here that many incidents reported by respondents happened in the mid to late eighties when all health professionals were struggling to understand and deal with HIV/AIDS. It is clear that practice throughout the health care system regarding HIV has improved and become more informed since that time.

It was not possible to find statistical evidence of an association between dissatisfaction with care and specific characteristics of respondents, due to the limited functions that can be performed using the Multiple Response facility in SPSS and the relatively small sample size. Scrutiny of the data, however, suggests that those who had been diagnosed longest reported most stigmatising incidents due to the fact that they had had more contact with HCWs during the course of their illness, and because they had acquired greater familiarity with hospitals, and therefore had greater confidence to complain when they were dissatisfied with their treatment. For both these reasons, respondents with haemophilia (who were mostly diagnosed in the mid eighties and had had contact with hospitals since a very young age) tended to be fairly critical of health care. Older respondents complained more than younger ones, but younger respondents and those who were neither drug users nor gay were the most affected emotionally by HIV-related stigma from HCWs. Those with an AIDS diagnosis and particularly those nearing death tended to be very complimentary about their care.

Some of the explanations given for dissatisfaction were not specifically related to HIV, but were the kind of complaints which are commonly expressed by consumers of health care. There was, for example, annoyance expressed about a lack of continuity of care and having consultations with constantly changing junior doctors. There were also complaints about having to wait for a long time to see a doctor despite having a fixed appointment time, and respondents felt they sometimes had problems getting sufficient information about the course and development of their condition. Some of the drug users reported having arguments with their physician about the level of methadone they were prescribed. There was some concern, especially among those offered AZT, that they were being used as 'guinea pigs'. Despite the counselling services set up to support people with HIV, eight respondents reported that psychosocial support was inadequate, although almost an equal number singled this aspect out for praise. GPs were criticised for lack of knowledge or for complaining about the cost of certain treatments, but more often they were praised by respondents for their caring attitude or their willingness to learn and for 'doing their best'. Ninety-two (72 per cent) of the 127 specific incidents cited were related to the stigma of HIV, including issues concerning confidentiality.

Fear of contagion

HCWs were reported to show fear of infection in a number of settings and procedures. Respondents reported many incidents where HCWs had tried to avoid bodily contact with them either by refusing to treat them adequately, or by their wearing protective clothing. Some respondents also reported being placed in physical isolation in order to prevent them having contact with other patients.

Refusal to treat adequately
Two prisoners reported that non-essential surgical operations had been cancelled after the HCWs treating them were informed they were HIV-positive, and six respondents said they had been refused treatment by a GP and seven by a dentist. All these refusals were believed by respondents to be in response to their HIV-status. Refusals to treat were often subtle, as for example when a GP insisted a respondent move to another practice when she moved to another house. They were usually relatively polite, *e.g.* many community dentists routinely referred respondents to hospital dental departments after disclosure of HIV-status. Occasionally, however, rejection was reported to be overt and brutal, exemplified in the extract below, taken from an interview with an ex-drug user and recovering alcoholic, who was trying to find a GP:

R35:   Well I needed a doctor because I had moved into the area and I
went down to the doctor's surgery and I asked if I could become a
patient and the lady started to hand me, you know, like a form to
fill in and I says to her 'Oh I'm HIV positive' and she says 'oh I
don't know if Doctor will see you but take a seat'. So I sat down
beside the rest of the patients and this doctor comes just right
across to me, got me by here, the collar, and he says to me 'you'll
have to leave the surgery'.

This quotation is a good example of the need to adopt a critical approach
to the interpretation of respondents' accounts. This woman is reporting an
incident which happened many years previously. There is no mention of
whether or not she had been using drugs or alcohol at the time of the
incident nor whether she had been a previous patient at this GP surgery when
she was using drugs. Issues such as these need to be considered in all the
quotations cited in this paper, although this does not detract from the fact that
the quotes provide verbatim accounts of the perceptions of people with HIV.

Reluctance to treat was also reported by respondents, as illustrated by the
extract below from an ex-drug user who had sought treatment for an ear
infection at an Accident and Emergency Department and disclosed his
HIV-status to the doctor:

R1:   He did not want to touch me after that. He just said 'I am writing
you a prescription for antibiotics. Go to the Infectious Diseases
Hospital or your own doctor. I don't want anything to do with you
because I don't know anything about HIV.' I said 'I am not here
about HIV I am here about my ears.'

Respondents frequently reported HCWs' fear of touching them or their
bodily fluids, sometimes leaving them overnight in sheets bloodied from
treatment the previous day. Sleeping in sheets 'all covered in blood' was
reported by one woman after delivery of her baby. One prisoner, after such
an experience in a general hospital where he had had teeth extracted,
remarked 'I have never been so glad to get back to prison in my life.'

The 'spacemen'

Fear of infection was most dramatically illustrated by respondents' reports
of receiving treatment from HCWs 'dressed like spacemen'. Twenty one
individuals cited incidents which had involved HCWs either wearing what
was seen to be an unnecessary amount of protective clothing (far exceeding
gloves and a mask), or for their insensitivity in letting them see such clothing.

HCWs wearing space suits were most often reported where there was a
high risk of bodily contact with respondent's bodily fluids. The two extracts
below are from interviews with women, the first having teeth extracted in
jail, and the second with a gynaecological problem.

R30:   I've been in the jail to a dentist and he was like a spaceman.
That was before I got all my teeth out. He was all – all you could
see were his eyes through a wee plastic, like a wee windscreen thing
and it was all big boots and – but that was years ago.

R10:   They had on like these big masks, they had like big space suits on
and I was just thinking you know this is all because I'm HIV
positive and they must be terrified of it . . . I didn't agree with
the treatment I had got. OK if they want to take precautions
fine but why don't they put you to sleep before letting me actually
see that.

Respondents often reported that the use of protective clothing was unnecessary and cited, for example, having routine dental treatment by HCWs
'all gowned up like they were going to do a major operation'. They also
reported HCWs wearing spacesuits in situations where there was no risk of
infection:

R55:   When I went to the dentist there was this frigging nurse,
she never came anywhere near me and was all gowned up.
She wasn't even treating me and she was wearing two pairs of
gloves and wellingtons.

Fear of infection was thus reported as manifest among HCWs concerned in
procedures which involved contact with bodily fluids, but also was sometimes
reported in very low risk and no-risk situations. This fear was reported as
affecting all levels of HCWs from consultants to auxiliary staff. A gay man
reported that the surgeon operating on him was concerned that the theatre
porters might insist on wearing full protective clothing to wheel him to and
from the theatre.

Respondents were aware that during some medical procedures there was a
small risk of HIV transmission and they were concerned that HCWs should
take reasonable precautions. Sometimes they expressed concern that HCWs
did not protect themselves sufficiently. Two respondents, for example, felt
they had to disclose their seropositive status when a HCW started to take
blood or to examine their teeth, without gloves on.

Isolation
Respondents who were admitted to hospital also reported instances where
they had been isolated from other patients. They reported being put in single
rooms 'it was more like a broom cupboard actually' and having markers
such as a red dot put on the door to signify 'infectious disease'. There were
also a number of reports of being given 'paper sheets and plastic plates to
eat my dinner off' and having to use a different toilet designated 'out of
order' to other patients.

Loathing

Another source of stigma reported by respondents related to the 'double stigma' of HIV and its association with gay men, injecting drug use and sexual promiscuity. Respondents reported many instances where HCWs treated them with distaste which they interpreted as being related to the perceived route of transmission of HIV. They also reported being treated in stigmatised institutions.

Routes of transmission

Respondents reported being treated badly by HCWs because they assumed that they were gay or used drugs. Even respondents who had not been infected by either of these routes reported this to have occurred, and that HCWs had 'just presumed things . . . and automatically thought I was a drug user'. The quotation below is from a heterosexual woman who had been infected by her fiancee:

> R10:   Em, and then actually being taken to the operating theatre was horrible because one of the doctors said 'oh, you're the junkie aren't you'. Well I was just about to get in due to fall asleep, em, and it's just that I remember falling asleep but crying and and kind of saying you know 'no I'm not, I'm not'.

An ex-drug user who had not used drugs for many years complained that he was never able to shake off the 'drug-using' image in his interactions with HCWs. He described his relationship with HCWs in a hospital ward where he had been admitted:

> R1:   If you're straight [*no longer using drugs*] and you're straight a long period of time you can be trusted, you're no gonnae dae anything oot of order or make drug deals or anything like that.
>
> GG: So are you still treated like an injecting drug user when you go in there?
>
> R1:   Uhu. I just don't like it. It shows nae respect fur me and what I've tried tae dae wae ma life and they've known me over a period of time now and they take ma blood all the time and they find traces of nothing in it so I mean it would come up if I was using anything and they'd be able to tell fae even ma physical appearance that I wis using and abusing d'you know what I mean and I feel quite bad about that.

Drug users complained that they were not given enough pain killers because HCWs thought 'I was looking for a free stone of something,' and consequently sometimes had to endure severe pain. 'Loathing' related to a gay identity was less often reported, although HCWs' attitudes were sometimes criticised:

> G5:   As soon as I told them I was a gay man with HIV the yes sirs were
> dropped and now uhu mm right and just go and sit there.

Treatment centres stigmatised

Respondents generally spoke warmly about specialist treatment centres
where they had been admitted and they were generally thought to be 'a good
thing'. A gay man argued that specialist units offer 'people secure space and
in some ways if you're in a specialist unit at least you're going to feel OK
about it rather than hiding in your room, you know, frightened to come out.'
This opinion was not shared by all respondents, however, particularly those
who reported that they had not been infected by gay sex or drug injecting.
A heterosexual male said he 'hated the stigma' attached to being a patient
at the HIV out-patient clinic. He attended the clinic during sessions in which
drug users were the principal attendees to minimise the possibility of being
recognised. A man with haemophilia also complained that at this hospital
'there's druggies all over the place', and most people with haemophilia
expressed a preference for receiving HIV treatment at the general hospital
where they were already being treated for haemophilia.

'Confidentiality's a joke'

An inevitable consequence of the highly stigmatising nature of HIV disease
is concern about confidentiality. Although the majority of respondents were
clearly reasonably satisfied with confidentiality procedures, one-fifth of those
who had been in-patients in hospital were not, and a number of breaches
of confidentiality were reported also at out-patient clinics, GP and dental
surgeries. Occasional gross breaches of confidentiality were reported. A gay
respondent said he had disclosed his HIV status to his dentist who was also
gay and that his dentist had informed a mutual friend. A drug user said his
GP had told his mother about his diagnosis without asking his permission
or informing him that he had told her. A prisoner said he was informed of
his diagnosis in a loud voice in a room with an open door so that all the
prisoners in the adjoining room heard. A man with haemophilia was unwittingly informed of his HIV-status by an HCW despite making it clear that,
although he knew his blood had been tested for HIV antibodies, he did not
want to be informed of the results. More normally, however, breaches of confidentiality were less serious and viewed by some respondents to be inevitable,
being largely attributable to informal information networks among HCWs.

Information sharing among HCWs about patients was the reason that
several respondents described confidentiality to be 'a joke'. Although they
were mostly able to rationalise that HCWs needed to share information about
them to improve care, they often felt that HCWs 'bandied information
about' and were not sufficiently careful with that information, as illustrated
by the quotation below from a respondent with haemophilia:

R20:   And they don't seem to treat it in a serious manner, it's just
        another bit of useless information that they've been given. That's
        the impression that one gets and, as I say, it doesn't help when your
        files go missing between departments.

A major problem reported by in-patients related to hospital files which they
felt were not sufficiently protected from on-lookers. There was concern that
anyone in the hospital could read the file and one man said that he had
'caught an auxiliary' reading his. Another man said that when he was in
hospital his file was 'lying on a desk with a big sticker saying "HIV positive"
on it. Anybody could have walked past and lifted it up.'
  One man was outraged that his confidentiality was threatened by the
information network among HCWs which is described below.

R24:   I can remember when I was diagnosed and I knew a member of
        the staff up there, I'd known him for some time, we'd worked
        together, and I felt very unsure at the time and I really didn't
        want him to know. So I said to the counsellor 'I really don't
        want him to know' and she said 'well we have regular team
        meetings where, you know, new cases are discussed.' And
        I said 'Well I don't want you to mention my name at the team
        meeting', and she said 'oh but we always do that' and I said
        'but I forbid you to do that'. And she was quite shocked at that
        because there is an assumption in professional circles that
        you can pass on information willy-nilly, and I don't think that's
        proper.

This quotation also illustrates the added confidentiality problems for seropositives receiving treatment in small communities. One man who lived in
a small town changed his GP to a practice in another town as although he
did not 'doubt their confidentiality . . . things do slip now and again'.
Glasgow and Edinburgh, the cities where most respondents were resident,
both have sizeable populations but the gay and drug-using communities
in both cities are not large and a number of respondents reported that
they had seen someone they knew at the HIV clinic or specialist HIV ward.
This rarely caused a great deal of anxiety, and in at least two cases was
the basis of a much deeper friendship, but it made people uneasy about
confidentiality.
  Another issue affecting confidentiality was a lack of privacy in hospitals.
Although some respondents complained about feeling stigmatised if they
were put in a private room, there were also drawbacks to a general ward. A
respondent with haemophilia, for example, was concerned that the patient
in the neighbouring bed would know his HIV status when the nurse
reminded him in a loud voice to take his AZT. A gay man with AIDS found
that the lack of privacy stifled open communication with his doctor.

Respondents were aware that great efforts had been taken in health care settings to preserve confidentiality but were sceptical that these procedures were ever watertight.

The impact

Mental strain

Anger, indignation and hurt to respondents typically resulted from incidents such as those described above. One man with haemophilia claimed to have 'suffered far more mental strain and humiliation in hospital than physical pain.' Many of the above incidents were reported with humour, less because they were experienced by respondents as funny than as a symptom of the emotive reaction they unleashed. In order to cope psychologically with stigmatising incidents it was important for many respondents to 'make light' of them or challenge stigmatising behaviour by laughing at the HCWs. Likewise the term 'spacemen' was often used to describe HCWs as they experienced such incidents as somewhat surreal, and perhaps to imply that 'the spacemen' not they were the 'aliens'. In general stigmatisation in health care settings had a very negative impact upon respondents.

Don't go

Physical avoidance of health care was only reported rarely by respondents, although some in retrospect said that they 'wished they had stayed at home.' In general, they felt they had to take advantage of the health care offered to them in order to maintain their health for as long as possible. All but three out of 40 respondents followed-up after one year were registered with a GP and in all but one case the GP was aware of their HIV status. Many prisoners, however, reported that when in the community they did not attend an out-patient clinic for routine check-ups, and one woman in the sample had had no contact whatsoever with the HIV clinic. Many attendees reported that they found attending a regular clinic a strain as it was 'a constant reminder' of their condition, and they chose to attend at infrequent, irregular intervals. Similarly visits to the dentist tended to be reduced to absolutely necessary treatment rather than routine 6-monthly visits, and one man had stopped going as he did not wish to disclose his HIV status to his dentist but he felt he had to do so if he continued to receive treatment.

Don't tell

In many health care settings, respondents' HIV status was known prior to consultation, largely as a result of the informal HCW information network whereby clinic consultants would often inform patients' GPs and/or vice versa, usually with the patient's consent. This information web did not normally extend to hospital departments to which the patient referred themselves, *e.g.* Accident and Emergency departments, or to community dental practices.

In such settings, respondents had to decide whether or not to disclose and six people cited instances where they had not disclosed during treatment. One such incident is described in the quotation below:

R19:   . . . what I really wanted was decent teeth. The dentist I go
       to . . . he doesn't know I am a haemophiliac and he doesn't know
       I am HIV, but he wears gloves.
GG: Right. So you have not told him that you have got the virus?
R19:   It would make it all too complicated . . . I would not get the job
       done the way I have got it done. I tried for two years to get it done
       at the hospital and it is two years that I have wasted. My teeth just
       deteriorated.

The actual number of incidents where respondents chose not to disclose their HIV status was probably rather higher as the social taboo surrounding non-disclosure may have led to under-reporting. The fact that some seropositives do not disclose, and many more are themselves not aware of their status having never been tested, meant that some respondents who received stigmatising treatment after disclosure felt they had been treated unfairly. A gay man who had disclosed his HIV status to his dentist and as a result been asked to attend for treatment always at the last appointment of the day complained that 'I may have not known. I may have decided not to tell them, so it is ridiculous'.

Discussion

There is clearly evidence that seropositives in this study encountered what they felt to be fear and loathing from HCWs. It is, however, important to qualify this statement in a number of ways. First, this analysis has focused upon negative experiences as respondents were asked about difficulties and problems they had encountered in the course of their health care. In fact, Table 2 shows that most respondents were satisfied most of the time with the health care that they received; many had no complaints whatsoever and spoke warmly about many aspects of their care. Specialist units such as a hospice and respite care centre, specialist HIV-hospital wards and out-patient clinics were singled out for particular praise. Individual HCWs were often spoken about warmly, particularly the consultants and nurses in HIV clinics, GPs and health visitors. Some respondents clearly felt that they had established a relationship over time with HCWs in these settings. Second, it is important to emphasise that the incidents reported here occurred between 1983 and the time of the second interview in 1992. The most florid examples of stigmatisation, *e.g.* women's treatment during labour, mostly occurred in the more distant past. Respondents themselves reported that things had improved and their recounting of many incidents ended by saying 'but that was a long time ago'. Thus this paper should not be taken as a description of the current situation. Nevertheless, some of the reports of stigma were among the newly diagnosed, and stigmatisation in health care settings remains a concern of people with HIV and professional bodies of HCWs.

Another important consideration is that this sample may not be representative of all people with HIV. Over 50 per cent were recruited from hospital clinics and all except one were recruited from organisations involved in providing support for people with HIV, or from institutions. Thus seropositives not in contact with any organisation or institution were under-represented, and it is possible that these people are the most stigmatised. They may have sought health care and then stopped as a result of a stigmatising incident, or they may not have sought any care because they feared the stigmatising treatment they might receive. It is therefore possible that this study has underestimated HIV-related stigma in health care settings.

A further qualification is that the data, based on self-reports by seropositives, are highly subjective. Whereas a seropositive respondent may have felt that protective clothing worn by an HCW was excessive and their attitude moralistic, it could be that the HCW was taking sensible precautions. In this manner, incidents may have been experienced and interpreted as 'stigmatising' due to 'felt stigma'. Avoidance of health care to avoid potential stigmatisation, failure to disclose HIV status to HCWs, or dislike of the attitude of some HCWs cannot be categorised as overt stigmatisation. Rather, they emanate from a fear of enacted stigma or from respondents' internalisation of stigmatising attitudes whereby they 'feel' devalued as a result of their HIV status, *i.e.* felt rather than enacted stigma. There are, however, also many incidents which one would categorise as overtly stigmatising even if one takes account of the possible bias in the reporting.

Many of the reported incidents relate to HCW's fear of infection from treating seropositives. This was identified by respondents as the principal source of stigma in health care settings. In this respect the views of seropositives in this study were in accordance with the attitudes of HCWs described in the literature (see introduction).

The level of fear and precautions reportedly taken by HCWs were generally related to the level of risk of HIV transmission. For example, full protective clothing was normally worn for invasive surgery whereas gloves alone were more common for simple procedures such as taking blood. Fear tended to be greater in procedures involving symbolically important areas of entry to the body, such as the mouth, throat or the vagina. Procedures performed without a general anaesthetic which required that the HCW came into contact with such areas were the most frequent cause of fear of infection and therefore stigma as patients were able to witness that fear.

There were a number of reported instances where the level of fear appeared to be unrelated to the actual procedure, *e.g.* the dental nurse who wore full protective clothing. Such incidents tended to occur in settings where the HCW was not familiar with HIV and had little or no experience in treating seropositives. Although this information was not systematically collected, it was clear that fear was greatest in non-specialist units such as general hospitals. It is not surprising that interactions between seropositives and HCWs unfamiliar with HIV are strained, uncomfortable and tense, as social disruption is part of the process and product of stigmatisation (see Goffman 1963, and also Albrecht *et al.* 1982). Continued contact, however, tends to reduce the saliency of the abnormal characteristic by a process of 'normalization' (Davis 1964) and the stigmatised individual is eventually accepted as 'normal', or at least ascribed an identity based on the person and not the stigmatising characteristic. HCWs who have regular contact with seropositives over time are likely to achieve normalised interactions and these individuals (*e.g.* HCWs in specialist HIV centres or clinics) were most frequently praised by seropositives in this study.

The fear of HCWs was probably based less upon ignorance about HIV transmission than upon the dirty and fearful image associated with HIV/ AIDS, particularly in the 1980s. Although all HCWs were no doubt aware that you could not 'catch' HIV by skin contact, touch of the stigmatised person was nevertheless tainted as s/he possessed a deeply discrediting attribute. This is the hallmark of stigma as defined by Goffman (1963) and it was no doubt the metaphorical 'otherness' of people with HIV which prompted the use of spacesuits by HCWs in low or no-risk situations. In addition, due to the dramatic manner in which AIDS entered the public consciousness, the risk of transmission tends to be greatly exaggerated (see for example Klepinger *et al.* 1993). Help lines which are set up after health professions disclose their seropositivity, for example, attract thousands of calls from worried former patients although the only recorded incident of a HCW infecting patients, was that of the dentist in Florida who somehow transmitted the virus to six identified patients (Scully and Mortimer 1994). It is likely that HCWs also exaggerated the risk of transmission from treating seropositives, at least in the 1980s, and were fearful about caring for them.

This analysis also provides further evidence of the 'double stigma' of HIV. Even respondents who had not been infected sexually or through injecting drugs reported occasionally being put into these categories and feeling stigmatised because of the association between HIV and gay men or drug injectors. The 'double stigma' of HIV thus affects all sufferers, however they were infected, and this potentially makes HIV-related stigma more acute for people with HIV who are neither gay nor drug injectors. Due to the double stigma of HIV, people with haemophilia or those infected heterosexually are particularly vulnerable to developing disapproval of self. To use Crawford's (1994) terminology, they represent the breakdown of the boundary between 'self' and 'other' because the 'stigmatising self ' has become the 'unhealthy other'; their identity is thus fractured.

Given that seropositives who are receiving treatment have, to some extent, placed trust in health care to maximise the quality and quantity of their lives, negative attitudes are potentially particularly damaging in a health care setting as they may erode any such trust. Also, relations with HCWs are very important for the adjustment of people with stigmatised illnesses, particularly if the illness is concealed and generally not disclosed to other people. HCWs may be among the few people who know about the illness and a negative reaction may lead to negative identity formation through an internalisation of the externally imputed stereotypical role. For example, the woman cited earlier whose experience with HCWs dressed as 'spacemen' led her to believe that 'they must be terrified of me'. This was confirmation to her of her 'terrifying identity'. Many asymptomatic seropositives conceal their HIV status due to fear of enacted stigma. Their interactions with HCWs, who are aware of their condition, are thus vital in shaping their management of the so-called stigma trajectory (Alonzo and Reynolds 1995) which unfolds during the course of the disease. In some of the scenarios described above the HIV status of the individual seems to have achieved 'master status' (Hughes 1945) and the HCWs treat the seropositive and not the person. Such a response can only reinforce the seropositive identity at the expense of personhood.

Conclusion

As the rate of new infections with HIV has stabilised, the panic associated with HIV has decreased and attitudes towards people with HIV have softened (Green 1995a). HCW organisations have issued guidelines about the treatment of seropositives, there are many specialist units treating seropositives, and HCWs have become more familiar with treating them. There is therefore every reason to suppose that enacted stigma towards seropositives in health care settings is becoming rarer, at least in areas where HIV prevalence is quite high. In time this should 'trickle down' and decrease felt stigma also, although it is likely that this may be a lengthy process. Whilst attitudes to seropositives may have softened in the last few years, such a change has yet to be perceived by people with HIV (Green 1995a). The memory of a harsh word from a HCW or being treated by a 'spaceman' lingers, and incidents which occurred several years ago still loom large in the consciousness of many seropositives today.

Many HCWs have tried to provide a stigma-free environment for the health care of seropositives. It is important that they continue to seek ways of achieving this goal in order to encourage seropositives to attend or treatment, to feel comfortable about disclosure and to believe that HCWs do not see them as 'social lepers'. Seropositives usually respect HCWs and look to them to maintain their health for as long as possible. Stigmatising behaviour towards the seropositive patient threatens the relationship between HCW and patient, and the patient may respond by avoiding contact or by losing faith in the HCWs' competence to heal.

In the biomedical model of disease stigma is not attached to disease and the reality of stigma may thus be ignored or neglected by the medical profession

(Williams 1987). It is clear that, at least in the 1980s, many HCWs were unaware of the extraordinary power of HIV-related stigma in the shaping of social relationships for people with HIV. As HIV is a disease in which the social impact is high, many HCWs have, however, gradually become aware of the social dimension of seropositivity. Growing experience of treating seropositives by HCWs has reduced the number of negative experiences in health care settings reported by people with HIV. This suggests that greater awareness and training in the social, personal and emotional dimensions of a stigmatising illness condition would assist the social adjustment of sufferers.

Acknowledgements

This research was funded by the Medical Research Council of Great Britain and carried out at the MRC Medical Sociology Unit, Glasgow University where the authors were both formerly employed. We are extremely grateful to the respondents who were prepared to take part in the study, and to Ruchill hospital outpatients and counselling clinic, Glasgow Royal Infirmary, Perth and Saughton prisons, Positive Help Edinburgh and Body Positive for allowing us access. Thanks also to colleagues Graham Hart and Martin Dunbar for their helpful comments on an earlier draft of this paper.

References

Ablon, J. (1981) Dwarfism and social identity: self-help group participation, *ocial Science and Medicine*, 15B, 25–30.
Ablon, J. (1995) 'The Elephant Man' as 'self' and 'other': the psycho-social costs of a misdiagnosis, *Social Science and Medicine*, 40, 11, 1481–9.
Albrecht, G.L., Walker, V.G. and Levy, J.A. (1982) Social distance from the stigmatized: a test of two theories, *Social Science and Medicine*, 16, 1319–27.
Alonzo, A.A. and Reynolds, N.R. (1995) Stigma, HIV and AIDS: an exploration and elaboration of a stigma trajectory, *Social Science and Medicine*, 41, 3, 303–15.
Anon (1992) AIDS in the family, *British Medical Journal*, 304, 1639–40.
Cleary, P.D., Fahs, M.C., McMullen, W., Fulop, G., Strain, J., Sacks, H.S., Muller, C., Foley, M. and Stein, E. (1992) Using patient reports to assess hospital treatment of persons with AIDS: a pilot study, *AIDS Care*, 4, 3, 325–32.
Crawford, R. (1994) The boundaries of the self and the unhealthy other: reflections on health, culture and AIDS, *Social Science and Medicine*, 38, 10, 1347–65.
Davis, F. (1964) Deviance disavowal: the management of strained interaction by the visibly handicapped. In Becker, H. (ed) *The Other Side*. Illinois: Free Press.
De Jong, W. (1980) The stigma of obesity: the consequences of naive assumptions concerning the causes of physical deviance, *Journal of Health and Social Behavior*, 21, 75–87.
Dworkin, J., Albrecht, G. and Cooksey, J. (1991) Concern about AIDS among hospital physicians, nurses and social workers, *Social Science and Medicine*, 33, 3, 239–48.

Gallop, R.M., Taerk, G., Lancee, W.G., Coates, R., Fanning, M. and Keatings, M. (1991) Knowledge, attitudes and concerns of hospital staff about AIDS, *Canadian Journal of Public Health*, 82, 409–12.

Glaser, G. and Strauss, A.L. (1968) *The Discovery of Grounded Theory: Strategies for Qualitative Research*. Weidenfield and Nicolson, London.

Goffman, E. (1963) *Stigma: Notes on the Management of Spoiled Identity*. Prentice-Hall: Englewood Cliffs.

Green, G. (1995a) Attitudes towards people with HIV: are they as stigmatising as people with HIV think they are? *Social Science and Medicine*, 41, 4, 557–68.

Green, G. (1995b) Processes of stigmatisation and impact on the employment of people with HIV. In Fitzsimmons, D. Hardy, V. and Tolley, K. *The Economic and Social Impact of AIDS in Europe*. Cassell: London.

Herek, G.M. and Glunt, E.K. (1988) An epidemic of stigma: public reactions to AIDS, *American Psychology*, 43, 11, 886–91.

Hospital Infection Society and the Surgical Infection Study Group (1992) Risks to surgeons and patients from HIV and hepatitis: guidelines on precautions and management of exposure to blood or body fluids, *British Medical Journal*, 305, 1337–43.

Howarth, G. (1993) AIDS and undertakers: the business of risk management, *Critical Public Health*, 4, 3, 47–53.

Hughes, E.C. (1945) Dilemmas and contradictions of status, *American Journal of Sociology*, 50, 353.

Jones, E.E., Farina, A., Hastorf, A.H., Markus, H., Miller, D.T., Scott, R.A. and French, R. de S. (1984) *Social Stigma – the Psychology of Marked Relationships*. W.H. Freeman: New York.

Klepinger, D.H., Billy, J.O.G., Tanfer, K. and Grady, W.R. (1993) Perceptions of AIDS risk and severity and their association with risk-related behavior among US men, *Family Planning Perspectives*, 25, 74–82.

Kowalewski, M.R. (1988) Double stigma and boundary maintenance: how gay men deal with AIDS, *Journal of Contemporary Ethnography*, 17, 2, 211–28.

Kunzel, C. and Sadowsky, D. (1993) Predicting dentists' perceived occupational risk for HIV infection, *Social Science and Medicine*, 36, 12, 1579–84.

Morin, M., Obadia, Y., Moatti, J-P. and Souville, M. (1995) Commitment, value conflicts and role strains among French GPs in care for HIV positive patients, *AIDS Care*, 7, Suppl 1, S79–S84.

Norusis, M.J./SPSS Inc. (1993) *SPSS for Windows: Base System User's Guide Release 6.0*. SPSS Inc: Chicago.

Richardson, A. and Bolle, D. (1992) *Wise before their Time: People with AIDS and HIV Talk about their Lives*. Harper Collins: London.

Robinson, P. and Croucher, R. (1994) The satisfaction of men with HIV infection attending a dedicated dental clinic: a controlled study, *AIDS Care*, 6, 1, 39–48.

Ross, M.W. and Hunter, C.E. (1991) Dimensions, content and validation of the fear of AIDS schedule in health professionals, *AIDS Care*, 3, 2, 175–80.

Scambler, G. (1984) Perceiving and coping with stigmatising illness. In Fitzpatrick, R., Hunton, J., Newman, S., Scambler, G. and Thompson, J. (eds) *The Experience of Illness*. Tavistock Publications: London.

Scambler, G. and Hopkins, A. (1986) Being epileptic: coming to terms with stigma, *Sociology of Health and Illness*, 8, 26–43.

Seidel, J.V., Kjolseth, R. and Seymour, E. (1988) *The Ethnograph: a User's Guide*. Qualis Research Associates: Colorado.

Scully, C. and Mortimer, P. (1994) Gnashings of HIV, *Lancet*, 334, 904.

Taerk, G., Gallop, R.M., Lancee, W.J., Coates, R.A. and Fanning, M. (1993) Recurrent themes of concern in groups for health care professions, *AIDS Care*, 5, 2, 215–22.

Wadsworth, E. and McCann, K. (1992) Attitudes towards and use of general practitioner services among homosexual men with HIV infection or AIDS, *British Journal of General Practice*, 42, 107–10.

Weyant, R.J., Bennett, M.E., Simon, M. and Palaisa, J. (1994) Desire to treat HIV-infected patients: similarities and differences across health-care professions, *AIDS* 8, 117–21.

Williams, S. (1987) Goffman, interactionism, and the management of stigma in everyday life. In Scambler, G. (ed) *Sociological Theory and Medical Sociology*. Tavistock Publications: London.

'They're not the same as us': midwives' stereotypes of South Asian descent maternity patients

Isobel Bowler

Introduction

This paper presents findings from a small-scale ethnographic study of the delivery of maternity care to South Asian descent maternity patients. The stereotypes of these women held by health service staff (in particular midwives) are examined and set in the context of observational data. The South Asian descent women were generally referred to and regarded as 'Asian' women by midwives and other personnel. This term is also common in the literature (*e.g.* Rathwell 1984: 123), but it masks heterogeneity in national, religious, and cultural background. However, because of the lack of differentiation by the midwives, their category of 'Asian' will be used in this paper.

The research[1] was carried out in the maternity department of a teaching hospital in Britain in 1988. All the women received shared consultant directed care[2]. The hospital serves a city in southern England which has a South Asian descent population estimated[3] around 8 per cent, or 8,000 people. The largest group, about half of the Asian population, is of Pakistani descent. This group has a younger age structure and higher fertility rate than the British population as a whole (Coleman and Salt 1992, Diamond and Clarke 1989, C. Shaw 1988). This results in a greater consumption of maternity services than would be expected from a consideration of numbers alone.

During fieldwork it became apparent that patient typification and labelling were common. The categorisation of clients as 'good', or more usually 'bad', is a routine feature of bureaucracies (Lispsky 1980, Prottas 1979) and medical settings are no exception (Kelly and May 1982). In addition to individual patients being assigned a 'moral status', recognisable groups are likely to attract stereotypes. Midwives and other staff expressed stereotyped views of South Asian descent women which related to their customs and culture as well as their moral status as patients. The quotation in the title comes from an interview with a community midwife, and illustrates the common theme in the accounts: that 'they' are different from 'us'.

Midwives use stereotypes to help them pitch their interactions with women appropriately (Macintyre 1978) and to make assumptions about the kind of care which different women want (Green *et al.* 1990). In the present study both of these observations held true. In addition midwives used stereotypes to make assumptions about the kind of care different women deserve.

Midwives' views are contrasted with observational data which show that these were often contradicted by reality. However midwives did not always recognise (or acknowledge) that individual women did not fit the stereotype. Even where midwives acknowledged a contradiction between experience and stereotype this did not necessarily cause them to question their view, but rather to treat the mismatch as the exception which proves the rule.

Green *et al.* (1990) and Macintyre (1978) report typifications of white women. Midwives in the present study also expressed stereotyped views of white mothers, although few data on this were collected. Examples given were of the 'thick' women from the large council estate and the educated NCT (National Childbirth Trust) middle class university women. Some of the aspects of the 'working class' stereotypes (*e.g.* low intelligence, lack of compliance) are present in the 'Asian' stereotypes. Indeed, the Asian women in the present study were all working class. However this does not fully explain the extreme negative typification they suffered. The typifications go beyond class and echo the stereotypes of black and minority ethnic people common in wider society. The issue of racism (and anti-racism) is extremely complex (Gilroy 1987) and beyond the scope of the present paper. Implicit throughout, however, is a recognition of the power relations between black women and white staff (Pearson 1986).

Methods

The fieldwork with midwives[4] was carried out by the author alone over a three month period in the Summer of 1988. Access to the midwives and the maternity hospital was negotiated with the Director of Midwifery Services for the District Health Authority. The main method of data collection was observation which was supported by data from interviews with twenty-five midwives.

The majority of the women observed were Moslem (of either Pakistani or Bangladeshi descent) but there were also Hindus and Christians. All were married and working class. Husbands were employed in local factories or on the buses; underemployed in family-run restaurants and shops; unemployed. Most of the women were recent migrants from rural areas; did not work outside the home and had limited contacts with non-Asian British people. Television, present in all the homes visited during fieldwork, was primarily used for the viewing of Hindi or Urdu videos. The use of medical services was therefore one of the few encounters they had with 'dominant' cultural values in British society.

The secondary method of data collection was interviews, primarily with the midwives, but also with a small number of other personnel including hospital doctors and general practitioners, members of the local community health (CHC) and community relations (CRC) councils. The interviews were 'ethnographic' in character without a predetermined schedule but, instead, topics to be covered (Hammersley and Atkinson 1983: 113). One of these topics was the midwives' attitudes to and perceptions of Asian women. Both directive and non-directive questions were used, although for the exploration of views about Asian women I favoured open-ended non-directive questions (Spradley 1979). Questions used including the following: 'Would you say that there are different sorts/types of patients? Are some women more difficult to care for? Do some kinds of women have different needs?' There were two main types of interview. These may be characterised as *natural* and *formal* interviews.

The formal interviews with midwives were arranged in advance so that we would be able to talk at length. The *natural* interviews were interactions between myself and the midwives-which occurred during observation, and in the context of general conversation. I took any opportunity to solicit accounts on the categories of interest, in particular views of black, and minority ethnic women. These occurred in the main with midwives I was shadowing when it was possible to introduce the topic with reference to individual Asian patients and/or particular events. Indeed it was often encounters with Asian women which would trigger expression of stereotyped views. For example, in the case of a woman who had a low haemoglobin count and had not taken her iron medication I asked the midwife why she thought this was, whether it was a common problem, and so on.

Altogether ten formal interviews were conducted, which varied in length between 30 and 60 minutes, and fifteen *natural* interviews of significant length. Many of the comments about Asian women came, however, in shorter natural interviews, for example during a woman's labour or between patients in the antenatal clinic. In addition I recorded comments from midwives and other actors during observation which may be regarded as unsolicited accounts. Responses and other accounts were recorded longhand almost invariably as they occurred. During observation I always had a notebook in my hand and so this was not problematic. The majority of the data for this paper come from the natural interviews, and from unsolicited accounts.

The midwives' stereotypes of the women

The stereotypes of Asian women have four main themes: the difficulty of communication; the women's lack of compliance with care and abuse of the service; their tendency to 'make a fuss about nothing'; their lack of 'normal maternal instinct'.

Communication difficulties
The level of competence in English among the Asian women observed was generally low. This resulted in the women being characterised as unresponsive, rude and unintelligent. It also help to strengthen the stereotypes because it was difficult for women with little English to make a personal relationship with the midwives and therefore challenge the assumptions made about them.

One or two midwives had extreme opinions and felt the women's lack of English to be a 'moral' failing. They articulated the view common among white people in Britain that immigrants should be competent in English. For example, during observation on the labour ward a staff midwife commented with reference to a woman who had been in the city for eight years that 'It's disgusting not to speak English after so long in Britain'.

None of the midwives in the hospital was of Asian descent and the hospital did not employ interpreters or advocates. Some staff reported this as a problem, others felt that such facilities were not necessary since there were Asian men employed in the hospital who could interpret if necessary. However, during the period of the study, no one was ever used in such a way. An extreme attitude was expressed by a consultant. Asked if the hospital was considering employing interpreters he answered:

Of course not. We haven't even got enough nurses. If you ask me they shouldn't be allowed into the country until they can pass an English exam.

Women who tried to speak English frequently offended the midwives. The main complaint was that the women did not say 'please' or 'thank you' and that they 'gave orders'. I know from my own attempts to learn Urdu that although the language has words equivalent to please and thank you, they are rarely used. In fact my Urdu teacher had to remind me frequently not to use them, pointing out that it was rather strange to use these words all the time 'like you English people do'. Instead in Urdu there is a polite form of the imperative with the 'please' built into the verb. The use of the imperative (fetch my baby, bring my lunch) without 'please' is indeed very rude in English, but was not so intended by the women.

Use of language indicates not only a person's attitudes towards those around them but also their intellectual abilities. The nature and content of speech (*e.g.* accent, vocabulary, grammar, syntax, dialect) are indicators employed to assess the other's competence. Black maternity patients in another study said that staff made them feel that they were 'too thick' to understand (Larbie 1985: 19). In the present study some midwives described the Asian women as unintelligent. Commenting on their poor attendance at antenatal clinics (a part of the stereotype discussed below in the section on compliance with care) a clinic midwife remarked 'They're too stupid to remember when to come to the clinic.' One midwife remarked on Asian women's lack of intelligence in front of one, Asmat[5], who was in labour. The midwife had asked for permission to give her a vaginal examination and gained no response. She said:

Some Asian women are like blocks of wood, you know, thick [banging the side of her head]. Mind you others are delightful. It's impossible to know whether they've understood or not.

She used this as an example of how difficult it was to work with Asian women. Four other midwives told me that they found the women unrewarding to work with because they were unable to have a 'proper relationship' with them. Having a 'good relationship' with a mother was reported as an important part of a midwife's role.

The midwives were rarely motivated to take trouble with the women and to ensure that they understood. As a researcher I had far more time (and patience) to spend with individual women. For example with Asmat after the midwife had left I asked whether she had understood what had been said. She said that the midwives spoke too fast and were difficult to follow but she understood some of what they said. She had understood that the midwife thought that she was stupid. Many of the women in the sample said the same thing. They could understand a fairly simple conversation and would talk to me but not to the midwives.

Communication difficulties also stemmed from the use of colloquial language. It was common for staff to use culturally specific lay terms for symptoms and euphemisms for parts of the body which confused the Asian women. Terms such as 'waterworks', 'down there', 'the other end', 'tummy', and 'dizzy' are difficult even for those Asian women who are competent in English. Macintyre (1978) notes that in the antenatal clinic (and in other medical settings) staff modify their interactions with women according to the typifications made of them, based on such things as socioeconomic class, vocabulary and perceived intelligence. She argues that staff do this because they make the common sense assumption that standardised questions and vocabularies will not elicit standardised responses from patients in different categories. As she points out, the vocabulary used to those of low competence, social status and/or intelligence tends to be colloquial simplistic language. Ironically, these culturally specific terms were especially likely to be used with Asian women, who are of low status (by virtue of their ethnicity), were known to be of poor linguistic competence and perceived as being of low intelligence. This process can be seen in the following example.

I accompanied a community midwife on a home visit to a woman (Rubina). The midwife wanted to examine her to see if her fundus (*i.e.* uterus) had begun to contract back to its previous size. In order to do this examination properly (and to minimise discomfort) it is important that the woman's bladder is empty. Midwives therefore check with the woman first.

Midwife: Do you need to go to the toilet – pass water?
Rubina: Yes.
Midwife: Or have you just been?
Rubina: Yes.

Rubina looked confused and went out of the room, only to return immediately with an empty specimen bottle and an interrogative look on her face.

The midwife waved it away crossly, told Rubina to lie on the sofa and began to feel her stomach.

While expansion of the question about 'going to the toilet' to include the phrase 'pass water?' in an interaction with an indigenous white English woman with limited vocabulary is probably better at eliciting a correct response than a question about 'urination', both versions may be equally incomprehensible to a woman who has English as a second language.

After the examination, the following interchange occurred:

Midwife: Is everything else OK?
Rubina: Headaches.
Midwife: Take some pain killers and you'll be fine.
Rubina: [Looks blank].
Midwife: [Giving her packet of paracetamol].
           Take two with some water every four hours OK?
Rubina: [Still looking confused takes packet].
Midwife: Two every four hours, yes?

At this point the midwife left. It is not clear whether or not Rubina understood what the tablets were for or when to take them. The midwife remarked in the car afterwards that headaches were a common complaint of Asian women:

I don't suppose she'll take the pills but it'll sort itself out.

Some of the misunderstandings between women and midwives can be attributed to differences in social and cultural background rather than the women's poor grasp of English. One area of confusion came over date of birth (DOB). Bureaucratic records of all kinds rely on DOB for classification and filing purposes (*e.g.* social security records, passports, driving licences) and hospital records are no exception. For Asian women DOB is particularly important since (as described below) there was often confusion over their names, which did not fit the Western surname/first name categories.

At their first antenatal clinic visit all women have to give their DOB. For the majority of women this question was expected, understood, and easy to answer. Some of the Asian women, however, did not know their birth date (age and birthdays do not have social significance in South Asia as they do in Europe), and were unaware of why it mattered. Some of the midwives took this as another example of poor linguistic competence. For those who realised that the women understood, but could not answer the question, this lack of knowledge of what in western society is an everyday fact, and part of personal identity, was mystifying. This reinforced the view that the women were stupid (so stupid that they don't even know when their birthday is). Some of the women had solved the problem. They knew (or estimated) the year in which they were born. Telling officials the year only did not satisfy the bureaucratic requirements. Therefore they gave their DOB as the first of January that year. One midwife, in all innocence, remarked how surprising it was that 'all these women' are born on the first of January.

Lack of compliance with care and service abuse
In interviews Asian women were described as non compliant patients. Yet they were also (often simultaneously) characterised as service 'over-users' or even 'abusers'. Indeed in the midwives' accounts one often led to another. For example 'lack of compliance' with family planning advice led to increased fertility and therefore to 'over-use' and 'abuse' of the maternity service.

General examples of non-compliance given in interviews were that Asian women were poor attenders at antenatal clinics (*c.f.* the clinic midwife's comment about women being 'too thick' to know when to come, above) and did not go to parentcraft classes. Non-attendance could result from a variety of factors, including misunderstanding the date and time of the next appointment, and missing an appointment because of being called by the wrong name. Many of the Pakistani descent women gave the 'surname' Begum whereas Begum is a courtesy title, not unlike Mrs in English names (Henley 1982). A woman called as 'Mrs Begum' would not immediately respond. This also contributed to the idea that the women were all alike: clinic midwives remarked that 'all these women have the same name'.

Another theme in the comments on non-compliance was that women had poor diets, suffered from anaemia and vitamin D deficiency and then failed to follow nutritional advice or take supplements. Few instances were actually observed in antenatal clinics. However, one community midwife shadowed was visiting an Asian woman daily to give her iron injections. The woman had previously been prescribed iron tablets but her haemoglobin count remained low. The midwife remarked:

> These women are very irritating. They don't take the tablets and then have to have injections. It takes time and its not nice for them . . . they hurt these jabs.

Midwives gave the women's fertility as an example of service abuse. Larbie cites examples of black women in hospital being told they have too many children (Larbie 1985: 19). In the present study a staff midwife on the postnatal nursing ward remarked of an Asian patient, 'She's having her ninth baby. It's a disgrace. Talk about abuse of the service.' Midwives argued that Asian women were not motivated to use contraception. Discussing a woman on the postnatal ward a midwife remarked that her linguistic competence had disappeared when she had tried to talk to her about the topic. She told me that she had not pursued the point: 'She's not very interested in family planning is Mrs Begum.'

Several of the Asian women in the study had large families and women born in South Asia do have higher fertility than British born women (Diamond and Clarke 1989). The only material in the hospital which was available in

Asian languages was the information on Depo-Provera issued by the manu-
facturer. These were proudly shown to me by one of the consultants to
demonstrate that he did take account of language problems.

Both midwives and doctors were ready to assume that Asian women have
no interest in family planning. However from the data collected in the separate sample of women[4] I found that this was not always the case. In her
small scale study of Pathan women in Bradford, Currer (1983) found that
of the 17 questioned at least nine were using a method of contraception.
Nevertheless the assumption persists. The following example shows the
stereotype being employed in the face of communication difficulties.

During postnatal home visits midwives discuss plans for future birth
control with new mothers. The following exchange occurred in an Asian's
woman's home 5 days after the delivery of her son. The community midwife
asked the Asian woman (Saida) about her intended family planning practice.
The following conversation ensued:

Midwife: Do you want any more children?
Saida: [confusion]
Midwife: You know, any more babies?
Saida: Four children
Midwife: More babies? Do you want to have five babies?
Saida: Not five babies, four babies.
Midwife: Well go and see Dr Smith in five weeks with your husband and
           discuss not having any more babies.

The midwife did not pursue the point any further. Saida appears to be answering the question of 'how many children do you have?' rather than 'how many
children do you want?' Neither I nor the midwife could be certain either
way. After we left the midwife told me that she tried her best with encouraging family planning but 'these women are just not interested'.

Not all the Asian women in the study were opposed to fertility control.
In an antenatal clinic a consultation was observed between an obstetric
senior house officer (SHO) and an Asian couple with one child of under one
year and a second unwanted pregnancy. The referral letter from the women's
GP stated that she had been on the pill but had stopped taking it because
of breakthrough bleeding. The GP pointed out in the referral letter that the
pregnancy was the couple's fault: she had stressed that the husband must use
a sheath and yet they had failed to comply with this advice. The SHO asked
the husband about this and he said that he did not like the sheath. Both
the doctor and midwife told me that they thought this couple were being
unnecessarily difficult about the pregnancy. The SHO remarked, 'Its only
her second baby. I thought these people liked large families.' The possibility
of a termination was not discussed.

The second main issue which was cited in connection with 'service abuse'
was circumcision, which was not provided on the NHS in the study hospital.

One Asian couple observed had just had a second son. The first had been delivered in the hospital and circumcised, but they had not paid the bill for the operation. The ward sister told the father that this time he must pay in advance. He was not pleased, but paid up. A staff midwife told me that she was glad that they had been made to pay:

> These people will try anything. He tried to tell me that he didn't understand that he had to pay, but he knew full well. He was just trying it on.

A second midwife remarked:

> I'm sympathetic but I get fed up with the repeated abuse of the service by these people.

This unwillingness to pay was not common to all Asian couples. In another case, a paediatrician apologised to a father for the charge, and remarked that he thought it was discriminatory. The father disagreed and said that he was quite happy to pay:

> I am a guest in this country. This country has been very good to me, why shouldn't I pay if I want something different?

The debate became quite heated with the doctor and a midwife arguing with the father over whether or not he should have to pay. The paediatrician thought that circumcisions should be available in all health districts on the NHS. In addition to the fact that he thought that it was racist (because particular religious groups including Moslems have their sons circumcised) he had seen the results of circumcisions by traditional practitioners which had ended up in the accident and emergency department.

Associated with comments about service abuse, midwives reported that Asian women were demanding and complaining. During interviews with midwives on postnatal nursing wards a major complaint was that Asian women refused to be physically active after delivery of their babies and, a lesser complaint, did not do the recommended toning exercises. A quotation from one midwife which illustrates an extreme of this view is that the women just 'lie in bed all day and expect to be waited on hand and foot'. This last example brings the discussion to the next major category in the stereotype: what the midwives reported as Asian women's tendency to make a fuss about nothing.

Making a fuss about nothing
'Making a fuss about nothing' was a phrase which recurred in interviews and was particularly applied to the intra- and postnatal behaviour of women. This view of black women has been reported in other studies. Larbie (1985: 22) found that black women were told by staff that they make too much

noise when in pain or discomfort. Brent Community Health Council (1981: 13) reports the stereotype of black people having a low pain threshold and Rakusen (1981: 81) mentions this specifically with reference to Asian women. Homans and Satow (1982: 17) note that some health workers hold the belief that black patients are likely to 'make a fuss about nothing' and suggest that this will limit the health workers' willingness to try to communicate effectively with such patients.

In the present study Asian women were characterised as 'attention seeking'; making too much noise and 'unnecessary fuss' during labour (because of 'low pain thresholds') and constantly complaining of minor symptoms (particularly headaches, see example of Rubina above) in the postnatal period. The issues of noise during labour and low pain thresholds were mentioned in interviews by all the midwives who worked on the labour ward. In response to a question about whether there were different sorts of patients who needed different sorts of treatment a typical response (from a labour ward midwife) was:

Well, these Asian women you're interested in have very low pain thresholds. It can make it very difficult to care for them.

Six Asian and four white women's deliveries were observed. None of the Asian women made a great deal of noise or had pain control and yet one of the white women had pethidine and another an epidural for pain (although this latter case was a premature labour of an older and very frightened woman). It may be that this was partly observer effect. Two of the husbands of Asian women thanked me for being with their wives during labour because it had stopped them being frightened. One midwife noted that women who are frightened make noise:

We perceive Asian women as whinging when they are just frightened. They just make more noise than we do.

This shows that it is possible to hold a stereotyped view without necessarily being unsympathetic to the stereotyped group.

Despite the fact that there was variation between women (and that non-Asian women also make a noise in labour) midwives saw making a noise in labour as the norm (although deviant behaviour) for Asian women. One woman (Shakila) expecting her eighth baby, had a long induced labour during which she vomited several times. On the postnatal ward she complained of a sore throat. The midwife said:

I expect you were shouting a lot during labour. That's why your throat hurts.

I had been with the woman in labour and said that actually this was not the case. The midwife then went on to report a story to me which was the exception which proves the rule:

I have a friend whose a Moslem. She's a GP's wife. She had a section and she had a lot of pain. But you know how much fuss they make. No one took very much notice. But I knew her so I knew that it really hurt. I made sure she got taken seriously.

This example provides circumstantial evidence that ethnicity is more important than class in the framing of typifications.

The noise Asian women were reported to make in labour was considered doubly inexcusable because they were perceived to have easier deliveries than Caucasian women. Some midwives cited this as a major (ethnic) difference. Others (and doctors I spoke to) pointed out that length of labour was primarily affected by parity (*i.e.* number of previous deliveries). Asian women have higher fertility and therefore make up a large proportion of the women of high parity delivered in maternity hospitals. For many of the midwives, however, ethnicity became the overriding factor. This is illustrated in the following example from my field notes. I was looking for an Asian woman on the antenatal nursing ward and a midwife told me that she had gone down to the labour ward. She was being induced and it was her first baby. Nevertheless the midwife remarked 'Oh, she'll be back in an hour, they're always quick'. In the event the woman had a slow and long labour. This example further demonstrates how a woman's ethnicity becomes her master status. The midwife knew that it was an induction and a first baby, both factors which indicated a longer labour, and yet the woman's ethnicity was seen as the overriding factor.

On the postnatal ward the Asian women were unwilling to get up and therefore the midwives had to nurse them in bed. This made them unpopular. The following comments from a midwife were overheard in the ward coffee room:

Mrs Kajoo is being difficult again. She wants me to bring her bottle [for the baby] but I'm not doing it. They're always ordering us around. Bring me my bottle indeed. [To a second midwife]. You're not to do it either.

Some of the older midwives felt, however, that all mothers were asked to get up too soon in modern midwifery practice. One, a community midwife who remembered the days when women were encouraged to have bed rest after delivery, argued that there were not enough staff on the postnatal wards and that women (of all ethnicities) were not being properly cared for. She felt that women who wanted to stay in bed should be allowed to:

If a woman isn't feeling very good her [baby's] bottle should be brought to her [so that she doesn't have to get up to get it].

In support of her view she cited the example that two of the women we had visited that day (both white) had breastfeeding problems:

The problem is the girls [*i.e.* the midwives] on the wards just don't have time to look after them properly. In the old days mums came out of hospital having had this kind of thing sorted out.

Community midwives too cited examples of women 'making a fuss about nothing'. In the coffee room in the GPU two community midwives were discussing a woman who had been discharged from postnatal midwifery care. One midwife remarked to the other:

I went to see Mrs Iqbal yesterday and finally got rid of her. She didn't want to be discharged . . . said she'd got a headache. These women they make such a fuss. In their own culture they get so much attention they have to invent it. I think it's pathetic.

Lack of normal maternal instinct
A theme running through accounts of Asian women given by midwives was that 'they're not the same as us'. In particular they were described as lacking normal maternal instinct and feelings. This was in part attributed to their large numbers of children and 'unhealthy' preference for sons.

In the everyday world in our society there is a concept of 'maternal instinct' which implies that humans (especially women) have instinctive drives towards reproduction. Macintyre (1976: 151–2) has pointed out that this and other aspects of 'normal' reproduction are socially constructed. However, she argues that although the majority of sociologists recognise the social construction of reproduction, most studies have defined 'normal' reproduction as occurring exclusively inside the statistically common nuclear family unit. The household formation (and different attitudes to marriage) of many Asian families (A. Shaw 1988) puts them outside this Western normality. A more recent analysis of the psychological research into mother-hood notes that the construction of 'normal' motherhood is based on white middle class behaviours (Phoenix and Woollett 1991). Psychological studies have omitted black and working class mothers from studies of normal processes, but included them in studies of deviance. Phoenix and Woollett (1991) argue that the narrow focus of these studies has helped to maintain negative social constructions of black mothers (1991: 25). In addition, mothers from minority ethnic groups are themselves socially constructed as 'other' and hence by definition viewed as deviating from 'good/normal' mothering (1991: 17).

Thus constructions of normal reproduction and motherhood take no account of structural differences between mothers. Some of the Asian women's behaviours did not conform to the prevailing (Western) model of motherhood. For example, of the six South Asian women observed during labour two reacted badly when the midwives delivered their baby onto their stomach, and three did not want to hold their new-born baby straight away. All those observed did not want to breastfeed immediately after delivery, and the majority of women in the study were likely to choose to bottle feed.

Midwives were also upset by the preference for sons expressed by women (and related to the importance of male offspring in Islamic culture). Some of the women's behaviours could be interpreted positively in the light of dominant models: for example none of the women in the sample worked outside the home, none smoked. However not one midwife mentioned this as a positive characteristic of Asian women although these issues were discussed with reference to mothers in general.

Models of childbirth and motherhood vary by culture. Many of the behaviours described above do not conflict with the South Asian Islamic models of motherhood described in Currer's (1983) study of Pathan women in Bradford. However they caused midwives, with their different cultural perspective, to characterise women as lacking normal maternal instinct and feelings[6].

Discussion

The examples above demonstrate how individual women's behaviours were interpreted within the stereotypes of 'Asian women' held by the midwives. This is not surprising since typifications of patients are common in medical settings. Menzies' (1960) classic paper on the defence against anxiety among nurses gives some indication of why this should be. She argues that depersonalisation and categorisation of patients (as, for example, bed numbers or illnesses) reduces the possibility of emotional attachment between carer and patient, and thus reduces anxiety and stress for the former. Green et al. (1990: 125) write that midwives on the labour ward commonly use stereotypes 'to make assumptions about what a particular woman is likely to want in labour and delivery'. In the present study midwives also used stereotypes to make judgements about the kind of care women deserved. When a woman speaks little English, stereotypes will be particularly likely to be employed in this way by the midwives.

The practice of typification described by Menzies leads to staff forming, transmitting and accepting stereotyped views of certain groups. For example the 'well-educated middle-class National Childbirth Trust type' or the 'uneducated working class woman' (Green et al. 1990) 'the demanding Jew' and the 'difficult Asian woman'. If an individual patient is easily categorised as a member of such a group she is more likely to suffer the effects of negative stereotyping. Black and minority ethnic women are particularly vulnerable to such typification because the colour of their skin makes it easy for staff to 'recognise them' and to assign them to a (negatively typified) group. 'Communication difficulties' were a major theme of the 'Asian' stereotype. The negative typifications were reinforced if women had poor English because midwives could more readily apply stereotypes to women with whom they could not communicate. Furthermore, women were unable to challenge the view that 'they're all the same'.

Communication difficulties: linguistic and cultural differences

Communication difficulties occur at two levels: the linguistic and the cultural. As demonstrated in the examples above language is a problem for some women. Their lack of English infuriated the midwives, and was one of the main 'problems with Asian women' mentioned by staff. More importantly, lack of English made the experience of hospital mystifying and often frightening for the women. However language was not the sole cause of misunderstanding. Even women who spoke good English experienced culturally-based communication difficulties.

Schutz (1976: 95) discusses the difficulty of the 'stranger', particularly (although not exclusively) an immigrant to a country, trying to interpret the cultural pattern of a social group which she or he approaches. He argues that the 'approached' (*i.e.* dominant) group has a system of knowledge, albeit 'incoherent, inconsistent and only partially clear', which allows anybody a reasonable chance of understanding and being understood. He describes this in terms of 'recipes' for interpreting the social world and expressing oneself within it. Garfinkel paraphrases this as 'common sense knowledge of social structures' (Garfinkel 1967: 76). The stranger does not share the dominant recipes for communication. As Schutz puts it, 'He becomes essentially the man who has to place in question nearly everything that seems to be unquestionable to the members of the approached group' (Schutz 1976: 96).

Applying these arguments to a medical setting, Hughes (1977) examines the way in which doctors in a casualty department use everyday knowledge to categorise patients: those needing immediate care; those who can wait; those who are deviant (drunk, down and out) and so on. He observed that overseas doctors had difficulty in typing patients and suggests that this may stem from their lack of 'conventional knowledge' (as opposed to medical expertise). It is possible to reverse this argument and to say that one reason why first generation black patients may become negatively typified is a result of the same phenomenon: they lack conventional 'common sense' knowledge about the system.

Ardener (1972, 1975, 1989) has discussed (with particular reference to the accounts of women rendered by (male) anthropologists in their monographs) how a subordinate group may become 'muted' in interactions with the dominant order. She argues not that they are dumb, but that when such groups become incorporated into dominant models and have to speak using dominant modes of expression then their meanings may become lost. They are muted because they are not listened to, or if listened to, not understood. Of course this argument can apply to all women using the maternity services: the dominant mode of expression is medical. However black and minority ethnic women will be doubly muted because they will be dealing with two degrees of dominance: the white British and the male medical.

In social interaction between any two (or more) parties offences against dominant social norms can occur. If offence occurs individuals usually engage in 'ritual remedial work': 'accounts, apologies and requests' (Goffman 1969:

365). Those from a minority cultural background are more likely, because of their unfamiliarity with majority culture, to offend these dominant norms. The offence is compounded because as they are less likely to have 'recipes' for social interaction they are therefore less likely to recognise the need for, or know how to carry out, remedial work.

Asian women as 'bad' patients

Stereotyping can be seen in the context of the research on patient typification. (See Kelly and May 1982 for a detailed review.) The characteristics of Asian women included in the midwives' stereotypes echo the negatively typified characteristics cited in this literature. In addition the women's ethnicity (which was never cited as a negative characteristic: no midwife told me that she didn't like black people) almost certainly plays a direct role in their typification as 'bad' patients.

Race, ethnicity and nationality have several effects. Patients who are not Caucasian, born outside Britain and who have poor command of English are likely to be unpopular. Several authors (Brown 1966, Papper 1970, Stockwell 1972) cite these characteristics as leading to negative client assessment by health professionals. In addition, a patient's ethnicity makes her more likely to be classified as an undesirable patient because her knowledge and expectations of the medical services are different to those of indigenous patients. Goffman (1969: 366), in his analysis of the sick role, writes that the proper enactment of this role involves a characteristic etiquette, for example entailing (in western culture) the belittling of discomfort, physical cooperation with carers and proper presentation of self. He notes that there are 'appreciable ethnic differences in the management of the sick role'.

There is evidence that patients become unpopular if they are perceived as constantly complaining (Armitage 1980, Lorber 1975, Stockwell 1972); malingering; and receiving treatment under false pretences (Kelly and May 1982). Those who fail to conform to the clinical regime are also regarded unfavourably (Basque and Merige 1980, Gillis and Biesheuvel 1988, Spitzer and Sobel 1962).

A theme running through the data reported above is the role of communication difficulties which may be seen as a major factor in negative typification of Asian women. Because of these problems it can be more difficult and time consuming for midwives to care for them. Menzies (1960) leads us to expect that patients who cause a high level of anxiety or who cause staff to feel ineffective or angry (such as women who cannot communicate to staff that they are all right) may become negatively typified. This is supported by other studies (*e.g.* Gillis and Biesheuvel 1988, Holderby and McNulty 1979, Orlando 1961, Schwartz 1958, Ujhely 1963). In addition Kelly and May (1982) point out that some patients are defined as difficult because they hinder staff in their work. Finally perceived patient intelligence has been shown to influence staff's evaluation of them (Gillis and Biesheuvel 1988, MacGregor 1960, Papper 1970).

Accepting a rigid stereotyped view of Asian women may act as a defence against the anxiety generated in staff who cannot communicate with them. Stereotyping can allow staff to make assumptions about the care women need (or deserve). In the context of the present study, a midwife does not need to feel too anxious about the noise an Asian woman makes in labour because, according to the stereotyped view such women have 'a low pain threshold' and therefore do not need pain relief. In addition they 'make a fuss about nothing' and so do not deserve it either. Asian women's problems with English become part of the stereotype and so staff's willingness to try to communicate with them is reduced.

There is a second set of explanations for the prevalence of stereotyping associated with the different attitudes and behaviour (real or perceived) of the women. Several authors note that patients who are judged to be attention-seeking (Gillis and Biesheuvel 1988, Jeffery 1979, Lorber 1975, MacGregor 1960); demanding (Brown 1966, Gillis and Biesheuvel 1988, Jeffery 1979, Papper 1970, Schwartz 1958); or who are thought to disrupt clinical routine unnecessarily (Lorber 1975, Orlando 1961) are negatively typified by staff. Those who are seen as manipulative (Armitage 1980, Ujhely 1963) are particularly unpopular.

In their review of the research on 'good and bad patients' Kelly and May (1982) comment that the criteria cited for negative typification tend to be treated as objective facts, having a concrete reality independent of the observer. This is to deny the essentially subjective nature of stereotyping. Stereotypes are socially constructed. For example certain behaviours are defined by midwives as 'making a fuss about nothing' whereas other behaviours are considered to be legitimate. This typology is not objective but is affected by the attitudes, both personal and professional, of the staff.

As Murcott emphasises, when typifying patients 'staff's concerns with getting through the day's work are of more immediate relevance then general moral concerns' (Murcott 1981: 129). Second, and more subtly, women are unpopular if they prevent the midwives from fulfilling their role. This includes everything from carrying out their work well to feeling positive about themselves. Once a midwife has had several difficult encounters with women of Asian descent it is not surprising if, by virtue of their visibility, all Asian women become perceived by her as 'difficult patients'. In this way stereotypes form and are transmitted to other staff.

In another paper May and Kelly (1982) discuss typifications of patients in psychiatric nursing. They contrast two patients with disruptive behaviour. One is excused (she can't help it/ it's part of her illness), whilst the other is negatively typified (she knows what she's doing). The authors argue that negative typification results when patients prevent staff from fulfilling activities which are a necessary part of self esteem and professional image. They go on to suggest that often it is the desire to censure a patient which results in the deviant being held responsible for his/her behaviour. Thus staff classify the patient's behaviour as good or bad after they have formed an impression of the patient's moral status. For black and minority ethnic women their moral status may (for some staff) be already compromised because they are black. Racist attitudes are not unknown among health service staff (Brent Community Health Council 1981, Larbie 1985, Phoenix 1990). Midwives could employ a stereotype to allow them to practice discrimination based on ethnicity without having to admit that to themselves, or appearing to others to be racist.

The effect of stereotypes
The data demonstrate the presence and construction of stereotypes of Asian women, but it is beyond the scope of the study to investigate fully their effect. The data strongly suggest that women are disadvantaged by the assumptions made about them by midwives. The two clearest cases concern family planning and pain control. In the examples of Mrs Begum and Saida neither midwife endeavoured to overcome language difficulties and talk about fertility control because they 'knew' that the women were not interested. Yet the example of the young couple with the unwanted pregnancy shows that this assumption should not be made. In that case it cannot be known whether termination would have been discussed with a similar white British couple.

None of the six Asian women observed during labour was offered pain control other than gas and air. Of the four white women observed two had intervention to control their pain. The sample is not matched and so no direct comparison is possible. The only indication is that in the case of Shakila, who suffered a long and painful labour, the registrar who saw her several hours after induction told me that pethidine could not be given because it was too close to the delivery. In the cases of the white women who had pain control this was at the suggestion of a midwife. The midwife looking after Shakila, who could have offered pethidine at an appropriate time, did not.

Stereotypes of Asian maternity patients, and black and ethnic minority patients generally, cannot be dissociated from the racist attitudes of many white people in Britain (one third of the sample in the 1984 *British Social Attitudes* survey admitted to being racially prejudiced, Jowell and Airey 1984). Space does not allow for a discussion of how the midwives' stereotypes reflect or feed into racist discourse but the following point can be made. Although it cannot be known whether the midwives were consciously or overtly racist *any* stereotype based on a racial or ethnic group is discriminatory, regardless of the stated attitudes of those holding the view.

Conclusion

This analysis has revealed several different ways in which stereotypes affect the interaction between staff and women, and how this interaction can reinforce the negative views of women. Lipsky (1980), citing the examples of the education and judicial systems, notes that the reification of stigmatised views of a client into facts about a client is common. This process affects the client's future encounters with the bureaucracy.

Individuals are typed according to a variety of criteria, cited in the literature review above. Macintyre (1978: 599) notes that staff revise their typification in the light of interactions with patients. It is difficult for women to assert their 'moral status' (and so get the typification revised) because language difficulties and cultural differences make it hard for them to make individual relationships with midwives.

There is evidence that ethnicity is a powerful criterion for typification, made stronger by its very visibility. Jeffery (1979: 90) shows how certain sorts of patients are unable to achieve entry into the legitimate career of sickness. The stereotypes emphasised the deviance of Asian women. If it is the women's ethnicity which causes them to be negatively typified then they are being disadvantaged because of ascribed ethnicity and not on the basis of individual action.

This analysis has implications for 'cultural awareness training' which can lead to static stereotyped views. It can encourage staff to make assumptions about ethnic difference based upon physical (racial) difference. If an Asian woman makes a noise in labour this is not because she is in pain but because Asian women in general have low pain thresholds and make fuss about nothing. There is therefore a difference in kind between stereotypes of black women and those of white women based on class. Race is a very hard boundary to cross. Stereotypes of Asian women can be applied purely on the basis of physical appearance and are therefore potentially racist.

A midwife in the present study asked me if I could recommend some information to help her understand her Asian patients. I suggested the booklets by Alix Henley (e.g. Henley, 1982, Caring for Muslims and Their Families). The midwife looked surprised 'I don't have time to read books,' she said, 'What we need is an A4 bit of paper with it all on so we can look things up when we need them'. This attitude to ethnicity is that all we need is some kind of cultural recipe book. Her reaction is similar to that of many health professionals to the complexities of other ethnicities: they're different to us (we need a map) but they're all the same (so one map will do).

Midwives were inclined to accept a view of 'Asian women' as a homogeneous group. In fact they were heterogeneous, not only in their cultural and religious background, but also in their relationships with staff. In other words the midwives held a rigid homogeneous view of these women, based on their physical appearance, in a way they did not for white British women. The behaviours and characteristics which led to negative typification of the women by midwives were not, therefore, common to all women of Asian descent. However characteristics of *some* women led to a stereotyped view which was attached to *all* women who were (or, more significantly, *looked* as if they were) of 'Asian' ethnic origin. As Phoenix (1990: 228) writes, 'The propensity to see black women as being 'all the same' is not only inaccurate but also racially discriminatory in that it can mask individual black women's needs'.

Acknowledgements

Some of the data and analysis in this paper were presented at the BSA conference, *Society and Health*, 1991. The author would like to thank Paul Atkinson, Robert Dingwall, David Hughes and the anonymous referees for their comments on earlier drafts of this paper.

Notes

1   The fieldwork was carried out whilst the author was an ESRC-funded graduate student. The views expressed in this article are those of the author, not the ESRC.
2   Women are booked for care with a consultant obstetrician and delivered in the hospital labour ward. However their routine antenatal checks are carried out by their GP and community midwife, *i.e.* the antenatal care is shared. This compares with GP directed care where all care is community based and the woman is delivered by community midwives in the General Practitioner Unit.
3   Estimated by the city council. The 1981 census did not collect data on ethnic origin, data from the 1991 census is not yet available.
4   This study is part of a wider project which also included a separate study of South Asian descent women who were recruited from an English language class and by snowball sampling. It is from this second study that the background information on the Asian women is derived.
5   Asmat is a pseudonym, as are all other names of respondents.
6   For a more detailed analysis of these issues see Currer (1983), Donovan (1986), Homans (1980).

References

Ardener, E. (1972) Belief and the problem of women. Reprinted in Ardener, S. (ed.) (1975) *Perceiving Women*. London: Dent.
Ardener, S. (1975) The problem of women revisited. In Ardener, S. (ed.) (1975) *Perceiving Women*. London: Dent.
Ardener, E. (1989) *The Voice of Prophesy*. (Edited by Malcolm Chapman). Oxford: Blackwell.
Armitage, S. (1980) Non-compliant recipients of health care. *Nursing Times Occasional Papers*, 76, 1.
Basque, L.O. and Merige, J. (1980) Nurses' experiences with dangerous behaviour: implications for training. *J. Continuing Education in Nursing*, 11, 47–51.
Brent Community Health Council (1981) *Black Women and the Maternity Services*. London: Brent Community Health Council.
Brown, E.L. (1966) Nursing & patient care. Reprinted in Davis, A. (ed.) (1978) *Relationships between Doctors and Patients*. Farnborough: Saxon House.
Coleman, D.A. and Salt, J. (1992) *The British Population*. Oxford: Oxford University Press.
Currer, C. (1983) *The Mental Health of Pathan Mothers in Bradford: A Case Study of Migrant Asian Women*. Coventry: University of Warwick.

Diamond, I. and Clarke, S. (1989) Demographic patterns among Britain's Ethnic Groups. In Joshi, H. (ed.) (1989) *The Changing Population of Britain.* Oxford: Blackwell.

Donovan, J. (1986) *We Don't Buy Sickness It Just Comes.* Aldershot: Gower.

Garfinkel, H. (1967) *Studies in Ethnomethodology.* Englewood Cliffs, NJ: Prentice-Hall.

Gillis, L. (with Biesheuvel, S.) (1988) *Human Behaviour in Illness.* London: Faber & Faber.

Gilroy, P. (1987) *There Ain't No Black in the Union Jack.* London: Hutchinson.

Goffman, E. (1969) The insanity of place. *Psychiatry* 32, 357–87. Reprinted in Black, N. *et al.* (eds) *Health and Disease: A Reader.* Milton Keynes: Open University Press.

Green, J. *et al.* (1990) Stereotypes of childbearing women: a look at some evidence. *Midwifery* 6, 125–32.

Hammersley, M. and Atkinson, P. (1983) *Ethnography: Principles in Practice.* London: Tavistock.

Henley, A. (1982) *Caring for Muslims and their Families: Religious Aspects of Care.* Cambridge: National Extension College.

Holderby, R.A. and McNulty, E.G. (1979) Feeling feelings: how to make a rational response to emotional behaviour. *Nursing.* October, 39–43.

Homans, H. (1980) *Pregnant in Britain. A Sociological Approach.* Unpublished PhD thesis: University of Warwick.

Homans, H. and Satow, A. (1982) Can you hear me? Cultural variations in communication. *J. Community Nursing.* January 1982, 16–18.

Hughes, D. (1977) Everyday medical knowledge in categorising patients. In Dingwall, R. *et al.* (eds) *Health Care and Health Knowledge.* London: Croom Helm.

Jeffery, R. (1979) Normal Rubbish: deviant patients in casualty departments. *Sociology of Health and Illness* 1, 90–107.

Jowell, R. and Airey, C. (1984) *British Social Attitudes.* London: Gower.

Kelly, M.P. and May, D. (1982) Good & bad patients: a review of the literature and a theoretical critique. *J. Advanced Nursing* 7, 147–56.

Larbie, J. (1985) *Black Women and the Maternity Services.* London: Training in Health and Race.

Lipsky, M. (1980) *Street-level Bureaucracy. Dilemmas of the Individual in Public Service.* New York: Russell Sage Foundation.

Lorber, J. (1975) Good patients and problem patients: conformity and deviance in a general hospital. *J. Health and Social Behavior* 16: 213–25.

MacGregor, F. (1960) *Social Science in Nursing: Applications for the Improvement of Patient Care.* New York: Russell Sage.

Macintyre, S. (1976) 'Who wants babies?' The social construction of 'Instincts'. In Leonard, D.L. and Allen, S. (eds) (1976) *Sexual Divisions and Society: Process and Change.* London: Tavistock.

Macintyre, S. (1978) Some notes on record taking, and making in an antenatal clinic. *Sociological Review* 26, 595–611.

May, D. and Kelly, M.P. (1982) Chancers, pests and poor wee souls: problems of legitimation in psychiatric nursing. *Sociology of Health and Illness* 4, 279–300.

Menzies, I.E.P. (1960) A case study in the functioning of social systems as a defence against anxiety. A report on a study of the nursing service of a general hospital. *Human Relations* 13, 95–121.

Murcott, A. (1981) On the typifications of 'bad' patients. In Atkinson, P. and Heath, C. (eds) (1981) *Medical Work: Realities and Routines.* London: Gower.

Orlando, I. (1961) *The Dynamic Nurse-Patient Relationship: Function, Process and Principles*. New York: G.P. Putnam's Sons.

Papper, S. (1970) The undesirable patient. *J. Chronic Diseases* 22, 777–9.

Pearson, M. (1986) The politics of ethnic minority health studies. In Rathwell, T. and Phillips, D. (eds) (1986) *Health, Race and Ethnicity*. Beckenham: Croom Helm.

Phoenix, A. (1990) Black women and the maternity services. In Garcia, J. *et al.* (eds) *The Politics of Maternity Care: Services for Childbearing Women in Twentieth-Century Britain*. Oxford: Clarendon Press.

Phoenix, A. and Woollett, A. (1991) Motherhood: Social construction, politics and psychology. In Phoenix, A. *et al.* (eds) (1991) *Motherhood. Meanings, Practices and Ideologies*. London: Sage.

Prottas, J.M. (1979) *People-Processing*. Lexington MA, USA: Lexington Books.

Rakusen, J. (1981) Depo-Provera: the extent of the problem. A case study in the politics of birth control. In Roberts, H. (ed.) *Women: Health and Reproduction*. London: Routledge & Kegan Paul.

Rathwell, T. (1984) General Practice, ethnicity and health services delivery. *Social Science and Medicine* 19, 123–30.

Schutz, Alfred (1976) The stranger: an essay in social psychology. In Schutz, A. *Collected Papers II. Studies in Social Theory*. Edited by Arvid Brodersen. The Hague, Netherlands: Martinus Nijhoff.

Schwartz, D. (1958) Uncooperative patients? *Amer. J, Nursing* 58, 75–7.

Shaw, A. (1988) *A Pakistani Community in Britain*. Oxford: Basil Blackwell.

Shaw, C. (1988) Components of growth in the ethnic minority population. *Population Trends* 52, 26–30.

Spradley, J.P. (1979) *The Ethnographic Interview*. New York: Holt, Reinhart & Winston.

Spitzer, S. and Sobel, R. (1962) Preferences for patients and patient behaviour. *Nursing Research* 11, 233–5.

Stockwell, F. (1972) *The Unpopular Patient*. Royal College of Nursing Research project. Series 1 no 2. London: Royal College of Nursing.

Ujhely, G.B. (1963) *The Nurse and her Problem Patient*. New York: Springer Verlag.

4.5

Doctor–patient negotiation of cultural assumptions

Sue Fisher and Stephen B. Groce

Introduction

Social action is a basic concept in sociology. Through time questions have been asked about how individuals come to behave appropriately and explanations have been generated which link norms or rules for behaviour with action. Parsons (1951) accounted for this phenomenon by positing that individuals internalize a shared set of norms. For Durkheim (1938), it was a collective consciousness that was shared in an external and constraining social world. And for Marx (1964), economic conditions provided the primary basis of the explanation.

These theorists lead us to believe that norms govern action – a position that has a long history of revision and criticism (see for example Gurwitsch 1964, Winch 1958, Wittgenstein 1952, among others). In this tradition Garfinkel and Cicourel have redefined and extended the concept of normative action. Garfinkel (1967) contends that individuals actively construct their behaviour. Rather than being 'judgmental dopes' who internalize deterministic norms into their cognitive systems, individuals are 'secret apprentices', ferreting from their daily interactions the information needed to act appropriately. While Garfinkel alludes to the context of action, he does not specify the relationship between norms and actual situations in the construction of behaviour. Mehan and Wood (1975) call this neglect of the social situation in which behaviour is constructed a 'constitutive bias'. It is this bias which Cicourel (1973) addresses when discussing the relationship between structure and process. Cicourel asks how individuals decide which norms are operating or relevant for the negotiation of social situations and concludes that general rules or policies (norms) must be interpreted within emergent, constructed action scenes. Meaning is constructed in this process of interpretation.

In this paper we simultaneously examine the relationship between norms as features of the social structure and norms as interactional accomplishments. We do so by analyzing medical conversations in a specific setting – a model family practice resident training programme in the southeastern part of the United States. In this setting, resident doctors diagnose illness and treat patients under the supervision of attending staff physicians. The patients are women who are using the clinic for the first time. Although the patients come from varied socioeconomic backgrounds, the residents and staff physicians in this hospital, as in most medical settings in the United States, are predominantly white, middle-class men (Navarro 1976).

We explore how cultural assumptions about patients as women emerge, develop and are negotiated and displayed as doctor and patient communicate over the course of an initial medical interview. Although at one level the argument can be taken as self-evident – the literature on the delivery of health care to women documents the pervasive use of medical domination in the form of sexism (*c.f.* Scully 1980, Ruzek 1978) – our point here is more subtle. We first examine *how* medical domination in the form of sexism is enacted and then we quantify our description. By posing cultural definitions of patients as women in a reflexive relationship with the interactional work participants do in a specific setting to construct action we can shed light on how doctors act as secret apprentices, ferreting from their medical interactions with new women patients cultural assumptions (or norms) about these patients as 'good' or 'bad' women. Once assumptions about women develop interactionally, they are evident in the discourse, structure the remaining exchange of information between doctor and patient and have consequences for the delivery of health care.

A growing body of literature suggests that doctors typify their clientele as either 'good' or 'problem' patients. Lorber (1975) finds that doctors evaluate those patients as 'good' who do not make trouble for the hospital staff and who do not interrupt established medical routines. Those who violate these norms of the medical relationship are considered 'problem' patients. Biener (1983) adds that factors such as the social distance between doctors and patients, the seriousness of presenting complaint and perceived patient co-operation influence doctors' perceptions and evaluations of their patients. Finally, Barr (1983) suggests that the perceived seriousness of presenting complaint is the strongest predictor of doctors' responses to patients.

The afore-mentioned studies (and many others like them) locate doctors' evaluations of patients within the normative framework of the doctor–patient relationship and the medical encounter itself. These studies suggest that 'patient' is the master status operating when a person visits the doctor. Macintyre (1977) has also discussed doctors' categorizations of patients, but has located the source of doctors' categorizations *outside* the framework of the doctor–patient relationship. She argues that during the course of consultations concerning unwanted pregnancies, doctors typify their clients as 'good' or 'bad' *women* rather than 'good' or 'bad' *patients*. Doctors ferret from the culturally produced collage of norms governing gender–role behaviour, sexuality and family interactions information which allows them to categorize their patients as 'good' or 'bad' women.

Following Macintyre, we suggest that *woman* emerges as the master status and overrides the status of *patient* in the interactional production of doctors' categorizations and evaluations of their clients. However, whether the master status is patient or woman, extant studies all take the negotiation of categorizations as unproblematic. Not only do we focus on woman as the master status, but we also analyze the *process* through which patients are identified as good or bad women and discuss how this identity, once formed, structures the discourse and influences the delivery of health care.

Cultural assumptions and medical dominance

Cultural assumptions about women take on increased significance when considered in the context of the structure of the medical relationship. Navarro
(1976) argues that the social and political factors woven into the fabric of
society are mirrored in the shape of the health care system. In this system,
class and gender interplay to give predominantly white, male physicians top
position in the medical hierarchy. Physicians, as the top 6 per cent in this
hierarchy, are the highest earners in the United States (see Conrad and Kern
1981, for a more complete discussion of these points). While 85 per cent of all
physicians are men, 75 per cent of all medical workers are women, and there
is almost no movement from one category of medical jobs to another, because
each has its own education and requires its own set of skills (Caress 1975, 1977).

The issue of control by a predominantly white, middle-class, male professional
group carries over to the doctor–patient relationship. Sociological examinations
of the medical relationship describe it as asymmetrical. Early discussions point
out the imbalance between the role of doctor and that of patient (Szasz and
Hollender 1956). Patients are described as passive dependent; doctors as active
and dominant (Parsons 1951). This asymmetry is ascribed to doctors' specialized medical knowledge, their technical skill, the professional prestige of their
role (Parsons 1951), and the organization of the profession and the practice
of medicine (Freidson 1970), as well as other demographic and interactional
variables (Zola 1972, Mechanic 1968, Davis 1963, Roth 1963).

Waitzkin and Waterman (1974) claim that most patients lack the medical
knowledge to be equal partners in the medical situations. Furthermore,
they describe this gap as widening at the lower end of the socioeconomic
spectrum. Patients at the lower end of the spectrum not only share different
life experiences, have less medical knowledge, and have fewer choices over
the medical setting in which they receive care, but they are also perceived as
irresponsible and forgetful (Ehrenreich and Ehrenreich 1970). Patients who
seek help in relative ignorance assume a subordinate position, while doctors
assume a superordinate one (Waitzkin and Waterman 1974). The woman's
role also contributes to being powerless. Ehrenreich and Ehrenreich (1970)
report that doctors assume women are difficult, neurotic, emotional, and
unable to understand complex explanations.

The asymmetry in the doctor–patient relationship, whether criticized or
accepted, is widely acknowledged by social scientists, medical providers, and
patients alike. Less well documented is whether doctor–patient interaction
in this asymmetrical relationship influences medical discourse and shapes
the delivery of health care. Recently a few researchers have taken the doctor–
patient relationship as a topic in its own right and begun to investigate
how doctor and patient transmit information during medical interviews. For
example, Strong (1979) suggests that the medical relationship is responsive
to a variety of medical factors: the nature of the medical problem, the

perceived social class of the patient, and the organization of the setting. Frankel (forthcoming) examines the details of doctor–patient communications and points out a 'dispreference' for patient-initiated questions during medical interviews. Others (Todd 1983, 1982, Fisher 1982, West 1982, Silverman 1981) argue that the lack of reciprocity in the practitioner–patient relationship creates gaps and misunderstandings in medical communication. They explore why the medical relationship is characterized by this lack of reciprocity and how the asymmetry in the medical relationship and the institutional authority of the physician's role influence medical decision-making in ways which have the potential to negatively influence the delivery of health care. In each of these analyses, the assumption, whether explicated or not, is that the asymmetry or paternalism which characterizes physician–patient discourse creates problems in the delivery of health care.

Medical interactions are social and micro political (Henley 1977, Waitzkin and Stoeckle 1976). They reflect and sustain cultural, structural and institutional factors and, in turn, are shaped by them. While medical encounters are interactions between individuals, the interactants – doctor and patient – are not equal interactional partners. Doctors have knowledge and skills that patients lack. By virtue of the authority vested in their professional role, doctors act as gatekeepers dominating the medical process. Since patients live in the same social world and frequently share a reciprocal view of the appropriate roles for doctors and patients, it is not too surprising that they often accept the subordinate role without question.

The issue here is *not* that the patient never has any power or that the doctor always has all of the power. Patients can and do ask questions, interrupt, change topics and claim and/or maintain the floor. Doctors' styles of communication can and do vary – some being more dominant and others more equalitarian. It is the institutional authority of the medical role and the control it provides for medical practitioners that does not change.

When doctors are men and patients are women, this imbalance is heightened[1]. In our society, the man–woman and the doctor–patient relationships recapitulate and reinforce each other, locking male physician and female patient in an asymmetrical relationship – a relationship in which female patients are dependent on their male physicians' judgments about them as women[2]. These judgments are often abstracted from the daily lives of women and frequently coloured by traditional assumptions about the appropriate roles for women in today's society.

The negotiations of cultural assumptions about women

Our data were gathered during the summer of 1981 in a model family practice clinic of a teaching hospital. Forty-three medical interviews of residents' initial visits with new women patients were audio and video taped and transcribed for later analysis. As we reviewed the transcripts we noticed a recurrent pattern: doctors were relying on cultural assumptions to categorize and evaluate their patients. In some cases the actual assumptions were directed toward the women *qua* patient and in other cases they are directed toward the woman *qua* women. The following examples, while showing the different forms cultural assumptions may take, all indicate this 'sizing-up' procedure:

Initiation	Response	Comment
P: I did put iodine on it. A lady told me it was good for ringworm so I thought it was ringworm	D: don't think this is ringworm	P: I don't think it is either

Later
P: I read up on it and I thought I had ringworm	D: well it didn't quite fit with ringworm	P: no I didn't think so

And later
D: what I would do is just keep an eye on this if it starts to spread a lot more if it's not getting better starts itching something like that let us see you again otherwise it should start fading over the next few weeks or it might take a month or more but it ought to go away//okay you want me to write that down for you	P: no I its all in that medical book at home I//	P: //uhhuh
D: //I'll write it down for you so you can remember what it is uh you have any other questions	P: nuhuh not that I know of	
D: alright otherwise we'll just see you back as we need to uh if a problem comes up		

This example illustrates cultural assumptions of woman *qua* patient. The patient says, 'I put iodine on it. A lady told me it was good for ringworm.' And later she continues, 'I read up on it and I thought I had ringworm.' In each case the doctor signals the inappropriateness of her behaviour by discounting her 'diagnosis' of ringworm. Finally, near the end of the interview, the patient tells the doctor that he need not write anything down for her because it's all in her medical book at home. The doctor interrupts her to say: 'I'll write it down for you so you can remember' (*c.f.* Groce and Fisher 1984 for a discussion of doctors' reactions to patient deviance as manifestations of social control). In each instance the woman displays behaviour inconsistent with the norms for 'good' patients, *i.e.* that patients allow the doctor to make diagnoses and treatment decisions and in each instance the doctor let the patient know that her behaviour is in some way inappropriate. In the end, the patient is cut off rather abruptly.

These transcripts also highlight assumptions or norms concerning woman *qua* women:

Initiation	Response	Comment
D: are you and your husband still having relations?	P: no no	
D: how long has that been	P: oh honey it's been I don't know I don't even know it's not a problem for either one of us	
D: oh so neither one of you care about that anymore	P: no no no	
D: he doesn't say if you'd like to	P: no no//he's sick too he's sick people you just	D: //okay
D: so that's not a problem	P: no nuhhub	
D: so that's not a part of what's making you sad	P: lord no honey lord no	

In this example, despite the patient's assurance that the absence of sexual relations in her marriage is *not* a problem to either her or her husband, the doctor repeatedly asks a variation of the same question; namely, is the absence of sex a problem. The patient's 'Lord no, honey, Lord no', provides an emphatic denial. In this case the doctor seems to be operating on the normative expectation (cultural assumption) that married women *should* engage in sexual relations with their husbands and if they do not, problems *should* result.

We found that the negotiation of cultural assumptions was a pervasive pattern that occurred in the majority of transcripts in our data set. There were

instances, particularly in briefer medical interviews, where these negotiations were less evident. Overall twenty-eight (67.4%) interviews contained
evidence of the negotiation of norms. In twelve (27.8%) norms about women
qua patient emerged and were negotiated against a background of cultural
expectations about patients. These occurred somewhat less frequently and
were not for us the most interesting. While doctors interrupted women
who were not acting like good patients and even evidenced some mild disapproval, we could find little evidence of how this behaviour influenced
medical outcomes. In sixteen (36.0%) norms about woman *qua* women
emerged and were negotiated against a background of cultural expectations
about women. In these instances doctors' behaviour seemed to indicate that
they 'liked' or 'did not like' patients as women and these evaluations, once
triggered, emerged more clearly as the medical interview unfolded to
influence the delivery of care. To illustrate this relationship we chose two
archetypal cases with the same doctor as examples – one in which the
picture of woman *qua* women that emerged was not consistent with cultural
norms about good women and another in which there was consistency. Since
it was our purpose to shed light on the intricacies of the reflexive relationship between cultural assumptions or norms about women and the communicational work doctors and patients do to produce and sustain them, we
analyze these two interviews in depth. A detailed comparison of them not
only reveals divergent sets of cultural assumptions, but how these assumptions emerge, structure and are expressed in the discourse, and influence the
delivery of health care.

   In each case, we explore how cultural assumptions are negotiated over the
course of the medical interview and comment on the relationship between
these assumptions and the delivery of health care. Then we examine the
ways in which these assumptions structure the discourse. The analysis
extends beyond the linguistic boundaries of the transcripts to blend linguistic data with more impressionistic ethnographic data. It seems reasonable
that neither residents nor patients say aloud all that contributes to the medical interview process. For example, patients rarely say aloud that they do
not trust their medical practitioners or that they feel unheard, manipulated,
and dissatisfied with the medical care they have received. Similarly, residents
do not say aloud that patients look like poor women or talk like uneducated
women. They do not say that the way patients talk, act, or dress leads them
to believe that they are 'good' or 'bad' women and influences the medical
interview and ultimately the delivery of health care. Yet while they are not
said in so many words, our observations suggest that these factors and a
host of similar ones are expressed in the discourse and contribute to the
diagnostic-treatment process.

   The first patient is Maria, a 24-year-old, unmarried, overweight Mexican-
American woman. She moved to this region from the far west, accompanying the boyfriend she currently lives with. Maria arrives for the interview
dressed in a pair of jeans and a loose-fitting shirt. Her presenting complaint

is a leg injury sustained during a motorcycle accident. While discussing the circumstances surrounding the accident, the resident's questions and his comments begin to display the unfolding of his cultural assumptions about Maria's 'character', *i.e.*, what kind of woman she is:

Initiation		*Response*		*Comment*	
D:	All right now let's see you were on your motorcycle and what happened	P:	well I was . . .		
D:	were you on the back	P:	no I was driving	D:	you were driving
D:	what kind do you drive	P:	a 450 . . . it's too big	D:	//a 450
D:	that's a big hod ain't it	P:	yeah it's too big// it's an older model and it's too heavy//so it took off and left me behind	D:	//uhhuh
				D:	//uhhuh
D:	so you fell off	P:	yeah, I fell off	D:	hhmmff

The negotiation of cultural assumptions has begun. In the second exchange the resident asks, 'Were you on the back?' Maria responds that she was driving the motorcycle and the resident recycles this information repeating, 'You were driving'. And continues by asking, 'What kind do you drive?' Maria tells him that she drives a big motorcycle – 'a 450' and again the resident recycles the information repeating, 'a 450'. While these exchanges might indicate the resident's awe, Maria has not successfuly managed the bike. She is at the clinic because of a leg injury. We suggest instead that the structure of the discourse provides time for the resident to regroup and displays a disjuncture between the norms or cultural assumption about the appropriate roles for women and the behaviour of this woman as it has emerged in the medical interview. This disjuncture is highlighted in the next exchange. The resident 'code switches' (Bernstein 1973). His 'ain't it' combines with the way he has recycled information and his emphatic 'hhmmff' to display the disjuncture further. As cultural members we would agree that it is more common for women to ride on the back of a motorcycle, not to drive one – especially such a big one. Maria displays her shared understanding that her behaviour was somehow inappropriate. The issue for her is the size of the motorcycle. Twice she acknowledges that the motorcycle is 'too big'.

During an exchange later in the interview, the picture of Maria is developed further:

Initiation	Response	Comment
	P: ... when I put the alcohol on it ((her leg)) I thought I was going to pass out from the pain//and I can take pain too	D: //oh
D: so you needed to take the alcohol internally and not ...	P: yeah, I tried that and that didn't work either no not a bit	

And later:

Initiation	Response	Comment
D: how much alcohol do you drink	P: uhm ...	
D: do you drink every day	P: uhm no no//about a few times a month	D: //no

Maria explains that when she washed her injured leg with alcohol the pain was so severe that she thought she was going to pass out. She makes her point more emphatic by boasting that she can tolerate high levels of pain. The resident takes alcohol used externally – to wash a wound – and switches to alcohol used internally – to ease pain. Later in the medical history phase of the interview the resident returns to the topic of alcohol use – drinking.

In a conservative Bible belt area where many people do not drink and some would be offended if asked about drinking, it is most unusual to hear questions phrased in such ways that seem to presume alcohol consumption – 'How much alcohol do you drink?' – and even more unusual to suggest that this behaviour occurs daily – 'Do you drink every day?' Nowhere else in our data do we see questions about alcohol use phrased in this way. The more typical question is, 'Do you drink alcohol?' If answered affirmatively, this question is on some occasions followed by another more specific one – 'How much alcohol do you drink?' Why the switch from a medicinal to a more social concept of use, why the change in the form of the questions asked about alcohol consumption and why the suggestion that the patient needs to drink alcohol for her leg pain?

This resident is a fundamentalist Christian raised in a 'Bible Belt' area[3]. His conservative attitudes toward drinking are well known in the clinic. We speculate that jostling Maria about drinking displays his religious beliefs as well as his developing picture of her as a woman. The structure of the discourse developed thus far suggests that he is coming to see her as an unfeminine, hard-drinking, motorcycle-riding woman who can take pain. The emerging picture of Maria is increasingly discrepant with traditional assumptions about women.

As the medical interview unfolds, Maria contributes further to the assumptions building about her:

Initiation	Response	Comment
D: have you ever been in the hospital	P: yeah	
D: what for	P: abortion	D: abortion
D: okay, how many times have you been pregnant	P: four	D: four times
D: what happened to all the pregnancies	P: three abortions and one miscarriage	D: one miscarriage
P: and I have a question too	D: uhhuh	
P: I feel that I might be again do you perform that kind of thing here	D: abortions, no no we don't	

And later:

Initiation	Response	Comment
D: what kind of birth control are you on	P: well I was on the pill for the longest time and I quit//and I just been going without for a few months	D: //uhhuh
P: I was spotting on that ((the birth control pills))	D: spotting on that okay well that's another subject//but I'll be glad to work with you on that//anyway I'll want to talk to you about all the different forms of birth control and explain all the	P: //yeah P: //okay

Initiation	Response	Comment
	different side effects of the pill // and some	P: //okay
	of the good effects and then	P: //okay
	go from there	
D: when was the last time you were at Planned Parenthood	P: uhm about 16 months ago	
D: well you need another Pap smear//*as many times as you've been pregnant*//has your foot been hurting		P: //yeah definitely
		P: //definitely

In answer to a standard question usually asked while taking a medical history, 'Have you ever been in hospital?' Maria tells the doctor that she has had three abortions and one miscarriage. The doctor recycles each piece of information, 'abortion', 'four times', and 'one miscarriage'. Each recycle provides time for him to reformulate and continue and each expresses a disjuncture between commonly held norms or cultural assumptions about women and the picture of herself this woman presents.

Once again Maria illustrates her shared understanding. She says, 'I feel I *might be again* do you perform *that kind of thing here.*' The elliptical way she refers to her suspicion that she might be pregnant and need another abortion further supports our suggestion that both doctor and patient recognize her pregnancies and abortions as somehow at odds with generally accepted cultural norms. Maria then goes on to justify her lack of birth control by saying that she spotted (bled) on the birth control pill so she stopped taking them and has '. . . been going without for a few months'.

The medical attitude toward abortion is common knowledge at the hospital. Doctors who perform them are talked about disparagingly and patients are often told that abortions can be obtained more inexpensively from an outpatient abortion clinic in the community. When placed in this conservative Bible belt context, the data are easier to understand. When asked about abortions, the resident claims that he cannot provide them. And the grounds stated by the resident to establish the need for Pap smear are, . . . 'as many times as you've been pregnant'. Again common medical assumption is displayed in the discourse: the increased sexual activities of today's population of young women plus the added strain of multiple abortions place women at a greater risk from cervical cancer (see Spletter 1983, Fisher 1982a for a more complete discussion of the social assumptions associated with cervical cancer).

In the next sequence, medication for Maria's leg is discussed and we begin to see how the resident's picture of her as a woman influences the delivery of health care:

Initiation	Response	Comment
D: well I'm really hesitant about medication//you're not, sure even though you know you might say have an abortion ((while he reads the label on some medicine))	P: definitely	P: //yeah
D: you may uh well the medication I want to use it's not recommended during pregnancy for treating nursing mothers or during pregnancy, tell you what to do what kind of if you just don't do anything you're alright	P: oh alright	

In this sequence, there is more concern with protecting an unborn foetus than there is with treating the pain from Maria's leg injury. The resident says, 'the medication I want to use, it's not recommended during pregnancy', and decides against *any* medication. He reaches the decision in spite of the fact that Maria has indicated that she had intense pain. Although an unwillingness to prescribe medicine that is unsafe for pregnant women is laudable, we question why the resident neither looks further for safer medication, nor takes Maria's statement that she 'definitely' wants an abortion into consideration.

Over the course of the medical interview, personal information about Maria has been gathered piece by piece. She not only rides motorcycles, she *drives* them – and rather large ones at that; she is a strong woman with an ability to withstand pain; she drinks; she has a history of abortions – not one, but three plus the possibility of another one in the near future; she lives, unmarried, with her boyfriend; and, while sexually active, she is not using birth control. This view of Maria, obtained over the course of the medical interview, influences the delivery of health care. Maria left the clinic without the Pap smear that both she and the resident agreed she needed, without the birth control information which the resident told her he would provide, without the abortion information that she requested, and without *any* medication to treat her leg pain. Finally, in closing the interview, Maria is not encouraged to return to the clinic:

Initiation	Response	Comment
D: it was nice meeting you	P: same to you I'll come back whenever I need to see a doctor . . .	
D: hopefully 24 year old ladies don' need many doctors	P: yeah okay thanks a lot bye bye	

Before discussing further the relationship between cultural assumption and the delivery of health care, we examine a case which contrasts with Maria's. The patient, Sarah, is a shy, 23-year-old. She is well-dressed in conservative, middle-class attire. As the medical interview unfolds, Sarah displays herself very differently than Maria did.

Initiation	Response	Comment
D: . . . we'll do a Pap smear and a pelvic today . . . well//		
P: //what's a pelvic	D: . . . the big thing is feeling your uterus and your ovaries and uh Pap smear is the scraping uh//	P: //of the uterus?
D: you had that before	P: no I never have	
D: never had it before	P: nuh uh ((no))	D: well how did//
P: //well I just never had it I heard that it wasn't necessary actually	D: nah I don't think anybody would tell you that it's not necessary	
P: well someone told me that as long as you weren't sexually active it isn't necessary	D: uhm//there may be a little in that//but it's not really true	P: //but then P: //but

Early in the interview, as the resident reviews the upcoming procedures, Sarah interrupts him to ask, 'What's a pelvic?' After explaining a pelvic examination and Pap smear, the resident says, 'You had that before'. Sarah indicates her sexual inexperience by saying that she has never had a Pap smear. Again the resident signals a disjuncture. He recycles this information and repeats his question. Sarah explains that she had heard that it was not necessary if a woman was not sexually active.

As the interview unfolds, both the doctor's assumptions about women and Sarah become more evident:

Initiation	Response	Comment
D: you ever been on birth control	P: no I haven't	
P: but that's something else I want to talk to you about	D: okay	
D: let's see are you married	P: no I'm not	
D: okay what do you do	P: what do I . . . I've just been using over-the-counter suppositories	

Sarah has never used prescription birth control, but wants to talk about it during this visit. Birth control may, in fact, be the reason for her visit – her hidden agenda. This request signals her emerging status as a sexually active woman and elicits the next question. The resident asks, 'Are you married?' and Sarah replies that she is not.

The resident's next question, 'Okay, what do you do?' is ambiguous. He could be asking for her occupational status, or asking how she manages sexual relationships outside of marriage so as not to get pregnant. He could be checking his cultural assumptions about women and constructing a view of Sarah in the process. If she is unmarried and sexually active, is she responsible? Even if she is without the social acceptability that sexual relationships within marriage provide, if she used some birth control measure to prevent unwanted pregnancy, her behaviour may still be consistent with commonly held cultural assumptions – although sexual behaviour is changing, responsible people use some form of birth control. He could, in addition, be making a more subtle assumption about the relationship between responsibility and social class. The resident's question, 'Okay, what do you do', could signal his conclusion that Sarah is an intelligent and responsible middle-class women who would be using birth control. The phrasing of the question leaves Sarah momentarily confused. She responds, 'What do I . . . ?' After a brief hesitation, she validates the resident's conclusion: 'I've just been using over-the-counter suppositories'.

Later in the interview, more evidence is presented that Sarah has a good background. She comes from a 'normal', middle-class family:

Initiation	Response	Comment
D: you just had your normal sore throats	P: uhhuh	
D: and all that and your childhood shots	P: uhhuh	
D: how about your *daddy is* he healthy	P: he's healthy, he's taking medication for	

Initiation	Response	Comment
	high blood pressure	D: uhm
D: how about your *mama*	P: she's healthy	

Underlying the phrasing of questions in this exchange are assumptions about Sarah's background. She comes from an intact nuclear family and she received the necessary childhood immunizations: Sarah's answers validate these assumptions. It is particularly interesting to us that questions of this sort were not included in Maria's interview. The resident asks no questions about childhood diseases or immunizations and did not inquire as to the existence or the condition of Maria's parents[4].

At this point, there is a picture of Sarah as a shy, newly sexually active, middle-class woman using over-the-counter contraceptives and inquiring about a more effective form of birth control. The resident summarizes the advantages and disadvantages of the available methods of contraception – birth control pills, diaphragms, IUDs, condoms, and spermicides. Throughout this discussion, an assumption is displayed: Sarah, although unmarried, cannot risk an unwanted pregnancy – she is a 'good' woman. To protect her a case for the birth control pill as the preferred contraceptive method is developed (see Fisher and Todd, forthcoming for a more complete discussion of this point):

Initiation	Response	Comment
D: you plan to get married sometime soon	P: uhhuh//it wouldn't be until I get out of school which should be next summer	D: //okay
D: well what would be perfectly acceptable for me if I was in your shoes is to be on the birth control pills until next summer for sure and uh that time you see how you did on them		

Once again, assumptions are reflected in the communication. If Sarah is sexually active, she will marry soon. As an intelligent and responsible woman, until she marries she will use an effective contraceptive. The resident declares that it is acceptable to him for her to use the birth control pill until she marries. Notice the use of authority. The doctor relies on the institutional authority of his role to control the flow of information and to 'help' the patient reach her decision about which method of contraception to use[5]. This institutionally based authority allows him to act as a gatekeeper, providing options to Sarah which were not provided to Maria.

Summary

The medical interviews just discussed produce two very different pictures of Maria and Sarah. In so doing, they illustrate commonly held cultural assumptions (norms) about women as well as how these norms are interactional accomplishments negotiated and displayed over the course of the medical interview. Assumptions about these patients emerged and were developed as doctor and patient discussed medical and social topics. In the first case, as the interview unfolded a negative picture of Maria developed. In the second case a positive picture of Sarah developed.

In each case, the delivery of health care was shaped by norms about the patients that were negotiated as the medical interviews unfolded. Maria came to the clinic with a painful leg injury. While this was her presenting complaint, several other medical problems emerged over the course of the medical interview. She left the clinic without having either her presenting complaint or the other problems which emerged during the medical interview dealt with. She received no prescription for pain and was encouraged not to return.

By comparison, Sarah came to the clinic requesting a Pap smear and a pelvic examination. Over the course of the medical interview, her need for information about menstrual pain and her interest in birth control information emerged. She left the clinic after both her presenting complaint and her emergent problems had been dealt with. She received a Pap smear and a pelvic examination as well as information about and prescriptions for menstrual pain and birth control. Again, the institutional authority of the medical role gave the resident control. He could provide medical services to Sarah (information and prescriptions) while denying them to Maria.

While the negotiation of norms about women and medical outcomes were interactional accomplishments, the institutional authority of the doctor's role gave the resident an interactional edge, which was expressed in the communication. Patients came to the clinic with what they perceived as medical problems. When the resident asked questions and they responded, presenting a social as well as a medical picture of themselves, patients may not have been aware of either the picture of themselves that was being developed or the consequences for them of that picture. Yet the data suggest that this information influenced the resident's conception of them as women as well as the health care he delivered.

We suspected that as a medical provider and a middle-class man the resident would hold certain culturally shared assumptions about women learned in society and reinforced in medical school (Scully 1980, Ruzek 1978, Scully and Bart 1973). This suspicion has been taken as the topic under study. The data suggest that as the medical interview unfolded the resident matched his cultural assumptions about women with the information the patient presented about herself – he acted like a secret apprentice ferreting out and interpreting information and developing a picture of the kind of woman the patient was. When there was a disjuncture between the norms about the appropriate ways for women to behave and the ways the patient described her behaviour, the discrepancy was marked in the discourse: the resident recycled information. Information was recycled with both Maria and Sarah. In each case the resident expressed disapproval and incredulity: Maria drove such a big motorcycle and had repeated abortions; Sarah did not know that women, even if they were not sexually active, needed Pap smears.

The negotiation of cultural assumptions was marked in the discourse in another way as well: the resident switched codes to a less formal, less medically appropriate way of talking. Code switching was only done with Maria. The resident's 'ain't it' spoke down to Maria and, we claim, displayed his developing redefinition of her.

As norms about women patients were negotiated they structured the remaining exchange of information and the delivery of health care. Although Sarah received the care for which she came to the clinic, Maria did not. Not only did Maria not have her presenting complaint cared for, but, perhaps even more importantly, none of the medical problems which emerged as the medical interview unfolded were dealt with. This raises a question about the adequacy of the care she received. The resident's authority allowed him to control medical outcomes, at least in part, by controlling the structure of the discourse. The finding is clearer when the structure of the discourse is examined more closely.

Cultural assumptions, medical authority, and the structure of discourse

Fisher (1984) identifies four phases of medical interviews – opening, medical history, physical examination, and closing phases[6]. Each phase has a characteristic form and specific task function. She suggests that during the opening phase the task is to get the patient's story – why she initiated the medical visit. It is during this phase that patients have the most input into the medical interview. The task of the medical history and physical examination phases is to gather the medical and social information necessary to treat the presenting complaint, gaining sufficient background information to provide quality medical care. During the closing phase, the task is for the doctor to sum up his/her findings, make treatment recommendations, prescribe medications, and, in general, to present the information the patient needs to reach a medical decision.

She finds that the asymmetry in the doctor–patient relationship is reflected in the phase structure of medical interviews. Doctors initiate topics and control access to the floor (who speaks when) as well as the flow of medical information. Although patients initiate less and ask fewer questions, they do ask questions and initiate exchanges of information which call for responses from physicians. While it could be argued that the doctor's word output over the course of the medical interview is influenced by both personality and context variables, we make a different argument. To validate our quantification of doctor-patient

Table 1 *Doctor's work output across medical interview phases*

	Maria		Sarah	
Phase	Words/ initiation	Words/ response	Words/ initiation	Words/ response
Opening	6.4	5.0	17.7	14.0
History	6.7	16.4	47.4	111.8
Closing	13.9	16.7	31.5	–*

* The patient made no initiations during this phase.

communication we point to research which demonstrates a positive correlation between doctors' raw word output and outcome variables such as patient compliance and satisfaction (*c.f.* Pfefferbaum *et al.* 1982, Slavin *et al.* 1982, Freemon *et al.* 1971). These and other studies show repeatedly that the more a doctor talks with/to a patient, the more satisfied the patient is with the medical encounter and the more likely s/he will be to comply with the prescribed regimen. Table 1 presents a numerical view of how information is exchanged across the phases of the interview and suggests that the ways the resident came to see Maria and Sarah affected the structure of the discourse.

Table 1 indicates a quantitative difference in the way information is both offered and responded to in the two interviews. The resident communicates more with Sarah than he does with Maria. In the opening phase, he responds to Sarah with an average of 14.0 words per response, while he responds to Maria with an average of only 5.0 words per response. In Maria's interview, the resident initiates at an average of only 6.4 words per initiation; in Sarah's interview, he initiates at 17.7 words per initiation. The resident's initiations are roughly two and one-half times longer in Sarah's interview. During the opening phase, the doctor both gathers and provides more information with Sarah than with Maria. This finding is consistent with and reinforces an earlier one: the way the resident came to see the two women is reflected in the structure of the discourse as well as the delivery of care.

This pattern continues through the medical history phase. In a phase typically characterized by short resident initiations, the table indicates a significant difference in the doctor's words per initiation. With Maria, he is short and to the point – only 6.7 words per initiation; with Sarah, though, his average words per initiation increases to 47.4. In terms of resident responses, we see a similar pattern. While he responds to Maria with only 16.4 words per response, he responds to Sarah with an average of 111.8 words per response. We once again argue that the doctor's typifications of Sarah and Maria influence the discourse, limiting the exchange of information[7].

Since Sarah made no initiations during the closing phase of the interview, the only category with comparable figures is the resident's words per initiation.

Table 2 *Patients' word output by topic*

	Maria		
Topic	*Words per initiation*	*Words per response*	*Words per utterance*
Presenting complaint	9.0	12.9	10.9
Birth control	5.8	10.5	8.2
Abortion	18.5	26.5	22.5
	Sarah		
Topic	*Words per initiation*	*Words per response*	*Words per utterance*
Presenting complaint	10.7	2.5	6.6
Birth control	17.7	5.8	11.8
Menstrual cycle	7.5	11.3	9.4

Here again, the developing pattern persists. Typically, the closing phase is characterized by a high incidence of doctor initiations as he sums up his findings and provides the patient with the information she needs to reach a medical decision. However, even here we see a discrepancy between the two interviews. The resident initiates exchanges with Sarah at an average of 31.5 words per initiation, a figure that suggests that he is providing information to her. His words per initiation average with Maria is only 13.9, which suggests that he provides her with less information. The lack of information provided to Maria is consistent with the limited health care which was delivered.

Our data indicate that cultural assumptions about these patients as women have an impact on how the resident manages both the patient's presenting complaint and the medically relevant topics that emerge during the course of the interview. Table 2 displays the patient's word outputs for topics that arise during the interview.

These tables indicate that both Maria and Sarah have preferences for certain topics. Maria clearly would rather discuss the availability of abortions than her motorcycle injury – her stated reason for coming to the clinic. Her words per utterance averages of 22.5 and 10.9 reflect her interest in the topics of abortion and the presenting complaint, respectively. Similarly, Sarah is least interested in discussing her presenting complaint (6.6 words per utterance). She is an unmarried, newly sexually active woman interested in contraceptive information and in obtaining a prescription for birth control pills. Her words per utterance average for this topic – 11.8 reflects such an interest.

Table 3 *Doctor's word output by topic*

Topic	Maria		
	Words per initiation	*Words per response*	*Words per utterance*
Presenting complaint	11.4	39.0	25.2
Birth control	14.2	17.5	15.9
Abortion	13.0	22.5	17.6
Topic	Sarah		
	Words per initiation	*Words per response*	*Words per utterance*
Presenting complaint	36.8	18.3	27.6
Birth control	90.1	141.6	115.9
Menstrual cycle	43.2	3.0	23.1

Now that we have an idea of what topics the patients wish to pursue, how do they compare with the topics discussed by the resident? Table 3 shows the resident's word output for the topics discussed with Maria and Sarah.

Table 3 indicates a significant difference in the resident's approach to the two interviews. He exhibits the highest words per utterance average while attending to Maria's presenting complaint (25.2 words per utterance). His output for the remaining two topics is roughly similar – 17.6 words per utterance for the abortion topic and 15.9 words per utterance for the birth control topic. This pattern displays the asymmetry in the resident–patient relationship. The resident, not the patient, controls the flow of information and the topics under discussion. In addition, it reinforces the suggestion that the resident has adopted a narrow health care orientation, *i.e.*, he primarily focuses his attention on Maria's presenting complaint.

When the typification of the woman is negative, as in Maria's case, the authority of the resident's role is reflected in the structure of the discourse. In turn, the structure of the discourse organizes the delivery of health care. When the typification of the woman is more positive, as in Sarah's case, both discourse and delivery of health care are organized differently. In Sarah's case, the resident not only generates a higher words per utterance average for Sarah's presenting complaint than he does for *any* topic of discussion with Maria (27.6 words per utterance), but he also demonstrates a willingness to generate the most substantial amount of discourse toward Sarah's hidden agenda, her desire for birth control (115.9 words per utterance).

Table 4 *Comparison of patients' initiations and doctor's responses by topic*

Topic	Maria		
	Words per initiation	*Words per response*	*RIR*
Presenting complaint	9.0	39.0	4.3
Birth control	5.8	17.5	3.0
Abortion	18.5	22.5	1.2
Topic	Sarah		
	Words per initiation	*Words per response*	*RIR*
Presenting complaint	10.7	18.3	1.7
Birth control	17.7	141.6	8.0
Menstrual cycle	7.5	3.0	0.4

This pattern suggests that, although the asymmetry in the resident–patient relationship has not lessened, the resident has adopted a broad health care orientation, *i.e.*, he treats her present complaint as well as focuses on emergent topics so as to provide the most comprehensive care.

We observe this phenomenon once more when we examine how the resident responds to initiations by both patients. We have created a statistic, the RIR, to highlight such a comparison. This response–initiation ratio is computed by dividing the resident's words per response by the patient's words per initiation. This demonstrates the resident's willingness to provide information in response to patients' questions – a willingness which we argue influences the adequacy of the health care he is able to deliver. The interpretation of the RIR provides a view of how many words the resident utters in response to every 1.0 words of patient initiation. Table 4 presents the resident's RIR for the topics discussed during the medical interviews.

Table 4 indicates the resident's preference for discussing Maria's presenting complaint. His RIR for her presenting complaint was 4.3 compared to an RIR of 1.2 for the abortion topic, the very topic that Maria wanted to discuss. Perhaps this reflects his abhorrence of abortion, his typification of Maria or, in this case, his narrow orientation toward her health care needs.

Sarah's case is just the opposite. The resident generates 8.0 words of response for every word of initiation by Sarah during the discussion of birth control. He is apparently quite willing to pursue topics important to Sarah other than the presenting complaint. Perhaps birth control is more consistent with his belief system, more congruent with his typification of Sarah or more compatible with his broader health care orientation.

Summary

We have argued that norms about women as features of the social system are in a reflexive relationship with the communicational work participants do in specific settings to construct them. Cultural assumptions and communication function as context and ground in the social production of both medical discourse and medical outcomes. Although discourse and outcomes are interactional accomplishments, doctors dominate in these interactions. Doctors have the institutional authority to orchestrate the medical interview and the delivery of health care. In the cases just discussed, norms about woman *qua* women and communicational processes between resident and patient produced two very different pictures of Maria and Sarah. These pictures, once developed, structured the discourse, organized the flow of information, and influenced the delivery of health care.

As the medical interview unfolded, the resident talked more with Sarah than with Maria. Not only did he talk more and provide more information for Sarah, but he evidenced more willingness to discuss with her the topics that emerged over the course of the medical interview. While both Maria and Sarah came to the clinic with presenting complaints – an injured leg and request for a Pap smear and pelvic examination, respectively – both also had hidden agendas which emerged as the interview progressed. These agendas were reflected in the talk. For Maria, the primary agenda, aside from her presenting complaint, was her need for information about abortions and for Sarah it was her desire for information about birth control.

The patients' presenting complaints and hidden agendas were treated differently by the resident. With Maria his behaviour indicated that he was more interested in talking about her presenting complaint than he was in talking about her preferred topic – abortion. Although he talked extensively with Sarah about her presenting complaint, he talked even more with her about birth control – her preferred topic. These differences in the structure of the discourse and the flow of information influenced medical outcomes. Even with a narrow definition of her medical problem, Maria left the clinic with less than she bargained for. Her leg injury was not treated, her hidden agendas were not dealt with, and it was questionable whether she received adequate medical care. In contrast, Sarah received all she bargained for and more. Her presenting complaint was dealt with as were her hidden agendas. Even if we were to take issue with how they were dealt with, for example, the persuasion used in the decision to use birth control pills (see Fisher and Todd forthcoming), the medical knowledge, and technical skill at the resident's disposal were used to address all the issues raised during the medical interview.

Social and political production of cultural assumptions

An analysis of the reflexive relationship between cultural assumptions and the communicational work which produces them creates a link between what are traditionally characterized as two disparate view-points. Often in the history of sociology, the analysis of social structure and social interaction has been characterized as incompatible (Knorr-Cetina & Cicourel 1981). By placing discourse between physicians and patients in its broader social and political contexts, these seemingly incompatible macro and micro approaches are recast so that social structure and social interaction are each seen to flow from and be part of the other (Mehan & Wood 1975). On the one hand, the social and political milieu of the culture we live in informs the discussion of the social production of medical discourse and medical outcomes. On the other hand, an understanding of the social production of medical discourse and outcomes illuminates how these are shaped by larger structural and institutional forces which in turn reproduce them. The analysis of discourse during medical interviews is strengthened by posing social structure and social interaction, context and ground, in a reflexive relationship with one another.

From the structural perspective there is work that describes the medical relationship as a *product* of particular features of the social structure. The assumption here is that the asymmetry in the doctor–patient relationship is *caused* by structural or institutional factors. Similarly, for some researchers, medical communication is a mechanism for reinforcing and maintaining the power differentials produced in a society dominated by class and gender and a medical profession which mirrors this domination (Wallen *et al.* 1979, Navarro 1976). Medical communication too is seen as a *product caused* by the structural and institutional arrangements of society.

Moving from a structural to an interactional approach, the doctor–patient relationship, and medical communication are presented as social productions. In each case, the focus is on process. In specific contexts, actors use language to produce meaning (*c.f.* Bosk 1979, Millman 1976, Davis 1963). The interrelationships of roles, values and attitudes are described as creating social realities (*c.f.* Scully 1980, Luker 1975). In addition, there is work in medical settings which addresses the social organization of doctor–patient communication – how physician and patient, in concert, produce medical discourse (*c.f.* Frankel 1983).

In this paper, we have recast the problem. Rather than posing social structure and social interaction as separate analyses, we suggest that each flows from and is part of the other – a reflexive analysis. At the structural level, we accept the premise that society is male dominated – a domination reflected in the organization and practice of medicine – and characterized by sexist assumptions about women. As cultural members these social facts are part of our common stock of knowledge. We are also committed to the belief that both male domination and sexist assumptions are socially produced realities constructed by participants as they communicate over the course of events such as medical interviews. Participants engage in an ongoing process of negotiation and interpretation.

Revealed in an examination of the communication between resident and patient over the course of the medical event are the means by which language is used to actualize the resident's power. The analysis illuminates how the structure of the medical relationship and cultural assumptions about women are, at one and the same time, social facts and socially produced, emergent realities. In the medical interviews just discussed, the resident evidenced a knowledge of the cultural assumptions (norms) about patients as 'good' or 'bad' women – knowledge of social facts. Over the course of the medical event the communicational work participants did to negotiate these norms is also displayed. The medical interview provides the context in which norms emerge, are displayed, interpreted and acted upon – a socially organized production accomplished through the situated activities of the participants.

The medical interviews also revealed how the asymmetrical structure of the medical relationship is, at one and the same time, a social fact and a socially accomplished reality. As Freidson (1970) points out, the medical profession is autonomous. As a profession physicians monitor the education, licensure and conduct of their fellow practitioners. Physicians also have a state-supported monopoly over the right to practise medicine and thus are guaranteed top position among health care providers. With autonomy and monopoly comes social control. When combined with their financial resources, the medical profession and the medical corporate enterprises that market health-related services – the pharmaceutical companies, health insurance companies, and medical supply industries as well as proprietary hospitals and nursing homes – have powerful political lobbies with tremendous legislative clout. Those who are reaping the benefits from the system as it is currently organized have a vested interest in preserving it and have been successful in resisting and limiting change. These are the social facts of the medical relationship; however, they do not tell the whole story.

Doctors not only have medical knowledge and technical expertise, but during medical interviews they have the ability to control patients' access to information and to health care services. Their power is enacted as the medical interview unfolds. This upper hand was evidenced in the ways the resident defined the patients, structured the discourse, controlled the flow of information and influenced the medical outcomes. This is the socially accomplished reality of the medical interviews just discussed.

There are social and political factors woven into the definition of health and illness as well as into the fabric of the health care delivery system. While providing health care, physicians also engage in an activity that is both social and political in nature. Since medical work occurs during face-to-face interaction and is an infinitely practical activity, it is social in that sense. Medical work also reflects, helps to sustain, and reproduces the status quo, and as such is micro-political. In the process of doing their work, doctors, who are predominantly men, control access to medical knowledge and technical skill, legitimate illness and help to maintain the existing social order.

Acknowledgements

Acknowledgements and thanks for providing helpful comments in the preparation of this manuscript go to Hugh Mehan, Alexandra Todd and Donna Eder. An earlier version of the paper was presented at the annual meeting of the Southern Sociological Society, Atlanta (April 1983).

Notes

1 At present we are aware of *no* studies which examine interactions between doctors and men patients. In hopes of remedying this situation, the junior author is currently engaged in research which examines how doctors and men patients communicate to reach medical treatment decisions.

2 While there is new research on the differential influence of a patient's gender and social class, the present study focuses solely on gender. This is due primarily to restraints of the research setting. First, since the setting is a resident training facility, we can assume that very few of the community's affluent members come for treatment. Second, since it is a *model* family practice clinic established to mirror the practice of medicine, the patient population is limited much as it is in a private fee-for-service practice. Most of the patients have private insurance. Only about 25 per cent of the patients are on Medicare or Medicaid and patients who cannot pay are rarely seen. The result is that the patient social class range is limited at both extremes and is concentrated on the middle.

3 This information surfaced during the gathering of background data at the model family practice clinic. As residents, staff doctors, and support personnel sat around discussing everyday topics, they often displayed attitudes and values which supported this analysis. For example, it was common knowledge that this doctor did not drink and would not perform abortions. The reasons stated were his religious beliefs.

4 Although it might be argued that the absence of history-taking in Maria's interview is justified on the basis of the presenting complaint (why take a full medical history for someone with a leg injury from a motorcycle accident?) a brief look at the organization of the family practice clinic suggests otherwise. As part of their training, residents are continually encouraged to obtain a full medical history from each patient on his/her initial visit. The logic of this practice is inescapable. Since the majority of the patients do return to the clinic at some future time and since classes of residents continue to enter and leave the programme, the patient's medical history, if taken during the initial visit, and duly recorded provides a needed foundation for future care. Furthermore, although a patient's medical history may have no immediate bearing on the presenting complaint, it is common practice for issues to emerge during the medical interview for which a more detailed history would be helpful, if not essential. We could speculate that perhaps a less detailed history was required with a presenting complaint of leg injury than with a presenting complaint of a pelvic examination. However, as the interviews unfolded, both women displayed medical issues that make a detailed history seem appropriate. One was done with Sarah and not with Maria, suggesting that the

doctor's assumptions structured the discourse as well as the delivery of health care.

5   Sarah is not such a responsible woman that she does not need to be protected. In the discussion of birth control, the resident makes it clear that diaphragms, which may be left in the drawer, and condoms, which may not be intact, are too risky to keep her safe until she is married. He recommends the birth control pill (see Fisher & Todd, forthcoming).

6   In these two cases, we have no data on the physical examination. For Maria's leg injury, none was performed. With Sarah, the doctor asked us not to tape, assuming that since she was shy and this was her first pelvic examination, she would be distressed.

7   A claim made stronger when the topic is considered. When responding to Sarah during the medical history phase, the doctor is primarily providing information about birth control – a topic he does not discuss with Maria.

References

Barr, Judith K. (1983), 'Physicians' Views of Patients in Prepaid Group Practice: Reasons for Visits to HMOs', *Journal of Health and Social Behavior*, 24: 244–55.

Bernstein, Basil (1973), 'Class, Codes and Control', In Gerald Berreman (ed.), *Toward a Theory of Educational Transmission*, London: Routledge & Kegan Paul.

Biener, Lois (1983), 'Perceptions of Patients by Emergency Room Staff: Substance Abusers Versus Non-Substance Abusers', *Journal of Health and Social Behavior*, 24: 264–75.

Bosk, Charles L. (1979), *Forgive and Remember: Managing Medical Failure*, Chicago: University of Chicago Press.

Caress, Barbara (1975), 'Sterilization', *Health-Pac Bulletin* 62, January/February, 1–13.

Caress, Barbara (1977), 'Womb-boom', *Health-Pac Bulletin*, July/August.

Cicourel, Aaron (1973), *Cognitive Sociology, Language and Meaning in Social Interaction*, London: Macmillan.

Conrad, Peter and Rochelle Kern (eds) (1981), *The Sociology of Health and Illness*, New York: St Martin's Press.

Davis, Fred (1963), *Passage Through Crisis*, Indianapolis: Bobbs-Merrill.

Durkheim, Emile (1938), *The Rules of Sociological Method*, Chicago: University of Chicago Press.

Ehrenreich, Barbara and John Ehrenreich (1970), *The American Health Empire*, Health-Pac Book, New York: Vintage.

Fisher, Sue (1982), 'The decision-making context: how doctors and patients communicate', in Robert J. Di Pietro (ed.), *Linguistics and the Professions*, Norwood, NJ: Ablex, pp. 51–81.

Fisher, Sue (1984), 'Doctor–patient communication: a social and micro-political performance', *Journal of Health and Illness*, 6(3): (March).

Fisher, Sue and Alexandra Dundas Todd (forthcoming), 'Friendly persuasion: the negotiation of the decisions to use oral contraception', In *Discourse and Institutional Authority*, Sue Fisher and Alexandra Dundas Todd (eds), Norwood, NJ: Ablex.

Frankel, Richard M. (forthcoming), 'Talking in interviews: A dispreference for patient initiated questions in coming physician–patient encounters', in George Psathas and Richard Frankel (eds) *Interactional Competence*, Norwood, NJ: Ablex.

Frankel, Richard M. (1983), 'The laying on of hands: aspects of the organization of gaze, touch and talk in a medical encounter', in Sue Fisher and Alexandra Tood (eds) *The Social Organization of Doctor–Patient Communication*, Washington D.C.: Center for Applied Linguistics, pp. 19–54.

Freemon, B., V.F. Negrette, M. Davis, *et al.* (1971), 'Gaps in doctor–patient communication: Doctor–patient interaction analysis', *Pediatric Research*, 5: 298–311.

Freidson, Eliot (1970), *Profession of Medicine*, New York: Dodd, Mead.

Garfinkel, Harold (1967), *Studies in Ethnomethodology*, Englewood Cliffs, NJ: Prentice-Hall.

Groce, Stephen B. and Sue Fisher (1984), 'Doctor-Talk/Patient-Talk: Patients' Accounting Practices and Doctors' Social Control Strategies as Interactional Accomplishments', Paper presented at the Annual Meeting of the Southern Sociological Society, Knoxville, TN (April).

Gurwitsch, Aaron (1964), *The Field of Consciousness*, Pittsburg: Duquesne University Press.

Henley, Nancy (1977), *Body Politics: Power, Sex and Nonverbal Communication*, Englewood Cliffs, NJ: Prentice-Hall.

Knorr-Cetina, K. and A.V. Cicourel (eds) (1981), *Advances in Social Theory and Methodology: Toward an Integration of Micro- and Macro-Sociologies*, London and Boston: Routledge & Kegan Paul.

Lorber, Judith (1975), 'Good Patients and Problem Patients: Conformity and Deviance in a General Hospital', *Journal of Health and Social Behavior*, 16: 213–25.

Luker, Kristin (1975), *Taking Chances: Abortion and the Decision Not To Contracept*, Berkeley: University of California Press.

Macintyre, Sally (1977), *Single and Pregnant*, New York: Prodist.

Marx, Karl (1964), *The Economic and Philosophic Manuscripts of 1844*, Trans. Martin Milligan, Ed. with an introduction by Dirk Streuch, New York: International Publishers.

Mechanic, David (1968), *Medical Sociology*, New York: Free Press.

Mehan, High and Houston Wood (1975), *The Reality of Ethnomethodology*, New York: Wiley.

Millman, Marcia (1976), *The Unkindest Cut: Life In the Backrooms of Medicine*, New York: William Morrow.

Navarro, Vincente (1976), *Medicine Under Capitalism*, New York: Prodist.

Parsons, Talcott (1951), *The Social System*, New York: Free Press.

Pfefferbaum, B., P.M. Levenson and J. Van Eys (1982), 'Comparison of physician and patient perceptions of communications issues', *Southern Medical Journal*, 75: 1080–3.

Roth, J.A. (1963), *Timetables*, Indianapolis: Bobbs-Merrill.

Ruzek, Sheryl Burt (1978), *The Women's Health Movement*, New York: Praeger.

Scully, Diana (1980), *Men who Control Women's Health*, Boston: Houghton-Mifflin.

Scully, Diana and Pauline Bart (1973), 'A funny thing happened on the way to the orifice: women in gynecological textbook', *American Journal of Sociology*, 78: 1045–0.

Silverman, David (1981), 'The child as a social object: Down's Syndrome children in a paediatric cardiology clinic', *Sociology of Health and Illness*, 3(3): 254–74.

Slavin, L.A., J.E. O'Malley, G.P. Foocher and D.J. Foster (1982), 'Communication of the cancer diagnosis to pediatric patients: Impact on long-term adjustment', *American Journal of Psychiatry*, 139: 179–83.

Spletter, Mary (1983), 'How important is a Pap test?' *Parade Magazine* (September 4): 10.

Strong, P.M. (1979), *The Ceremonial Order of the Clinic: Parents, Doctors and Medical Bureaucracies*, London: Routledge & Kegan Paul.

Szasz, T.S. and M.H. Hollender (1956), 'A contribution to the philosophy of medicine: the basic models of doctor–patient relationship', *A.M.A. Archives of Internal Medicine*, 97: (May): 585.

Todd, Alexandra Dundas (1983), 'A diagnosis of doctor–patient discourse in the prescription of contraception' in Sue Fisher and Alexandra Dundas Todd (eds) *The Social Organization of Doctor–Patient Communication*, Washington, D.C.: The Center for Applied Linguistics.

Todd, Alexandra Dundas (1982), 'The Medicalization of Reproduction: Scientific Medicine and the Diseasing of Healthy Women', Unpublished doctoral dissertation, University of California, San Diego.

Waitzkin, Howard, B. and John D. Stoeckle (1976), 'Information Control and the micropolitics of health care: summary of an ongoing research project, *Social Science and Medicine*, 10: 263–76.

Waitzkin, Howard and Barbara Waterman (1974), *The Exploitation of Illness in Capitalist Society*, Indianapolis: Bobbs-Merrill.

Wallen, Jacqueline, Howard Waitzkin and John D. Stoeckle (1979), 'Physician stereotypes about female health and illness', *Women & Health*, 4: 135–46.

West, Candace (1982), 'When the doctor is a lady: power, status and gender in physician–patient conversations', in Ann Stromberg (ed.), *Women, Health and Medicine*, Palo Alto, CA: Mayfield.

Winch, Peter (1958), *The Idea of a Social Science and its Relation to Philosophy*, London: Routledge & Kegan Paul.

Wittgenstein, Ludwig (1953), *Philosophical Investigations*, London: Basil Blackwell & Mott.

Zola, Irving (1972), 'Medicine as an institution of social control', *Sociological Review* 20, 487.

Openness and specialisation: dealing with patients in a hospital emergency service

Nicolas Dodier and Agnès Camus

Introduction

The functioning of hospital emergency services is at the heart of a recurring question in hospitals, a question that is becoming increasingly acute: how to reconcile the principle of openness to the very heterogeneous demands for medical care that are spontaneously directed to the hospital, with the concern to select patients in terms of their match with the medical specialties? The hospital's openness to spontaneous demands has taken many forms: the association with charity under the Ancien Régime; the creation of a 'public assistance' scheme for the care of the indigent in the 19th century; the emergence, after the second world war, of the concept of the hospital as 'a public service open to all' and adapted to users' demands[1]. This openness coexists, particularly in teaching hospitals, with the need to specialise to a high degree in fields at the cutting edge of medicine and biomedical research (Jamous 1969, Lejonc *et al.* 1993, Vassy and Renard 1992). The hospital's dual role generates an increasingly tense situation. On the one hand, because of its openness to all types of demands, the hospital tends more and more to be solicited by people affected by the growing importance of the social question in contemporary societies (Castel 1995). On the other hand, hospital services are tending to select their patients on ever more stringent criteria, either to ensure a patient profile adapted to harsh budget restrictions, or to recruit patients that correspond to the trend towards biomedical innovation (Dodier and Camus 1997).

This dual function of the hospital can be seen at several levels, first of all, in a polarisation of settings. On the one hand are places that we might describe as 'open': services dealing with internal or general medicine (Herzlich 1973, Lejonc *et al.* 1993), and the emergency room, which in large hospitals is organised as a genuinely independent service. These services receive all sorts of demands, many of them associated with their role as a 'neighbourhood' service for the district in which the hospital is located. Conversely, there are also 'selective' areas, such as services associated with specialties dealing with a limited range of pathological conditions. They are anchored in medical-scientific networks, of the same type as the sociotechnical networks studied by Michel Callon (1989) and Bruno Latour (1989). The notion of 'neighbourhood' is no longer meaningful, in that their relationship to space is not with an actual territory, but with a network (Mol and Law 1994). However, the dual role of the hospital also affects the internal organisation of certain services. It can be seen again at the very core of the ambiguity surrounding the role of the emergency hospital service. On the one hand, these services are characterised by their *accessibility*, as implied by the very concept of emergency. A person who applies to a service 'in an emergency' must be able to do so rapidly and take priority over other demands. An emergency service must be able to bypass the usual formalities for gaining access to medical attention: the need to make an appointment, deadlines for treatment, the relevant administrative formalities, opening hours. However, at the same time, the emergency service, as a specialised service, must also answer to another concept of emergency: *a restricted range of conditions* or symptoms generating a more or less serious life-threatening situation. In this sense, emergency services belong to a set of specialised networks using specific skills and equipment (Peneff 1992): the SAMU (mobile medical emergency unit); the fire brigade; the '999' or emergency police unit; general practitioners (GPs) specialising in emergency medicine; intensive care units. This applies even if emergency medicine itself does not exist as a specialty in the same sense as the other specialties taught in the course of medical training.

The flow of demands attracted by the accessibility of emergency services is documented in many works. Some of these confirm the heterogeneous nature of these demands (Béland *et al.* 1991, Mannon *et al.* 1987); others highlight the function of this accessibility for deprived persons (Béland *et al.* 1990), people in danger of becoming disconnected from society (Genell and Rosenqvist 1987a), in contact with psychiatric services or in a situation of solitude (Genell and Rosenqvist 1987b). The effect of this duality on the actual work undertaken by emergency services has also been examined in several studies carried out from an ethnographic standpoint (Roth 1972a, 1972b, Mannon 1976, Jeffery 1979, Roth and Douglas 1983, Dingwall and Murray 1983, Hughes 1988, 1989, all in the English-speaking countries; Peneff 1992 in France). This research shows that the way in which patients are dealt with depends on the way in which they are *categorised*, in situ, by staff, much more than on exclusively clinical criteria. The analytical frameworks adopted to understand the way in which patients are dealt with in emergency services raises questions on several different levels. The first is related to the intention behind this categorisation. Some research emphasises the distinction made by staff between 'good patients' and 'bad patients'. For example Roth and Douglas (1983) suggest, on the one hand, that patients are 'deserving' or 'undeserving' depending on the social worth attributed to them and, on the other, that they are 'legitimate' or 'non-legitimate' depending on whether or not their demand matches the concept which personnel have of their own work. Jeffery (1979) distinguishes between 'good patients' and 'rubbish' patients'. The merits of this approach is that it shows that the reception given to patients in the emergency service reflects sharply contrasting reactions: on the one hand, there are patients for whom mobilisation is immediate and unequivocal; on the other, there are patients for whom everything in the reaction of staff tends to cast doubt on the very legitimacy of their presence. The drawback of this approach is that it tends to 'congeal' the work of categorisation by creating a dichotomy. It reflects only one aspect of staff's reactions, since through these categories of good and bad patients, it refers to the two extremes of a much more complicated range of mobilisation. Categorisation of patients by staff does not only concern questions of eligibility, but also the constant establishing of orders of precedence between patients, via a series of small operations, in the framework of management of a flow of demands distributed between the different actors in the department (physicians, nurses, nursing auxiliaries, etc). Barring obvious exceptions, nothing in our own observations, at least, suggests, for example, that the very long wait that must sometimes be endured by certain patients results necessarily from an intentional decision made by staff at the outset, categorising them straight away as bad patients. In many cases, their having to wait is more a result of being pushed down the order of precedence by new priorities established between cases in the course of time and as new patients arrive. In order to understand these gradients of mobilisation, we shall start with the notion of *mobilising worth*, by which we mean what, in each patient, triggers the particular degree of mobilisation of staff with respect to him/her, in gradually establishing his/her place in the order of precedence.

The second question concerns the different dimensions involved in categorising patients. These dimensions are heterogeneous, given the openness of emergency services to all types of demands, which makes analysis rather difficult. If we seek, as Jeffery did (1979) separately to reconstruct criteria for the origin of the categories of good patients and bad patients, we run into problems of consistency, as Dingwall and Murray (1983) have pointed out. When the comparison adopted is too simple, such as between a judgment made on social grounds and a judgment made on clinical grounds (Roth and Douglas 1983, Dingwall and Murray 1983), we may end up lumping very different cases together in a single category. For example, Roth and Douglas (1983) lump together in the category of patients who are negatively perceived in terms of their social worth, attempted suicides, hysterical and bizarre behaviour, vague complaints, dirty, smelly patients, hippies, women with scanty clothing, young unmarried pregnant women who have attempted an abortion, drunks, pelvic inflammatory disease. In Jeffery's (1979) work, we find a hotchpotch of the same type between rubbish patients – trivia, drunks, overdoses, tramps – but also nutcases, smelly, dirty, obese patients. Mannon (1976) distinguishes three categories among 'problem patients': helpless, drunk and drugged, regulars. In terms of clinical judgment, the authors obviously have difficulty in identifying a single dimension in the judgment made about patients: hence, although they believe that outpatient cases, that is, cases that are not real emergencies, are not legitimate for staff, they also note that some of them have high mobilising worth, since they arouse interesting clinical problems (Roth and Douglas 1983: 85). This discordance can only pose a problem for the framework of an analysis that treats the clinical aspect of judgment as an indivisible whole.

In this article, we attempt to define distinctions between the different dimensions that go to make up the patient's mobilising worth, and to undertake a systematic analysis of each of them. To avoid casting our net too wide, we evaluate the respective weight of these dimensions in the actual work, finally retaining only the most important. For this article we have chosen four of them. The first two can be lumped together under clinical judgment, but arouse reactions of different types: the degree to which the case can be seen as a life-and-death situation, and the intellectual interest of the case. The third is related to the social aspects of the demand and the fourth to the responsibilities of physicians who send patients to the emergency service. The patient's worth is made up of several dimensions. Various authors have mentioned this point during their observations (*e.g.* Roth and Douglas 1983: 94). Here, it should be used as a theoretical central point of the analytical framework: Several markers may potentially contribute to this mobilising worth; each may arouse different reactions, some of which tend to accelerate and others to delay mobilisation.

The complexity of staff reactions is not only a question of the combination of different dimensions whose effects may be quite contradictory, but an internal characteristic of the judgment made within the framework of each dimension. We suggest that for certain dimensions – and notably, as we shall see, for the intellectual interest of the case and the social aspects of the demands – staff reactions are not unequivocal. Rather they should be seen as a complex of reactions which are not without internal contradictions, even for each person who is called on to deal with a given patient. This situation is not specific to the emergency services. On the contrary, much is to be gained by looking at it in the light of theoretical developments contributed in the last ten years in terms of the sociological approach to action. As recent works tend to suggest[2], we shall here look at the general assumption whereby people wishing to make judgments in a given situation can refer to a large number of possible justifications. Far from forming a theoretically coherent whole, these justifications must be combined according to more or less complex formulae, with the same people being likely to switch between different forms of commitment from one situation to another. Our assumptions about the many dimensions of mobilising worth and the complexity of staff reactions with respect to each dimension taken separately should be seen as related to this framework. Hence, rather than immediately presuming a shared basis of reactions, either within the framework of a common 'culture' (Hughes 1989), or because the people holding them occupy identical positions in the organisation (Peneff 1992), the point of the situational approach, at least to begin with, is to be very attentive to those aspects of reactions to patients that stem from possibly differentiated or even fluctuating reactions, perhaps later and with caution looking at what might be likely to stabilise and align these reactions.

The field inquiry

To highlight the way in which the mobilising worth of patients is built up during the course of the action, we have used ethnographic inquiry methods. We chose a monographic approach focusing on a medical emergency service in a French teaching hospital. This service has high patient flows: 17,134 consultations in 1993. The fieldwork was carried out between October 1992 and December 1993, in the form of direct observations of the work done in the service, and interviews (19) with staff: four with permanent consultants, four nurses, three supervisors, three residents, two social workers, one head of clinic, one clinic student and one nursing auxiliary – altogether 11 women and eight men. It is a genuine emergency service, not just a partial service delegated to deal with emergency cases, as in smaller hospitals. The permanent physicians in the service may be more insistent than others on the point that working in the emergency service calls for specialist skills, even if emergency medicine is not recognised as a separate medical specialty. In addition, as a teaching hospital, it has many very specialised services (neurology, cardiology, hematology . . .). Residents from those services, on duty in the emergency service, often refer – and here again perhaps more than elsewhere – to their determination to learn anything that has a bearing on their original speciality, up to and including the tensions that this may create in the course of their work in the emergency service. The importance of specialisation also comes into play when patients are to be transferred from the emergency service into one of these specialised services. On the other hand, the hospital is located in a Paris neighbourhood which has quite a large proportion of inhabitants who are attracted first and foremost by the accessibility of the service (open 24 hours a day, no appointment needed, possibility of free treatment . . .). So, the service in which we carried out our fieldwork is an interesting area in which to view this dual movement of biomedical specialisation of hospital services and their exposure to the effects of the social question.

Our study is based on the way in which personnel refer *explicitly*, by word and judgment, to what attracts their attention in patients. It does not aim to throw light on the silent influence of factors, only actual reference to these factors in the course of action, or retrospectively in comments or accounts. This provides a guarantee against misleading interpretations, but it is also a limitation, since it forces us to focus on the overt aspects of mobilisation around patients, to the exclusion of anything that is not said or not conscious. We observed in turn the major points of the patients' trajectory: the actual reception; treatment dispensed by the service itself, which is dealt with in this article; and transfer to other services (Dodier and Camus 1997). More precisely, we rely on three sources: observation in situ of a series of cases dealt with in the treatment cubicles (n = 60); observation of 'sketches', that is, comments or brief moments, in isolation from the actual cases but instructive for understanding the order of precedence (n = 23); interviews in which the actors deliver more comprehensive opinions about aspects of general arrangements (n = 16). After describing the general framework for establishing the order of precedence between patients in the service, we shall look one by one at the main dimensions of the mobilising worth of patients.

Establishing orders of precedence

The general organisation of the waiting list is closer to a 'distributed' than a 'planned' model of coordination. This means that no actor can be seen as a central authority with an overview of the whole process, and that this process results from a series of operations involving actors, each engaged in initiatives which partly escape the others (Perrow 1984, Star 1989, Thévenot 1993, Dodier 1995b). In a typical day, it mobilises, to varying degrees, three nurses, three nursing auxiliaries, three clinical students, two residents and one consultant. This organisation hinges on two tools kept in one of the treatment cubicles: the chronological entry register and the file tray. In the entry register, a large ledger that is always on view on a table, we find a list of patients by name, in their chronological order of arrival, along with the following indications: date and time of entry, nurse's diagnosis on arrival, diagnosis when leaving the treatment cubicle, time at which the patient was transferred or left the hospital. From time to time, someone appears – a nurse, a nursing auxiliary or a consultant, sometimes a resident – and reviews the overall situation: Who is still waiting in the corridor? How long has this person been waiting? What are his/her symptoms? There is no codified procedure for choosing patients and chronological order is not necessarily important. It is even more distributed than the organisation described by Hughes (1988, 1989): it is quite common for reception staff – by which we mean a nursing auxiliary or a nurse, not a clerical employee – to make an immediate technical judgment. Nurses write down in the register a specific form of diagnosis, the nurse's diagnosis, and any member of the staff can at any time bring a patient to the attention of one of the doctors.

The second tool is the file tray, in which files are placed one on top of the other by reception staff as they register a patient. There is no attempt at chronological order – the time of arrival is mentioned only in the file, on the labels. The patient's mobilising worth, as evaluated by the doctor from information written in the file by reception staff, is of prime importance. From time to time, a doctor reaches into the tray, leafs through the files and decides to take a particular patient. The choice of patient is generally made in silence, without the doctor having to justify his or her decision. Hence, the information written in the file by the first person to see the patient on reception is vital.

A female consultant mentions the following case: 'This case really made an impression on me. It was at night and we had a young woman of 27 who arrived with a high temperature after returning from a tropical country. Basically, when someone writes that down in the patient's file, you think "malaria". We were frantically busy on that particular ward. She had to wait an hour in the corridor. After an hour, I take all the papers, all the observations about patients to be seen and have a closer look. I see: "High temperature on return from a tropical country"; I say to myself: "Aha, it's probably a case of malaria, I'll go and see how she is", telling myself that if it's a serious bout, she's been waiting rather a long time already. I spy her on a stretcher, covered right up to here (. . .). Then I start to panic: she's covered with purpura – obviously a meningococcal meningitis, an extreme medical emergency!'

An important factor is the verbal announcement made by reception staff. When placing a file in the basket, the nurse or nursing auxiliary makes a comment repeating the words written in it and indicating the degree of mobilisation required by the case. The staff can also decide to put the file into the tray in silence, make a general announcement to the people present, who may be involved in other activities, or address a doctor directly to call his or her attention to the case. All these mini-procedures have an effect on the doctor's degree of mobilisation. Fire brigade or SAMU staff, who bring patients directly into the department on stretchers, are obliged to present them to the treatment cubicles and have them entered in the current 'work lines', according to the usual process of negotiation in the hospital described more generally by Strauss et al. (1985), thereby bypassing the slower process of the register or the file tray. However, this verbal announcement does not necessarily mobilise doctors – it is simply a way of attracting their attention. Announcement of a new case can easily attract no response at all. Here again, the key element is the mobilising worth of the patient as far as the doctor is concerned.

Another factor that comes into play is that of the reminders made to physicians concerning patients waiting to be seen. When personnel circulate in the corridor, they look around, depending on how preoccupied they are, to check the condition of waiting patients and any changes in their condition. They may even be reminded by patients themselves, who may complain about the length of time they have been waiting and the pain or discomfort they are feeling, or who express their anxiety. In some cases, patients or the people accompanying them may go to the treatment cubicles to remind staff of their presence. All these indicators may increase the patient's mobilising worth for nurses or nursing auxiliaries, who may then pass on the information, if they consider it vital, to the doctors in the cubicles. Finally, consultants, nurses and nursing auxiliaries have access to pointers concerning the overall flow of patients: they estimate the number of people waiting in the corridor, they check the entry register in order to evaluate the patients waiting to be seen, the number of patients waiting and the different stages they have reached in the process. As a function of these observations, they call to order the doctors dispensing this treatment, particularly residents, to get them to expedite their current work or transfer their attention to another patient. The panoramic view enjoyed by the staff other than doctors is another reason, on top of those already identified by Hughes (1989), for them to feel authorised to intervene with the residents, who are involved in the actual clinical work on a case-by-case basis and are not concerned with fluctuations in flow[3].

Hence, establishing the order of precedence is a process distributed between numerous actors. It is the result of a whole series of micro-operations carried out by all personnel involved with a patient. Chronological order, as in the entry register, has a role to play, but it is a comparatively minor role compared with moments in which it is the patient's mobilising worth that determines the degree to which staff concerned at that particular moment direct their efforts to ensuring that the patient moves further up the order of precedence. There is no specific procedure to be respected, but rather a series of individual initiatives based on the notes written in the file, quick evaluations of the state of waiting patients, and attempts by patients themselves to attract attention – this last initiative has a high failure rate. A person's 'rank' is not fixed once and for all, as it is in much more codified procedures of sequencing (Elster and Herpin 1992). But it depends at all times on new arrivals in the service and changes in the state of existing patients. We look one by one at the aspects that are most frequently encountered. (See appendix 1.)

Closeness to life-threatening emergency

In emergency manuals, as in spoken language, cases that are closest to the core of life-threatening emergencies are described as 'real emergencies'. Evaluations made within the emergency service put the proportion of real emergencies at 18 per cent of all the patients registered in the department. They are consistent with broader data on hospitals in France (Steg 1989). The status of a particular case concerning the core of life-threatening emergencies has an effect on the quantity of resources mobilised: the number of persons, their professional capacity, the equipment employed. It also determines whether the case is serious enough to interrupt current work lines. At one extreme of mobilisation, there is the patient for whom other patients are immediately removed from the resuscitation cubicle without anyone protesting and where all the people required to prevent the death of the patient immediately abandon the treatment on which they are currently engaged. The actual therapeutic gestures are not necessarily more rapid (Timmermans 1995) but the different stages: waiting in the corridor, waiting for a cubicle to become free, even the diagnostic examination – since in general we are concerned with the therapeutic gestures implemented before an exact diagnosis can be made – are bypassed.

   The further we depart from the life-threatening emergency and even from
the 'real' emergency, the more likely we are to see the emergence of resistance to mobilisation of resources. The patient has to wait longer and has
more difficulty entering into the work lines. At an even lower degree of
mobilisation, questions will be voiced about the patient's rights in light of
his or her condition: the person will be treated but will not be given an
ambulance for the return home; staff will agree to give painkillers but will
not extract a tooth in the middle of the night; staff will listen to the worried
person's complaints but without paying great attention. At an even lower
level of mobilisation, the patient will be reproached for having applied to
the emergency service. In this case, the patient is definitely a 'bad patient',
who is assumed to have infringed a certain number of rules governing his/
her role (Jeffery 1979).

> The cubicles are very calm. There are few patients. The reception nurse
> places a file in the tray. The clinical student takes it and goes off to see
> the patient in a cubicle. According to the file, this 19-year-old man
> has come to consult a doctor for 'vesiculate, pruriginous lesions in the
> right arm and left lumbar region'. The resident arrives in the cubicle.
> He asks the man: 'You don't have a temperature? How long has it been
> going on?'
> – 'Since last week.'
> – *'And you've only decided to come in now, when it's practically finished!*
> (to the clinical student) We'll give him some ointment. (to me) *He should
> never have come to the emergency service!*

In this case, note that the reproach is based on the idea that only recent pain
justifies recourse to the emergency service. If the pain is not recent, the
patient's condition is not seen as a real emergency[4].

   Patients whose condition is well removed from this core of real emergencies also arouse recriminations during the actual treatment. There is a
tangible atmosphere of dissatisfaction around cases not considered to be real
emergencies, cases that should have been dealt with by a GP or in a hospital
consultation, as shown by Roth and Douglas (1983: 84) in surveys carried
out in the United States, UK and Australia. In this manner, personnel
express their belief that the patient could just as well have consulted a general practitioner or made an appointment in another hospital service rather
than turning up at the emergency service: 'But why isn't she in the neurology
service?' 'It would be better for your daughter to be seen by a GP'; 'That's
exactly the sort of case that shouldn't be seen in the emergency service; He's
come here for a nephrological check-up, what are we supposed to do?'

   Two dimensions are evident in the words used by staff when expressing
this attitude: the feeling of being useful and the concept of taking pleasure
in one's work. This is particularly evident in the responses to questions we
asked in interviews concerning the degree of interest in emergency cases.

AC:	What is your idea of an interesting case?
Female consultant:	My idea of an interesting case? *An interesting case is one where I have the feeling of being useful*, where we've arrived at a diagnosis and found a suitable treatment, that's an interesting case (interview notes enclosed).

AC:	Practically speaking, what's your idea of an interesting case?
Male consultant:	*First of all, a case where I feel useful*, where I can apply everything I've learned over the last few years. That's what I call an interesting case – a situation where I feel involved and useful (interview notes enclosed).

These excerpts refer to a general feeling on the part of doctors of being useful. But this feeling may also be related much more closely to a logic of specialisation, as indicated by the following excerpt:

> What I have to offer is specific skills in the field of emergency medicine – *if it's not an emergency, anyone else could do it as well as me*, and maybe better, since that person would have more time and would feel more involved (interview notes enclosed).

Doctors feel they have done something useful when they have been able to mobilise a particular skill and not just the skills possessed by any doctor. This dimension provides a very strong basis for mobilisation, combining a personal interest in the case, an awareness of possessing a rare skill (the doctor belongs to a small group of people who are alone capable of solving this type of problem) and the feeling of acting for the good of another person. Arguments stemming from both individual interest and the general interest are reconciled through the logic of hospital specialisation. This feeling corresponds to a vision of work in the emergency service based on gestures of resuscitation.

> Say someone comes in with severe respiratory distress. I'll have to intubate and oxygenate the patient, hook her up to the machine, that's something I find interesting. Or say it's chest pain with an infarction, I will initiate a treatment, and if I don't do it, or some other doctor doesn't do it, then the patient will die. What I really like is to feel that the patient's life is in my hands – it makes me feel useful, as if I have a real mission in life (interview notes enclosed).

In this scheme of things, the patient's mobilising worth for the doctor increases in line with his or her feeling of usefulness; that is, the extent to which the doctor can anticipate a visible improvement in the patient's state thanks to his or her expertise in an area of medical treatment not within the scope of an ordinary doctor. Hence, patients who consult the emergency service but are not considered real emergencies may succeed in obtaining immediate access to medical care – thanks to the emergency service's accessibility – but are then dependent on the doctor's decision either to avoid dealing with the case or to make it his or her business to treat the patient.

Social demands

In this category we have put patients who consult the emergency service because of their inability to obtain what they need elsewhere (Béland *et al.* 1990): difficulties in gaining access to medical care; difficulty in satisfying the minimum requirements of life (accommodation, protection against cold, food . . .). This category of patient arouses complex reactions, which can range from a very negative attitude to a deliberate mobilisation around the problem, with differences or even conflicts arising between personnel about the right attitude to adopt. Negative reactions can fall into several different groupings. First come recriminations of the same type as we noted earlier, when it is suggested that it would be more appropriate for the case to be treated by a GP than in an emergency service: criticisms concerning the difference between the patient's actual case and a 'real' emergency, or even the absence of a genuine medical problem, anticipation of difficulties in placing the patient. The principle of a service open to all the spontaneous demands of users is accepted in terms of actual behaviour but is criticised verbally.

> The telephone rings in the cubicles and is answered by the consultant. He explains that it concerns a young man of 23, a drug addict, a 'social problem' with a huge dental abscess. 'I *can't refuse him*', he says, 'and I know there's no room for him in the relevant service, so . . .'

Apart from simple verbal recriminations, negative reactions may take the form of delayed or limited mobilisation during treatment. For example, homeless people are often pushed further down the waiting list.

> We are in the cubicle where the entry register is kept. The resident for that afternoon is leafing through the book: 'I'll wait for a bit before I take that homeless fellow. I'm never in a hurry to see those people!' She adds: 'What's wrong with him?', then looks at the file and says: 'Nothing'. She looks at the fireman's sheet on which is written: 'Fit of faintness'. She comments: 'They feel faint all the time, they come here to be in the warm, that's all.'

These patients may also arouse suspicion as to the possibility that they are manipulating the emergency service to obtain certain advantages by simulating or exaggerating medical problems. As in many other medical contexts, the medical decision is at the same time a decision concerning allocation of rights, that influences how doctors deal with an individual's complaints (Dodier 1994).

> A homeless man is brought in by the fire brigade 'in an advanced state of drunkenness'. The residents tell me that in this sort of case, they 'do a dextro, look at the pupils and that's it.' Another resident says that he 'doesn't waste time giving them a complete check-up'. A nurse walks by: 'So who's going to see him?' No decision is made. A clinical student finally decides to examine the patient.

These reactions obviously delay treatment of such patients, who are often made to wait for quite a long time, until there are only a few people waiting to be seen.

The low mobilising worth of these patients is also reflected in the way the interaction is initiated, with staff tending to take a moralising tone: the person is reproached for having applied to the emergency service or for being drunk. The following case shows a whole range of negative reactions in the comments made, the speed of mobilisation and the interaction with the patient, more or less transcended by attempts at humour or joking with the other doctors.

> This is the homeless person brought in by the fire brigade, the one referred to in the observation repeated above, whom the resident said she was in no hurry to see. I asked the resident if patients from the emergency department could easily be transferred to her department. She answered that she was 'a neurology resident and didn't like dealing with emergency patients[5], the emergency service always has these social cases, there are always problems to do with discharging patients and the social problems compounded the medical problems. However,' she added, 'sometimes interesting things crop up and you have to be careful not to miss them (. . .) In fact, the Clinical Director in Neurology comes down every morning to check out the emergency service[6]. He'll say: "Okay, we'll take two, but only those two there . . .". You have to be able to see whether there's something interesting going on'. Then she says: 'One thing that influences the quality of a hospital service is not having a whole lot of these emergency patients.'
>
> In a joking voice, this resident asks a consultant: 'So, what are we going to do with this homeless fellow? Chuck him out?' (that is, refuse to admit him to the emergency service). The consultant replies that 'we've had problems before, you have to see them.' The resident resigns herself, puts on some gloves and approaches the man whom she ushers into the cubicle. The resident is obviously disgusted by the homeless man, she pinches her nose when talking to him, looks past him at the others and makes faces etc.

She speaks roughly to him. She asks him to move his legs, stretch out his arms: 'Come on, come on, no messing about, do what I tell you, it's an order!' In the file she writes: 'breath impregnated ++++, no motor deficit, general feeling of weakness over the last three days.' When first questioned, the homeless man says he is really exhausted, that he wants to stay in the emergency service. At this point the resident replies 'it's understandable given the amount he puts away, but he can't stay here.' The homeless man replies 'Put me in detox.' She replied: 'The emergency service isn't a detox unit.'

She asks for a hemogram and blood electrolyte, sugar and alcohol tests. She tells the man 'we are going to check your blood sugar, you can stay a while in the corridor to rest up and then you have to go.' The man replies: 'So I don't have a choice.' The resident says: 'No, you don't have a choice.'

The resident's attitude in this sequence shows that her reaction to the patient is also governed by certain aspects – drunken behaviour and physical characteristics, particularly smell – that may be associated, in certain patients, with their 'social' demands, but which are not the same order.

Alongside this tendency to become demobilised when confronted with so-called social problems, we can also see efforts to remobilise, which can create conflicting and tense situations among staff. Some reminders made to doctors, notably residents, by nurses and nursing auxiliaries, which we mentioned earlier, can be seen in this light. We can even observe, in contrast with 'non-social' demands, moments of active mobilisation when patients, even those whose problems should have been dealt with by consulting a GP or a specialist, find in the hospital emergency service a place that responds to their distress. Here, the patient's social problem gives him or her greater mobilising worth than an ordinary patient suffering from a similar medical problem. These observations converge with what Strong (1979: 41–5) calls the 'charity format' in doctor/patient interaction. It is quite common for doctors to examine and treat without recrimination patients who are obviously using the emergency service as a place for free consultations, or for these doctors to call to order colleagues who overtly display a lack of willingness to treat this type of patient.

We will refer back to the case of the homeless man brought in by the fire brigade as mentioned above. I asked the consultant what he thought of the presence of such people in the emergency service. Should they be treated? He replied: 'You have to see these people. Because of the life they lead – living out of doors, wandering about, alcoholism – they often have conditions that require hospitalisation. They can't consult a doctor because you have to pay before the visit, even in dispensaries they have to pay out 20 francs. There is this Paris-santé (health) card, but they have to be registered somewhere, they have to have an address, so the hospital is the only place that they can be seen and treated for free'. This consultant also believed that it was useful to hospitalise homeless people since hospitalisation tended to improve their general condition.

In some cases, staff may even propose treatment or services which the person did not request. An example is a resident and a surgical consultant offering a homeless German woman the possibility of having her bandages checked in the emergency service – for free, they added, knowing that the woman had no money or medical insurance.

Some personnel explicitly refer to the hospital's 'social function', bringing up the historic tradition whereby the hospital is open to all types of demands. In this way, they justify responding positively to social demands that are rejected by others.

A.C.:	Talking of all these social problems and so on: in your opinion, should they be dealt with in the emergency service? These people who . . . come here because they don't know where else to go . . .
Clinical student:	Strictly speaking, given that this is an emergency service, no, they shouldn't be here. But where else can they go? The dispensaries aren't open – they are open at specific times but closed at night. . . I don't know, I find it easier to accept some down-and-out coming here for treatment than some lady who comes in and says. 'I've had this pain for three weeks now, so I've come to the emergency service.' It bothers me less, I don't know why, it puts me out less. I believe this is one of the functions of the hospital, this social function. This idea of integration was one of the things behind the creation of hospitals, so I think it's quite logical to hold onto this idea of inclusion (interview).

In this excerpt, the clinical student highlights the principle of positive mobilisation around social demands, where the emergency service performs a function appropriate to the hospital ('I believe this is one of the functions of the hospital, this social function'), even if it contradicts the strict definition of emergency ('given that this is an emergency service, no, they shouldn't be here').

The social demands made here on emergency services are not always a source of criticism or systematic lowering of mobilisation, as work carried out in the United Kingdom and the United States have indicated (Jeffery 1979, Roth and Douglas 1983). They are highly variable and very much dependent on circumstances. On the one hand, as for all cases which diverge sharply from the core of genuine emergencies, the way in which the patient is treated will depend on the particular flow of patients at the time.

It's morning. The consultant is talking in the cubicles about a man in the corridor, lying on a stretcher, who wants to stay in the hospital because they're disinfecting the place where he lives and it triggers asthma attacks. The consultant explains to the male nurse that this man is staying in the corridor because he can't be hospitalised. The nurse suggests that he stay on the stretcher *as long as there aren't too many people* and that he leave afterwards. The consultant goes to explain to the man that he can't be hospitalised because that would take a bed from someone who was really sick, but that he can stay on the stretcher and that he should inform someone when he wants to leave.

The greater the flow of patients, the longer it will take for medical staff to mobilise around social demands or the more limited this mobilisation will be.

In the absence of a stabilised and explicit arrangement, in other words a 'policy', treatment of social demands is also dependent on variations in individual response. We have already observed sharp contrasts between different personnel. It is also possible that a given individual's reaction to social demands may vary, in that this reaction can be dictated as much by temporary feelings (pity, mood) as by a set reaction to the problem (individual policy). In any case, this variability of reaction came to light in the interviews and discussions which we carried out. In the interview excerpt below, a resident makes the following point:

AC: And homeless people, those poor people who are rather . . . yes, what do you think of . . . ?

Resident: It's completely open. . . .

AC: Yes, open, you mean. . . . ?

Resident: You can't do anything . . . already, it depends a great deal on their attitude. If they inspire pity in people, it will be okay, they'll get a meal tray, they'll be dealt with . . . but if they're aggressive, if they stink, if they're drunk, no-one will have anything to do with them.

AC: Yes, I suppose that generally speaking, you have to see people who must be rather unpleasant to examine, physically speaking, because they smell bad, or, as we saw this morning, they have body lice. However, it seems to me that people do in fact agree to treat them. . . .

Resident: Okay, *they agree to treat them, but on a scale of zero to 100 per cent*. From time to time in the overnight stay section, you see homeless people hospitalised just so they can spend the night indoors. You might be better off paying a hotel room for them so they could watch TV . . . all because that night the head nurse was in a good mood or the resident felt sorry for them, so, they give them a bed in the overnight stay section even though there's nothing much wrong with them. So, they won't spend the night in the cold. They'll have a good sleep, they'll spend the night in the warm, but the next day they'll be thrown out like undesirables. *So it really depends a lot on the particular day.* (interview with resident).

The intellectual interest of the case

What we mean here by intellectual interest is the extent to which a case presents a challenge in terms of the diagnosis. This dimension is close to what Dingwall and Murray call the 'rule of clinical priority': 'We would there characterize the doctors as working under what we have called a rule of clinical priority. What they want is a steady flow of interesting cases with sufficient time to savour each one' (1983: 143). They are cases that are difficult to solve, but where there is a hope of clarification, which excludes rather poorly differentiated conditions such as alterations in the general state of elderly people – unusual cases, cases that teach the doctor something. How do doctors actually express their reaction to the intellectual interest of a case? Intellectual interest generates a higher degree of mobilisation in terms of treating the patient. The difference in treatment between an interesting condition and an uninteresting condition can be seen when choosing the next patient from the entry register or the file tray.

A clinical student is standing in front of the register. He remarks: 'I'd like to have a look at that: epigastric pain, decompensation, very interesting!' He walks off into the corridor and sees an elderly woman lying on a stretcher: 'Ah! it must be her!'

An interesting condition can increase the doctor's level of commitment in terms of case follow-up and defending the case against other players, particularly since the patient will also be easier to transfer, given that the other people involved will also consider it to be interesting (Dodier and Camus 1997).

The telephone rings for Doctor N, a resident. Someone goes to find her. She picks up the phone with a contented look. We hear only her half of the conversation: 'So, what was wrong with her? (. . .)[7] What? (. . .) But I thought there were one or two nodules. (. . .) But I thought that . . . (. . .) What? (. . .) *Interesting!* (. . .) She should come back, we'll hospitalise her here, I'm very pleased (. . .) but generally there is some arthralgia, isn't there? (. . .) Okay, so you'll send her back?'
      She speaks to the consultant, who has just arrived: '*I'm pleased, it's an erythema nodosum. Its not the first time I've seen that, but you usually get one big nodule, here's it's lots of small nodules!* They're going to send her back.'

The consultant says: 'Why are they sending her back? Can't they hospitalise her over there? He's a big dumb, that dermatologist!' 'No, he's nice.' The resident calls the dermatologist back: 'It's the resident in the medical emergency service. I have a young woman with an erythema nodosum. Can you take her? *It's interesting, huh?* (. . .) Great!' A nurse goes past and asks whether the lady in question wants to be hospitalised. The doctor continues with her telephone conversation. 'I'll call you back. She's come to us from a medical consultation, I'm going to ask her if she agrees to be hospitalised.' She goes off in the cubicle alongside and asks, very excited, to be informed immediately the patient gets back.

In this example, we can see that the resident is so enthusiastic about hospitalising this very interesting case that the nurse has to remind her discreetly that the lady may not in fact want to be hospitalised. Other examples of interest can be noted throughout the treatment procedure: the ease with which a doctor will move onto a new case, the energy and effort devoted to consulting books to find the information for an unusual diagnosis, the time it takes for other doctors to come and check out the case, the rank of the persons mobilised (a particularly interesting case will attract doctors high up in the hierarchy: chief residents, heads of service).

Another thing that enters into this category is any aspect of pedagogical interest for young doctors. Faced with an interesting case, clinical students and residents all examine the patient, dropping by one after the other to check out the symptoms for themselves. The case is then discussed in a staff meeting and commented on by the chief resident for the edification of all the doctors in the service. Conversely, uninteresting cases may trigger expressions of disappointment, grimaces, recriminations or even jokes about stratagems for getting rid of the case.

A resident pulls a face when confronted with a patient brought in by the fire brigade and presented by them as epileptic whereas the patient himself believed he had asthma.

A consultant comments on the files when coming on duty and stops at one that says: 'Very high transaminase count, no platelets.' He looks amazed: 'So what do they expect me to do?' He asks the nurse: 'So what's he doing here?' The nurse replies that he was found lying in the subway. The consultant attending replies, ironically: '*How exciting!*' Nevertheless, he goes off to examine the man in a cubicle.

Here again, signs of lack of interest in a patient may be translated into action, but are also reflected in the words accompanying the different levels of action, even if the actual therapeutic gestures for treating the patient are not necessarily modified.

Intellectual interest can take a number of forms: in the short term, the immediate interest of a complicated case to be solved; in the longer term, the feeling of having acquired new knowledge through a case that added to the individual's personal 'log-book' of cases; in the even longer term, interest in terms of later publication. Here, concepts of intellectual pleasure, interest in knowledge and the search for credit or fame through publication are very closely related. They refer notably to the growing role of medical research in the activity of hospital doctors (Jamous 1969, Berg 1995, Löwy 1996).

This said, the concept of 'an interesting case' has a complex status in the language of doctors. The idea itself is part of their spontaneous language. But at the same time, when we routinely asked the following question in interviews: 'What constitutes an interesting case for you?', we noted a reluctance to use the concept itself. The following example with a female resident is instructive:

AC: What, in your opinion, is an interesting case?
Resident: Don't go any further! I mean that's a personal judgment,
           there's no such thing as an interesting case.
AC: Be honest, there must be moments, there must be cases that
           you find more interesting than others . . .
Resident: Well actually, you really don't have the right . . .
AC: What?
Resident: Well, you're not supposed to think in those terms . . .
AC: Sure, you're not supposed to, but you can't help being
           human . . . and doctors are more interested in some cases than
           in others, that's obvious.
Resident: Yes, I would say there are interesting shifts and less interesting
           shifts.

Degrees of mobilisation according to the intellectual interest of the condition can generate a contradictory relationship between doctors and patients. This reason for mobilisation exists, it can be observed and the doctors themselves admit it. At the same time, it contradicts the doctor's duty to act, first and foremost, in the patient's interests. The interests of the doctor, even if intellectual, should remain secondary. This general duty is sometimes mentioned – in our survey, primarily during the interviews – as a way of placing the intellectual interest of the case on a secondary plane.

Shifting responsibility to the emergency service

Some of the demands made on the emergency service correspond to the desire of other players – general practitioners, other hospital services, other hospitals (see appendix 2) – to shift responsibility. These situations create a problem, which is that of the agreement or refusal of the emergency service to accept this transfer of responsibility for patients who have already been admitted but who are then caught between two medical authorities. From the point of view of the GP, the hospital emergency service can be used as a sort of buffer zone between the outside world and the hospital. It has the advantage of being accessible without the need to make preliminary arrangements. The task of transferring the patient to a particular place for hospitalisation can then be carried out by the staff of the emergency service, which is seen as sufficiently non-specialist to avoid the doctor having to specify a particular specialty and give reasons for the transfer, which he may find difficult. Patients can be sent straight away without being allocated to any specific service. We will now look at emergency staff's reaction to this category of transfer to the emergency service. When these cases are not seen as belonging to the core of real emergencies, in the strict sense of the term, medical staff tend primarily to react by criticising the doctor who sent the patient. However, the patient is there and has to be examined. Some criticisms merely comment on an error of judgment by a general practitioner as to the degree of urgency of the case.

> The consultant is on the telephone. She is seeking advice from the neurologist concerning a patient that she has just examined in a cubicle: '*I want to know if you can see a patient, not an emergency, but just to give your opinion.* He hasn't been able to grasp objects for three weeks. The neurological examination seems to be normal, but his doctor sent him to the emergency service (. . .) *Well, yes, as I said at the beginning, it's not an emergency.* I'll send him for a neurological consultation.' She hangs up and says to the nurse: 'I'm going to do a blood electrolyte to check his potassium level all the same.' Then she says to the man 'I spoke to the neurologist. There's nothing to be worried about. We'll make an appointment for you in the neurology service tomorrow.'

Other criticisms go further with suspicions of a deliberate intention behind the transfer. The doctor is suspected of taking advantage of the ease of gaining admittance to the emergency service in order to avoid all the organisational tasks involved in transferring a patient to the hospital or to some other place: making contact with the relevant service for a consultation or admittance, making contact with the technical services for additional examinations, as if emergency service personnel were there solely to take care of this type of work.

> This is the case in the following interview excerpt, where a consultant talks about a diabetic patient suffering from migraines, who has been sent to the emergency service by his GP:

> Consultant: It could be a perfectly ordinary migraine, but we should at least do a routine scan so we don't miss something

                      important. But as you saw, I questioned him first, then examined him and afterwards asked for a scan. I didn't ask for a scan straight away.

AC: So here the scan is more to . . . more to define a condition more exactly, but there was also the idea of covering yourself against something . . .

Consultant: Oh, absolutely. It was to make sure – not from the medical-legal point of view, because that's not the point – but to make sure I hadn't missed something important. That's it really, because I'd be quite astonished if . . . finally, it's really so as not to miss something important . . . and then, one reason is that you can do that kind of thing in the emergency service. However, this is an atypical patient, this young man, *who in my opinion could easily have been dealt with through the normal medical channels*, and I was able to request a scan quickly. That said, he might have been able to get it quicker going through his doctor, than in . . .

AC: So, what happens when a patient goes through a GP and gets sent off to the hospital . . .

Consultant: *Ah no, that's because GPs unfortunately won't . . . don't want to take the trouble,* but a GP *who really wants to do the job properly* will question the patient like I did . . . he'll ask the same questions as me and will send him . . . he'll telephone a private diagnostic centre and within three hours his patient will have a scan. You can probably get a scan more quickly in the private sector than going through the public hospital. In my opinion, he'll have to wait several hours – he might not have his scan until 8 o'clock tonight.

AC: So it's strange that these GPs send patients to the emergency service, whereas . . . ,

Consultant: *Because it's a lot easier for them to do this in Paris.* In Paris, people are only 10 minutes away from the nearest hospital, but when you're in the provinces, you can't just systematically send your patients off to the hospital – you have to take responsibility for things. In this case, the patient was not suffering from any serious distress.

AC: No, apparently not.

Consultant: Right, so . . . but the GP couldn't be bothered, *it's so much easier to just send the patient to the emergency service.*

In this interview, the criticism of general practitioners is reinforced by their error in believing that it is easier to gain access to technical services in the hospital: the emergency service is very accessible, but obtaining a scan in the hospital is apparently not as easy as getting one in a private laboratory. This situation further complicates the task of emergency service staff, since they have to deal with the problem arising for patients who arrive without an appointment but for whom they have to make an appointment with the hospital's technical services.

GPs who wish to allocate their patients to a specific service in the hospital must make some kind of prior diagnosis. In some cases, emergency service personnel suspect these doctors of not being willing or able to do this work and to be using the emergency service to do this preliminary spadework on their behalf.

> In one cubicle, a resident shows me a letter from a GP who has sent a women for a psychiatric problem. The letter is addressed to the psychiatrist, but the patient has been sent to the emergency service. According to the resident, the GP is trying to cover himself but doesn't want to be thought ridiculous by sending the patient directly to the psychiatrist. The GP no doubt believes the problem to be a psychiatric one, but is not completely certain, and wants the emergency service to do the preliminary spade-work for him.

Other recriminations reflect suspicions that the GP is dissociating him or herself from a patient with low mobilising worth. Here the transfer is seen as a way of abandoning the patient. From the point of view of emergency staff, the doctor, by shrugging off responsibility, has not respected the minimal obligation to follow up the patient to which he had committed himself in practice. This criticism is formulated in terms such as: 'getting rid of the patient', 'palming a patient off', 'losing interest in a patient', 'abandoning a patient'. This is the exact counterpart, from the viewpoint of the emergency department, of the process for which residents are socialised in other services under the generic term of 'Getting Rid of the Patient' (Mizrahi 1985).

> Morning visit on a Friday. A resident brings up the case of a woman sent in with a sudden rise in blood pressure. The doctors look at the letter accompanying this woman, who was sent by a retirement home. Resident: This lady is in a very excited state, she's been really putting on a show! She was on Catapressan when she arrived. This morning her blood pressure suddenly shot up to 24, I put her on Loxene. Assistant – *What's the point of sending someone to the emergency department for that!* She has high blood pressure which is not very well controlled. . . . *Why send her off here when the problem has been going on for days. The problem is she was overexcited and they couldn't deal with it anymore.*
> The doctors go to the patient's bedside. She confirms that she has sudden rises in blood pressure, complains of backache and says that 'it's horrible' back there (in the home). She would like to be someplace where she could be alone, because she feels very tired. She also mentions arthritis in her left arm. Back in the corridor, the assistant very strongly criticises the treatment she was given at the retirement home and suggests a new treatment. He also suggests keeping her at the hospital where at

least there are competent medical staff. Once again he criticises this way of sending people to the emergency service. *According to him, 'she must have been "very excited" and they wanted to send her off to emergency so as to have a quiet weekend.'*

The situation of patients send off to the emergency service when they are already being followed in another service is quite similar. Here again, the emergency service is seen as an easily accessible buffer zone, but the decision to send the patient is a little more specific than in the preceding case, in that the patient is already being followed in one of the services in the hospital, which justifies sending him or her to this particular hospital. There are fewer recriminations than in the preceding cases. In fact, some of the preliminary work of admittance has already been done and is therefore not the responsibility of the emergency service, even if the work of placing the patient will not necessarily correspond to the principle of follow-up. This type of case could include patients suffering from chronic conditions but subject to regular flare-ups, who are quite routinely treated by the emergency services before going back to the service which usually treats them. Here, the transfer formalities are fairly cut and dried.

Another channel concerns patients sent to the emergency service from a service in the same hospital. They may first of all be patients who should in fact be hospitalised or treated in a particular service, and who were sent to this service, but without any prior preparation for admittance. For lack of a bed, they are sent on to the emergency service. Here, the emergency service is used as a rallying point for remedying problems in transfers between the outside world and the hospital. Another category might concern patients who were already hospitalised in a hospital service, but whose condition has evolved in such a way that the service in question believes it no longer has the capacity to deal with the new problems that have arisen.

> For example, surgical emergency staff will visit the medical emergency service for a patient whose condition calls more for their particular specialty, but will make an arrangement with the medical emergency service to admit the patient to the medical section if there are no beds free in the surgical ward. In another case, the pneumology service sends a patient who needs an oxygen bottle if there is not one available in their service, or to have hormonal tests done.

The main criticism levelled against these services is the suspicion that they have abandoned a patient with little mobilising worth and have reneged on their obligation to follow up the patient. The admitting specialty describes the patients as not being 'suitable' for the service, or claims that there are no resources available to treat them. Emergency personnel see these arguments as pretexts concealing a loss of interest in the patient, which the service in question is not able to admit overtly – and which is in any case difficult to admit given that the patient is already being treated by the service – and see this as getting rid of a person who is already 'its patient'. The criticism will be even sharper if the patient also has low mobilising worth for the emergency service itself. A typical cause of conflict between hospital services is the arrival at the emergency service of people in terminal phase, already being treated in the hospital, but not accepted by their usual service. These patients have entered what Sudnow (1967) calls the phase of 'social death', which is primarily reflected in the lack of interest shown in them by the staff of this service.

> A man comes into the cubicle and says to the resident: 'I've brought you a little lady with a possible pleural problem, sent by R.' The resident goes to see the woman, who is lying on a stretcher and is 'much worse' than the woman with thoracic pain he was in the middle of examining in the cubicle. Since the resuscitation cubicle is already taken, he decides to put her in cubicle M3. He tells me with a certain irony: '*If the lady is already in terminal phase, of course we'll be able to save her here! That's R's great specialty: palming their patients off on the emergency service!*' He says to the nurse: 'Do a blood electrolyte, anyway', then goes into cubicle M3. Here, several people with the SAMU initials on the back of their coats are busily dealing with the lady, who is extremely thin. They hook her up to an oxygen bottle. The lady asks for a cushion. According to the SAMU doctor, the GP indicated that the lady's heart had stopped, that he did a cardiac message and that it 'started up again'. He indicates that the tests done yesterday showed a sodium level at 128, potassium at 5 and calcium at 80. The resident explains that the reasoning behind the service not wanting to keep this woman who had come in to die was that '*it would take up a bed for nothing, so they think they might as well palm her off on the emergency service*'. He says that he's not going to leave her there, because 'it could last a quarter of an hour, or it could last several days'. He starts of towards the telephone. Walking in front of the scope, he sees that the woman is no longer breathing. The trace is flat. He feels her neck, fails to find a pulse and listens with his stethoscope. He tells the nurse that the scope is flat and that he can remove the drip. The nurse initiates the process of dealing with a dead person (closing the eyes, shutting the mouth, making a report etc.)

Transferring patients who are close to death creates tensions between services. Such a transfer can be justified by the fact that the emergency service has resuscitation equipment. But this particular case concerned a patient whose death was pretty much inevitable. From the point of view of the oncology department, if there is a lack of beds, giving a bed to a patient for whom the treatment dispensed has little chance of being effective, is considered to be 'taking up a bed for nothing'. But at the same time, the service is exporting a difficult situation to emergency and breaching its commitment to 'its patient'.

The reference to 'an obligation of follow-up' is definitely inherent in criticisms of abandonment of patients. But the exact limits of this obligation raise many questions. The obligation to follow up a patient may be in contradiction with the concept of specialisation. This is the case when a patient's problems evolve in such a way that they come within the scope of another specialty. Where does the obligation to follow up the patient give way to the need to redirect the case to the relevant specialty? At what point does the emergency service change from being a place equipped with specific resources enabling it to deal better than other services with patients in crisis, to a place to 'stock' patients not wanted or not placeable elsewhere? These are the terms of a recurrent debate that can make moments of transfer particularly difficult.

The reaction can go beyond verbal recriminations to a refusal to admit a patient when a transfer to emergency is requested.

> We are in the office of the ward sister in the overnight stay section of the emergency service. The head nurse of another service rings up to ask if a patient can be admitted to emergency since her service is full. Pauline, the head sister in emergency, gives out the phone number of a clinic. She explains that she keeps a list of clinic numbers because 'unfortunately, they tend to transfer patients at the drop of a hat.' I ask why the person had requested a bed in the emergency service. Pauline explains that it was a patient who had been seen by a specialist resident on duty in the emergency service, who had asked the patient to consult his particular service. The patient did so, but it turned out there was no bed in this service and so the head nurse believes that the patient should be sent back to the emergency service. Pauline tells the supervisor that she should tell the resident: 'You accepted the patient, now you deal with him'.

In this example, the moral commitment made by the resident to the patient on duty in the emergency service was confirmed by his transferring the patient to his own service. Sending the patient back to emergency, with another transfer on the cards, is unacceptable from the ward sister's point of view. It is obviously easier to refuse by telephone than if the patient had already come back to the emergency service.

When we look at all these transfers of responsibility, we can see that the emergency service plays three major roles: (1) it is a place for absorbing cases that have not yet been placed in the hospital but which are directed to it (the hospital's 'front door'); (2) it is a holding area for mistaken referrals and for patients who are present but not wanted by the different departments; (3) and more generally, as an easily accessible service, the emergency service acts as a buffer zone for those difficult moments of transfer from one place to another. The latter function forces staff to take on the work involved in the transfer, which they accept without comment (26 per cent of the cases in our study), with recriminations (65 per cent of the cases) or may even refuse (9 per cent). In the event of disagreement (with or without a refusal), the dispute will centre on the fact that people are delegating to the emergency service tasks that are part of the duties incumbent on a doctor who accepts responsibility for a patient: organising the patient's transfer to the hospital, ensuring treatment even when the case no longer has any mobilising worth – in other words, they must not seek to 'get rid of patients' whose mobilising worth has been lowered. Evaluation of the scope and limits of this obligation to follow up a case is the main cause of tensions between the protagonists.

Concluding remarks

In this article, we have identified the main actors that explicitly influence the differing degrees of mobilisation of staff around the flow of demands to be dealt with in an emergency department: closeness to the core of real emergencies, social demands, the intellectual interest of the pathology, questions raised by transfers of responsibility. Other aspects also play a – more secondary – role in our observations and we will mention them here for purposes of information: bodily contact, a dimension which has been analysed quite methodically in Peneff's study (1992); anticipation of failure in dealing with the patient; the degree to which the patient cooperates; specific questions around drunkenness; anticipation of difficulties in placing the patient; social category (Camus and Dodier 1994). In this French example, our observations confirm that the logics of specialisation and openness are both strongly present, simultaneously, within an emergency service. The three major categories (closeness to a real emergency, social demands, the intellectual interest of the case) are associated directly with one or other of them. The fact that budget criteria are not brought into play in judging patients, unlike what can be observed in other services (Dodier and Camus 1997), is related to the fact that the emergency service budget is calculated on the number of patients treated, and is not modulated, as in other hospital services, by more precise considerations concerning the individual patient and, notably, the time of his/her stay. Our observations confirmed the existence of a whole range of mobilising arguments that cannot be easily reduced to a dichotomy between good and bad patients. Work in the emergency service can be seen as the task of controlling a variable flow of patients, each of which has a different mobilising worth. Systematic work on the different sources of this worth suggests three comments.

1. Reference to specialisation of treatment raises not one, but two – very different – types of reaction: closeness to life-threatening emergency and the intellectual interest of the case. This distinction comes into play in terms of the degree of mobilisation: it shows that patients whose case does not really fall into the category of an emergency – outpatient cases

or GP cases – can be highly mobilising to emergency staff if they are clinically interesting, a factor observed several times in earlier studies (for example, Roth and Douglas 1983: 95), but not systematically analysed there. This distinction also brings into play qualitatively different reactions: the concept of emergency is associated with what the doctor brings to the patient, and what the patient brings to him/her, in the present moment; the intellectual interest of the case is associated with the doctor's investment in the future, through what it teaches him, through the accumulation of medical-scientific observations and publications. As concerns the degree of urgency of the case, we observe that staff's reactions are straightforward and that they react as a unit: the closer the case is to a real emergency, the more the feeling of usefulness and spontaneous interest increases on the part of all staff. This is not so in terms of reference to other specialties, via the concept of the intellectual interest of the case. Here, reactions are much more complex. On the one hand, for doctors on duty in the emergency service, there is a tension between taking an interest in things related to their original specialty and things related to the different tasks of an emergency service. But on the other hand, the intellectual interest in the case – as an interest in what the patient brings the doctor in terms of learning, publications, recognition by other doctors – is likely to come into contradiction with what the doctor gives the patient in terms of treatment.

2. Social demands arouse very mixed reactions: some refer to the concept of the emergency service as a specialised service and relegate social problems further down the order of precedence; conversely, others refer directly to the hospital's tradition of openness in order to defend the need to respond to these demands without pushing the patient down the waiting list. In this respect, the function of the emergency service is far from being fixed. The duality of the hospital, between specialisation and openness, is a source of very different reactions on the part of its personnel. The position of the different players is important here: specialty residents tend to give social problems lesser importance, whereas certain nurses and nursing auxiliaries, and even non-specialist consultants, call their attention to this question. At the same time, we believe that in the absence of an explicit policy concerning the social question, personnel construct their own individual policies or express varying attitudes at different times. This variety of reactions means that people who apply to the emergency service because of its accessibility are exposed to great uncertainty as to the degree to which staff will mobilise around their case, either as a function of the flow of simultaneous demands, or because of the impossibility of predicting individual attitudes at a given time.

This complexity of reactions to social demands is a new finding with respect to earlier observations. This mixture of reactions seems to be much more a feature of the French example than observations concerning English or American hospitals, where the aspects that we identify as related to social demands are placed in the same category as 'bad patients' – the convergence between all these studies is quite striking. We might suggest two interpretations, which call for further and systematic comparative work. Either the difference is linked to analytical frameworks: in other words, the dichotomy between good and bad patients on which these works are based tends to flatten out complex reactions, and presupposition of a certain homogeneity tends to diminish the variety of these reactions, in which case, certain stances in favour of social demands would not have been picked up by these studies. Alternatively, there really do exist national differences, in that the mobilisation of staff in emergency departments around the social question in France – more than in the United States and the United Kingdom – appears to have been more diffuse, more closely intermingled with everyday work, running counter to the spontaneous movement towards specialised selection of patients.

This taking into account of the social aspects of demands refers back to the social question, and must be clearly distinguished, analytically, from what Roth and Douglas (1983), in their extension to several earlier works on the hospital and more generally on relationships with a clientele, call judgments on the social worth of patients. It is rare to find any reference to patients' social worth in our body of cases, a point that is particularly obvious if we use a very circumscribed definition based on socio-professional category. Here again, and for lack of any complementary work, we might examine two quite different possibilities for interpreting this difference: either this categorisation of patients plays a very negligible role in the everyday work of staff in the service which we studied, or indeed more generally, in French emergency services; or it belongs to that category of judgments, which, although having a genuine influence on activity, is not expressed and acts silently, in which case, given the way our study was organised, it remained outside our grasp.

3. Finally, there is another aspect of dealing with patients which earlier ethnographic studies have barely touched on: the question of transfer of patients between doctors. When looking at this question, these studies simply mentioned that patients sent on by doctors have greater legitimacy than patients arriving from other sources. Here, our observations highlight a more complex web of relationships built up between the people responsible for treatment. They are faced with the following question: to what extent is the transfer of a patient from one doctor to another justified by the division of tasks between specialties, and to what extent does it result from an advanced stage of demobilisation, an abandonment of a patient with particularly low mobilising worth? Here, the moral judgment no longer concerns the patient, but the agency responsible for his/her transfer to the emergency service. Our observations show

the complexity of the work done by members of the emergency service to define, for each case, the responsibilities for following up their own patients incumbent on the other services. As Bosk and Frader (1990) suggest, the debate about how far doctors are obliged to go in dealing with patients in hospital is becoming more and more acute. Uncertainties here reflect questions about the way these questions are decided and the role of agencies outside the services themselves, notably hospital administration (see Green and Armstrong 1993). We might think that certain important trends in contemporary hospitals tend to accentuate tensions between services around these questions. Under the influence of budget restrictions and the increasing emphasis on the scientific aspects of medicine, each hospital service tends to tighten up its patient profile around selective criteria. However, on this question, we can merely note the limitations of an inquiry strategy based on an ethnographic study of a service. The organisational repercussions of specialisation tend to influence sociological methods. In a situation in which specialties are becoming increasingly interdependent, arrangements for ensuring circulation of patients between services take on capital importance. Studying them implies the need for transversal approaches – as well as ethnographic studies based on services – designed to recognise, right along the flow of patients, instances of solidarity and confrontation between the different actors making up together their access to treatment.

Appendix 1 *Factors explicitly influencing the mobilisation of staff*

Total cases observed: 79 patients, or 113 items[8]

Breakdown of cases by source of mobilisation	*Number of cases*
Degree of urgency of the case	33
Social demands	22
Intellectual interest of the case	13
Transfer of responsibility to the emergency service	13
Bodily contact	8
Anticipation of care failure	6
Patient's degree of cooperation	4
Drunkenness	4
Anticipation of placement difficulties	3
Other	5

Appendix 2 *Transfer by other doctors to the emergency service*

Total cases observed	34
Patients sent to the hospital by general practitioners but not expected in a department	14

Patients sent to the hospital by general practitioners,
    already followed by a service, but sent without previous contact
    being made with this service   7
Patients sent to the emergency service by another hospital service   13

Notes

1   For France, see particularly Castel (1995), Faure (1982) Foucault (1979), Imbert (1982), Maillard (1988).
2   See notably the research of Luc Boltanski and Laurent Thévenot on the ordinary sense of justice (Boltanski 1990, Boltanski and Thévenot 1991). For a presentation of the analytical framework thus created and its extension to other fields of investigation, see Dodier (1993, 1995a). Indications about the consequences in terms of ethnographic work may be found in Baszanger and Dodier (1997).
3   Nurses' injunctions to residents to work faster is described by Mizrahi (1985), although he does not suggest a link between the panoramic work of managing patient flows and clinical attention to individual cases.
4   For further remarks on antagonism between users and staff on this point at reception, with users finding it difficult to understand that a persistent pain can generate a refusal to admit them to the emergency service, see Camus and Dodier (1994). In English hospitals, this reference to the time when the symptoms first appeared is used as a criterion of eligibility, in an even more codified manner, since it is explicitly mentioned at the entrance that injuries must not be more than 48 hours old (Hughes 1989).
5   This is an example of a 'specialist' resident, assigned to services other than emergency, but who is nevertheless obliged to work shifts in the emergency service.
6   Patients can remain no longer than 24 hours in the service. After the morning visit, those who are to remain hospitalised must be placed in other services. Here, the clinical student is referring to the fact that during the daily morning visit in the emergency service, emergency doctors solicit the opinion of the chief resident in the neurology service.
7   The three dots between brackets (. . .) indicate the unheard part of the telephone call.
8   The same patient may simultaneously present several characteristics.

References

Baszanger, I. and Dodier, N. (1997) Ethnography: relating the part to the whole. In Silverman, D. (ed.) *Qualitative Analysis: Issues of Theory and Method.* London: Sage.
Béland, F., Philibert, L., Thouez, J.P. and Maheux, B. (1990) Socio-spatial perspectives on the utilization of emergency hospital services in two urban territories in Quebec, *Social Science and Medicine*, 30, 1, 53–66.
Béland, F., Lemay, A., Philibert, L. and Maheux, B. (1991) Elderly patients' use of hospital-based emergency services, *Medical Care*, 29, 408–18.
Berg, M. (1995) Turning a practice into a science: redrawing the nature and flaws of postwar medical practice, *Social Studies of Science*, 25, 437–76.

Boltanski, L. (1990) *L'Amour et la Justice Comme Compétences. Trois Essais en Sociologie de l'Action.* Paris: Métailié.

Boltanski, L. and Thévenot, L. (1991) *De la Justification. Les Économies de la Grandeur.* Paris: Gallimard.

Bosk, C. and Frader, J. (1990) AIDS and its impact on medical work: the culture and politics of the shop floor, *The Milbank Quarterly*, 68 supp. 2, 257–79.

Camus, A. and Dodier, N. (1994) *L'Intérêt pour les Patients à l'Entrée de l'Hôpital. Enquête Sociologique dans un Service d'Urgences Médicales.* Paris: CERMES-GSPM.

Callon, M. (ed.) (1989) *La Science et ses Réseaux.* Paris: La Découverte.

Castel, R. (1995) *Les Métamorphoses de la Question Sociale. Une Chronique du Salariat.* Paris: Fayard.

Dingwall, R. and Murray, T. (1983) Categorization in accident departments: 'good' patients, 'bad' patients and 'children', *Sociology of Health and Illness*, 5, 2, 127–48.

Dodier, N. (1993) Acting as a combination of 'common words', *The Sociological Review*, 41, 3, 556–71.

Dodier, N. (1994) Dealing with complaints in expert medical decision: a sociological analysis of judgment, *Sociology of Health and Illness*, 16, 4, 489–514.

Dodier, N. (1995a) The conventional foundations of action: elements of a sociological pragmatics, *Réseaux. The French Journal of Communication*, 3, 2, 147–66.

Dodier, N. (1995b) *Les Hommes et les Machines. La Conscience Collective dans les Sociétés Technicisées.* Paris: Métailié.

Dodier, N. and Camus, A. (1997) L'admission des malades. Histoire et pragmatique de l'accueil à l'hôpital, *Annales. Histoire, Sciences Sociales*, 4, 733–63.

Elster, J. and Herpin, N. (ed.) (1992) *Ethique des Choix Médicaux.* Poitiers: Actes Sud.

Faure, O. (1982) *Genèse de l'Hôpital Moderne: les Hospices Civils de Lyon de 1802 à 1845.* Lyon: Presses Universitaires de Lyon.

Foucault, M. (ed.) (1979) *Les Machines à Guérir.* Bruxelles. Pierre Mardaga.

Genell Andrén, K. and Rosenqvist, U. (1987a) Heavy users of an emergency department – a two year follow-up study, *Social Science and Medicine*, 25, 7, 825–31.

Genell Andrén, K. and Rosenqvist, U. (1987b) An ecological study of the relationship between risk indicators for social disintegration and use of a somatic emergency department, *Social Science and Medicine*, 25, 10, 1121–7.

Green, J. and Armstrong, D. (1993) Controlling the 'bed state': negotiating hospital organisation, *Sociology of Health and Illness*, 15, 3, 337–52.

Herzlich, C. (1973) Types de clientèle et fonctionnement de l'institution hospitalière, *Revue Française de Sociologie*, 14, 41–59.

Hughes, D. (1988) When nurses know best: some aspects of nurse/doctor interactions in a casualty department, *Sociology of Health and Illness*, 10, 1, 1–22.

Hughes, D. (1989) Paper and people: the work of the casualty reception clerk, *Sociology of Health and Illness*, 11, 4, 382–408.

Imbert, J. (ed.) (1982) *Histoire des Hôpitaux en France.* Toulouse: Privat.

Jamous, H. (1969) *Sociologie de la Décision. La Réforme des Études Médicales et des Structures Hospitalières.* Paris: Editions du CNRS.

Jeffery, R. (1979) Normal rubbish: deviant patients in casualty departments, *Sociology of Health and Illness*, 1, 1, 90–107.

Latour, B. (1989) *La Science en Action.* Paris: La Découverte.

Lejonc, J.L., Amselem, J., Marchalot-Leclercq, G., De Saxce, A-M., Fleury, M-N. and Marsault, C. (1993) L'Hôpital universitaire peut-il assurer sa mission d'hôpital général? L'expérience du service des urgences et de l'unité de médecine générale de l'hôpital Henri-Mondor (Créteil), *Gestions Hospitalières*, 328, 489–93.

Löwy, I. (1996) *Between Bench and Bedside: Science, Healing and Interleukin-2 in a Cancer Ward.* Cambridge and London: Harvard University Press.

Maillard, C. (1988) *Histoire de l'Hôpital de 1940 à nos Jours. Comment la Santé est Devenue une Affaire d'Etat.* Paris: Dunod.

Mannon, J., Green, L., Levine, M., Gibson, G. and Gurlay, H. (1987) Using the emergency department as a screening site for high blood pressure, *Medical Care*, 25, 770–80.

Mannon, J. (1976) Defining and treating 'problem patients' in a hospital emergency room, *Medical Care*, 14, 12, 1004–13.

Mizrahi, T. (1985) Getting rid of patients: contradictions in the socialisation of internists to the doctor-patient relationship, *Sociology of Health and Illness*, 7, 214–35.

Mol, A. and Law, J. (1994) Regions, networks and fluids: anaemia and social topology, *Social Studies of Science*, 24, 641–71.

Peneff, J. (1992) *L'Hôpital en Urgence. Etude par Observation Participante.* Paris: Métailié.

Perrow, C. (1984) *Normal Accidents. Living with High Risk Technologies.* New York: Basic Books.

Roth, J. (1972a) Some contingencies of the moral evaluation and control of clientele: the case of the hospital emergency service, *American Journal of Sociology*, 77, 5, 839–56.

Roth, J. (1972b) Staff and client control strategies in urban hospital emergency, *Urban Life and Culture*, 1, 39–60.

Roth, J. and Douglas, D. (1983) *No Appointment Necessary. The Hospital Emergency Department in the Medical Services World.* New York: Irvington.

Star, S.L. (1989) The structure of ill-structured solutions: boundary objects and heterogeneous distributed problem solving. In Gasser, L. and Huhns, M. (eds) *Distributed Artificial Intelligence, vol. 2.* London: Pitman.

Steg, A. (1989) *Rapport Pour le Conseil Économique et Social sur la Situation des Services d'Urgences.* Paris: La Documentation Française.

Strauss, A., Fagerhaugh, S., Suczeck, B. and Wiener, C. (1985) *The Social Organization of Medical Work.* Chicago: University of Chicago Press.

Strong, P. (1979) *The Ceremonial Order of the Clinic.* London: Routledge and Kegan Paul.

Sudnow, D. (1967) *Passing on. The Social Organization of Dying.* Englewood Cliffs: Prentice Hall.

Thévenot, L. (1993) Les formes de savoir collectif selon les régimes pragmatiques: des compétences attribuées ou distribuées. In Dupuy, J.P., Livet, P. and Reynaud, B. (eds) *Limitations de la Rationalité et Constitution du Collectif.* Paris: La Découverte.

Timmermans, S. (1995) La déconstruction/reconstruction oles 'soi' dans les techniques de réanimation, *Techniques et Culture* 25–6, *Les Objets de la Médecine*, 245–61.

Vassy, C. and Renard, F. (1992) Quels malades pour l'hôpital public? Deux stratégies de segmentation, *Annales des Mines*, coll. *Gérer et Comprendre*, June, 29–39.

Index